ETHICS ACROSS THE PROFESSIONS

ETHICS ACROSS THE PROFESSIONS

PROFESSIONS

A Reader for Professional Ethics

Clancy Martin
University of Missouri, Kansas City

Wayne Vaught
University of Missouri, Kansas City

Robert C. Solomon
University of Texas at Austin

New York Oxford
OXFORD UNIVERSITY PRESS
2010

Oxford University Press, Inc., publishes works that further Oxford University's
objective of excellence in research, scholarship, and education.

Oxford   New York
Auckland   Cape Town   Dar es Salaam   Hong Kong   Karachi
Kuala Lumpur   Madrid   Melbourne   Mexico City   Nairobi
New Delhi   Shanghai   Taipei   Toronto

With offices in
Argentina   Austria   Brazil   Chile   Czech Republic   France   Greece
Guatemala   Hungary   Italy   Japan   Poland   Portugal   Singapore
South Korea   Switzerland   Thailand   Turkey   Ukraine   Vietnam

Published by Oxford University Press, Inc.
198 Madison Avenue, New York, New York 10016

www.oup.com

Oxford is a registered trademark of Oxford University Press

Library of Congress Cataloging-in-Publication Data
Ethics across the professions : a reader for professional ethics / [compiled by]
   Clancy Martin, Wayne Vaught, Robert C. Solomon.
      p.   cm.
Includes bibliographical references.
ISBN 978-0-19-532668-0
1. Professional ethics.   I. Martin, Clancy W.   II. Vaught, Wayne.   III. Solomon, Robert C.
BJ1725.E762 2011
174—dc22

                                                                2009032245

Printed in the United States of America
on acid-free paper

This book is dedicated to the memory of
Robert C. Solomon

CONTENTS

PREFACE

This is a reader in professional ethics, intended for undergraduate, graduate, and executive courses on that subject. It consists of classic and recent articles that address the broad range of ethical issues and dilemmas that occur in professional life. Our desire is to offer a text that will genuinely help the student who is training to be a professional to be better prepared when she or he comes across the moral problems that are inevitable in the real world of working as a professional. We hope also to provide frameworks that the professional in training will use to understand her or his chosen profession—that is, how to think about oneself as a professional, how to understand professionalism as one integrates it into one's life. The professions, perhaps more than any other kind of work, have a tendency to embrace one's entire personality. This fact makes it particularly urgent for the student to take the time—and to have the tools—to consider the moral status, the moral virtues, and the possible moral pitfalls of her or his chosen profession.

Because of the diversity of the professions—doctors, lawyers, nurses, accountants and other businesspersons, teachers, journalists, engineers, and many more—we have organized the book around topics, rather than around specific professions. The benefit of this approach is, it turns out, that many of the professions have precisely the same moral concerns—or that their concerns are similar enough that they can helpfully learn from one another. An article on what makes an honest lawyer can be useful to a medical student who is considering what it means to be a truthful doctor. An article showing the conflicts of interest faced by nurses can be illuminating for a young accountant, in whose profession conflicts of interest are common and so important to know how to deal with. We have also tried to focus the book as much as possible on *you*, the reader of the book. That is, in the case of every article, we have asked ourselves not "Does this contribute to the scholarly issue at hand?" but rather "Would this help the student who was actually facing a moral dilemma?" We have tried to make this a kind of handbook for professional ethics that will, we hope, stay on your bookshelf long after you have left the university as a real aid when you are thinking about professionalism and ethics in the future.

The book could have been twice as long as it is, and we would have been that much happier: there is so much to think about when it comes to morality, the good life, and the professions. We will not review every chapter here, but there are a few chapters that bear particular mention. The first chapter introduces the idea of what it is to be a professional and discusses the importance of the professional as a leader. The first chapter, with its consideration of several different kinds of professionals and some straightforwardly philosophical pieces that are independent of any particular professional, will give the student a good idea of what is to come in the rest of the book. Some instructors may see fit to omit chapter two, which is a quick survey of what the great philosophers of the Western tradition have had to say about morality and the good life. There are good tools here, though, for thinking about what it means to be moral, and we provided the material in the hope that it would be a useful source for an instructor to refer back to throughout the course, even if she or he did not go straight through chapter two in a particular class or series of classes. The chapters that follow these two chapters address the "classic" problems of professionalism: duties and rights, truthfulness, privacy and confidentiality, conflicts of interest, social welfare, and integrity and loyalty. Again, we could have added eight more chapters and would still have had more to say. But there is only so much time in a class, and we tried to create a book that can be taught more or less completely in a single semester.

The chapters, you will notice, more or less stand alone, so the instructor is free to move around the book as she or he sees fit: we do not think there is a particular order the chapters ought to be taught in (although we think chapter one does a nice job of introducing a lot of the central issues). But you will also notice that the chapters flow together: issues that arise in one chapter rearise, often in a slightly different form, in another chapter, and as the student reads the chapters, we expect that she or he will become more and more capable at anticipating the central moral problems and at solving them. Because this is, above all, a practical subject and a practical nook, we are attempting to show you the concrete moral problems you are likely to face, how to anticipate and avoid these problems, and when they cannot be avoided how best to handle them.

We won't solve all your moral problems here. But we hope that, with the crucial help of your instructor, we can help you learn some ways to think about them more intelligently.

For their invaluable comments on the manuscript of this book, we'd like to thank: William E. Abshire, Bridgewater College; Kenneth G. Ferguson, East Carolina University; Richard W. Field, Northwest Missouri State University; Glenn C. Graber, University of Tennessee, Knoxville; Mitchell R. Haney, University of North Florida; Errol G. Katayama, Ohio Northern University; Patricia Kazan, York University; Christopher Meyers, California State University, Bakersfield; Andy Piker, Texas A&M University; Michael S. Pritchard, Western Michigan University; and William Sweet, St. Francis Xavier University.

During the course of the creation of this book, one of its creators, Robert C. Solomon, died unexpectedly. We have tried to do justice to him, but his help was sorely missed. Among his many other virtues, Bob was a true professional.

ETHICS ACROSS THE PROFESSIONS

1

What Is It to Be a Professional?

The Professions, Leadership, and Work

Introduction

When you think of noble work, work truly worth doing, you think of the professional. The doctor performing a coronary bypass surgery that adds twenty years to a life; the lawyer defending an innocent client; the engineer who invents a new way to purify water and thus saves thousands of lives.

All of us have to work. But only a few of us will become professionals. To choose to enter a profession is to take on a distinct and important set of new responsibilities. A professional will never be able to separate his or her work life from his or her personal, private life. Your personality will be crucial to your success as a professional, and your professional life will influence and change how you interact with your friends and family and even your self-definition. As a consequence of your professional training and, eventually, your career as a professional, you will look at yourself in the mirror a bit (or maybe a lot) differently. Are you ready for it?

More and more fields are becoming "professionalized." Only recently, for example, have businesspeople been considered professionals—and the emergence of professional codes of conduct for businesspeople is a relatively new (and actively evolving) phenomenon. Think of the diversity of the professions and their roles. Lawyers, doctors, advertising executives, educators, nurses, pharmacists, athletes, computer scientists: these are all called "professionals." So what do they have in common? Why is it that being a professional in our society is a mark of honor? Another way of asking what is really the same question is (a question you may never have asked yourself, but should): why do you want to be a professional?

To be a professional is to be a paid expert. It is to claim a high degree of competence in an area of knowledge that others will not claim. It is a way of saying: "trust me. I know what I am doing here. I have spent years learning how to do this. I take pride in it. You don't have to fact-check all my claims because this is the thing I really know how to do. I know it so well that I am willing to make promises, and to take your money, on the basis of my expertise. I may not know everything, but on this subject, I am the person you need."

The reason you should put real thought into the ethics of your profession—and how your personal ethics will come into play in your professional life—is that many other people will be relying on you in a new way. As you enter and grow within your profession, your impact on others and your importance to them will increase. People will be trusting you with their money, with their careers, quite possibly with their own lives and the lives of their loved ones. What does that mean for your conduct? For your understanding of yourself and your life? When, why, and how much should your new role as a professional impact your personal life?

You have surely noticed that professionals, unlike many other workers, serve an interesting role in our society: they are often taken to be models of ethical behavior. We rely upon professionals for good judgment and, what is often even more important, we rely upon them for the truth. We expect professionals to be both sincere and accurate. When a reporter calls an expert for an opinion, that expert opinion usually comes from a professional. In our society, professionals often serve as the collective conscience for the rest of us.

Professionals are leaders. As such, they need to consider the principles of good leadership. A professional does not have the luxury of pretending that his or her life and actions do not extend beyond their immediate sphere of influence. A professional recognizes that younger professionals around her, her clients, and other professionals she knows look to her as a role model in how to conduct oneself not merely as an expert, but as a person. More obviously, professionals these days are also usually called upon to lead others in their everyday work environments. Accountants, teachers, lawyers, nurses, business executives, doctors: none of them works alone, and their work cannot be accomplished without the support of the teams they lead.

This chapter introduces some of the issues that arise when we ask: what does it mean to be a professional? And, perhaps even more important, what does it mean to be a good (as opposed to an average, or a mediocre, or even a bad) professional?

Henry Mintzberg | # The Professional Organization

Henry Mintzberg is Cleghorn Professor of Management Studies at McGill University.

I work in a professional organization, and probably chose to do so initially because it is the one place in the world where you can act as if you were self-employed yet regularly receive a paycheck. These seemingly upside-down organizations, where the workers sometimes appear to manage the bosses, are fascinating in the way they work. As the nursery rhyme goes, when they're good, they're very, very good, but when they're bad, they're horrid. It all hinges on that fine line between collegiality (working for the common good) and politics (working for self-interest). We need professional organizations to carry out highly skilled yet highly stable tasks in society, such as replacing someone's heart or auditing a company's books. But as a society we have yet

From Henry Mintzberg and James B. Quian, *The Strategy Process*, Prentice Hall, NY, 1995.

to learn how to control their excesses: professionals who mistreat their clients, professional organizations that mistreat their supporters. . . .

THE BASIC STRUCTURE

An organization can be bureaucratic without being centralized. This happens when its work is complex, requiring that it be carried out and controlled by professionals, yet at the same time remains stable, so that the skills of those professionals can be perfected through standardized operating programs. The structure takes on the form of *professional* bureaucracy, which is common in universities, general hospitals, public accounting firms, social work agencies, and firms doing fairly routine engineering or craft work. All rely on the skills and knowledge of their operating professionals to function; all produce standardized products or services. . . .

Control over their work means that professionals work relatively independently of their colleagues but closely with the clients they serve—doctors treating their own patients and accountants who maintain personal contact with the companies whose books they audit. Most of the necessary coordination among the operating professionals is then handled automatically by their set skills and knowledge—in effect, by what they have learned to expect from each other. During an operation as long and as complex as open-heart surgery, "very little needs to be said [between the anesthesiologist and the surgeon] preceding chest opening and during the procedure on the heart itself . . . [most of the operation is] performed in absolute silence." The point is perhaps best made in reverse by the cartoon that shows six surgeons standing around a patient on an operating table with one saying, "Who opens?" . . .

But no matter how standardized the knowledge and skills, their complexity ensures that considerable discretion remains in their application. No two professionals—no two surgeons or engineers or social workers—ever apply them in exactly the same way. Many judgments are required.

Training, reinforced by indoctrination, is a complicated affair in the professional organization. The initial training typically takes place over a period of years in a university or special institution, during which the skills and knowledge of the profession are formally programmed into the students. There typically follows a long period of on-the-job training, such as internship in medicine or articling in accounting, where the formal knowledge is applied and the practice of skills perfected. On-the-job training also completes the process of indoctrination, which began with the formal education. As new knowledge is generated and new skills develop, of course (so it is hoped) the professional upgrades his or her expertise.

All that training is geared to one goal, the internalization of the set procedures, which is what makes the structure technically bureaucratic . . . : The professional bureaucracy differs markedly from the machine bureaucracy. Whereas the latter generates its own standards—through the technostructure, enforced by its line managers—many of the standards of the professional bureaucracy originate outside its own structure, in the self-governing associations its professionals belong to with their colleagues from other institutions. These associations set universal standards, which they ensure are taught by the universities and are used by all the organizations practicing the profession. So whereas the machine bureaucracy relies on authority of a hierarchical nature—the power of office—professional bureaucracy emphasizes authority of a professional nature—the power of expertise. . . .

The Pigeonholing Process

When we understand how the professional organization functions at the operational level, it is helpful to think of it as a set of standard programs—in fact, the repertoire of skills the professionals stand ready to use—that are applied to known situations, called contingencies, and are also standardized. Weick notes of one case in point, "schools are in the business of molding and maintaining categories." The process is sometimes known as *pigeonholing*. In this regard, the professional has two basic tasks: (1) to categorize, or "diagnose," the client's need in terms of one of the contingencies, which indicates which standard program to apply, and (2) to apply, or execute, that program....

It is in the pigeonholing process that the fundamental differences among the machine organization, the professional organization, and the innovative organization (to be discussed next) can best be seen. The machine organization is a single-purpose structure. Presented with a stimulus, it executes its one standard sequence of programs, just as we kick when tapped on the knee. No diagnosis is involved. In the professional organization, diagnosis is a fundamental task, but one highly circumscribed. The organization seeks to match a predetermined contingency to a standardized program. Fully open-ended diagnosis—that which seeks a creative solution to a unique problem—requires the innovative form of organization. No standard contingencies or programs can be relied upon there.

The Administrative Structure

Everything we have discussed so far suggests that the operating core is the key part of the professional organization. The only other part that is fully elaborated is the support staff, but that is focused very much on serving the activities of the operating core. Given the high cost of the professionals, it makes sense to back them up with as much support as possible. Thus, universities have printing facilities, faculty clubs, alma mater funds, publishing houses, archives, libraries, computer facilities, and many, many other support units.

The technostructure and middle-line management are not highly elaborated in the professional organization. They can do little to coordinate the professional work. Moreover, with so little need for direct supervision of, or mutual adjustment among, the professionals, the operating units can be very large. For example, the McGill Faculty of Management functions effectively with fifty professors under a single

manager, its dean, and the rest of the university's academic hierarchy is likewise thin....

Because of the power of their professional operators, these organizations are sometimes described as inverse pyramids, with the professional operators on top and the administrators down below to serve them—to ensure that the surgical facilities are kept clean and the classrooms well supplied with chalk. Such a description slights the power of the administrators of professional work, however, although it may be an accurate description of those who manage the support units. For the support staff—often more numerous than the professional staff, but generally less skilled—there is no democracy in the professional organization, only the oligarchy of the professionals. Such support units as housekeeping in the hospital or printing in the university are likely to be managed tightly from the top, in effect as machine-like enclaves within the professional configuration. Thus, what frequently emerges in the professional organization are parallel and separate administrative hierarchies, one democratic and bottom-up for the professionals, a second machinelike and top-down for the support staff.

The Roles of the Administrators of Professional Work

Where does all this leave the administrators of the professional hierarchy, the executive directors and chiefs of the hospitals and the presidents?... Are they powerless? Compared with their counterparts in the entrepreneurial and machine organizations, they certainly lack a good deal of power. But that is far from the whole story. The administrator of professional work may not be able to control the professionals directly, but he or she does perform a series of roles that can provide considerable indirect power.

First, this administrator spends much time handling disturbances in the structure. The pigeonholing process is an imperfect one at best, leading to all kinds of jurisdictional disputes between the professionals. Who should perform mastectomies in the hospitals, surgeons who look after cutting or gynecologists who look after women? Seldom, however, can one administrator impose a solution on the professionals involved in a dispute. Rather, various administrators must often sit down together and negotiate a solution on behalf of their constituencies.

Second, the administrators of professional work—especially those at higher levels—serve in key roles at the boundary of the organization, between the professionals inside and the influencers outside: governments, salient associations, benefactors, and so on. On the one hand, the administrators are expected to protect the professionals' autonomy, to "buffer" them from external pressures. On the other hand, they are expected to woo those outsiders to support the organization, both morally and financially. And that often leads the outsiders to expect these administrators, in turn, to control the professionals, in machine bureaucratic ways. Thus, the external roles of the manager—maintaining liaison contacts, acting as figurehead and spokesman in a public relations capacity, negotiating with outside agencies—emerge as primary ones in the administration of professional work.

Some view the roles these administrators are called upon to perform as signs of weakness. They see these people as the errand boys of the professionals, or else as pawns caught in various tugs of war—between one professional and another, between support staffer and professional, between outsider and professional. In fact, however, these roles are the very sources of administrators' power. Power is, after all, gained at the locus of uncertainty, and that is exactly where the administrators of professionals sit. The administrator who succeeds in raising extra funds for his or her organization gains a say in how they are distributed; the one who can reconcile conflicts in favor of his or her unit or who can effectively buffer the professionals from external influence becomes a valued, and therefore powerful, member of the organization.

We can conclude that power in these structures does flow to those professionals who care to devote effort to doing administrative instead of professional work, so long as they do it well. But that, it should be stressed, is not laissez-faire power; the professional administrator maintains power only as long as the professionals perceive him or her to be serving their interests effectively.

CONDITIONS OF THE PROFESSIONAL ORGANIZATION

The professional form of organization appears wherever the operating work of an organization is dominated by skilled workers who use procedures that are difficult to learn yet are well defined....

The prime example of the professional configuration is the personal-service organization, at least the one with complex, stable work not reliant on a fancy technical system. Schools and universities, consulting firms, law and accounting offices, and social work agencies all rely on this form of organization, more or less, so long as they concentrate not on innovating in the solution of new problems but on applying standard programs to well-defined ones. The same seems to be true of hospitals, at least to the extent that their technical systems are simple. (In those areas that call for more sophisticated equipment—apparently a growing number, especially in teaching institutions—the hospital is driven toward a hybrid structure, with characteristics of the innovative form. But this tendency is mitigated by the hospital's overriding concern with safety. Only the tried and true can be relied upon, which produces a natural aversion to the looser innovative configuration.)

So far, our examples have come from the service sector. But the professional form can be found in manufacturing too, where the above conditions hold up. Such is the case of the craft enterprise, for example the factory using skilled workers to produce ceramic products. The very term *craftsman* implies a kind of professional who learns traditional skills through long apprentice training and then is allowed to practice them free of direct supervision. Craft enterprises seem typically to have few administrators, who tend to work, in any event, alongside the operating personnel. The same would seem to be true for engineering work oriented not to creative design so much as to modification of existing dominant designs.

———————

...Some writers have traditionally associated professional organizations with a *collegial* model, where decisions are made by a "community of individuals and groups, all of whom may have different roles and specialties, but who share common goals and objectives for the organization." *Common interest* is the guiding force, and decision-making is therefore by consensus. Other writers instead propose a *political* model, in which the differences of interest groups are irreconcilable. Participants thus seek to serve their *self-interest*, and political factors become instrumental in determining outcomes.

Clearly, neither common interest nor self-interest will dominate decision processes all the time; some combination is naturally to be expected. Professionals may agree on goals yet conflict over how they should be achieved; alternatively, consensus can sometimes be achieved even where goals differ—Democrats do, after all, sometimes vote with Republicans in the U.S. Congress. In fact, we need to consider motivation, not just behavior, in order to distinguish collegiality from politics. Political success sometimes requires a collegial posture—one must cloak self-interest in the mantle of the common good. Likewise, collegial ends sometimes require political means. Thus, we should take as collegial any behavior that is *motivated* by a genuine concern for the good of the institution, and politics as any behavior driven fundamentally by self-interest (of the individual or his or her unit).

A third model that has been used to explain decision-making in universities is the *garbage can*. Here decision-making is characterized by "collections of choices looking for problems, issues and feelings looking for decision situations in which they may be aired, solutions looking for issues to which they might be an answer, and decision makers looking for work." Behavior is, in other words, nonpurposeful and often random, because goals are unclear and the means to achieve them problematic. Furthermore, participation is fluid because of the cost of time and energy. Thus, in place of the common interest of the collegial model and the self-interest of the political model, the garbage can model suggests a kind of *disinterest*.

The important question is not whether garbage can processes exist—we have all experienced them—but whether they matter. Do they apply to key issues or only to incidental ones? Of course, decisions that are not significant to anyone may well end up in the garbage can, so to speak. There is always someone with free time willing to challenge a proposal for the sake of so doing. But I have difficulty accepting that individuals to whom decisions are important do not invest the effort necessary to influence them. Thus, like common interest and self-interest, I conclude that disinterest neither dominates decision processes nor is absent from them.

Finally, *analysis* may be considered a fourth model of decision-making. Here calculation is used, if not to select the best alternative, then at least to assess the acceptability of different ones. Such an approach seems consistent with the machine configuration, where a technostructure stands ready to calculate the costs and benefits of every proposal. But, in fact, analysis figures prominently in the professional configuration too, but here carried out mostly by professional operators themselves. Rational analysis structures arguments for communication and debate and enables champions and their opponents to support their respective positions. In fact, as each side seeks to pick holes in the position of the other, the real issues are more likely to emerge....

———————

SOME ISSUES ASSOCIATED WITH THE PROFESSIONAL ORGANIZATION

The professional organization is unique among the different configurations in answering two of the paramount needs of contemporary men and women. It is democratic, disseminating its power directly to its workers (at least those lucky enough to be professional). And it provides them with extensive autonomy, freeing them even from the need to coordinate closely with their colleagues. Thus, the professional has the best of both worlds. He or she is attached to an organization yet is free to serve clients in his or her own way, constrained only by the established standards of the profession.

The result is that professionals tend to emerge as highly motivated individuals, dedicated to their work and to the clients they serve. Unlike the machine organization, which places barriers between the operator and the client, this configuration removes them, allowing a personal relationship to develop. Moreover, autonomy enables the professionals to perfect their skills free of interference, as they repeat the same complex programs time after time.

But in these same characteristics, democracy and autonomy, lie the chief problems of the professional organization. For there is no evident way to control the work, outside of that exercised by the professior itself, no way to correct deficiencies that the professionals choose to overlook. What they tend to overlook are the problems of coordination, of discretion, and of innovation that arise in these configurations.

Problems of Discretion

Pigeonholing raises another serious problem. It focuses most of the discretion in the hands of single professionals, whose complex skills, no matter how standardized, require the exercise of considerable judgment. Such discretion works fine when professionals are competent and conscientious. But it plays havoc when they are not. Inevitably, some professionals are simply lazy or incompetent. Others confuse the needs of their clients with the skills of their trade. They thus concentrate on a favored program to the exclusion of all others (like the psychiatrist who thinks that all patients, indeed all people, need psychoanalysis). Clients incorrectly

sent their way get mistreated (in both senses of that word).

Various factors confound efforts to deal with this inversion of means and ends. One is that professionals are notoriously reluctant to act against their own, for example, to censure irresponsible behavior through their professional associations. Another (which perhaps helps to explain the first) is the intrinsic difficulty of measuring the outputs of professional work. When psychiatrists cannot even define the words *cure* or *healthy*, how are they to prove that psychoanalysis is better for schizophrenics than chemical therapy?

Discretion allows professionals to ignore not only the needs of their clients but also those of the organization itself. Many professionals focus their loyalty on their profession, not on the place where they happen to practice it. But professional organizations have needs for loyalty too—to support their overall strategies, to staff their administrative committees, to see them through conflicts with the professional associations. Cooperation is crucial to the functioning of the administrative structure, yet many professionals resist it furiously.

Problems of Innovation

In the professional organizaton, major innovation also depends on cooperation. Existing programs may be perfected by the single professional, but new ones usually cut across the established specialties—in essence, they require a rearrangement of the pigeonholes—and so call for collective action. As a result, the reluctance of the professionals to cooperate with each other and the complexity of the collective processes can produce resistance to innovation. These are, after all, professional *bureaucracies*, in essence, performance structures designed to perfect given programs in stable environments, not problem-solving structures to create new programs for unanticipated needs.

The problems of innovation in the professional organization find their roots in convergent thinking, in the deductive reasoning of the professional who sees the specific situation in terms of the general concept. . . . As Lucy once told Charlie Brown, great art cannot be done in half an hour; it takes at least forty-five minutes!

The fact is that great art and innovative problem-solving require *inductive* reasoning—that is, the inference of the new general solution from the particular experience. And that kind of thinking is *divergent*; it breaks away from old routines or standards rather than perfecting existing ones. And that flies in the face of everything the professional organization is designed to do.

Public Responses to these Problems

. . . Change in the professional organization does not *sweep* in from new administrators taking office to announce wide reforms, or from government officials intent on bringing the professionals under technocratic control. Rather, change *seeps* in through the slow process of changing the professionals—changing who enters the profession in the first place, what they learn in its professional schools (norms as well as skills and knowledge), and thereafter how they upgrade their skills. Where desired changes are resisted, society may be best off to call on its professionals' sense of public responsibility or, failing that, to bring pressure on the professional associations rather than on the professional bureaucracies.

A Note on the Unionization of Professionals

Professionals subjected to dysfunctional administrative pressures have sometimes been driven to unionization. . . .

The key to the effective functioning of the professional organization is *individual* responsibility: the dedication of the professional to his or her client. Individual responsibility is often based on a personal working relationship between the professional and the client—the professor with the students, the physician with the patient. A subtle but crucial point must be stressed here. Professional bureaucracy may be a highly decentralized structure in which the professionals hold a good deal of the power. But they do so, first individually and then in small specialist units, but not in one homogeneous collectivity. Professional organizations typically house all kinds of professionals, each with his or her own needs and interests.

Unionization, by blurring professional and sub-unit differences and by undermining *individual* control of the operating work, can seriously damage professional responsibility. It provides collective action instead, but that can never replace individual responsibility in the professional organization. Unionization can also damage another characteristic critical to the effective functioning of these organizations, a close coordination of operating and administrative efforts through the involvement of the same professionals in both. Unionization assumes a conflict of interest between these two levels. It takes a we–they attitude, which views administrators as authority figures or "bosses" instead of colleagues. The result is that unionization either drives a wedge between the operating core and the administrative structure or else drives an existing wedge in deeper.

Note that many union demands amount to standards, in the form of rules and regulations, imposed on the entire organization—not professional standards, but machinelike ones. In other words, though ostensibly imposed on behalf of the professionals, these demands serve to formalize the structure and strengthen the senior administration, which, ironically, implements the standards negotiated by the union. Thus, the direct effect of unionization is to drive whatever is left of professional bureaucracy toward machine bureaucracy, which may be precisely opposite of the reasons professionals unionized in the first place. Everyone loses in the bargain, save a few union officials and some weak members who should never have been allowed into the profession in the first place. The other professionals would have been better off to fight through the administrative system for the reinstatement of collegiality instead.

Michael D. Bayles | # The Professions

Michael D. Bayles was Professor of Philosophy at Florida State University.

...No generally accepted definition of the term *profession* exists, yet a working concept is needed for our study of professional ethics. Because the purpose of this study is to consider common ethical problems raised by and within professions, a good definition will delineate characteristics of occupations with similar ethical problems. (These characteristics may prove to be related to some of those problems in important ways.) One need not characterize professions by a set of necessary and sufficient features possessed by all professions and only by professions.[1] The variety of professions is simply too great for that approach. Rather, some features can be taken as necessary for an occupation to be a profession, and others as simply common to many professions and as raising similar ethical concerns.

Three necessary features have been singled out by almost all authors who have characterized professions. First, a rather extensive training is required to practice a profession. Lawyers now generally attend law school for three years, and in the past they underwent years of clerkship with an established lawyer. Many, if not most, professionals have advanced academic degrees, and one author has plausibly contended that at least a college baccalaureate is necessary to be a professional.[2]

Second, the training involves a significant intellectual component.[3] The training of bricklayers, barbers, and craftspeople primarily involves physical skills. Accountants, engineers, lawyers, and physicians are trained in intellectual tasks and skills. Although physical skill may be involved in, for example, surgery or dentistry, the intellectual aspect is still predominant. The intellectual component is characteristic of those professionals who primarily advise others about matters the average person does not know about or understand. Thus, providing advice rather than things is a characteristic feature of the professions.

Third, the trained ability provides an important service in society. Physicians, lawyers, teachers, accountants, engineers, and architects provide services important to the organized functioning of society—which chess experts do not. The rapid increase in the numbers of professions and professionals in the twentieth century is due to this feature. To function, technologically complex modern societies require a greater application of specialized knowledge than did the simpler societies of the past. The production and distribution of energy requires activity by many engineers. The operation of financial markets requires accountants, lawyers, and business and investment consultants. In short, professions provide important services that require extensive intellectual training.

Other features are common to most professions, although they are not necessary for professional status. Usually a process of certification or licensing exists. Lawyers are admitted to the bar and physicians receive a license to practice medicine. However, licensing is not sufficient to constitute an occupation a profession. One must be licensed to drive a car, but a driver's license does not make one a professional driver. Many professionals need not be officially licensed. College teachers are not licensed or certified, although they must usually possess an advanced university degree. Similarly, many accountants are not certified public accountants, and computer scientists are not licensed or certified.

Another feature common to professions is an organization of members.[4] All major professions have organizations that claim to represent them. These organizations are not always open to all members of a profession, and competing organizations

From *Professional Ethics* (Belmont, CA: Wadsworth Publishing Co., 1981), pp. 7–11.

sometimes exist. Some bar associations, at least in the past, did not admit all lawyers. The organizations work to advance the goals of the profession—health, justice, efficient and safe buildings, and so on—and to promote the economic well-being of their members. Indeed, one author has stated that "the ethical problem of the profession, then, is . . . to fulfill as completely as possible the primary service for which it stands while securing the legitimate economic interest of its members."[5] If this claim is even approximately correct, one must expect professional organizations to be deeply involved in securing the economic interests of their members. Nevertheless, such organizations do generally differ from trade unions, which are almost exclusively devoted to members' economic interests. One does not expect to find carpenters' or automobile workers' unions striking for well-designed and constructed buildings or automobiles, yet public school teachers do strike for smaller classes and other benefits for students, and physicians and nurses for improved conditions for patients.

A third common feature of the professional is autonomy in his or her work. . . . How far such autonomy would extend is an open question. The minimum lies perhaps in the tasks of the work itself.[6] For example, surgeons are free to use their own judgment about the details of operating procedure and lawyers to use their judgment about how to draft a contract, provided they remain within the bounds of acceptable professional practice. If professionals did not exercise their judgment in these aspects, people would have little reason to hire them. However, many professionals now work in large bureaucratic organizations in which their autonomy is limited by superiors who direct their activity and overrule their judgments. Nurses are often thought to have an equivocal status as professionals simply because their superiors can overrule their judgments about specific aspects of their work. In these cases, however, an element of autonomy remains since the professionals are expected to exercise a considerable degree of discretionary judgment within the work context. Thus, an element of autonomy is a common and partially defining feature of a profession, though it might not be a

necessary feature and the extent of such autonomy is debatable.

————————

Distinctions among kinds of professions are usually related to the kinds of activities pursued by most but not all members of the professions. An important distinction in professional ethics is between *consulting* and *scholarly* professions.[7] The consulting professions, such as law, medicine, and architecture, have traditionally practiced on a fee-for-service basis with a personal, individual relationship between client and professional. A consulting professional (or a professional in a consulting role) acts primarily in behalf of an individual client. A scholarly professional, such as a college teacher or scientific researcher, usually has either many clients at the same time (students) or no personal client (jobs assigned by superiors in a corporation). A scholarly professional usually works for a salary rather than as an entrepreneur who depends on attracting individual clients. Of course, this distinction is blurred in many cases. For example, a junior lawyer in a large law firm is more like a scientific researcher, and nurses have individual clients even though they usually work for a large organization (hospital). Among the consulting professionals are physicians, lawyers, accountants, consulting engineers, architects, dentists, psychiatrists, and psychological counselors. Other persons with tasks similar to some of the consulting professions include nurses, pharmacists, stockbrokers, the clergy, insurance brokers, social workers, and realtors. Among the scholarly professions are nonconsulting engineers, teachers, scientists, journalists, and technicians.

These differences between the roles of consulting and scholarly professionals are crucial in defining the kinds of ethical problems each confronts. The economic considerations of the consulting professional—fees, advertising, and so on—are not important problems for the professional employed by a large organization on a salary. Although consulting architects and accountants have many ethical problems in the professional–client relationship, research scientists or engineers in large organizations do not normally deal with clients. University teachers do have clients, but they typically confront them in a group and have fewer problems of confidentiality, and so forth. . . .

Three salient features of the role of the consulting professions in the United States during the last half of the twentieth century lie at the heart of the problem of their positions in a liberal society. First, they all provide an important service. Consulting engineers and architects design the structures and facilities essential and architects design the structures and facilities essential to modern life—buildings, houses, power stations, transportation systems, and so on. Most of us depend on the medical and dental professions to protect our health and well-being, even our lives. The legal profession provides services essential for justice and equality before the law. Accountants, as auditors, testify to the financial integrity of institutions and keep track of the wealth in society. The services of professionals are important for individuals to realize the values they seek in their personal lives—health, wealth, justice, comfort, and safety.

Second, not only do the professions serve basic values, they also have a monopoly over the provision of services. In many professions, one must be legally certified to practice. Laws often make it a criminal offense to practice a profession without a license. Attempting to do without professionals or to be one's own professional can realistically have only minimal success. If one decides to be one's own physician, one cannot obtain access to the most useful medicines and technology; most drugs can only be obtained legally with a prescription from a licensed physician and from another professional, a pharmacist. Although one may legally represent oneself, the legal profession has waged continuous war against allowing people access to information that would enable them to handle their own legal problems, such as divorce and probate of wills.

The monopolistic aspect of professional practices has frequently brought profession into conflict with each other and with other occupational groups over the provision of services. Architects and engineers have long debated their respective spheres of practice, as have lawyers and accountants. The legal profession has also been anxious to define the respective spheres of practice of realtors and insurance and title companies. The medical profession now confronts questions concerning the services provided by nurse practitioners and physician's assistants. A little noticed battle has concerned the practice of midwives, especially lay midwives, at home births. In many states, delivering a child is considered the practice of medicine and only licensed physicians may offer to do so.[8] In a recent California case, three lay midwives were prosecuted for the unlicensed practice of medicine, and the Supreme Court of California upheld the constitutionality of the law with respect to childbirth.[9] A woman's right of privacy, it held, does not extend to the choice of the manner and circumstances in which her baby is born.

The legal monopoly of professional services has an important implication for professional ethics. Professionals do not have a right to practice; it is a privilege conferred by the state. One must carefully distinguish between a right and a privilege in this context. A right is a sound claim that one be permitted (or assisted) to act in some manner without interference. A privilege is a permission to perform certain acts provided specified conditions are fulfilled. With a privilege, the burden is upon the person obtaining it to demonstrate that he or she has the necessary qualifications. For example, one must pass tests for the privilege of driving a car. In the case of a right, the burden is upon anyone who fails to respect it, for example, by prohibiting the publication of one's opinions. Individual professionals have only a privilege to practice; in addition, the profession as a whole is a privileged activity created by the state to further social values.

A third feature of the consulting professional's role is that although some professions have secured legally protected monopolies, none of them has been subject to much public control. Monopolies such as public utilities that provide essential services have usually been subject to strict public control as to the conditions and types of services provided. In contrast, the professions have claimed and been accorded a large degree of self-regulation. They have claimed that because of the intellectual training and judgment required for their practice, nonprofessionals are unable to properly evaluate their conduct. Thus, in addition to control over membership and the disciplining of members, the professions also control the conditions of practice (including until recently the setting of fees and the regulation of advertising). . . .

NOTES

1. Wilbert E. Moore, in *The Professions: Rules and Rules* (New York: Russell Sage Foundation, 1970), pp. 4–5, recognizes this point and offers a scale of professionalism. The definitional technique used here could be modified to a scale system by assigning points to the possession of those characteristics that are not necessary but are often found in professions. Both the scale system and that used here agree that an occupation may be a profession yet lack some features found in most professions.

2. Ibid., p. 11.

3. Professionals "profess to know better than others the nature of certain matters, and to know better than their clients what ails them or their affairs. This is the essence of the professional idea and the professional claim." Everett C. Hughes, "Professions," in *The Professions in America*, ed. Kenneth S. Lynn and the editors of *Daedalus* (Boston: Houghton Mifflin, 1965 [Beacon pbk., 1967]. p. 2). [Rpt. chap. 2, sel. 2, *EIPL*.—ED.]

4. See Moore, op. cit., pp. 9–10, and Roscoe Pound, "What is a Profession? The Rise of the Legal Profession in Antiquity," *Notre Dame Lawyer* 19 (1944): 204.

5. R. M. Maciver, "The Social Significance of Professional Ethics," in *Cases and Materials on Professional Responsibility*, 2nd ed., ed. Maynard E. Pirsig (St. Paul, MN: West, 1965), p. 48.

6. See Eliot Freidson, *Profession of Medicine: A Study of the Sociology of Applied Knowledge* (New York: Harper and Row, 1970), pp. xviii, 42, 70, 82.

7. Freidson, op. cit., pp. 70, 75, 188.

8. George J. Annas, "Childbirth and the Law: How to Work Within Old Laws, Avoid Malpractice, and Influence New Legislation in Maternity Care." In *21st Century Obstetrics Now!*. 2 vols., ed. David Stewart and Lee Stewart, (Chapel Hill, NC: NAPSAC, 1974), vol. 2, p. 588.

9. *Bowland v. Municipal Ct. for Santa Cruz City*, 18 Cal. 3d 479, 556 P. 2d 1081, 134 Cal. Rptr. 630 (1976).

Michael Davis

Professional Responsibility: Just Following the Rules?

Michael Davis is Senior Fellow at the Center for the Study of Ethics in the Professions, Illinois Institute of Technology.

INTRODUCTION[1]

My subject is a criticism of conduct which runs something like this: "That's not acting responsibly, that's just following the rules." The criticism appears as an attack on "legalism" in both business and professional ethics. . . .

Legalism (it is said) reduces professional responsibility to doing as the profession's code of ethics requires; professional responsibility, like moral responsibility generally, is more open-ended, including (among other things) certain virtues.[2] . . .

My thesis is that following "the rules," while not all there is to professional ethics, is generally enough for responsible conduct (or, at least, is so when the profession's code of ethics is reasonably well-written, as most are). Rules set the standard of professional conduct; just following those rules, in a relatively robust but not unusual sense of "following those rules," just is acting as a responsible professional.

SOME PRELIMINARIES

The attack on legalism need not be put in terms of rules. One can make it in terms of "just satisfying one's obligations [or duties]" or "just respecting others' rights." ...

Consider this brief rule of engineering ethics having its counterpart in the code of ethics of most professions: "Engineers shall perform services only in areas of their competence.[3] Sometimes engineers do not need discretion or even much technical knowledge to know that the service in question is beyond their competence. (Think of an engineer asked to do brain surgery because she has a doctorate—in engineering.) Often, however, engineers do need discretion, technical knowledge, and an understanding of the values inherent in engineering's conception of competence to decide whether a certain service is within their competence. For example, whether writing a certain computer program is within the competence of an engineer may depend in part on whether the errors she is likely to commit given her skill would create substantial risks for users or third parties. Deciding whether a risk is substantial combines technical judgments (such-and-such errors are likely) with judgements of value (the risks are, or are not, substantial).

... We are, then, in no position to decide whether her criticism of rules—or the similar criticism of others—is justified until we understand what "just following the rules" leaves out. And we are not likely to understand that until we understand what just following the rules might be.... I devote the body of this paper to considering seven different interpretations of "just following the rules," all that I have found in the literature, noticed in conversation, or made up on my own: blind obedience, strict obedience, malicious obedience, negligent obedience, accidental obedience, stupid obedience, and interpretative obedience. Having examined these seven, I conclude that, for professional ethics at least, the criticism of just following the rules is unjustified. Under all but one interpretation of "just following the rules," the rules are not in fact being followed. Under that one (the interpretative), there is nothing obviously wrong with just following the rules.

FOLLOWING RULES BLINDLY OR STRICTLY

... Rules, especially the rules of professional ethics, are more than nonsense syllables. They mean something. That meaning is not merely linguistic (like the meaning of most puns) or merely propositional (like the meaning of a scientific law). What rules generally mean, and what rules of professional ethics always mean, are acts required, allowed, or forbidden. Rules are guides to conduct (and, so, also standards for evaluating conduct). No one has learned a rule of professional ethics (in any robust sense of "learned a rule") who has not understood it as a guide to conduct, indeed, who does not have a pretty good idea how to guide her conduct by the rule. Those who learn the rules of professional ethics without understanding how they guide conduct have taken only a small step toward learning them.

We should, of course, not set the standard for learning a rule too high. We should not, for example, require perfect knowledge before we admit that someone has learned the rule. If knowing a rule meant knowing exactly what it required in every circumstance, who among us could claim to know any important rule? There must be room for occasional uncertainty, mistake, and even being totally at a loss what to do. To know a rule is not necessarily to know it perfectly.

———

... Mere rule-following is doing what the rule says without concern for context or consequence—a "mechanical" or "blind" obedience. Finding a clear example of such obedience is hard. Here is the best I have (blind obedience, though not exactly to a rule): One day, at age two, my son was having trouble opening a cabinet door because of a safety latch.

Instead of opening the door for him, I advised him to "use his head." He immediately obeyed, giving the door a hard rap with his forehead, apparently without thought to any alternative interpretation of my advice or even to past experience of banging his head against a hard surface. He has not given me such blind obedience since.

I doubt adults ever offer blind obedience. Typical examples turn out to be something more measured, what we might call "strict obedience." In strict obedience, we allow our own judgment to be short-circuited by someone else's. The military provides the most dramatic example of strict obedience (though, again, not precisely of obedience to rules). Consider these lines from Tennyson's "Charge of the Light Brigade":

"Forward, the Light Brigade!"
Was there a man dismayed?
Not though the soldier knew
    Someone had blundered.
Theirs not to make reply,
Theirs not to reason why,
Theirs but to do or die.
Into the valley of death
    Rode the six hundred.

The Light Brigade did not charge into the enemy's massed cannon with the instinctive abandon with which my son rapped his head on the cabinet door in obedience to my (misunderstood) advice. The members of the Brigade could "reason why" even if doing so was not their job. They did in fact understand what was wrong with what they had been told to do: "Someone had blundered." (The Brigade will probably be shot to pieces, without effect, well before reaching the enemy.) The Brigade's members may have been entitled to "make reply." Many armies have procedures allowing subordinates to object to an order judged ill-advised; in some armies, even the ordinary soldier has a duty to refuse an order he believes unlawful. But, unlawfulness aside, once a subordinate has questioned the order, been heard out, and been overruled, he has no right to disobey, whatever his final opinion of the order. He must put aside what he knows and do as ordered.

This putting-aside-of-what-one-knows may, in certain contexts, be rational (and so, not "blind"). The division of labor between those who are to "reason why" and those who are only to "do or die" may, taking into account the costs and probabilities of error, make the best overall use of available information. So, for example, the Light Brigade may have ridden into the valley of death because its members believed that, on the battlefield, acting on individual judgment generally does more harm than obeying orders, even orders obviously mistaken. Strict obedience, though not unthinking in the way blind obedience is, is still unthinking in a straightforward way: it ignores the individual's thinking to an unusual degree.

MALICIOUS OBEDIENCE

Sometimes the description, "I was just following the rules," occurs in defense of conduct. To have acted according to the rules, however bad the outcome and however foolish the rules, is to have acted in a way insulating one from (full) responsibility. The most common use of "just following rules" in this sense, or at least the most visible, is when employees "strike" their employer by "working to rule" or "going by the book." This form of strike is particularly satisfying to employees and maddening for the employer. The employees continue to be paid, though they are costing their employer money, time, and grief. The employer cannot complain without admitting that "the book" is wrong. For many employers, the point of having "the book" is to have a basis for disciplining employees when they fail to do as they should. So, working to rule catches the employer in his own trap. One way or another, the employer must "eat his words." Think, for example, how the police can bring traffic to a halt on a busy highway simply by ticketing every traffic violation they observe—as many police manuals require.

What does working to rule leave out? Another name for working to rule, "malicious obedience," suggests an answer. What working to rule leaves out is the good will employees otherwise give their employer. Ordinarily, employees interpret the rules to take into account the inability of general language to anticipate special cases; they try to understand what the employer is trying to achieve by laying down such rules; they use "common sense."

Working to rule resembles strict obedience. In both, there is an obvious disconnect between what a reasonable person would think should be done, all else equal, and what the person in question is doing. In both, too, there is a reason, though not the same reason, for the disconnect. The difference between strict obedience and working to rule is that, in strict obedience, the reason for the disconnect is the overall good of the enterprise; in working to rule, the reason is the exact opposite. The employee takes into account what would be good for the employer only in order to choose an interpretative strategy to defeat it.

We may distinguish a weak sense and a strong sense of malicious obedience. In the weak sense, malicious obedience is the malicious adoption of an interpretative strategy that is not itself malicious. For example, the principle "Be literal" might be adopted for reasons other than malice. But, in working to rule, it is adopted maliciously, that is, with the intent, expectation, or hope that literalness will make trouble for the employer. Malicious obedience in the strong sense carries malice one step further. Not only is the interpretative strategy adopted maliciously but what is adopted also has malice built into it, for example, "Choose the most damaging interpretation the language allows."

What do these two forms of working to rule have to do with just following a code of professional ethics? For most of these codes, the answer must be: little. The codes themselves contain rules of interpretation. Often gathered at the front under the heading "preamble," "principles," or "canons" to distinguish them from less general directives, these rules of interpretation effectively rule out malicious obedience. For example, the NSPE's "Code of Ethics for Engineers" includes at least two "Fundamental Canons" that seem to rule out malice:

Engineers, in the fulfillment of their professional duties, shall:

Hold paramount the safety, health, and welfare of the public in the performance of their professional duties.... [and]

Act in professional matters for each employer or client as faithful agents or trustees.[4]

Specific rules of practice must then be read to protect the public welfare and to serve the employer as a faithful agent or trustee. An engineer cannot simply work to rule.

But, it might be argued, engineers can still read these fundamental canons more or less maliciously. Indeed they can. The question, however, is whether a malicious interpretation of such interpretative rules can generate the damaging conduct that malicious interpretation of more specific rules can. I doubt it often can. How malicious can one be about, for example, holding the public welfare paramount in the interpretation of the rules of practice? Clearly, there is much less room for effective malice. But, even if the fundamental canons could—by themselves—be given an effectively malicious interpretation, the NSPE code has a fail-safe feature. Its preamble contains a principle for interpreting the canons: "In the practice of their profession, engineers must perform under a standard of professional behavior which requires adherence to the highest principles of ethical conduct on behalf of public, employers, and the profession."[5]

I do not claim that such general principles of interpretation make following the rules easy. On the contrary, I admit that they make following the rules hard. My point is that, as they do, they also rule out most, perhaps all, of the malicious interpretations of rules necessary for malicious obedience.

Or, to be more precise, that is *one* of my points. Malicious obedience requires a conscious misunderstanding of the rules; there can also be unconscious misunderstanding. For example, engineers have been known to argue that the rule requiring them to serve each client or employer as a faithful agent or trustee imposes a professional obligation to cut costs even when doing so endangers the public. These engineers neither reject the obligation to the public welfare nor misinterpret it. They just do not think of it as they try to do what they should. They fail to

exercise reasonable care in interpreting their professional code. If malicious obedience is a conscious
failure to exercise reasonable care in interpreting
the rules, then what we are now contemplating
is an *unconscious* failure. We must now consider
three forms of unconscious failure to just follow
the rules.

NEGLIGENT AND ACCIDENTAL OBEDIENCE

... In the common law, both American and English,
negligence is, almost by definition, a failure to exercise due care in our relations with others. In negligence law, the interesting question is *not* whether
anyone, especially a professional, should be held to
the due-care standard. Due care is the minimum standard even for a child or a madman. The interesting
question is what due care requires. ...

Any distinction between what one's profession
requires and what is merely legally required cannot
be made in terms of "due care"—or, at least, cannot
be so made without inviting confusion. A profession
does not need a code of ethics to be held to the standard of due care. The law already does that; any
malpractice suit (for negligence) will allege a failure of due care. What a code of professional ethics
does, if it does anything beyond restating existing
legal obligations, is to set a new standard of care,
one higher than existed before. That new standard
can, in virtue of the code, become what may reasonably be expected of members of the profession, since
it is reasonable to expect members of a profession
to do what they commit themselves to doing. Some
dangers that had been reasonable before would then
become unreasonable, raising the legal minimum for
members of the profession and thereby turning into
malpractice conduct previously allowed to the profession (and still allowed to others). A profession's
code of ethics helps define what care is due from
members of that profession and, in doing that, sets
the standard of malpractice for them. But, whatever
the standard, anything less than good practice is
malpractice. ...

Negligent obedience is, then, a failure to exercise due care in following the relevant rules, whether
the failure unreasonably risks harm to others or is in
some other way faulty. Negligent obedience differs
from (what we shall call) stupid obedience in that
the failure need not arise from an inability to act as
one should. Stupid obedience is a matter of competence; negligent obedience is not (or, at least, need
not be). ...

Negligent obedience is always a failure to follow
the rule; accidental obedience, while not a failure to
follow the rule, is at least a failure to follow the rule
for the right reason, that is, because one has understood it properly. Negligent failure to understand the
rule properly may arise from lack of the appropriate
virtue (such as carefulness). But it need not. Lack of
virtue is neither necessary nor sufficient for negligent
obedience.

———————

... Even a relatively careless person can (sometimes) exercise due care—though she may have to
try hard to do it. Her trying hard enough may, as
a matter of fact, arise (in part) from other virtues,
such as practical wisdom or concern for others; but,
it might also arise from less noble grounds, such as
greed or fear of punishment. Whatever the ground,
if she tries hard, she may be able to do as the rule
requires; doing that, she does not act negligently,
however lacking in the virtue of care she may be. Nor
is her obedience merely accidental; it is the ordinary
consequence of her deliberate effort.

———————

STUPID OBEDIENCE

Those who obey stupidly resemble the negligent
in unconsciously failing to exercise due care in
interpreting the relevant rules. They differ from the
negligent only in the cause of failure. Unlike the
negligent, the stupid fail because they do not know
better. The cause of not knowing better may be original, that is, a lack of native wit, or educational,

for example, never having been taught how to interpret the rule in question. In law, the most common form of stupid obedience is the layman's trying to follow a statute without considering how case law may have made the statute's simple language treacherous. In professional ethics, the most common form of stupid obedience is, I think, reading a code of ethics as if each rule were independent of the others.

The stupid have an excuse the negligent do not. They are not therefore free of blame. One can blame another for an act or for its consequences. To blame someone for an act is to declare the act bad and his; to blame him for some state of affairs is to declare the state of affairs bad and some act or omission of his the cause. To excuse someone's failure to follow a rule by saying. "He doesn't know better," does not save him from blame; it only changes the terms. Whether the change of terms even amounts to a reduction in blame is a matter of opinion; many of us might prefer to be thought malicious or negligent rather than stupid. In any case, for a professional, stupidity is as objectionable as malice.

Perhaps many of those professionals who seek to excuse themselves for misconduct with the answer, "I was just following the rules," are pleading stupidity. It is therefore worth pointing out that whenever this plea is necessary, the professional in question was not in fact following the rules (even if she was doing her best to follow them). In this respect, stupid obedience resembles the other forms of rule-following discussed so far. It is a failure to follow the rules.

INTERPRETATIVE OBEDIENCE

Except for blind obedience, all the forms of rule-following discussed so far acknowledged, however implicitly, that rules must be interpreted. In strict obedience, the interpretation is largely left to others ("higher authority"). In malicious obedience, interpretation is deliberately abused; in negligent or accidental obedience, interpretation is not given the attention it deserves; and, in stupid obedience, interpretation is not done skillfully enough, whether from

lack of wit or learning. This list of ways in which one can fall to follow the rules suggests that just following the rules is not simple....

––––––––––––––

What must we teach students in order to teach them how to follow the code of ethics of their hoped-for profession? We must, of course, teach them the context in which the code is to be applied, that is, something of the history of the profession, of the organizations in which members of the profession work, of the expectations other members of the profession will have of their colleagues, and of what members do (and the effect what they do can have on others). We must also teach something about the purpose of the rules, the structure of the code (the relation of one rule to another), the interpretative strategies considered appropriate, and the consequences of certain mistakes in interpretation. We should help students to see their profession's code of ethics as the work of human beings much like themselves, human beings who have specific purposes in developing such rules and should therefore be open to revising them, or standing interpretations of them, as new information comes in. Last, and perhaps most important, we should give practice in following the rules, that is, in analyzing specific "fact situations," applying the rules to those facts, reaching conclusions about what is required, allowed, or forbidden, making arguments in defense of the conclusions, and inventing ways to do as the rules so interpreted say. One does not know how to follow a rule unless one knows how to develop, state, defend, and carry out workable courses of action in accord with the rule in contexts in which the rule ordinarily applies.

LEFT OUT?

This (interpretative) way of understanding "just following the rules" leaves us with the question with which we began: what does just following the rules leave out? What I have argued so far is that the rules of professional ethics themselves exclude certain forms of "just following the rules" (malicious, negligent, accidental, and stupid obedience); other forms (blind and strict obedience) are not following the rules at all. Only one interpretation of just following the rules of professional ethics, the interpretative, seems robust enough to count as just following the rules (without some apologetic qualification). That interpretation seems to leave nothing important out.

My argument, even admitting its soundness, may seem to miss what underlay the objection to "*just* following the rules" with which we began, the idea (introduced by "just") of trying to get by with the minimum, a failure to make room for the "spirit" of the rules as well as the "letter." To this fundamental objection, I have two replies, one general and one particular. The general reply is that "the spirit of the rule" is a metaphor. By itself, it tells us little. My own view is that the appropriate interpretative strategy is the rule's spirit. It is what gives life to the otherwise dead letters of a rule. Those who try to follow a rule without the appropriate interpretative strategy may think of themselves as "just following the rule," but they are likely to fail to follow it. That is the lesson of negligent and stupid obedience. Those who have criticized "just following the rules," seem not to have realized how much goes into following a rule. That is not to say that virtue is not relevant to following the rules. It is, instead, to point to a particular rarely-mentioned virtue, the disposition to interpret rules correctly, as crucial to responsible professional conduct (though not defining it), to come a long way down from the airy world in which rules are hardly worth mention to one in which teaching the rules is central to developing the crucial virtue.

That is my general reply. My particular reply is a challenge to individual critics: show me a clear case of professional responsibility that is not just following the profession's code of ethics. By "clear case," I mean one that most members of the profession would agree is uncontroversial.

I feel safe making this challenge because I think the critics of legalism badly underestimate what rules can do. Rules can set high standards; set positive standards as well as negative; and provide guidance on when to make exceptions to otherwise binding rules. Rules can also require virtues such as competence and caring. There is no reason, except oversight, why a profession's code should leave out anything most members of the profession consider important.

NOTES

1. I presented versions of this paper to the Philosophy Colloquium, Illinois Institute of Technology, to the Philosophy Department, University of South Florida, at Colorado School of Mines, as the Phipps' Lecture, Davis and Elkins College, at a session of Annual Meeting of the Society for Business Ethics, and at the University of St. Francis. I should like to thank those present—as well as David Coogan—for helpful discussions.

2. See, for example, Charles E. Harris, Michael S. Pritchard, and Michael J. Rabins, *Engineering Ethics: Concepts and Cases* (Wadsworth: Belmont, 1995), 67–68: "We have suggested that professional responsibility can include virtues that go beyond fulfilling the basic duties typically found in a professional code of ethics. Virtues are normally understood to include attitudes and dispositions, not just conduct. . . . One of the attractions of restricting the idea of moral responsibility of professionals to basic duties is that this makes responsibility seem more precisely stateable and thereby more manageable. However, . . . moral responsibility is more open-ended and admits of varying degrees and stringency."

3. The seminal work in the criticism of legalism in professional ethics is John Ladd, "Legalism and Medical Ethics," *Contemporary Issues in Bioethics*, eds. John W. Davis, Barry Hoffmaster, and Sarah Shorten (Humana Press: Clifton, N. J., 1979), 1–35. Ladd there defines "legalism" much as I have: "By 'legalism' I shall mean: 'the ethical attitude that holds moral conduct to be a matter of rule-following and of moral relationships to consist of duties and rights determined by rules' " (Ladd, 4). It is odd, therefore, that Ladd in fact has little to say about legalism in that article. Most of his criticism explicitly concerns rights (rather than rules). While I agree with most, perhaps all, of his criticism of making rights central to medical (or professional) ethics, I regard "legalism" as a poor label for that criticism. Rules are a category not only larger than rights but immune to much of his criticism of rights.

The term "legalism" confuses his argument. His choice of term is nonetheless understandable: the more appropriate term, "rightism," would have been an ugly (even if helpful) neologism.

4. National Society of Professional Engineers, *Code of Professional Ethics* (1997), II.2.

5. National Society of Professional Engineers, *Code of Professional Ethics* (1997), II.2. The equivalent of the preamble for corporate codes of conduct is, of course, (often) those much maligned "value statements" and "vision statements."

| C. S. Lewis | # The Inner Ring |

C. S. Lewis was an Irish novelist, academic, and playwright. He was a professor at Cambridge University.

May I read you a few lines from Tolstoi's *War and Peace*?

When Boris entered the room, Prince Andrey was listening to an old general, wearing his decorations, who was reporting something to Prince Andrey, with an expression of soldierly servility on his purple face. "Alright. Please wait!" he said to the general, speaking in Russian with the French accent which he used when he spoke with contempt. The moment he noticed Boris he stopped listening to the general who trotted imploringly after him and begged to be heard, while Prince Andrey turned to Boris with a cheerful smile and a nod of the head. Boris now clearly understood what he had already guessed—that side by side with the system of discipline and subordination which were laid down in the Army Regulations, there existed a different and more real system—the system which compelled a tightly laced general with a purple face to wait respectfully for his turn while a mere captain like Prince Andrey chatted with a mere second lieutenant like Boris. Boris decided at once that he would be guided not by the official system but by this other unwritten system.

In the passage I have just read from Tolstoi, the young second lieutenant Boris Dubretskoi discovers that there exist in the army two different systems or hierarchies. The one is printed in some little red book and anyone can easily read it up. It also remains constant. A general is always superior to a colonel, and a colonel to a captain. The other is not printed anywhere. Nor is it even a formally organised secret society with officers and rules which you would be told after you had been admitted. You are never formally and explicitly admitted by anyone. You discover gradually, in almost indefinable ways, that it exists and that you are outside it; and then later, perhaps, that you are inside it.

There are what correspond to passwords, but they are too spontaneous and informal. A particular slang, the use of particular nicknames, an allusive manner of conversation, are the marks. But it is not so constant. It is not easy, even at a given moment, to say who is inside and who is outside. Some people are obviously in and some are obviously out, but there are always several on the borderline. And if you come back to the same Divisional Headquarters, or Brigade Headquarters, or the same regiment or even the same company, after six weeks' absence, you may find this secondary hierarchy quite altered.

There are no formal admissions or expulsions. People think they are in it after they have in fact been

From C. S. Lewis, "The Memorial Lecture," King's College, University of London, 1944.

pushed out of it, or before they have been allowed in: this provides great amusement for those who are really inside. It has no fixed name. The only certain rule is that the insiders and outsiders call it by different names. From inside it may be designated, in simple cases, by mere enumeration: it may be called "You and Tony and me." When is very secure and comparatively stable in membership it calls itself "we." When it has to be expanded to meet a particular emergency it calls itself "all the sensible people at this place." From outside, if you have dispaired of getting into it, you call it "That gang" or "they" or "So-and-so and his set" or "The Caucus" or "The Inner Ring." If you are candidate for admission you probably don't call it anything. To discuss it with the other outsiders would make you feel outside yourself. And to mention talking to the man who is inside, and who may help you if this present conversation goes well, would be madness. . . .

. . . I wonder whether you will say the same of my next step, which is this. I believe that in all men's lives at certain periods, and in many men's lives at all periods between infancy and extreme old age, one of the most dominant elements is the desire to be inside the local Ring and the terror of being left outside. This desire, in one of its forms, has indeed had ample justice done to it in literature. I mean, in the form of snobbery. Victorian fiction is full of characters who are hag-ridden by the desire to get inside that particular Ring which is, or was, called Society. But it must be clearly understood that "Society," in that sense of the word, is merely one of a hundred Rings, and snobbery therefore only one form of the longing to be inside.

People who believe themselves to be free, and indeed are free, from snobbery, and who read satires on snobbery with tranquil superiority, may be devoured by the desire in another form. It may be the very intensity of their desire to enter some quite different Ring which renders them immune from all the allurements of high life. An invitation from a duchess would be very cold comfort to a man smarting under the sense of exclusion from some artistic or communistic côterie. Poor man—it is not large, lighted rooms, or champagne, or even scandals about peers and Cabinet Ministers that he wants: it is the

sacred little attic or studio, the heads bent together, the fog of tobacco smoke, and the delicious knowledge that we—we four or five all huddled beside this stove—are the people who *know*.

I must now make a distinction. I am not going to say that the existence of Inner Rings is an Evil. It is certainly unavoidable. There must be confidential discussions: and it is not only a bad thing, it is (in itself) a good thing, that personal friendship should grow up between those who work together. And it is perhaps impossible that the official hierarchy of any organisation should coincide with its actual workings. If the wisest and most energetic people held the highest spots, it might coincide; since they often do not, there must be people in high positions who are really deadweights and people in lower positions who are more important than their rank and seniority would lead you to suppose. It is necessary: and perhaps it is not a necessary evil. But the desire which draws us into Inner Rings is another matter. A thing may be morally neutral and yet the desire for that thing may be dangerous. As Byron has said:

Sweet is a legacy, and passing sweet
The unexpected death of some old lady.

My main purpose in this address is simply to convince you that this desire is one of the great permanent mainsprings of human action. It is one of the factors which go to make up the world as we know it- this whole pell-mell of struggle, competition, confusion, graft, disappointment and advertisement, and if it is one of the permanent mainsprings then you may be quit sure of this. Unless you take measures to prevent it, this desire is going to be one of the chief motives of your life, from the first day on which you enter your profession until the day when you are too old to care. That will be the natural thing—the life that will come to you of its own accord. Any other kind of life, if you lead it, will be the result of conscious and continuous effort. If you do nothing about it, if you drift with the stream, you will in fact be an "inner ringer." I don't say you'll be a successful one; that's as may be. But whether by pining and moping outside Rings that you can never enter, or by passing triumphantly further and further in—one way or the other you will be that kind of man.

I have already made it fairly clear that I think it better for you not to be that kind of man. But you may have an open mind on the question. I will therefore suggest two reasons for thinking as I do.

It would be polite and charitable, and in view of your age reasonable too, to suppose that none of you is yet a scoundrel. On the other hand, by the mere law of averages (I am saying nothing against free will) it is almost certain that at least two or three of you before you die will have become something very like scoundrels. There must be in this room the makings of at least that number of unscrupulous, treacherous, ruthless egotists. The choice is still before you: and I hope you will not take my hard words about your possible future characters as a token of disrespect to your present characters.

And the prophecy I make is this. To nine out of ten of you the choice which could lead to scoundrelism will come, when it does come, in no very dramatic colours. Obviously bad men, obviously threatening or bribing, will almost certainly not appear. Over a drink, or a cup of coffee, disguised as triviality and sandwiched between two jokes, from the lips of a man, or woman, whom you have recently been getting to know rather better and whom you hope to know better still—just at the moment when you are most anxious not to appear crude, or naïf or a prig—the hint will come. It will be the hint of something which the public, the ignorant, romantic public, would never understand: something which even the outsiders in your own profession are apt to make a fuss about: but something, says your new friend, which "we"—and at the word "we" you try not to blush for mere pleasure—something "we always do."

And you will be drawn in, if you are drawn in, not by desire for gain or ease, but simply because at that moment, when the cup was so near your lips, you cannot bear to be thrust back again into the cold outer world. It would be so terrible to see the other man's face—that genial, confidential, delightfully sophisticated face—turn suddenly cold and contemptuous, to know that you had been tried for the Inner Ring and rejected. And then, if you are drawn in, next week it will be something a little further from the rules, and next year something further still, but all in the jolliest, friendliest spirit. It may end in a crash, a scandal, and penal servitude; it may end in millions, a peerage and giving the prizes at your old school. But you will be a scoundrel.

That is my first reason. Of all the passions, the passion for the Inner Ring is most skillful in making a man who is not yet a very bad man do very bad things.

My second reason is this. The torture allotted to the Danaids in the classical underworld, that of attempting to fill sieves with water, is the symbol not of one vice, but of all vices. It is the very mark of a perverse desire that it seeks what is not to be had. The desire to be inside the invisible line illustrates this rule. As long as you are governed by that desire you will never get what you want. You are trying to peel an onion: if you succeed there will be nothing left. Until you conquer the fear of being an outsider, an outsider you will remain.

This is surely very clear when you come to think of it. If you want to be made free of certain circle for some wholesome reason—if, say, you want to join a musical society because you really like music—then there is a possibility of satisfaction. You may find yourself playing in a quartet and you may enjoy it. But if all you want is to be in the know, your pleasure will be short lived. The circle cannot have from within the charm it had from outside. By the very act of admitting you it has lost its magic.

Once the first novelty is worn off, the members of this circle will be no more interesting than your old friends. Why should they be? You were not looking for virtue or kindness or loyalty or humour or learning or wit or any of the things that can really be enjoyed. You merely wanted to be "in." And that is a pleasure that cannot last. As soon as your new associates have been staled to you by custom, you will be looking for another Ring. The rainbow's end will still be ahead of you. The old ring will now be only the drab background for your endeavor to enter the new one.

And you will always find them hard to enter, for a reason you very well know. You yourself, once you are in, want to make it hard for the next entrant, just as those who are already in made it hard for you. Naturally. In any wholesome group of people which holds together for a good purpose, the exclusions are in a sense accidental. Three or four people who are together for the sake of some piece of work exclude others because there is work only for so many or because the others can't in fact do it. Your little musical group limits its numbers because the rooms they meet in are only so big. But your genuine Inner Ring exists for exclusion. There'd be no fun if there were no outsiders. The invisible line would have no meaning unless most people were on the wrong side of it. **Exclusion is no accident; it is the essence.**

The quest of the Inner Ring will break your hearts unless you break it. But if you break it, a surprising result will follow. If in your working hours you make the work your end, you will presently find yourself all unawares inside the only circle in your profession that really matters. You will be one of the sound craftsmen, and other sound craftsmen will know it. This group of craftsmen will by no means coincide with the Inner Ring or the Important People or the People in the Know. It will not shape that professional policy or work up that professional influence which fights for the profession as a whole against the public: nor will it lead to those periodic scandals and crises which the Inner Ring produces. But it will do those things which that profession exists to do and will in the long run be responsible for all the respect which that profession in fact enjoys and which the speeches and advertisements cannot maintain.

Joanne B. Ciulla | # What Is Good Leadership?

Joanne B. Ciulla is Professor and Coston Family Chair in Leadership and Ethics at the University of Richmond.

The moral triumphs and failures of leaders carry a greater weight and volume than those of nonleaders. In leadership we see morality and immorality magnified, which is why ethics is fundamental to our understanding of leadership. Ethics is about right and wrong and good and evil. It's about what we should do and what we should be like as human beings, members of a group or society, and in the different roles that we play in life. Leadership entails a particular kind of role and moral relationship between people. By understanding the ethics of leadership we gain a better understanding of what constitutes good leadership.

The point of studying leadership is to answer the question. What is good leadership? The point of teaching it is to develop good leaders. The use of the word *good* here has two senses: morally good and technically good (or effective). The problem with this notion of good leadership is that it is sometimes difficult to find both qualities in the same person. Some people are ethical, but not very effective; others are effective, but not very ethical. History only makes things more difficult. Historians don't write about the leader who was ethical but didn't do anything of significance. They rarely write about a general who was a very moral person but never won a battle. Most historians write about leaders who were winners or who changed history, for better or for worse. While leaders usually bring

From Joanne B. Ciulla, "What is Good Leadership?" Center for Public Leadership Working Papers, John F. Kennedy School of Government, Harvard University, Spring, 2004, pp. 116–122. (Author holds copyright.)

about change or are successful at doing something, the ethical questions waiting in the wings are: What were the leader's intentions? How did the leader go about bringing change? And was the change itself good? Leadership educators and educators in professional schools face the challenge of seamlessly teaching students to do things right and do the right thing.

OUR FASCINATION WITH PIZZAZZ

Leadership scholars have spilled a lot of ink about the effectiveness of charismatic leaders. But as Rakesh Khurana argues in his book *Searching for a Corporate Savior: The Irrational Quest for Charismatic CEOs*, the mythical belief in the powers of charismatic leaders is overestimated when it comes to their actual effect on corporate performance.[1] Our fascination with charismatic leaders blurs the line between leaders and celebrities. As we have seen in politics, it is almost impossible for a highly competent but dry and boring person to be elected. It's certainly more fun to work with charismatic leaders, and they are more interesting to study, but it's not clear that they are always more effective than leaders with less pizzazz.

American writers used to pay more attention to the moral virtues of leaders than to their personality traits. Benjamin Franklin argued that good character was necessary for success. In his autobiography he listed eleven virtues needed for success in business and in life: temperance, silence, order, resolution, sincerity, justice, moderation, cleanliness, tranquility, chastity, and humility.[2] This list does not describe the ideal political candidate or the business leaders who frequently grace the cover of *Fortune* magazine.

In the nineteenth century, William Makepeace Thayer specialized in biographies of business and political leaders. His books focused on how the moral values that leaders formed early in life contributed to their success. Thayer summed up the moral path to success this way: "Man deviseth his own way, but the Lord directeth his steps."[3] Other eighteenth- and nineteenth-century writers preached that strong moral character was the key to leadership

and wealth. By the early twentieth century the emphasis on moral character shifted to an emphasis on personality. In Dale Carnegie's 1936 classic *How to Win Friends and Influence People*, personality, not morality, was the key to success in business.[4] Until recently, this was true in the leadership research as well. Scholars were more interested in studying the personality traits of leaders than their ethics.

IT'S GREAT TO BE KING!

When you really think about it, the issue is not that leaders should be held to a *higher* moral standard, but that they should be held to the *same* standards as the rest of us. What we want and hope for are leaders who have a higher rate of success at living up to those standards than the average person. History is littered with leaders who didn't think they were subject to the same rules and standards of honesty, propriety, etc., as the rest of society. Leaders sometimes come to think that they are exceptions to the rules. It's easy to see why, given the perks and privileges that we give to leaders, whether in business, politics, or government. For example, Tyco's former CEO L. Dennis Kozlowski didn't seem to think that he should have to pay $1 million in New York State taxes on $13 million worth of art that he bought for his Fifth Avenue apartment. He simply arranged to have empty boxes and the invoices for the artwork sent to the Tyco headquarters in Exter, New Hampshire.[5] Commentators have described Kozlowski's behavior in terms of an overblown sense of entitlement or plain and simple greed. But he may have decided that he no longer had to live by the rules.

THE CHALLENGE OF CONSISTENCY

There are some areas, such as moral consistency, where leaders have to be more meticulous than ordinary people—first, because a leader's moral inconsistencies are public and more noticeable than other people's, and second, because a leader's credibility rests on some level of consistency. When leaders' actions do not match their espoused values, they lose the trust they need to be effective with various stakeholders.

Moral consistency is so important to a leader that moral *inconsistency* is the weapon of choice for character assassination. Consider the case of Tim Eyman, leader of the citizen group Permanent Offence. This group has sponsored a number of successful citizen ballot initiatives aimed at holding politicians accountable for how they spent taxpayers' dollars. In February 2002, the *Seattle Post-Intelligencer* revealed that Eyman had paid himself $45,000 of the money raised for one of his ballot initiatives. While this is not illegal, the politicians whom Eyman had often called "corrupt" seized on the issue to damage his credibility and the credibility of the causes that his organization supported. Eyman must have realized how hypocritical he looked because when confronted with the allocations, he denied that he had paid himself the money. He later confessed, saying, "I was in lie mode."[6] We generally think of hypocrites as people who express strong moral values that they do not hold and then act against them. But hypocrites are not always liars. Some really want to live up to the values they talk about, but fail to do so; either intentionally or unintentionally. This may have been Eyman's problem. Sometimes people find it difficult to live up to their own values.

MACHIA VELLIANISM AND ROBINHOODISM

We characterize effective leaders largely in terms of their ability to bring about change, for better or worse. This creates a divide between the ethics of a leader and the ethics of what the leader does. Machiavelli was disgusted by Cesare Borgia the man, but impressed by Borgia as the resolute, ferocious, and cunning prince. Borgia got the job done, but the way he did it was morally repugnant.[7] This is the classic problem of the ends justifying immoral means. Leaders don't have to be evil, greedy, or power hungry to have this moral problem. It even rears its head in charitable organizations. The fact that Robin Hood stole from the rich to give to the poor doesn't get him off the moral hook. Stealing for a good cause looks better than stealing for a bad one, but stealing is still stealing. Robinhoodism is simply Machiavellianism for nonprofits.

There are cases where leaders use appropriate means to serve the needs of some of their constituents effectively, but their beliefs are morally suspect in other areas. Trent Lott's departure as Senate majority leader offers a compelling example of this. Lott was forced to step down from his position because of insensitive racial comments that he made during a speech at the late Senator Strom Thurmond's birthday party. After the incident, some of his African American constituents were interviewed on the news. Several of them said that they would vote for Lott again, regardless of his racist beliefs, because Lott had used his power and influence in Washington to bring jobs and money to the state. In politics, the old saying "He may be a son-of-a-bitch, but he's *our* son of a bitch," captures the trade-off between ethics and effectiveness. In other words, as long as Lott accomplishes the part of the job we're interested in, we don't care about his ethics in other areas. This morally myopic view of a leader explains why people sometimes get the leaders they deserve when their "son-of-a-bitch" turns out to be a *real* son-of-a-bitch.

THE INTERSECTION OF ETHICS AND EFFECTIVENESS

The distinction between ethics and effectiveness is not always a crisp one. In certain cases being ethical *is* being effective and sometimes being effective *is* being ethical. Sometimes simply being regarded as ethical and trustworthy makes a leader effective, and at other times simply being effective makes a leader ethical. Given the limited power and resources of the secretary-general of the United Nations, it would be very difficult for someone in this position to be effective on the job if he or she did not behave ethically. In some jobs, personal integrity is a leader's sole or primary currency of power and influence. Business leaders have other sources of power that allow them to be effective, but in some situations acting ethically boosts their effectiveness. In the famous Tylenol case, manufacturer Johnson and Johnson actually increased sales of Tylenol by pulling the product off the shelves after some Tylenol had been poisoned. The leaders at Johnson and Johnson were effective at boosting sales of Tylenol *because* of the ethical way that they handled the problem.

In other cases the sheer competence of a leader has a moral effect. There were many examples of heroism in the aftermath of the terrorist attack on the World Trade Center. The most inspiring and frequently cited were the altruistic acts of rescue workers. Yet consider the case of Alan S. Weil, whose law firm, Sidley, Austin, Brown, & Wood, occupied five floors of the World Trade Center. Immediately after watching the towers fall to the ground and checking to see whether his employees got out safely, Weil got on the phone and within three hours had rented four floors of another building for his employees. By the end of the day he had arranged for an immediate delivery of eight hundred desks and three hundred computers. The next day the firm was open for business with a desk for almost every employee who wanted to work.[8] We don't know whether Mr. Weil's motives were altruistic or avaricious. Mr. Weil may have worked quickly to keep his law firm going because he didn't want to lose a day of billing, but in doing so he also filled the firm's obligations to various stakeholders. We may not like his personal reasons for acting, but in this scenario, the various stakeholders might not care because they benefited.

UNETHICAL OR STUPID?

So what can we say about leaders who do ethical things but for selfish or unethical reasons? In modernity we often separate the inner person from the outer person. John Stuart Mill saw this split between an individual's ethics and the ethics of his or her actions clearly. He said the intentions or reasons for an act tell us something about the morality of the person, but the ends of an act tell us about the morality of the action.[9] This solution doesn't really solve the ethics-and-effectiveness problem. It simply reinforces the split between the personal morality of a leader and what he or she does as a leader. If the various stakeholders knew that Weil had selfish intentions, they

would, as Mill said, think less of him but not less of his actions. This is sometimes the case in business. When a business runs a campaign to raise money for the homeless, it may be doing so to sell more of its products or improve its public image. Yet it would be harsh to say that the business shouldn't hold the charity drive and raise needed funds for the homeless. Sometimes it is unethical (and just mean spirited) to demand perfect moral intentions. Nonetheless, personally unethical leaders who do good things for their constituents are still problematic. Even though they might provide for the greatest good, once their unethical intentions are public, people can never really trust them, even if they benefit.

In some situations it is difficult to tell whether leaders are unethical or stupid. They can be incompetent in terms of their knowledge or skill or incompetent in terms of their ability to identify, solve, or prioritize moral problems. There are times when leaders get their facts wrong or think that they are acting ethically when, in fact, they are not. For example, in 2000, President Thabo Mbeki of South Africa issued a statement saying that it was not clear that HIV caused AIDS. He believed the pharmaceutical industry was just trying to scare people so that it could increase its profits.[10] Coming from the leader of a country where about one in five people tests positive for HIV, this was a shocking statement. His stance outraged public health experts and other citizens. Mbeki understood the scientific literature but chose to put political and philosophical reasons ahead of scientific knowledge. (He has since backed away from this position.) When leaders do things like this, we want to know whether they are unethical or misinformed. Mbeki was not misinformed. He knew the AIDS literature but chose to focus on work by researchers who held this minority opinion. His actions appeared unethical, but he may have thought he was taking an ethical stand; however, it was the wrong ethical stand on the wrong ethical issue. His comments demonstrated a misplaced sense of moral priorities. Political concerns about big business and the way the world sees South Africa may have led him to recklessly disregard his more pressing obligations to stop the AIDS epidemic.

In other situations leaders act with moral intentions, but because they are incompetent, the way they solve a problem creates an unethical outcome. For instance, consider the unfortunate case of the Swiss charity Christian Solidarity International. Its goal was to free an estimated 200,000 Dinka children who were enslaved in Sudan. The charity paid between $35 and $75 a head to free the enslaved children. The unintended consequence of their actions was that by creating a market for slavery, they actually encouraged it. The price of slaves and the demand for them went up. Also, some cunning Sudanese found that it paid to pretend that they were slaves; they could make money by being liberated again and again.[11] This deception made it difficult for the charity to distinguish those who really needed help from those who were faking it. Here the charity's intent and the means it used to achieve its goals were not unethical in relation to alleviating suffering in the short run: however, in the long run, the charity inadvertently created more suffering.

BLINDING MORALITY

We want leaders who possess strong moral convictions, but there are times when leaders' moral convictions are too strong and they undercut both their ethics and their effectiveness. Leaders with overzealous moral convictions can be far more dangerous than amoral or immoral leaders. Consider the recent response of the Catholic Church hierarchy to cases of sexual abuse. Many Church leaders still held the medieval view that they could play by different rules than the rest of society, in part because they were the "good guys." The sexual abuse of children is one of the most heinous crimes in our society; however, some church leaders treated it differently because it involved people who "do God's work." Overly moralistic leaders sometimes confuse working for God with being God, usually with disastrous results.

Self-righteousness can also blind leaders to the more mundane things that they need to do in order to be effective. They become so impassioned with the moral rightness of their cause that they forget what they have learned in other areas of life or fail to get the expertise they need to do their job. This is as true today as it was in the past. The story of Magellan, the first navigator to circumvent the globe, is one such case. Magellan led his three ships down the South American coast and on a 12,600-mile journey across the Pacific Ocean. When he arrived in the Philippines, he took up the Spanish cause of spreading Christianity. He began baptizing native leaders and gaining their allegiance to Spain. Magellan's religious fervor became so great that he started to think that he could perform miracles. He then took up the cause of a baptized chief in an unnecessary battle against an unbaptized chief on the island of Mactan. Magellan's seasoned marines would not join him in the battle, so he organized a ragtag group of cooks and other apprentices to fight. The battle was a disaster. Before attacking the island, Magellan failed to get information on the tides. Hence, one of the greatest navigators in the world met his demise waist deep in water, weighed down by heavy armor and unprotected by his ships, which were helplessly anchored outside the reef, too far away to provide him with cover.[12] All this because he thought mundane details and planning were not necessary when you had God on your side.

The story of Magellan shows us how even brilliant leaders can believe so much in the moral rightness of their goals that they don't listen to others or take mundane precautions to achieve their goals. This case is a dramatic way to think about the mistakes that nonprofit leaders sometimes make, such as having earnest but unqualified volunteers keep the books or assuming that when providing meals for the homeless, it is not necessary to follow standard health procedures in the kitchen. Leaders have a moral obligation to consult with experts, get their facts straight, and take care in planning. This is where ethics and effectiveness converge. The line between being incompetent and unethical is often very thin.

Professional schools are good at teaching students what they know, but they are not as good at teaching them what they don't know. Leadership requires a mixture of confidence and humility. It is about how well leaders understand the limitations of their knowledge and personal perspective.

Good leadership calls for people who are confident enough to ask for help, admit they are wrong, and invite debate and discussion. Good leadership also requires humility. Leaders are imperfect human beings who are put in jobs where the moral margin of error is much smaller because the effect of their actions on others is greater. That is why good leaders need knowledge, self-knowledge, ethics, confidence, humility, and a lot of help from people who will tell them the truth.

NOTES

1. Khurana, Rahesh. (2002). *Searching for the Corporate Savior/The Irrational Quest for Charismatic CEOs*. (Princeton): Princeton University Press.

2. Franklin, Benjamin (1964). *The Autobiography of Benjamin Franklin*, ed. Leonard W. Larabee, et al. (New Haven): Yale University Press.

3. Thayer, quoted in Huber, R. M. (1971). *The American Idea of Success* (New York): McGraw-Hill, p. 53.

4. Carnegie, Dale. (1981). *How to Win Friends and Influence People*. (New York): Pocket Books.

5. Maremont, M., & Markon, J. "Ex-Tyco Chief Evaded S1 Million in Taxes on Art, Indictment Says," *Wall Street Journal*, June 5, 2002, A1.

6. "A Watchdog Who Got Watched," *The Economist*, February 9, 2002, p. 29.

7. Prezzolini Giuseppe. (1928). Ralph Roeder (trans.) *Nicolo Machiavelli, the Florentine*. (New York): Brentanos.

8. Schwartz, J. "Up from the Ashes, One Firm Rebuilds." *New York Times*, September 16, 2001: Section 3, p. 1.

9. Mill, John Stuart (1987). "What Utilitarianism Is." Alan Ryan (ed). *Utilitarianism and Other Essays*, (New York): Penguin Books, 276–297.

10. Garrett, L. "Added Foe in AIDS War: Skeptics," Newsday, March 29, 2000: News Section, A6.

11. "A Funny Way to End the Slave trade: Slavery in Sudan," *The Economist*, February 9, 2002, p. 42.

12. Manchester, W. (1993). *A World Lit Only by Fire*. (Boston): Little, Brown.

Richard A. Wasserstrom

Lawyers as Professionals: Some Moral Issues

Richard A. Wasserstrom was Professor of Philosophy at The University of California, Santa Cruz.

In this paper I examine two moral criticisms of lawyers. . . .

The first criticism centers around the lawyer's stance toward the world at large. The accusation is that the lawyer-client relationship renders the lawyer at best systematically amoral and at worst more than occasionally immoral in his or her dealings with the rest of mankind.

The second criticism focuses upon the relationship between the lawyer and the client. Here the charge is that it is the lawyer-client relationship which is morally objectionable because it is a relationship in which the lawyer dominates and in which the lawyer typically, and perhaps inevitably, treats the client in both an impersonal and paternalistic fashion.

To a considerable degree these two criticisms of lawyers derive, I believe, from the fact that the lawyer is a professional. And to the extent to which this is the case, the more generic problems I will

From *Human Rights 5:1* (1975): 1–24.

be exploring are those of professionalism generally. But in some respects, the lawyer's situation is different from that of other professionals. The lawyer is vulnerable to some moral criticism that does not as readily or as easily attach to any other professional. . . .

. . . One central feature of the professions in general and of law in particular is that there is a special, complicated relationship between the professional and the client or patient. For each of the parties in this relationship, but especially for the professional, the behavior that is involved is, to a very significant degree, what I call role-differentiated behavior. And this is significant because it is the nature of role-differentiated behavior that it often makes it both appropriate and desirable for the person in a particular role to put to one side considerations of various sorts—and especially various moral considerations—that would otherwise be relevant if not decisive. . . .

Being a parent is, in probably every human culture, to be involved in role-differentiated behavior. In our own culture, and once again in most, if not all, human cultures, as a parent one is entitled, if not obligated, to prefer the interests of one's own children over those of children generally. That is to say, it is regarded as appropriate for a parent to allocate excessive goods to his or her own children, even though other children may have substantially more pressing and genuine needs for these same items. If one were trying to decide what the right way was to distribute assets among a group of children all of whom were strangers to oneself, the relevant moral considerations would be very different from those that would be thought to obtain once one's own children were in the picture. In the role of a parent, the claims of other children vis-à-vis one's own are, if not rendered morally irrelevant, certainly rendered less morally significant. In short, the role-differentiated character of the situation alters the relevant moral point of view enormously.

A similar situation is presented by the case of the scientist. For a number of years there has been debate and controversy within the scientific community over the question of whether scientists should participate in the development and elaboration of atomic theory, especially as those theoretical advances could then be translated into development of atomic weapons that would become a part of the arsenal of existing nation-states. The dominant view, although it was not the unanimous one, in the scientific community was that the role of the scientist was to expand the limits of human knowledge. Atomic power was a force which had previously not been utilizable by human beings. The job of the scientist was, among other things, to develop ways and means by which that could now be done. And it was simply no part of one's role as a scientist to forego inquiry, or divert one's scientific explorations because of the fact that the fruits of the investigation could be or would be put to improper, immoral, or even catastrophic uses: The moral issues concerning whether and when to develop and use nuclear weapons were to be decided by others; by citizens and statesmen; they were not the concern of the scientist *qua* scientist.

In both of these cases it is, of course, conceivable that plausible and even thoroughly convincing arguments exist for the desirability of the role-differentiated behavior and its attendant neglect of what would otherwise be morally relevant considerations. Nonetheless, it is, I believe, also the case that the burden of proof, so to speak, is always upon the proponent of the desirability of this kind of role-differentiated behavior. For in the absence of special reasons why parents ought to prefer the interests of their children over those of children in general, the moral point of view surely requires that the claims and needs of all children receive equal consideration. But we take the rightness of parental preference so for granted, that we often neglect, I think, the fact that it is anything but self-evidently morally appropriate. My own view, for example, is that careful reflection shows that the *degree* of parental preference systematically encouraged in our own culture is far too extensive to be morally justified.

All of this is significant just because to be a professional is to be enmeshed in role-differentiated behavior of precisely this sort. One's role as a doctor, psychiatrist, or lawyer alters one's moral universe in a fashion analogous to that described above. Of special significance here is the fact that the professional *qua* professional has a client or patient whose interests must be represented, attended to, or looked after by the professional. And that means that the role of the professional (like that of the parent) is to prefer in a variety of ways the interests of the client or patient over those of individuals generally.

Consider, more specifically, the role-differentiated behavior of the lawyer. Conventional wisdom has it that where the attorney-client relationship exists, the point of view of the attorney is properly different—and appreciably so—from that which would be appropriate in the absence of the attorney-client relationship. For where the attorney-client relationship exists, it is often appropriate and many times even obligatory for the attorney to do things that, all other things being equal, an ordinary person need not, and should not do. What is characteristic of this role of a lawyer is the lawyer's required indifference to a wide variety of ends and consequences that in other contexts would be of undeniable moral significance. Once a lawyer represents a client, the lawyer has a duty to make his or her expertise fully available in the realization of the end sought by the client, irrespective, for the most part, of the moral worth to which the end will be put or the character of the client who seeks to utilize it. Provided that the end sought is not illegal, the lawyer is, in essence, an amoral technician whose peculiar skills and knowledge in respect to the law are available to those with whom the relationship of client is established. The question, as I have indicated, is whether this particular and pervasive feature of professionalism is itself justifiable. At a minimum, I do not think any of the typical, simple answers will suffice.

One such answer focuses upon and generalizes from the criminal defense lawyer. For what is probably the most familiar aspect of this role-differentiated character of the lawyer's activity is that of the defense of a client charged with a crime. The received view within the profession (and to a lesser degree within the society at large) is that having once agreed to represent the client, the lawyer is under an obligation to do his or her best to defend that person at trial, irrespective, for instance, even of the lawyer's belief in the client's innocence. There are limits, of course, to what constitutes a defense: A lawyer cannot bribe or intimidate witnesses to increase the likelihood of securing an acquittal. And there are legitimate questions, in close cases, about how those limits are to be delineated. But, however these matters get resolved, it is at least clear that it is thought both appropriate and obligatory for the attorney to put on as vigorous and persuasive a defense of a client believed to be guilty as would have been mounted by the lawyer thoroughly convinced of the client's innocence. I suspect that many persons find this an attractive and admirable feature of the life of a legal professional. I know that often I do. The justifications are varied and, as I shall argue below, probably convincing.

But part of the difficulty is that the irrelevance of the guilt or innocence of an accused client by no means exhausts the altered perspective of the lawyer's conscience, even in criminal cases. For in the course of defending an accused, an attorney may have, as a part of his or her duty of representation, the obligation to invoke procedures and practices which are themselves morally objectionable and of which the lawyer in other contexts might thoroughly disapprove. And these situations, I think, are somewhat less comfortable to confront. For example, in California, the case law permits a defendant in a rape case to secure in some circumstances an order from the court requiring the complaining witness, that is the rape victim, to submit to a psychiatric examination before trial. For no other crime is such a pretrial remedy available. In no other case can the victim of a crime be required to undergo psychiatric examination at the request of the defendant on the ground that the results of the examination may help the defendant prove that the offense did not take place. I think such a rule is wrong and is reflective of the sexist bias of the law in respect to rape. I certainly do not think it right that rape victims should be singled out by the law for this kind of special pretrial treatment, and I am skeptical about the morality of any involuntary psychiatric examination of witnesses. Nonetheless, it appears to be part of the role-differentiated obligation of a lawyer for a defendant charged with rape to seek to take advantage of this particular rule of law—irrespective of the independent moral view he or she may have of the rightness or wrongness of such a rule.

Nor, it is important to point out, is this peculiar, strikingly amoral behavior limimted to the lawyer involved with the workings of the criminal law. Most clients come to lawyers to get the lawyers to help them do things that they could not easily do without the assistance provided by the lawyer's special competence. They wish, for instance, to dispose of their property in a certain way at death. They wish to contract for the purchase or sale of a house or a business. They wish to set up a corporation which will manufacture and market a new product. They wish to minimize their income taxes. And so on. In each case, they need the assistance of the professional, the lawyer, for he or she alone has the special skill which will make it possible for the client to achieve the desired result.

And in each case, the role-differentiated character of the lawyer's way of being tends to render irrelevant what would otherwise be morally relevant considerations. Suppose that a client desires to make a will disinheriting her children because they opposed the war in Vietnam. Should the lawyer refuse to draft the will because the lawyer thinks this a bad reason to disinherit one's children? Suppose a client can avoid the payment of taxes through a loophole only available to a few wealthy taxpayers. Should the lawyer refuse to tell the client of a loophole because the lawyer thinks it an unfair advantage for the rich? Suppose a client wants to start a corporation that will manufacture, distribute and promote a harmful but not illegal substance, for example, cigarettes. Should the lawyer refuse to prepare the articles of incorporation for the corporation? In each case, the accepted view within the profession is that these matters are just of no concern to the lawyer *qua* lawyer. The lawyer need not of course agree to represent the client (and that is equally true for the unpopular client accused of a heinous crime), but there is nothing wrong with representing a client whose aims and purposes are quite immoral. And having agreed to do so, the lawyer is required to provide the best possible assistance, without regard for his or her disapproval of the objective that is sought.

The lesson, on this view, is clear. The job of the lawyer, so the argument typically concludes, is not to approve or disapprove of the character of his or her client, the cause for which the client seeks the lawyer's assistance, or the avenues provided by the law to achieve that which the client wants to accomplish. The lawyer's task is, instead, to provide that competence which the client lacks and the lawyer, as professional, possesses. In this way, the lawyer as professional comes to inhabit a simplified universe which is strikingly amoral—which regards as morally irrelevant any number of factors which nonprofessional citizens might take to be important, if not decisive, in their everyday lives. And the difficulty I have with all of this is that the arguments for such a way of life seem to be not quite so convincing to me as they do to many lawyers. I am, that is, at best uncertain that it is a good thing for lawyers to be so professional—for them to embrace so completely this role-differentiated way of approaching matters.

More specifically, if it is correct that this is the perspective of lawyers in particular and professionals in general, is it right that this should be their perspective? Is it right that the lawyer should be able so easily to put to one side otherwise difficult problems with the answer: But these are not and cannot be my concern as a lawyer? What do we gain and what do we lose from having a social universe in which there are professionals such as lawyers, who, as such, inhabit a universe of the sort I have been trying to describe?

One difficulty in even thinking about all of this is that lawyers may not be very objective or detached in their attempts to work the problem through. For one feature of this simplified, intellectual world is that it is often a very comfortable one to inhabit.

To be sure, on occasion, a lawyer may find it uncomfortable to represent an extremely unpopular client. On occasion, too, a lawyer may feel ill at case invoking a rule of law or practice which he or she thinks to be an unfair or undesirable one. Nonetheless, for most lawyers, most of the time, pursuing the interests of one's clients is an attractive and satisfying way to live in part just because the moral world of the lawyer is a simpler, less complicated, and less ambiguous world than the moral world of ordinary life. There is, I think, something quite seductive about being able to turn aside so many ostensibly difficult moral dilemmas and decisions with the reply: But that is not my concern; my job as a lawyer is not to judge the rights and wrong of the client or the cause: it is to defend as best I can my client's interests. For the ethical problems that can arise within this constricted point of view are, to say the least, typically neither momentous nor terribly vexing. Role-differentiated behavior is enticing and reassuring precisely because it does constrain and delimit an otherwise often intractable and confusing moral world.

It is good, so the argument goes, that the lawyer's behavior and concomitant point of view are role-differentiated because the lawyer *qua* lawyer participates in a complex institution which functions well only if the individuals adhere to their institutional roles.

For example, when there is a conflict between individuals, or between the state and an individual, there is a well-established institutional mechanism by which to get that dispute resolved. The mechanism is the trial in which each side is represented by a lawyer whose job it is both to present his or her client's case in the most attractive, forceful light and to seek to expose the weaknesses and defects in the case of the opponent.

When an individual is charged with having committed a crime, the trial is the mechanism by which we determine in our society whether or not the person is in fact guilty. Just imagine what would happen if lawyers were to refuse, for instance, to represent persons whom they thought to be guilty. In a case where the guilt of a person seemed clear, it might turn out that some individuals would be deprived completely of the opportunity to have the system determine whether or not they are in fact guilty. The private judgment of individual lawyers would in effect be substituted for the public, institutional judgment of the judge and jury. The amorality of lawyers helps to guarantee that every criminal defendant will have his or her day in court.

In addition, of course, appearances can be deceiving. Persons who appear before trial to be clearly guilty do sometimes turn out to be innocent. Even persons who confess their guilt to their attorney occasionally turn out to have lied or to have been mistaken. The adversary system, so this argument continues, is simply a better method than any other that has been established by which to determine the legally relevant facts in any given case. It is certainly a better method than the exercise of private judgment by any particular individual. And the adversary system only works if each party to the controversy has a lawyer, a person whose institutional role it is to argue, plead and present the merits of his or her case and the demerits of the opponent's. Thus if the adversary system is to work, it is necessary that there be lawyers who will play their appropriate, professional, institutional role of representative of the client's cause.

Nor is the amorality of the institutional role of the lawyer restricted to the defense of those accused of crimes. As was indicated earlier, when the lawyer functions in his most usual role, he or she functions as a counselor, as a professional whose task it is to help people realize those objectives and ends that the law permits them to obtain and which cannot be obtained without the attorney's special competence in the law. The attorney may think it wrong to disinherit one's children because of their views about the Vietnam war, but the attorney's complaint is really with the laws of inheritance and not with his or her client. The attorney may think the tax provision an unfair, unjustifiable loophole, but once more the complaint is really with the Internal Revenue Code and not with the client who seeks to take advantage of it. And these matters, too, lie beyond the ambit of the lawyer's moral point of view as institutional counselor and facilitator. If lawyers were to substitute their own private views of what ought to be legally permissible and impermissible for those of the legislature, this would constitute a surreptitious and undesirable shift from a democracy to an oligarchy of lawyers. For given the fact that lawyers are needed to effectuate the wishes of clients, the lawyer ought to make his or her skills available to those who seek them without regard for the particular objectives of the client.

...I do believe that the amoral behavior of the *criminal* defense lawyer is justifiable. But I think that justification depends at least as much upon the special needs of an accused as upon any more general defense of a lawyer's role-differentiated behavior. As a matter of fact I think it likely that many persons such as myself have been misled by the special features of the criminal case. Because a deprivation of liberty is so serious, because the prosecutorial resources of the state are so vast, and because, perhaps, of a serious skepticism about the rightness of punishment even where wrongdoing has occurred, it is easy to accept the view that it makes sense to charge the defense counsel with the job of making the best possible case for the accused—without regard, so to speak, for the merits. This coupled with the fact that it is an adversarial proceeding succeeds, I think, in justifying the amorality of the criminal defense counsel. But this does not, however, justify a comparable perspective on the part of lawyers generally. Once we leave the peculiar situation of the criminal defense lawyer, I think it quite likely that the role-differentiated amorality of the lawyer is almost certainly excessive and at times inappropriate. That is to say, this special case to one side, I am inclined to think that we might all be better served if lawyers were to see themselves less as subject to role-differentiated behavior and more as subject to the demands of the moral point of view. In this sense it may be that we need a good deal less rather than more professionalism in our society generally and among lawyers in particular.

...First, all of the arguments that support the role-differentiated amorality of the lawyer on institutional grounds can succeed only if the enormous degree of trust and confidence in the institutions themselves is itself justified. If the institutions work well and fairly, there may be good sense to deferring important moral concerns and criticisms to another

time and place, to the level of institutional criticism and assessment. But the less certain we are entitled to be of either the rightness or the self-corrective nature of the larger institutions of which the professional is a part, the less apparent it is that we should encourage the professional to avoid direct engagement with the moral issues as they arise. And we are, today, I believe, certainly entitled to be quite skeptical both of the fairness and of the capacity for self-correction of our larger institutional mechanisms, including the legal system. To the degree to which the institutional rules and practices are unjust, unwise or undesirable, to that same degree is the case for the role-differentiated behavior of the lawyer weakened if not destroyed.

Second, it is clear that there are definite character traits that the professional such as the lawyer must take on if the system is to work. What is less clear is that they are admirable ones. Even if the role-differentiated amorality of the professional lawyer is justified by the virtues of the adversary system, this also means that the lawyer *qua* lawyer will be encouraged to be competitive rather than cooperative; aggressive rather than accommodating; ruthless rather than compassionate; and pragmatic rather than principled. This is, I think, part of the logic of the role-differentiated behavior of lawyers in particular, and to a lesser degree of professionals in general. It is surely neither accidental nor unimportant that these are the same character traits that are emphasized and valued by the capitalist ethic—and on precisely analogous grounds. Because the ideals of professionalism and capitalism are the dominant ones within our culture, it is harder than most of us suspect even to take seriously the suggestion that radically different styles of living, kinds of occupational outlooks, and types of social institutions might be possible, let alone preferable.

Third, there is a special feature of the role-differentiated behavior of the lawyer that distinguishes it from the comparable behavior of other professionals. What I have in mind can be brought out through the following question: Why is it that it seems far less plausible to talk critically about the amorality of the doctor, for instance, who treats all patients irrespective of their moral character than it does to talk critically about the comparable amorality of the lawyer? Why is it that it seems so obviously sensible, simple and right for the doctor's behavior to be narrowly and rigidly role-differentiated, that is, just to try to cure those who are ill? And why is it that at the very least it seems so complicated, uncertain, and troublesome to decide whether it is right for the lawyer's behavior to be similarly role-differentiated?

The answer, I think, is twofold. To begin with (and this I think is the less interesting point) it is, so to speak, intrinsically good to try to cure disease, but in no comparable way is it intrinsically good to try to win every lawsuit or help every client realize his or her objective. In addition (and this I take to be the truly interesting point), the lawyer's behavior is different in kind from the doctor's. The lawyer— and especially the lawyer as advocate—directly says and affirms things. The lawyer makes the case for the client. He or she tries to explain, persuade and convince others that the client's cause should prevail. The lawyer lives with and within a dilemma that is not shared by other professionals. If the lawyer actually believes everything that he or she asserts on behalf of the client, then it appears to be proper to regard the lawyer as in fact embracing and endorsing the points of view that he or she articulates. If the lawyer does not in fact believe what is argued by way of argument, if the lawyer is only playing a role, then it appears to be proper to tax the lawyer with hypocrisy and insincerity. To be sure, actors in a play take on roles and say things that the characters, not the actors, believe. But we know it is a play and that they are actors. The law courts are not, however, theaters, and the lawyers both talk about justice and they genuinely seek to persuade. The fact that the lawyer's words, thoughts, and convictions are, apparently, for sale and at the service of the client helps us, I think, to understand the peculiar hostility which is more than occasionally uniquely directed by lay persons toward lawyers. The verbal, role-differentiated behavior of the lawyer *qua* advocate puts the lawyer's integrity into question in

a way that distinguishes the lawyer from the other professionals.

Fourth, and related closely to the three points just discussed, even if on balance the role-differentiated character of the lawyer's way of thinking and acting is ultimately deemed to be justifiable within the system on systemic instrumental grounds, it still remains the case that we do pay a social price for that way of thought and action. For to become and to be a professional, such as a lawyer, is to incorporate within oneself ways of behaving and ways of thinking that shape the whole person. It is especially hard, if not impossible, because of the nature of the professions, for one's professional way of thinking not so dominate one's entire adult life.... The nature of the professions—the lengthy educational preparation, the prestige and economic rewards, and the concomitant enhanced sense of self—makes the role of professional a difficult one to shed even in those obvious situations in which that role is neither required nor appropriate. In important respects, one's professional role becomes and is one's dominant role, so that for many persons at least they become their professional being. This is at a minimum a heavy price to pay for the professions as we know them in our culture, and especially so for lawyers. Whether it is an inevitable price is, I think, an open question, largely because the problem has not begun to be fully perceived as such by the professionals in general, the legal profession in particular, or by the educational institutions that train professionals.

The role-differentiated behavior of the professional also lies at the heart of the second of the two moral issues I want to discuss, namely, the character of the interpersonal relationship that exists between the lawyer and the client. As I indicated at the outset, the charge that I want to examine here is that the relationship between the lawyer and the client is typically, if not inevitably, a morally defective one in which the client is not treated with the respect and dignity that he or she deserves.

There is the suggestion of paradox here. The discussion so far has concentrated upon defects that flow from what might be regarded as the lawyer's excessive preoccupation with and concern for the client. How then can it also be the case that the lawyer *qua* professional can at the same time be laxed with promoting and maintaining a relationship of dominance and indifference vis-à-vis his or her client? . . .

One way to begin to explore the problem is to see that one pervasive, and I think necessary, feature of the relationship between any professional and the client or patient is that it is in some sense a relationship of inequality. This relationship of inequality is intrinsic to the existence of professionalism. For the professional is, in some respects at least, always in a position of dominance vis-à-vis the client, and the client in a position of dependence vis-à-vis the professional. To be sure, the client can often decide whether or not to enter into a relationship with a professional. And often, too, the client has the power to decide whether to terminate the relationship. But the significant thing I want to focus upon is that while the relationship exists, there are important respects in which the relationship cannot be a relationship between equals and must be one in which it is the professional who is in control. As I have said, I believe this is a necessary and not merely a familiar characteristic of the relationship between professionals and those they serve. Its existence is brought about by the following features.

To begin with, there is the fact that one characteristic of professions is that the professional is the possessor of expert knowledge of a sort not readily or easily attainable by members of the community at large. Hence, in the most straightforward of all senses the client, typically, is dependent upon the professional's skill or knowledge because the client does not possess the same knowledge.

Moreover, virtually every profession has its own technical language, a private terminology which can only be fully understood by the members of the profession. The presence of such a language plays the dual role of creating and affirming the membership of the professionals within the profession and of preventing the client from fully discussing or understanding his or her concerns in the language of the profession.

These circumstances, together with others, produce the added consequence that the client is in a poor position effectively to evaluate how well or badly the professional performs. In the professions, the professional does not look primarily to the client to evaluate the professional's work. The assessment of ongoing professional competence is something that is largely a matter of self-assessment conducted by the practising professional. Where external assessment does occur, it is carried out not by clients or patients but by other members of the profession, themselves. It is significant, and surely surprising to the outsider, to discover to what degree the professions are self-regulating. They control who shall be admitted to the professions and they determine (typically only if there has been a serious complaint) whether the members of the profession are performing in a minimally satisfactory way. This leads professionals to have a powerful motive to be far more concerned with the way they are viewed by their colleagues than with the way they are viewed by their clients. This means, too, that clients will necessarily lack the power to make effective evaluations and criticisms of the way the professional is responding to the client's needs.

In addition, because the matters for which professional assistance is sought usually involve things of great personal concern to the client, it is the received wisdom within the professions that the client lacks the perspective necessary to pursue in a satisfactory way his or her own best interests, and that the client requires a detached, disinterested representative to look after his or her interests. That is to say, even if the client had the same knowledge or competence that the professional had, the client would be thought to lack the objectivity required to utilize that competency effectively on his or her own behalf.

Finally, as I have indicated, to be a professional is to have been acculturated in a certain way. It is to have satisfactorily passed through a lengthy and allegedly difficult period of study and training. It is to have done something hard. Something that not everyone can do. Almost all professions encourage this way of viewing oneself; as having joined an elect group by virtue of hard work and mastery of the mysteries of the profession. In addition, the society at large treats members of a profession as members of an elite by paying them more than most people for the work they do with their heads rather than their hands, and by according them a substantial amount of social prestige and power by virtue of their membership in a profession. It is hard, I think, if not impossible, for a person to emerge from professional training and participate in a profession without the belief that he or she is a special kind of person, both different from and somewhat better than those, nonprofessional members of the social order. It is equally hard for the other members of society not to hold an analogous view of the professionals. And these beliefs surely contribute, too, to the dominant role played by a professional in any professional–client relationship.

———————

… But the point is not that the professional is merely dominant with the relationship. Rather, it is that from the professional's point of view the client is seen and responded to more like an object than a human being, and more like a child than an adult. The professional does not, in short, treat the client like a person; the professional does not accord the client the respect that he or she deserves. And these, it is claimed, are without question genuine moral defects in any meaningful human relationship. They are, moreover, defects that are capable of being eradicated once their cause is perceived and corrective action taken. The solution, so the argument goes, is to "deprofessionalize" the professions; not do away with the professions entirely, but weaken or eliminate those features of professionalism that produce these kinds of defective, interpersonal relationships.

———————

It is … fairly easy to see how a number of the features already delineated conspire to depersonalize the client in the eyes of the lawyer *qua* professional.

To begin with, the lawyer's conception of self as a person with special competencies in a certain area naturally leads him or her to see the client in a partial way. The lawyer, *qua* professional is, of necessity, only centrally interested in that part of the client that lies within his or her special competency. And this leads any professional including the lawyer to respond to the client as an object—as a thing to be altered, corrected, or otherwise assisted by the professional rather than as a person. At best the client is viewed from the perspective of the professional not as a whole person but as a segment or aspect of a person—an interesting kidney problem, a routine marijuana possession case, or another adolescent with an identity crisis.

———————

The forces that operate to make the relationship a paternalistic one seem to be at least as powerful. If one is a member of a collection of individuals who have in common the fact that their intellects are highly trained, it is very easy to believe that one knows more than most people. If one is a member of a collection of individuals who are accorded high prestige by the society at large, it is equally easy to believe that one is better and knows better than most people. If there is, in fact, an area in which one does know things that the client doesn't know, it is extremely easy to believe that one knows generally what is best for the client. All this, too, surely holds for lawyers.

In addition there is the fact, also already noted, that the client often establishes a relationship with the lawyer because the client has a serious problem or concern which has rendered the client weak and vulnerable. This, too, surely increases the disposition to respond toward the client in a patronizing, paternalistic fashion. The client of necessity confers substantial power over his or her well-being upon the lawyer. Invested with all of this power both by the individual and the society, the lawyer *qua* professional responds to the client as though the client were an individual who needed to be looked after and controlled, and to have decisions made for him or her by the lawyer, with as little interference from the client as possible.

Now one can, I think, respond to the foregoing in a variety of ways. One could, to begin with, insist that the paternalistic and impersonal ways of behaving are the aberrant rather than the usual characteristics of the lawyer–client relationship. One could, therefore, argue that a minor adjustment in better legal education aimed at sensitizing prospective lawyers to the possibility of these abuses is all that is required to prevent them. Or, one could, to take the same tack described earlier, regard these features of the lawyer–client relationship as endemic but not as especially serious. One might have a view that, at least in moderation, relationships having these features are a very reasonable price to pay (if it is a price at all) for the very appreciable benefits of professionalism. The impersonality of a surgeon, for example, may make it easier rather than harder for him or for her to do a good job of operating successfully on a patient. The impersonality of a lawyer may make it easier rather than harder for him or for her to do a good job of representing a client. The paternalism of lawyers may be justified by the fact that they do in fact know better—at least within many areas of common concern to the parties involved—what is best for the client. And, it might even be claimed, clients want to be treated in this way.

But if these answers do not satisfy, if one believes that these are typical, if not systemic, features of the professional character of the lawyer–client relationship, and if one believes, as well, that these are morally objectionable features of that or any other relationship among persons, it does look as though one way to proceed is to "deprofessionalize" the law—to weaken, if not excise, those features of legal professionalism that tend to produce these kinds of interpersonal relationships.

The issue seems to me difficult just because I do think that there are important and distinctive competencies that are at the heart of the legal profession. If there were not, the solution would be simple. If there were no such competencies—if, that is, lawyers didn't really help people any more than (so it is sometimes claimed) therapists do—then no significant social goods would be furthered by the maintenance of the legal profession. But, as I have said, my own view is that there are special competencies and that they are valuable. This makes it harder to determine what to preserve and what to shed. The question, as I see it, is how to weaken the bad consequences of the role-differentiated lawyer–client relationship without destroying the good that lawyers do.

Without developing the claim at all adequately in terms of scope or detail. I want finally to suggest the direction this might take. Desirable change could be brought about in part by a sustained effort to simplify legal language and to make the legal processes less mysterious and more directly available to lay persons. The way the law works now, it is very hard for lay persons either to understand it or to evaluate or solve legal problems more on their own. But it is not at all clear that substantial revisions could not occur along these lines. Divorce, probate, and personal injury are only three fairly obvious areas where the lawyers' economic self-interest says a good deal more about resistance to change and simplification than does a consideration on the merits.

The more fundamental changes, though, would, I think, have to await an explicit effort to alter the ways in which lawyers are educated and acculturated to view themselves, their clients, and the relationships that ought to exist between them. It is, I believe, indicative of the state of legal education and of the profession that there has been to date extremely little self-conscious concern even with the possibility that these dimensions of the attorney-client relationship are worth examining—to say nothing of being capable of alteration. That awareness is, surely, the prerequisite to any serious assessment of the moral character of the attorney-client relationship as a relationship among adult human beings.

I do not know whether the typical lawyer–client relationship is as I have described it; nor do I know to what degree role-differentiation is the cause; nor do I even know very precisely what "deprofessionalization" would be like or whether it would on the whole be good or bad. I am convinced, however, that this, too, is a topic worth taking seriously and worth attending to more systematically than has been the case to date.

Samuel Gorovitz

Good Doctors

Samuel Gorovitz is Professor of Philosophy at Syracuse University.

... The behavior of physicians can fail to meet the expectations that patients and the public might reasonably impose on them. But ... the burdens faced by physicians are severe, the problems complex, and the expectations sometimes unreasonable. In this [essay] I will offer an account of what is involved in being a good doctor and some recommendations about how medical training could increase the likelihood that doctors will turn out that way. So the [essay] will focus on medical education. ...

———

An independent reason for attending to the training of physicians, especially to their preparation for dealing with moral issues, is that we have good reason to be concerned about the professions generally, and the medical profession can be an instructive case study for those whose concerns lie elsewhere. Whether it is a mark of increased social complexity, greater public awareness, or other causes, all our professions are having to grapple with the ethical dimensions of their professional lives. Scientists, teachers, lawyers, jurists, politicians, and others have come under the same sort of moral scrutiny that has been brought to bear more visibly on the more visible profession of medicine. To the extent that we can gain an increased understanding of what is involved in being a good doctor and what is likely to make doctors good, we will also have gained a model for the illumination of professional standards and professional training more generally. It is with this broader agenda in mind that I invite you now to consider the question, in both its senses, What makes a good doctor?

———

The objective of medical education is primarily the training of good physicians. It is not possible to provide an uncontroversial definition of the species. But I will emphasize those characteristics that are central to the concerns of this discussion. ... I then want to consider how the goal of producing such physicians can be more successfully achieved.

Primary among the characteristics that I associate with the good physician are these: The good physician

—has and maintains a high level of technical competence, including both the knowledge and the skills appropriate to his specialty;

—is unfailingly thorough and meticulous in his approach to his specialty;

—is aware of the dependence of clinical medicine on medical research and equally aware of the experimental nature of clinical medicine;

—sees patients as persons with life stories, not merely as bodies with ailments;

—sees beyond simplistic slogans about health, nature, and life to the complexity involved in selecting goals for treatment;

—has a breadth of understanding that enables transcending the parochialism of his own specialty;

—understands his own values and motivation well enough to recognize that they can be in conflict with the patient's interests;

From *Doctors' Dilemmas: Moral Conflict and Medical Care* (New York: Macmillan, 1982; reissued New York: Oxford University Press, 1985), pp. 191–224.

—is sensitive to the diversity of cultural, inter-personal, and moral considerations that can influence a patient's view of what is best, in process or outcome, in the context of medical care, and has the judgment to respect that diversity without undermining the integrity of his own moral commitments;

—has a respect for persons that shapes his interactions with patients, staff, and colleagues alike;

—has the humility to respect patient autonomy, the dedication to promote it through patient education, and the courage to override it when doing so seems justified;

—has the honesty to be truthful both with himself and with his patients about his own fallibility and that of his art; and

—has the sensitivity to recognize moral conflict where it exists, the motivation to face it where it is recognized, the understanding to consider it with intelligent reflection where it is faced, and the judgment to decide wisely following such consideration.

It is a tall order. But many physicians meet it, and more approximate to it reasonably well. The question is whether it is possible to increase the extent to which physicians on the whole are of this character.

A good physician obviously must know a great many things. Medical schools are notorious for requiring the assimilation of an enormous mass of factual material and for requiring little in the way of reflection. This is not peculiar to medical schools, of course, but is characteristic of professional training generally. As Daniel Callahan and Sissela Bok write, in their 1980 report *The Teaching of Ethics in Higher Education*:

> It is striking how few professional schools offer students an opportunity to examine the nature of their profession—its historical roots, its function in society, its sociological characteristics, and its assumptions about the political and social order. Such questions will of course arise during a professional education, but few professional schools seem to think it valuable to confront them in any systematic fashion.[1]

This phenomenon led one of my college roommates, an outrageously bright man who went on to a leading medical school, to enroll simultaneously, after one semester of medicine, in a graduate program in another discipline; this he reported doing to temper the tedium of medical education with something conceptually interesting.

It should be clear that acquiring the characteristics listed above does not, in the main, depend on the accumulation of information. Rather, they are largely dispositions to behave in certain ways—aspects of character, not merely of mind. Recall that Plato held right actions to be a matter of understanding: To know the good is to seek the good. But for Aristotle, understanding alone would not suffice: Right action flows from the will, not from the understanding alone. It was perhaps the Watergate story that most effectively brought to the public consciousness the wisdom of Aristotle's view, for the Watergate rogues were largely intelligent and highly trained professionals. As Arjay Miller (former dean of the Stanford Business School and previously head of the Ford Motor Company) put it in a newspaper interview, "It is a problem of motivation and basic human values. There are a lot of people in jail today who have passed ethics courses."[2]

No wonder, then, that there is dispute about the possibility of increasing the extent to which physicians have these characteristics. In one view it is beyond the reach of education. One hopes the admissions process will select only people of sterling character, for with those of sterling character no moral education is needed, whereas for those who lack it, nothing can be done. A second view holds that character and moral judgment are, in fact, subject to educational influence, even though they may not be wholly a matter of cognitive understanding; it then becomes incumbent upon medical schools to provide the right kinds of educational influences. And here the sides divide again, on the matter of effective pedagogy.

Aristotle saw habituation as the only effective route to moral improvement: If you would become virtuous, act as a virtuous man does until the patterns of behavior that make him virtuous become habit with you. Then you, too, will have become a man of virtue.[3] This viewpoint is defended by many medical educators. Students learn not merely what they are taught explicitly but also what they gather from the behavior of teachers who serve as role models. A kind of imprinting goes on, apart from the transactions of textbook and classroom, that determines a student's approach to people and decisions. No other method of teaching morality or character should be employed, the argument goes, because no other method works. One must instead rely on the selection processes for students and faculty, so that the students are inclined to develop the proper habits of behavior and their faculty mentors will present exemplary standards of behavior.

This view has strengths and weaknesses. Surely much learning and patterning of behavior do result from the implicit influence on us of the people we admire. The power of the faculty member as a role model is often underestimated by teachers, perhaps because it is more comfortable to concentrate on the presentation of one's discipline than to concentrate on the presentation of oneself. But it is a failure of responsibility to rely solely on this phenomenon, for various reasons. First, faculty members are selected primarily for disciplinary expertise and are not all exemplars of the good physician. Secondly, there is the obvious problem of selecting the paragons of virtue from among the panoply of behavioral types that are available as models. If one does not yet understand what virtue is, how is one to know which behavior to emulate? For Aristotle, it is a matter of parental responsibility and of legislation. The ideal state will constrain people, through its system of laws, to act in accordance with virtue until such actions become so much a matter of habit that they persist even in the absence of constraint. Only then is virtue achieved, in Aristotle's view.[4] But it is plainly impossible to write rules of specific behavior that will habituate students of medicine to the behavior of the good physician. Nor does it suffice to tell them to model themselves after those who exemplify whatever sense they have already developed of excellence in clinical behavior. Rather, there must be an interplay between the understanding that can be achieved through thinking about questions of morality and the internalization of standards that does

come from a repeated pattern of behavior. Virtue is not a purely cognitive capacity, but neither is it wholly independent of the understanding.

I once presented to a class a case that was hypothetical but based on cases that are real. At issue was the treatment of the irreversibly comatose. The patient was a young child, hopelessly ill, devoid of sentience, capable of an indeterminate life with the support of medical treatment, but threatened with a curable infection that would end the life if left untreated. This is a standard sort of class exercise in grappling with problems of medical ethics. As expected, the class debate centered on questions of the right to life, whether considerations of the quality of a life could be legitimately taken into account, why life has value, what the physician's obligations are, whether considerations of what consequences would be "for the best" should settle the matter, whether the high costs of sustaining the life had any bearing on the case, and the like. Some members of the class were uncertain about what to do, but many of them thought it was quite clear what to do. They divided, of course, into two camps—those who thought it obvious that this child's life must be preserved and those who thought that this former child, now but a vegetating relic of humanity, should be dispatched as promptly as circumstances would allow. Each group viewed the other with uncomprehending horror. We discussed the case at length, reached what common understanding we could, made as much sense as possible of the remaining conflict, and moved on.

A year later the hypothetical case came to life. A physician presented an actual case in which the circumstances of the patient were essentially the same. The discussion and debate were replayed. But then the physician arranged for us all to go into the hospital to see the patient. We discussed the case in a conference room for a while, and then the child was brought in. She was barely three, a beautiful little blond girl, sleeping deeply without concern for the tubes that linked her to the surrounding outside world. She breathed unaided, and responded to nothing. She had been in such a state for months, her condition was one of slow but inexorable decline, and no physician held out any hope for recovery.

Moments before, the debate had been spirited and positions had been emphatic. Now the class was subdued, awed almost into silence by the presence of a tragedy that shredded their arguments into irrelevance, shattered their confidence, and terrified them. With tears in their eyes they stared mutely into the face of the horrible, hopeless reality. Then, slowly, they began to challenge that reality. Couldn't this be tried, or that, they wondered. But there was no escape; the medical evidence was overwhelming. And as they gradually accepted the reality of the case they had so easily discussed when it did not confront them, there was very little certainty in the air. Those who had argued for a calculated, coldly consequentialist case for withdrawing support were struck by the obvious humanity, by the beauty, by the seeming peace of the sleeping child. One student volunteered that she would never again refer to any patient as a vegetable, that although she had argued for the withdrawal of treatment, she now had no idea what was right. But another, who had argued for continued treatment, was overcome with the hopelessness that he so reluctantly came to accept. He'd always had a respect for life, he explained, but this life was so impoverished, so limited, so searingly painful for all those around it that he was no longer certain what he would do either.

At the next class meeting the discussion revealed that a number of students, including several who had offered opinions previously, were uncertain about what should be done. And among those who were able to take a side, there were several who had switched from the position they had previously taken to the one they had previously opposed; this crossing over had occurred both ways. Yet no additional information of any substantial sort had been imparted to the class in the interim—none, that is, of the sort that can be apprehended by the intellect alone. Instead, the feelings of many students had been powerfully engaged in a way that influenced their beliefs about what ought to be done. They were then challenged to consider the extent to which this impact of feelings on their judgment was legitimate. For on one account, the best decision is most likely to emerge from a dispassionate analysis based on the relevant factors that can be abstracted from a situation

without regard to the emotionalism that can distort the judgment of those immediately involved in a case. Yet the feelings of the involved parties are among the relevant facts, and it is irrational not to give due weight to the nonrational factors that swirl around a tragic situation. So we discussed how the students' feelings arose, what effect those feelings had on their judgments, and whether their judgments were likely to be better or worse when they were thus influenced by an emotional response to a situation they had previously been able to discuss in a more detached way. I believe that the students gained an enhanced appreciation of the interplay of emotions and judgment; in any event, I gained an enhanced sense of the shallowness of discussion that is wholly detached from the emotional impact, and the attendant stresses, of the situation in question.

The phenomenon of detachment is central in medical practice, and it may in part explain some of the interpersonal failings that physicians often exhibit under close scrutiny. For physicians must do terrible things to people, and it may be a psychological necessity to maintain a certain degree of detachment from the patient when such things are being done. The clearest case is that of surgery; surgeons are notoriously more remote and aloof than the practitioners of other specialties and often strike their patients as being brusque, mechanical, calculating, or cold. But think of what they have to do! A surgeon who identifies sensitively with the patient on the operating table may be less effective for it, to the ultimate disadvantage of the patient. The apparent detachment of the surgeon may be a mechanism which, by defending the surgeon against the natural sentiments that could arise from and impede the doing of surgery, makes it possible to do it well. A certain amount of detachment is also a necessary consequence of the professionalization of the physician—of the development of a sense of identification with a peer group from which standards and conventions of behavior are derived over the course of a career. It is impossible to march to the beat of one's profession's drum without at least partially distancing oneself from other constituencies.

Yet this comes at a price. For he who usefully adopts the mechanisms of detachment cannot be expected to exhibit sensitive identification with the patient on passing through the operating room door. As Aristotle noted, the patterns of behavior we adopt shape the character we assume, and we become what we do. The physician who suffers along with each patient, however, will not likely be any more successful than the one for whom the patient is merely an object presenting a challenge to technical expertise. There is thus a tension between detachment and sensitivity that calls upon the physician to strike a balance between letting emotions run rampant and suppressing them to a point that dehumanizes the physician beyond the point of successful interpersonal interactions.

To learn to strike such a balance, one must experience a range of emotional responses to the highly charged situations that clinicians face—the repugnance of delivering a monstrosity, the elation of a dramatic intervention, the revulsion of mutilating surgery, the frustration of dealing with an uncooperative patient, the discomfort of reporting a death to a spouse, the anger and humiliation of botching a case, the satisfaction of doing a difficult procedure well, and all the rest. It does not suffice simply to learn in the classroom that such responses occur and can influence the way one makes decisions. But neither does it suffice simply to experience such responses along the way to becoming an independent practitioner, for it takes an understanding of the essence of good medical practice to develop the ability to strike the elusive balance. So, unsurprisingly, there are both cognitive and affective dimensions to learning to be a good physician, and there is a constant interplay between them. This has consequences for the way medical education should be structured.

Thinking about moral conflicts in medicine will not by itself prepare physicians to deal with them; the case of the comatose girl illustrates this point. Neither will feeling the impact of such cases by itself enhance the capacity to confront them wisely. Rather, what is required is a prolonged interplay of thinking about problems, facing them (in reality or through as realistic a simulation as possible), and then thinking about them again with others who can bring critical scrutiny to bear on the quality of that thought. At first the result is likely to be the kind of

confusion felt by the students who saw the comatose girl. But eventually a habit of response can emerge—a pattern of thinking and feeling about cases in a reflective and informed way that strikes many balances at once: between consequentialist and non-consequentialist values, between the patient's desires and the physician's medical knowledge, between the demands of the physician's moral integrity and those of the patient's values, between detachment from the patient and identification with the patient, and between the affective and cognitive factors that influence how one decides what to do. This pattern is a large part of what in the end is called clinical judgment, but it doesn't just happen. It is cultivated with greater or less success, depending on the qualities both of the student and of the educational experience that is provided.

If we assume that what makes a good physician is not merely factual knowledge and technical skill but is, beyond that, a kind of character and quality of judgment that comes only from reflection on the interplay of cognitive and affective learning, it follows that certain lines of approach to the improvement of medical education will be more promising than others. Let me consider a few.

There is nothing like being a patient to open the eyes of a physician to the perils and indignities associated with receiving medical care. Testimony to this effect is eloquently presented in the medical literature, in which physicians report on their own experiences as patients. Much the same message appears in conversations with physicians who have recovered from major illnesses, many of whom see themselves as better physicians because of the experience of life on the receiving end. Rarely does the experience provide them with technical data or other factual knowledge about medical care that was not previously known to them. Rather, what they gain is a sense of what it feels like to be a patient—to undergo the fears, confusions, angers, and hopes that even they face when cast in the patient's role.

This awareness of what it is like to be ill and to be treated—of the phenomenology of illness—is hard to come by in any indirect way. Descriptive lectures in medical school are perhaps better than nothing, but probably just barely. To be told that illness is boring, indeed, to know that fact and to bear it in mind in managing the treatment of a patient, still falls far short of having endured the long, empty hours waiting for the physician's brief and perhaps all-too-facile visit to a patient's room, after which the long, empty hours begin again. To be told that postoperative patients can become discouraged and depressed, as they impatiently wait for their strength to return to a level that allows the resumption of work, still falls far short of living with the irrational anxiety of fearing that one's career is over, while a glib physician, oozing confidence, uncomprehendingly says that there is nothing to worry about because these things always take a bit of time. And so on.

The pedagogical point should be obvious: A prerequisite for receipt of the medical degree should be having fallen victim to and survived a serious illness and its treatment! I have no doubt that medical care would be the better for it. But the proposal is unrealistic to the point of seeming whimsical. Yet we can approximate the benefits that would result with milder measures. Medical training incorporates a small bit of patient experience already. Students learn to draw blood samples by drawing them from one another, and various other relatively innocuous procedures are learned this way. The students are sometimes provided with material that is descriptive of patients' experiences, they spend some time talking with patients or hearing them talk during rounds, and some students will inevitably have been patients at one time or another. Still, many students reach the end of their formal training without having so much as spent a day in a hospital bed.

Why not require that each student spend a forty-eight-hour period in a hospital ward, in a bed, playing a patient role as a participant-observer of the full hospital day in the life of an inpatient? This could be done late in the clinical years and scheduled on the basis of availability of beds. Since it is hard to predict when vacant beds will be available in a teaching hospital, or in what wards, the students would receive their hospitalization assignments on short notice. They would be unable to tell before the last moment where they would be placed, or when, and the assignment would in all likelihood be

disruptive of their otherwise busily scheduled lives. So much the better; so much the move valid the experience. (The incremental cost to the hospital of filling otherwise empty beds would *not* be a serious barrier.)

Additional appreciation of the phenomenology of illness can be gained through the judicious use of films or videotapes, and medical schools have developed some fine materials of this sort. One of the best tells the story of, shows an interview with, and shows the treatment of a man who was badly burned, blinded, and crippled in a gas leak explosion. The man pleads to be allowed to die; he asks that treatment be terminated and he presents an articulate and reasoned defense of his position. He even seeks legal redress, but to no avail; the forces of medical intervention press on inexorably, and his treatment continues. The film provokes lively debate about the right to refuse treatment, the value of life, and related issues. But that is not the point here. Rather, it is the impact that such a film can have. It captures the attention of the viewer, who becomes drawn into it, wholly absorbed in it, and often deeply affected by it. It can prompt nausea, rage, and tears; viewers tend to to identify with the patient, to begin in a limited way to feel his frustration and despair, to share in his experience. The film has this capacity because in addition to being a documentary, it is good drama—despite its reality, it commands belief like a work of art.[5]

What gives the film its impact is its quality as art, rather than its literal veracity. This suggests a way to enhance the physician's understanding of the patient's perspective through simulated experience. For there is a rich heritage of literature that illuminates the phenomenology of illness as nothing else can short of illness itself. Yet it is rare indeed for a medical school to provide for any significant exposure to such material. One reform that would improve medical education is precisely the incorporation of the literary perspective on illness and treatment, despite its apparent remove from the day-to-day practicalities of clinical treatment or laboratory research.

Consider this passage on reactions to illness, from Hicks's *Patient Care Techniques*. (Note that this text is primarily for allied health workers; one searches in vain for any discussion of the patient's reaction to illness in such classical medical texts as *Price's Textbook of the Practice of Medicine*,[6] *Conybeare's Textbook of Medicine*,[7] or the massive fifteenth edition of the *Cecil Textbook of Medicine*.[8])

It is generally accepted that illness poses a threat to which persons respond with behavior like that associated with mourning. The process of mourning can be divided into four sequential phases: denial, anger, grief-depression, and acceptance.... It is often difficult to determine the difference between the normal range of behaviors in the phases of mourning and those behaviors which might indicate a pathological response that requires professional help. Careful attention should be given to a patient's behavior so that expert assistance can be sought to maintain mental health....

Denial is described as a defensive behavior unconsciously used by a person to cope with thoughts and feelings that he is unable to face consciously. The denial phase is considered a necessary reaction to give the patient time to absorb the emotional shock of illness and to mobilize the constructive behavior needed to cope with the condition. This is especially true in critical illness or severe disability.

In working with patients during this phase it is important to give emotional support by showing concern for them and acceptance of them as persons....

Anger or hostility is a sign that the patient can no longer completely deny his condition. This state is frequently one of the most difficult with which families and health care personnel must deal. The patient may direct his anger in many directions, such as toward those who are caring for him, toward the institution, and toward the family. He may become demanding and make frequent, and sometimes conflicting, requests.

When caring for angry patients, it is helpful to try to understand the reason for their anger. Illness interrupts a person's life—the plans for the future. The individual is afraid....

Grief-depression is the normal manifestation of a recognized loss. It is part of an increased awareness by the patient of the reality of his condition. He may be quiet and withdrawn, or may give the appearance of sadness. He may cry or may talk about past experiences when he was able to function more ably.[9]

These observations are reasonable and important. But compare the impact of Solzhenitsyn's description of Pavel Nikolayevich's (Rusanov's) first day of hospitalization, in *The Cancer Ward*:

He needed support, but instead he was being pushed down into a pit. In a matter of hours he had as good as lost all his personal status, reputation and plans for the future—and had turned into one hundred and fifty-four pounds of hot, white flesh that did not know what tomorrow would bring....

The lump of his tumor was pressing his head to one side, made it difficult for him to turn over, and was increasing in size every hour. Only here the doctors did not count the hours. All the time from lunch to supper no one had examined Rusanov and he had had no treatment. And it was with this very bait that Dr. Dontsova had lured him here—immediate treatment. Well, in that case she must be a thoroughly irresponsible and criminally negligent woman. Russnov had trusted her, and had lost valuable time in this cramped, musty, dirty ward when he might have been telephoning and flying to Moscow.

Resentment at the delay and the realization of having made a mistake, on top of the misery of his tumor, so stabbed at Pavel Nikolayevich's heart that he could not bear anything from the noise of dishes scraped by spoons, to the iron bedsteads, the rough blankets, the walls, the lights, the people. He felt that he was in a trap, and that until the next morning any decisive step was impossible.

Deeply miserable, he lay there covering his eyes from the light and from the whole scene with the towel he had brought form home.[10]

Or consider his account of the psychological impact of hospital dress:

It was the shabby gray dressing gowns of rough cotton, so untidy-looking even when perfectly clean, as well as the fact that they were about to undergo surgery, that set these women apart, deprived them of their womanliness and their feminine charm. The dressing gowns had no cut whatever. They were all enormous, so that any woman, however fat, could easily wrap one around her. The drooping sleeves looked like wide, shapeless smoke-stacks.

The men's pink and white striped jackets were much neater, but the women were never issued dresses, only those dressing gowns without buttons or buttonholes. Some of them shortened the dressing gowns, others lengthened them. They all had the same way of tightening the cotton belt to hide their nightdresses and of holding the flaps across their breasts. No woman suffering from disease and in such a drab dressing gown had a chance of gladdening anyone's eye, and they all knew it.[11]

A sympathetic understanding of the patient's perspective is necessary for the good doctor, but not sufficient. Some address to the moral dimensions of medical practice is needed as well. But what sort? There are basically four positions. The first is that there is no point to a formal consideration of ethical issues. This view can result from the belief that the diversity and confusion in ethical argumentation make complete moral skepticism the only reasonable position, so that there is nothing to discuss.... [But] this is overly pessimistic and ... enough light can be shed by a systematic inquiry into matters of morality to make the undertaking worthwhile. Opposition also arises from the belief that the behavior of physicians depends on the moral outlook they have established prior to their medical training. This, too, I see as overly pessimistic; given an initial disposition on the part of the student to take matters of morality seriously, the quality of moral judgment can be enhanced by a systematic and guided exploration of the issues.

Three remaining positions hold that the consideration of ethics should take place early, late, and throughout the curriculum. As Callahan and Bok report:

A common problem in professional schools is whether it is better, comparatively, to introduce ethics at the beginning of a professional education, or to wait until the end. The main argument for introducing it at the beginning is to alert students to the ethical problems they will encounter in other courses, and to serve notice of the importance of ethical concerns. The argument for putting it at the end of a professional education is that, by then, students will better understand the nature of their profession and its problems, and thus be in a stronger position to appreciate the moral dilemmas—something not always possible when students, at the very beginning, have yet to really discover the nature of the professional problems themselves....

A frequent comment, at both the undergraduate and especially the professional school level, is that ethics ought not to be taught in a specific course at all, but should be built into all other courses in the curriculum.[12]

Providing formal consideration of ethical issues at the start of professional training is the inoculation method. Give them a good dose at the outset, and they will be immune from moral crisis thereafter! The odd booster shot may be needed from time to time, but basic protection should be provided.

This method is unlikely to succeed. The initial dose is often small and dilute—a few guest lectures in the first-year program, a series of lunch-hour discussions, or something of the kind. More important, there is a mismatch between the methods and the goals. For there are two distinct stages of ethical sophistication [that are] often conflated. One is the heightening of moral sensitivity—making the physician aware of value assumptions, value conflicts, and perhaps different theoretical accounts of the nature and origin of values. This much may well be accomplished in a single course. But the other objective is the more crucial, and that is to go beyond a heightened awareness of ethical issues to an enhanced capacity to exercise ethical judgment. And this requires the internalization of a habit of mind that can come only through prolonged and reflective grappling with the issues. Even a large and potent single dose cannot accomplish that.

For the same reason, the single dose will fail when administered at the end of a professional program. Further, such late administration lets pass the opportunity to provide an enriched perspective for viewing the experiences to be encountered throughout a medical school career. So it may seem that the method of building ethical consideration into all the courses—what has come to be known as the pervasive method—is the method of choice. But it is even less satisfactory than the others.

What is everyone's responsibility too easily becomes no one's, and the time devoted to ethical issues in the context of other pursuits is likely to be insignificant. Worse, what consideration does occur is likely to be untutored, providing the form without the substance. One cannot expect the entire faculty of a medical school to be competent in the analysis of ethical issues—any more than one should expect them all to be competent in, say, anesthesiology. But whereas no one without qualifications in anesthesiology would consider trying to teach it, anyone can conduct a meandering discussion of some moral dilemma or other or can ruminate aloud about ethical conflicts faced and conquered. As likely as not, the result will be, at best, to increase the student's awareness of the reality of moral conflict and, at worst, to give the consideration of ethical issues a bad name.

I favor the intermittent method. Students should be sensitized to the reality and importance of ethical issues as early as possible in their medical training. And surely at the end, before they go on to residencies, there should be another systematic exploration of ethical issues, linked to the clinical experiences they will have confronted. Along the way there should be some thread of continuity—structuring and guiding the reflections that the students bring to bear on ethical matters. For the point is not to provide information, but to cultivate habits of mind and attitude. Only if the students' exposure to ethical reflection is a continuing presence in their consciousness will this result be achieved.

The details are where such proposals come to grief because of battles about who has to give up what to transform them from noble plans into operating programs. A medical school would have to go to some lengths to make such a program a reality, but some have already done it, thereby demonstrating their collective concern with the humanistic dimensions of medical practice.

Every discussion of curriculum reform comes rapidly to dispute about whether new programs should be required. Many medical schools offer courses in medical ethics and related areas as electives to interested students. However, they play little role in increasing the likelihood that the school will produce good physicians. For the students who elect them tend to be those who need them least. The chap who is most likely to become a cold medical technician will give such courses wide berth.

In a recent BBC series on the British public schools one headmaster put his position well. "Any lad worth 'is salt," he said, "will find the easy path. That's why they must be coerced into valuable experience." The point has broad applicability, for higher education generally has suffered a crisis of confidence and a failure of responsibility in the planning of educational programs. In the tumultuous period from 1964 through the mid-1970s, many long-overdue educational reforms were adopted at colleges and universities, but some excesses were embraced along the way. One of them was an over-ready acceptance of the notion that students know enough to determine not only what general course of studies they wish to pursue but what the fine structure of that pursuit should be. They do not. The faculty has no infallible insight into such matters, but it does have a broader base of judgment and a responsibility to exercise it. On the basis of that responsibility, medical schools should require a sustained consideration of the moral issues in clinical practice.

Increasingly, matters of medical practice become entangled with matters of public policy. Whenever there are issues to decide about such matters as expansion of hospital beds, the financing of medical care, or the establishment of environmental or industrial safety standards, physicians are called upon in the deliberation. Although their role may in principle be thought of as value-free, providing just the relevant technical facts, it is not possible in reality to separate the issues as sharply as that. The physician as a citizen is called upon to exercise judgment in hearings, at civic meetings, on committees, and at the ballot box, on matters that pertain to medicine and health. Yet there is typically nothing in the training of a physician to provide for an informed sense of social responsibility where such matters are concerned. This, too, needs redress in the curriculum.

I have argued against the position that the morality of medical students is wholly determined by the selections of the admissions committee. I believe that students who have the moral capacity and inclination to become good physicians are far more likely to do so if they are exposed to the kinds of influences I have been describing. Of course, some students will become good physicians, as many have before them, independently of the content of their training. And others will be interpersonal thugs no matter what they are exposed to in or after medical school. But that is no argument against reforms—no more than it is an argument against driving safely that doing so only modifies the likelihood of survival.

The extent to which students benefit from such programs along the way to becoming good doctors will depend to a great degree on who they are at the outset. So, although I reject the view that admissions decisions wholly determine the moral character of the class, I want to focus now on the importance of such decisions. There is probably no greater influence on the products of any educational institution than the raw material on which it exercises its influence—the students chosen for admission. Much of their ultimate character is already shaped, and they constitute one of the primary influences on one another. Present circumstances make medical school admissions highly competitive, and admissions decisions are often made on the basis of marginal considerations. There is a substantial literature concerning admissions policies, and medical sociologists strive to understand what sort of policies have what sorts of results. My views on the matter are not offered as the results of any study, but rather as suggestions for consideration.

Some years ago I was privy to admissions deliberations at a prestigious medical school. There were more than five thousand applications for just over one hundred seats. Most of the applications were from very good students, and perhaps the top ten percent—five hundred or so—were indistinguishably excellent. There were even two hundred applicants who already held the Ph.D. In a situation like that, an admissions committee can be very fussy. In the scramble to gain admission, the premedical student will do whatever there is a hint that admissions committees look on with favor. So if it were known that a particular school needed a new kettle-drum player for its anatomy lab band, drum sales would boom near college campuses across the land. And if an admissions committee rather favored fans of surrealistic art, campus book-stores would be stripped overnight of posters by Magritte. Because of this immense power, admissions policies must be fashioned and promulgated with great care.

Typically a candidate must have taken courses in mathematics, biology, and chemistry. But there is no requirement to have specialized in such subjects. Rather, the student may have taken a degree in linguistics, art history, philosophy, or anything else, so long as the premedical requirements are met. Yet most premedical students do major in biological or natural sciences largely because of the belief that doing so will enhance their prospects for admission. Further, they show no particular propensity to study such areas as abnormal psychology, moral philosophy, or sociology of the family, which have potential bearing on the practice of medicine. The quest for the perfect grade dominates all decisions, and the quest for breadth of learning takes a back seat.

A handful of medical schools could modify this pattern by explicitly favoring, among those with superb records in the premedical requirements, students who demonstrate an active concern with the humanistic dimensions of health care, manifested in the sustained pursuit of programs in the humanities or social sciences or in other ways. Such students do gain admission to medical school now, but increasing their number—a transformation that could be accomplished in short order—could substantially alter the intellectual climate within medical education and increase receptivity to the programs most likely to nurture the character traits that make good physicians good. No diminution of technical competence would result; selections would still be from among the technically superior. But parochialism might well diminish, and better clinical judgment could result. The experiment could be safely tried, given the strength of the admissions committees' position in the marketplace. Of course, the occasional brilliant psychopath would continue to slip through the net, but not likely any more often.

Medical schools do not have the sole responsibility for confronting issues in medical ethics. On the contrary, training in the early postgraduate years is of comparable importance, and it is gratifying to see new programs designed to help physicians learn to grapple with the moral problems they face in these early years of practice. Nor are these matters for the medical profession alone. I have argued that a good physician must develop moral sensitivity and good ethical judgment. But as I argued earlier, the moral problems in clinical practice, although they may center on what the physician does, are the proper concern of others as well. The exploration of these issues should not be limited to physicians because such issues are also the burden of the rest of us. Those who practice medicine should be good physicians, and that is too seldom the case. But good physicians should have the support of a broader community that understands the problems they face and accepts the responsibility of sharing them.

Medical science proceeds, answering old questions and replacing them with new, often harder questions, so that it becomes impossible to conceive of the enterprise's ever reaching an end. So, too, does medical ethics change and grow. Issues in medical ethics can be explored in medical training, but medical ethics cannot be taught as if it were a body of information any more than the skills of philosophical reflection can. For new problems arise to humble old conclusions, and only an appropriately reflective individual can confront them insightfully. So no amount of change in medical education or public education will solve the moral problems in medicine; at best it can merely increase the quality of thought that is brought to bear on them.

NOTES

1. Daniel Callahan and Sissela Bok, *The Teaching of Ethics in Higher Education* (Hastings-on-Hudson, NY: Hastings Center, 1980), p. 37.

2. Arjay Miller, quoted in Edward B. Fiske, "Ethics Courses Now Attracting More U.S. College Students," *New York Times* (February 20, 1978).

3. Aristotle, *Nichomachean Ethics*, Bk. II, many translations.

4. Ibid.

5. The videotape "Please Let Me Die" was developed by Dr. Robert White of the University of Texas Medical Branch at Galveston (1974).

6. Ronald B. Scott, ed. *Price's Textbook of the Practice of Medicine* (New York: Oxford University Press, 1978).

7. W. N. Mann, *Conybeare's Textbook of Medicine*, 16th ed. (New York: Churchill, 1975).

8. Paul B. Berson et al., *Cecil Textbook of Medicine*, 2 vols., 15th ed. (Philadelphia: Saunders, 1979).

9. Dorothy J. Hicks, *Patient Care Techniques* (Indianapolis, IN: Bobbs-Merrill, 1975), pp. 12–13.

10. Alexander Solzhenitsyn, *The Cancer Ward*, trans. Nicholas Bethell and David Berg (New York: Farrar, Straus and Giroux, 1969), pp. 11, 15.

11. Ibid., p. 42.

12. Callahan and Bok, *The Teaching of Ethics in Higher Education*, p. 74.

CASES

CASE 1.1
Professionalism and Nursing

Diane MacIntyre has two years of experience as a staff nurse on a general medical floor that serves many diabetic and stroke patients. As a team leader, she both gives direct patient care and plans basic

Case adapted from Martin Benjamin and Joy Curtis, *Ethics in Nursing* (New York: Oxford University Press, 1981), p. 122.

care for other nursing personnel to carry out. In the past, when she worked extra hours at home or in the hospital library writing procedures, the other nurses (especially another team leader, Arlene Estes, who is a single parent with three children) have said that Diane (who is single and has no children) was foolish to work without pay. During the last few months Diane's attendance at weekly meetings of a multidisciplinary team—composed of professionals from physical therapy, occupational therapy, and social services who are active in rehabilitation efforts on her floor—has strained her relationships with some nursing coworkers. According to Diane, "These other nurses think I'm crazy to come in on my own time. I go to practically every weekly meeting, which take place mainly on my days off. I get a lot of positive reinforcement from being with that group of people, and I think they have a little better impression of professionalism in nursing because of my participation."

Diane's decision to participate with the multidisciplinary team stems from her desire to get more out of her job than just a paycheck. She wants to show that "nursing is an important profession and that nurses have more to contribute than passing meds and giving baths." Despite her justification for working extra hours, Diane, nevertheless, feels hurt by the other nurses' reactions, especially those of her friend, Arlene, whose skills and integrity she has always admired.

Diane and Arlene have lunch one day with Peggy Sayre, a nurse from a different unit, and the topic of Diane's extra hours comes up. Peggy asks them both to explain their views. Diane defends her coming in on her day off by pointing out that her involvement with the interdisciplinary team and working on hospital procedures will lead to better care for a larger number of clients. But Arlene argues that Diane's functioning as a "super nurse" puts those who have other responsibilities in a bad light. What is more, she argues, Diane's doing this sort of thing without pay simply increases the expectation that nurses (who are always in danger of being disadvantaged by the "compassion trap") will work overtime without pay. But such work, Arlene argues, is unfair to staff nurses, who are paid an hourly wage. Working overtime without pay, she argues, amounts to being paid less than one's contract provides and is unfair. Arlene finishes defending her position by arguing that nurses like Diane actually hold nurses down by contributing to exploitation rather than helping to raise nursing to the status of a profession because professionals like physicians and lawyers get paid (and paid well) for their professional work.

Questions

1. In taking the position she does, has Arlene in any way failed to understand the proper role of altruism in professionalism in general and in nursing in particular? Why or why not?

2. Is Arlene's position fully coherent with the provisions of the American Nurses' Association Code for Nurses? Why or why not? (See appendix I, sample code 3, *EIPL*.)

3. Arlene suggests that the fact staff nurses get paid an hourly wage is relevant to deciding whether what Diane is doing is a fair treatment of a nurse by the hospital administration. Is this correct? Explain the reasons for your answer. Is it unfair for nurses who must consistently work ten or fifteen minutes extra each day not to be paid for that time? Why or why not?

4. Is Arlene correct in believing that activities, such as Diane's coming in on her day off and taking work home, holds nurses down? Why or why not?

5. Since Diane's work with the team seems to depend on the willingness of a nurse to work extra time without pay, does Diane jeopardize the positive gains of her work by not pressing for a paid, regular, institutionalized position to ensure that the work is carried on if she should move to another position? Why or why not?

CASE 1.2
Less Heat, More Light
Nick Denton

State of the Union: My next company will be different. No more late nights. No more monomaniac workaholics. Less heat, more light. Call it the 80% company.

My first job over here was with a company of 120%-ers. It said so on the web site, without further explanation, as if it were self-evident that employees of a successful startup would work more than humanly possible.

"Are you a 120%-er?" I was asked in my interview. Intoxicated with stories of kids with sleeping bags under their desks and a mission to change the world, I answered unhesitatingly: yes, totally. Just as I later put aside my awkward English reserve and joined in on the high-five celebratory greeting when the incompetent programmers produced another line of code.

That particular company went bankrupt; the frenetic activity of the dot.com years has produced about a dozen lasting companies and a generation of burned-out cynics. They will never again believe that a business can be built on enthusiasm—and venture capital—alone.

And this is why I intend my next company to be different. No more late nights. No more monomaniac workaholics. Less heat, more light. If I keep my nerve, I'm going to institute a four-day week as the norm. Call it the 80% company.

It is a controversial notion, particularly in the U.S., where people work longer hours than anywhere else in the developed world. In Silicon Valley, the connection between success and long hours is so much assumed that venture capitalists are said to make investment decisions, in part, on the number of cars at night in a company's parking lot.

I could say that I have come to that conclusion from a study of international productivity statistics.

The International Labour Organization points to labour productivity growth—that is, productivity growth allowing for the impact of capital spending.

In the 1980s and 1990s, as U.S. workers put in longer and longer hours—1,966 per annum compared with 1,560 in Germany—labour productivity rose much more rapidly in western Europe. This

From Nick Denton, Less Heat, More Light: No More Workaholics, "State of the Union," *Management Today*, Haymarket Business Publications January 4, 2002. © Copyright 2002 Haymarket Business Publications Ltd. *Reprinted with permission.*

is despite the fact that annual working hours have been going up in the U.S., while they've been on the decline or remained steady in Germany, France and other western European countries.

One could draw conclusions from France's Loi Aubrey, which legislated for a 35-hour week. France outstrips the U.S. in output per man-hour. When workers in the UK had to work three days a week in the 1970s to save power, production dropped only marginally.

But I've dug out these statistics only to justify a gut feeling: that part-timers are simply more effective, and just plain nicer to have around.

At Moreover Technologies, we employed a marketing writer called Eric who did not really want the job. He was, and is, a novelist, but reluctantly supplements his income with part-time commercial work. Open about his lack of commitment, Eric would achieve more in three days than others in a week, and with much less fuss.

Generalizing a little, part-timers are better employees first of all because they are more disciplined. It is an item of faith among part-timers with young children that they are more efficient than their full-time (usually male) counterparts, because they can't procrastinate. They simply have to get everything done by 5.30 p.m. in order to relieve the child care.

Second, part-timers focus on the job rather than their own psychological needs. Someone who writes a novel out of hours—or looks after children, or scales cliffs on Fridays—is less likely to have a mental breakdown over the company's decision to target larger corporate customers.

Third, part-timers are more loyal. It is so hard in corporate America to find a part-time job with real status that no-one can easily afford to leave. Once an employee has tasted the delights of another 52 days off each year, they will not want to go back to the U.S. norm: most working Americans get less than three weeks of paid vacation each year.

It is true, that part-timers lack single-minded drive. To which I would counter: yes, thank God. The creative and driven individuals who populated the management of most dot.coms spent far too much of their time arguing strategy, concluding meaningless deals and politicking. Give me someone who is in it for the wage cheque, any day.

There is just one problem with hiring part-timers. The obsessive full-timers. They dislike the idea that someone else has a life outside work; they complain about absent part-time colleagues; and, above all, they resent reporting to someone who puts in fewer hours. That means, in practice, that it is difficult to put part-timers into management positions, even though they often have the right, calm and organized temperament.

So my solution: employ only 80%-ers. Close down on Fridays. That way an employer can hire people with a life outside work, and give them a career path. Yes, you too can become a CEO one day. An 80% CEO, that is.

Questions

1. What is the difference between a workaholic and someone who works hard?

2. Do you think that reducing the workweek or hiring more part-time workers will improve people's lives and make the workplace more productive?

3. What is the relationship between the meaning of work and moral behavior in the workplace?

CASE 1.3
The Professional Engineer
Michael C. Loui

Characteristics of engineers

- Technical competence: creativity, innovation, intellect, intelligent, resourcefulness, techniques, solve problems, education in math and science, complete tasks, scientific knowledge, technical knowledge, knowledgeable.
- Work ethic: conscientious, dedicated, determination, diligent, efficiency, patience, persistence, hard work, thorough, do the best job possible.
- Accuracy and precision: concerned with details, no tolerance for errors or mistakes, attention to detail, meticulous, careful.
- Communication and team-work: leadership, collaborate, cooperate, present ideas clearly, work well with others, friendliness, relations between people, diplomacy, social skills.
- Confidence and courage: stand up for ideas, brave, pride, independence.
- Moral standards: accountable, beyond reproach, candor, character, conduct, honest, honesty, impartiality, integrity, loyal, morals, respect, sense of right and wrong, tolerance, truthful, trustworthy, values.

Responsibilities of engineers

- Safety: should not harm the general public, public safety, protect the public.
- Social responsibility: welfare of the public, responsibility to the community, understand impact of solution on the community, decisions for the public good, social conscience, social awareness, improve society, betterment of society, serve the public interest.

Sources of understandings

- Relatives and co-workers: father, mother, parent, uncle, friend, peer, supervisor, manager, boss, engineers.
- Academics: course, professor.

Criteria for determining a professional engineer

- Internal qualities: can solve a difficult problem, embody these characteristics and qualities.
- External approval: recognized for expertise, consulted for advice, projects assigned to me, others see me, respect of peers.

Questions

1. Do any of the characteristics of engineers conflict with each other?
2. How does the list of engineering characteristics support the list of engineering responsibilities?
3. Can you think of other virtues of engineers?
4. What might be a list of ten vices of engineers?

From "Ethics and the Development of Professional Identities of Engineering Students," *Journal of Engineering* 94.4 (October 2005): 383.

2

How to Be Ethical

Introduction

In the course of an average weekday, working professionals are likely to encounter a wide range of ethical issues. In many cases, the choices demanded in these situations may seem trivial, with the correct answer ready at hand. Should I deliberately mislead a client about the need or benefits of a product for my own financial gain? Should I embezzle money from my employer so that I may buy a new car? Should I fabricate billable hours to a client to generate greater profits for my firm? When asked, most professionals are likely to insist that the answer to these ethical questions is a resounding No. It is wrong, in each and every case, to engage in deceptive practices that cause harm to those who have placed their trust in a given professional.

But if I were to ask you why such acts are wrong, what answer would you give? Why is it wrong to lie, to cheat, and to steal? What argument might you give to someone who suggested that, in some of these cases, it might not be so bad after all? When you encounter a real ethical challenge in the workplace, where do you turn for a critical assessment and moral insight?

For some, the answer may simply be that this is the way I was raised. These were the moral values I learned from my parents, in my church, through my teachers, and with my friends. It is wrong to steal because stealing is wrong. Answered in this way, it may seem to be so basic that no further justification can be given. But these questions are not so easily answered. Oftentimes, appeals to one's personal beliefs or religious traditions prove inadequate. In these situations, when one encounters competing ethical obligations and diverse systems of moral appraisal, professionals must begin to ponder the question, "How to be ethical?"

This chapter provides an overview of major theories and principles in moral philosophy. Underlying each piece rests a central concern: how are we to understand moral behavior? For some, like Aristotle, morality is best understood in terms of character traits. What character traits, or virtues, are essential to living a moral life? For Aristotle, we are able to identify the character traits that should govern our actions only by first identifying the ultimate goal, or end, of human existence. That goal, or *telos*, Aristotle claims, is to achieve happiness (*eudaimonia*). Virtues consist of a set of specific behavioral traits that effectively propel us in the direction of happiness. Vices are behavioral traits that tend to lead us away from happiness. Aristotle provides a theoretical foundation for virtue theory. Robert Solomon provides examples of how virtue theory may inform professional practice.

From Hobbes, we are introduced to an amoral world in the original state of nature. According to Hobbes, in the state of nature, there are no moral restrictions. Everyone is entitled to everything, including the possessions of others. It is only due to the brutish existence to which we would be exposed in a state of nature that we ultimately opt to form a social contract, agreeing to be bound by certain moral constraints that ultimately work to our advantage. Are morals merely a matter of social convention? Apart from a tacit contract with others, would there be no true sense of what is morally right or wrong?

Another theoretical approach to moral reasoning, Utilitarianism, shares some similarities with virtue theory in that it has a teleological focus (emphasizing the ends of human action) and identifies happiness as the ultimate aim of the moral life. It differs, however, significantly from virtue theory in that instead of focusing on internal character traits, it focuses on specific actions and their consequences. Jeremy Bentham, one of the chief architects of Utilitarian thought, believed the happiness with which we are to be concerned can be readily understood in terms of pleasures and pains. According to Bentham, "nature has placed mankind under the governance of two sovereign masters, pain and pleasure. It is for them alone to point out what we ought to do, as well as to determine what we shall do." Acts are right, according to Utilitarianism, if they tend to promote happiness, wrong if they diminish happiness and increase pain.

On the one hand, Utilitarianism seems to have identified something central to our moral beliefs, that pleasure is a good and pain is a bad. In fact, it would be difficult for us to imagine meaningful conversations about the moral life were it not for the capacity to experience pleasure and pain. If you could lie, steal, cheat, maim, and kill, all without causing anyone pain, we probably wouldn't consider such behaviors morally wrong. So, it seems clear that pain and pleasure are connected to our understanding of the moral life. On the other hand, the fact that something may cause considerable happiness for some, even the majority, does not necessarily make the action morally praiseworthy.

In this chapter, John Stuart Mill develops his version of Utilitarian theory. Like Bentham, Mill acknowledges that pain and pleasure provide the foundation for moral appraisal. However Mill goes further than Bentham to distinguish between competing types of pleasures. According to Mill some pleasures are more valuable than others. Intellectual pleasures, for example, are rated as inherently more valuable than mere sensual pleasures. So, in calculating the moral appropriateness of a given course of action, one must consider not only whether the action tends to promote happiness, but the type of happiness being promoted.

Providing an alternative to Utilitarian thought, Immanuel Kant offers a Deontological perspective on moral reasoning. Deontology stems from the Greek root referring to duties. Deontological theories are not concerned with the consequences of one's actions, as we find in Utilitarianism, but rather on what one's moral duty is independent of such concerns. Kant rightly acknowledges that pleasure and pain can, at times, be a poor guide for moral behavior. In some situations, doing the right thing may cause considerable pain. Does one, for example, have a duty to "blow the whistle" on inappropriate behavior when it may cost jobs for a lot of innocent people? According to Kant, when evaluating such questions we should turn not to our sensual capacities for pleasure and pain but, rather, toward our capacity to reason. Harris then explores the relationship between professional codes and Kantian ethics.

As you read through these selections, consider how you might apply them to ethical situations you have encountered. What are the strengths and weaknesses of each system? Do you find you actions reflecting one or more of these moral systems?

Aristotle	# On the Good Life

Aristotle was one of the two greatest Greek philosophers of ancient times. His ethics is devoted to an examination of happiness (*eudaimonia*) and the good life.

Each man judges well the things he knows, and of these he is a good judge. And so the man who has been educated in a subject is a good judge of that subject, and the man who has received an all-round education is a good judge in general. Hence a young man is not a proper hearer of lectures on political science; for he is inexperienced in the actions that occur in life, but its discussions start from these and are about these; and further, since he tends to follow his passions, his study will be vain and unprofitable, because the end aimed at is not knowledge but action. And it makes no difference whether he is young in years or youthful in character; the defect does not depend on time, but on his living, and pursuing each successive object, as passion directs. For to such persons, as to the incontinent, knowledge brings no profit; but to those who desire and act in accordance with a rational principle knowledge about such matters will be of great benefit.

These remarks about the student, the sort of treatment to be expected, and the purpose of the inquiry, may be taken as our preface.

What is the highest of all goods achievable by action [as opposed to mere good fortune and those achievable by pure thought and contemplation]?

Verbally, there is very general agreement; for both the general run of men and people of superior refinement say that it is happiness, and identify living well and doing well with being happy; but with regard to what happiness is they differ, and the many do not give the same account as the wise. For the former think it is some plain and obvious thing, like pleasure wealth, or honour; they differ, however, from one another—and often even the same man identifies it with different things, with health when he is ill, with wealth when he is poor, but, conscious of their ignorance, they admire those who proclaim some great ideal that is above their comprehension.

To judge from the lives that men lead, most men, and men of the most vulgar type, seem (not without some ground) to identify the good, or happiness, with pleasure; which is the reason why they love the life of enjoyment. For there are, we may say, three prominent types of life—that just mentioned, the political, and thirdly the contemplative life. Now the mass of mankind are evidently quite slavish in their tastes, preferring a life suitable to beasts, but they get some ground for their view from the fact that many of those in high places share the tastes of Sardanapallus. A consideration of the prominent types of life shows that people of superior refinement and of active disposition identify happiness with honour; for this is, roughly speaking, the end of the political life. But it seems too superficial to be what we are looking for, since it is thought to depend

From the *Nicomachean Ethics* (translated by W. D. Ross, Oxford University Press, 1915).

on those who bestow honour rather than on him who receives it, but the good we divine to be something proper to a man and not easily taken from him. Further, men seem to pursue honour in order that they may be assured of their goodness; at least it is by men of practical wisdom that they seek to be honoured, and among those who know them, and on the ground of their virtue; clearly, then according to them, at any rate, virtue is better. And perhaps one might even suppose this to be, rather than honour, the end of the political life. But even this appears somewhat incomplete; for possession of virtue seems actually compatible with being asleep, or with lifelong inactivity, and, further, with the greatest sufferings and misfortunes; but a man who was living so no one would call happy, unless he were maintaining a thesis at all costs. But enough of this; for the subject has been sufficiently treated even in the current discussions. Third comes the contemplative life, which we shall consider later.

The life of money-making is one undertaken under compulsion, and wealth is evidently not the good we are seeking; for it is merely useful and for the sake of something else. And so one might rather take the aforenamed objects to be ends; for they are loved for themselves. But it is evident that not even these are ends; yet many arguments have been thrown away in support of them.

The function of man is an activity of the soul which follows or implies a rational principle, and the function of a good man is the good and noble performance of these in accordance with the appropriate virtue or excellence, so the good for man turns out to be an activity of soul in accordance with virtue, and if there are more than one virtue, in accordance with the best and most complete. But we should add, "in a complete life." For one swallow does not make a summer, nor one day; and so too one day, or a short time, does not make a man blessed or happy.

So the argument has reached this point; Since there are evidently more than one end, and we choose some of these (e.g. wealth, flutes, and in general instruments) for the sake of something else, clearly not all ends are final ends: but the chief good is evidently something final. Therefore, if there is only one final end, this will be what we are seeking, and if there are more than one, the most final of these will be what we are seeking. Now we call that which is in itself worthy of pursuit more final than that which is worthy of pursuit for the sake of something else, and that which is never desirable for the sake of something else more final than the things that are desirable both in themselves and for the sake of that other thing, and therefore we call final without qualification that which is always desirable in itself and never for the sake of something else.

Now such a thing happiness, above all else, is held to be; for this we choose always for itself and never for the sake of something else, but honour, pleasure, reason, and every virtue we choose indeed for themselves (for if nothing resulted from them we should still choose each of them), but we choose them also for the sake of happiness, judging that by means of them we shall be happy. Happiness, on the other hand, no one chooses for the sake of these, nor, in general, for anything other than itself.

From the point of view of self-sufficiency the same result seems to follow; for the final good is thought to be self-sufficient. Now by self-sufficient we do not mean that which is sufficient for a man by himself, for one who lives a solitary life, but also for parents, children, wife, and in general for his friends and fellow citizens, since man is born for citizenship. But some limit must be set to this; for if we extend our requirement to ancestors and descendants and friends' friends we are in for an infinite series. Let us examine this question, however, on another occasion; the self-sufficient we now define as that which when isolated makes life desirable and lacking in nothing; and such we think happiness to be; and further we think it most desirable of all things, without being counted as one good thing among others—if it were so counted it would clearly be made more desirable by the addition of even the least of goods; for that which is added becomes an excess of goods, and of goods the greater is always more desirable. Happiness, then, is something final and self-sufficient and is the end of action.

We must take as a sign of states of character the pleasure or pain that ensues on acts; for the man who abstains from bodily pleasures and delights in this very fact is temperate, while the man who is annoyed at it is self-indulgent, and he who stands his ground against things that are terrible and delights in this or at least is not pained is brave, while the man who is pained is a coward. For moral excellence is concerned with pleasures and pains; it is on account of the pleasure that we do bad things, and on account of the pain that we abstain from noble ones. Hence we ought to have been brought up in a particular way from our very youth, as Piato says, so as both to delight in and to be pained by the things that we ought; for this is the right education.

Again, if the virtues are concerned with actions and passions, and every passion and every action is accompanied by pleasure and pain, for this reason also virtue will be concerned with pleasures and pains. This is indicated also by the fact that punishment is inflicted by these means; for it is a kind of cure, and it is the nature of cures to be effected by contraries.

———————

After these matters we ought perhaps next to discuss pleasure. For it is thought to be most intimately connected with our human nature, which is the reason why in educating the young we steer them by the rudders of pleasure and pain; it is thought, too, that to enjoy the things we ought and to hate the things we ought has the greatest bearing on virtue of character. For these things extend right through life, with a weight and power of their own in respect both to virtue and to the happy life, since men choose what is pleasant and avoid what is painful; and such things, it will be thought, we should least of all omit to discuss, especially since they admit of much dispute. For some say pleasure is the good, while others, on the contrary, say it is thoroughly bad—some no doubt being persuaded that the facts are so, and others thinking it has a better effect on our life to exhibit pleasure as a bad thing even if it is not; for most people (they think) incline towards it and are the slaves of their pleasures, for which reason they ought to

lead them in the opposite direction, since thus they will reach the middle state. But surely this is not correct. For arguments about matters concerned with feelings and actions are less reliable than facts: and so when they clash with the facts of perception they are despised, and discredit the truth as well; if a man who runs down pleasure is once seen to be aiming at it, his inclining towards it is thought to imply that it is all worthy of being aimed at; for most people are not good at drawing distinctions. True arguments seem, then, most useful, not only with a view to knowledge, but with a view to life also; for since they harmonize with the facts they are believed, and so they stimulate those who understand them to live according to them.

Eudoxus thought pleasure was the good because he saw all things, both rational and irrational, aiming at it, and because in all things that which is the object of choice is what is excellent, and that which is most the object of choice the greatest good; thus the fact that all things moved towards the same object indicated that this was for all things the chief good (for each thing, he argued, finds its own good, as it finds its own nourishment); and that which is good for all things and at which all aim was *the* good. His arguments were credited more because of the excellence of his character than for their own sake; he was thought to be remarkably self-controlled, and therefore it was thought that he was not saying what he did say as a friend of pleasure, but that the facts really were so. He believed that the same conclusion followed no less plainly from a study of the contrary of pleasure; pain was in itself an object of aversion to all things, and therefore its contrary must be similarly an object of choice. And again that is most an object of choice which we choose not because or for the sake of something else, and pleasure is admittedly of this nature; for no one asks to what end he is pleased; thus implying that pleasure is in itself an object of choice. Further, he argued that pleasure when added to any good, e.g. to just or temperate action, makes it more worthy of choice, and that it is only by itself that the good can be increased.

This argument seems to show it to be one of the goods, and no more a good than any other; for every good is more worthy of choice along with another good than taken alone. And so it is by an argument of this kind that Plato proves the good *not* to be pleasure; he argues that the pleasant life is more desirable with wisdom than without, and that if the mixture is better, pleasure is not the good; for the good cannot become more desirable by the addition of anything to it. Now it is clear that nothing else, any more than pleasure, can be the good if it is made more desirable by the addition of any of the things that are good in themselves. What, then, is there that satisfies this criterion, which at the same time we can participate in? It is something of this sort that we are looking for.

In reply to those who bring forward the disgraceful pleasures one may say that these are not pleasant; if things are pleasant to people of vicious constitution, we must not suppose that they are also pleasant to others than these, just as we do not reason so about the things that are wholesome or sweet or bitter to sick people, or ascribe whiteness to the things that seem white to those suffering from a disease of the eye. Or one might answer thus—that the pleasures are desirable, but not from *these* sources, as wealth is desirable, but not as the reward of betrayal, and health, but not at the cost of eating anything and everything. Or perhaps pleasures differ in kind; for those derived from noble sources are different from those derived from base sources, and one cannot get the pleasure of the just man without being just, nor that of the musical man without being musical, and so on. . . .

No one would choose to live with the intellect of a child throughout his life, however much he were to be pleased at the things that children are pleased at, nor to get enjoyment by doing some most disgraceful deed, though he were never to feel any pain, in consequence. And there are many things we should be keen about even if they brought no pleasure, e.g. seeing, remembering, knowing, possessing the virtues. If pleasures necessarily do accompany these, that makes no odds; we should choose these even if no pleasure resulted. It seems to be clear,

then, that neither is pleasure the good nor is all pleasure desirable, and that some pleasures *are* desirable in themselves, differing in kind or in their sources from the others. So much for the things that are said about pleasure and pain.

Since every sense is active in relation to its object, and a sense which is in good condition acts perfectly in relation to the most beautiful of its objects (for perfect activity seems to be ideally of this nature; whether we say that *it* is active, or the organ in which it resides, may be assumed to be immaterial), it follows that in the case of each sense the best activity is that of the best-conditioned organ in relation to the finest of its objects. And this activity will be the most complete and pleasant. For, while there is pleasure in respect of any sense, and in respect of thought and contemplation no less, the most complete is pleasantest, and that of a well-conditioned organ in relation to the worthiest of its objects is the most complete; and the pleasure completes the activity. But the pleasure does not complete it in the same way as the combination of object and sense, both good, just as health and the doctor are not in the same way the cause of a man's being healthy. (That pleasure is produced in respect to each sense is plain; for we speak of sights and sounds as pleasant. It is also plain that it arises most of all when both the sense is at its best and it is active in reference to an object which corresponds; when both object and perceiver are of the best there will always be pleasure, since the requisite agent and patient are both present.) Pleasure completes the activity not as the corresponding permanent state does, by its immanence, but as an end which supervenes as the bloom of youth does on those in the flower of their age. So long, then, as both the intelligible or sensible object and the discriminating or contemplative faculty are as they should be, the pleasure will be involved in the activity; for when both the passive and the active factor are unchanged and are related to each other in the same way, the same result naturally follows.

Plato | # Ring of Gyges

Plato was one of the two greatest Greek philosophers of ancient times. This is the "Ring of Gyges" story from his dialogue, *The Republic*, told by one of Socrates philosophical sparring partners, Glaucon.

GLAUCON (TO SOCRATES): I have never yet heard the superiority of justice to injustice maintained by anyone in a satisfactory way. I want to hear justice praised in respect of itself; then I shall be satisfied, and you are the person from whom I think that I am most likely to hear this; and therefore I will praise the unjust life to the utmost of my power and my manner of speaking will indicate the manner in which I desire to hear you too praising justice and censuring injustice. Will you say whether you approve of my proposal?

SOCRATES: Indeed I do; nor can I imagine any theme about which a man of sense would oftener wish to converse.

GLAUCON: I am delighted to hear you say so, and shall begin by speaking, as I proposed, of the nature and origin of justice.

They say that to do injustice is, by nature, good: to suffer injustice, evil; but that there is more evil in the latter than good in the former. And so when men have both done and suffered injustice and have had experience of both, any who are not able to avoid the one and obtain the other, think that they had better agree among themselves to have neither; hence they began to establish laws and mutual covenants; and that which was ordained by law was termed by them lawful and just. This, it is claimed, is the origin and nature of justice;—it is a mean or compromise, between the best of all, which is to do injustice and not be punished, and the worst of all, which is to suffer injustice without the power of retaliation; and justice, being at a middle point between the two, is tolerated not as a good but as the lesser evil, and honoured where men are too feeble to do injustice. For no man who is worthy to be called a man would ever submit to such an agreement with another if he had the power to be unjust; he would be mad if he did. Such is the received account Socrates, of the nature of justice, and the circumstances which bring it into being.

Now that those who practise justice do so involuntarily and because they have not the power to be unjust will best appear if we imagine something of this kind: having given to both the just and the unjust power to do what they will, let us watch and see whither desire will lead them; then we shall discover in the very act the just and unjust man to be proceeding along the same road, following their interest, which all creatures instinctively pursue as their good; the force of law is required to compel them to pay respect to equality. The liberty which we are supposing may be most completely given to them in the form of such a power as is said to have been possessed by Gyges, the ancestor of Croesus the Lydian. According to the tradition, Gyges was a shepherd in the service of the reigning king of Lydia; there was a great storm, and an earthquake made an opening in the earth at the place where he was feeding his flock. Amazed at the sight, he descended into the opening, where, among other marvels which form part of the story, he beheld a hollow brazen horse, having doors, at which he stooping and looking in saw a dead body of stature, as appeared to him, more than human; he

From *Republic*, Book 2, trans. Benjamin Jowett (Oxford University Press, 1924).

took from the corpse a gold ring that was on the hand, but nothing else, and so reascended. Now the shepherds met together, according to custom, that they might send their monthly report about the flocks to the king: into their assembly he came having the ring on his finger, and as he was sitting among them he chanced to turn the collet of the ring to the inside of his hand, when instantly he became invisible to the rest of the company and they began to speak of him as if he were no longer present. He was astonished at this, and again touching the ring he turned the collet outwards and reappeared; when he perceived this, he made several trials of the ring, and always with the same result—when he turned the collet inwards he became invisible, when outwards he was visible. Whereupon he contrived to be chosen one of the messengers who were sent to the court; where as soon as he arrived he seduced the queen, and with her help conspired against the king and slew him, and took the kingdom. Suppose now that there were two such magic rings, and the just put on one of them and the unjust the other; no man can be imagined to be of such an iron nature that he would stand fast in justice. No man would keep his hands off what was not his own when he could safely take what he liked out of the market, or go into houses and lie with any one at his pleasure, or kill or release from prison whom he would, and in all respects be like a god among men. Then the actions of the just would be as the actions of the unjust; they would both tend to the same goal. And this we may truly affirm to be a great proof that a man is just, not willingly or because he thinks that justice is any good to him individually, but of necessity; for wherever anyone thinks that he can safely be unjust, there he is unjust. For all men believe in their hearts that injustice is far more profitable to the individual than justice and he who argues as I have been supposing will say that they are right. If you could imagine anyone obtaining this power of becoming invisible, and never doing any wrong or touching what was another's, he would be thought by the lookers-on to be an unhappy man and a fool, although they would praise him to one another's

faces, and keep up appearances with one another from a fear that they too might suffer injustice. Enough of this.

Now, if we are to form a real judgement of the two lives in these respects, we must set apart the extremes of justice and injustice; there is no other way; and how is the contrast to be effected? I answer: Let the unjust man be entirely unjust, and the just man entirely just; nothing is to be taken away from either of them, and both are to be perfectly furnished for the work of their respective lives. First, let the unjust be like other distinguished masters of craft; like the skillful pilot or physician, who knows intuitively what is possible or impossible in his art and keeps within those limits, and who, if he fails at any point, is able to recover himself. So let the unjust man attempt to do the right sort of wrongs, and let him escape detection if he is to be pronounced a master of injustice. To be found out is a sign of incompetence; for the height of injustice is to be deemed just when you are not. Therefore I say that in the perfectly unjust man we must assume the most perfect injustice; there is to be no deduction, but we must allow him, while doing the most unjust acts, to have acquired the greatest reputation for justice. If he has taken a false step he must be able to recover himself; he must be one who can speak with effect, if any of his deeds come to light, and who can force his way where force is required, by his courage and strength and command of wealth and friends. And at his side let us place the just man in his nobleness and simplicity, wishing, as Aeschylus says, to be and not to seem good. There must be no seeming, for if he seems to be just he will be honoured and rewarded, and then we shall not know whether he is just for the sake of justice or for the sake of honours and rewards; therefore, let him be clothed in justice only, and have no other covering; and he must be imagined in a state of life the opposite of the former. Let him be the best of men, and let him be reputed the worst then he will have been put to the test and we shall see; whether his justice is proof against evil reputation and its consequences. And let him continue thus to the hour of death; being just and seeming to be unjust. When both have reached the uttermost extreme, the one of justice and the other of injustice, let judgement be given which of them is the happier of the two.

SOCRATES: Heavens! my dear Glaucon...how energetically you polish them up for the decision, first one and then the other, as if they were two statues.

Norman E. Bowie	# Business Codes of Ethics: Window Dressing or Legitimate Alternative to Government Regulation?

Norman Bowie is a Professor of Philosophy at the University of Minnesota.

The problem is to find some mechanism for ensuring that *all* corporations adhere to the minimum conditions of business ethics. Most corporations believe that it is clearly in the enlightened self-interest of the free enterprise system to ensure adherence to ethical standards through self-regulation. Unethical conditions should not be allowed to develop to the point where government regulation takes over. Government regulation of corporate ethics is viewed on a scale from distrust to horror. There are several reasons why government regulation is opposed. These include:

1. A recognition that government regulation would diminish the power and the prestige of corporate officials.
2. A fear that government officials would interfere with incentives and efficiency and hence reduce profit.
3. A judgment that government officials do not understand business and hence that its regulations would be unrealistic and hence unworkable.

4. A judgment that government officials are in no position to comment on the ethics of others.
5. A judgment that the federal government is already too powerful in a pluralistic society so that it is inappropriate to increase the power of government in this way.
6. A judgment that government regulation violates the legitimate freedom and moral rights of corporations.

When compared to the spectre of government regulations, codes of ethics at least deserve a second look. Codes of good business practice do serve a useful function and are not new. After all, one of the purposes of the Better Business Bureau is to protect both the consumer and the legitimate business operator from the "fly-by-night operator." The lesson we learn from the Better Business Bureau is that business ethics is not simply in the interest of the consumer, it is in the vital interest of the business community as well. Business activity depends on a high level of trust and confidence. If a firm or industry loses the confidence of the public, it will have a difficult time in selling its products. Kenneth Arrow has made this point in an earlier selection. An important result follows from the argument that business codes are in the general interest of business. To be effective, codes of business ethics must be adopted industry-wide. Otherwise, it is not to the competitive advantage of the individual firm to follow them. For example, it would not make sense for Bethlehem Steel to initiate the installation of anti-pollution devices for their own plants. In the absence of similar initiatives on the part of other steel companies, Bethlehem's steel would become more expensive and hence Bethlehem would suffer at the hands of its competitors.

An industry-wide code based on rational self-interest would help rebut a frequent criticism of the codes of individual firms. Often the cynical reaction of the public to any individual code is that it is a mere exercise in public relations. For arguments already given, there is good reason for that public reaction. An individual code by a particular firm on matters of industry-wide significance runs the danger of being nothing but window dressing if the firm is not to be at a competitive disadvantage. However an industry-wide code designed to protect legitimate businesses from the unethical acts of their competitors is not mere public relations; it is designed to preserve the trust and confidence of the public which is necessary for the survival of the industry itself. For the purpose of protecting the consumer and hence ultimately for the protection of industry itself, industry-wide codes of ethics are in theory a viable alternative to government regulation.

If industry-wide codes of ethics make sense on grounds of self-interest, why don't we have more successful examples? Two factors explain the basic situation. The first has to do with the scope of the regulations, and the second has to do with enforcement.

First, it is hard to make regulations flexible enough to meet a wide variety of situations, especially new situations, and yet simple enough to guide people's behavior in ways that will hold them accountable. Many criticize professional codes of ethics because they are too broad and amorphous. For example, consider four of the first six standards of the Public Relations Society of America.

1. A member has a general duty of fair dealing towards his clients or employees, past and present, his fellow members and the general public.
2. A member shall conduct his professional life in accord with the public welfare.
3. A member has the affirmative duty of adhering to generally accepted standards of accuracy, truth, and good taste.
4. A member shall not engage in any practice which tends to corrupt the integrity of channels of public communication.

By using such terms as "fair dealing," "public welfare," "generally accepted standards," and "corrupt the integrity," the code of standards of the PRSA could be charged with being too general and vague.

Before giving up on codes on this account, a few comments about the nature of language are in order. Except in the use of proper names, language is always general and is always in need of interpretation. Consider a municipal law: "No vehicles are allowed in the park." What counts as a vehicle? A bicycle? A skateboard? A baby carriage? Moreover, whenever we have a definition, there are certain borderline cases. When is a person bald or middle-aged? I used to think 35 was middle-aged. Now I am not so sure. The point of these comments is to show that some of the criticisms of business codes are really not criticisms of the codes but of language itself.

One should note, however, that none of these remarks refutes the criticism that business codes of ethics are too general and amorphous. Indeed these codes must be supplemented by other forms of self-regulation. First, the codes must provide procedures for interpreting what the code means and what it requires. Just as the Constitution needs the Supreme Court, a code of business ethics needs something similar. A serious code of business ethics can have its vagueness and generality corrected in ways not dissimilar from the mechanisms used by the law to correct vagueness problems in statutes and precedents. Perhaps a professional association could serve as the necessary analogue. Business codes of ethics do not have unique problems here.

Now we come to the second basic factor underlying the lack of successful existing codes of ethics: the difficulty of adequate enforcement procedures.

There is a validity to the saying that a law which is unenforceable is really not a law at all. Any code of ethics worth having is worth enforcing and enforcing effectively.

First, the codes must be taken seriously in the sense that failure to follow them will carry the same penalties that failure to meet other company objectives carries. The trouble with many corporate codes of ethics is that employees see the codes as peripheral to their main concerns. After all, what is important is the bottom line. Experience demonstrates that when the crunch comes, ethics takes a back seat.

If they were philosophers, the employees could put their point in the form of a syllogism. (1) If management is serious about a policy, management will enforce it; (2) management doesn't enforce its codes of ethics; (3) therefore management isn't really serious about its codes of ethics.

If codes of ethics are to work they must be enforced, and the first step in getting them enforced is to get them taken seriously by the management. How is that to be done? Phillip T. Drotning of Standard Oil of Indiana puts it this way:

> Several generations of corporate history have demonstrated that any significant corporate activity must be locked into the mainstream of corporate operations or it doesn't get done. Social policies will remain placebos for the tortured executive conscience until they are implemented with the same iron fisted management tools that are routinely employed in other areas of activity to measure performance, secure accountability, and distribute penalties and rewards.[1]

In a home where discipline is taken seriously a certain atmosphere pervades. I submit that in a company where ethics is taken seriously, a certain atmosphere will also pervade. Since I do not work in a business corporation, I cannot identify all the signs which indicate that the right atmosphere exists, but I can mention some possibilities discussed in the literature. These include:

1. Recognition that ethical behavior transcends the requirements of the law. The attitude that if it's not illegal it's okay is wrong. It's wrong first because at most the law prescribes minimum standards of ethical behavior. The public desires higher standards and the desire of the public is legitimate although I will not argue for this point here. Moreover, the attitude "if it's not illegal, it's okay" is wrong because it is ultimately self-defeating. By depending upon the law, one is encouraging the government regulations most business persons strongly object to. The American Institute for Certified Public Accountants recognizes this point when it describes its code of professional ethics as a voluntary assumption of self-discipline above and beyond the requirements of law.

2. A high level officer, presumably a vice-president, with suitable staff support, being empowered to interpret and enforce the code. This vice-president should have the same status as the vice-presidents for marketing, production, personnel, etc. The vice-president should also be responsible for measuring performance.

3. Utilization of the device of the corporate social audit as part of the measurement of performance. The corporate social audit has come to have a number of different meanings. What I have in mind, however, is a revision of the corporation's profit and loss statement and balance sheet. Following the ideas of David Linowes, on the credit side all voluntary expenditures not required by law aimed at improving the employees and the public would be entered. On the debit side would be known expenditures which a reasonably prudent socially aware management would make, but didn't make. Such debit entries represent lost opportunities which the company should not have lost.

I recognize that many of these suggestions are highly controversial and I do not want the discussion to shift away from our main topic. This discussion does reiterate, however, an important point made before. Codes of ethics by themselves are not sufficient devices to provide the climate for a desirable record on business ethics. Codes of ethics must be buttressed by internal mechanisms within the corporation if they are to be effective. They must be adequately interpreted and effectively enforced.

Given these criticisms, we should remind ourselves why written codes, both legal and moral, are viewed as desirable despite their inadequacies. Laws or codes of conduct provide more stable permanent guides to right or wrong than do human personalities. As you recall, God recognized that the charismatic leadership of Moses needed to be replaced by the Ten Commandments. Codes of ethics or rules of law provide guidance especially in ethically ambiguous situations. When one is tempted to commit a wrong act, laws also provide the basis for appeal in interpersonal situations. Professor Henry P. Sims, Jr., Professor of Organizational Behavior at Penn State, has done some research with graduate students confronted with decision-making opportunities. His results show that a clear company policy forbidding kickbacks lowers the tendency of the graduate students to permit kickbacks. A business code of ethics can provide an independent ground of appeal when one is urged by a friend or associate to commit an unethical act. "I'm sorry, but company policy strictly forbids it," is a gracious way of ending a conversation about a "shady" deal.

Codes of ethics have another advantage. They not only guide the behavior of average citizens or employees, they control the power of the leaders and employers. For Plato, questions of political morality were to be decided by philosopher kings. Plato had adopted this approach after observing the bad decisions of the Athenian participatory democracy. Aristotle, however, saw the danger that Plato's elitism could easily lead to tyranny. The actions of human beings needed to be held in check by law. The English and American tradition is similar. One means for controlling the king or other governing officials is through a constitution. The Bill of Rights of our own Constitution protects the individual from the tyranny of the majority. A strict company code of ethics would help provide a needed defense for an employee ordered by a superior to do something immoral. "I'm sorry but company regulations forbid that" does have some bite to it.

Finally, during the time when conflicting standards of ethics are being pushed on the business community, a code of ethics would help clarify the ethical responsibilities of business. One of the most frustrating aspects of the current debate about business ethics is that no one knows what the rules are. Most business leaders recognize that the social responsibilities of business must expand and that businessmen and women will be held to higher ethical standards than in the past. However there are some obvious limits. A blanket ethical demand that business solve all social problems is arbitrary and unrealistic. Business codes of ethics acceptable both to the business community and to the general public would help bring some order out of the chaos.

Let me conclude by providing some suggestions for writing an effective code of ethics. I am taking these suggestions directly from an article by Neil H. Offen, Senior Vice-President and Legal Counsel of the Direct Selling Association.

1. Be clear on your objectives, and make sure of your constituent's support. It is important to get the commitment from the president of each company.
2. Set up a realistic timetable for developing and implementing your code.
3. Know the costs of running a code program, and be sure you have long-term as well as short-term funding.
4. Make sure to provide for changing the code to meet new situations and challenges. It should be a living document.
5. Gear your code to the problems faced by your industry or profession.
6. Be aware of the latest developments and trends in the area of self-regulation. Pay particular attention to FTC, Justice Department, and Congressional activities.
7. Make sure legal counsel is consulted and the code is legally defensible.
8. Get expert advice on how to promote the code and how to go about educating the public.
9. Watch your rhetoric. Don't promise more than you can deliver.
10. Write it as simply as possible. Avoid jargon and gobbledygook.
11. Be totally committed to being responsive and objective.
12. Select an independent administrator of unquestionable competence and integrity.

13. Be patient, maintain your perspective, and don't lose your sense of humor.[2]

NOTES

1.   Phillip T. Drotning, "Organizing the Company for Social Action," in S. Prakash Sethi, *The Unstable Ground: Corporate Social Policy in a Dynamic Society* (Los Angeles: Melville Publishing Co., 1974), p. 259.

2.   Neil H. Offen, "Commentary on Code of Ethics of Direct Selling Association," in *The Ethical Basis of Economic Freedom* (Chapel Hill, N.C.: American Viewpoint, Inc. 1976), pp. 274–75.

Thomas Hobbes

Of the Natural Condition of Mankind as Concerning Their Felicity and Misery

Thomas Hobbes was one of the most important political philosophers of the Enlightenment.

Nature hath made men so equal, in the faculties of the body, and mind; as that though there be found one man sometimes manifestly stronger in body, or of quicker mind than another; yet when all is reckoned together, the difference between man, and man, is not so considerable, as that one man can thereupon claim to himself any benefit, to which another may not pretend, as well as he. For as to the strength of body, the weakest has strength enough to kill the strongest, either by secret machination, or by confederacy with others, that are in the same danger with himself.

And as to the faculties of the mind, setting aside the arts grounded upon words, and especially that skill of proceeding upon general, and infallible rules, called science; which very few have, and but in few things; as being not a native faculty, born with us; nor attained, as prudence, while we look after somewhat else, I find yet a greater equality amongst men, than that of strength. For prudence, is but experience; which equal time, equally bestows on all men, in those things they equally apply themselves unto.

That which may perhaps make such equality incredible, is but a vain conceit of one's own wisdom, which almost all men think they have in a greater degree, than the vulgar; that is, than all men but themselves, and a few others, whom by fame, or for concurring with themselves, they approve. For such is the nature of men, that howsoever they may acknowledge many others to be more witty, or more eloquent, or more learned; yet they will hardly believe there be many so wise as themselves; for they see their own wit at hand, and other men's at a distance. But this proveth rather that men are in that point equal, than unequal. For there is not ordinarily a greater sign of the equal distribution of any thing, than that every man is contented with his share.

From this equality of ability, ariseth equality of hope in the attaining of our ends. And therefore if any two men desire the same thing, which nevertheless they cannot both enjoy, they become enemies; and in the way to their end, which is principally their own conservation, and sometimes their delectation only, endeavour to destroy, or subdue one another. And from hence it comes to pass, that where an invader hath no more to fear, than another man's single power; if one plant, sow, build, or possess a convenient seat, others may probably be expected to come prepared with forces united, to dispossess, and deprive him, not only of the fruit of his labour, but also of his life, or liberty. And the invader again is in the like danger of another.

And from this difference of one another, there is no way for any man to secure himself, so reasonable, as anticipation; that is, by force, or wiles, to master the persons of all men he can, so long, till he see no other power great enough to endanger him: and this is no more than his own conservation requireth, and is generally allowed. Also because there be some, that taking pleasure in contemplating their own power in the acts of conquest, which they pursue farther than their security requires; if others, that otherwise would be glad to be at ease within modest bounds, should not by invasion increase their power, they would not be able, long time, by standing only on their defence, to subsist. And by consequence, such augmentation of dominion over men being necessary to a man's conservation, it ought to be allowed him.

Again, men have no pleasure, but on the contrary a great deal of grief, in keeping company, where there is no power able to over-awe them all. For every man looketh that his companion should value him, at the same rate he sets upon himself: and upon all signs of contempt, or undervaluing, naturally endeavours, as far as he dares (which amongst them that have no common power to keep them in quiet, is far enough to make them destroy each other), to extort a greater value from his contemners, by damage; and from others, by the example.

So that in the nature of man, we find three principal causes of quarrel. First, competition; secondly, diffidence; thirdly, glory.

The first, maketh men invade for gain; the second, for safety; and the third, for reputation. The first use violence, to make themselves masters of other men's persons, wives, children, and cattle; the second, to defend them; the third, for trifles, as a word, a smile, a different opinion, and any other sign of undervalue, either direct in their persons, or by reflection in their kindred, their friends, their nation, their profession, or their name.

Hereby it is manifest, that during the time men live without a common power to keep them all in awe, they are in that condition which is called war; and such a war, as is of every man, against every man. For WAR, consisteth not in battle only, or the act of fighting; but in a tract of time, wherein the will to contend by the battle is sufficiently known; and therefore the notion of *time*, is to be considered in the nature of war, as it is in the nature of weather. For as the nature of foul weather, lieth not in a shower or two of rain; but in an inclination thereto of many days together: so the nature of war, consisteth not in actual fighting; but in the known disposition thereto, during all the time there is no assurance to the contrary. All other time is PEACE.

Whatsoever therefore is consequent to a time of war, where every man is enemy to every man; the same is consequent to the time, wherein men live without other security, than what their own strength, and their own invention shall furnish them withal. In such condition, there is no place for industry; because the fruit thereof is uncertain: and consequently no culture of the earth; no navigation, nor use of the commodities that may be imported by sea; no commodious building; no instruments of moving, and removing, such things as require much force; no knowledge of the face of the earth; no account of time; no arts; no letters; no society; and which is worst of all, continual fear, and danger of violent death; and the life of man, solitary, poor, nasty, brutish, and short.

It may seem strange to some man, that has not well weighed these things; that nature should thus dissociate, and render men apt to invade, and destroy one another: and he may therefore, not trusting to this inference, made from the passions, desire perhaps to have the same confirmed by experience. Let him therefore consider with himself, when taking a journey, he arms himself, and seeks to go well accompanied; when going to sleep, he locks his doors; when even in his house he locks his chests; and this when he knows there be laws, and public officers, armed, to revenge all injuries shall be done him; what opinion he has of his fellow-subjects, when he rides armed; of his fellow citizens, when he locks his doors; and of his children, and servants, when he locks his chests. Does he not there as much accuse mankind by his actions, as I do by my words? But neither of us accuse man's nature in it. The desires, and other passions of man, are in themselves no sin. No more are the actions, that proceed from those passions, till they know a law that forbids them: which till laws be made they cannot know: nor can any law be made, till they have agreed upon the person that shall make it.

It may peradventure be thought, there was never such a time, nor condition of war as this; and I believe it was never generally so, over all the world: but there are many places, where they live so now. For the savage people in many places of America, except the government of small families, the concord whereof dependeth on natural lust, have no government at all; and live at this day in that brutish manner, as I said before. Howsoever, it may be perceived what manner of life there would be, where there were no common power to fear, by the manner of life, which men that have formerly lived under a peaceful government, use to degenerate into, in a civil war.

But though there had never been any time, wherein particular men were in a condition of war one against another; yet in all times, kings, and persons of sovereign authority, because of their independency, are in continual jealousies, and in the state and posture of gladiators; having their weapons pointing, and their eyes fixed on one another; that is, their forts, garrisons, and guns upon the frontiers of their kingdoms; and continual spies upon their neighbours; which is a posture of war. But because they uphold thereby, the industry of their subjects; there does not follow from it, that misery, which accompanies the liberty of particular men.

To this war of every man, against every man, this also is consequent; that nothing can be unjust. The notions of right and wrong, justice and injustice have there no place. Where there is no common power, there is no law: where no law, no injustice. Force, and fraud, are in war the two cardinal virtues. Justice, and injustice are none of the faculties neither of the body, nor mind. If they were, they might be in a man that were alone in the world, as well as his senses, and passions. They are qualities, that relate to men in society, not in solitude. It is consequent also to the same condition, that there be no propriety, no dominion, no *mine* and *thine* distinct; but only that to be every man's that he can get; and for so long, as he can keep it. And thus much for the ill condition, which man by mere nature is actually placed in; though with a possibility to come out of it, consisting partly in the passions, partly in his reason.

The passions that incline men to peace, are fear of death; desire of such things as are necessary to commodious living; and a hope by their industry to obtain them. And reason suggesteth convenient articles of peace, upon which men may be drawn to agreement. These articles, are they, which otherwise are called the Laws of Nature: whereof I shall speak more particularly, in the following chapters.

Of the First and Second Natural Laws and of Contracts

The right of nature, which writers commonly call *jus naturale*, is the liberty each man hath, to use his own power, as he will himself, for the preservation of his own nature; that is to say, of his own life; and consequently, of doing any thing, which in his own judgement, and reason, he shall conceive to be the aptest means thereunto.

By liberty, is understood, according to the proper signification of the word; the absence of external impediments: which impediments, may oft take away part of a man's power to do what he would; but cannot hinder him from using the power left him, according as his judgment, and reason shall dictate to him.

A law of nature, *lex naturalis*, is a precept or general rule, found out by reason, by which a man is forbidden to do that, which is destructive of his life, or taketh away the means of preserving the same; and to omit that, by which he thinketh it may be best preserved. For though they that speak of this subject, use to confound *jus*, and *lex*, *right* and *law*: yet they ought to be distinguished; because RIGHT, consisteth in liberty to do, or to forbear; whereas LAW, determineth, and bindeth to one of them: so that law, and right, differ as much, as obligation, and liberty, which in one and the same matter are inconsistent.

And because the condition of man, as hath been declared in the precedent chapter, is a condition of war of every one against every one: in which case every one is governed by his own reason; and there is nothing he can make use of, that may not be a help unto him, in preserving his life against his enemies; it followeth, that in such a condition, every man has a right to every thing; even to one another's body. And therefore, as long as this natural right of every man to every thing endureth, there can be no security to any man, how strong or wise soever he be, of living out the time, which nature ordinarily alloweth men to live. And consequently it is a precept, or general rule of reason, *that every man, ought to endeavour peace, as far as he has hope of obtaining it; and when he cannot obtain it, that he may seek, and use, all helps, and advantages of war.* The first branch of which rule, containeth the first, and fundamental law of nature; which is, to *seek peace, and follow it.* The second, the sum of the right of nature; which is, *by all means we can, to defend ourselves.*

From this fundamental law of nature, by which men are commanded to endeavour peace, is derived this second law; *that a man be willing, when others are so too, as far-forth, as for peace, and defence of himself he shall think it necessary, to lay down this right to all things; and be contented with so much liberty against other men, as he would allow other men against himself.* For as long as every man holdeth this right, of doing any thing he liketh; so long

are all men in the condition of war. But if other men will not lay down their right, as well as he; then there is no reason for any one, to divest himself of his: for that were to expose himself to prey, which no man is bound to, rather than to dispose himself to peace. This is that law of the Gospel; *whatsoever you require that others should do to you, that do ye to them.* And that law of all men, *quod tibi fieri non vis, alteri ne feceris.*

To *lay down* a man's *right* to any thing, is to *divest* himself of the *liberty*, of hindering another of the benefit of his own right to the same. For he that renounceth, or passeth away his right, giveth not to any other man a right which he had not before; because there is nothing to which every man had not right by nature: but only standeth out of his way, that he may enjoy his own original right, without hindrance from him; not without hindrance from another. So that the effect which redoundeth to one man, by another man's defect of right, is but so much diminution of impediments to the use of his own right original.

Right is laid aside, either by simply renouncing it; or by transferring it to another. By *simply* RENOUNCING; when he cares not to whom the benefit thereof redoundeth. By TRANSFERRING; when he intendeth the benefit thereof to some certain person, or persons. And when a man hath in either manner abandoned, or granted away his right; then is he said to be OBLIGED, or BOUND, not to hinder those, to whom such right is granted, or abandoned, from the benefit of it: and that he *ought*, and it is his DUTY, not to make void that voluntary act of his own: and that such hindrance is INJUSTICE, and INJURY, as being *sine jure*; the right being before renounced, or transferred. So that *injury*, or *injustice*, in the controversies of the world, is somewhat like to that, which in the disputations of scholars is called *absurdity*. For as it is there called an absurdity, to contradict what one maintained in the beginning: so in the world, it is called injustice, and injury, voluntarily to undo that, which from the beginning he had voluntarily done. The way by which a man either simply renounceth, or transferreth his right, is a declaration, or signification, by some voluntary and sufficient sign, or signs, that he doth so renounce, or transfer; or hath so renounced, or transferred the same, to him that accepted it. And these signs are either words only, or actions only; or, as it happenneth most often, both words, and actions. And the same are the BONDS, by which men are bound, and obliged: bonds, that have their strength, not from their own nature, for nothing is more easily broken than a man's word, but from fear of some evil consequence upon the rupture.

Whensoever a man transferreth his right, or renounceth it; it is either in consideration of some right reciprocally transferred to himself; or for some other good he hopeth for thereby. For it is a voluntary act: and of the voluntary acts of every man, the object is some *good to himself*. And therefore there be some rights, which no man can be understood by any words, or other signs, to have abandoned, or transferred. As first a man cannot lay down the right of resisting them, that assault him by force, to take away his life; because he cannot be understood to aim thereby, at any good to himself. The same may be said of wounds, and chains, and imprisonment; both because there is no benefit consequent to such patience; as there is to the patience of suffering another to be wounded, or imprisoned: as also because a man cannot tell, when he seeth men proceed against him by violence, whether they intend his death or not. And lastly the motive, and end for which this renouncing, and transferring of right is introduced, is nothing else but the security of a man's person, in his life, and in the means of so preserving life, as not to be weary of it. And therefore if a man by words, or other signs, seem to despoil himself of the end, for which those signs were intended; he is not to be understood as if he meant it, or that it was his will; but that he was ignorant of how such words and actions were to be interpreted.

The mutual transferring of right, is that which men call CONTRACT.

There is difference between transferring of right to the thing: and transferring, or tradition, that is delivery of the thing itself. For the thing may be delivered together with the translation of the right; as in buying and selling with ready-money; or exchange of goods, or lands: and it may be delivered some time after.

Again, one of the contractors, deliver the thing contracted for on his part, and leave the other to perform his part at some determinate time after, and in the mean time be trusted; and then the contract on his part, is called PACT, or COVENANT: or both parts may contract now, to perform hereafter: in which cases, he that is to perform in time to come, being trusted, his performance is called *keeping of promise*, or faith: and the failing of performance, if it be voluntary, *violation of faith*. . . .

These are the laws of nature dictating peace for a means of the conservation of men in multitudes, and which only concern the doctrine of civil society. There be other things tending to the destruction of particular men—as drunkenness and all other parts of intemperance—which may therefore also be reckoned among those things which the law of nature has forbidden, but are not necessary to be mentioned nor are pertinent enough to this place.

And though this may seem too subtle a deduction of the laws of nature to be taken notice of by all men—whereof the most part are too busy in getting food and the rest too negligent to understand—yet to leave all men inexcusable they have been contracted into one easy sum, intelligible even to the meanest capacity, and that is *Do not that to another which you would not have done to yourself*; which shows him that he has no more to do in learning the laws of nature but, when weighing the actions of other men with his own they seem too heavy, to put them into the other part of the balance and his own into their place, that his own passions and self-love may add nothing to the weight, and then there is none of these laws of nature that will not appear unto him very reasonable. . . .

The laws of nature are immutable and eternal, for injustice, ingratitude, arrogance, pride, iniquity, acception of persons, and the rest can never be made lawful. For it can never be that war shall preserve life and peace destroy it.

The same laws, because they oblige only to a desire and endeavor—I mean an unfeigned and constant endeavor—are easy to be observed. For in that they require nothing but endeavor, he that endeavors their performance fulfills them; and he that fulfills the law is just.

And the science of them is the true and only moral philosophy. For moral philosophy is nothing else but the science of what is *good* and *evil* in the conversation and society of mankind. *Good* and *evil* are names that signify our appetites and aversions, which in different tempers, customs, and doctrines of men are different; and divers men differ not only in their judgment on the senses of what is pleasant and unpleasant to the taste, smell, hearing, touch, and sight but also of what is conformable or disagreeable to reason in the actions of common life. Nay, the same man in divers times differs from himself, and one time praises—that is, calls good—what another time he dispraises and calls evil; from whence arise disputes, controversies, and at last war. And therefore so long as a man is in the condition of mere nature, which is a condition of war, private appetite is the measure of good and evil; and consequently all men agree on this: that peace is good, and therefore also the way or means of peace, which, as I have showed before, are *justice, gratitude, modesty, equity, mercy*, and the rest of the laws of nature, are good—that is to say, *moral virtues*—and their contrary *vices* evil. Now the science of virtue and vice is moral philosophy; and therefore the true doctrine of the laws of nature is the true moral philosophy. But the writers of moral philosophy, though they acknowledge the same virtues and vices, yet, not seeing wherein consisted their goodness nor that they come to be praised as the means of peaceable, sociable, and comfortable living, place them in a mediocrity of passions; as if not the cause but the degree of daring made fortitude, or not the cause but the quantity of a gift made liberality.

These dictates of reason men used to call by the name of laws, but improperly, for they are but conclusions or theorems concerning what conduces to the conservation and defense of themselves, whereas law, properly, is the word of him that by right has command over others. But yet if we consider the same theorems as delivered in the word of God, that by right commands all things, then are they properly called laws....

Immanuel Kant

FROM Fundamental Principles of the Metaphysics of Morals

Immanuel Kant is often considered to be, with Plato and Aristotle, one of the three greatest philosophers in history.

Nothing can possibly be conceived in the world, or even out of it, which can be called good without qualification, except a *good will*. Intelligence, wit, judgment, and other *talents* of the mind, however they may be named, or courage, resolution, perseverance, as qualities of temperament, are undoubtedly good and desirable in many respects; but these gifts of nature may also become extremely bad and mischievous if the will which is to make use of them, and which, therefore, constitutes what is called *character*, is not good. It is the same with the *gifts of fortune*. Power, riches, honor, even health, and the general well being and contentment with one's condition which is called *happiness*, inspire pride and often presumption, if there is not a good will to correct the influence of these on the mind, and with this also to rectify the whole principle of acting, and adapt it to its end. The sight of a being who is not

From Immanuel Kant, *Fundamental Principles of the Metaphysics of Morals*, trans. T. K. Abbott, New York: Longmans, Green, 1898.

adorned with a single feature of a pure and good will, enjoying unbroken prosperity, can never give pleasure to an impartial rational spectator. Thus a good will appears to constitute the indispensable condition even of being worthy of happiness.

A good will is good not because of what it performs or effects, not by its aptness for the attainment of some proposed end, but simply by virtue of the volition—that is, it is good in itself, and considered by itself is to be esteemed much higher than all that can be brought about by it in favor of any inclination, nay, even of the sumtotal of all inclinations. Even if it should happen that, owing to special disfavor of fortune, or the niggardly provision of a step-motherly nature, this will should wholly lack power to accomplish its purpose, if with its greatest efforts it should yet achieve nothing, and there should remain only the good will (not, to be sure, a mere wish, but the summoning of all means in our power), then, like a jewel, it would still shine by its own light, as a thing which has its whole value in itself. Its usefulness or fruitlessness can neither add to nor take away anything from this value. It would be, as it were, only the setting to enable us to handle it the more conveniently in common commerce, or to attract it to the attention of those who are not yet connoisseurs, but not to recommend it to true connoisseurs, or to determine its value.

There is, however, something so strange in this idea of the absolute value of the mere will, in which no account is taken of its utility, that notwithstanding the thorough assent of even common reason to the idea, yet a suspicion must arise that it may perhaps really be the product of mere high-flown fancy, and that we may have misunderstood the purpose of nature in assigning reason as the governor of our will. Therefore we will examine this idea from this point of view.

[Our] existence has a different and far nobler end, for which and not for happiness, reason is properly intended, and which must, therefore, be regarded as the supreme condition to which the private ends of man must, for the most part, be postponed. . . .

I omit here all actions which are already recognized as inconsistent with duty, although they may be useful for this or that purpose, for with these the question whether they are done *from duty* cannot arise at all, since they even conflict with it. I also set aside those actions which really conform to duty, but to which men have *no* direct *inclination*, performing them because they are impelled thereto by some other inclination. For in this case we can readily distinguish whether the action which agrees with duty is done *from duty* or from a selfish view. It is much harder to make this distinction when the action accords with duty, and the subject has besides a *direct* inclination to it. For example, it is always a matter of duty that a dealer should not overcharge an inexperienced purchaser; and wherever there is much commerce the prudent tradesman does not overcharge, but keeps a fixed price for everyone, so that a child buys of him as well as any other. Men are thus *honestly* served; but this is not enough to make us believe that the tradesman has so acted from duty and from principles of honesty; his own advantage required it; it is out of the question in this case to suppose that he might besides have a direct inclination in favor of the buyers, so that, as it were, from love he should give no advantage to one over another. Accordingly the action was done neither from duty nor from direct inclination, but merely with a selfish view.

On the other hand, it is a duty to maintain one's life; and, in addition, everyone has also a direct inclination to do so. But on this account the often anxious care which most men take for it has no intrinsic worth, and their maximum has no moral import. They preserve their life *as duty requires*, no doubt, but not *because duty requires*. On the other hand, if adversity and hopeless sorrow have completely taken away the relish for life, if the unfortunate one, strong in mind, indignant at his fate rather than desponding or dejected, wishes for death, and yet preserves his life without loving it—not from inclination or fear, but from duty—then his maxim has a moral worth.

HOW TO BE ETHICAL 71

To be beneficent when we can is a duty; and besides this, there are many minds so sympathetically constituted that, without any other motive of vanity or self-interest, they find a pleasure in spreading joy around them, and can take delight in the satisfaction of others so far as it is their own work. But I maintain that in such a case an action of this kind, however proper, however amiable it may be, has nevertheless no true moral worth, but is on a level with other inclinations, for example, the inclination to honor, which, if it is happily directed to that which is in fact of public utility and accordant with duty, and consequently honorable, deserves praise and encouragement, but not esteem. For the maxim lacks the moral import, namely, that such actions be done *from duty*, not from inclination. Put the case that the mind of that philanthropist was clouded by sorrow of his own extinguishing all sympathy with the lot of others, and that while he still has the power to benefit others in distress he is not touched by their trouble because he is absorbed with his own; and now suppose that he tears himself out of this dread insensibility and performs the action without any inclination to it, but simply from duty, then first has his action its genuine moral worth. Further still, if nature has put little sympathy in the heart of this or that man, if he, supposed to be an upright man, is by temperament cold and indifferent to the sufferings of others, perhaps because in respect of his own, he is provided with the special gift of patience and fortitude and supposes, or even requires, that others should have the same—and such a man would certainly not be the meanest product of nature—but if nature had not specially framed him for a philanthropist, would he not still find in himself a source from whence to give himself a far higher worth than that of a good-natured temperament could be? Unquestionably. It is just in this that the moral worth of the character is brought out which is incomparably the highest of all, namely, that he is beneficent, not from inclination, but from duty.

pressure of many anxieties and amidst unsatisfied wants, might easily become a great *temptation to transgression of duty*. But here again, without looking to duty, all men have already the strongest and most intimate inclination to happiness, because it is just in this idea that all inclinations are combined in one total. But the precept of happiness is often of such a sort that it greatly interferes with some inclinations, and yet a man cannot form any definite and certain conception of the sum of satisfaction of all of them which is called happiness. It is not then to be wondered at that a single inclination, definite both as to what it promises and as to the time within which it can be gratified, is often able to overcome such a fluctuating idea, and that a gouty patient, for instance, can choose to enjoy what he likes, and to suffer what he may, since, according to his calculation, on this occasion at least, he has [only] not sacrificed the enjoyment of the present moment to a possibly mistaken expectation of a happiness which is supposed to be found in health. But even in this case, if the general desire for happiness did not influence his will, and supposing that in his particular case health was not a necessary element in this calculation, there yet remains in this, as in all other cases, this law—namely, that he should promote his happiness not from inclination but from duty, and by this would his conduct first acquire true moral worth.

It is in this manner, undoubtedly, that we are to understand those passages of Scripture also in which we are commanded to love our neighbor, even our enemy. For love, as an affection, cannot be commanded, but beneficence for duty's sake may, even though we are not impelled to it by any inclination—nay, are even repelled by a natural and unconquerable aversion. This is *practical* love, and not *pathological*—a love which is seated in the will, and not in the propensions of sense—in principles of action and not of tender sympathy; and it is this love alone which can be commanded.

To secure one's own happiness is a duty, at least indirectly; for discontent with one's condition, under a

The second proposition is: That an action done from duty derives its moral worth, *not from the purpose* which is to be attained by it, but from the maxim by which it is determined, and therefore does not depend on the realization of the object of the action, but merely on the *principle of volition* by which the action has taken place, without regard to any object of desire. It is clear from what precedes that the purposes which we may have in view in our actions, or their effects regarded as ends and springs of the will cannot give to actions any unconditional or moral worth. In what, then, can their worth lie if it is not to consist in the will and in reference to its expected effect? It cannot lie anywhere but in the *principle of the will* without regard to the ends which can be attained by the action. For the will stands between its *a priori* principle, which is formal, and its *a posteriori* spring which is material, as between two roads, and as it must be determined by something, it follows that it must be determined by the formal principle of volition when an action is done from duty, in which case every material principle has been withdrawn from it.

The third proposition, which is a consequence of the two preceding, I would express thus: *Duty is the necessity of acting from respect for the law.* I may have *inclination* for an object as the effect of my proposed action, but I cannot have *respect* for it just for this reason that it is an effect and not an energy of will. Similarly, I cannot have respect for inclination, whether my own or another's; I can at most, if my own, approve it; if another's, sometimes even love it, that is, look on it as favorable to my own interest. It is only what is connected with my will as a principle, by no means as an effect—what does not subserve my inclination, but overpowers it, or at least in case of choice excludes it from its calculation—in other words, simply the law of itself, which can be an object of respect, and hence a command. Now an action done from duty must wholly exclude the influence of inclination, and with it every object of the will, so that nothing remains which can determine the will except objectively the *law*, and subjectively *pure respect* for this practical law, and consequently the maxim that I should follow this law even to the thwarting of all my inclinations.

Thus the moral worth of an action does not lie in the effect expected from it, nor in any principle of action which requires to borrow its motive from this expected effect. For all these effects—agreeableness of one's condition, and even the promotion of the happiness of others—could have been also brought about by other causes, so that for this there would have been no need of the will of a rational being; whereas it is in this alone that the supreme and unconditional good can be found. The pre-eminent good which we call moral can therefore consist in nothing else than *the conception of law* in itself, *which certainly is only possible in a rational being*, in so far as this conception, and not the expected effect, determines the will. This is a good which is already preset in the person who acts accordingly, and we have not to wait for it to appear first in the result.

By what sort of law can that be the conception of which must determine the will, even without paying any regard to the effect expected from it, in order that this will may be called good absolutely and without qualification? As I have deprived the will of every impulse which could arise to it from obedience to any law, there remains nothing but the universal conformity of its actions to law in general, which alone is to serve the will as a principle.

———————

I am never to act otherwise than so, *that I could also will that my maxim should become a universal law.* Here, now, it is the simple conformity to law in general, without assuming any particular law applicable to certain actions, that serves the will as its principle, and must so serve it if duty is not to be a vain delusion and a chimerical notion. The common reason of men in its practical judgments perfectly coincides with this, and always has in view the principle here suggested. Let the question be, for example: May I when in distress make a promise with the intention not to keep it? I readily distinguish here between the two significations which the question may have; whether it is prudent or whether it is right to make a false promise? The former may undoubtedly often be the case. I see clearly indeed that it is not enough to extricate myself from a present difficulty by means of this subterfuge, but it must be well considered whether there may not hereafter spring from this lie much greater inconvenience than that from which I now free myself, and as, with all my supposed *cunning*, the consequences cannot be so beneficial that credit once lost may be much more injurious to me than any mischief which I seek to avoid at present, it should be considered whether it would not be more *prudent* to act herein according to a universal maxim, and to make it a habit to promise nothing except with the intention of keeping it. But it is soon clear to me that such a maxim will still only be based on the fear of consequences. Now it is a wholly different thing to be truthful from duty, and to be so from apprehension of injurious consequences. In the first case, the very notion of the action implies a law for me; in the second case, I must first look about elsewhere to see what results may be combined with it which would affect myself. For to deviate from the principle of duty is beyond all doubt wicked; but to be unfaithful to my maxim of prudence may often be very advantageous to me, although to abide by it is certainly safer. The shortest way, however, and an unerring one, to discover the answer to this question whether a lying promise is consistent with duty, is to ask myself. Should I be content that my maxim (to extricate myself from difficulty by a false promise) should hold good as a universal law, for myself as well as for others; and should I be able to say to myself, "Every one may make a deceitful promise when he finds himself in a difficulty from which he cannot otherwise extricate himself"? Then I presently become aware that, while I can will the lie, I can by no means will that lying should be a universal law. For with such a law there would be no promises at all, since it would be in vain to allege my intention in regard to my future actions to those who would not believe this allegation, or if they over-hastily did so, would pay me back in my own coin. Hence my maxim, as soon as it should be made a universal law, would necessarily destroy itself.

———————

Now all *imperatives* command either *hypothetically* or *categorically*. The former represent the practical necessity of a possible action as means to something else that is willed (or at least which one might possibly will). The categorical imperative would be that which represented an action as necessary of itself without reference to another end, that is, as objectively necessary.

Since every practical law represents a possible action as good, and on this account, for a subject who is practically determinable by reason as necessary, all imperatives are formulae determining an action which is necessary according to the principle of a will good in some respects. If now the action is good only as a means *to something else*, then the imperative is *hypothetical*: if it is conceived as good *in itself* and consequently as being necessarily the principle of a will which of itself conforms to reason, then it is *categorical*.

———————

There is therefore but one categorical imperative, namely, this: *Act only on that maxim whereby thou canst at the same time will that it should become a universal law.*

Now if all imperatives of duty can be deduced from this one imperative as from their principle, then, although it should remain undecided whether what is called duty is not merely a vain notion, yet at least we shall be able to show what we understand by it and what this notion means.

Since the universality of the law according to which effects are produced constitutes what is properly called *nature* in the most general sense (as to form)—that is, the existence of things so far as it is determined by general laws—the imperative of duty may be expressed thus: *Act as if the maxim of thy action were to become by thy will a universal law of nature.*

We will now enumerate a few duties, adopting the usual division of them into duties to ourselves and to others, and into perfect and imperfect duties.

1. A man reduced to despair by a series of misfortunes feels wearied of life, but is still so far in possession of his reason that he can ask himself whether it would not be contrary to his duty to himself to take his own life.

Now he inquires whether the maxim of his action could become a universal law of nature. His maxim is: From self-love I adopt it as a principle to shorten my life when its longer duration is likely to bring more evil than satisfaction. It is asked then simply whether this principle founded on self-love can become a universal law of nature. Now we see at once that a system of nature of which it should be law to destroy life by means of the very feeling whose special nature it is to impel to the improvement of life would contradict itself, and therefore could not exist as a system of nature; hence that maxim cannot possibly exist as a universal law of nature, and consequently would be wholly inconsistent with the supreme principle of all duty.

2. Another finds himself forced by necessity to borrow money. He knows that he will not be able to repay it, but sees also that nothing will be lent to him unless he promises stoutly to repay it in a definite time. He desires to make this promise, but he has still so much conscience as to ask himself: Is it not unlawful and inconsistent with duty to get out of a difficulty in this way? Suppose, however, that he resolves to do so, then the maxim of his action would be expressed thus: When I think myself in want of money, I will borrow money and promise to repay it, although I know that I never can do so. Now this principle of self-love or of one's own advantage may perhaps be consistent with my whole future welfare; but the question now is, Is it right? I change then the suggestion of self-love into a universal law, and state the question thus: How would it be if my maxim were a universal law? Then I see at once that it could never hold as a universal law of nature, but would necessarily contradict itself. For supposing it to be a universal law that everyone when he thinks himself in a difficulty should be able to promise whatever he pleases, with the purpose of not keeping his promise, the promise itself would become impossible, as well as the end that one might have in view in it, since no one would consider

that anything was promised to him, but would ridicule all such statements as vain pretenses.

3. A third finds in himself a talent which with the help of some culture might make him a useful man in many respects. But he finds himself in comfortable circumstances and prefers to indulge in pleasure rather than to take pains in enlarging and improving his happy natural capacities. He asks, however, whether his maxim of neglect of his natural gifts, besides agreeing with his inclination to indulgence, agrees also with what is called duty. He sees then that a system of nature could indeed subsist with such a universal law, although men (like the South Sea islanders) should let their talents rest and resolve to devote their lives merely to idleness, amusement, and propagation of their species—in a word, to enjoyment; but he cannot possibly *will* that this should be a universal law of nature, or be implanted in us as such by a natural instinct. For, as a rational being, he necessarily wills that his faculties be developed, since they serve him, and have been given him, for all sorts of possible purposes.

4. A fourth, who is in prosperity, while he sees that others have to contend with great wretchedness and that he could help them, thinks: What concern is it of mine? Let everyone be as happy as Heaven pleases, or as he can make himself; I will take nothing from him nor even envy him, only I do not wish to contribute anything to his welfare or to his assistance in distress! Now no doubt, if such a mode of thinking were a universal law, the human race might very well subsist, and doubtless even better than in a state in which everyone talks of sympathy and good-will, or even takes care occasionally to put it into practice, but, on the other side, also cheats when he can, betrays the rights of men, or otherwise violates them. But although it is possible that a universal law of nature might exist in accordance with that maxim, it is impossible to *will* that such a principle should have the universal validity of a law of nature. For a will which

resolved this would contradict itself, inasmuch as many cases might occur in which one would have need of the love and sympathy of others, and in which, by such a law of nature, sprung from his own will, he would deprive himself of all hope of the aid he desires.

These are a few of the many actual duties, or at least what we regard as such, which obviously fall into two classes on the one principle that we have laid down. We must be *able to will* that a maxim of our action should be a universal law. This is the canon of the moral appreciation of the action generally. Some actions are of such a character that their maxim cannot without contradiction be even *conceived* as a universal law of nature, far from it being possible that we should *will* that it *should* be so. In others, this intrinsic impossibility is not found, but still it is impossible to *will* that their maxim should be raised to the universality of a law of nature, since such a will would contradict itself. It is easily seen that the former violate strict or rigorous (inflexible) duty; the latter only laxer (meritorious) duty. Thus it, has been completely shown by these examples how all duties depend as regards the nature of the obligation (not the object of the action) on the same principle.

———————

Now I say: man and generally any rational being *exists* as an end in himself, *not merely as a means* to be arbitrarily used by this or that will, but in all his actions, whether they concern himself or other rational beings, must be always regarded at, the same time as an end. All objects of the inclinations have only a conditional worth; for if the inclinations and the wants founded on them did not exist, then their object would be without value. But the inclinations themselves, being sources of want, are so far from having an absolute worth for which they should be desired that, on the contrary, it must be the universal wish of every rational being to be wholly free from them. Thus the worth of any object which is *to be acquired* by our action is always conditional. Beings whose existence depends not on our will but

on nature's, have nevertheless, if they are not rational beings, only a relative value as means, and are therefore called *things;* rational beings, on the contrary, are called *persons*, because their very nature points them out as ends in themselves, that is, as something which must not be used merely as means, and so far therefore restricts freedom of action (and is an object of respect). These, therefore, are not merely subjective ends whose existence has a worth *for us* as an effect of our action, but *objective ends*, that is, things whose existence is an end in itself—an end, moreover, for which no other can be substituted, which they should subserve *merely* as means, for otherwise nothing whatever would possess *absolute worth;* but if all worth were conditioned and therefore contingent, then there would be no supreme practical principle of reason whatever.

If then there is a supreme practical principle or, in respect of the human will, a categorical imperative, it must be one which, being drawn from the conception of that which is necessarily an end for everyone because it is *an end in itself*, constitutes an *objective* principle of will, and can therefore serve as a universal practical law. The foundation of this principle is: *rational nature exists as an end in itself*. Man necessarily conceives his own existence as being so; so far then this is a *subjective* principle of human actions. But every other rational being regards its existence similarly, just on the same rational principle that holds for me; so that it is at the same time an objective principle from which as a supreme practical law all laws of the will must be capable of being deduced. Accordingly the practical imperative will be as follows: *So act as to treat humanity, whether in thine own person or in that of any other in every case as an end withal, never as means only.* We will now inquire whether this can be practically carried out.

To abide by the previous examples:

First, under the head of necessary duty to oneself: He who contemplates suicide should ask himself whether his action can be consistent with the idea of humanity *as an end in itself*. If he destroys himself in order to escape from painful circumstances, he uses a person merely as *a mean* to maintain a tolerable condition up to the end of life. But a man is not a thing, that is to say, something which can be used merely as means, but must in all his actions be always considered as an end in himself. I cannot, therefore, dispose in any way of a man in my own person so as to mutilate him, to damage or kill him. (It belongs to ethics proper to define this principle more precisely, so as to avoid all misunderstanding, for example, as to the amputation of the limbs in order to preserve myself; as to exposing my life to danger with a view to preserve it, etc. This question is therefore omitted here.)

Secondly, as regards necessary duties, or those of strict obligation, towards others: He who is thinking of making a lying promise to others will see at once that he would be using another man *merely as a mean*, without the latter containing at the same time the end in himself. For he whom I propose by such a promise to use for my own purpose cannot possibly assent to my mode of acting towards him, and therefore cannot himself contain the end of this action. This violation of the principle of humanity in other men is more obvious if we take in examples of attacks on the freedom and property of others. For then it is clear that he who transgresses the rights of men intends to use the person of others merely as means, without considering that as rational beings they ought always to be esteemed also as ends, that is, as beings who must be capable of containing in themselves the end of the very same action.

Thirdly, as regards contingent (meritorious) duties to oneself: It is not enough that the action does not violate humanity in our own person as an end in itself, it must also *harmonize with it*. Now there are in humanity capacities of greater perfection which belong to the end that nature has in view in regard to humanity in ourselves as the subject; to neglect these might perhaps be consistent with the *maintenance of* humanity as an end in itself, but not with the *advancement* of this end.

Fourthly, as regards meritorious duties towards others: The natural end which all men have is their own happiness. Now humanity might indeed subsist although no one should contribute anything to the happiness of others, provided he did not intentionally withdraw anything from it; but after all,

this would only harmonize negatively, not positively, with *humanity as an end in itself*, if everyone does not also endeavor, as far as in him lies, to forward the ends of others. For the ends of any subject which is an end in himself ought as far as possible to be *my* ends also, if that conception is to have its *full* effect with me.

This principle that humanity and generally every rational nature is *an end in itself* (which is the supreme limiting condition of every man's freedom of action), is not borrowed from experience, *first*, because it is universal, applying as it does to all rational beings whatever, and experience is not capable of determining anything about them; *secondly*, because it does not present humanity as an end to men (subjectively), that is, as an object which men do of themselves actually adopt as an end; but as an objective end which must as a law constitute the supreme limiting condition of all our subjective ends, let them be what we will; it must therefore spring from pure reason.

Looking back now on all previous attempts to discover the principle of morality, we need not wonder why they all failed. It was seen that man was bound to laws by duty, but it was not observed that the laws to which he is subject are *only those of his own giving*, though at the same time they are *universal*, and that he is only bound to act in conformity with his own will—a will, however, which is designed by nature to give universal laws. For when one has conceived man only as subject to a law (no matter what), then this law required some interest, either by way of attraction or constraint, since it did not originate as a law from *his own will*, but this will was according to a law obliged by *something else* to act in a certain manner. Now by this necessary consequence all the labor spent in finding a supreme principle of *duty* was irrevocably lost. For men never elicited duty, but only a necessity of acting from a certain interest.

Nigel G. E. Harris

Professional Codes and Kantian Duties

Nigel G. E. Harris writes widely about professional ethics and duties.

A professional body may introduce a code of conduct for one or more of several different reasons. Doing so may be viewed as a useful public relations exercise which will enhance the profession's status. Where the professional body has been criticized for failing to control the actions of maverick members it may help counter those seeking to have self-regulation replaced by statutory control. Having a code can assist members to defend themselves against clients, particularly in litigation where malpractice is claimed, by delimiting responsibilities. But these and some other possible uses to which codes may be put are not their purported ones. It would be a rash professional body which dared to admit publicly that these were the only or even the main reasons for having a code. Taken at face value a code presents a set of principles of action to which it is desirable that members of the profession should conform.

There are two ways in which prescribed professional behaviour may be desirable. Many codes contain clauses which set out a preferred method of carrying out some task. In many professional situations it is advantageous to have standardized procedures, since this will improve efficiency, yet the choice of standard taken may be arbitrary. Codes which consist largely or entirely of such clauses—what I shall refer to as "standardizing clauses"—are often called codes of practice. There are, however, many professional codes which contain clauses which are not aimed at achieving standardization, but purport to have more direct ethical force. They say do this or do that, not because it is good to have everyone do things the same way, but because this is how one ought to act if one is to act ethically.

Now either the apparent moral content of these "ethical" clauses is just a sham, or it really is something that can be taken as giving them status as moral precepts. If the clauses of a code are thought of as having genuine ethical content then a question has to be faced, namely, what is the basis for that content? In traditional thinking about ethics principles of the level of generality found in codes of conduct are not self-justifying, but need to be seen as applied principles of some general moral theory. But what moral theory could be taken as backing these claims?

I shall start by showing that given their terminology, the matters covered by them, and the situations in which appeal is made to them, "ethical" clauses from codes appear to fit most easily into a deontological moral theory of the Kantian kind. I shall argue that they are more easily reconciled with a Kantian ethics than with alternative theories. However, I shall then show that even trying to provide a deontological basis raises problems. Why these problems are serious is that they bring into question whether the principles set out in the codes can rightly be treated as ethical at all.

WHY A KANTIAN INTERPRETATION IS THE MOST PLAUSIBLE

A check I made through the codes of nearly 150 professions in Britain showed that all consisted of a series of clauses expressed as imperatives or as what members have undertaken to do. Two-thirds said that members "shall" do certain things and "shall not" do others. Other expressions frequently used in

From Ruth Chadwick (ed.) *Ethics and the Professions*, Amesbury, 104–115.

this context are: "must," "should," "are obliged to," "undertake to," "agree to."

Some typical clauses are:

A member shall perform only those services which are within the member's competence (Harris, 1989, p. 168).

A member shall at all times uphold the principle that equal consideration should be given to all regardless of gender, marita status, sexual orientation, creed, colour, race or ethnic origin, religion disablement or nationality (Harris, 1989, p. 219).

A member *shall* at all times take care to avoid waste of natural resources, damage to the environment, and damage or destruction of the products of human skill and industry (*The Production Engineer*, 1975, p. 2).

Similar clauses to each of these are found in many other codes.

These and most other clauses from codes are categorical rather than hypothetical imperatives. They say of actions of some type that they are what ought to be done, but they do not say do this, or do not do this, because such-and-such will result. From their linguistic structure they conform to the Kantian idea of the sorts of moral rule we should take to govern our actions.

Of course, this does not imply that those who adopt a code must have a Kantian ethics. Any moral theory can be expressed in imperatives or using deontological terminology. For example, a utilitarian could say we all have a duty to promote the greatest general happiness. But when we try to formulate more specific rules of action, then the utilitarian has to claim that we have a duty, say, to refrain from lying except in limited circumstances, because of its felicific benefits. At the level of specificity about actions found in codes of conduct, the consequentialist would have to adopt hypothetical, not categorical, imperatives.

It is not that clauses from codes never mention consequences. For instance, damage to the environment could result from some of the actions production engineers might carry out, and their code requires them to take all reasonable steps to avoid it.

An unharmed environment is something for which an engineer may strive, yet in the Institution of Production Engineers' code it is not treated as an ultimate end, but rather—in the Kantian way—as something a rational will could happily envisage being effected by all actions, and so a possible basis for a principle of action.

It might be objected that it is wrong to reject a consequentialist basis for the principles in codes on the grounds that the principles themselves do not require individual justification. Rather, we should seek a justification only for a code as a whole, and that justification can be found in the benefits from increased efficiency and cooperation that result from the adoption of a code. This view has been argued for by Michael Davis, who writes:

> . . a profession is a group of persons who want to cooperate in serving the same ideal better than they could if they did not cooperate. Engineers, for example, might be thought to serve the ideal of efficient design, construction, and maintenance of safe and useful objects. A code of ethics would then prescribe how professionals are to pursue their common ideal so that each may do the best she can at minimal cost to herself and those she cares about (including the public, if looking after the public is part of what she cares about). The code is to protect each professional from certain pressures (for example, the pressure to cut corners to save money) by making it reasonably likely (and more likely than otherwise) that most other members of the professional code of conduct. A code protects members of a profession from unreasonable consequences of competition. A code is a solution to a coordination problem (Davis, 1991, p.2).

One of the more obvious troubles with this account is that it makes it hard to explain why so much space in codes is devoted to the protection of clients, since many of these safeguards will not decrease competition between members of the profession. Another is that the notion of "ideal" used is extremely wide. The engineers who designed the ovens at Auschwitz used to cremate Holocaust victims could well have claimed that they conformed to it (the ovens being safe to those operating them and useful for disposing of corpses, whatever their source). Efficiency and cooperative endeavour may serve the public good, but in some cases they may do the opposite. Suppose, for instance, drug dealers came together and drew up a code of conduct which, if followed, would enable them to ply their trade more effectively. This would hardly make their trade more ethical.

Davis is not unaware of this problem. He asks:

> What if most engineers were moral monsters or just self-serving opportunists? What then? Interpreting their codes would certainly be different, and probably harder. We could not understand it as *professional* code. We would have to switch to principles interpretation we reserve for mere folkways, Nazi statues, or the like. We would have to leave the presuppositions of ethics behind (Davis, 1991, pp. 163–4).

1. General adherence to this clause increases efficiency or cooperation;
2. Efficiency or cooperation enables the profession in question to do more work;
3. The work of the profession in general brings public good; therefore,
4. Adherence to the clause will bring more public good.

I want to suggest that few professionals would, or indeed should, be happy with the idea that the only ethical force in the principles in their codes comes indirectly through the possible promotion of cooperative endeavour, where having such cooperation is generally beneficial and in accordance with "the presuppositions of ethics." For instance, recklessly or maliciously injuring another member's reputation may well inhibit cooperation and lead to a loss of efficiency, but it is not bad only because it has those consequences, it would be a morally bad thing to do whether, it had those consequences or not. To point out that in a particular case such injury had not, in fact, destroyed any cooperation or reduced efficiency would not be an adequate defence. Thus, I suggest that the kind of consequentialist view advocated by Davis fails to acknowledge

just what it is about some of the clauses in codes of conduct that makes people want to describe them as "ethical."

WHY SHOULD CODES BE NEEDED?

Having explained why, prima facie, it is plausible to give a Kantian interpretation to the principles in codes of conduct, I now want to discuss, whether such a view can be sustained. In doing this I shall try to avoid raising contentious questions about how Kant's own views are to be interpreted. I shall argue that professional codes as they exist at present can be reconciled only with a corrupted version of Kant's theory, but that they could be improved by making them more compatible with his actual doctrines.

On a pure Kantian view why do we need codes at all? Surely a professional should make up his or her mind about how to act in good faith. There are two quite separate points here.

Firstly, Kant is not at all averse to setting down maxims in print. Notoriously, some of the examples he gives, such as the duty never to lie (Kant, 1979, p.363) are questionable candidates for what a rational will would adopt as universal laws of action. But my point here is that he does give examples and nothing he says would rule out our setting down a list of duties in a code as an aide-mémoire.

One of the troubles about having a code is that, however long, its set of clauses will not be comprehensive and, in particular, will not cover unprecedented sorts of unethical behaviour. Of course, new clauses can be added, but this takes time, and until it has been done the novel sort of unprofessional action will not be outlawed. It may even lead to a loophole-seeking mentality amongst some members of the profession. This is particularly likely to occur when behaving unethically can produce rich financial rewards.

RESTRICTED SCOPE OF APPLICATION

Another questionable feature about trying to fit codes of conduct into a Kantian ethics is that the categorical imperative is supposed to be applied by every human agent. But a code is designed to be applied by members of a profession and by noone else. Of course, some Kantian precepts may be such that only a section of society can put them into practice. For instance, obligations to one's own children cannot be acted upon except by those who have become parents. But it is not that the codes for accountants or engineers apply to everyone, but are only acted upon by members of those professions; the codes have no force on anyone unless and until they become accountants or engineers.

The answer is, perhaps, that we should not see the contents of codes as Kantian moral principles, but rather as a set of guidelines about what maxims of action professional members should adopt, with the guidance being targeted only at them. Not maliciously harming the reputation of another is a plausible candidate for a moral imperative that everyone should follow, whether a professional or not. However, a professional body which puts a clause in its code about not harming another's reputation can address only its own members and may further limit its guidance to the time when members are acting in a professional capacity and the reputation being harmed is that of another member.

One of the reasons professional ethics is seen as important is that the relationship between a member of a profession and a client is an unequal one. The professional is hired because he or she has expertise not possessed by the client. In the short term it may be impossible for the client to determine whether or not the expertise is being used competently or for his or her benefit. So those who seek professional help are forced to put their trust in those from whom they seek it. The interests of professionals will not be the same as those of their clients, but the latter should be able to trust the professionals not to act against their interests.

Clients who doubt whether professional codes do genuinely protect their interests could question the way most codes are drawn up. It is normal practice for codes to be drafted by committees consisting entirely of members of the profession concerned and so lacking representatives of clients or others who could be affected by professional action. Yet, who better to ensure that codes are worded so as to safeguard their interests than those whose interests they are?

A code should help to reconcile the interests of professionals and the clients and others whose actions they affect. This idea of acting in harmony with the interests of other people surfaces in Kant's conception of a "kingdom" or "commonwealth" of ends, which he describes as "a whole of all ends in systematic conjunction," "both of rational beings as ends in themselves and also of the personal ends which each may set before himself." The guiding principle of this "kingdom" is that a rational being "should treat himself and all others, *never merely as a means*, but always *at the same time as an end in himself*" (Kant, 1785, p. 95). A high proportion of the clauses from codes may be seen as applications of this rule, particularly regarding not treating clients as a means to advance personal ends of the professional.

The Kantian idea of treating another as an end in himself (or herself) carries the idea of doing the best one can for that other person within the constraints of universalisability. This, however, is not easy to reconcile with the way clauses in codes of conduct are, in practice, interpreted by at least some professionals. The trouble is that there can be clauses which are open to being interpreted as laying down *minimum* standards of conduct, rather than ones which will ensure the best possible treatment of the client.

Suppose, for instance, that a clause in a code requires a member who gives financial advice "to declare any personal interest he or she has in any business referred to in the advice." The scope of the word "personal" here is open to different possible interpretations. Narrowly, it might be taken to apply only to the member's own financial affairs and not to those of his or her wife or husband. If it is to be interpreted more widely, say, to include the interests of close relatives, how far is this to be taken? Often with such clauses conventions are established about how adjectives like "personal," "substantial," "adequate," etc., are to be interpreted.

Imagine then that in my hypothetical case the convention is established that "personal interest" encompasses the affairs of spouses and immediate blood relatives. This would then allow a member of the profession to refrain from disclosing a business interest of a live-in partner or of a step-daughter. Yet the existence of such an interest could, in a particular case, be just as relevant as those "professionally required" to be disclosed. Here, rigid adherence to a conventionalized interpretation of the wording in a clause will produce a situation in which the interests of some clients will not be served in the best way possible, and hence doing so will mean treating the clause as other than a maxim expressing the categorical imperative. That is not to say that a member of the profession might not act as a good Kantian and declare an interest beyond the conventional scope, but my point is that the tendency to conventionalize interpretation of clauses encourages lower standards of conduct than those required by a pure Kantian ethics.

A final feature about most codes that demonstrates their limited application is that few have much to say about cases where someone in his or her leisure time acts in a way which, had he or she been at work, would have constituted unprofessional conduct. A noteworthy exception is the guide to conduct issued by the General Medical Council which states: "The public reputation of the medical profession requires that every member should observe proper standards of personal behaviour, not only in the professional activities *but at all times*" [my italics]. (General Medical Council, 1987, p. 13). The Scottish Faculty of Advocates also takes as principle that a lawyer should be worthy of the trust of those who do with him or her to apply to "an advocate's non-professional activities since his conduct

there may affect the trust which others have in him in the professional capacity" (Faculty of Advocates, 1988, p. 3). The relative widely used requirement not to bring a profession "into disrepute," if taken to include non-professional activities, is likely to be seen as applicable only in respect of the most flagrant and well publicized misdeeds.

CONCLUSION

In the previous two sections I have argued that the clauses in professional codes, despite their imperatival form, are formulate applied in ways which are hard to reconcile with Kantian moral theory: But given that it is even less plausible to base them on other types of moral theory, we might be led to the conclusion that they cannot be given any moral justification at all. This, I think, would be a mistake.

The defects or limitations in codes as they are now applied should not be taken to show that their clauses are not to be treated as Kantian principles at all, but rather that as Kantian principles they are flawed. So we should not look for a different theoretical basis, but try to ensure that codes fit the Kantian model better by seeking to rectify their current shortcoming.

REFERENCES

Davis, Michael (1991), "Thinking like an engineer: the place of a code of ethics in the practice of a profession", Philosophy and public Affairs, vol. 20.

Faculty of Advocates (1988), *Guide to the Professional Conduct of Advocates*, Faculty of Advocates, Edinburgh.

General Medical Council (1987), *Professional Conduct and Discipline: Fitness to Practise*, General Medical Council, London.

Harris, N. (1989), *Professional Codes of Conduct in the United Kingdom: A Directory*, Mansell, London.

Kant, Immanuel (1797), *Uber ein vermeintes Recht aus Menschenliebe zu lügen*, translated by Thomas K. Abbot (1909) in *Kant's Critique of Practical Reason and Other Works*, 6th edition, Longmans, London.

Kant, Immanuel (1785), *Grundlegung zur Metaphysik der Sitten*, translated by H. J. Paton (1956) in *The Moral Law*, 3rd edition, Hutchinson, London.

Press Council (1990), *The Press and the People: 36th Annual Report (1989)*, The Press Council, London.
Production Engineer (1975), vol. 54.

John Stuart Mill | # FROM Utilitarianism

John Stuart Mill was one of the most important philosophers and public intellectuals of the nineteenth century.

Our moral faculty, according to all those of its interpreters who are entitled to the name of thinkers, supplies us only with the general principles of moral judgments; it is a branch of our reason, not of our sensitive faculty; and must be looked to for the abstract doctrines of morality, not for perception of it in the concrete. The intuitive, no less than what may be termed the inductive, school of ethics, insists on the necessity of general laws. They both agree that the morality of an individual action is not a question of direct perception, but of the application of a law to an individual case. They recognise also, to a great extent, the same moral laws; but differ as to their evidence, and the source from which they derive their authority. According to the one opinion, the principles of morals are evident a priori, requiring nothing to command assent, except that the meaning of the terms be understood. According to the other doctrine, right and wrong, as well as truth and falsehood, are questions of observation and experience. But both hold equally that morality must be deduced from principles; and the intuitive school affirm as strongly as the inductive, that there is a science of morals. Yet they seldom attempt to make out a list of the a priori principles which are to serve as the premises of the science; still more rarely do they make any effort to reduce those various principles to one first principle, or common

ground of obligation. They either assume the ordinary precepts of morals as of a priori authority, or they lay down as the common groundwork of those maxims, some generality much less obviously authoritative than the maxims themselves, and which has never succeeded in gaining popular acceptance. Yet to support their pretensions there ought either to be some one fundamental principle or law, at the root of all morality, or if there be several, there should be a determinate order of precedence among them; and the one principle, or the rule for deciding between the various principles when they conflict, ought to be self-evident.

To inquire how far the bad effects of this deficiency have been mitigated in practice, or to what extent the moral beliefs of mankind have been vitiated or made uncertain by the absence of any distinct recognition of an ultimate standard, would imply a complete survey and criticism of past and present ethical doctrine. It would, however, be easy to show that whatever steadiness or consistency these moral beliefs have attained, has been mainly due to the tacit influence of a standard not recognised. Although the non-existence of an acknowledged first principle has made ethics not so much a guide as a consecration of men's actual sentiments, still, as men's sentiments, both of favour and of aversion, are greatly influenced by what they suppose to be the effects of things upon their happiness, the principle of utility, or as Bentham latterly called it, the greatest happiness principle, has had a large share in forming the moral doctrines even of those who most scornfully reject its

John Stuart Mill, *Utilitarianism*, London: J.M. Dent, 1910.

authority. Nor is there any school of thought which refuses to admit that the influence of actions on happiness is a most material and even predominant consideration in many of the details of morals, however unwilling to acknowledge it as the fundamental principle of morality, and the source of moral obligation. I might go much further, and say that to all those a priori moralists who deem it necessary to argue at all, utilitarian arguments are indispensable. It is not my present purpose to criticise these thinkers; but I cannot help referring, for illustration, to a systematic treatise by one of the most illustrious of them, the *Metaphysics of Ethics*, by Kant. This remarkable man, whose system of thought will long remain one of the landmarks in the history of philosophical speculation, does, in the treatise in question, lay down a universal first principle as the origin and ground of moral obligation: it is this:—"So act, that the rule on which thou actest would admit of being adopted as a law by all rational beings." But when he begins to deduce from this precept any of the actual duties of morality, he fails, almost grotesquely, to show that there would be any contradiction, any logical (not to say physical) impossibility, in the adoption by all rational beings of the most outrageously immoral rules of conduct. All he shows is that the *consequences* of their universal adoption would be such as no one would choose to incur.

On the present occasion, I shall, without further discussion of the other theories; attempt to contribute something towards the understanding and appreciation of the, Utilitarian or Happiness theory, and towards such proof as it is susceptible of, it is evident that this cannot be proof in the ordinary and popular meaning of the term. Questions of ultimate ends are not amendable to direct proof. Whatever can be proved to be good must be so by being shown to be a means to something admitted to be good without proof. The medical art is proved to be good by its conducing to health; but how is it possible to prove that health is good? The art of music is good, for the reason, among others, that it produces pleasure; but what proof is it possible to give that pleasure is good?

If, then, it is asserted that there is a comprehensive formula, including all things which are in themselves good, and that whatever else is good, is not so as an end, but as a mean, the formula may be accepted or rejected, but is not a subject of what is commonly understood by proof. We are not, however, to infer that its acceptance or rejection must depend on blind impulse, or arbitrary choice. There is a larger meaning of the word proof, in which this question is as amenable to it as any other of the disputed questions of philosophy. The subject is within the cognisance of the rational faculty; and neither does that faculty deal with it solely in the way of intuition. Considerations may be presented capable of determining the intellect either to give or withhold its assent to the doctrine; and this is equivalent to proof.

A passing remark is all that needs be given to the ignorant blunder of supposing that those who stand up for utility as the test of right and wrong, use the term in that restricted and merely colloquial sense in which utility is opposed to pleasure. An apology is due to the philosophical opponents of utilitarianism, for even the momentary appearance of confounding them with any one capable of so absurd a misconception; which is the more extraordinary, inasmuch as the contrary accusation, of referring everything to pleasure, and that too in its grossest form, is another of the common charges against utilitarianism; and, as has been pointedly remarked by an able writer, the same sort of persons, and often the very same persons, denounce the theory "as impracticably dry when the word utility precedes the word pleasure, and as too practically voluptuous when the word pleasure precedes the word utility." Those who know anything about the matter are aware that every writer, from Epicurus to Bentham, who maintained the theory of utility, meant by it, not something to be contradistinguished from pleasure, but pleasure itself, together with exemption from pain; and instead of opposing the useful to the agreeable or the ornamental, have always declared that the useful means these, among other things. Yet the common herd, including the herd of writers, not only in newspapers and periodicals, but in books of weight and pretension, are perpetually falling, into this shallow mistake. Having caught up the word utilitarian, while knowing nothing whatever about it but its sound, they habitually express by it the rejection, or the neglect, of pleasure in some of its forms; of beauty, of ornament, or of amusement. Nor is the term thus ignorantly misapplied solely in disparagement, but occasionally in compliment; as though it implied superiority to frivolity and the mere pleasures of the moment. And this perverted use is the only one in which the word is popularly known, and the one from which the new generation are acquiring their sole notion of its meaning. Those who introduced the word, but who had for many years discontinued it as a distinctive appellation, may well feel themselves called upon to resume it, if by doing so they can hope to contribute anything towards rescuing it from this utter degradation.

The creed which accepts as the foundation of morals. Utility or the Greatest Happiness Principle, holds that actions are right in proportion as they tend to promote happiness, wrong as they tend to produce the reverse of happiness. By happiness is intended pleasure, and the absence of pain: by unhappiness, pain, and the privation of pleasure. . . .

———————

Now, such a theory of life excites in many minds, and among them in some of the most estimable in feeling and purpose, inveterate dislike. To suppose that life has (as they express it) no higher end than pleasure—no better and nobler object of desire and pursuit—they designate as utterly mean and grovelling; as a doctrine worthy only of swine, to whom the followers of Epicurus were, at a very early period, contemptuously likened; and modern holders of the doctrine are occasionally made the subject of equally polite comparisons by its German, French, and English assailants.

When thus attacked, the Epicureans have always answered, that it is not they, but their accusers, who represent human nature in a degrading light; since the accusation supposes human beings to be capable of no pleasures except those of which swine are

capable. If this supposition were true, the charge could not be gainsaid; but would then be no longer an imputation; for if the sources of pleasure were precisely the same to human beings and to swine, the rule of life which is good enough for the one would be good enough for the other. The comparison of the Epicurean life to that of beasts is felt as degrading, precisely because a beast's pleasures do not satisfy a human being's conceptions of happiness. Human beings have faculties more elevated than the animal appetites, and when once made conscious of them, do not regard anything as happiness which does not include their gratification. I do not, indeed, consider the Epicureans to have been by any means faultless in drawing out their scheme of consequences from the utilitarian principle. To do this in any sufficient manner, many Stoic, as well as Christian elements require to be included. But there is no known Epicurean theory of life which does not assign to the pleasures of the intellect, of the feelings and imagination, and of the moral sentiments, a much higher value as pleasures than to those of mere sensation. It must be admitted, however, that utilitarian writers in general have placed the superiority of mental over bodily pleasures chiefly in the greater permanency, safety, uncostliness, etc., of the former—that is, in their circumstantial advantages rather than in their intrinsic nature. And on all these points utilitarians have fully proved their case; but they might have taken the other, and, as it may be called, higher ground, with entire consistency. It is quite compatible with the principle of utility to recognise the fact, that some *kinds* of pleasure are more desirable and more valuable than others. It would be absurd that while, in estimating all other things, quality is considered as well as quantity, the estimation of pleasures should be supposed to depend on quantity alone.

If I am asked, what I mean by difference of quality in pleasures, or what makes one pleasure more valuable than another, merely as a pleasure, except its being greater in amount, there is but one possible answer. Of two pleasures, if there be one to which all or almost all who have experience of both give a decided preference, irrespective of a feeling of moral obligation to prefer it, that is the more desirable pleasure. If one of the two is, by those who are competently acquainted with both, placed so far above the other that they prefer it, even though knowing it to be attended with a greater amount of discontent, and would not resign it for any quantity of the other pleasure which their nature is capable of, we are justified in ascribing to the preferred enjoyment a superiority in quality, so far outweighing quantity as to render it, in comparison, of small account.

Now it is an unquestionable fact that those who are equally acquainted with, and equally capable of appreciating and enjoying, both, do give a most marked preference to the manner of existence which employs their higher faculties. Few human creatures would consent to be changed into any of the lower animals, for a promise of the fullest allowance of a beast's pleasures; no intelligent human being would consent to be a fool, no instructed person would be an ignoramus, no person of feeling and conscience would be selfish and base, even though they should be persuaded that the fool, the dunce, or the rascal is better satisfied with his lot than they are with theirs. They would not resign what they possess more than he for the most complete satisfaction of all the desires which they have in common with him. If they ever fancy they would, it is only in cases of unhappiness so extreme, that to escape from it they would exchange their lot for almost any other, however undesirable in their own eyes. A being of higher faculties requires more to make him happy, is capable probably of more acute suffering, and certainly accessible to it at more points, than one of an inferior type; but in spite of these liabilities, he can never really wish to sink into what he feels to be a lower grade of existence. We may give what explanation we please of this unwillingness; we may attribute it to pride, a name which is given indiscriminately to some of the most and to some of the least estimable feelings of which mankind are capable; we may refer it to the love of liberty and personal independence, an appeal to which was with the Stoics one of the most effective means for the inculcation of it; to the love of power, or to the love of excitement, both of which do really enter into and contribute to it; but its most appropriate appellation is a sense of dignity, which all human beings possess in one form

or other, and in some, though by no means in exact, proportion to their higher faculties, and which is so essential a part of the happiness of those in whom it is strong, that nothing which conflicts with it could be, otherwise than momentarily, an object of desire to them. Whoever supposes that this preference takes place at a sacrifice of happiness—that the superior being, in anything like equal circumstances, is not happier than the inferior—confounds the two very different ideas, of happiness, and content. It is indisputable that the being whose capacities of enjoyment are low, has the greatest chance of having them fully satisfied; and a highly endowed being will always feel that any happiness which he can look for, as the world is constituted, is imperfect. But he can learn to bear its imperfections, if they are at all bearable; and they will not make him envy the being who is indeed unconscious of the imperfections, but only because he feels not at all the good which those imperfections qualify. It is better to be a human being dissatisfied than a pig satisfied; better to be Socrates dissatisfied than a fool satisfied. And if the fool, or the pig, are of a different opinion, it is because they only know their own side of the question. The other party to the comparison knows both sides.

It may be objected, that many who are capable of the higher pleasures, occasionally, under the influence of temptation, postpone them to the lower. But this is quite compatible with a full appreciation of the intrinsic superiority of the higher. Men often, from infirmity of character, make their election for the nearest goal though they know it to be the less valuable; and this no less when the choice is between two bodily pleasures, than when it is between bodily and mental. They pursue sensual indulgences to the injury of health, though perfectly aware that health is the greater good. It may be further objected, that many who begin with youthful enthusiasm for everything noble, as they advance in years sink into indolence and selfishness. But I do not believe that those who undergo this very common change, voluntarily choose the lower description of pleasures in preference to the higher. I believe that before they devote themselves exclusively to the one, they have already become incapable of the other. Capacity for the nobler feelings is in most natures a very tender plant, easily killed, not only by hostile influences, but by mere want of sustenance; and in the majority of young persons it speedily dies away if the occupations to which their position in life has devoted them, and the society into which it has thrown them, are not favourable to keeping that higher capacity in exercise. Men lose their high aspirations as they lose their intellectual tastes, because they have not time or opportunity for indulging them; and they addict themselves to inferior pleasures, not because they deliberately prefer them, but because they are either the only ones to which they have access, or the only ones which they are any longer capable of enjoying. It may be questioned whether any one who has remained equally susceptible to both classes of pleasures, ever knowingly and caimly preferred the lower, though many, in all ages, have broken down in an ineffectual attempt to combine both.

From this verdict of the only competent judges, I apprehend there can be no appeal. On a question which is the best worth having of two pleasures, or which of two modes of existence is the most grateful to the feelings, apart from its moral attributes and from its consequences, the judgment of those who are qualified by knowledge of both, or, if they differ, that of the majority among them, must be admitted as final. And there needs be the less hesitation to accept this judgment respecting the quality of pleasures, since there is no other tribunal to be referred to even on the question of quantity. What means are there of determining which is the acutest of two pains, on the intensest of two pleasurable sensations, except the general suffrage of those who are familiar with both? Neither pains nor pleasures are homogeneous, and pain is always heterogeneous with pleasure. What is there to decide whether a particular pleasure is worth purchasing at the cost of a particular pain, except the feelings and judgment of the experienced? When, therefore, those feelings and judgment declare the pleasures derived from the higher faculties to be preferable *in kind*, apart from

the question of intensity, to those of which the animal nature, disjoined from the higher faculties, is suspectible, they are entitled on this subject to the same regard.

I have dwelt on this point, as being a necessary part of a perfectly just conception of Utility or Happiness, considered as the directive rule of human conduct. But it is by no means an indispensable condition to the acceptance of the utilitarian standard; for that standard is not the agent's own greatest happiness, but the greatest amount of happiness altogether; and if it may possibly be doubted whether a noble character is always the happier for its nobleness, there can be no doubt that it makes other people happier, and that the world in general is immensely a gainer by it. Utilitarianism, therefore, could only attain its end by the general cultivation of nobleness of character, even if each individual were only benefited by the nobleness of others, and his own, so far as happiness is concerned, were a sheer deduction from the benefit. But the bare enunciation of such an absurdity as this last, renders refutation superfluous.

According to the Greatest Happiness Principle, as above explained, the ultimate end, with reference to and for the sake of which all other things are desirable (whether we are considering our own good or that of other people), is an existence exempt as far as possible from pain, and as rich as possible in enjoyments, both in point of quantity and quality; the test of quality, and the rule for measuring it against quantity, being the preference felt by those who in their opportunities of experience, to which must be added their habits of self-consciousness and self-observation, are best furnished with the means of comparison. This, being, according to the utilitarian opinion, the end of human action, is necessarily also the standard of morality; which may accordingly be defined, the rules and precepts for human conduct, by the observance of which an existence such as has been described might be, to the greatest extent possible, secured to all mankind; and not to them only, but, so far as the nature of things admits, to the whole sentient creation.

| Robert Solomon | # The Basic Business Virtues: Honesty, Fairness, Trust, and Toughness |

Robert C. Solomon was Professor of Philosophy at the University of Texas in Austin.

Business is a social activity, specifically, the activity of exchanging money, goods, and services. It may be, at its most primitive, mere barter, or it may involve the extremely sophisticated sale and purchase of stock or futures options on the commodities exchange. But the very idea of exchange in business has built into it the requirement of mutual agreement, the expectation of an honest accounting, and a fair exchange. Of course, an exchange can be mutually agreed upon without being honest, but then one rightly questions (possibly in court) whether the exchange has then actually even taken place. So, too, one can have a mutually agreed upon exchange that is not fair, but this is reason for just complaint and, again, a plausible cause for litigation. In one sense, the whole point of mutual agreement is fairness, and it is often assumed by legal and political thinkers that an agreement between knowledgeable, intelligent, informed, and consenting adults is thereby fair, even if (from outside eyes) the balance of exchange is by no means equal and one person is getting a much better deal than the other. Of course, such an agreement may be compromised by duress or what Hobbes called "force," but so long as the agreement itself is not extorted or compelled, the deal is generally considered valid. (There are extreme exceptions, such as the high price of life-prolonging medicine for the desperately ill.) The importance of mutual agreement in business is absolutely essential. It is the first premise in the logic of personal freedom upon which the entire edifice of free enterprise thinking is built. My surreptitiously replacement of your worn-out radio with a brand new digital clock-radio that I know you want is not a business transaction, no matter how delighted you may be at the outcome. There has been no mutual agreement. A transaction with a child or someone mentally deficient, a "deal" with your dog or a friendly cow is not a business transaction, no matter how well intended. There has been no mutual agreement because there can be no assumption of mutual knowledge or understanding. An exchange with a stranger holds all sorts of pitfalls; assumptions of mutual knowledge and understanding that may well not be the case. (Consider a cab driver counting out change for a first-time foreign tourist.) The virtues of business are just those traits of character that make mutual knowledge or understanding possible.

In other words, the very nature of business is to be open and honest, to make one's goods or service available to others and to make them known for what they are, with a positive "spin," no doubt, but with considerable accuracy nonetheless. The precondition of business is the virtue of the participants. This is not to make an extraordinarily naive suggestion that we should trust everyone. It is only to say that without a modicum of trust and a general practice of candor and honesty there could be no exchange and no business. There are also any number of instrumental virtues involved here, which only come to our attention when suddenly we notice their absence. There is the mutual recognition of equal worth, the value of a commodity or service, the ability to recognize, count, and value money (a skill often amusingly lacking in children). There are communications skills assumed, to be able to talk, negotiate, phone, write, or fax, and with all such exchanges of information the virtue of honesty (and secondarily truthfulness) is essential. Immanuel Kant gives the example of a false promise to pay back borrowed money, and reflectively considers the consequences if everyone did that. He quickly concludes that such promises would be greeted, with ridicule as vain pretenses.[1] Indeed, we don't have to ponder the overwhelming (and ultimately nonsensical) thought that "everyone did that." It would be quite enough if it happened more than once in a while. Witness the normal reaction to being taken advantage of in a shop or a mail-order catalog: "I'll never shop with them again!" Being stranded once without help by an airline or burned once with excessive rent-a-car charges may be enough to switch brand loyalties for life, and a single bank failure even on the other end of the country is enough to shake the trust of depositors. In other words, trustworthiness is not a sign of naiveté but one of the presuppositions of the business world, and dependability is not an extraordinary gesture on the part of a business but the basic criterion for its continued existence. Of course, here we always find the exceptions, the "fly-by-night" companies and the one-shot deals, but, as we argued in our discussion of "game theory" in business, such exceptions are not to be taken as the general rule.

As I have stated, such notions as "honest advertising" and "truth in lending" are not simply legal impositions upon business life nor are they saintly ideals that are unrealistic for people in business. They are rather the preconditions of business and, as such, the essential virtues for any business dealing. Along with these cardinal business virtues goes a network of communicative and logical virtues as well, notably demands of relevance, coherence and consistency, the demands of clear unambiguous expression, the ability to speak and to listen—not just as a sales tool but as an essential. The loud and just complaints against so much of advertising these days (especially political advertising) is not that they spout falsehoods but rather that they spew irrelevancies, including a great many in poor taste. The standard repulsed reaction against the aggressive salesman is not so much because of what he says (as if one really listens), but because of the manner of presentation, the repetitiveness, and, most of all, the clearly intentional aim of preventing the buyer from having a moment to think things through and make an intelligent decision. Not that purchases (especially large, personal purchases) are normally made

with very much rationality or intelligence, but the aggressive salesman interferes with one of our basic rights as consumers—and, again, one of the presuppositions of business as such—namely, the right to make our own stupid decisions without interference or the use of force by anyone.

So, too, one of the basic virtues of business is that broad notion that we call *fairness*. We will have more to say about fairness later on, under the more philosophically proper title of "justice." But for now, it is enough to say that fairness isn't so much an ideal in business as a basic expectation. It has to do with honesty, dependability, and trust, insofar as mutual agreement is, in business, the hallmark of fairness. It also has to do with the notion of equivalence or "equity," the equal value of what is exchanged, whether it be goods, work, or wages. But it is not as if "fair price" and "fair wages" and "reasonable returns" are marked in heaven, which once again brings us back to the importance of mutual agreement, which, writ large, is what we call "market value." What counts as "fair," accordingly, is always in some sense a subjective judgment, based not just on the individual feelings and needs of the immediate participants but on the larger collective consciousness as well. It is remarkable, however, how vigorously this sense of market has been and still is resisted. Aristotle and Aquinas really did write as if prices and the wages of labor were somehow written into the nature of things, and even Adam Smith (and after him Karl Marx) tried to tack down "intrinsic values" above and beyond market values in order to insist that some things (such as human labor) had their true worth even if certain commodities were left to the vicissitudes of supply and demand. True, there is such a thing as an "inflated market," but typically this refers not to some transcendental value behind the market but the recognition that prices and real demand (as opposed to artificial stimulation) are out of sync.

Fairness in business, in other words, is a certain kind of "attunement," a sense of value and a willingness to exchange value for value in a market that provides no ultimately objective guideposts. It also means that negotiation skills are not nearly so incidental or special as we are often lead to believe.

We are mislead, I think, by the "microeconomic" fact that most of the goods and services we buy are offered to us beforehand with a price tag, as if the value were already set (which we notice especially, of course, when it is set too high). But the nature of the free market is that even the most "set" prices are the outcome of a grand negotiation, often of thousands of consumers acting as a block even as they think of themselves acting only as individuals. The point is more obvious in many foreign bazaars, where the very idea of a fixed price (as opposed to a fair price) is nonsensical. But again, the point of all of this is that the notion of fairness in the market is ultimately a function of mutual agreement. The virtues of facilitation, or what we have called the congenial virtues (the basic Aristotelean virtues), are the essential virtues of business activity.

Honesty is the first virtue of business life. Honesty, to put it sweet and simple, means telling the truth, being told what you are getting or, at least, what you are letting yourself in for. Honesty does not, however, mean "full disclosure," and there are certain aspects of every transaction that are expected to be unknown and undisclosed. Every transaction involves a certain amount of risk and uncertainty, and that risk and uncertainty may even be the focus of the deal itself (as in certain forms of gambling and, of course, in may "securities" and commodities exchanges). If someone buys a used car or an old house, he or she cannot possibly be expected to be told everything about the liabilities about to be obtained. Indeed, the practice of buying used cars (and to a lesser extend old houses) is already riddled with high expectations about risk and low expectations about disclosure. But there are limits, of course, and a great many expectations nevertheless. A seller may not tell about a shaky transmission or a potentially leaky roof, but he or she is bound to tell the truth if asked. (The Roman philosopher Cicero worried about leaky roofs two thousand years ago, and where roofs are involved, business ethics seems not to have changed much since then.) Not knowing the answer to a direct question may sometimes be an excuse for not answering, but not always. There are some things that the buyer can be expected to ask and has the right to know, which

means the seller has an obligation to find out in turn. (A record of automobile mileage, for example, is tightly regulated by law, and house-termite inspection is now built into madated purchase agreements in most states in the United States.) "Good faith" provisions often dictate what is relevant to a business transaction, but it would be a mistake to think of these as spelled out explicitly, much less formulated into law. "Buyer beware" may be a now-archaic piece of micro-economic advice, but the importance of general awareness of the specifics of the particular practice in which one is participating is an essential virtue on the purchasing side of the deal. There are others, of course—paying on time, but bouncing checks—but asking the right questions and having the knowledge to come to an informed mutual agreement is the complement of the basic virtues expected of the seller. Indeed, one of the most frustrating issues in business ethics is convincing the consumer, and not just the person in business, that he or she too has obligations and responsibilities, and knowledge—and acting on that knowledge—is first and foremost among them.

Not disclosing is different from a refusal to disclose, and this is different again from dishonesty. As so often in matters of ethics, distinctions are made in black and white, and so any adequate understanding is closed to us.[2] The contrast between honesty and dishonesty is not a simple black-and-white contrast between right and wrong but (to extend the metaphor) they are two extremes in a rich colorful spectrum, in which the presence of risk and uncertainty as well as the frequent need to not tell all render both black and white a painterly and often illusory surface of many mixed colors. Insofar as every transaction involves some risk, it also precludes total honesty, even the seemingly straightforward "I don't know." The tolerance for risk varies, of course. What the pharmacist or the surgeon says to a patient has protections and constraints that are not present for the television consumer who calls a toll-free number to buy the "surprise value of the week." Often, not disclosing means simply not having been asked the right question ("you never asked me"), but sometimes the question can be taken for granted, even if never thought of ("well, you never asked me if the automobile had an engine"). Refusal to disclose when asked is not necessarily unethical, of course, but it certainly changes the nature of the transaction. Risk then moves from being an ordinary but marginal liability to the center stage of the bargain. Thus Carr on business bluffing is at best talking about the kind of transaction that has already gone partially sour or is from the first a special case.[3] Business (like much else in life) may involve bluffing but ordinary business presumes the very opposite, candor and straightforward information. . . .

Dishonesty, finally, is not refusal to inform but the giving of false information. This is, perhaps, straightforwardly a vice—even in poker—but it does not follow that it is always a vice. Like all vices it may become a virtue in extreme circumstances, the standard example is lying about the presence of your friend who is hiding from the Gestapo, or, in business, lying to a customer to *discourage* a purchase that might be ill-afforded or dangerous. What's more, the lie may be virtuous even if (and not because) it should turn out to be true.[4] But in any ordinary business circumstances, dishonesty undermines and invalidates the agreement. The very nature of an agreement after all, presupposes that all parties know *to what* they are agreeing. Dishonesty, accordingly, undoes the very idea of a business exchange, and despite the routine charges of rampant and widespread dishonesty in the business world there can in fact be relatively little dishonesty if that world is to continue to function at all.

Honesty isn't everything, however. One of the odder complications of honesty and truth telling is the fact that people often have vices that work against (or for, depending on your point of view) the effort to be honest. First and foremost among these is *self-deception*, that uncanny ability that we have to fool ourselves as well as (often better than) other people. When one is self-deceived, one honestly tells what he or she thinks to be the truth. Is the resulting falsehood a lie? So, too, people who are honest are sometimes weak-willed[5] and, accordingly, do not deliver on what they quite sincerely promised. And then again, some people change their minds. They meant it when they said it, but now they wouldn't say it at all. Thus dependability ranks along with honesty as one of the cardinal business virtues, particularly given the time-lag nature of most business deals. In a barter system or in small market transactions, exchanges may be simultaneous ("give it to me, and I'll give this to you"). But we often order products in advance, even have them made up especially for us, and with the time lapse between the order and the delivery, and the delivery and the payment, dependability makes all of the difference. It is not enough for the deal to be good. It has to actually come about as well. Many a sucker has been taken in by the offer of a bargain "too good to be believed" just because it was. The deal was terrific but the product advertised never arrived. . . .

Finally, trust is not the same as naiveté, a point that often has to be made again and again for both distrustful consumers and self-styled hardheaded business types. Trust is an attitude, a working presupposition. It is not a principle, much less the principle that one ought to trust everyone. But, mixed with experience and judgment and open to the possibility that sometimes we all get "burned," one needs trust in order to enter into even the simplest transactions and activities, indeed, even to walk down the street. It is trust that makes the system work, the fundamental supposition that most of the people are honest and dependable most of the time. That is not to say that you cannot fool or be fooled, but that network of community and shared expectations that we have taken to be the heart of the Aristotelean view of business might just as well be called "trust." Indeed, if Aristotle did not mention it as one of his virtues (and he was by no means naive about the treachery that pervaded the Athenian *polis*), it was rather because he took it for granted. No practice and no community could even begin to survive without it.

This brings us to the perhaps most misunderstood virtue in business life, the virtue of *toughness*. The word "tough" is typically used by way of admiration, though often coupled with a shake of the head and an expression of frustration. Sometimes, it is used as a euphemism, in place of or in conjunction with various synonyms for a nasty or odious human being. Not infrequently, it simply means stubborn, impossible, or meanspirited. But toughness is generally and genuinely perceived as a virtue, albeit a virtue that is often misplaced and misconceived. Insofar as business consists of bargaining and dealing with other people, toughness is essential, and its opposite is not so much weakness as incompetence. But much of what is called toughness is neither a virtue nor a vice. It is not a character trait so much as it is a skill, whether cultivated or "natural." In certain central business practices, notably negotiating, toughness is not so much a personal virtue as it is a technique or set of techniques, an acquired manner and an accomplished strategy, "knowing when to hold 'em, knowing when to fold 'em." Toughness includes knowing how to bluff and when to keep silent, when to be cooperative and when not to be. But such a skill is not, contra Carr, unethical or divorced from ordinary morals; it is a legitimate part of a certain kind of obviously legitimate activity. Yet, as a specific skill or set of skills, being a tough negotiator is not sufficiently personal or general to count as a virtue, which is not to say, of course, that it is not therefore admirable or necessary.

Very often, what "toughness" means is simply "smart," that is, knowing the business, knowing one's competitors and dealings, knowing how to get things done. Again, this is an admirable and necessary set of business qualifications but not, as such, a virtue. But toughness also means perseverance, which is a personal as well as a business virtue. As always, Aristotle's standard of moderation comes into play here, for there is such a thing as too much perseverance, which then becomes mere obstinacy or stubborness. Of course, what seemed like obstinacy to those of little faith may well turn out to be richly rewarded by the results, and what was indeed healthy perseverance may nevertheless turn to failure in the vicissitudes of the market. But too little "stick-to-it-iveness" makes success virtually impossible and makes life intolerable for those investors, employees, and other stakeholders who naturally depend on a full-blooded effort rather than a halfhearted try. Toughness as perseverance means nothing other than having a goal and a purpose, seeing its worthiness and pursuing it to the end. What makes it "tough" is facing up to setbacks and obstacles that would discourage lesser beings; indeed, it is only in the face of failure that such toughness is truly tested, for it is

no virtue to "persevere" when the market is handing you nothing but success.

Toughness in an executive also has an ethically painful element. Sometimes it is necessary to do something wrong in order to do what is right. Powerful politicians, of course, face such dilemmas all of the time, giving rise to a substantial literature on the controversial virtues of toughness and ruthlessness and the allegedly opposed domains of public and private morality.[6] Sometimes, to reach a higher goal, one must do what one otherwise would not and should not even consider. For example, in the face of debts or deficiencies that will very likely capsize the company, a chairman may need to let go perfectly qualified, hard-working, loyal employees. Viewed as an action isolated from the circumstances, letting people go for no reason whatever—that is, for no fault of their own—would be the height of injustice. But if it is a matter of saving the company, then this otherwise-unjust act may nevertheless be necessary. Toughness is being able and willing to undertake such measures. This is not to say, however—and this cannot be emphasized enough—that such decisions can or should be made without guilt or pain or had feelings. It does not mean that what one has done is not, despite its necessity, wrong. The chief executive of a large corporation once told me that "downsizing" his company was the most painful thing he had ever had to do. His toughness lay not in callousness or indifference but in his willingness to do what was necessary and in his insistence on doing it as humanely as possible. Indeed, callousness and indifference are not themselves signs of toughness but the very opposite, indications of that form of weakness that can face moral issues only by denying them. Toughness is a virtue, but callousness and indifference are not, and the two should never be confused.

In politics, toughness is the phenomenon that is sometimes called "dirty hands."[7] It is the need to do what is painful or awful, even (in a small frame of reference) immoral in order to do what is right or necessary. One chief executive was asked point-blank by an elderly stockholder if his holdings in the company were safe and secure. The CEO, knowing full well that a slash in the dividend would be announced later that week, could not help but tell a lie or, at least, seriously circumnavigate the truth. Again, his personal pain and guilt were considerable, but prevarication was unavoidable. Of course, profits alone are not sufficient as an excuse, and one might thus understand the popularity and indignation surrounding Michael Moore's movie *Roger and Me*, about the closing of GM plants in Flint, Michigan. If the reason was company survival, combined with some well-publicized cutbacks in executive positions, perks, and salaries, such closings would have hardly made a movie. But when profits and perks are the motivation, toughness is not a virtue—or, in this case, toughness is callousness.

Like almost all of the virtues, toughness is not simply self-interested, but neither can it be considered an altruistic or self-sacrificing trait of character. Toughness is ultimately having a vision and persevering in the long-term plans and strategies necessary to achieve that vision. It means not being dissuaded by threats and temptations. But it does not mean an easy willingness to step on other people or violate the basic rules of morality or sacrifice the other basic virtues of business. Toughness has its place in the constellation of virtues, and sometimes it needs to yield to compassion or generosity, to trust or fairness. Again, this is no defense of naiveté, but what toughness certainly does not mean—and is far too often taken to mean—is meanspiritedness and indifference, lack of care and concern for others. Toughness is a true business virtue, and in tough businesses it may even emerge as the primary business virtue, but it is not opposed to integrity. Indeed, one might well argue that it is ultimately equivalent to integrity. Toughness is a proper sense of purpose, insulated against greed as well as weakness. As such, much of what is called toughness might better be called moral courage.

NOTES

1. Immanuel Kant, *Grounding of the Metaphysics of Morals*, sec. 11.

2. See, for example, Ezra Bowen's essay on "business and literacy" in *Business Ethics: The State of the Art*, ed. R. Edward Freeman (New York: Oxford University Press, 1991), p. 186, "the fact is that ethics, or accountability, comes in two decorator colors: black and white." I recommend Joanne Cinlla's reply in the same book.

3. Alfred Carr, "Is Business Blufling Ethical?" *Harward Business Review* (Jan.–Feb. 1968).

4. Jean-Paul Sartre wrote an early short story called "The Wall," in which a captured resistance fighter lies about the whereabouts of his good friend, who will no doubt be tortured and killed if caught. It turns out, however, that the friend has moved to the place mentioned in the lie, and so he is caught after all. The virtue of the lie, however, remains, though Sartre's character is, needless to say, less than self-righteous about the outcome. See *The Well and Other Stories* (New York: New Directions, 1948).

5. What Aristotle called *akrasia*, or "incontinence."

6. See, for example, Stuart Hampshire, ed., *Public and Private Morality* (Cambridge: Cambridge University Press, 1978), and his own *Innocence and Experience* (Cambridge: Harvard University Press, 1989). See also Bernard Williams, "Politics and Moral Character," in his *Moral Luck* (Cambridge: Cambridge University Press, 1981), and Thomas Nagel, "Ruthlessness in Public Life" in the Hampshire collection.

7. The need to do wrong in order to do good was one of the enduring obsessions of the great German sociologist, Max Weber. See his "Politics as a Vocation," in *From Max Weber: Essays in Sociology*, ed. H. Gerth and C. Mills (New York: Oxford University Press, 1946). The term "dirty hands" was popularized by Jean-Paul Sartre in his play of that name. It can be found in the volume *No Exit and Three Other Plays* (New York: Vintage, 1946). See also Michael Stocker on "The Problem of Dirty Hands," in his *Plural and Conflicting Values* (Oxford: Oxford University Press, 1990).

CASES

CASE 2.1
The Prisoner's Dilemma
James Rachels

James Rachels was Professor of Philosophy at the University of Alabama.

Suppose you live in a totalitarian society, and one day, to your astonishment, you are arrested and charged with treason. The police say that you have been plotting against the government with a man named Smith, who has also been arrested and is being held in a separate cell. The interrogator demands that you confess. You protest your innocence; you don't even know Smith. But this does no good. It soon becomes clear your captors are not interested in the truth; for reasons of their own, they merely want to convict someone. They offer you the following deal:

- If Smith does not confess, but you confess and testify against him, they will release you. You will go free, whereas Smith, who did not cooperate, will be put away for 10 years.
- If Smith confesses and you do not, the situation will be reversed—he will go free while you get 10 years.
- If you both confess, however, you will each be sentenced to 5 years.
- But if neither of you confesses, there won't be enough evidence to convict either of you. They can hold you for a year, but then they will have to let both of you go.

Finally, you are told that Smith is being offered the same deal; but you cannot communicate with him and you have no way of knowing what he will do.

The problem is this: Assuming that your only goal is to spend as little time in jail as possible, what should you do? Confess or not confess? For the purposes of this problem, you should forget about maintaining your dignity, standing up for your rights, and other such notions. That is not what this problem is about. You should also forget about trying to help Smith. This problem is strictly about calculating what is in your own interests. The question is: What will get you free the quickest? Confessing or not confessing?

At first glance it may seem that the question cannot be answered unless you know what Smith will do. But that is an illusion. The problem has a perfectly clear solution: No matter what Smith does, you should confess. This can be shown by the following reasoning.

1. Either Smith will confess or he won't.
2. Suppose Smith confesses. Then, if you confess you will get 5 years, whereas if you do not confess you will get 10. Therefore, if he confesses, you are better off confessing as well.
3. On the other hand, suppose Smith does not confess. Then you are in this position: If you confess you will go free, whereas if you do not

From James Rachels, *The Elements of Moral Philosophy*, 4th ed. (New York: McGraw Hill, 2003).

confess you will remain imprisoned for a year. Clearly, then, even if Smith does not confess, you will still be better off if you do.

4. Therefore, you must confess. That will get you out of jail the soonest, regardless of what Smith does.

So far, so good. But there is a catch. Remember that Smith is being offered the same deal. Assuming that he is not stupid, he will also conclude from the very same reasoning that he should confess. Thus the outcome will be that you will both confess, and this means that you will both be given 5-year sentences. *But if you had both done the opposite, each of you could have gotten out in only one year.* That's the catch. By rationally pursuing your own interests, you both end up worse off than if you had acted differently. That is what makes the Prisoner's Dilemma a dilemma. It is a paradoxical situation: You and Smith will both be better off if you simultaneously do what is *not* in your own individual self-interests.

If you could communicate with Smith, of course, you could make an agreement with him. You could agree that neither of you would confess; then you could both get the one-year detention. By cooperating you would both be better off than if you acted independently. Cooperating will not get either of you the optimum result—immediate freedom—but it will get both of you a better result than either of you could obtain if you did not cooperate.

It would be vital, however, that any agreement between you be enforceable, because if he reneged and confessed, while you kept the bargain, then you would end up serving the maximum 10 years while he went free. Thus, in order for it to be rational for you to keep your part of such a bargain, you would have to be assured that he will have to keep his part. (And of course he would have the same worry about you reneging.) Only an enforceable agreement could provide a way out of the dilemma, for either of you.

Questions

1. How does this dilemma pertain to everyday situations? Should we act with or without our own self interests in mind?

2. The author alludes to paranoia in regard to cooperation. How can this contract between you and "Smith" be enforced?

CASE 2.2
George, Jim, and Utilitarianism
Bernard Williams

...(1) George, who has just taken his Ph.D. in chemistry, finds it extremely difficult to get a job. He is not very robust in health, which cuts down the number of jobs he might be able to do satisfactorily. His

From "George, Jim and Utilitarianism," in Bernard Williams *Utilitarianism: For and Against* (London: Cambridge University Press, 1973).

wife has to go out to work to keep them, which itself causes a great deal of strain, since they have small children and there are severe problems about looking after them. The results of all this, especially on the children, are damaging. An older chemist, who knows about this situation, says that he can get George a decently paid job in a certain laboratory, which pursues research into chemical and biological warfare. George says that he cannot accept this, since he is opposed to chemical and biological warfare. The older man replies that he is not too keen on it himself, come to that, but after all George's refusal is not going to make the job or the laboratory go away; what is more, he happens to know that if George refuses the job, it will certainly go to a contemporary of George's who is not inhibited by any such scruples and is likely if appointed to push along the research with greater zeal than George would. Indeed, it is not merely concern for George and his family, but (to speak frankly and in confidence) some alarm about this other man's excess of zeal, which has led the older man to offer to use his influence to get George the job ... George's wife, to whom he is deeply attached, has views (the details of which need not concern us) from which it follows that at least there is nothing particularly wrong with research into CBW. What should he do?

(2) Jim finds himself in the central square of a small South American town. Tied up against the wall are a row of twenty Indians, most terrified, a few defiant, in front of them several armed men in uniform. A heavy man in a sweat-stained khaki shirt turns out to be the captain in charge and, after a good deal of questioning of Jim which establishes that he got there by accident while on a botanical expedition, explains that the Indians are a random group of the inhabitants who, after recent acts of protest against the government, are just about to be killed to remind other possible protestors of the advantages of not protesting. However, since Jim is an honoured visitor from another land, the captain is happy to offer him a guest's privilege of killing one of the Indians himself. If Jim accepts, then as a special mark of the occasion, the other Indians will be let off. Of course, if Jim refuses, then there is no special occasion, and Pedro here will do what he was about to do when Jim arrived, and kill them all. Jim, with some desperate recollection of schoolboy fiction, wonders whether if he got hold of a gun, he could hold the captain, Pedro and the rest of the soldiers to threat, but it is quite clear from the set-up that nothing of that kind is going to work: any attempt at that sort of thing will mean that all the Indians will be killed, and himself. The men against the wall, and the other villagers, understand the situation, and are obviously begging him to accept. What should he do?

Questions

1. Based on the previous readings in this chapter, how would a utilitarian respond to these cases? Likewise, how would a non-utilitarian?

2. How does personal integrity play a role in the decisions of each of these men?

3. What other considerations must be dealt with in pondering these cases?

3

Professional Duties, Clients' Rights

Introduction

Perhaps the most important aspect of professional life is the relationship a professional has with his or her clients. How you understand and define the relationship between yourself and your client will, in large measure, determine the success of your future career and your happiness (or unhappiness—regrettably, that happens, too!) within it.

Professional relationships, unlike relationships in many work environments and types of work, tend to be long term. Most of the people you spend your money with are people who you know briefly, if at all: restaurant servers, cashiers, the anonymous salespeople at the end of a phone line or, more likely, at the other end of a computer server. But your interactions with professionals and your interactions as a professional are for the long haul. Generally speaking, you don't want a new doctor or a new attorney every time you have a new problem. Even when you have to call in "a specialist," you will undoubtedly rely upon your established relationships with your "regular person" when you do so. And when you are a professional, you will want to cultivate similarly long-term relationships with your clients: not just because it makes for a successful professional life, but because the better you know your clients, the more successfully you can serve their needs.

What does it mean to have a "duty"? A duty is something we "ought" to do. We have to fail in "our duty." But where do those duties come from? And why do they have such a strong force over us? Is there ever a time when you should refuse to do your duty? When it may be part of your duty to refuse to act in accordance with some other professional duty?

Clients have a right to expect certain things from their relationships with professionals. They have a right to expect expertise. They have a right to expect honesty. They have a right to be fully informed of what will directly impact them: in many situations, they have a right to demand information—and to be given that information even if they do not demand it—before consenting to certain professional actions or procedures. But they cannot demand everything, can they? What limits exist on the rights of your clients? Another way of putting this is: where do your client's rights end and your own rights begin? What are the tensions between a client's rights and the professional's rights?

A client has a right to expect that a professional will share his or her concerns in a personal way. The professional relationship with a client is a little bit like the relationship between family members: the professional and the client understand one another as part of the same group, with shared concerns and interests.

But professionals must also know how to establish boundaries when it comes to their clients' concerns. Knowing how and when to help a client and how and when to say "this is no longer within the boundaries of our professional relationship" can be one of the most difficult calls for a professional to make. And there may be times when your responsibilities to your client seem in direct conflict with what you personally feel you should do. For example, many pharmacists have confronted the difficult choice of prescribing "morning after" pills—which some pharmacists consider a form of abortion—even though they are personally opposed to the use of such medications.

This chapter explores the intersections of the client's rights and the professional's duties to the client.

| Michael D. Bayles | # The Professional–Client Relationship |

Michael D. Bayles was Professor of Philosophy at Florida State University.

... Many analyses have been offered of the professional–client relationship. Some analyses are empirical; they describe the relationship as it normally exists. That is not the purpose of this section. Rather, the purpose here is to develop an ethical model that should govern the professional–client relationship. However, ethical models and norms often assume certain facts. For example, an ethical model of the appropriate relationship between parent and child makes certain assumptions about a child's abilities. A model of full equality would not work for very young children simply because they lack the physical and mental abilities to engage in such a relationship. Thus, although an ethical model of the professional–client relationship is not simply to describe it, a model can be inappropriate because it makes false empirical assumptions about one or the other parties.

———————

To develop an ethical model that has the broadest scope, the model should not be based on unusual situations, such as a defendant charged with a capital crime or an unconscious patient. Unusual situations are so simply because they lack features, of the usual or have additional features. An analysis based on unusual situations is therefore likely to distort normal situations. Professional ethics should be based on the usual sort of contact average clients have with professionals. Individual citizens are most likely to see lawyers in connection with real estate transactions, divorces, making wills, and personal injury negligence cases. Lawyers also spend much time drafting commercial contracts and advising about

From *Professional Ethics* (Belmont, CA: Wadsworth Publishing Co., 1981), pp. 60–70.

business matters. The average client will probably have a physician's attendance during a fatal illness or injury, but most physician–patient contacts are for more mundane matters such as a bacterial infection or a broken bone. Only gross neglect by the patient or physician—for example, the failure of a patient to take any medicine at all or of a physician to ask whether the patient is allergic to penicillin before prescribing it—is apt to turn these matters into seriously life-threatening illnesses or injuries. Engineers are apt to be consulted by companies or governments that want a project designed. Similarly, certified public accounts are most often hired to audit the books of a corporation. Both accountants and architects also deal with individuals for such purposes as income tax preparation and designing houses.

The central issue in the professional–client relationship is the allocation of responsibility and authority in decision making—who makes what decisions. The ethical models are in effect models of different distributions of authority and responsibility in decision making. One may view the professional–client relationship as one in which the client has most authority and responsibility in decision making, the professional being his employee; one in which the professional and client are equals, either dealing at arm's length or at a more personal level; or as one in which the professional, in different degrees, has the primary role. Each of these conceptions has been suggested by some authors as the appropriate ethical model of the relationship. Each has some commonsense support.

AGENCY

According to this view, the client has most of the authority and responsibility for decisions; the professional is an expert acting at the direction of the client.[1] The client hires a professional to protect or act for some interest; the professional provides services to achieve the client's goal—purchase of a house, removal of a gallbladder, design of a building. According to this conception, not only does the professional act for or in behalf of the client, but also acts under the direction of the client as in bureaucratic employer–employee relationships. This conception is especially plausible for lawyers. In filing a complaint or arguing for a client, a lawyer acts for and in behalf of the client. According to some people, a lawyer is merely a "mouthpiece" or "hired gun." It is not a plausible view of accountants performing public audits, for they are supposed to provide an independent review and statement of the clients' financial conditions.

In some contexts, professionals are prone to adopt the agency view of the professional–client relationship. Professionals are sometimes "identified" with their clients and charged with the client's alleged moral failings. Lawyers offer the defense that in representing clients, they do not thereby ascribe to or support clients' goals or aims.[2] They are merely employees hired to perform a specific task. If the projects are bad or immoral, the fault lies with the clients, or perhaps with the legal system for permitting them.

The agency model most clearly exemplifies what has been called the "ideology of advocacy." This ideology has two principles of conduct: (1) that the lawyer is neutral or detached from the client's purposes, and (2) that the lawyer is an aggressive partisan of the client working to advance the client's ends.[3] This ideology is readily applicable to physicians, architects, and engineers. A physician, for example, should not evaluate the moral worth of patients but only work to advance their health. The second element of the ideology does not apply to accountants performing audits, for they are to present independent statements of clients' financial conditions. It applies in other accounting activities though. For example, an accountant preparing a client's income tax statement should try to take every plausible deduction on behalf of the client.

Some aspects of this ideology appear inescapable in professional ethics. If professionals accepted only clients whose purposes they approved of and did not consider clients' interests any more than those of others, many persons with unusual purposes (such as wanting an architectural style of a building that is completely inconsistent with those nearby) might be unable to obtain professional services. And even if they did, the services might not be worth much, as no special consideration would be paid to their interests.[4] The chief problem with the ideology of advocacy, where it does become an ideology, is that sometimes devotion to a client's interests is thought to justify any lawful action advancing the client's ends, no matter how detrimental the effect on others.

The agency view of the professional–client relationship is unduly narrow. A number of considerations indicate limits to a professional's proper devotion to a client's interests, and consequently to a client's authority in decision making.

1. ... Professionals have obligations to third persons that limit the extent to which they may act in behalf of client interests.

2. The agency view arises most often in the context of defending professionals, especially lawyers, from attribution of client sins. This focus is too narrow to sustain a general account of the professional–client relationship. It best pertains to an adversarial context in which two opposing parties confront one another. In counseling, a lawyer's advice "need not be confined to purely legal considerations.... It is often desirable for a lawyer to point out those factors which may lead to a decision that is morally just as well as legally permissible."[5]

3. Professionals emphasize their independence of judgment. Unlike a soldier who is not expected to think for himself but to do things the army's way, professionals should exercise their training and skills to make objective judgments. The agency view ignores this feature.

4. Except in cases of dire need—medical emergencies, persons charged with crimes—professionals may accept or reject specific clients. With a few restrictions, they may also stop the relationship. Consequently, the agency view is too strong. Professionals must also be ethically free and responsible persons. For their own freedom and the protection of others, they should not abdicate authority and responsibility in decision making.

The strongest possible claim of supremacy has been suggested, namely, that, like the common law doctrine of the merging of the identity of the husband and wife, the attorney and client are similarly merged in the identity of the client.[6] The proposal was made

in the context of attempts by the Internal Revenue Service to obtain possibly incriminating documents from a client's attorney. By the Fifth Amendment to the U.S. Constitution, clients need not surrender possibly incriminating documents in their own possession. The IRS contends this Fifth Amendment privilege does not extend to lawyers, just as it does not extend to tax accountants. If the identities of client and attorney are merged, then the rights and privileges of a client would apply to the attorney.

Although this "legal fiction" could be useful in this narrow context, strong reasons are against adopting it. Fictions should be avoided in law and ethics if straightforward arguments lead to similar results. Once admitted, fictions can bewitch the understanding and lead to unjustifiable results in other areas. The analogy with the common law doctrine of the identity of husband and wife is quite weak. Except for dowry and a few other matters, the identities of husband and wife were completely merged for legal purposes. In contrast, the merger of attorney and client identities would be very limited. As the considerations against the agency view indicate, good grounds exist for separating the attorney and client in many contexts. Even with respect to incriminating materials, professionals should be permitted or even required to reveal confidences indicating a client's intention to commit a crime.[7]

CONTRACT

If a client ought not to be viewed as having most authority and responsibility, then perhaps the authority and responsibility should be shared equally. In law, a professional–client relationship is based on a contract, and the ethical concept of a just contract is of an agreement freely arrived at by bargaining between equals. If the relationship is a contractual one, then there are mutual obligations and rights, "a true sharing of ethical authority and responsibility."[8] As it recognizes the freedom of two equals to determine the conditions of their relationship, the contract model accords well with the liberal values of freedom and equality of opportunity.

However, no gain results from treating as equals people who are not relevantly equal in fact or from assuming a nonexistent freedom. The history of contracts of adhesion (the standard forms offered by monopolies or near monopolies such as airlines) indicates the injustice that can result from falsely assuming contracting parties have equal bargaining power. Many commentators have noted relevant inequalities between professionals and clients, especially in the medical context.[9] First, a professional's knowledge far exceeds that of a client. A professional has the special knowledge produced by long training, knowledge a client could not have without comparable training. Second, a client is concerned about some basic value—personal health, legal status, or financial status—whereas a professional is not as concerned about the subject matter of their relationship. The client usually has more at stake. Third, a professional often has a freedom to enter the relationship that a client lacks. A professional is often able to obtain other clients more easily than a client can obtain another professional. Especially if a potential client has an acute illness or has just been charged with a crime, he or she is not free to shop around for another professional. From this point of view, the bargaining situation is more like that between an individual and a public utility.

These considerations are not as important for the usual situation in architecture, accounting, and engineering. The clients of these professionals are often better informed about the subject matter of the transaction than are clients of lawyers and physicians. For example, businesses and corporations have accountants working for them who can give advice about auditors. Often firms hiring consulting engineers have had previous experience working with engineers in that field. Governments, even local ones, frequently have one or two engineers working for them who can advise and help. Moreover, they are freer than the professional to conclude an arrangement with another firm. Thus, in these situations the factual basis for the contract model is most nearly present. However, the consulting engineer or architect has some special knowledge and ability the client lacks, or else a professional would probably not be hired, so the contract model's empirical assumptions do not quite hold even in these cases.

FRIENDSHIP

Instead of viewing the relationship as one between two free and equal persons dealing at arm's length, some authors suggest that the relationship is more personal. One does not relate to a professional as one does to a grocer or public utility. The personal element is most closely captured by viewing the relationship as one of pals or friends. According to this view, professional and client have a close relationship of mutual trust and cooperation; they are involved in a mutual venture, a partnership.

Perhaps the most sophisticated version of this conception is that proposed by Charles Fried.[10] He is primarily concerned with the legal and medical professions. Fried seeks to justify professionals devoting special attention and care to clients and sometimes seeking ends and using means that they would not seek or use for themselves. Friends are permitted, even expected, to take each others' interests seriously and to give them more weight than they do those of other persons. Fried suggests that the attorney–client relationship is analogous to a one-way limited friendship in which the lawyer helps the client secure legal rights. The lawyer helps the client assert his autonomy or freedom within the bounds society permits. Others have suggested that the physician–patient relationship should similarly be viewed as a cooperative effort of friends or pals to deal with the patient's illness or injury.

The many dissimilarities between friendship and the professional–client relationship, however, destroy the analogy. First, as Fried recognizes, the professional–client relationship is chiefly in one direction; the professional has a concern for the client's interests but not vice versa. Second, friendship is usually between equals. Even in friendships between employer and employee, the employer's superiority in the office is changed to a position of equality in the bar for a drink. As the above discussion of the contract model indicates, professionals and clients are not equals. Third, the affective commitment of friendship is usually lacking.[11] Professionals accept clients for a fee, not out of concern for individuals. Thus, one commentator concludes that "Fried has described the classical notion, not of friendship, but of prostitution."[12] As the factual assumptions of this model are incorrect and the analogy supporting it is weak, its ethical implications are unfounded.

The friendship analogy is not needed to justify a professional paying special attention to a client's interests. The role of a professional is to provide services to clients, and the acceptance of a client is sufficient to justify the special attention. A barber who accepts a customer pays special attention to a customer's hair over that of others who need a haircut more. One need not postulate the barber as friend to justify this attention. It is presupposed by any system of services for a fee.

PATERNALISM

Once one abandons models that assume the professional and client are equal and accepts that the professional is to some extent in a superior position to the client, one faces the problem of the proper extent of professional authority and responsibility in decision making. Parents have knowledge and experience that children lack, and it is often ethically appropriate for them to exercise their judgment on behalf of their children. Similarly, as a professional has knowledge and experience a client lacks and is hired to further the client's interests, perhaps the relationship should be viewed as one of paternalism.

Three arguments are often offered to justify paternalism.

1. The agent has superior knowledge as to what is in a person's best interest. Because the agent knows better than the person what is best, the agent is justified in acting to avoid significant harm to, or to procure a significant benefit for, the person. This argument is perhaps the central one in favor

of paternalism by professionals. As noted before, a professional possesses a relevant knowledge the client lacks, so he or she is better able to perceive the advantages and disadvantages of alternative actions. Consequently, the professional rather than the client should have primary authority and responsibility for decisions.

2. The client is incapable of giving a fully free and informed consent. By "fully free" is meant without duress, psychological compulsion, or other emotional or psychological disturbance. By "informed" is meant with appreciation of the consequences of a course of conduct and its alternatives. If people cannot give such consent, then their decisions will not adequately reflect their reasonable desires and will not be expressions of their "true selves." This argument, which in some respects is a subcase of the previous one, is also popular in the professions, especially medicine. It is often claimed that people who are ill have a strong feeling of dependency, are worried by their illness, and are in a weakened state, and so lack their usual mental command. A somewhat similar argument can be made about lawyers' clients. If charged with a criminal offense, a person is fearful and disturbed. Even in civil suits, a client's emotions might be aroused, preventing an objective view of the situation.

3. A person will later come to agree that the decision was correct. Although the person does not now consent, he will later. For example, an unconscious accident victim with a broken limb will agree that a physician was correct to set the bone. Parents often require their children to do things, such as take music lessons, on the ground that later the children will be glad they did—"You'll thank me later!" An engineer might see a way to improve an agreed-upon rough design to better serve a client's needs, although it involves a significant alteration from the rough design. She might make the change in the belief that the client will agree when he sees the completed design.

To decide whether these justifications support viewing the professional–client relationship as paternalistic, it is useful to consider when reasonable people would allow others to make decisions for them. First, a person might not wish to bother making decisions because the differences involved are trivial. For example, an executive authorizes a secretary to order any needed office supplies, because the differences between brands of paper clips and so forth are not important. Second, the decisions might require knowledge or expertise a person does not possess. For example, an automobile mechanic knows whether a car's oil filter needs changing. One goes to a mechanic for knowledge and service. Third, a person might allow others to make judgments if he or she is or will be mentally incompetent. Some people voluntarily enter mental hospitals.

The first of these reasons does not directly relate to the arguments for paternalism, but the second and third do relate to the first two arguments for paternalism. Reasonable persons would allow others to make decisions for them when they lack the capacity to make reasonable judgments. However, most clients do not have sufficiently impaired judgment to reasonably allow others to make important decisions for them. This incapacity argument has little or no plausibility for the common clients of architects, engineers, and accountants. Business and corporate clients of lawyers are unlikely to have significantly impaired judgment, even if they are biased. Moreover, even with individuals, the view is not plausible for the common legal and medical cases. A person who wants to purchase a house or make a will, or who has the flu or an infection, is rarely so distraught as to be unable to make reasonable decisions. Consequently, the argument from incapacity does not support adopting a paternalistic conception of the professional–client relationship for most cases, although it supports using that conception in special cases.

The first argument for paternalism, that from superior knowledge, fits with reasonable persons allowing others to make decisions when they lack knowledge.

Moreover, clients go to professionals for their superior knowledge and skills: such knowledge and skill is a defining feature of a profession. However, many decisions require balancing legal or health concerns against other client interests. As many authors have noted, crucial professional decisions involve value choices.[13] They are not simple choices of technical means to ends, and even choices of means have a value component. Professionals have not had training in value choices. Even if they had, they might not know a client's value scheme sufficiently to determine what is best for him when everything is considered. An attorney might advise a client that he or she need not agree to such large alimony or child support payments, but the client might decide that for personal relations with the former spouse or the welfare of the children, the larger payments are best. Similarly, a physician can advise bed rest, but because of business interests a client can decide her overall interests are best promoted by continuing to work on certain matters. The client might especially need the income or be on the verge of completing a business deal that will earn a promotion. Physicians sometimes fail to realize that a patient's other concerns, even a vacation trip with the family, can precede health. They write and speak of the problem of patient noncompliance just as parents speak of noncompliance by children. Yet, one does not have everything when one has health. Similarly, a client might want an engineering or architectural design to use one type of construction rather than another because its subsidiary supplies such materials.

Although a professional and client are not equals, sufficient client competence exists to undermine the paternalistic model as appropriate for their usual relationship. Clients can exercise judgment over many aspects of professional services. If they lack information to make decisions, professionals can provide it. Sometimes professionals argue that clients can never have the information they have. This is true, but not directly to the point. Much of the information professionals have is irrelevant to decisions that significantly affect client values. The precise name of a disease and its manner of action are not relevant to deciding between two alternative drug therapies, but the fact that one drug reduces alertness is. Similarly, clients of engineers do not need to know the full weight a structure will bear, only that it is more than sufficient for all anticipated stress. To deny clients authority and responsibility by adopting the paternalistic model is to deny them the freedom to direct their own lives. Clients are not capable of determining the precise nature of their problem, or of knowing the alternative courses of action and predicting their consequences or carrying them out on their own. They need and want the technical expertise of a professional to do so. However, they are capable of making reasonable choices among options on the basis of their total values. They need professionals' information in order to make wise choices to accomplish their purposes.

Finally, when the professional–client relationship is conducted on the paternalistic model, client outcomes are not as good as when the client has a more active role. Douglas E. Rosenthal studied settlement awards in personal injury cases.[14] The actual awards received were compared to an expert panel's judgments of the worth of the claims. The less the client participated in the case by not expressing wants or seeking information from the lawyers, and so on, the more the awards fell short of the panel's estimates of the worth of claims. Not only does the paternalistic model sacrifice client freedom and autonomy, but as a result client values and interests are also often sacrificed.

FIDUCIARY

As a general characterization of what the professional–client relationship should be, one needs a concept in which the professional's superior knowledge is recognized, but the client retains a significant authority and responsibility in decision making. The law uses such a conception to characterize most professional–client relationships, namely, that of a fiduciary. In a fiduciary relationship, both parties are responsible and their judgments given consideration. Because one party is in a more advantageous position, he or she has special obligations to the other. The weaker party depends upon the stronger in ways in which the other does not and so must *trust* the stronger party.

In the fiduciary model, a client has more authority and responsibility in decision making than in the paternalistic model. A client's consent and judgment are required and he participates in the decision-making process, but the client depends on the professional for much of the information upon which

he gives or withholds his consent. The term *consents* (the client consents) rather than *decides* (the client decides) indicates that it is the professional's role to propose courses of action. It is not the conception of two people contributing equally to the formulation of plans, whether or not dealing at arm's length. Rather, the professional supplies the ideas and information and the client agrees or not. For the process to work, the client must trust the professional to accurately analyze the problem, canvass the feasible alternatives, know as well as one can their likely consequences, fully convey this information to the client, perhaps make a recommendation, and work honestly and loyally for the client to effectuate the chosen alternatives. In short, the client must rely on the professional to use his or her knowledge and ability in the client's interests. Because the client cannot check most of the work of the professional or the information supplied, the professional has special obligations to the client to ensure that the trust and reliance are justified.

This is not to suggest that the professional simply presents an overall recommendation for a client's acceptance or rejection. Rather, a client's interests can be affected by various aspects of a professional's work, so the client should be consulted at various times. The extent of appropriate client participation and decision making can be determined by advertence to the reasons for allowing others to make decisions for one. Professionals do not have expertise in a client's values or in making value choices. Their superior knowledge and expertise do not qualify them to make value choices significantly affecting a client's life plans or style. However, they do have knowledge of technical matters. A patient will certainly let a physician determine the dosage of medicines. A client can reasonably allow an engineer to determine the general specifications of materials for a job. A lawyer may decide whether to stipulate facts, object to testimony, or agree to a postponement.[15] Clients allow professionals to make these judgments, because the effects on their values are small and they do not wish to be bothered. In short, client consent and involvement are not necessary when (1) the matter is chiefly a technical one or (2) the value effect is not significant.

The appropriate ethical conception of the professional–client relationship is one that allows clients as much freedom to determine how their life is affected as is reasonably warranted on the basis of their ability to make decisions. In most dealings of business and corporate clients with accountants, architects, engineers, and lawyers, the relationship is close to a contract between equals. As clients have less knowledge about the subject matter for which the professional is engaged, the special obligations of the professional in the fiduciary model become more significant. The professional must assume more responsibility for formulating plans, presenting their advantages and disadvantages, and making recommendations. Because of the increased reliance on the professional, he or she must take special care to be worthy of client trust. Thus, although the fiduciary model is appropriate throughout the range of competent clients and services, the less a client's knowledge and capacity to understand, the greater the professional's responsibilities to the client.

Finally, some clients are not competent to make decisions. In this case, the paternalistic model becomes appropriate. These cases of an incompetent client will almost always be restricted to members of the legal and health professions. Even then it does not follow that the professional should make the decisions. If a client is incompetent, a legal guardian should be appointed to make decisions. When this is done, the professional has a fiduciary relationship to the guardian. Consequently, the appropriate occasions for professionals to adopt a paternalistic role are restricted to those in which a client is incompetent and a guardian has not yet been appointed. . . .

NOTES

1. See Robert M. Veatch, "Models for Ethical Medicine in a Revolutionary Age." *Hastings, Center Report* 2:3 (June 1972): 5–7, p. 5. Veatch calls this the engineering model of the physician, but this assumes it is appropriate for engineers. [See chap. 4, sel. 10, *EIPL.*—ED.]

2. See American Bar Association (ABA) Commission on Evaluation of Professional Standards, *Model Rules of Professional Conduct: Proposed Final Draft* (Chicago:

American Bar Association, 30 May 1981), 1.2(b). [For the final draft, see appendix 1, sample code 1, *EIPL.*—ED.]

3. See William A. Simon, "The Ideology of Advocacy: Procedural Justice in Professional Ethics," 1978 *Wisconsin Law Review*: 29–144, p. 36.

4. Simon's [op. cit.] proposed alternative to the ideology of advocacy suffers these defects to some extent. He does not allow for professional roles. Thus, all professional obligations are at best specifications of ordinary norms. "The foundation principle of non-professional advocacy is that problems of advocacy be treated as a matter of *personal* ethics. . . . Personal ethics apply to people merely by virtue of the fact that they are human individuals. The obligations involved may depend on particular circumstances or personalities, but they do not follow from social role or station." Ibid., p. 131.

5. ABA, *Code of Professional Responsibility and Code of Judicial Conduct* (Chicago: ABA, 1979), EC [Ethical Consideration] 7–8; see also ABA Commission, *Proposed Model Rules*, op. cit., 2.1 and comment.

6. Roger M. Grace, "Invading the Privacy of the Attorney-Client Relationship." *Case and Comment* 81 (July-August 1976): 46–49, p. 47.

7. ABA, *Code of Professional Responsibility*, DR [Disciplinary Rule] 4–101(C)(3); ABA Commission, *Proposed Model Rules* 1.6(b).

8. Veatch, op. cit., p. 7.

9. See, for example, Roger D. Masters, "Is Contract an Adequate Basis for Medical Ethics?" *Hastings Center Report* 5:6 (December 1975): 24–28, p. 5; William F. May, "Code, Covenant, Contract, or Philanthropy?" *Hastings Center Report* 5:6 (December 1975): 29–38, p. 35 [see chap. 4, sel. 11, *EIPL*—ED.]; H. Tristram Englehardt, Jr. "Rights and Responsibilities of Patients and Physicians," in *Medical Treatment of the Dying: Moral Issues*, ed. Michael D. Bayles and Dallas M. High (Cambridge, MA: G. K. Hall and Schenkman, 1978), pp. 16–17; Richard Wasserstrom, "Lawyers as Professionals: Some Moral Issues," in *1977 Conference on Teaching Moral Responsibility: Pre-Conference Materials*, ed. Stuart C. Goldberg (Detroit: University of Detroit Law School, 1977), pp. 122–22 [rpt. chap. 4, sel. 6, *EIPL*—ED.].

10. Charles Fried, "The Lawyer as Friend: The Moral Foundations of the Lawyer-Client Relation," in Goldberg, op. cit., pp. 129–58; and Fried, *Right and Wrong* (Cambridge, MA: Harvard University Press, 1978) chap. 7; see also Veatch, op. cit., p. 7.

11. Edward A. Dauer and Arthur Allen Leff, "The Lawyer as Friend," in Goldberg, op. cit., p. 164.

12. Simon, op. cit., p. 108.

13. See, for example, Glenn C. Graber, "On Paternalism and Health Care," in Davis et al., eds., op. cit., p. 239; Allen E. Buchanan, "Medical Paternalism," *Philosophy and Public Affairs* 7:4 (1978): 370–90, p. 381; and Alan H. Goldman, *The Moral Foundations of Professional Ethics* (Totowa, NJ: Rowman and Littlefield, 1980), pp. 179–86.

14. Douglas E. Rosenthal, *Lawyer and Client: Who's in Charge?* (New York: Russell Sage Foundation, 1974), chap. 2.

15. See ABA, *Code of Professional Responsibility*, op. cit., EC7–7; but see ABA Commission, *Proposed Model Rules*, op. cit., 1.2(a), 1.4.

Autonomy and the Very Limited Role of Advocacy in the Classroom

Joel J. Kupperman

Joel J. Kupperman writes widely on ethics and philosophy.

My thesis is that advocacy in the classroom is rarely appropriate with regard to live (i.e., contentious) moral, political, or social issues, and for that matter not always appropriate with regard to issues within a discipline. By advocacy I mean a teacher's presenting a view as her or his own in a way that might well elicit students' agreement....

... The classic study of undergraduate intellectual and ethical development is William G. Perry, Jr.'s (1970) Forms of Intellectual and Ethical Development in the College Years. Perry's subjects arrived in college looking for right answers, which they then could give back on tests to their instructors. In many cases they were frustrated by instructors' refusal to give them right answers and by their insistence instead on exposing students to a variety of perspectives on controversial issues. Overcoming their disappointment, students passed through a phase of relativism, in which conflicting perspectives were thought to be equally valid. At a yet higher level lay the realization that it can both be true with regard to a particular issue that there is no answer on which all reasonable people must agree and also false that any opinion (however unconsidered) is as good as any other.

Plainly this reflects a style of teaching, at least at Harvard (where Perry's study was conducted), in which attention is given to competing points of view on the same issue, and students tend to be discouraged from thinking that there is a single definitively and clearly right answer to key questions. Some of Perry's subjects were led to ask whether, in the end, some of the competing claims had more to be said for them than their rivals do. This can lead the student to attempt to develop a considered personal point of view. This seems to me very important, not only as part of the student's development but also as a contribution to the actively committed (rather than passive) and reflective citizenry that our political culture requires.

There are many pitfalls here. The ideal is a sophisticated balance: a student who has arrived at a personal point of view but is able to appreciate opposing positions and also can entertain objections to her or his view. Less desirable is the opinionated student who has not been thoughtful enough about her or his position and does not fully hear anything that represents a different outlook. This is always a risk, but is especially one of teaching that heavily

From *The Monist* 79, 488–98 October 1996.

emphasizes the importance of personal points of view. Also less desirable–but much more likely to do well academically–is the student who becomes very good at balancing and comparing points of view without at the same time committing much to a personal and independent approach. This is especially a risk of teaching that heavily emphasizes the task of comparing and analyzing competing perspectives. Having what is sometimes called a "card index mind" is perhaps better than opinionated ignorance, but we should hope to do still better and to produce students who have minds of their own which are organized and receptive.

There are various ways in which a teacher can try to promote this desirable balance between personal independent thought and appreciation of the ideas of others. Sympathetic presentation of ideas that might at first seem repugnant to many students can play an important role in promoting the appreciation of other perspectives: the goal is getting the student to see how someone who is not a fool could come to accept what at first had seemed unpalatable. One device that I have found useful in promoting personal reflection, and that I think could work well in most humanities subjects or in policy-oriented social sciences is this. There is a pause in the middle of an undergraduate class in which each student is handed a sheet of lined paper and is given ten minutes or so to state a clear position on a contentious question and to give at least one argument for this position or against opposing views. It is important that the question genuinely be one on which reasonable people can differ, and on which one could imagine two or more positions that can be supported by good arguments. Ideally, also, the question should be such that most students would have to pause first to think out a response rather than having a kneejerk reaction; and it is a bad sign if all or almost all of the brighter students in the class take pretty much the same position. What students write is returned later to them with comments and queries and a number grade based on the clarity, coherence, and quality of argument of what they wrote. In my experience, most students are appreciably better at the third or fourth of these exercises than they were at first.

For this to work, there can be no thought that the instructor will favor one position over its rivals. Because of this I generally keep my own views out of play in the classroom, and do not use or mention books that I have written. This is especially important in undergraduate courses; but even in graduate seminars there should be, in my view, an "anxiety of influence" on the part of the possible influencer. It is a bad sign when some well-known figure produces students who are essentially clones of himself or herself.

II

There is a good deal to be said about the political importance of producing college graduates who both have reflective personal commitments and are good at understanding opposing points of view. If there is anything to the tradition of civic humanism, these will be bulwarks of a free society. In this paper, though, we can concentrate on the importance of this educational goal in personal development. The key value that needs to be looked at and emphasized is that of autonomy

––––––––

There are practical reasons,... for treating the normal adult human being as autonomous.... In moral and legal systems, autonomy is linked with responsibility: we tend to hold people responsible for their actions if and only if we can regard them as in charge of their lives. In order viably to fulfill their social functions, moral and legal systems must be designed for the broad use of people with varying capacities and degrees of sensitivity, and for people furthermore who may be tempted to abuse nuances. The crucial distinctions therefore are painted with a broad brush. Although there are categories of diminished capacity, by and large there are sharp lines between groups of people who are held responsible for actions of a certain sort and groups that are not. What counts as "coming of age" is such a dividing line. Because of this feature of ordinary legal and moral thinking, it makes sense to regard autonomy as an all-or-nothing feature of someone's life.

———————

There is a sense also in which autonomy is harder to judge: this is in relation to how much someone is in control of her or his own life, is able to do what she or he really wants, or can think for herself or himself. Autonomy in this sense typically is not an all-or-nothing matter. As an abstraction of extreme autonomy, we might try to imagine someone who is entirely self-determining. Arguably God meets this standard; but no human being can, in that each of us is the product of influences (from parents, teachers, the spirit of the age, etc.) that leave their marks even when we rebel against them. Autonomy grows when we transform or reject these influences and/or accept elements of them in a way that makes them part of our own thinking (which involves a degree of whole-heartedness and spontaneity). Diana Meyers (1989) has developed an elaborate and searching account of the skills of autonomy that people can acquire: in her account, a high degree of autonomy is an achievement that may require insight, inventiveness, and strength. . . .

Autonomy . . . is not only a matter of degree, but also can vary from part to part of a person's life and thought. People can think for themselves on some kinds of issues and not on others, or can be whole-hearted in some parts of their lives and not in others. To become more autonomous in major areas of one's life, knowing what one really thinks and choosing what one really wants, has something to do with the development of a self. It is not farfetched to see the college years as especially important in this for most students. During this period they may come to a much better sense of who they are. They also may come to a better sense of where they stand on major social, political, and moral issues. What happens in the classroom is, of course, especially relevant to this latter element in growing autonomy.

. . . The most obvious threats to autonomy involve coercion; and advocacy can involve a subtle form of coercion if a student worries that a professor will be able to infer, from facial expressions in class or from answers on an exam, that she or he does not fully agree with the professor's views and that the professor will grade accordingly. This is serious enough that the case against advocacy in the class-room would be less strong in contexts in which (as in British universities) the functions of teaching and grading are separated than the case is in the context of the typical American college or university.

But there still would be a case, because coercion is far from being the only worry. Usually, in fact, manipulation is a far more serious worry, involving as it does the possibility that a self that is at an early stage of developing autonomy (especially in thought about moral, social, and political questions) can be overwhelmed by the influence of a much stronger and more definite point of view. Students should not come to college to become followers. No doubt the cynical can view what I am warning against as a collusion between those who, because of weakness of personality, want to become followers, and those who, because of a weakness of personality, want to have followers. But this would be too facile a gen-eralization, especially as regards the students. There is no reason not to assume the following: that there are many students who can be educated to think for themselves and to develop the skills associated with this element of autonomy, but who—if they are intel-lectually overpowered at an early stage—may not develop these skills as fully as they might.

III

. . . Some prescriptions of how one should or should not behave are specific to members of a group or of a profession. Thus one has codes of ethics for doctors, for lawyers, etc. Many of the imperatives that these codes yield will also be moral imperatives; but it is arguable that there can be cases in which a doctor or lawyer, all things considered, should do some-thing that violates her or his professional code of ethics. In any event, the code of ethics of a profes-sion helps to define what amounts to good practice of the profession. It is natural to wonder whether there should be a professional ethics for college teachers, also, along the lines of medical and legal ethics.

Prescriptions within a professional ethics, however, can function in two different ways. Some prescriptions are designed to be enforced by regularly constituted bodies following established procedures. Thus some rules of legal ethics are linked to disciplinary committees that can censure or move to disbar someone; and some rules of medical ethics are connected, also, with procedures by which a doctor can have his or her license taken away.

By and large, when we think of medical or legal ethics we think of rules that are linked to formal sanctions. There is no reason though not to think that the ethics specific to doctors could contain other kinds of prescriptions: e.g., that one should when possible take the time to understand the role of a disease in a patient's life, or that one should not officiously prolong the life of someone who is in great pain, has no hope, and wishes to die. Lawyers could be generally enjoined not to make public relations work on behalf of a client's image in the media too great a part of legal representation, and not to badger emotionally upset "hostile" witnesses (especially rape victims or children) excessively. Such prescriptions would not be linked to formal sanctions. Indeed, to link them would be both intrusive and subject to abuse. To have professional bodies that monitored the degree to which a lawyer's work consisted of public relations or the time that a doctor spent in thinking about the broader context of patients' cases would be extremely cumbersome. It could easily lend itself, also, to intimidation of people who were disliked by their colleagues.

Linkage to formal sanctions carries with it a limitation on discretion. To say, "This violates the rules of your professional association and can lead to censure or the loss of your license" is a way of saying "Don't think twice." It leaves no room for treatment of unusual cases as exceptions, unless of course there are explicit categories of exception built into the rule itself and the unusual case fits one of these categories.

One example of this feature of a rule, linked to formal sanctions, in a professional ethics is the case of two court-appointed defense attorneys who refused to tell the parents of one of their client's victims what had happened to their daughter, even though they knew where she was buried. . . . Attorney–client privilege was at stake, and there certainly is room for argument about this case. But it is possible to think both that the general protection of attorney–client privilege is desirable, and also that in an occasional extreme case there can be countervailing needs that outweigh it. It is very hard to see, though, how just this position could be woven effectively into a legal ethics linked to formal sanctions. Once one says, "There are exceptions; you may have to judge for yourself," the rule loses most of its power. An alternative approach is to say, in effect, "For purposes of enforcement the rule does not have exceptions; there may be cases in which your conscience will tell you that you ought to make an exception, but no matter how reasonable this is you will be punished all the same." This may seem a counter-intuitive combination of judgments. But one needs to distinguish between "Was that the best thing to do?" and "What is the best verdict on someone who has done it?" Sometimes it is imperative that one deter people from emulating rule-breaking behavior, even though in an unusual case such behavior turned out (perhaps, in that case, predictably) to have good results. Thus there are occasional cases in the military in which someone is (legitimately) court-martialed for having done what is generally agreed to have been the right thing.

There is no reason why a professional ethics cannot consist both of rules that are linked to formal sanctions and rules that are not so linked. Rules for college professors of the first sort might include such things as rules against plagiarism, selling grades for money, sexual involvement with students, violence against colleagues, etc. But there might also be rules of the second sort, analogous to the recommendations to doctors and lawyers to pursue professional activities in some of the ways that separate good from mediocre or shabby practice. The recommendation for which this paper argues is intended to be of this sort.

REFERENCES

Kipnis, Kenneth (1986) Legal Ethics (Englewood Cliffs, NJ: Prentice-Hall).

Kupperman, Joel J. (1975) "Precision in History," Mind 84, 374–89.

Kupperman, Joel J. (1983) Foundations of Morality (London: George Allen & Unwin).

Meyers, Diana T. (1989) Self, Society, and Personal Choice (New York: Columbia University Press).

Perry, William G., Jr. (1970) Forms of Intellectual and Ethical Development in the College Years: A Scheme (New York: Holt, Rinehart & Winston).

John Wesley Hall, Jr.

Professional Responsibility for Lawyers

John Wesley Hall, Jr., is a lawyer who is a well-known expert on professionalism and ethics.

One of the great marvels of the American legal system is the way it seeks to balance important interests of both the government and the accused. Sometimes the balance is marked by irony.

Perhaps the greatest irony, at least for nonlawyers, is how the system balances the lawyer's duty of honesty, candor, and fairness, discussed in this chapter, with the lawyer's duties of zealousness in representation of the client and of loyalty and the duty to maintain client confidences.

"There is no gainsaying that arriving at the truth is a fundamental goal of our legal system."[1] As will be seen, the truth in any one case, however, is secondary to the larger policy interests of the adversary system. Lawyers have all sorts of duties that run counter to the truth. For example, criminal defense lawyers are expected to: defend the guilty client to put the government to its proof; cross-examine witnesses that they may believe are telling the truth to expose bias or possible mistakes; put on client perjury when the client cannot be dissuaded from it; and of course, keep the client's confidences. In each of these examples; there are higher interests involved than the transient need of one client. Even though

a lawyer has all these duties to clients which run counter to their more generalized duties to the system, a lawyer can and must still be honest, candid, and fair.

II. DUTY OF HONESTY

A lot has been said about lawyers as professional liars. This is one separate fact from fiction or half-truth? Which lawyers do not earn our trust? Do we muddle on, giving every lawyer the benefit of the doubt until we have caught them in a lie (or we hear of those who have), or do we make every lawyer we deal with prove his or her integrity?

We have to give them the benefit of the doubt until they have proved they are no longer trustworthy or the system will not operate smoothly. The system depends upon trust, and it and the lawyers who are victims need to deal harshly with any breach of that trust, including those who simply do not care about the truth in their relations rather than just putting forth a complete lie.

Your Word Is Your Bond

"An honest man's word is as good as his bond." Next to a lawyer's courtroom or negotiating skills, one's

From *Search and Seizure*, Criminal Law Library, 1982.

credibility with the courts and other lawyers has to be a lawyer's greatest asset. A lawyer who cannot be trusted or believed by judges and lawyers does not serve his or her clients, the system of justice, or him or herself.

When a lawyer gives his or her word about something, the lawyer must follow through unless there is a vitally compelling reason for not. Then, the reason may have to be revealed to the other persons involved so they know why a promise had to be broken to preserve the lawyer's integrity.

Integrity is everything. Without it, you are nothing.

Ethical Responsibilities

Ethical rules prohibit lawyers generally from conduct involving dishonesty, fraud, deceit, or misrepresentation. Further, no lawyer shall commit a crime that reflects adversely on the lawyer's honesty, trustworthiness, or fitness to be a lawyer.

The rules of professional responsibility also have more specific provisions. There are separate rules for fairness toward the opposing party and counsel, which also include conduct nominally or actually obstructing justice, and for candor toward the tribunal, including the use of perjury and concealing and fabricating evidence. These, of course, also constitute crimes from which lawyers are not immune from prosecution merely because they are lawyers.

Honesty to One's Self

A lawyer has a duty to be honest with himself or herself and any personal moral values. "Integrity, in other words, is a kind of substantive honesty, or honesty to one's self."[2] "[W]hen a lawyer takes a position, files a claim, or makes a statement which violates his conscience, he is lying to himself."[3] Ethical rules implicitly recognize this duty.

This duty, however, goes beyond the law. Any lawyer who can lie to himself that what he is doing for a client is right and just when it really is not will devalue his or her worth to him or herself and become a mere "hired gun" for the client. Ultimately, this course has to pervert or dilute the lawyer's own sense of values.

If there is any doubt about the moral correctness of planned conduct on behalf of a client, the lawyer can either refuse to do it or withdraw. Whichever course is taken, the lawyer cannot lie to him or herself about it.

Lawyers' Criminal Responsibility in General

Lawyers are not generally immune from prosecution for crimes committed on behalf of clients or themselves, except perhaps where the law is unclear and the lawyer acts in good faith. Lawyers have been prosecuted for all kinds of offenses as accessories and conspirators with their clients or for offenses against the administration of justice for obstruction of justice, tampering with evidence, suborning or aiding perjury, and tampering with witnesses, and for money laundering. They always have and they always will—lawyers have no immunity. Indeed, they make a bigger target for the police officer or prosecutor wanting to make a name for himself. Also, lawyers are treated more harshly under the U.S. Sentencing Guidelines.

Personal and Moral Influences on the Law of Professional Responsibility

The law and ethics of criminal defense transcends the law and what it requires or disapproves. A lawyer should also include any personal moral or ethical considerations in determining whether conduct is appropriate. Just because the law does not prohibit particular conduct does not mean that the lawyer has to do it.

Checklist: A criminal defense analysis of ethical issues should follow the following format.

1. **Sixth Amendment:** What does the Sixth Amendment duty of zealous and loyal counsel require in a particular situation?
2. **Other law:** What does the law otherwise permit or prohibit, and does that law permit what the lawyer proposes to do?
3. **Moral considerations:** What does the lawyer's personal moral code dictate in the situation?

4. **Ethics rules**: What do the ethics rules permit or prohibit? If the lawyer feels that the ethics rule violates the lawyer's Sixth Amendment duty, can the lawyer violate the ethics rules in pursuit of a higher duty? I submit that, in the proper circumstance, the lawyer can, and I have done so myself. The ethics rules recognize that an ethical duty may be conditioned upon complying with other law. Therefore, the ethics rules must be read through the lens of the Sixth Amendment and the duty of zealous advocacy.

AMENDMENT G TO THE UNITED STATES CONSTITUTION

In all criminal prosecutions, the accused shall enjoy the right to a speedy and public trial, by an impartial jury of the state and district wherein the crime shall have been committed, which district shall have been previously ascertained by law, and to be informed of the nature and cause of the accusation; to be confronted with the witnesses against him; to have compulsory process for obtaining witnesses in his favor, and to have the assistance of counsel for his defense.

NOTES

1. U.S. v. Havens, 446 U.S. 620, 626, 100 S. Ct. 1912, 64 L. Ed. 2d 559, 6 Fed. R. Evid. Serv. 1 (1980), citing Oregon v. Hass, 420 U.S. 714, 722, 95 S. Ct. 1215, 43 L. Ed. 2d 570 (1975).
2. RPC Rule 3.4; CPR DR 7-102(A). See § 3:16.
3. See also Chs 16, 21, and 22 dealing with obstruction of justice and relations with witnesses.

John K. Davis

Conscientious Refusal and a Doctor's Right to Quit

John K. Davis is a Professor at the Brody School of Medicine.

I. INTRODUCTION

When a patient requests a procedure the doctor considers immoral, why can't the doctor simply *quit*? The usual approaches to conscientious refusal ask whether a doctor's professional duties require fulfilling such requests, and if so, whether those duties are outweighed by other moral considerations. Those are legitimate approaches. However, if a doctor simply quits the doctor-patient relationship, wouldn't that dodge the problem by *cancelling* the doctor's professional duties towards that patient, thereby eliminating any conflict between those duties and other moral considerations?

At the risk of sounding flippant, this is essentially what I argue. There is such a thing as an ethics of quitting—the moral constraints on terminating of curtailing a doctor–patient relationship. With qualifications, a doctor may refuse a patient's request provided the refusal leaves the patient no worse off than the patient would have been had the patient never met that doctor in the first place. Sometimes refusal is not enough to put the patient in that position, and the doctor must take extra steps to ensure

From *Journal of Medicine and Philosophy*, 2, 104, Vol. 29, No. 1, pp 75–91.

that the patient is no worse off: I call those extra steps "restitution."

The "restitution approach" is important also because it provides a framework for answering a number of questions concerning the ethics of quitting, such as whether a refusing doctor must refer the patient, whether a doctor may provide "moral counseling" to a patient, and the significance of an ethical consensus in the medical profession. . . .

II. THE RESTITUTION APPROACH

Sometimes doctors have moral objections to fulfilling patient requests for certain procedures—"conscience cases," I'll call them. The best-known examples concern prolife doctors who object to counseling and referring patients to abortionists, or providing abortifacient drugs or performing antenatal diagnoses of nonremediable fetal defects that might be managed with elective abortion. Even a pro-choice doctor might object to the selective abortion of female fetuses, perhaps because the doctor believes sex selection is demeaning to women, or bad social policy.

Of course, the range of possible moral conflicts between physicians and patients extends well beyond abortion. A doctor may have moral objections to fulfilling a patient's request for physician-assisted suicide, or providing reproductive assistance to a 60-year-old single woman who wants help conceiving and gestating a child, or providing futile life support at the request of a surrogate decisionmaker, or to terminating life support when the doctor believes the patient's competent request for it is premature.

Conscience cases can also involve disagreements between doctors and those with whom they have a contract for employment or reimbursement. For example, a resident must follow the orders of an attending physician, but may believe that will not serve the patient's best interest. This can also happen in a group practice and in managed care settings.

One way for a doctor to resolve conscience cases is to terminate or curtail the doctor–patient relationship, so that the doctor is no longer that patient's doctor (either entirely, or at least for the procedure

in question). To "terminate" a doctor–patient relationship is to end it completely. To "curtail" it is to limit it so that a particular procedure is not available within that relationship. To say the relationship is "repealed" is to say it is terminated and/or curtailed.

To motivate this way of thinking about conscientious refusal, consider a couple who came to a maternal-fetal specialist and requested an ultrasound so they can abort the fetus if it is female. The doctor is morally opposed to abortion for sex selection, and thinks, "Why did they have to come to *me?*" Well, they didn't and had matters gone differently, they might not have. If this couple had never come to this doctor, this doctor would have no moral obligation to them. Moreover, if they *had* gone to some other doctor, this doctor would have no business interfering with their plans. This suggests two premises:

1. If you're not this patient's doctor, you need not do anything for this patient.
2. If this patient is the patient of some *other* doctor, you have no right to interfere with what they do.

The second premise has a qualification that is very important for conscientious refusal. There are degrees of immorality. In general we do not have a right to stop other people from doing something *merely* on the grounds that what they do is immoral. To justify interference with their actions, those actions have to be *sufficiently* immoral. Otherwise, the immorality means merely that *you* cannot do the act, not that you can actively prevent someone *else* from doing it. For example, if your neighbors are committing mild psychological abuse of their child, you probably would judge that the wrong did not rise to the level where it would be appropriate to take actions to stop them. (Assume they would not listen to reason.)

Degrees of immorality are possible in the refusal cases mentioned earlier. For example, on a gradualist view, abortion is less wrong early in gestation and more wrong as the fetus develops. On this view, it is possible to believe that, although it is wrong for people to abort early in a pregnancy, it is not wrong enough that anyone should stop them at that stage. To take another example, the wrongness of a

60-year-old woman getting reproductive assistance to conceive and gestate a child may be a function of her qualifications as a mother. It may never be morally right, but its degree of wrongness may depend on her qualities and situation. Depending on which, moral positions are correct, similar points can be made about life support for dying patients and physician-assisted suicide.

These examples show that we should qualify the second premise: "Unless what the patient wants is sufficiently wrong." This qualification to the second premise means that there are some cases where you are morally justified in interfering with another person's wrongful act, and other cases where, even though the act is wrongful, you are *not* morally justified in interfering with it. A lot will hang on this distinction.

These two premises support an argument for a qualified right of conscientious refusal:

1. If you're not this patient's doctor, you need not do anything for this patient.
2. If this patient is the patient of some *other* doctor, you have no right to interfere with what they do, unless what they do is sufficiently wrong.
3. Therefore, in any case where premises 1 and 2 are met (and their exceptions are not met), you do not have to provide the requested procedure, but you may not stop the patient from getting that procedure elsewhere.
4. Therefore, if you can transform your existing relationship with a patient into a sufficiently close approximation of what would have happened had that patient gone to some other doctor, then you do not have to provide the procedure, but you may not stop the patient from getting the procedure done elsewhere.

The fourth step in this argument says, in effect, that a doctor can refuse to provide a procedure on moral grounds, provided the doctor does not thereby make the patient worse off than she would have been had she never gone to him in the first place. In effect, the doctor resolves the conflict by repealing his relationship with that patient, thereby canceling his or her duty to that patient. . . .

Now things get complicated, and the complications flow from two possibilities. First, it is possible that the qualification to premise 2 is met: what the patient wants is so immoral that the doctor *is* morally justified in interfering with the patient's efforts to get it from another doctor. If this is true, then the third and fourth steps of the argument are different— the doctor does *not* have to transform her existing relationship with a patient into a sufficiently close approximation of what would have happened had that patient gone to some other doctor. For example, if the patient wants help enacting Munchausen's syndrome by proxy on her child, the fact that *some* doctor will do it (for a price) does not obligate her current doctor to refer her to the willing doctor.

The second complication concerns this condition in the fourth step of the argument: "if you can transform your existing relationship with a patient into a sufficiently close approximation of what would have happened had that patient gone to some other doctor." The complication is the possibility that this condition cannot be met. For example, the patient's situation may have changed since he first came to that doctor, and simple refusal might not leave him where he would have been had he not come to that doctor in the first place either because his condition has progressed, or because time is running out, or both. If this happens, then, in order to transform the relationship into what would otherwise have been the case, the doctor must do more than simply refuse.

I call this the "restitution approach" because we can think of the doctor's efforts to make the patient no worse off as a kind of restitution: if refusing makes the patient worse off than she would have been had she not gone to that doctor in the first place, then the refusing doctor must (subject to qualifications mentioned below) *make restitution* by making her situation roughly what it would have been had she not come to him at all. (More later about what this involves.) The restitution approach comprises the four-step argument presented above and the following statement of the right of conscientious refusal:

Right of conscientious refusal: To refuse a patient request on moral grounds, ask what the patient's situation would have been had she chosen another doctor, and put her there—unless you'd be morally justified in interfering with her getting that procedure even when another doctor provides it.

If you can't meet these conditions, then you must give her what she wants—*unless she would not have found another doctor to do so....*

Earlier I mentioned many kinds of conscience cases, including abortion, futile treatment requests, 60-year-old would-be mothers, assisting an AIDS patient's suicide, and many more. Can one approach handle such a diverse set of problems? The answer is that refusal is justified by restitution (or the fact that restitution is not necessary to put the patient where she would have been had she never gone to the refusing doctor). On this approach, refusal in not justified by the nature, sufficiency, or weight of the doctor's reasons for refusing. Thus, the doctor's reasons for refusing—and their nature, weight, or sufficiency—are irrelevant to the justification. So long as either the doctor provides restitution, or restitution is unnecessary (because a simple refusal will leave the patient where she would have been had she not gone to that doctor in the first place), the refusal is justified even if 1) the refusal is sincere but the doctor's moral analysis is mistaken, or 2) the doctor's refusal is based on a nonmoral concern, such as a personality conflict.

———————

Of course, sometimes restitution is necessary, but the doctor either will not or cannot provide it. In such cases, justifying a refusal does require a sufficient moral objection, for the restitution approach says that restitution need not be made when the doctor would be "morally justified in interfering with [the patient] getting that procedure even when another doctor provides it." To be morally justified in interfering with another doctor providing a procedure to that doctor's patient probably requires a moral objection to what they are doing; the objecting bystanders' own distress or convenience seems insufficient....

Long-standing doctor–patient relationships characterized by considerable trust and commitment on both sides call for separate discussion, for those characteristics affect what it takes to make full restitution. Suppose a doctor in general practice has seen a patient for 30 years, the patient trusts her deeply she feels highly responsible for him, and they feel some attachment to each other. Had he seen another doctor 30 years ago, he might have an equally close relationship with a doctor willing to provide the procedure, but there is now no way to achieve that close a relationship with another doctor soon enough to get the procedure done. If so, then the patient loses something when his long-term doctor refuses, and the refusing doctor must compensate for that "something" as part of the restitution.

It's nearly impossible for the refusing doctor to make up for the loss of 30 years of trust and familiarity. However, she may not have to. Consider the interference clause again: restitution need not be provided when fulfilling the request would be sufficiently immoral that the refusing doctor would be justified in interfering with another doctor and patient who attempt to fulfill a similar request. If we construe refusal to provide the procedure, together with refusal to put a patient where he would have been, as a kind of interference, we should also construe refusal to provide the procedure, together with *inability* to put him there, as a kind of interference. In the case of the 30-year doctor–patient relationship, the doctor is *unable* to put her patient where he would have been—that would take years. Therefore, to justify a refusal to provide the procedure when the refusing doctor is unable to entirely replace the current relationship, the procedure must be immoral enough to justify a degree of interference equivalent to somehow taking the trust and familiarity out of the relationship between another doctor and another patient. In short, the more the patient loses by the refusal, the more restitution the doctor must make, and the more the doctor is unable to completely restitute, the more immoral the procedure must be to justify her failure to provide complete restitution. Thus, the degree of immorality matters not only to *whether* restitution must be paid, but also to *how much* restitution must be paid—sometimes partial restitution is enough. This means that, unless the procedure is sufficiently immoral, the doctor will not be justified in refusing her long-term patient his request, even though she would be justified in refusing that procedure to a relatively new patient.

III. FIVE QUESTIONS ABOUT REFUSAL

A. **Referral inconsistency:** Can it be consistent to refuse to do a procedure on moral grounds, yet refer the patient so someone else will do it?

B. **Majority limitation:** What moral significance, if any, should we attribute to a majority consensus about what is morally acceptable medical practice?

C. **The only available doctor:** Can the absence of other available doctors mean that a doctor must perform an objectionable procedure?

D. **"Moral counseling":** To what extent should a doctor discuss with a patient the doctor's moral reasons for refusing?

E. **Avoiding the field:** When, if ever, do a doctor's moral beliefs obligate the doctor to stay out of a specialty?

A. Duty to refer and referral inconsistency

There is a widely-held view that refusing doctors have a duty to refer patients who are leaving for one reason or another. This view reflects the fact that the patient's situation may have changed since she first came to see her doctor, either because her condition has progressed, or time is running out, or both. This may create a duty to refer and perhaps otherwise facilitate a transfer, for if the patient's condition has changed, she may need another doctor quickly and be unable to go out and look for one. If she had not come to that doctor in the first place, she might very well have another doctor who, right now, would be treating her condition the way she wants. Therefore, in order put her in the situation she would otherwise have found, her doctor must refer her to another doctor.

What about referral inconsistency? The inconsistency is that it's permissible for the doctor to refuse to do the procedure only if the procedure is immoral, but if the procedure is immoral, then it's immoral for any *other* doctor to do the procedure. Thus, it seems the doctor should neither perform the procedure nor refer the patient to anyone else. The solution to this inconsistency stems from the interference exception (italicized below) to the right of conscientious refusal:

> Ask what the patient's situation would have been had she chosen another doctor, and put her there— *unless you'd be morally justified in interfering with her getting that procedure even when another doctor provides it.*

If what the patient wants is *not* immoral enough to justify the refusing doctor in interfering with her efforts to get it from another doctor, and she would have found another doctor had she not come to that doctor, then given that the doctor must restore her to the situation that would have happened *had* she gone to another doctor, her doctor must see to it that she *gets* another doctor. Her doctor must refer her to a doctor willing to do the procedure. If referral is not enough, then her doctor must take further steps to facilitate her to another doctor. Thus there is no inconsistency: the duty to refer exists only if the procedure is too immoral to perform, but not immoral enough to justify interfering with someone else's performance of it. In cases where the procedure *is* immoral enough to justify interference, there is no duty to refer (refusal to refer being a kind of interference).

B. The majority limitation

Earlier I questioned the common view that what the majority of doctors in the relevant specialty consider appropriate is relevant to whether a referral should be provided, or conscientious refusal is justified, or a doctor should stay out of a field. I question this because what a majority believes is irrelevant to what is moral. Why, then, do so many people believe it is relevant here? The answer is that majority consensus is not irrelevant to a doctor's duties *in those cases where* fulfilling the patient's request is immoral but not immoral enough to justify interference. The consensus among doctors is relevant because, if the patient had sought out some other doctor in the first place, the odds are high that she would have encountered a doctor whose views are consistent with the majority.

Consider refusal: if most other doctors would do the procedure, then the patient probably would have found a willing doctor had she not come to the refusing doctor first. In that case, the refusing doctor must refer her (provided the procedure is not sufficiently immoral to justify interference), for her position has changed since she came to him. If, however, most other doctors would not do the procedure (whether their reasons for refusing are moral or otherwise), then the refusing doctor has no duty to refer. After all, the patient will be no worse off than she would have been had she never come to that doctor in the first place. This reasoning explains the last clause to my specification of the right of conscientious refusal:

> If you can't meet [all the above] conditions, then you must give her what she wants—*unless she would not have found another doctor to do so.*

How large must the majority be before we can say that the patient would not have found another doctor to provide the procedure, and that her doctor may therefore refuse to refer? Suppose 90% of all available doctors would have refused to provide the procedure. The patient might still have kept looking until she found a doctor in the 10% minority who would provide the procedure. The majority of unwilling doctors must be *very* large, or to put it another way, the patient's odds of finding a willing doctor must be *very* small, before her doctor may refuse to refer a patient whose request is not immoral enough to justify interference.

I used referral to explain this analysis. The majority limitation will come up again in the next subsection, concerning refusal when no other doctor is available, and in the last subsection, concerning when doctors should stay out of a field.

C. When no other doctor is available to do a procedure, must the doctor who finds it morally objectionable do it anyway?

Now suppose that the procedure is *not* immoral enough to justify interference (and hence refusal to refer). Suppose further that no other doctor will take this patient because her condition has progressed too far, but that one of them would have taken her earlier and given her the procedure she requests. Referral and transfer are no longer possible, interference is not justified, and the majority consensus is such that the patient had a reasonable chance of finding a willing doctor had she not come to the refusing doctor in the first place. From this combination of factors it follows that the refusing doctor must provide the requested procedure. If, however, the procedure is immoral enough to justify interference, then the refusing doctor does not have to provide the procedure whether or not another doctor is available.

D. Limited moral counseling is required

Our fourth question is whether doctors may—or should—reveal their moral reasons for refusing to provide a requested procedure. I answer that doctors have a duty to reveal their moral reasons for refusal because, if they do not, patients may mistakenly conclude that there are medical reasons for the refusal. In that event, the patient is worse off because she came to the refusing doctor: she now has a false belief that may limit her perceived options. In order to avoid making patients worse off in this way, doctors not only may but *should* reveal their moral objections to providing a given treatment.

There are limitations, of course. A doctor's persuasive ability can overwhelm patients who tend to defer to doctors and other authority figures, or who cannot compete with the doctor in reasoning and verbal ability. The doctor should communicate his objection in a way that does not diminish the patient's ability to exercise her own moral judgment.

This does not mean that a doctor may not persuade a patient to revoke her request for the procedure, but if he does, he must do so by helping the patient to see another point of view, and not by overwhelming and effectively coercing the patient.

E. When doctors should stay out of a field

Some writers suggest that doctors who cannot bring themselves to provide treatments considered acceptable in a given specialty should stay out of that field. Once again, what the majority believes is irrelevant to whether a procedure is morally acceptable. And once again, a majority consensus is relevant here in another way.

Doctors should stay out of fields where they cannot provide procedures most other specialists deem acceptable—*in those cases where the procedure is so immoral that interference is justified*. However, if interference *is* justified, then they can enter a field where they will routinely refuse to provide procedures other specialists consider routine—a form of interference.

Suppose a pro-life maternal-fetal doctor practices in a location where prochoice maternal-fetal specialists are not hard to find, and where many patients hold pro-choice views. Under those conditions, if the nature and strength of her pro-life views are such that she is not justified in interfering, then she has a duty to refer patients to doctors who perform abortions. Why can't she stay in the field and simply refer all patients who want abortions? She probably can provided that her routine refusals and referrals do not interfere unduly with her patients or her community of specialists.

However, on what I will call the "aggregation principle," under certain conditions a doctor *is* obligated to stay out of a field. Although each referral may not inconvenience a given patient unduly, the cumulative volume of terminations and referrals might produce a large volume of patient inconvenience. If so, over time our maternal-fetal doctor will create a lot of interference (in the form of inconvenience), albeit distributed over many people and not very heavily on any one of them. One way to avoid all that inconvenience is for the doctor to routinely disclose her pro-life views at the outset, make sure the patient understands that other doctors are pro-choice, and advise the patient that she may later want a procedure which that doctor will not provide, but which the other doctors will. Depending on the nature of the doctor's practice, that may be enough. However, if disclosures up front do not sufficiently reduce the total volume of inconvenience, that volume may, constitute more total harm to others than the harm the doctor would suffer by staying out of that specialty.

It can be argued that harms distributed over many people, none of whom suffer unduly as individuals, can be aggregated for purposes of determining whether a pattern of behavior over time is morally permissible. If so, then the total volume of interference can be weighed against the harm the doctor suffers by staying out of her chosen field. On the ethical principle that harms can be aggregated in this way, the doctor should stay out of the field. If, however, we reject that principle, then even in the circumstances described above, the doctor is not obligated to stay out of the field. I do not know whether the aggregation principle is true, so I will leave this issue unresolved. Readers with stronger views about aggregation can draw the proper conclusions about when, if ever, doctors are obligated to stay out of fields.

IV. CONCLUSION

Doctors have a qualified right to conscientious refusal because they have a qualified right to quit, a right to repeal all or part of their relationship with a patient. The qualifications stem from the principle that a doctor's refusal should not make the patient *worse* off than he would have been had he never gone to that doctor in the first place. A doctor's refusal is justified provided (1) restitution is unnecessary to ensure the patient is no worse off, or (2) the doctor makes full restitution, or (3) what the patient wants is sufficiently immoral to justify interference. This restitution approach enables us to settle several controversies about conscientious refusal: when there is a duty to refer, why the moral consensus among doctors seems relevant even though it does not determine what is morally acceptable, whether doctors must provide objectionable procedures when no other doctor is available, whether "moral counseling" is permissible, and whether doctors should stay out of fields whose standard procedures they find immoral.

	Solicitation of Clients: The Professional Responsibility to Chase Ambulances
Monroe H. Freedman	

Monroe H. Freedman is a Professor of Law at Hofstra University.

INTRODUCTION

A five-year-old boy named Ernest Gene Gunn was seriously injured when he was hit by a car driven by John J. Washek. Shortly after the accident, the boy's mother was visited at home by an adjuster from Washek's insurance company. The adjuster told Ms. Gunn that there was no need for her to hire a lawyer, because the company would make a settlement as soon as Ernest was out of his doctor's care. If Ms. Gunn was not satisfied at that time, he explained, she could get a lawyer and file suit.

Ernest's injuries were sufficiently severe to require a doctor's care for twenty-three months. During that time, the adjuster was regularly in touch with Ms. Gunn. At the end of Ernest's medical treatment, however, despite several efforts on her part to reach him, the adjuster was unavailable. Finally, she retained a lawyer, who promptly filed suit for her. Ernest Gunn never had his day in court, however, because the insurance company successfully pleaded a two-year statute of limitations.

From Lexis Nexis, 3rd edition, June 2004.

USING THE STATUTE OF LIMITATIONS UNJUSTLY

A lawyer is not required to represent a client whose claim or defense is morally offensive to the lawyer. In fact, if the lawyer's feelings are sufficiently strong, she should decline the case on conflict of interest grounds. . . . because the lawyer is required to "abide by" the client's decision with regard to "objectives" of the representation, but need only "consult" with the client with regard to the "means" of pursuing the client's ends.

HOW THE LEGAL PROFESSION FAILED ERNEST GUNN

The legal profession failed in its responsibilities when a plaintiff's lawyer was not at Ms. Gunn's doorstep at least as soon as the insurance adjuster.

The response of the organized bar to the plight of the aggrieved individuals has been to denounce as "ambulance-chasers" the lawyers who seek to give them their day in court before it is too late.

Illustrative of the bar's attitude is a $125,000 study of lawyers' ethics undertaken by the Philadelphia Bar Association not long after *Gunn v. Washek* was decided. The resulting report recognized the need "to counter the activity of [insurance] carriers' adjusters." It suggested, however, that the problem could be dealt with "by the exercise of restraint on the part of carriers." There was no reference in the report to any professional responsibility on the part of those lawyers who are house counsel to insurance carriers or who regularly represent them in litigation. On the contrary, the substance of the report was dedicated to the need to stamp out "ambulance chasing."

Ironically, the report did acknowledge the "social value" of automobile wrecking companies listening to police calls in order to be the first to arrive at accident scenes to carry off the damaged vehicles. The report found no social value, however, in a similar effort by lawyers to protect the rights of the injured people (which would include the preservation of relevant evidence that might be hauled off and destroyed by the wrecking companies).

ADVERTISING FOR CLIENTS—"THIS NEW REVOLUTION IN LAW PRACTICE"

The first attack on the Model Code restrictions on advertising and solicitation was in 1970. The Stern Community Law Firm in Washington, D.C., a public-interest law firm of which Freedman was Director, advertised in newspapers, magazines, and on the radio seeking clients for two cases that the firm wanted to litigate. The first of these cases related to child adoption. At that time the District of Columbia kept a larger proportion of its homeless children in public institutions than did any other American city. These institutions were notoriously overcrowded and understaffed, and the children were being neglected and abused. Nevertheless, many people who wanted to adopt the children were being barred from doing so solely because

they were single, because both parents were working, or because they were white (virtually all of the homeless children were African American). The firm therefore advertised for clients who wanted to adopt children but who wanted to adopt children but who were unable to do so because of these rules.

Similarly, when the Food and Drug Administration refused to take action regarding toys that presented a risk of maiming and killing children, the firm published a list of the toys and their manufactures and offered to represent anyone who had bought one of the toys and was having difficulty getting a refund.

Complaints by judges and lawyers about the Stern Firm's advertisements resulted in a proceeding against Freedman and the firm before the Bar's Committee on Legal Ethics and Grievances. In its brief to the Grievance Committee, the firm argued that advertising and solicitation by lawyers is protected under the First Amendment as freedom of speech by the attorney and as an essential aspect of the client's right to petition for redress of grievances. The firm also argued that it is important to the profession as well as to the public that lawyers be seen reaching out to serve members of the community and not just corporations and other wealthy clients. Although the Committee began with an openly hostile attitude, it ultimately issued the first Bar Association opinion in the country approving advertisements for clients by public interest lawyers serving without fees.

Despite this limitation, Fred Graham wrote in the *New York Times* that "for a profession that has forbidden lawyers to wear tie clasps bearing their state bar emblem or to send Christmas cards to prospective clients, on the ground that such activities were unethical 'advertising,' the activities approved in the new ruling are unprecedented." In introducing federal legislation to override the Bar's decision, a member of Congress complained that "[c]lient soliciting, this new revolution in law practice ... can be expected to usher in a new era of encouraged litigation from so-called poor people, class action by groups, and idealists in the areas of consumerism and ecology, etc."

LAWYER ADVERTISING IN THE SUPREME COURT

It did that and more. Six years later, in *Bates v. State Bar of Arizona*, the Supreme Court agreed that advertising by lawyers is protected under the First Amendment.

In response to the contention that advertising has an adverse effect on professionalism, the Court found any connection between advertising and the erosion of "true professionalism" to be "severely strained." Because "professionalism" is frequently a euphemism for public image, the Court pointed out that the failure of lawyers to advertise may be viewed by the public as a professional failure to reach out and serve the community. Elaborating on that point, the Court noted that "cynicism with regard to the profession may be created by the fact that it long has publicly eschewed advertising, while condoning the actions of the attorney who structures his social or civic associations so as to provide contacts with potential clients."

Nor did the Court find persuasive the contention that advertising is "inherently misleading." "[W]e view as dubious," the Court said, "any justification that is based on the benefits of public ignorance." In any event, "the bar retains the power to correct omissions that have the effect of presenting an inaccurate picture." "If the naivete of the public will cause advertising by attorneys to be misleading," the Court added, "then it is the bar's role to assure that the populace is sufficiently informed as to enable it to place advertising in its proper perspective."

Further, the Court said, "we cannot accept the notion that it is always better for a person to suffer a wrong silently than to redress it by legal action.". . .

Because advertising by lawyers for fee-paying clients is "commercial speech," however, the Court held that those attacking the bar's restrictions could not rely on the First Amendment "overbreadth" doctrine. That is, the disciplinary rule at issue could not be attacked on its face on the ground that speakers not before the court might be chilled in the exercise of First Amendment rights by the statute's breadth.

Since the bar did not have to cope with an overbreadth attack on its disciplinary rules, it could have

prevailed simply by carrying the burden of proving that the advertisement at issue was misleading. The bar attempted to do this on the ground that the ad used the title "legal clinic," that it referred to "very reasonable" prices, and that it omitted the fact that a lawyer is not needed in order to obtain a name change (one of the legal services offered in the ad). The Court found, however, that the bar had failed to carry its burden of showing "unambiguously" that the advertising at issue had been misleading in any of those respects and reversed the disciplinary sanctions against the lawyers.

Using a test that comes from *Central Hudson Gas & Electric Corp. v. Public Service Comm'n of New York*, the opinion in *R.M.J.* explained the burden on the state in a case involving a limitation on commercial speech. As the *Central Hudson* test has evolved, it provides a two-part test of "intermediate scrutiny" of restrictions on commercial speech. The first part of the *Central Hudson* test posits that the government may freely regulate commercial speech that concerns unlawful activity or that is misleading. The second part of the test has three "prongs." First, the state must assert a "substantial interest" in support of its regulation. Second, the government must show that the restriction on commercial speech "directly and materially advances that interest." Third, the regulation must be "narrowly drawn." Inherent in these is the requirement of *Bates* that the state must carry the burden of proving "unambiguously" that the evils that justify the regulation are in fact present in the particular advertising that the state seeks to suppress.

The next Supreme Court decision on lawyer advertising after *R.M.J.* was *Zauderer v. Office of Disciplinary Counsel*. Again the bar sought to discipline a lawyer on petty grounds, this time that he had solicited clients in an advertisement that explained the rights of women who had been injured, some of them severely, through the use of the Dalkon Shield intrauterine device. The bar was also concerned that the advertisement had contained an illustration of the Dalkon Shield, under which was the question, "Did you use this IUD?" Two women who had retained the lawyer to represent them testified that they would not have known of their legal rights had it not been for the lawyer's ad. The Supreme Court reversed the state's disciplinary action against the lawyer with respect to these charges.

The Court upheld the state's power to discipline the attorney on two other grounds, however, with respect to advertising statements that were in fact misleading. The Dalkon Shield ad said that the client would not be responsible for any fees unless she recovered a judgement in the case. This was misleading to those members of the public who would not realize that the client would be responsible for costs (which could be substantial). Also, in an ad for clients charged with drunk driving, the same lawyer had said that legal fees would be returned in full if the client were "convicted of drunk driving." What the ad failed to say was that most drunk driving defendants plead guilty to a lesser offense than drunk driving, in which event the fee would not be refundable. Accordingly, the Court upheld a rule requiring the inclusion of clarifying information in such advertisements.

Not long after, in *Shapero v. Kentucky Bar Association*, the Supreme Court again struck down bar restrictions on truthful advertising. Shapero had sought permission to send a letter to members of the public whose homes were the subject of foreclosure suits. The letter was found to be neither false nor misleading. Nevertheless, the Kentucky Supreme Court held that it would be unethical to advise people who were about to lose their homes that Federal law might allow them additional time to pay, and then to represent those people to enforce their rights.

The Supreme Court's response had a sardonic edge. "Generally, unless the advertiser is inept, the latter group would include members of the former," the Court said, adding, "the First Amendment does not permit a ban on certain speech merely because it is more efficient; the State may not constitutionally ban a particular letter on the theory that to mail it only to those whom it would most interest is

somehow inherently objectionable." In short, the bar cannot categorically forbid targeted mailings that are neither false nor misleading.

In 1995, in *Florida Bar v. Went For it, Inc.*, the Supreme Court limited the scope of *Shapero. Went For It* involved a challenge to provisions in Florida's Rules of Professional Conduct that prohibited direct mail advertising of legal services to victims or victims' relatives within thirty days of an accident or disaster. A lawyer and his referral service (Went For It, Inc.) challenged the new rules on First Amendment grounds.

Justice Sandra Day O'Connor wrote a five-to-four majority opinion upholding Florida's thirty-day limitation on solicitation. She was joined by Chief Justice Rehnquist and Justices Scalia, Thomas, and Breyer. Applying the *Central Hudson* test, O'Connor first found that the state has a substantial interest, both in regulating the practice of professions and in protecting the privacy of citizens from intrusion.

With respect to the second prong of *Central Hudson*, O'Connor held that the thirty-day limitation directly and materially advances the state's interest. She based this holding on a 106-page summary of a two-year study of lawyer advertising and solicitation submitted by the Florida Bar, which concluded that a majority of the public views direct mail solicitation immediately after an accident as "an intrusion on privacy that reflects poorly on the profession." O'Connor acknowledged that the Bar, which had the burden of proof, failed to provide crucial backup information regarding sample size, selection procedures, and copies of the actual surveys. Without that support information, a summary of the results of a survey is worthless. Nevertheless, O'Connor found the data to be "sufficient" to show that the restriction "targets a concrete, nonspeculative harm."

Turning to the third prong of *Central Hudson*, O'Connor held the Bar's rule to be "reasonably well-tailored to its stated objective of eliminating targeted mailings whose type and timing are a source of distress to Floridians, distress that has caused many of them to lose respect for the legal profession." She also noted that there are other ways for lawyers to reach potential clients, including advertising on prime-time television and radio, newspapers and other media, and by renting billboards; she referred also to the allowable use of "untargeted letters to the general population."

This last point (the fact that untargeted mailings are permitted) undercuts the reasoning in *Went For It*, because, as the Court noted in *Shapero*, unless the advertiser is inept, the untargeted general public will include all of the same targeted accident victims. The result would therefore be the identical asserted invasion of privacy and impairment of the image of the bar. The only practical difference appears to be that a general mailing (like prime-time television, billboards, etc.) are likely to be prohibitively expensive for most lawyers.

Justice Anthony Kennedy dissented, joined by Justices Stevens, Souter, and Ginsburg. Kennedy pointed out (and the majority did not disagree) that "when an accident results in death or injury, it is often urgent at once to investigate the occurrence, identify witnesses, and preserve evidence." Accordingly, the banned communications may be "vital to the recipients' right to petition the courts for redress of grievance" under the First Amendment. Also, quoting *Zauderer*, he noted that "the mere possibility that some members of the population might find advertising . . . offensive cannot justify suppressing it. The same must hold true for advertising that some members of the bar find beneath their dignity."

Kennedy also pointed to the bar's failure to carry its burden of demonstrating the reality of the asserted harm. Noting the lack of backup information for the survey summary, Kennedy observed that the anecdotal evidence (which the majority had found "noteworthy for its breadth and detail") was "noteworthy for its incompetence."

Perhaps Kennedy's strongest point is the practical one, that the problem asserted by the state is "largely self-policing." That is, if members of the public really find the banned solicitation to be offensive, such solicitation will stop because it will fail to attract clients. On the contrary, however, the fact that some 280,000 direct mail solicitations are sent to accident victims and their survivors in Florida each year is an indication of a positive public response to the practice.

Unfortunately, what may have been the most effective argument before this Supreme Court was not made in *Went For It*. Kennedy mentioned in his opinion that while plaintiffs' personal injury lawyers were barred from contacting victims or their survivors, there is no similar ban against potential defendants, their lawyers, and their adjusters. This, he said, "makes little sense." Actually, this discriminatory treatment between the two adverse sides is more serious than that, and the constitutional authority for striking it down is significant.

Just as there is anecdotal evidence that some people resent the intrusion of a plaintiffs' lawyer on their privacy, there is evidence that people similarly resent intrusion by insurance adjusters. One source for this is the Wall Street Journal (not a friend to plaintiffs' lawyers). For example, an adjuster for Liberty Mutual Group knocked on the door of the family of a New Jersey woman, just thirteen hours after she had been killed in a wreck, to discourage them from getting a lawyer and to propose settlement with a waiver of their rights. The insurer defended the practice as a benefit to those solicited. In another case, this one from Florida, a woman briefly considered dealing directly with an adjuster but "became suspicious" after the claims representative repeatedly stressed that a lawyer wasn't necessary. And, of course, additional anecdotal evidence can be found in published cases, like the case of Ernest Gene Gunn, recounted above.

Discouraging victims and their survivors from retaining lawyers is a familiar practice of insurance companies. Here, for example, are questions and answers from a document distributed to victims and their survivors by Allstate Insurance Company:

1) AM I REQUIRED TO HIRE AN ATTORNEY TO HANDLE MY CLAIM?

No. In fact, each year Allstate settles claims directly with many accident victims with no attorneys involved in the claim settlement process.

2) WILL AN ATTORNEY MAKE THE CLAIM SETTLEMENT PROCESS FASTER FOR ME?

A recent study . . . found that people who settle insurance claims without and attorney generally settle their claims more quickly than those who have hired attorneys.

3) HOW MUCH ARE ATTORNEYS' FEES AND WHO PAYS FOR THEM?

Attorneys often take up to one-third of the total settlement you receive from an insurance company, plus expenses incurred. If you settle directly with Allstate, however, the total amount of the settlement is yours.

Clearly, this is a controversy of public importance — whether an accident victim should retain a lawyer to assert her First Amendment right of petition, and whether a particular settlement is in the interest of a particular victim. To speak, while the other is being gagged. This is "viewpoint discrimination," which was declared unconstitutional. . . .

"ACTUALLY," "INHERENTLY," AND "POTENTIALLY" MISLEADING

Another important Supreme Court decision on lawyer advertising is *Peel v. Attorney Registration and Disciplinary Commission of Illinois*. In *Peel*, the lawyer truthfully stated on his letterhead that he had been certified by the National Board of Trial Advocacy (NBTA). Illinois censured him under a disciplinary rule that categorically forbad a lawyer to hold himself out as certified or as a specialist.

The Supreme Court struck down the disciplinary rule as applied to Peel. In doing so, the Court discussed three kinds of misleading advertising — "actually," "inherently," and "potentially." We are not sure precisely what each of these terms means. What is clear, however, is that the state may categorically ban advertising that is either "actually" or "inherently" misleading. Together, these terms include situations in which the state shows that a "potential client or person was actually misled or deceived," and situations in which the statement is true but deceptive. An illustration of the latter category is where the state presents evidence that "the certification [has] been issued by an organization that [has] made no inquiry into [the lawyer's] fitness, or by one that [issues] certificates indiscriminately. . . ."

Peel's letterhead, however, was "neither actually nor inherently misleading" because "there is no dispute about the bona fides and the relevance of NBTA certification." Thus, the state's blanket proscription was unconstitutional as applied to Peel. The Court added that the state's concern about "the possibility of deception in hypothetical cases is not sufficient to rebut the constitutional presumption favoring disclosure over concealment." Nevertheless, a holding that a total ban is unconstitutional "does not necessarily preclude less restrictive regulation of commercial speech."

We understand the reference to "the possibility of deception" to mean that the statement was "potentially" misleading, in the sense, for example, that a member of the public might infer that the NBTA is affiliated with the state or federal government. Therefore, as emphasized in Justice Marshall's concurrence, the state could use "less restrictive measures" than a total ban to prevent deception. One way to do that would be to require a statement that the certifying organization is private.

IN-PERSON SOLICITATION

The real problem of the potential client who may feel overwhelmed by circumstances is illustrated by the following case. A woman arrives at a busy, crowded metropolitan courthouse holding a small boy by the hand. She speaks almost no English. She is intimidated by the imposing surroundings, and she is frightened and confused by the bustle and the noise. All she knows is that she is required to be some place in that building because her son has gotten into trouble or her landlord is attempting to evict her family. People brush by her, concerned with their own problems. Then a man appears, smiles at her, and asks her in her own language whether he can help her. Through him, the woman meets and retains the man's employer, a lawyer who gives her competent representation at a fair fee.

In our view, that lawyer should have been given an award as Attorney of the Year. Instead, Solomon Cohn, whose practice consisted of cases like that one, was prosecuted as a criminal and convicted of the misdemeanor of soliciting business on behalf of an attorney. Professional disciplinary proceedings then followed. Giving favorable weight to Cohn's "expressions of self-reproach and the humiliation he has already suffered," the court in the disciplinary case decided to treat him with "leniency." This meant humiliating him further by publicly censuring him on the front page of the *New York Law Journal*.

SOLICITATION AT THE BEDSIDE

The classic horror for those who decry ambulance-chasing is solicitation of a tort victim at the bedside. Consider, then, the following case.

Laura Eagle is a sole practitioner in a large city. One evening an acquaintance who is a social worker mentioned to Eagle the terrible conditions he had seen that day on a visit to a private nursing home in the city—filth, poor food, and neglect, even to the point of one patient who had maggots growing in her flesh. Because the patients are poor, elderly, bedridden, and rarely visited by anyone, they have no way to help themselves or to get help. Eagle asked the social worker to return to the nursing home, explain to some of the patients about the possibility of litigation on their behalf, and sign up one or more of them on a contingent fee. She made it clear that the social worker was not to mislead or pressure the patients in any way, and he followed her instructions.

As a result, Eagle became attorney for the patients. Before taking any action on their behalf, she discussed possible courses of action with them, explaining the advantages and disadvantages of each course. The patients unanimously decided on a class action against the nursing home. Eagle obtained a substantial recovery for the patients and a court order protecting their rights to adequate care. She also received a substantial fee on the normal one-third contingency basis.

At Eagle's disciplinary hearing ... she admitted that a significant motive for her taking the case was to earn the fee. She pointed out that she could not have afforded to handle such a difficult and time-consuming case on a *pro bono* basis.

Eagle was suspended from practice for one year, while the lawyer who represented the nursing home spent the same year serving as President of the State Bar Association.

The moral of the story, and of the bar's anti-solicitation rules, appears to be that it is better to have maggots feeding on your flesh than to have a lawyer sitting at your bedside.

A real-life variation on the Eagle hypothetical was subsequently provided in an opinion by the Alabama State Bar Disciplinary Commission. The facts, as accepted by the Commission were these. A lawyer represents twenty-five members of a class of people who had had experimental surgery performed on them without their consent by a surgeon who was acting on behalf of a company. There are about 150 other members of the class who do not know that they have rights and that their rights will be terminated shortly by a statute of limitations.

Because these potential clients are mostly elderly and uneducated, they are unlikely to understand or to be able to respond to a written communication about the case. The lawyer therefore proposed to speak with them directly to inform them of what he has discovered and to advise them that they may choose to do nothing, to seek the advice of other attorneys, or to become members of the class the lawyer represents. The lawyer does not want "to do anything unethical but cannot simply sit by and allow this injustice . . . to go unchallenged and unknown by most of the victims."

SOLICITATION AT THE DISASTER SITE

After a major disaster in the United States, two groups rush to the site. One group is comprised of members of the news media, the other of lawyers. Each group is there to further First Amendment rights and each has a financial interest in doing so. Not infrequently the reporters ask intrusive and offensive questions like, "How did you feel when you learned that your child was one of those that burned to death on the school bus?" In a letter to the editor, the parent of a student killed in the explosion of TWA Flight 800 complained of the abusive conduct by reporters: "We can endure no more."

Then, after they have tired of the story, the reporters and editorialists devote their attention to harsh criticism of the way in which lawyers invade the privacy of the victims and their grieving families by offering them legal services.

Consider, for example, a story in *The New York Times* relating to an accident in which twenty-one children drowned and sixty others were injured when a school bus plunged into a water-filled gravel pit in Alton, Texas. Fully four months after the accident, the *Times* ran a front-page story with a three column headline: "Where 21 Youths Died, Lawyers Wage a War." The story tells of a "parade of lawyers" that began almost immediately after the accident, and of "fierce competition" among the lawyers to represent the families. On page one, the *Times* identifies "one benefit, if that is what it is: a poor and undereducated community, made up largely of Hispanic field laborers, has acquired a new kind of sophistication." This questionable benefit, according to the *Times*, is that people who wanted to grieve without the intrusion of lawyers are now saying, "When this happens to you, you hire a lawyer and you get money."

The important part of the story is on an inside page, at the very end, and is written in a way that makes it appear to be unrelated to the main story that preceded it. There we learn that the 3,000 people who live in Alton have returned to "the anonymous, poverty-stricken lives they led before the bus crashed into the water." Because the students who died were among the poorest in the high school, the response among the other students was "much less than if it was the star quarterback."

With the filing of that story, the last of the reporters also left Alton. Although the *Times*' prominent and lengthy critique of the "parade of lawyers" did not mention the fact, only the lawyers remained, to serve the members of this "poor, undereducated community, made up largely of Hispanic field laborers." Subsequently, in a brief item buried on an inside page, the *Times* reported that the lawyers for

sixteen of the families whose children had been killed had obtained a settlement of $67.5 million for their clients.

In short, the legal system succeeded in providing equal protection and due process of law to poverty-stricken people whom all others were content to abandon. That is the story that deserved, but never received, a front-page headline.

Similarly, in a disaster in Bhopal, India, in 1984, 3,100 people were killed and 30,000 were severely disabled when poisonous gas was released from a Union Carbide pesticide plant. Predictably, Union Carbide mounted a legal defense at a cost of more than $7,000,000—per year. Its court documents have been described as mountainous. Nevertheless, the American lawyers who went to India to offer to take on this multinational conglomerate on behalf of its victims were frequently referred to as "vultures." Imagine: we have developed a system of justice in which some of the best lawyers in the world travel thousands of miles to offer their services to impoverished people, and instead of celebrating that fact, there are those who decry it.

SOLICITATION OF CLIENTS AND THE FIRST AMENDMENT

Unfortunately, those who condemn in-person solicitation in cases like those we have been discussing include the ABA and the state bars, which have uniformly adopted the anti-solicitation provisions. It is necessary to consider, therefore, the extent to which solicitation is protected under the First Amendment. In fact, lawyers who solicit clients in person, in fee-paying cases, have a significant degree of constitutional protection....

In *NAACP v. Button* the Supreme Court considered solicitation by the NAACP to recruit plaintiffs for school desegregation cases. The NAACP called a series of meetings, inviting not only its members and not only poor people, but all members of the community. At these meetings, the organization's staff attorneys took the platform to urge those present to authorize the lawyers to sue in their behalf. The lawyers had a clear pecuniary interest, because they were paid for the litigation they conducted. Also, the NAACP maintained the ensuing litigation by defraying all expenses, regardless of the financial means of any particular client. Further, as pointed out by the dissenting Justices, common-law prohibitions of champerty, barratry, and maintenance are of long standing.

Nevertheless, the Supreme Court held that "the State's attempt to equate the activities of the NAACP and its lawyers with common-law barratry, maintenance and champerty, and to outlaw them accordingly, cannot obscure the serious encroachment . . . upon protected freedoms of expression." The Court added that "it is no answer to the constitutional claims asserted by petitioner to say . . . that the purpose of these regulations was merely to insure high professional standards and not to curtail free expression. For a State may not, under the guise of prohibiting professional misconduct, ignore constitutional rights."

A year later, in *Brotherhood of Railroad Trainmen*, the Supreme Court considered a union's legal services plan that resulted in channeling all or substantially all of the union members' personal injury claims, on a private fee basis, to lawyers selected by the union and touted in its literature and at meetings. Asserting that this constituted unlawful solicitation, the Virginia State Bar obtained an injunction against the legal services plan. The Court again upheld the solicitation on constitutional grounds, despite the objections of the two dissenting Justices that by giving constitutional protection to the solicitation of personal injury claims, the Court "relegates the practice of law to the level of a commercial enterprise," "degrades the profession," and "contravenes both the accepted ethics of the profession and the statutory and judicial rules of acceptable conduct."

In the *United Mine Workers* case three years thereafter, the Court dealt with the argument that *Button* should be limited to litigation involving major political issues, like school desegregation, and not be extended to personal injury cases. The Court recognized that the litigation at issue was "not bound up with political matters of acute social moment," as in *Button*. It held, nevertheless, that "the First

Amendment does not protect speech . . . only to the extent that it can be characterized as political. 'Great secular causes, with small ones, are guarded.' "

The next case in this line was *United Transportation Union v. State Bar of Michigan*. At that time, commercial speech was still wholly without constitutional protection, and *United Transportation Union* presented a case of commercial speech by lawyers in a classic (if not extreme) form of in-person solicitation. As Justice John Marshall Harlan said, the state decree was designed "to fend against 'ambulance chasing,' an activity that I can hardly suppose the Court thinks is protected by the First Amendment."

The facts were that the United Transportation Union maintained a cadre of paid accident "investigators" (commonly referred to in the literature of solicitation as runners, cappers, or touters). Their job was to keep track of accidents, to visit the injured members, to make contingent fee contracts with them, and to urge the injured members to retain private attorneys who had been selected by the union. Even if the runners were unsuccessful in signing up victims, they were paid by the union for their time and expenses in transporting potential clients to the designated lawyers' offices, where the lawyers themselves could induce the victims to retain them.

In holding this conduct to be constitutionally protected, the Court reiterated that "collective activity to obtain meaningful access to the courts is a fundamental right within the protection of the First Amendment." What is important to bear in mind, however, is that: (1) the attorneys were not in-house counsel for the union, but were private practitioners; (2) the attorneys earned substantial fees; (3) the cases were ordinary personal injury cases; (4) the attorneys were retained as a result of the activities of runners paid by the union to find out where accidents had occurred, to visit the victims as promptly as possible after the accident, to "tout" the particular lawyers, and, if necessary, to take the victim to the lawyers' office so that the lawyer, in person, could solicit the victim to sign a retainer agreement.

In *Button* and the union cases the Court happened to be dealing with legal services provided by associations, and there are therefore references in those cases to the First Amendment right of association. However, the cases also recognized "the right of individuals" to be represented in lawsuits and to obtain "meaningful access to the courts." Again, the aggrieved person who has no association or union to turn to (perhaps because she has no job) is even more in need of information about her rights than one who has the advantages of association. Recognizing this, the Supreme Court has held that the "[u]nderlying . . . concern" of *Button* and the union cases was that "the aggrieved receive information regarding their legal rights and the means of effectuating them." This concern, the Court added, "applies with at least as much force to aggrieved individuals as it does to groups."

PRIMUS AND *OHRALIK* — TWO DIFFERENT LEVELS OF CONSTITUTIONAL PROTECTION

We have not yet considered two very important solicitation cases, *Primus* and *Ohralik*, which were decided by the Supreme Court in 1978, one year after *Bates*. On the facts of *Primus* (solicitation for a social cause) the Court reversed discipline of the lawyer, while on the facts of *Ohralik* (solicitation of a personal injury case) the Court affirmed discipline. *Ohralik* is frequently cited as holding that when solicitation is done for the lawyer's pecuniary gain, it is without any constitutional protection. However, that is a misinterpretation.

Primus involved an effort by the American Civil Liberties Union to litigate a case on behalf of pregnant mothers on public assistance who were being sterilized or threatened with sterilization as a condition of continued receipt of medical assistance under Medicaid. Edna Smith Primus was a cooperating (*i.e.*, unpaid) attorney with the ACLU. She met with a group of women who had been sterilized by Dr. Clovis H. Pierce, explained their rights to them, and suggested the possibility of a lawsuit. Primus then followed up this in-person contact by

writing to one of the women, Mary Etta Williams, asking her to become a plaintiff in an ACLU lawsuit against Pierce. As a result, Primus was subjected to professional discipline for soliciting a client.

In upholding the disciplinary action, the South Carolina Supreme Court noted that the ACLU "would benefit financially [through court-awarded fees] in the event of successful prosecution of the suit for money damages." In addition, Primus herself had a pecuniary interest in the sterilization case, because she acted in part in her capacity as a retained lawyer for the South Carolina Council on Human Relations (a private, nonprofit organization). Nevertheless, the Supreme Court described the case as one that was not in-person solicitation "for pecuniary gain," because Primus herself would not receive a share of any recovery.

The Supreme Court reversed the disciplinary action against Primus. The Court noted that the ACLU "engages in litigation as a vehicle for effective political expression and association, as well as a means for communicating useful information to the public." Accordingly, the Court held that Primus had been exercising "core First Amendment rights" in soliciting Williams, and that the state's action in punishing Primus had to withstand "exacting scrutiny." The state therefore had to carry the burden of demonstrating that it had a "subordinating interest which is compelling," and that the regulation used in furtherance of that interest is "closely drawn" to avoid unnecessary abridgment of First Amendment rights.

In response, South Carolina contended that it had a compelling interest in preventing such evils as undue influence, overreaching, misrepresentation, invasion of privacy, and conflict of interest. The Court replied, however, that "the Disciplinary Rules in question permit punishment for mere solicitation unaccompanied by proof of any of the substantive evils that [the state] maintains were present in this case." Moreover, even assuming that the Disciplinary Rules were not overbroad, the state had not carried its burden of proving the presence of the asserted evils. "The record does not support [the state's] contention that undue influence, overreaching, misrepresentation, or invasion of privacy *actually occurred* in this case."

Primus, therefore, illustrates the highest level of constitutional protection for "core" First Amendment speech — advertisement or solicitation where the lawyer is using litigation as a form of political expression. *Bates* illustrates the intermediate level of constitutional protection afforded to speech, in writing, that proposes a commercial transaction. In such a case, the *Central Hudson* test applies, including the requirement inherent in that test that the state carry the burden of proving "unambiguously" that the evils that justify the regulation are in fact present in the particular advertising that the state seeks to suppress.

Ohralik v. Ohio State Bar Association illustrates the third level of constitutional protection in the area of advertising and solicitation by lawyers. This lowest level of protection is accorded to commercial speech when it involves in-person solicitation, as distinguished from the core political speech in *Primus* (full First Amendment protection) and the written advertisements in *Bates, Shapero.* and *Went for It, Inc.* (intermediate, commercial-speech protection). At this third level of protection, the state need not prove that the evils that justify the regulation are present; rather the state enjoys a presumption that the evils are present, and the burden is shifted to the lawyer to prove that her solicitation was in fact free of those evils. Nevertheless, the important — and often overlooked — point is that even in-person solicitation enjoys some degree of First Amendment protection as commercial speech.

Ohralik arose under the Model Code. Having learned that a young woman named Carol McClintock had been injured in an automobile accident, an attorney named Albert Ohralik called her home and was told that she was in the hospital. When he suggested that he visit McClintock there, her parents requested that he first stop by to speak with them. In Ohralik's conversation with McClintock's parents, they told him that she had been driving the family car when she was hit by an uninsured motorist. They also told him that McClintock's passenger (Wanda Lou Holbert) had also been hospitalized. McClintock's parents expressed concern that they might be sued by Holbert, but Ohralik advised them that such an action would be precluded by Ohio's guest statute. He then suggested that they retain a lawyer for their

daughter, and they replied that their daughter should make that decision.

Ohralik then went to the hospital, where he found McClintock lying in traction in her room. He asked her to sign a retainer agreement, but she said that she would have to discuss it with her parents.

Ohralik next picked up a tape recorder, which he used to secretly record subsequent conversations with McClintock, her parents, and Holbert, both before and after the young women had retained him.

When Ohralik returned to McClintock's parents, they told him that their daughter had telephoned to say that he could represent her. (Although the opinion is unclear as to whether the parents considered themselves, along with their daughter, to be Ohralick's clients, they were at least acting as her agents in their relations with him.) Two days later Ohralik had McClintock sign a retainer agreement providing for a one-third contingent fee. While at the McClintock home, Ohralik reexamined their insurance policy and discovered that it provided benefits of up to $12,500 each for McClintock and Holbert under an uninsured-motorist clause. McClintock's mother again indicated to Ohralik that they did not want Holbert to make a claim against them or their policy, telling him that "Wanda swore up and down she would not do it."

Intending to solicit Holbert as a client to sue against the McClintocks' insurance policy, but telling them only that he had to ask Holbert some questions about the accident, Ohralik obtained her name and address from the McClintocks. In his visit to Holbert, Ohralik told her that he had a "little tip" for her — the McClintocks' insurance policy had an uninsured motorist clause that might provide her with up to $12,500.

During the same visit, Ohralik got Holbert to retain him on a one-third contingent fee. In doing so, he told her that if there was no recovery, she would not have to pay him anything. Holbert was eighteen years old and had not graduated from high school. The next day, Holbert's mother called Ohralik on her daughter's behalf and repudiated the agreement to retain him. Ohralik refused to withdraw as Holbert's lawyer, and advised his client through her mother that she could not get out of her agreement with him.

McClintock also discharged Ohralik, and another attorney represented her in concluding a settlement with the insurance company for the full $12,500. However, the insurance company refused to release the check to her because Ohralik was asserting a claim for $4,166 against the settlement.

All of these facts were reported to the Board of Commissioners on Grievances and Discipline of the Supreme Court of Ohio. We have catalogued over a dozen disciplinary violations, many of them clear and some involving dishonesty, fraud, deceit, or misrepresentation, as well as betrayal of his own client. Yet, consistent with the bar's long-standing preoccupation, the only charges against Ohralick were that he had engaged in solicitation of clients in violation of [professional conduct rules]. As a result, he was indefinitely suspended from the practice of law — a sanction that is more than justified by the charges that were *not* brought against him.

The Supreme Court affirmed the disciplinary action against Ohralik and used the case to refine the constitutional law applicable to in-person solicitation of clients in fee cases. Because the case involved commercial speech, Ohralik was unable to rely upon overbreadth analysis. That is, he could not argue that the statute on its face could be applied to cases of protected speech; rather, he had to argue that, as applied to him, the disciplinary rules were unconstitutional. Attempting to use the rule established in the advertising cases, therefore, Ohralik argued that the state had failed to carry its burden of proving that the evils said to be associated with solicitation were present in his case.

Ohralik conceded, and the Court agreed, that the state had a compelling interest in preventing "those aspects" of solicitation that involve fraud, undue influence, intimidation, overreaching, and other forms of "vexatious" conduct. That concession would end the case, the Court said, "but for his insistence that none of those evils was found to be present in his acts of solicitation." "We agree," the Court added, "that the appropriate focus is on [Ohralik's] conduct," which requires the Court to "undertake an independent review of the record to determine whether that conduct was constitutionally protected."

Ohralik lost, however, at the next point in his argument, in which he contended that the state had failed to prove "actual harm" to Carol McClintock or Wanda Lou Holbert. In response, the Court declined to apply the rule that imposes the burden on the state to demonstrate that the evils sought to be prevented by the disciplinary rules were in fact present in the case at issue. "Unlike the advertising in *Bates*," the Court explained, "in-person solicitation is not visible or otherwise open to public scrutiny." In such cases, therefore, it may be "difficult or impossible to obtain reliable proof of what actually took place." Accordingly, if the state had to carry the burden of proving actual injury to those solicited, "in-person solicitation would be virtually immune to effective oversight and regulation." For this reason, "the absence of explicit proof or findings of harm or injury is immaterial, because the state is entitled to a presumption of such harm." Nevertheless, in-person solicitation does enjoy First Amendment protection, although at a lower level of judicial scrutiny. This lower level of scrutiny involves shifting the burden to the lawyer to prove the absence of harmful conduct, rather than requiring the state to prove that harm was present.

Thus, although "the appropriate focus is on [Ohralik's] conduct," and the Court "must undertake an independent review of the record," Ohralik lost. The reason is that he failed to carry the burden of proof which had been shifted to him by the presumption of harm that is afforded the state in a case of inperson solicitation. This failure of proof was shown "[o]n the basis of the *undisputed* facts of record," which justified the conclusion that "the Disciplinary Rules *constitutionally could be applied to appellant* [Ohralik]." As the Court has subsequently explained, what justified disciplining Ohralik was "not so much that he solicited business for himself, but rather the circumstances in which he performed that solicitation and the means by which he accomplished it."

The Limits of Conscientious Objection—May Pharmacists Refuse to Fill Prescriptions for Emergency Contraception?

Julie Cantor and Ken Baum

Julie Cantor is a lawyer and expert on bioethics. Ken Baum is a doctor and lawyer who publishes widely on bioethics.

Health policy decisions are often controversial, and the recent determination by the Food and Drug Administration (FDA) not to grant over-the-counter status to the emergency contraceptive Plan B was no exception. Some physicians decried the decision as a troubling clash of science, politics, and morality.[1] Other practitioners, citing safety, heralded the agency's prudence.[2] Public sentiment mirrored both views. Regardless, the decision preserved a major barrier to the acquisition of emergency contraception—the need to obtain and fill a prescription within a narrow window of efficacy. Six states have lowered that hurdle by allowing pharmacists to dispense emergency contraception without a prescription.[3-8] In those states, patients can simply bypass physicians. But the FDA's decision means that patients cannot avoid pharmacists. Because emergency contraception remains behind the counter, pharmacists can block access to it. And some have done just that.

Across the country, some pharmacists have refused to honor valid prescriptions for emergency contraception. In Texas, a pharmacist, citing personal moral grounds, rejected a rape survivor's prescription for emergency contraception.[9] A pharmacist in rural Missouri also refused to sell such a drug,[10] and in Ohio, Kmart fired a pharmacist for obstructing access to emergency and other birth control.[11] This fall, a New Hampshire pharmacist refused to fill a prescription for emergency contraception or to direct the patron elsewhere for help. Instead, he berated the 21-year-old single mother, who then, in her words, "pulled the car over in the parking lot and just cried."[12] Although the total number of incidents is unknown, reports of pharmacists who refused to dispense emergency contraception date back to 1991[13] and show no sign of abating.

Though nearly all states offer some level of legal protection for health care professionals who refuse to provide certain reproductive services, only Arkansas, Mississippi, and South Dakota explicitly protect pharmacists who refuse to dispense emergency and other contraception.[14] But that list may grow. In past years, legislators from nearly two dozen states have taken "conscientious objection"—an idea that grew out of wartime tension between religious freedom and national obligation[15] and was co-opted into the reproductive-rights debate of the 1970s[16]—and applied it to pharmacists. One proposed law offers pharmacists immunity from civil lawsuits, criminal liability, professional sanctions, and employment repercussions.[17] Another bill, which was not passed, would have protected pharmacists who refused to transfer prescriptions.[18]

This issue raises important questions about individual rights and public health. Who prevails when the needs of patients and the morals of providers collide? Should pharmacists have a right to reject prescriptions for emergency contraception?...

From *New England Journal of Medicine* 351:19, Nov. 4, 2004.

ARGUMENTS IN FAVOR OF A PHARMACIST'S RIGHT TO OBJECT

Pharmacists Can and Should Exercise Independent Judgment

Pharmacists, like physicians, are professionals. They complete a graduate program to gain expertise, obtain a state license to practice, and join a professional organization with its own code of ethics. Society relies on pharmacists to instruct patients on the appropriate use of medications and to ensure the safety of drugs prescribed in combination. Courts have held that pharmacists, like other professionals, owe their customers a duty of care.[19] In short, pharmacists are not automatons completing tasks; they are integral members of the health care team. Thus, it seems inappropriate and condescending to question a pharmacist's right to exercise personal judgment in refusing to fill certain prescriptions.

Professionals Should Not Forsake Their Morals as a Condition of Employment

Society does not require professionals to abandon their morals. Lawyers, for example, choose clients and issues to represent. Choice is also the norm in the health care setting. Except in emergency departments, physicians may select their patients and procedures. Ethics and law allow physicians, nurses, and physician assistants to refuse to participate in abortions and other reproductive services.[14,20] Although some observers argue that active participation in an abortion is distinct from passively dispensing emergency contraception, others believe that making such a distinction between active and passive participation is meaningless, because both forms link the provider to the final outcome in the chain of causation.

Conscientious Objection is Integral to Democracy

More generally, the right to refuse to participate in acts that conflict with personal ethical, moral, or religious convictions is accepted as an essential element of a democratic society. Indeed, Oregon acknowledged this freedom in its Death with Dignity Act,[21] which allows health care providers, including pharmacists, who are disquieted by physician-assisted suicide to refuse involvement without fear of retribution. Also, like the draftee who conscientiously objects to perpetrating acts of death and violence, a pharmacist should have the right not to be complicit in what they believe to be a morally ambiguous endeavor, whether others agree with that position or not. The reproductive-rights movement was built on the ideal of personal choice; denying choice for pharmacists in matters of reproductive rights and abortion seems ironic.

ARGUMENTS AGAINST A PHARMACIST'S RIGHT TO OBJECT

Pharmacists Choose to Enter a Profession Bound by Fiduciary Duties

Although pharmacists are professionals, professional autonomy has its limits. As experts on the profession of pharmacy explain, "Professionals are expected to exercise special skill and care to place the interests of their clients above their own immediate interests."[22] When a pharmacist's objection directly and detrimentally affects a patient's health, it follows that the patient should come first. Similarly, principles in the pharmacists' code of ethics weigh against conscientious objection. Given the effect on the patient if a pharmacist refuses to fill a prescription, the code undermines the right to object with such broadly stated objectives as "a pharmacist promotes the good of every patient in a caring, compassionate, and confidential manner," "a pharmacist respects the autonomy and dignity of each patient," and "a pharmacist serves individual, community, and societal needs."[23] Finally, pharmacists understand these fiduciary obligations when they choose their profession. Unlike conscientious objectors to a military draft, for whom choice is limited by definition, pharmacists willingly enter their field and adopt its corresponding obligations.

Emergency Contraception is Not an Abortifacient

Although the subject of emergency contraception is controversial, medical associations,[24] government agencies,[25] and many religious groups agree that it is not akin to abortion. Plan B and similar hormones have no effect on an established pregnancy, and they may operate by more than one physiological mechanism, such as by inhibiting ovulation or creating an unfavorable environment for implantation of a blastocyst.[26] This duality allowed the Catholic Health Association to reconcile its religious beliefs with a mandate adopted by Washington State that emergency contraception must be provided to rape survivors.[27] According to the association, a patient and a provider who aim only to prevent conception follow Catholic teachings and state law. Also, whether one believes that pregnancy begins with fertilization or implantation, emergency contraception cannot fit squarely within the concept of abortion because one cannot be sure that conception has occurred.

Pharmacists' Objections Significantly Affect Patients' Health

Although religious and moral freedom is considered sacrosanct, that right should yield when it hinders a patient's ability to obtain timely medical treatment. Courts have held that religious freedom does not give health care providers an unfettered right to object to anything involving birth control, an embryo, or a fetus.[28,29] Even though the Constitution protects people's beliefs, their actions may be regulated.[30] An objection must be balanced with the burden it imposes on others. In some cases, a pharmacist's objection imposes his or her religious beliefs on a patient. Pharmacists may decline to fill prescriptions for emergency contraception because they believe that the drug ends a life. Although the patient may disapprove of abortion, she may not share the pharmacist's beliefs about contraception. If she becomes pregnant, she may then face the question of abortion—a dilemma she might have avoided with the morning-after pill.

Furthermore, the refusal of a pharmacist to fill a prescription may place a disproportionately heavy burden on those with few options, such as a poor teenager living in a rural area that has a lone pharmacy. Whereas the savvy urbanite can drive to another pharmacy, a refusal to fill a prescription for a less advantaged patient may completely bar her access to medication. Finally, although Oregon does have an opt-out provision in its statute regulating assisted suicide, timing is much more important in emergency contraception than in assisted suicide. Plan B is most effective when used within 12 to 24 hours after unprotected intercourse.[31] An unconditional right to refuse is less compelling when the patient requests an intervention that is urgent.

Refusal has Great Potential for Abuse and Discrimination

The limits to conscientious objection remain unclear. Pharmacists are privy to personal information through prescriptions. For instance, a customer who fills prescriptions for zidovudine, didanosine, and indinavir is logically assumed to be infected with the human immunodeficiency virus (HIV). If pharmacists can reject prescriptions that conflict with their morals, someone who believes that HIV-positive people must have engaged in immoral behavior could refuse to fill those prescriptions. Similarly, a pharmacist who does not condone extramarital sex might refuse to fill a sildenafil prescription for an unmarried man. Such objections go beyond "conscientious" to become invasive. Furthermore, because a pharmacist does not know a patient's history on the basis of a given prescription, judgments regarding the acceptability of a prescription may be medically inappropriate. To a woman with Eisenmenger's syndrome, for example, pregnancy may mean death. The potential for abuse by pharmacists underscores the need for policies ensuring that patients receive unbiased care.

TOWARD BALANCE

Compelling arguments can be made both for and against a pharmacist's right to refuse to fill prescriptions for emergency contraception. But even cogent ideas falter when confronted by a dissident moral code. Such is the nature of belief. Even so, most people can agree that we must find a workable and respectful balance between the needs of patients and the morals of pharmacists.

Three possible solutions exist: an absolute right to object, no right to object, or a limited right to object. On balance, the first two options are untenable. An absolute right to conscientious objection respects the autonomy of pharmacists but diminishes their professional obligation to serve patients. It may also greatly affect the health of patients, especially vulnerable ones, and inappropriately brings politics into the pharmacy. Even pharmacists who believe that emergency contraception represents murder and feel compelled to obstruct patients' access to it must recognize that contraception and abortion before fetal viability remain legal nationwide. In our view, state efforts to provide blanket immunity to objecting pharmacists are misguided. Pharmacies should follow the prevailing employment-law standard to make reasonable attempts to accommodate their employees' personal beliefs.[32] Although neutral policies to dispense medications to all customers may conflict with pharmacists' morals, such policies are not necessarily discriminatory, and pharmacies need not shoulder a heightened obligation of absolute accommodation.

Complete restriction of a right to conscientious objection is also problematic. Though pharmacists voluntarily enter their profession and have an obligation to serve patients without judgment, forcing them to abandon their morals imposes a heavy toll. Ethics and law demand that a professional's morality not interfere with the provision of care in life-or-death situations, such as a ruptured ectopic pregnancy.[29] Whereas the hours that elapse between intercourse and the intervention of emergency contraception are crucial, they do not meet that strict test. Also, patients who face an objecting pharmacist do have options, even if they are less preferable than having the prescription immediately filled. Because of these caveats, it is difficult to demand by law that pharmacists relinquish individual morality to stock and fill prescriptions for emergency contraception.

We are left, then, with the vast middle ground. Although we believe that the most ethical course is to treat patients compassionately—that is, to stock emergency contraception and fill prescriptions for it—the totality of the arguments makes us stop short of advocating a legal duty to do so as a first resort. We stop short for three reasons: because emergency contraception is not an absolute emergency, because other options exist, and because, when possible, the moral beliefs of those delivering care should be considered. However, in a profession that is bound by fiduciary obligations and strives to respect and care for patients, it is unacceptable to leave patients to fend for themselves. As a general rule, pharmacists who cannot or will not dispense a drug have an obligation to meet the needs of their customers by referring them elsewhere. This idea is uncontroversial when it is applied to common medications such as antibiotics and statins; it becomes contentious, but is equally valid, when it is applied to emergency contraception. Therefore, pharmacists who object should, as a matter of ethics and law, provide alternatives for patients.

Pharmacists who object to filling prescriptions for emergency contraception should arrange for another pharmacist to provide this service to customers promptly. Pharmacies that stock emergency contraception should ensure, to the extent possible, that at least one nonobjecting pharmacist is on duty at all times. Pharmacies that do not stock emergency contraception should give clear notice and refer patients elsewhere. At the very least, there should be a prominently displayed sign that says, "We do not provide emergency contraception. Please call Planned Parenthood at 800-230-PLAN (7526) or visit the Emergency Contraception Web site at www.not-2-late.com for assistance." However, a direct referral to a local pharmacy or pharmacist who is willing to fill the prescription is preferable. Objecting pharmacists should also redirect prescriptions for emergency contraception that are received by telephone to another pharmacy known to fill such prescriptions. In rural areas, objecting pharmacists should provide referrals within a reasonable radius.

Notably, the American Pharmacists Association has endorsed referrals, explaining that "providing alternative mechanisms for patients . . . ensures patient access to drug products, without requiring the pharmacist or the patient to abide by personal decisions other than their own."[33] A referral may also represent a break in causation between the pharmacist and distributing emergency contraception, a separation that the objecting pharmacist presumably seeks. And, in deference to the law's normative value, the rule of referral also conveys the importance of professional responsibility to patients. In areas of the country where referrals are logistically impractical, professional obligation may dictate providing emergency contraception, and a legal mandate may be appropriate if ethical obligations are unpersuasive.

Inevitably, some pharmacists will disregard our guidelines, and physicians—all physicians—should be prepared to fill gaps in care. They should identify pharmacies that will fill patients' prescriptions and encourage patients to keep emergency contraception at home. They should be prepared to dispense emergency contraception or instruct patients to mimic it with other birth-control pills. In Wisconsin, family-planning clinics recently began dispensing emergency contraception, and the state set up a toll-free hotline to help patients find physicians who will prescribe it.[34] Emergency departments should stock emergency contraception and make it available to rape survivors, if not all patients.

In the final analysis, education remains critical. Pharmacists may have misconceptions about emergency contraception. In one survey, a majority of pharmacists mistakenly agreed with the statement that repeated use of emergency contraception is medically risky.[35] Medical misunderstandings that lead pharmacists to refuse to fill prescriptions for emergency contraception are unacceptable. Patients, too, may misunderstand or be unaware of emergency contraception.[36] Physicians should teach patients about this option before the need arises, since patients may understand their choices better when they are not under stress. Physicians should discuss emergency contraception during office visits, offer prescriptions in advance of need, and provide education through pamphlets or the internet.

Web sites such as www.not-2-late.com allow users to search for physicians who prescribe emergency contraception by ZIP Code, area code, or address, and Planned Parenthood offers extensive educational information at www.plannedparenthood.org/library/birthcontrol/ec.html, including details about off-label use of many birth-control pills for emergency contraception.

Our principle of a compassionate duty of care should apply to all health care professionals. In a secular society, they must be prepared to limit the reach of their personal objection. Objecting pharmacists may choose to find employment opportunities that comport with their morals—in a religious community, for example—but when they pledge to serve the public, it is unreasonable to expect those in need of health care to acquiesce to their personal convictions. Similarly, physicians who refuse to write prescriptions for emergency contraception should follow the rules of notice and referral for the reason previously articulated: the beliefs of health care providers should not trump patient care. It is difficult enough to be faced with the consequences of rape or of an unplanned pregnancy; health care providers should not make the situation measurably worse.

Former Supreme Court Chief Justice Charles Evans Hughes called the quintessentially American custom of respect for conscience a "happy tradition"[37]—happier, perhaps, when left in the setting of a draft objection than when pitting one person's beliefs against another's reproductive health. Ideally, conflicts about emergency contraception will be rare, but they will occur. In July, 11 nurses in Alabama resigned rather than provide emergency contraception in state clinics.[38] As patients understand their birth-control options, conflicts at the pharmacy counter and in the clinic may become more common. When professionals' definitions of liberty infringe on those they choose to serve, a respectful balance must be struck. We offer one solution. Even those who challenge this division of burdens and benefits should agree with our touchstone—although health professionals may have a right to object, they should not have a right to obstruct.

NOTES

1. Drazen JM, Greene MF, Wood AJJ. The FDA, politics, and Plan B. N Engl J Med 2004; 350:1561–2.

2. Stanford JB, Hager WD, Crockett SA. The FDA, politics, and Plan B. N Engl J Med 2004; 350:2413–4.

3. Alaska Admin. Code tit. 12, § 52.240 (2004).

4. Cal. Bus. & Prof. Code § 4052(8) (2004).

5. Hawaii Rev. Stat. § 461–1 (2003).

6. N.M. Admin. Code § 16.19.26.9 (2003).

7. Wash. Rev. Code § 246–863–100 (2004).

8. Me. Rev. Stat. Ann. tit.32, §§ 13821–13825 (2004).

9. Pharmacist refuses pill for victim. Chicago Tribune. February 11, 2004:C7.

10. Simon S. Pharmacists new players in abortion debate. Los Angeles Times. March 20, 2004:A18.

11. Sweency JF. May a pharmacist refuse to fill a prescription? Plain Dealer. May 5, 2004:E1.

12. Associated Press. Pharmacist refuses to fill morning after prescription. (Accessed October 14, 2004, at http://www.thechamplainchannel.com/wnne/3761928/detail.html.)

13. Sauer M. Pharmacist to be fired in abortion controversy. St. Petersburg Times. December 19, 1991:1B.

14. State policies in brief: refusing to provide health services. New York: Alan Guttmacher Institute, September 1, 2004. (Accessed October 14, 2004 at http://www.guttmacher.org/statecenter/spibs/spib_RPHS.pdf.)

15. Seeley RA. Advice for conscientious objectors in the armed forces. 5th ed. Philadelphia: Central Committee for Conscientious Objectors, 1998:1–2 (Accessed October 14, 2004, at http://www.objector.org/Resources/adviceforcos.pdf.)

16. 42 U.S.C. § 300a-7 (2004).

17. Mich. House Bill No. 5006 (as amended April 21, 2004).

18. Oregon House Bill No. 2010 (as amended May 11, 1999).

19. Hooks Super X, Inc. v. McLaughlin, 642N.E. 2d 514 (Ind. 1994).

20. Section 2.01. In: Council on Ethical and Judicial Affairs. Code of medical ethics: current opinions with annotations. 2002–2003 ed. Chicago: American Medical Association, 2002.

21. Oregon Revised Statute § 127.885 § 4.01 (4) (2003).

22. Fassett WE, Wicks AC. Is pharmacy a profession? In: Weinstein BD, ed. Ethical issues in pharmacy. Vancouver, Wash.: Applied Therapeutics, 1996:1–28.

23. American Pharmacists Association. Code of ethics for pharmacists: preamble. (Accessed October 14, 2004, at http://www.aphanet.org/pharmcare/ethics.html.)

24. Hughes EC, ed. Obstetric-gynecologic terminology, with section on neonatology and glossary of congenital anomalies. Philadelphia: F.A. Davis, 1972.

25. Commodity Supplemental Food Program, 7 C.E.R. § 247.2 (2004).

26. Glasier A. Emergency postcoital contraception. N Engl J Med 1997;337:1058–64.

27. Daily reproductive health reports state politics & policy: Washington governor signs law requiring hospitals to offer emergency contraception to rape survivors. Menlo Park, Calif.: Kaisernetwork, April 2, 2002. (Accessed October 14, 2004, at http://www.kaisernetwork.org/daily_reports/rep_index.cfm?hint=2&DR_ID=10366.)

28. Brownfield v. Daniel Freeman Marina Hospital, 208 Cal. App. 3d 405 (Cal. Ct. App. 1989).

29. Shelton v. Univ. of Medicine & Dentistry, 223 F.3d 220 (3d Cir. 2000).

30. Tribe LH. American constitutional law. 2nd ed. Mincola, N.Y.: Foundation Press, 1988:1183.

31. Brody JE. The politics of emergency contraception. New York Times. August 24, 2004:F7.

32. Trans World Airlines v. Hardison, 432 U.S. 63 (1977).

33. 1997–98 APhA Policy Committee report: pharmacist conscience clause. Washington, D.C.: American Pharmacists Association, 1997.

34. Politics wins over science. Capital Times. May 13, 2004:16A.

35. Alford S, Davis L, Brown L, Pharmacists' attitudes and awareness of emergency contraception for adolescents. Transitions 2001; 12(4):1–17.

36. Foster DG, Harper CC, Bley JJ, et al. Knowledge of emergency contraception among women aged 18 to 44 in California. Am J Obstet Gynecol 2004;191:150–6.

37. United States v. Macintosh, 283 U.S. 605, 634 (1931) (Hughes, C.J., dissenting).

38. Elliott D. Alabama nurses quit over morning-after pill. Presented on All Things Considered. Washington, D.C.: National Public Radio, July 28, 2004 (transcript).

Alan Meisel and Mark Kuczewski

Legal and Ethical Myths About Informed Consent

Alan Meisel teaches at the Law School at the University of Pittsburgh. Mark Kuczewski teaches at the Medical School at the University of Pittsburgh.

Some physicians are still mistrustful of the doctrine of informed consent. It has been condemned in the medical literature as a myth and as bad medicine. It has been the subject of numerous parodies intended to illustrate the absurdities to which it can be carried. Most of these attacks are based on the idea that there is a fundamental incompatibility between the patient autonomy that informed consent is intended to promote and physician responsibility for a patient's well-being and on the fear that well-being will be severely compromised.

Recently, more subtle attacks on informed consent have come from well-intentioned medical ethicists. For instance, Veatch argues that modern medicine has too many treatments available for many conditions for a physician to be able to disclose relevant information about all of them—as would need to be done if the letter of the law were to be observed—and therefore, physicians should disclose only information about those treatments that are consistent with their own values. Veatch somewhat overoptimistically advocates delivery-of-care arrangements that pair physicians and patients who have similar values and treatment dispositions as the solution to this problem.

APPROACHES TO INFORMED CONSENT: RIGHTS VS. SHARED PROCESS

Patient autonomy began to grow as an antidote to physician paternalism—the supposed tendency of physicians to assume almost complete responsibility for determining what treatment patients would have—and in recognition of the fact that what treatment patients should have is a normative as well as a scientific determination. Its function in preserving a patient's liberties is probably responsible for the enthusiastic response lawyers have given to informed consent. However, too strong an emphasis on its legal origins and function eclipses the fact that informed consent is not merely a legal concept. Informed consent is a legal doctrine that also supports many of our cherished ideals about the rights of the individual. The law's rights-oriented approach to informed consent assumes that the individual patient is characterized by a set of personal values that no one but that patient can know. In deciding what treatment, if any, a patient is to receive, the physician is viewed as an expert who should leave his or her values aside and only bring technical expertise into play. In the standard rendition of informed consent, the physician's role is to explain the various possibilities for the diagnosis or treatment of a particular patient's condition, and the patient is to consider this information in the context of his or her own values and then choose a course of treatment suited to him or her.

This approach fits certain cases nicely, for example, religiously based treatment refusals by a competent adult patient. However, mindless application of this approach to all medical decision making is responsible for many of the myths that have developed about informed consent. In the clinical setting, rights often recede into the background, and it is more helpful to approach informed consent as a shared process of decision making. A shared process approach does not restrict the physician to providing facts and insists that the patient supply all the values. The physician and patient each have access to interrelated facts and values. The values and thinking of the physician and patient should gradually take shape. They should mutually monitor each other so that their goals, thoughts, and evaluations become transparent to each other.

Conceived as a process of shared decision making, informed consent can accommodate both patient autonomy and the physician's responsibility for the well-being of the patient. As we explore some of the myths about informed consent, we highlight how a balance should be struck to accommodate both autonomy and beneficence.

MYTH 1: A SIGNED CONSENT FORM IS INFORMED CONSENT

Perhaps the most fundamental and pervasive myth about informed consent is that informed consent has been obtained when a patient signs a consent form. Nothing could be further from the truth, as many courts have pointed out to physicians who were only too willing to believe this myth. Consent forms are used as a matter of routine in both treatment and research settings because many hospital administrators, physicians, and their attorneys see these forms as providing protection against liability, despite the fact that they actually provide little protection.

Consent forms do have some value. They create an inference that the patient at least had an opportunity to read the information on it. If the information presented in the consent form contains a description of the risk that actually came to pass and contains other information that is adequate for a patient to

make a decision, it will probably be helpful to a physician in the defense of a lawsuit.

On the other hand, if the information on the form is not adequate or is overly complex, the form may provide evidence to support the patient's case. If the form merely acknowledges that disclosure was made, but fails to recite the content of what should have been disclosed, it is unlikely to provide the physician with any advantage with respect to the main issue in a lawsuit: what was disclosed and whether it was adequate. Contemporary consent forms—often optimistically referred to as "informed consent forms" as if wishing would make it so—provide a false sense of security to physicians and hospital administrators who are led to believe that a signed consent form constitutes informed consent.

MYTH 2: INFORMED CONSENT IS A MEDICAL MIRANDA WARNING

As practiced, and certainly as symbolized by consent forms, informed consent is often no more than a medical Miranda warning. Just as police are required to tell criminal suspects that "you have a right to remain silent, you have a right to a lawyer, and if you choose to speak, anything you say can be used against you," some physicians believe that informed consent has been obtained if they warn patients of the risks of treatment.

Certainly, patients should be told about the risks of treatment. Admittedly, it is difficult to know what risks must be disclosed, but the approach to informed consent that we advocate makes this less important. Rather than focusing on risks, the focus needs to be on therapeutic options. For example, patients with ulcers need to know about medical treatment and surgical treatment. Patients with breast cancer need to know about different kinds and combinations of surgery, radiation, and chemotherapy. All patients always need to know that one of their options is to do nothing.

Knowledge of one's options alone, however, is not meaningful unless one also knows the range of consequences is choosing each option. One facet of information about consequences is the risks of treatment, but there are others such as information about the likely outcomes, including information about mortality, morbidity, and functioning.

MYTH 3: INFORMED CONSENT REQUIRES THAT PHYSICIANS OPERATE A MEDICAL CAFETERIA

A myth that contradicts the previous one, yet is sometimes held simultaneously with it, is that informed consent requires physicians to operate a medical cafeteria, in which they must set out all the therapeutic options and let patients choose, each according to his or her own appetite. The law clearly does not require this.

Some physicians feel that their ability to practice medicine "the way we used to in the good old days" has been impinged on not only by courts and lawyers but also by third-party payers, health facility administrators, Congress, the state legislature, governmental bureaucrats, and patients incited by Ralph Nader, the consumer advocate. In a sense, this myth about informed consent has arisen as an antidote to the previous one. It is not hard to envision a physician, who has been continually told to provide patients with information about medical options and their consequences, wringing his or her hands in disgust or discouragement and responding with, "Well, damn it, if informed consent is all about letting patients chart their own course in medical matters, then let them do it. And if things go wrong, well it's their own fault—both because they did the choosing, and because they didn't listen to us."

When this attitude is at work, there is a serious sin of omission. What is being omitted is a central part of the physician—patient relationship as both physicians and patients view it—namely, the physician's role as medical adviser.

Patients usually want more than information. They also want advice. They say, "Doctor, if you were in my position, what would you do?" That does not mean they are going to do what their physician would do, nor does it mean that they should have just let the physician decide from the outset. It does not mean that informed consent is a charade. What it means is that informed consent is a process and

part of the process is human interaction. Rather than thinking of informed consent as an abstract ideal, what we call informed consent should take the form of a conversation in which patients get information, ask questions, give information, and say "I want to think about it" or "I've thought about it and I can't decide. What do you think I should do?" Thus viewed, informed consent is a process of shared or collaborative decision making.

Another way of looking at the process of informed consent is that it must mix together treatment goals and particular treatments. Most of the confusion surrounding the cafeteria approach to informed consent assumes that patients wish to micromanage their care. This is rarely the case. However, patients are entitled to know the goals of therapeutic options and when that goal has changed. Too often, treatments are discussed in detail but patients are not really sure what the treatment is ultimately meant to do. Similarly, when new treatments are introduced and discussed, it is not always clear to the patient that the old goal is no longer realistic, e.g., cure is no longer possible, and that this new treatment is directed at a different goal such as minimizing disability or relieving pain. Patients are not experts at treatments; physicians are. However, patients' preferences are central to the choice of treatment goals. Thus, in selecting and revising treatment goals, physicians and patients need to form a partnership.

MYTH 4: PATIENTS MUST BE TOLD EVERYTHING ABOUT TREATMENT

Some believe that the law requires patients be told everything about treatment—the equivalent of giving them the Physicians' Desk Reference. Actually, the law requires only that patients be given a reasonable amount of information. In about half the states, the adequacy of disclosure is measured by customary professional practice, which means that patients must be given the information that a reasonable physician would disclose. In the remaining states, the adequacy of disclosure is measured by a so-called legal standard, which requires the provision of that amount and kind of information that a reasonable patient would find material to making a decision about treatment.

Because those rules are vague, lawyers cannot provide physicians with specific guidance about how to comply. Therefore, physicians sometimes feel driven back into the corner of disclosing everything, which is unnecessary. Further, it is unwise from a legal perspective because physicians could be held liable (though it is not likely) for intentionally inflicting emotional distress on patients by giving them too much information.

Our previous discussions of goals and treatments should provide a minimal checklist. Once a physician and patient have explored all the relatively realistic goals of treatment, the number of therapeutic options and amount of information about those options frequently become relatively minor issues.

MYTH 5: PATIENTS NEED FULL DISCLOSURE ABOUT TREATMENT ONLY IF THEY CONSENT

Information about therapeutic options and their consequences to be used by patients in making decisions needs to be provided before, not after, decisions are made. In practice, this is not always the case. One reason is the nature of the process by which physicians conceptualize and solve problems and formulate recommendations. Physicians acquire information about patients through examination, history, medical records, laboratory tests, and similar processes and then formulate a diagnosis. The physician makes a treatment recommendation to the patient in the form of, "Here's what's wrong with you and this is what we need to do."

Patients are expected to comply with the recommendation although some patients will ask questions, take some time to think about it, seek a second opinion, or even refuse the recommendation or any further medical attention. If the patient decides to follow the recommendation (i.e., consents), and especially if the physician has not yet provided much in the way of information, he or she might then receive more information because this decision provides an occasion to discuss the medical malady and its treatment. In other words, much of the

information relevant to making a decision actually comes after the decision is made. There is nothing wrong with continuing to provide, reiterate, or recast information at the time the patient consents to treatment. In fact, we recommend it. However, if informed consent was conceived of by physicians as a process of shared decision making, information might more readily flow earlier and more frequently.

The failure to make information available to patients before they decide whether to accept or reject a physician's recommendations is based on the premise that if the patient refuses treatment, it is unnecessary, if not paradoxical, to obtain informed consent. This illustrates how the use of the term informed consent is unfortunate, if not dangerous, for it assumes that the process of informing is to eventuate in consent. Physicians also assume that if in fact consent is not forthcoming, information need not be given to patients or if the patient refuses the recommended treatment and settles on an alternative treatment, no information need be provided about the rejected treatment.

In fact, physicians are obligated to obtain not only informed consent but also informed refusal. This is not as silly as it might at first appear, when one recalls that the most important part of informed consent is information about options and their consequences and a refusal of treatment is a choice to do nothing, which has predictable consequences too. This is not a resurrection of the cafeteria approach, nor are we recommending that the physician present the entire treatment menu. What we are saying is that when the physician examines the patient and says, for example, "We'll have to do bypass surgery," and omitted discussion of the choice of goals, he or she has assumed that the patient would agree about the treatment to meet that goal.

MYTH 6: PATIENTS CANNOT GIVE INFORMED CONSENT BECAUSE THEY CANNOT UNDERSTAND COMPLEX MEDICAL INFORMATION

The notion that informed consent is a myth and bad medicine is premised in part on the assumption that providing information to patients frightens them. These characterizations are also based on the assumed difficulty of transmitting technical information to patients. A typical unspoken thought might go, "Patients can't understand all this medical stuff. Why I have trouble keeping up with my own subspecialty, I've forgotten 95% of what I learned in medical school, and the 5% I remember is now outdated. Even worse, what about all those empirical studies that show that patients who have been given information don't remember it 6 months, 6 days, or even 6 hours or 6 minutes later?"

There are at least 2 errors in this reasoning. The first is the equation of recall with understanding. While it might be true that someone who cannot retain information for a few seconds might not be said to understand it, people often make reasonable decisions but cannot later recall the premises that supported the reasoning or the process that led to the conclusion. Nevertheless, they might well have understood it at the time.

The second error is the assumption that patients must understand information in the same way and to the same extent as the physician. It is true that a patient who is totally bereft of understanding lacks decision-making capacity and would be considered legally incompetent. In such a case, decision making would need to take place with a surrogate decision maker acting on the patient's behalf. The fact that a patient might put an odd gloss on information or might not have a completely accurate factual understanding of the information does not disqualify that patient as a decision maker. To have decision-making capacity, patients do not need to be Jonas Salk. They merely need to be able to understand their options and the potential risks and benefits of these options. Most assuredly the fact that the patient reaches a decision different from the one that the physician would have made does not mean that the patient does not understand the information.

What is critical is that patients be given information and that they have a chance to use it in formulating a decision, to ask questions about it, and to gather further information. It is essential that they be given the context for the proposed treatments, i.e., they must be told the physician's goals in making this treatment recommendation. However, within broad limits, patients have the right to set their own goals and to make their own decisions in their own way and for their own reasons, which includes the right not to use information that others might think relevant, rational, and even necessary to decision making.

We are steering a course between extremes. One extreme assumes that a patient just cannot understand medical information, and so we should give up on informed consent. On the other end of the spectrum resides the extreme rights-oriented view that a patient's treatment choices should not be challenged. We advocate the middle path: patients' choices should make sense in terms of their values and way of making sense of the world and these decisions should be made in the manner patients normally make similar choices. However, to require "understanding" in the same way and to the same extent that a physician understands the information is as paternalistic as not permitting patients to participate in decision making at all.

MYTH 7: PATIENTS MUST BE GIVEN INFORMATION WHETHER THEY WANT IT OR NOT

Some patients choose not to participate in the decision-making process at all or may wish to participate on a reduced basis. Withholding information from patients when they request that it not be given respects their autonomy as much as providing information to patients who want it. Enabling and permitting patients to make medical decisions is one way of fostering self-determination; respecting their wish not to participate is another. Compelling patients to receive information that they do not want or to make decisions that they do not wish to make is to fail to respect their dignity.

Withholding information from patients at their request is a legally recognized exception to informed consent referred to as waiver. Usually, only by initiating a conversation with a patient can a physician determine that a patient wishes to participate in only a limited way, or not at all, in the decision-making process. In some instances, patients may fully engage in such a conversation and only at the end declare that they do not know what to do and wish to leave the decision to a family member, the physician, or someone else. In such a case, a patient can be said to have waived the right to decide though not the right to be informed. Sometimes patients make it clear that they do not even want to talk about therapeutic options and consequences. They may be willing to make a decision on less, rather than more, information. In such a case, a patient can be said to have waived the right to be informed, though not necessarily the right to decide. Or patients may want neither information nor to decide, again preferring to leave it all to someone else.

Thus, the waiver exception parallels the 2 distinct but related rights that informed consent embodies, the right to be given information and the right to decide. Patients who waive their right to decide do not automatically waive their right to information. There may be good reasons to continue to provide information to such patients. One is that just because patients do not want to make a particular treatment decision does not mean that they will not wish to participate in the future. Furthermore, there are reasons to provide information other than for decision making. Patients also need information to facilitate compliance with treatment decisions. They deserve information about their treatment as a sign of respect and so that they can be prepared for what is to happen to them.

MYTH 8: INFORMATION MAY BE WITHHELD IF IT WILL CAUSE THE PATIENT TO REFUSE TREATMENT

It is ironic that physicians who profess not to know much about informed consent sometimes do know about the therapeutic privilege, which, like the waiver exception, allows information to be withheld from patients. When information is withheld under the waiver exception, patients decide that having information would not serve their ends. By contrast, when the therapeutic privilege is invoked to withhold information, the physician determines that providing the patient with information would undermine, rather than promote, the goals of informed consent.

The purpose of the therapeutic privilege is to allow physicians to honor their "primary duties" to do what is beneficial for the patients and to avoid inflicting harm on them. However, it is far less clear what circumstances justify the physician in withholding information. In general, physicians are permitted to withhold information when its disclosure would seriously harm the patient.

In practice, the therapeutic privilege may legitimate a physician's natural aversion to providing unpleasant information to patients—indeed, almost everyone's natural aversion to providing unpleasant information to anyone else. However, the therapeutic privilege is not a license for physicians to withhold information when they fear, rightly or wrongly, that providing it to patients will lead them to refuse recommended treatment. Such a view of the privilege is paternalistic in the extreme; it threatens to devour any obligation to provide information and would permit physicians to substitute their judgment for the patient's. The more appropriate formulation of the privilege permits physicians to tailor (and even withhold) information when, but only when, its disclosure would so upset a patient that he or she could not rationally engage in a conversation about therapeutic options and consequences.

CONCLUSION

A number of myths about what the law requires impede the practice of obtaining informed consent. If informed consent is viewed as a process of shared decision making, some of the seeming absurdities and excesses that can be associated with it disappear. In so doing, it might make the practice of medicine more rewarding for physicians. The doctrine of informed consent does not analogize physicians to waiters who take orders from customers. Rather, it recognizes the responsibility of the physician for the patient's well-being.

We are a litigious society, and physicians must be concerned with avoiding lawsuits. The best advice we can give is to treat patients like people, act sensitively and compassionately, and most of all, talk to patients. Have a conversation, have several;

remember that this is a process. In this process, you will gradually come to know your patient's decision-making style. Furthermore, do not press patients to decide quickly. Do not make them think that you do not have time for them. Because if you do, regardless of how much information they are given, they are going to be angry, and another name for an angry patient is plaintiff.

Judge Spotswood W. Robinson, III

Opinion in *Canterbury* v. *Spence*

Judge Robinson was Chief Judge of the U.S. Court of Appeals for the District of Columbia.

The record we review tells a depressing tale. A youth troubled only by back pain submitted to an operation without being informed of a risk of paralysis incidental thereto. A day after the operation he fell from his hospital bed after having been left without assistance while voiding. A few hours after the fall, the lower half of his body was paralyzed, and he had to operated on again. Despite extensive medical care, he has never been what he was before. Instead of the back pain, even years later, he hobbled about on crutches, a victim of paralysis of the bowels and urinary incontinence. In a very real sense this lawsuit is an understandable search for reasons. . . .

Suits charging failure by a physician adequately to disclose the risks and alternatives of proposed treatment are not innovations in American law. They date back a good half-century, and in the last decade they have multiplied rapidly. There is, nonetheless, disagreement among the courts and the commentators on many major questions, and there is no precedent of our own directly in point. For the tools enabling resolution of the issues on this appeal, we are forced to begin at first principles.

The root premise is the concept, fundamental in American jurisprudence, that "[e]very human being

of adult years and sound mind has a right to determine what shall be done with his own body. . . ."[1] True consent to what happens to one's self is the informed exercise of a choice, and that entails an opportunity to evaluate knowledgeably the options available and the risks attendant upon each.[2] The average patient has little or no understanding of the medical arts, and ordinarily has only his physician to whom he can look for enlightenment with which to reach an intelligent decision.[3] From these almost axiomatic considerations springs the need, and in turn the requirement, of a reasonable divulgence by physician to patient to make such a decision possible.[4]

A physician is under a duty to treat his patient skillfully[5] but proficiency in diagnosis and therapy is not the full measure of his responsibility. The cases demonstrate that the physician is under an obligation to communicate specific information to the patient when the exigencies of reasonable care call for it.[6] Due care may require a physician perceiving symptoms of bodily abnormality to alert the patient to the condition.[7] It may call upon the physician confronting an ailment which does not respond to his ministrations to inform the patient thereof.[8] It may command the physician to instruct the patient as to any limitations to be presently observed for his own welfare,[9] and as to any precautionary therapy

From U.S. Court of Appeals, District of Columbia Circuit, 19 May 1972. 464 *Federal Reporter*, 2nd Series, pp. 772–96. West Publishing Company.

he should seek in the future.[10] It may oblige the physician to advice the patient of the need for or desirability of any alternative treatment promising greater benefit than that being pursued.[11] Just as plainly, due care normally demands that the physician warn the patient of any risks to his well-being which contemplated therapy may involve.[12]

The context in which the duty of risk-disclosure arises is invariably the occasion for decision as to whether a particular treatment procedure is to be undertaken. To the physician, whose training enables a self-satisfying evaluation, the answer may seem clear, but it is the prerogative of the patient, not the physician, to determine for himself the direction in which his interests seem to lie.[13] To enable the patient to chart his course understandably, some familiarity with the therapeutic alternatives and their hazards becomes essential.[14]

A reasonable revelation in these respects is not only a necessity but, as we see it, is as much a matter of the physician's duty. It is a duty to warn of the dangers lurking in the proposed treatment, and that is surely a facet of due care. It is, too, a duty to impart information which the patient has every right to expect.[15] The patient's reliance upon the physician is a trust of the kind which traditionally has exacted obligations beyond those associated with arms-length transactions. His dependence upon the physician for information affecting his well-being, in terms of contemplated treatment, is well-nigh abject. As earlier noted, long before the instant litigation arose, courts had recognized that the physician had the responsibility of satisfying the vital informational needs of the patient.[16] More recently, we ourselves have found "in the fiducial qualities of [the physician—patient] relationship the physician's duty to reveal to the patient that which in his best interests it is important that he should know."[17] We now find, as a part of the physician's overall obligation to the patient, a similar duty of reasonable disclosure of the choices with respect to proposed therapy and the dangers inherently and potentially involved.

This disclosure requirement, on analysis, reflects much more of a change in doctrinal emphasis than a substantive addition to malpractice law. It is well established that the physician must seek and secure his patient's consent before commencing an operation or other course of treatment.[18] It is also clear that the consent, to be efficacious, must be free from imposition upon the patient. It is the settled rule that therapy not authorized by the patient may amount to a tort—a common law battery—by the physician.[19] And it is evident that it is normally impossible to obtain a consent worthy of the name unless the physician first elucidates the options and the perils for the patient's edification. Thus the physician has long borne a duty, on pain of liability for unauthorized treatment, to make adequate disclosure to the patient.[20] The evolution of the obligation to communicate for the patient's benefit as well as the physician's protection has hardly involved an extraordinary restructuring of the law.

There are, in our view, formidable obstacles to acceptance of the notion that the physician's obligation to disclose is either germinated or limited by medical practice. To begin with, the reality of any discernible custom reflecting a professional consensus on communication of option and risk information to patients is open to serious doubt.[21] We sense the danger that what in fact is no custom at all may be taken as an affirmative custom to maintain silence, and that physician-witnesses to the so-called custom may state merely their personal opinions as to what they or others would do under given conditions.[22] We cannot gloss over the inconsistency between reliance on a general practice respecting divulgence and, on the other hand, realization that the myriad of variables among patients[23] makes each case so different that its omission can rationally be justified only by the effect of its individual circumstances. Nor can we ignore the fact that to bind the disclosure obligation to medical usage is to arrogate the decision on revelation to the physician alone. Respect for the patient's right of self-determination on particular therapy demands a standard set by law for physicians rather than one which physicians may or may not impose upon themselves. . . .

Once the circumstances give rise to a duty on the physician's part to inform his patient, the next inquiry is the scope of the disclosure the physician is legally obliged to make. The courts have frequently confronted this problem but no uniform standard defining the adequacy of the divulgence emerges from the decisions. Some have said "full" disclosure,[24] a norm we are unwilling to adopt literally. It seems obviously prohibitive and unrealistic to expect physicians to discuss with their patients every risk of proposed treatment—no matter how small or remote—and generally unnecessary from the patient's viewpoint as well. . . .

The larger number of courts, as might be expected, have applied tests framed with reference to prevailing fashion within the medical profession.[25] Some have measured the disclosure by "good medical practice,"[26] others by what a reasonable practitioner would have bared under the circumstances,[27] and still others by what medical custom in the community would demand.[28] We have explored this rather considerable body of law but are unprepared to follow it. The duty to disclose, we have reasoned, arises from phenomena apart from medical custom and practice. The latter, we think, should no more establish the scope of the duty than its existence. Any definition of scope in terms purely of a professional standard is at odds with the patient's prerogative to decide on projected therapy himself. That prerogative, we have said, is at the very foundation of the duty to disclose, and both the patient's right to know and the physician's correlative obligation to tell him are diluted to the extent that its compass is dictated by the medical profession.[29]

In our view, the patient's right of self-decision shapes the boundaries of the duty to reveal. That right can be effectively exercised only if the patient possesses enough information to enable an intelligent choice. The scope of the physician's communications to the patient, then, must be measured by the patient's need, and that need is the information material to the decision. Thus the test for determining whether a particular peril must be divulged is its materiality to the patient's decision: all risks potentially affecting the decision must be unmasked.[30] And to safeguard the patient's interest in achieving his own determination on treatment, the law must itself set the standard for adequate disclosure.[31]

Optimally for the patient, exposure of a risk would be mandatory whenever the patient would deem it significant to his decision, either singly or in combination with other risks. Such a requirement, however, would summon the physician to second-guess the patient, whose ideas on materiality could hardly be known to the physician. That would make an undue demand upon medical practitioners, whose conduct, like that of others, is to be measured in terms of reasonableness. Consonantly with orthodox negligence doctrine, the physician's liability for nondisclosure is to be determined on the basis of foresight, not hindsight; no less than any other aspect of negligence, the issue on nondisclosure must be approached from the viewpoint of the reasonableness of the physician's divulgence in terms of what he knows or should know to be the patient's informational needs. If, but only if, the fact-finder can say that the physician's communication was unreasonably inadequate is an imposition of liability legally or morally justified.[32]

Of necessity, the content of the disclosure rests in the first instance with the physician. Ordinarily it is only he who is in position to identify particular dangers; always he must make a judgment, in terms of materiality, as to whether and to what extent revelation to the patient is called for. He cannot know with complete exactitude what the patient would consider important to his decision, but on the basis of his medical training and experience he can sense how the average, reasonable patient expectably would react.[33] Indeed, with knowledge of, or ability to learn, his patient's background and current condition, he is in a position superior to that of most others—attorneys, for example—who are called upon to make judgments on pain of liability in damages for unreasonable miscalculation.[34]

From these considerations we drive the breadth of the disclosure of risks legally to be required. The scope of the standard is not subjective as to either the physician or the patient; it remains objective with due regard for the patient's informational needs and with suitable leeway for the physician's situation. In broad outline, we agree that "[a] risk is thus material when a reasonable person, in what the physician knows or should know to be the patient's position, would be likely to attach significance to the risk or cluster of risks in deciding whether or not to forego the proposed therapy."[35]

The topics importantly demanding a communication of information are the inherent and potential hazards of the proposed treatment, the alternatives to the treatment, if any, and the results likely if the patient remains untreated. The factors contributing significance to the dangerousness of a medical technique are, of course, the incidence of injury and the degree of the harm threatened.[36] A very small chance of death or serious disablement may well be significant; a potential disability which dramatically outweighs the potential benefit of the therapy or the detriments of the existing malady ... summons discussion with the patient.

There is no bright line separating the significant from the insignificant; the answer in any case must abide a rule of reason. Some dangers—infection, for example—are inherent in any operation; there is no obligation to communicate those of which persons of average sophistication are aware. Even more clearly, the physician bears no responsibility for discussion of hazards the patient has already discovered, or those having no apparent materiality to patients' decision on therapy. The disclosure doctrine, like others marking lines between permissible and impermissible behavior in medical practice, is in essence a requirement of conduct prudent under the circumstances. Whenever non-disclosure of particular risk information is open to debate by reasonable-minded men, the issue is for the finder of the facts.

Two exceptions to the general rule of disclosure have been noted by the courts. Each is in the nature of a physician's privilege not to disclose, and the reasoning underlying them is appealing. Each, indeed, is but a recognition that, as important as is the patient's right to know, it is greatly outweighed by the magnitudinous circumstances giving rise to the privilege. The first comes into play when the patient is unconscious or otherwise incapable of consenting, and harm from a failure to treat is imminent and outweighs any harm threatened by the proposed treatment. When a genuine emergency of that sort arises, it is settled that the impracticality of conferring with the patient dispenses with need for it. Even in situations of that character the physician should, as current law requires, attempt to secure a relative's consent if possible. But if time is too short

to accommodate discussion, obviously the physician should proceed with the treatment.

The second exception obtains when risk-disclosure poses such a threat of detriment to the patient as to become unfeasible or contraindicated from a medical point of view. It is recognized that patients occasionally become so ill or emotionally distraught on disclosure as to foreclose a rational decision, or complicate or hinder the treatment, or perhaps even pose psychological damage to the patient.[37] Where that is so, the cases have generally held that the physician is armed with a privilege to keep information from the patient,[38] and we think it clear that portents of that type may justify the physician in action he deems medically warranted. The critical inquiry is whether the physician responded to a sound medical judgment that communication of the risk information would present a threat to the patient's well-being.

The physician's privilege to withhold information for therapeutic reasons must be carefully circumscribed, however, for otherwise it might devour the disclosure rule itself. The privilege does not accept the paternalisitc notion that the physician may remain silent simply because divulgence might prompt the patient to forego therapy the physician feels the patient really needs.[39] That attitude presumes instability or perversity for even the normal patient, and runs counter to the foundation principle that the patient should and ordinarily can make the choice for himself. Nor does the privilege contemplate operation save where the patient's reaction to risk information, as reasonably foreseen by the physician, is menacing.[40] And even in a situation of that kind, disclosure to a close relative with a view to securing consent to the proposed treatment may be the only alternative open to the physician.

NOTES

1. *Schloendorff* v. *Society of New York Hospital*, 211 N.Y. 125, 105 N.E. 92, 93 (1914). See also *Natanson* v. *Kline*, 186 Kan. 393, 350 P.2d 1093, 1104 (1960), clarified, 187 Kan. 186, 354 P.2d 670 (1960)....

2. See *Dunham* v. *Wright*, 423 F.2d 940, 943–946 (3d Cir. 1970) (applying Pennsylvania law); *Campbell* v.

Oliva, 424 F.2d 1244, 1250–1251 (6th Cir. 1970) (applying Tennessee law); *Bowers* v. *Talmage*, 159 So.2d 888 (Fla. App. 1963); *Woods* v. *Bramlop*, 71 N.M. 221, 377 P.2d 520, 524–525 (1962); *Mason* v. *Ellsworth*, 3 Wash.App. 298, 474 P.2d 909, 915, 918–919 (1970).

3. Patients ordinarily are persons unlearned in the medical sciences. Some few, of course, are schooled in branches of the medical profession or in related fields. But even within the latter group variations in degree of medical knowledge specifically referable to particular therapy may be broad, as for example, between a specialist and a general practitioner, or between a physician and a nurse. It may well be, then, that it is only in the unusual case that a court could safely assume that the patient's insights were on a parity with those of the treating physician.

4. The doctrine that a consent effective as authority to form therapy can arise only from the patient's understanding of alternatives to and risks of the therapy is commonly denominated "informed consent." See, *e.g.*, Waltz and Scheuneman, Informed Consent to Therapy, 64 Nw. U.L. Rev. 628, 629 (1970). The same appellation is frequently assigned to the doctrine requiring physicians, as a matter of duty to patients, to communicate information as to such alternatives and risks. See, *e.g.*, Comment. Informed Consent in Medical Malpractice, 55 Calif.L.Rev. 1396 (1967). While we recognize the general utility of shorthand phrases in literary expositions, we caution that uncritical use of the "informed consent" label can be misleading. See, *e.g.*, Plante, An Analysis of "Informed Consent," 36 Ford.L.Rev. 639, 671–72 (1968).

In duty-to-disclose cases, the focus of attention is more properly upon the nature and content of the physician's divulgence than the patient's understanding or consent. Adequate disclosure and informed consent are, of course, two sides of the same coin—the former a *sine qua non* of the latter. But the vital inquiry on duty to disclose relates to the physician's performance of an obligation, while one of the difficulties with analysis in terms of "informed consent" is its tendency to imply that what is decisive is the degree of the patient's comprehension.... [T]he physician discharges the duty when he makes a reasonable effort to convey sufficient information although the patient, without fault of the physician, may not fully grasp it.... Even though the factfinder may have occasion to draw an inference on the state of the patient's enlightenment, the factfinding process on performance of the duty ultimately reaches back to what the physician actually said or failed to say. And while the factual conclusion on adequacy of the revelation will vary as between patients—as, for example, between a lay patient and a physician–patient—the fluctuations are attributable to the kind of divulgence which may be reasonable under the circumstances.

5. *Brown* v. Keaveny, 117 U.S.App.D.C. 117, 118, 326 F.2d 660, 661 (1963); *Quick* v. *Thurston*, 110 U.S.App.D.C. 169, 171, 290 F.2d 350, 362, 88 A.L.R.2d 299 (en banc 1961); *Rodgers* v. *Lawson*, 83 U.S.App.D.C. 281, 282, 170 F.2d 157, 158 (1948).

6. See discussion in McCoid, The Care Required of Medical Practitioners, 12 Vand.L.Rev. 549, 586–97 (1959).

7. See *Union Carbide and Carbon Corp.* v. *Stapleton*, 237 F.2d 229, 232 (6th Cir. 1956); *Maertins* v. *Kaiser Foundation Hosp.*, 162 Cal.App.2d 661, 328 P.2d 494, 497 (1958); *Daty* v. *Lutheran Hosp. Ass'n*, 110 Neb. 467, 194 N.W.444, 445, 447 (1923); *Tredt* v. *Haugen*, 70 N.D. 338, 294 N.W. 183, 187 (1940). See also *Dietze* v. *King*, 184 F.Supp. 944, 948, 949 (E.D. Va. 1960); *Dowling* v. *Mutual Life Ins. Co.*, 168 So.2d 107, 116 (La.App.1964), writ refused, 247 La. 248, 170 So.2d 508 (1965).

8. See *Rahn* v. *United States*, 222 F.Supp. 775, 780–781 (S.D.Ga. 1963) (applying Georgia law); *Baldor* v. *Rogers*, 81 So.2d 658, 662, 55 A:L.R.2d 453 (Fla. 1955): *Manion* v. *Tweedy*, 257 Minn. 59, 100 N.W.2d 124, 128, 129 (1959); *Tvedt*. v. *Haugen*, supra note 7, 294 N.W. at 187; *Ison* v. *McFall*, 55 Tem.App. 326, 400 S.W.2d 243, 258 (1964); *Kelly* v. *Carroll*, 36 Wash.2d 482, 219 P.2d 79, 88, 19 A.L.R.2d 1174, cert. denied, 340 U.S. 892, 71 S.Ct. 208, 95 L.Ed. 646 (1950).

9. *Newman* v. *Anderson*, 195 Wis. 200, 217 N.W. 306 (1928). See also *Whitfield* v. *Damiel Constr. Co.*, 226 S.C. 37, 83 S.E.2d 460, 463 (1954).

10. *Beck* v. *German Klinik*, 78 Iowa 696, 43 N.W. 617, 618 (1889); *Pike* v. *Honsinger*, 155 N.Y. 201, 49 N.E. 760, 762 (1898); *Doan* v. *Griffith*, 402 S.W.2d 855, 856 (Ky. 1966).

11. The typical situation is where a general practitioner discovers that the patient's malady calls for specialized treatment, whereupon the duty generally arises to advise the patient to consult a specialist.... See also *Baldor* v. *Rogers, supra* note 8, 81 So.2d at 662; *Garafola* v. *Maimonides Hosp.*, 22 A.D.2d 85, 253 N.Y.S.2d 856, 858, 28 A.L.R.3d 1357 (1964); aff'd, 19 N.Y.2d 765, 279 N.Y.S.2d 523, 226 N.E.2d 311, 28 A.L.R.3d 1362 (1967); McCoid, The Care Required of Medical Practitioners, 12 Vand.L.Rev. 549, 597–98 (1959).

12. See, *e.g., Wall* v. *Brim*, 138 F.2d 478, 480–481 (5th Cir. 1943), consent issue tried on remand and verdict for plaintiff aff'd., 145 F.2d 492 (5th Cir. 1944), cert. denied, 324 U.S. 857, 65 S.Ct. 858, 89 L.Ed. 1415 (1945); *Belcher*

v. *Carter*, 13 Ohio App.2d 113, 234 N.E.2d 311, 312 (1967); *Hunter* v. *Barroughs*, 123 Va. 113, 96 S.E. 360 at 366: Plante. An Analysis of "Informed Consent," 36 Ford.L.Rev. 639, 653 (1968).

13. See text *supra* at notes 1–2.

14. See cases cited *supra* notes 3–4.

15. Some doubt has been expressed as to ability of physicians to suitably communicate their evaluations of risks and the advantages of optional treatment, and as to the lay patient's ability to understand what the physician tells him. Karchmer, Informed Consent: A Plaintiff's Medical Malpractice "Wonder Drug," 31 Mo.L.Rev. 29, 41 (1966). We do not share these apprehensions. The discussion need not be a disquisition, and surely the physician is not compelled to give his patient a short medical education: the disclosure rule summons the physician only to a reasonable explanation.... That means generally informing the patient in non-technical terms as to what is at stake: the therapy alternatives open to him, the goals expectably to be achieved, and the risks that may ensue from particular treatment and no treatment. See *Stinnett* v. *Price*. 446 S.W.2d 893, 894, 895 (Tex.Civ.App.1969). So informing the patient hardly taxes the physician, and it must be the exceptional patient who cannot comprehend such an explanation at least in a rough way.

16. See, *e.g.*, *Sheets* v. *Burman*, 322 F.2d 277, 279–280 (5th Cir. 1963); *Hudson* v. *Moore*, 239 Ala. 130, 194 So. 147, 149 (1940): *Guy* v. *Schuldt*, 236 Ind. 101, 138 N.E.2d 891. 895 (1956); *Perrin* v. *Rodriguez*, 153 So. 555. 556–557 (La.App. 1934); *Schmucking* v. *Mayo*. 183 Minn. 37, 235 N.W. 633 (1931): *Thompson* v. *Barnard*, 142 S.W.2d 238, 241 (Tex.Civ.App. 1940), aff'd, 138 Tex. 227, 158 S.W.2d 486 (1942).

17. *Emmett* v. *Eastern Dispensary and Cas. Husp.*, 130 U.S.App.D.C. 50, 54, 396 F.2d 931, 935 (1967). See also, Swan, The California Law of Malpractice of Physicians, Surgeons, and Dentists, 33 Calif.L.Rev. 248. 251 (1945).

18. Where the patient is incapable of consenting, the physician may have to obtain consent from someone else. See, *e.g.*, *Bonner* v. *Moran*, 75 U.S.App.D.C. 156, 157–158, 126 F.2d 121, 122–123, 139 A.L.R. 1366 (1941).

19. See. *e.g.*, *Bonner* v. *Moran*, *supra* note 18, 75 U.S.App.D.C. at 157, 126 F.2d at 122....

20. We discard the thought that the patient should ask for information before the physician is required to disclose. Caveat emptor is not the norm for the consumer of medical services. Duty to disclose is more than a call to speak merely on the patient's request, or merely to answer the patient's questions; it is a duty to volunteer, if necessary, the information the patient needs for intelligent decision.

The patient may be ignorant, confused, overawed by the physician or frightened by the hospital, or even ashamed to inquire. See generally Note, Restructuring Informed Consent: Legal Therapy for the Doctor Patient Relationship, 79 Yale L. J. 1533, 1545–51 (1970). Perhaps relatively few patients could in any event identify the relevant questions in the absence of prior explanation by the physician. Physicians and hospitals have patients of widely divergent socio-economic backgrounds, and a rule which presumes a degree of sophistication which many members of society lack is likely to breed gross inequities. See Note, Informed Consent as a Theory of Medical Liability, 1970 Wis.L.Rev. 879, 891–97.

21. See, *e.g.*, Comment, Informed Consent in Medical Malpractice, 55 Calif.L.Rev. 1396, 1404–05 (1967); Comment. Valid Consent to Medical Treatment: Need the Patient Know?, 4 Duquesne L.Rev. 450, 458–59 (1966); Note, 75 Harv.L.Rev. 1445, 1447 (1962).

22. Comment, Informed Consent in Medical Malpractice, 55 Calif.L.Rev. 1396, 1404 (1967): Note, 75 Harv.L.Rev. 1445, 1447 (1962).

23. For example, the variables which may or may not give rise to the physician's privilege to withhold risk information for thereapeutic reasons....

24. *E.g., Salgo* v. *Leland Standford Jr. Univ. Bd. of Trustees*, 154 Cal.App.2d 560, 317 P.2d 170, 181 (1957); *Woods* v. *Brumlop, supra* note 2, 377 P.2d at 524–525.

25. *E.g., Shetter* v. *Rochelle*, 2 Ariz.App. 358, 409 P.2d 74, 86 (1965), modified, 2 Ariz. App. 607, 411 P.2d 45 (1966); *Ditlow* v. *Kaplan*, 181 So.2d 226, 228 (Fla.App.1965); *Williams* v. *Menehan*, 191 Kan. 6. 379 P.2d 292, 294 (1963); *Kaplan* v. *Haines*, 96 N.J.Super, 242, 232 A.2d 840, 845 (1967) aff'd, 51 N.J. 404, 241 A.2d 235 (1968): *Govin* v. *Hunter*, 374 P.2d 421, 424 (Wyo, 1962)....

26. *Shetter* v. *Rochelle, supra* note 25, 409 P.2d at 86.

27. *E.g., Ditlow* v. *Kaplan, supra* note 25, 181 So.2d at 228; *Kaplan* v. *Haines, supra* note 25, 232 A.2d at 845.

28. *E.g., Williams*, v. *Menehan, supra* note 25, 379 P.2d at 294; *Gowin* v. *Hunter, supra* note 25, 374 P2d at 424.

29. For similar reasons, we reject the suggestion that disclosure should be discretionary with the physician. See Note, 109 U.Pa.L.Rev. 768, 772–73 (1961).

30. See Waltz & Scheuneman, Informed Consent to Therapy, 64 Nw.U.L.Rev. 628, 639–41 (1970).

31. See Comment, Informed Consent in Medical Malpractice, 55 Calif.L.Rev. 1396, 1407–10 (1967).

32. See Waltz & Scheuneman, Informed Consent to Theraphy, 64 Nw.U.L.Rev. 628, 639–40 (1970).

33. *Id.*

34. *Id.*

35. *Id.* at 640. . . .

36. See Comment, Informed Consent in Medical Malpractice, 55 Calif.L.Rev. 1396, 1407 n. 68 (1967).

37. See, *e.g., Salgo* v. *Leland Stanford Jr. Univ. Bd. of Trustees, supra* note 24, 317 P.2d at 181 (1957); Waltz & Scheuneman, Informed Consent to Therapy, 64 Nw.U.L.Rev. 628, 641–43 (1970).

38. *E.g., Roberts* v. *Wood*, 206 F.Supp. 579, 583 (S.D.Ala. 1962); *Nishi* v. *Hartwell*, 52 Haw. 188,

473 P.2d 116, 119 (1970); *Woods* v. *Brumlop, supra* note 2, 377 P.2d at 525; *Ball* v. *Mallinkrodt Chem. Works*, 53 Tenn.App. 218, 381 S.W.2d 563, 567–568 (1964).

39. *E.g., Scott* v. *Wilson*, 396 S.W.2d 532 at 534–535; Comment, Informed Consent in Medical Malpractice, 55 Calif.L.Rev. 1396, 1409–10 (1967); Note, 75 Harv.L.Rev. 1445. 1448 (1962).

40. Note, 75 Harv.L.Rev. 1445, 1448 (1962).

Thomas L. Carson | # The Ethics of Sales

Thomas L. Carson is Professor of Philosophy at Loyola University in Chicago.

PRELIMINARIES: A CONCEPTUAL ROADMAP

We need to distinguish between lying, deception, withholding information, and concealing information. Roughly, deception is intentionally causing someone to have false beliefs. Standard dictionary definitions of lying say that a lie is a false statement intended to deceive others. The *Oxford English Dictionary* (1989) defines a lie as: "a false statement made with the intent to deceive." *Webster's* (1963) gives the following definition of the verb *lie:* "to make an untrue statement with intent to deceive." The word *deception* implies success in causing others to have false beliefs, but lying is often unsuccessful in causing deception. A further difference between lying and deception is that, while a lie must be a false statement, deception needn't involve false statements; true statements can be deceptive and many forms of deception do not involve making statements of any sort. Thus, many instances of deception do not constitute lying. Withholding information does not constitute deception.

It is not a case of *causing* someone to have false beliefs; it is merely a case of failing to correct false beliefs or incomplete information. On the other hand, actively concealing information usually constitutes deception.

THE COMMON LAW PRINCIPLE OF CAVEAT EMPTOR

According to the common law principle of *caveat emptor,* sellers are not required to inform prospective buyers about the properties of the goods they sell. Under *caveat emptor,* sales and contracts to sell are legally enforceable even if the seller fails to inform the buyer of serious defects in the goods that are sold. Buyers themselves are responsible for determining the quality of the goods they purchase. In addition, English common law sometimes called for the enforcement of sales in cases in which sellers made false or misleading statements about the goods they sold (Atiyah 464–65).

Currently, all U.S. states operate under the Uniform Commercial Code of 1968. Section 2-313 of the code defines the notion of sellers' warranties (Preston 52). The code provides that all factual affirmations or statements about the goods being sold are warranties. This means that sales are not valid or legally enforceable if the seller makes false statements about the goods s/he is selling. The American legal system has developed the concept of an "implied" (as opposed to an express or explicit) warranty. Implied warranties are a significant limitation on the principle of *caveat emptor*. According to the Uniform Commercial Code, any transaction carries with it the following implied warranties: 1) that the seller owns the goods he is selling and 2) that the goods are "merchantable," i.e., suitable for the purposes for which they are sold (Preston 56–57). Many local ordinances require that people who sell real estate inform buyers about all known serious defects of the property they sell. These ordinances are also a significant limitation on the traditional principle of *caveat emptor*.

Deceptive sales practices also fall under the purview of the Federal Trade Commission (FTC). The FTC prohibits deceptive sales practices—practices likely to materially mislead reasonable consumers (FTC Statement 1983)....

HOLLEY'S THEORY

Holley's theory is based on his concept of a "voluntary" or "mutually beneficial" market exchange (Holley uses the terms *voluntary exchange* and *mutually beneficial exchange* interchangeably). He says that a voluntary exchange occurs "only if" the following conditions are met (Holley takes his conditions to be *necessary* conditions for an acceptable exchange):

1. Both buyer and seller understand what they are giving up and what they are receiving in return.
2. Neither buyer nor seller is compelled to enter into the exchange as a result of coercion, severely restricted alternatives, or other constraints on the ability to choose.
3. Both buyer and seller are able at the time of the exchange to make rational judgments about its costs and benefits. (Holley 463)

These three conditions admit of degrees of satisfaction. An ideal exchange is an exchange involving people who are fully informed, fully rational, and "enter into the exchange entirely of their own volition" (Holley 464). The conditions for an ideal exchange are seldom, if ever, met in practice. However, Holley claims that it is still possible to have an "acceptable exchange" if the parties are "adequately informed, rational, and free from compulsion."

According to Holley, "the primary duty of salespeople to customers is to avoid undermining the conditions of an acceptable exchange." He makes it clear that, on his view, acts of omission (as well as acts of commission) can undermine the conditions of an acceptable exchange (Holley 464).

Because of the complexity of many goods and services, customers often lack information necessary for an acceptable exchange. Careful examination of products will not necessarily reveal problems or defects. According to Holley, caveat emptor is not acceptable as a moral principle, because customers often lack information necessary for an acceptable exchange. In such cases, salespeople are morally obligated to give information to the buyer. The question then is: *What kind of information* do salespeople need to provide buyers in order to ensure that the buyer is adequately informed? Holley attempts to answer this question in the following passage in which he appeals to the golden rule:

> Determining exactly how much information needs to be provided is not always clear-cut. We must in general rely on our assessments of what a reasonable person would want to know. As a practical guide, a salesperson might consider, "What would I want to know, if I were considering buying this product?" (Holley 467)

This principle is very demanding, perhaps more demanding than Holley realizes. Presumably, most reasonable people would *want* to know a *great deal* about the things they are thinking of buying. They might want to know *everything* relevant to the decision whether or not to buy something (more on this point shortly).

CRITICISMS OF HOLLEY

First, when time does not permit it, a salesperson cannot be morally obligated to provide all information necessary to ensure that the customer is adequately informed (all the information that a reasonable person would *want* to know if she were in the buyer's position). In many cases, reasonable customers would *want* to know a great deal of information. Often salespeople simply don't have the time to give all customers all the information Holley deems necessary for an acceptable exchange. Salespeople don't always know all the information that the buyer needs for an acceptable exchange. It cannot be a person's duty to do what is impossible—that statement that someone *ought* to do a certain act implies that she *can* do that act. Further, in many cases, salespeople don't know enough about the buyer's state of knowledge to know what information the buyer needs in order to be adequately informed. A salesperson might know that the buyer needs certain information in order to be adequately informed but not know whether or not the buyer possesses that information. One might reply that salespeople *should* know all the information necessary for an adequate exchange. However, on examination, this is not a plausible view. A salesperson in a large retail store cannot be expected to be knowledgeable about every product he sells. Often, it is impossible for realtors and used car salesmen to know much about the condition of the houses and cars they sell or the likelihood that they will need expensive repairs.

Second, Holley's theory implies that a salesperson in a store would be obligated to inform customers that a particular piece of merchandise in her store sells for less at a competing store if she knows this to be the case. (Presumably, she would *want* to know where she can get it for the lowest price, were she herself considering buying the product.) Not only do salespeople have no duty to provide this kind of information, (ordinarily) it would be wrong for them to do so.

Third, Holley's theory seems to yield unacceptable consequences in cases in which the buyer's alternatives are severely constrained. Suppose that a person with a very modest income attempts to buy a house in a small town. Her options are severely constrained, since there is only one house for sale in her price range. According to Holley, there can't be an acceptable exchange in such cases, because condition number 2 is not satisfied. However, it's not clear what he thinks sellers ought to do in such cases. The seller can't be expected to remove these constraints by giving the buyer money or building more homes in town. Holley's view seems to imply that it would be wrong for anyone to sell or rent housing to such a person. This result is unacceptable.

TOWARD A MORE PLAUSIBLE THEORY ABOUT THE ETHICS OF SALES

I believe that salespeople have the following moral duties regarding the disclosure of information when dealing with *rational adult consumers* (cases involving children or adults who are not fully rational raise special problems that I will not try to deal with here):

1. Salespeople should provide buyers with safety warnings and precautions about the goods they sell. (Sometimes it is enough for salespeople to call attention to written warnings and precautions that come with the goods and services in question. These warnings are unnecessary if the buyers already understand the dangers or precautions in question.)

2. Salespeople should refrain from lying and deception in their dealings with customers.

3. As much as their knowledge and time constraints permit, salespeople should fully answer questions about the products and services they sell. They should answer questions forthrightly and not evade questions or withhold information that has been asked for (even if this makes it less likely that they will make a successful sale). Salespeople are obligated to answer questions about the goods and services they sell. However, they are justified in refusing to answer questions that would require them to reveal information about what their competitors are selling. They are not obligated to answer questions about competing goods

and services or give information about other sellers.

4. Salespeople should not try to "steer" customers toward purchases that they have reason to think will prove to be harmful to customers (financial harm counts) or that customers will come to regret.

These are prima facie duties that can conflict with other duties and are sometimes overridden by other duties. A prima facie duty is one's actual duty, other things being equal; it is an actual duty in the absence of conflicting duties of greater or equal importance. For example, my prima facie duty to keep promises is my actual duty in the absence of conflicting duties of equal or greater importance. The above is a *minimal list* of the duties of salespeople concerning the disclosure of information. I believe that the following are also prima facie duties of salespeople, but I am much less certain that these principles can be justified:

5. Salespeople should not sell customers goods or services they have reason to think will prove to be harmful to customers or that the customers will come to regret later, without giving the customers their reasons for thinking that this is the case. (This duty does not hold if the seller has good reasons to think that the customer already possesses the information in question.)

6. Salespeople should not sell items they know to be defective or of poor quality without alerting customers to this. (This duty does not hold if the buyer can be reasonably expected to know about the poor quality of what he is buying.)

I have what I take to be strong arguments for 1–4, but I'm not so sure that I can justify 5 and 6. I believe that reasonable people can disagree about 5 and 6. (I have very little to say about 5 and 6 in the present essay. See Carson [2001] for a discussion of arguments for 5 and 6.)

There are some important connections between duties 2, 4, and 6. Lying and deception in sales are not confined to lying to or deceiving customers about the goods one sells. Many salespeople misrepresent their own motives to customers/clients. Almost all salespeople invite the trust of customers/clients and claim, implicitly or explicitly, to be acting in the interests of customers/clients. Salespeople often ask customers to defer to their judgment about what is best for them. For most salespeople, gaining the trust of customers or clients is essential for success. Many salespeople are *not* interested in helping customers in the way they represent themselves as being. A salesperson who misrepresents her motives, and intentions to customers violates rule 2. This simultaneous inviting and betrayal of trust is a kind of treachery. In ordinary cases, rules against lying and deception alone prohibit salespeople from steering customers toward goods or services they have reason to think will be bad for them. It is difficult to steer someone in this way without lying or deception, e.g., saying that you believe that a certain product is best for someone when you don't believe this to be the case. Similar remarks apply to selling defective goods. Often, it is impossible to do this without lying to or deceiving customers. In practice, most or many violations of rules 4 and 6 are also violations of rule 2. . . .

The Golden Rule

I think that the golden rule is most plausibly construed as a consistency principle (those who violate the golden rule are guilty of inconsistency). The following version of the golden rule can be justified.

GR. Consistency requires that if you think that it would be morally permissible for someone to do a certain act to another person, then you must consent to someone else doing the same act to you in relevantly similar circumstances.

How the Golden Rule Supports My Theory

Given this version of the golden rule, any rational and consistent moral judge who makes judgments about the moral obligations of salespeople will have to accept rules 1–4 as prima facie duties. Consider each duty in turn:

1. All of us have reason to fear the hazards about us in the world; we depend on others to warn us of those hazards. Few people would survive to adulthood were it not for the warnings of

others about such things as oncoming cars, live electric wires, and approaching tornadoes. No one who values her own life can honestly say that she is willing to have others fail to warn her of dangers.

2. Like everyone else, a salesperson needs correct information in order to act effectively to achieve her goals and advance her interests. She is not willing to act on the basis of false beliefs. Consequently, she is not willing to have others deceive her or lie to her about matters relevant to her decisions in the marketplace. She is not willing to have members of other professions (such as law and medicine) make it a policy to deceive her or lie to her whenever they can gain financially from doing so.

3. Salespeople have questions about the goods and services they themselves buy. They can't say that they are willing to have others evade or refuse to answer those questions. We want our questions to be answered by salespeople or else we wouldn't ask them. We are not willing to have salespeople evade or refrain from answering our questions. (Digression. Rule 3 permits salespeople to refuse to answer questions that would force them to provide information about their competitors. Why should we say *this?* Why not say instead that salespeople are obligated to answer *all questions* that customers ask? The answer is as follows: A salesperson's actions affect *both* her customers and her employer. In applying the golden rule to this issue she can't simply ask what kind of information she would want were she in the customer's position [Holley poses the question in just this way]. Rule 3 can probably be improved upon, but it is a decent first approximation. A disinterested person who was not trying to give preference to the interests of salespeople, employers, or customers could endorse 3 as a policy for salespeople to follow. We can and must recognize the legitimacy of employers' demands for loyalty. The role of being an advocate or agent for someone who is selling things is legitimate within

certain bounds—almost all of us are willing to have real estate agents work for us. A rational person could consent to the idea that everyone follow principles such as rule 3.)

4. All of us are capable of being manipulated by others into doing things that harm us, especially in cases in which others are more knowledgeable than we are. No one can consent to the idea that other people (or salespeople) should manipulate us into doing things that harm us whenever doing so is to their own advantage. Salespeople who claim that it would be permissible for them to make it a policy to deceive customers, fail to warn them about dangers, evade their questions, or manipulate them into doing things that are harmful to them whenever doing so is advantageous to them are inconsistent because they are not willing to have others do the same to them. They must allow that 1–4 are prima facie moral duties.

Rules 1–4 are only prima facie duties. The golden rule can account for the cases in which 1–4 are overridden by other more important duties. For example, we would be willing to have other people violate rules 1–4 if doing so were necessary in order to save the life of an innocent person. In practice, violating 1, 2, 3, or 4 is permissible only in very rare cases. The financial interests of salespeople seldom justify violations of 1, 2, 3, or 4. The fact that a salesperson can make more money by violating 1, 2, 3, or 4 would not justify her in violating any of these unless she has very pressing financial obligations that she cannot meet otherwise. Often, salespeople need to meet certain minimum sales quotas to avoid being fired. Suppose that a salesperson needs to make it a policy to violate 1–4 in order to met her sales quotas and keep her job. Would this justify her in violating 1–4? *Possibly.* But, in order for this to be the case, the following conditions would have to be met: a) she has important moral obligations such as feeding and housing her family that require her to be employed (needing money to keep one's family in an expensive house or take them to Disney World wouldn't justify violating 1–4); and b) she can't find another job that would enable her to meet her obligations without violating 1–4 (or other equally important duties). Those salespeople who can't keep their jobs or make an adequate income without violating 1–4 should seek other lines of employment. . . .

EXAMPLES

I will discuss several cases to illustrate and clarify my theory.

Example A

I am selling a used car that I know has bad brakes; this is one of the reasons I am selling the car. You don't ask me any questions about the car, and I sell it to you without informing you of the problem with the brakes.

Example B

I am selling a used car that starts poorly in cold weather. You arrange to look at the car early in the morning on a very cold day. I don't own a garage so the car is out in the cold. With difficulty, I start it up and drive it for thirty minutes shortly before you look at it and then cover the car with snow to make it seem as if it hasn't been driven. The engine is still hot when you come and the car starts up immediately. You then purchase the car, remarking that you need a car that starts well in the cold to get to work, since you don't have a garage.

Example C

While working as a salesperson, I feign a friendly concern for a customer's interests. I say, "I will try to help you find the product that is best suited for your needs. I don't want you to spend any more money than you need to. Take as much time as you need." The customer believes me, but she is deceived. In fact, I couldn't care less about her welfare. I only want to sell her the highest priced item I can as quickly as I can. I don't like the customer; indeed, I am contemptuous of her.

In example A, I violate rule 1 and put the buyer and other motorists, passengers, and pedestrians at risk. In example B, I violate rules 2 and 5. In example C, I violate rule 2. In the absence of conflicting obligations that are at least as important as the rules I violate, my actions in cases A–C are morally wrong.

Example D: A Longer Case (an Actual Case)

In 1980, I received a one-year fellowship from the National Endowment for the Humanities. The fellowship paid for my salary, but not my fringe benefits. Someone in the benefits office of my university told me that I had the option of continuing my health insurance through the university if I paid for the premiums out of my own pocket. I told the benefits person that this was a lousy deal and that I could do better by going to a private insurance company. I went to the office of Prudential Insurance agent Mr. A. O. "Ed" Mokarem. I told him that I was looking for a one-year medical insurance policy to cover me during the period of the fellowship and that I planned to resume my university policy when I returned to teaching. (The university provided this policy free of charge to all faculty who were teaching.) He showed me a comparable Prudential policy that cost about half as much as the university's policy. He explained the policy to me. I asked him to fill out the forms so that I could purchase the policy. He then told me that there was a potential problem I should consider. He said roughly the following:

> You will want to return to your free university policy next year when you return to teaching. The Prudential policy is a one-year terminal policy. If you develop any serious medical problems during the next year, Prudential will probably consider you "uninsurable" and will not be willing to sell you health insurance in the future. If you buy the Prudential policy, you may encounter the same problems with your university policy. Since you will be dropping this policy *voluntarily*, they will have the right to underwrite your application for re-enrollment. If you develop a serious health problem during the next year, their underwriting

decision could be "Total Rejection," imposing some waivers and/or exclusions, or (at best) subjecting your coverage to the "pre-existing conditions clause," which would not cover any pre-existing conditions until you have been covered under the new policy for at least a year.

If I left my current health insurance for a year, I risked developing a costly medical condition for which no one would be willing to insure me. That would have been a very foolish risk to take. So, I thanked him very much and, swallowing my pride, went back to renew my health insurance coverage through the university. I never bought any insurance from Mr. Mokarem and never had occasion to send him any business.

I have discussed this case with numerous classes through the years. It usually generates a lively discussion. Most of my students do not think that Mr. Mokarem was morally obligated to do what he did, but they don't think that what he did was wrong either—they regard his actions as supererogatory or above and beyond the call of duty.

My View About Example D

On my theory, this is a difficult case to assess. If rules 1–4 are a salespersons's only duties concerning the disclosure of information, then Mr. Mokarem was not obligated to inform me as he did. (In this case, the information in question was information about a competing product—the university's health insurance policy.) If rule 5 is a prima facie duty of salespeople, then (assuming that he had no conflicting moral duties of greater or equal importance) it was his duty, all things considered, to inform me as he did. Since I am uncertain that 5 can be justified, I'm not sure whether or not Mr. Mokarem was

obligated to do what he did or whether his actions were supererogatory. This case illustrates part of what is at stake in the question of whether rule 5 is a prima facie duty of salespeople.

NOTE

This essay is a revised and abridged version of material from two earlier essays, "Deception and Withholding Information in Sales," *Business Ethics Quarterly* 11 (2001): 275–306, and "Ethical Issues in Selling and Advertising." *The Blackwell Guide to Business Ethics*, ed. Norman Bowie (Oxford: Blackwell, 2002), 186–205. Many thanks to Ivan Preston for his very generous and helpful advice and criticisms. Everyone interested in these topics should read his work.

REFERENCES

Atiyah, P. S. (1979) *The Rise and Fall of Freedom of Contract*. Oxford: The Clarendon Press.

Carson, Thomas. (1988) "On the definition of lying: a reply to Jones and revisions." *Journal of Business Ethics*, 7:509–14.

Carson, Thomas. (2001) "Deception and withholding information in sales." *Business Ethics Quarterly* 11:275–306.

FTC policy statement on deception. (1983—still current) Available on the Web at: http://www.ftc.gov/bcp/guides/guides.htm then click on FTC Policy Statement on Deception.

Gensler, Harry. (1986) "A Kantian argument against abortion." *Philosophical Studies* 49:83–98.

Holley, David. (1993) "A moral evaluation of sales practices." In Tom Beauchamp and Norman Bowie, eds., *Ethical Theory and Business*, fourth edition, 462–72. Englewood Cliffs, NJ: Prentice Hall.

CASES

CASE 3.1
The Booming Twenties
Edwin J. Perkins

...When the crash came in October 1929, the firm was prepared, having large reserves of ready cash on hand. Forewarned was indeed forearmed. Charlie had proved correct in his assessment of market conditions—probably more correct than even he had envisioned, given the magnitude of the downswing over the next three years. His partners, employees, and hundreds of loyal retail customers remained forever grateful for his wise counsel; he helped many of them avoid huge capital losses in a prolonged bear market that would drop more than 85 percent from its all-time high in September 1929 to its lowest point in March 1932. Charlie's reputation as a market forecaster was etched in stone after the crash and remains to this day one of the hallmarks of his career on Wall Street.

Charlie was not alone in his assessment of stock market conditions, but he was among the earliest and loudest voices crying in the wilderness. Moreover, he did not use his superior intuition merely to feather his own nest through secrecy, deceit, or manipulation. He never engaged in short selling the stocks of companies that his firm had underwritten, although he knew they were at risk.[1] (In short selling, a speculator borrows a stock certificate from a third party, sells it for cash, waits for an opportunity to repurchase at a lower price, and returns the certificate to the lender—retaining the profits if the market had fallen during the interim.) While brokers with most other firms were encouraging customers to borrow more money

to buy more securities, Charlie instructed his sales personnel to advise investors to exercise caution with regard to acquiring stocks on margin.

The firm had reduced its vulnerability in a sharp downturn, but Charlie retained a substantial number of shares in a select group of the companies that the partners had financed. The stocks of more than twenty-five companies with a market value of $30 million were listed on the partnership's balance sheet in January 1930. The stocks of just four companies accounted for more than 85 percent of the total: $14.8 million, Safeway Stores; $5.4 million, MacMarr Stores; $4.6 million, McCrory Stores; and $1.1 million, National Tea. The large positions in the equities of Safeway and MacMarr remained because the partnership had assumed a controlling interest in these two grocery chains on the West Coast, and Charlie wanted to maintain his voting power in forthcoming elections for the boards of directors. He had the voting strength to select the CEOs for both companies, and he planned to stay in complete control for the foreseeable future. As a consequence, those stocks were exempt from the pruning of the investment portfolio that occurred in 1929. Safeway and McMarr were the remnants of the partners' highly successful strategy of functioning as merchant bankers.

After dropping steadily for three weeks, the stock market rebounded over the next five months. Following a low of 248 in November, the Dow-Jones

From Edwin J Perkins, "The Booming Twenties," *Wall Street to Main Street: Charles Merrill and the Middle Class Investors* (Cambridge: Cambridge University Press, 1999), 105–108.

industrials rose to 294 in April—a climb of 18 percent. Many contemporaries breathed a sigh of relief, believing that the sell-off was merely a short-term correction rather than the beginning of a bear market. But Charlie remained dubious about the long term. Indeed, he was so pessimistic that he decided to curtail drastically his involvement in the financial services sector. On February 3, 1930, the firm announced that the brokerage portion of the business, namely, the six branch offices, had been transferred to E. A. Pierce, already the nation's leading brokerage house in terms of number of offices. Most of the employees in the six branches, primarily sales personnel and support staff, agreed to join the Pierce organization and continue in their current positions. Some of the junior partners at the main office also accepted an invitation to join Pierce, including Sumner Cobb and Winthrop Smith, two men who had been with Charlie almost from the very start.

Announced in the press as a sale of assets, the arrangement was closer in its dimensions to one of the firm's earlier merchant banking transactions. Pierce took over the bulk of the firm's property and personnel, but Charlie and Lynch received no payment in return. Instead, they and their departing juniors agreed to invest $5 million in. E. A. Pierce to strengthen its capital base. The two principals put up $1.9 million each, and their former partners contributed $1.2 million. Charlie believed strongly in the concept of a large-scale, geographically diversified brokerage house with thousands of retail accounts. Pierce had been in the securities business since 1901 and had established an outstanding record as managing partner of the firm that bore his name after 1926.

Merrill, Lynch was not formally dissolved in this shake-up. A skeleton staff moved into much smaller quarters at 40 Wall Street. The new strategy was to restrict future operations to investment banking. Henceforth, there would be no retailing of securities and no merchant banking commitments. The partners planned to continue underwriting securities for former corporate clients at the wholesale level and to join syndicates with other houses when opportunities arose. But the search for new corporate clients ceased. The retrenchment proved sensible as events unfolded, since the number of companies going public for the first time in the depressed 1930s was minuscule.

Lynch went into quasi retirement. With millions in the bank and millions more invested in safe bonds and preferred stocks, he spent most of the next seven years, until his untimely death in 1938, living a life of leisure and luxury. He came to the office occasionally, as did Charlie, and sometimes they met with executives of companies that the firm had financed in the past. Business and recreational activities increasingly overlapped. Deals were arranged on tennis courts, on the golf course, at the country club. Charlie joined from time to time in his partner's hedonistic pursuits.

Charlie's dramatic decision to shift careers from financial services to groceries at the age of forty-four was based on several considerations—both negatives and positives. The main negative was that he had lost confidence in his partners as a result of their foot-dragging in 1928 and 1929 with regard to the realization of paper profits on investments in common stocks. His goal was to emphasize safety in uncertain times; they were driven more strongly by greed and the avoidance of income taxes. Even Lynch had proved recalcitrant. Although Charlie ultimately prevailed, the stress of constant conflict with his business associates had tried his patience. He never wanted to go through a similar experience. Henceforth, he wanted total control of an enterprise, with no dissenting partners.

NOTE

1. Lynch may have engaged in some short selling after the crash, but he may not have profited since the market recovered some of its losses over the next six months, climbing sharply from the low in November 1929 to the high in April 1930.

Questions

1. What do you think Kenneth Lay of Enron would have done in this situation?

2. Beyond the legal duties surrounding the acts of buying and selling stock, what ethical duties does a man in a position as Charles Merrill have to his investors?

3. After the devastating market crash in 1929, what decisions did Charlie make that helped the market and his business, and were any decisions made that were detrimental to his business and the market's financial security?

CASE 3.2

An Apple a Day

Megan Rickel

We all have heard the stories of nightmarish doctor's visits: the doctor is dismissive and rude, patronizing, rushed and annoyed, or even prejudiced on some level. The advent of new technology has replaced long discussions with more accurate tests and scans. Some doctors' attitudes have driven away clients and have become hotbeds for malpractice lawsuits. Others feel the pressure to see more and more patients, thus reducing the time allowed for each individually. While, of course, accurate diagnoses are beneficial, is the seeming decrease in personal concern in doctors cause for alarm?

A patient can rate their doctor on such sites as WebMD.com, but most doctors either are never aware of such surveys, or they don't take them seriously, as these surveys are totally unmoderated. There are medical practice groups who perform medical surveys, and take the results very seriously; even docking the pay of low-ranking physicians. Because of an increase of such requests, insurance companies are now adopting their own physician rating systems; and will offer bonuses to highly rated physicians.

While these incentives may not cure the case of the distant doctor, they may, at least, create awareness in the medical community regarding a patient's personal expectations.

Questions

1. Are doctors treating their jobs as just that, jobs, or do physicians have an ethical duty to go beyond diagnosis and treatment? Do patients have a right to expect personal treatment?

2. Is the financial reward offered by health insurers an ethically feasible solution in addressing the patient satisfaction problem?

3. Most doctors never hear the complaints of their patients and most don't take online rating systems seriously, what could be a realistic solution to this problem?

CASE 3.3

Target at the Center of Battle over Plan B

Allison Stevens

WASHINGTON, D.C. (WOMENSENEWS)–Rachel Pourchot, a 27-year-old social worker who lives with her longtime boyfriend, left her office near St. Louis for what she thought would be a routine errand to fill prescriptions for contraceptives.

But instead of walking away with both of her prescribed medications, Pourchot wound up inciting a scuffle between Target, the Minneapolis-based retail giant, and Planned Parenthood Federation of America, the New York-based reproductive rights organization.

That's because Pourchot left Target with only one medication: a packet of the hormonal contraceptive Ortho Tri-Cyclen. She alleges that a Target pharmacist refused to fill her second prescription, for an emergency contraceptive commonly known as Plan B.

She "said something like, 'That's my right. I don't have to fill it,' " Pourchot recalled in a recent telephone interview. "She was so self-righteous about it. I remember being stunned. I honestly didn't believe she would say no."

Target, however, has denied Pourchot's version of events.

"Regarding the alleged event in St. Louis, we will not go into any details, other than to say that we differ in the portrayals of what happened," Target spokesperson Lena Michaud told Women's eNews. "Target maintains that there was no refusal to fill the prescription for Plan B."

In a November statement, Planned Parenthood's interim president, Karen Pearl, accused Target of "attempting to cover up a misguided corporate policy that denies women access to contraception." Pearl will step down as acting president in mid-February, when the group's new president, Cecile Richards, steps into the position.

The alleged incident in Missouri is the latest in a series of at least 12 refusals that Planned Parenthood has tracked over the past 12 months.

ESCALATING STRUGGLE

The counter-charges have become part of an escalating struggle over access to emergency birth control.

In Pourchot's home state, Missouri Gov. Matt Blunt announced Thursday he would support legislation allowing pharmacists to refuse prescriptions for emergency contraception, according to recent news reports.

Some women's rights activists say that whoever's story is more accurate—that of Target or that of Pourchot—they are troubled that any kind of controversy surrounds a routine trip to the drug store for contraceptives.

"Contraceptive pills have been on the market since the 1960s," said Feminist Majority Foundation President Eleanor Smeal. "We thought we put this behind us."

In describing Plan B as a contraceptive pill, Smeal is backed by the American College of Obstetricians and Gynecologists. The Washington, D.C.-based organization defines the onset of pregnancy as the moment a fertilized egg is implanted in the uterus. Plan B, they say, is a contraceptive because it prevents implantation from occurring.

Opponents of abortion rights, however, define pregnancy as the moment an egg and sperm are united and therefore view emergency contraception as an abortion pill.

This debate over emergency contraception has emerged as a new frontier in the ongoing war over women's reproductive rights.

In addition to pharmacists' refusals, the Bush administration has presided over expansions of federal funding for abstinence-only sex education programs and a delayed decision by the Rockville, Md.-based Food and Drug Administration over whether to grant emergency contraception over-the-counter status. Meanwhile, Bush spokesperson Scott McClellan has declined to define the administration's position on birth control, Smeal said.

The White House did not return calls on the subject.

POLICY IS TO REFUSE BUT REFER

Target's policy allows its pharmacists to refuse to fill prescriptions for moral and religious reasons. If they take this option, pharmacists are required to ensure that the prescription is filled in a timely and respectful manner by another Target pharmacist or at a different pharmacy.

Target's Michaud would not amplify about why the company denies that a refusal occurred, even though Pourchot's account does not suggest the pharmacist broke the store's stated policy.

The pharmacy department at the Fenton, Mo., store declined to comment on the matter and referred a call for comment to the company's public relations office.

Hoping to use public pressure to compel Target to change its refuse-and-refer policy, Planned Parenthood supporters held demonstrations outside Target stores around the country on Dec. 17, a key Christmas shopping day. Planned Parenthood is also encouraging consumers to write letters and sign an online petition to get the store to change its policy.

The hope is that Target will join a group of stores—including Eckerd Corporation, Costco, CVS, Fagen's, Harris Teeter, Kmart, Price Chopper Supermarkets and Super Valu—that, according to Planned Parenthood, have implemented policies to ensure prescriptions of emergency contraception are filled on site and without delay.

Aside from Target, chains that have not implemented policies guaranteeing rapid, onsite filling of emergency contraception prescriptions include Rite Aid, Walgreens, Wal-Mart Stores Inc. and Winn Dixie Stores, according to Planned Parenthood.

Thirty-four corporations—including Duane Reade, Giant, Piggly Wiggly and Safeway—have not made their policies regarding pharmacist refusals known to Planned Parenthood.

A FRIEND TOLD A FRIEND

Planned Parenthood became aware of the allegation through word of mouth. Pourchot said she told her story to a friend, who told another friend who worked at Planned Parenthood.

Pourchot says she is bewildered by the store's denial of her story.

She says a medical technician told her she would have to wait a day or two before obtaining Plan B because the store did not have it in stock. Pourchot wanted to have the medication on hand in case her daily medication failed to prevent a pregnancy. If taken within 72 hours of unprotected sex, Plan B—also known as the "morning-after pill"—is 89 percent effective in preventing pregnancy, according to the medication's manufacturers.

Pourchot says she then asked if she would have any other problems getting the prescription filled, a question that prompted a nearby pharmacist to inform her that she would not fill the prescription. A medical technician then told Pourhcot she could get the prescription filled at a different drugstore, she said.

She left Target and switched her prescription to Walgreens, where she says a computerized record shows her prescription for Plan B was transferred from Target on Sept. 30.

Questions

1. What professional responsibility does a pharmacist have in filling prescriptions for their clients? What rights do they have in maintaining a personal ethical standard that may contradict their professional responsibility?

2. Should large companies, like Target or Walgreens, regulate these actions of their pharmacists, or leave it up to the personal branches to reach a decision in this matter?

3. What rights does a woman have in filling a plan B contraceptive? Should the dissenting pharmacy ensure a transfer to a participating pharmacy in these cases? Does this inherently undermine the pharmacists' original refusal, or does a transfer allow for an adherence to both professional responsibility and to the clients' rights?

4

Truth, Lies, and Deception

Introduction

Everybody lies. Anyone who tells you otherwise is lying to you. And many lies look harmless—or even helpful. Think about the many "little white lies" required by ordinary politeness. If your roommate asks you how her haircut or her new pair of jeans look it, is sometimes kinder, and almost always easier, simply to tell her what you know she wants to hear, even if that is not exactly the truth. And don't forget about the lies you tell yourself! The great American psychologist and philosopher William James (1842–1910) pointed out that many of our greatest achievements—including, he thought, the act of falling in love—could never be attained if we could not lie to ourselves in the course of pursuing them. And maybe, on the way, lie a little bit to other people too.

But the truth is tremendously important. We have to be able to trust one another—and it is hard to see how we could trust one another, and especially what we say to one another, unless we supposed that we were mostly being honest with each other most of the time. It is particularly important that a client can trust a professional: imagine a lawyer who regularly lied to his clients, or a doctor who lied to his patients. But already we might pause and ask: must a doctor always tell the cold, hard truth to a patient who is dying of cancer, especially if she suspects that the truth might hasten her patient's death? And yet, if the doctor lies, couldn't her patient complain that she was prevented from making certain important decisions because she did not have access to the truth? Which would you prefer: the truth if it meant you would die in a month by knowing it, or a lie if it meant you would live three months longer by believing it?

We also want clients to tell the truth to their professionals. We can hardly expect a professional to make expert decisions without knowing all of the facts. But are there some facts a professional need not know? Is a client sometimes permitted to lie to his or her professional representative? And, even more interestingly, could a client sometimes be morally required to lie to the professional who represented her interests?

Is it the case that lying is always wrong? Are some lies justifiable? Is the truth always a good thing? Or are some truths bad news—bad news we could do without? And are some lies worse than others?

The fact is that most of us consider ourselves to be truthful people—and maybe we are. But in professional contexts, in particular, we have to *know* that we are being truthful. And that means doing some difficult work. One of the tough questions we have to ask ourselves is: am I being honest with myself? The German philosopher Friedrich Nietzsche (1844–1900) argued that what most people do is lie to themselves first, and then they can lie to others with a clean conscience (of course, one could even do this unconsciously). So part of the struggle of truthfulness is avoiding self-deception, or having that notoriously difficult thing, self-knowledge.

Some of us think that in order to be truthful, one need only report the facts. And indeed, reporting the facts as one knows them is part of the art of truthfulness. But one must also do a diligent job of investigating the facts. The accountants who audited Enron reported that they were simply crunching the numbers that they were being given. They didn't feel they were doing anything wrong. But the problem was they were not sufficiently scrupulous in chasing down the facts. Discovering the facts, the genuinely relevant facts, is not as easy as one might think—and yet it is a crucial part of being truthful.

And it doesn't end there. Even once one has the relevant facts, one must report them sincerely. Because there are many different ways of reporting facts, and unless they are reported with sincerity the facts themselves can be misleading. Consider a fellow who wants to sell his car because it had a bad radiator. He could take it to a good radiator repair shop, but that would be expensive, so he takes it to a fellow he knows who will patch it for almost nothing, even though the patch won't last more than a week or two. A customer arrives, now, to buy his car. He says, "I plan on taking a long drive through the desert in this car, I'll be gone for three weeks, how's the radiator?" Well, the fellow selling the car could say, quite truthfully, and reporting the facts, "I just had it repaired." But the point is he wouldn't be telling the truth in the appropriate way—he wouldn't be telling the truth with real sincerity. And so he would be making an obvious moral mistake.

This chapter examines the many moral intricacies of lying and truth telling. Lying and truth telling are absolutely crucial to the life of the professional, and we encourage you to take the problems presented here very seriously.

Robert C. Solomon | # Is It Ever Right to Lie?

Robert Solomon taught philosophy and business at the University of Texas at Austin.

Is it ever right to lie?
   No.

Reprinted with the permission of the author.

Now, let's get down to business.

It may never be right to tell a lie, but nevertheless it is often prudent, preferable, and—if the way people behave is any indication at all of morals—popular as well.

Consider the familiar dilemma of HGT sales representative John G., who is asked whether his product is in fact as good as a Xerox. One curious fact is that John G. owns a Xerox himself, but another not insignificant fact is that he is employed by the HGT company to sell their line of products, not to express his personal preferences or conduct a neutral survey of product quality. What does he do? What can he do? Of course, he says, "Yes—and better besides." Is he lying? Or just doing his job? He is doing both, of course, but should we say that he is thereby doing wrong?

"Truth" and "falsehood" are evasive qualities even in an academic seminar or a scientist's laboratory; they are even more so in the real world. Is a lover lying to himself when he says that his love is the "most wonderful woman in the world"? Is a salesman lying to a customer when he praises an imperfect product? To be sure, there is such a thing as outright deception—the standard case in which a used-car salesman insists that an old convertible is in excellent mechanical condition, knowing full well that the unhappy new owner will be lucky to get the heap off the lot. But one can also argue that shopping at certain used-car lots (the kind advertised by a hand-painted sign that says "Honest Harry Has the Bargains") carries with it the knowledge of risk on the part of the buyer, risking a trade-off for the bargain. What counts as "honest" is already put into question. Of course, there are outright lies—falsification of the odometer reading or the false claim that the engine was overhauled 3,000 miles ago, but there is a certain latitude in lying that depends on the context, the customer, and the costs. Not only lying but giving misleading information is intolerable in the health-care industry—for example, not mentioning the side effects of a new drug. Showing hyperdramatic demonstrations of "action" toys to children or giving technical information to people who cannot possibly understand it may involve neither false nor misleading information but nevertheless may be morally dubious (given the huge proportion of the adult population that can be swayed by mere adjectives such as "scientific" or "natural"). Cost counts, too. Exaggerated claims for the cleaning powers of an inexpensive soap product or the convenience of a household gadget advertised on TV for (inevitably) $19.95 are more easily forgiven than even mildly bloated praise for the value of a new house or bulldozer. On the other hand, it is clear that it is not only self-defeating but cruel to tell a customer *everything* horrible that might befall him with his product, (Imagine the warnings that would have to accompany even such a simple household appliance as a food processor.)

Lying may always be wrong, but some lies are much more wrong than others. Truth may always be desirable, but the "whole truth and nothing but the truth" is just as likely to be a nightmare.

To say that it is never right to lie is not the same as to say that one should never lie. It is rather to say that a lie is always a later resort, a strategy that is not a first choice. If the salesman could sell his wares by saying nothing but the truth, he could, should, and would do so. But one must always excuse a lie, by showing that some greater evil would result from telling the truth or, most often, simply by showing that there is minimal harm done by lying and that, in this context, the lie was not wholly inappropriate. The one thing that a person cannot do is to think that telling a lie—*any* lie—is just as good or right as telling the truth, and so needs no special justification for doing so.

Lying has almost always been considered a sin or an immoral act. In a best-selling book, Sissela Bok has argued that lying is always wrong because, in a variety of ways, it always has bad consequences—worse, that is, than if the lie had not been told. Common experience indicates otherwise, perhaps, for the general attitude both in business and in society is that lies have a perfectly proper social place. Indeed there are clearly contexts in which it would be wrong *not* to lie. Lies can prevent family fights and quarrels among couples. They can prevent bad feelings and help avoid misunderstandings. And, often, they can help an employee keep his or her job. ("I was caught in traffic" is a transparent lie but sometimes an acceptable excuse for being late; "I hated the idea of coming to work so much that I forgot to set the alarm" is, though true, utterly unacceptable.)

We can all agree, looking only at short-term and immediate benefits, that the harm done by some lies is considerably less than the harm that would be done by telling the "unvarnished truth." An employer forced to fire a mediocre worker is certainly not to be blamed for saying that "financial exigencies" have forced him to lay off several low-seniority personnel, instead of telling the truth, which is that the fellow borders on incompetence and doesn't have either the charm or the imagination of a pocket calculator. An advertiser would be judged an idiot, not honest, if he baldly stated that this pain remedy is no more nor less effective than any other on the market, though its packaging is prettier. Nevertheless, there are reasons for saying that lying is always wrong.

The first reason has to do with the enormous amount of effort involved in telling a lie—any lie. The truth—even the incomplete truth—is an enormously complex network of interlocking facts. Anyone who has found himself caught in the nervous web of fabrications involved in even such a simple lie as "We don't know a thing about what our competitors are doing" ("Then how do you know that . . . ?") knows how many seemingly disparate facts can come crashing in when a lie has torn just a small piece out of the truth. As recent national politics has so prominently displayed, the cost of a cover-up is often many times more than the damage done by the lie itself, even if the cover-up is successful.

The second reason looks beyond the short-term benefits of lying to the longer-term damage, which may be harder to see. Every lie diminishes trust. A lie discovered is guaranteed to undermine faith in the liar, but, more subtly, *telling* a lie diminishes one's trust in others. ("If I'm lying to them, they are probably lying to me as well.") Most Americans now look at television advertising as if it were nothing but a tissue of lies—ironically making the more successful ads just those that ignore substantial content and concentrate on memorable associations and effects. A businessman may make many a profit through deception—for a while—but unless one wants to keep on the road for the rest of one's life (sounds good at twenty, not so good at forty), deception almost always catches up and destroys just the

business it used to ensure. As long-term investments, lies are usually a bad risk.

The third and strongest reason for thinking that it is never right to lie was suggested by Kant. He asked himself the question, "What would happen if lying were generally accepted? For example, what would happen if it were an everyday and unexceptional feature of the business world that one person would borrow money from another with no intention whatever of repaying the loan?" His answer was that telling the truth and, in the example, borrowing money would both become impossible, so that if I were to approach you and ask for a $10,000 loan, which I would promise to repay on the first of the year, you would simply laugh in my face, since everyone by then would know that such promises were not to be taken seriously. Lying, in other words, must always be wrong, since to treat lying as acceptable undermines just that trust that makes telling the truth meaningful.

Does this mean that one should never lie? Well, no. But it does mean that it is never right to tell a lie; that telling a lie always requires extra thought and some very good reasons to show that this cardinal violation of the truth should be tolerated.

This said, perhaps we should clear up a few common misconceptions about the place of lying in business. It is sometimes suggested that advertising is always a lie, since it tells only one side of the story and that side, needless to say, in the best possible light. But now it is important to distinguish—in facing any such accusation—among the following:

1. telling less than the whole truth;
2. telling a biased truth, with one's own interests in mind;
3. idealizing one's products or services;
4. giving misleading information; that is, true statements that are intended to be misunderstood or misinterpreted;
5. stating obvious falsehoods;
6. stating vicious falsehoods.

An obvious falsehood, for example, is the displayed claim of some toothpaste manufacturers—that use of a certain gel will overnight convert Shy Sam or Plain Jane to Fabulous Fred or Super Sally, the heartthrob of the high-school prom. One might object to other aspects of such advertising, but "It isn't true" seems too silly to say.

Vicious falsehoods, on the other hand, are those that are not at all obvious and are a deliberate and possibly dangerous form of deception. Saying that a product will do such and such when it will not is vicious deception, as is intentionally withholding information—for example, the flammability of children's pajamas or the side effects of a popular over-the-counter drug. Misleading information can be as vicious as false information—indeed it is only a matter of logical nuance that allows us to distinguish between the two.

It is impossible to tell the "whole story," especially in the limited time of a fifteen-second radio or TV slot or in the small space available on a paper package. But advertising isn't supposed to be a scientific study, even if it utilizes some (more or less) scientific evidence on the product's behalf. Of course advertising expresses a bias on the behalf of the product. Of course it idealizes the product in its presentation. But neither bias nor idealization is lying, and it is surely foolish to insist that advertising, unlike almost every other aspect of social life, be restricted to the simple, boring truth—that is, that this product is not much different from its competitors and that people have lived for hundreds of thousands of years without any of them.

It is often challenged—these days with Orwellian overtones—that advertising in general and TV advertising in particular have turned the American consumer into something of a supermarket zombie, without a will of his or her own, without judgment, buying hundreds of innocuous but sometimes tasteless products that no one really needs. But the zombie image contradicts precisely what lies beneath the whole discussion of truth—namely, the confidence that we are, more or less, capable of making value judgments on our own, and that

if we buy or even need to buy products that are of no particular cosmic importance, this does not signal either the end of civilization or the disintegration of the human mind. Encouraging someone to buy a product that is only a fad or a mark of status is not deception, and to call it that tends to undermine the ethical distinction that is of enormous importance—between vicious false-hoods and any number of other "varnishings" of the truth. These may be vulgar. They may encourage us to compete for some pretty silly achievements—the shiniest (and most slippery) floor, a car that can win the grand prix (to be driven in bumper-to-bumper traffic up and down the freeway), a soap that makes one speak in a phony Irish brogue. But to condemn all advertising is to make it impossible to attack vicious advertising and thus to bring about the logical conclusion imagined by Kant—an entire world in which no one believes anything, in which advertising serves at most as a source of amusement and seduction of the feebleminded.

Let's end our discussion of lying by commenting once again on Alfred Carr's suggestion that business is like poker, that it has its own rules, which are different from ordinary ethics. One of these rules, supposedly, is the permissibility of lying. But business (like poker) forbids lying. Contrary to Carr, a generally accepted practice of lying would undermine the business world faster than any external threat that has ever faced it. Promises and contracts, if not good faith, are the presuppositions of all business. The exact nature of truth in advertising may be controversial, but advertising in general must be not only based on fact but believable and trustworthy. If it were not, the commercial world in America would be about as effective as the provocations of Hari Krishnas in America's airports—an annoyance to be ignored as we all go on with the rest of our lives.

Honesty isn't just the best policy in business; it is, in general, the only possible policy.

Joseph S. Ellin

Special Professional Morality and the Duty of Veracity

Joseph S. Ellin is Professor of Philosophy at Western Michigan University.

TWO THEORIES OF SPECIAL PROFESSIONAL MORALITY

Are there special rules and principles which govern professionals in their professional conduct? This question has been called (by Alan Goldman) "the most fundamental question for professional ethics."[1] But what exactly is being asked? Are we supposed to imagine the possibility of a fundamental conflict between ordinary morality and the special standards of the professions?[2] It certainly seems as if the standards of professional morality do not necessarily correspond with those of ordinary morality: lawyers, for example, are required to defend vigorously the interests of unsavory characters who by ordinary moral standards are entitled to no assistance from anyone. But the question is not whether professionals subscribe to such special standards, but whether such standards would amount to a departure, within certain limited circumstances, from ordinary moral rules. But departures from ordinary moral rules, it seems, can only be justified by reference to other, more basic, principles of morality. We must have good moral reasons for allowing such exceptions to our general principles. Where there are apparent conflicts between ordinary and special morality, these conflicts can generally be adjudicated by moral reasoning based on large moral considerations.

This view, which we may call "the priority of ordinary reflective morality," gives to ordinary morality a double function. First, ordinary reflective morality imposes the rules and standards which govern all of us in our ordinary, that is non-special, life encounters. Second, ordinary reflective morality plays an adjudicating role, resolving apparent conflicts between obligations in ordinary contexts and those in special contexts, such as those of professional life.

To hold the priority view is not, of course, to hold that in cases of apparent conflict, one's ordinary obligations always override, as if professionals could have no obligations inconsistent with those imposed on everybody by ordinary morality: There might be good moral reasons why we would want to impose special obligations on professionals in their professional life. Nor is it necessarily to hold that there can not be fundamental or irreconcilable moral conflicts which arise in the course of one's professional activities. The crux of the "priority" view is that whether there are such special obligations, and such irreconcilable conflicts, is to be determined by ordinary moral considerations. At bottom, no conflict can occur between an ordinary moral norm and a norm drawn from some special context; such conflicts that do occur are conflicts between the norms of ordinary morality itself. Suppose, for example, a professional finds a conflict between an obligation to tell the truth and an obligation to protect a client from a foolish blunder. The professional might conclude that he or she is forced simply to decide between inconsistent norms. On the priority view, such a conflict might be possible, but when it occurs, it does not arise because ordinary morality the other, but rather because ordinary morality supports both norms and provides no deeper principle of reconciliation.

The priority view holds that, since ordinary reflective morality is the only source of moral obligation, there is no such thing as a morality that is "internal" to special contexts such as professional life. The morality of the professions, rather, is imposed on

From *Business and Professional Ethics Journal* 1:2 (1982): 75–90.

them from above, by our usual values and common principles. Professional morality is, thus, [comprised of] a set of rules which is, in a sense, purely external to the professions. [These rules] do not grow out of any conception of professional life. The obligations of professionals must be assessed and determined strictly in accordance with our usual moral standards.

The priority view, then, gives us our first theory of special professional morality. According to it, there may well be special rules which govern professionals, and which impose duties inconsistent with the duties imposed on everybody in ordinary life. But the sole justification for imposing such special duties is that, judged by the norms of ordinary morality, "better moral consequences" (as Goldman puts it) will result.[3] Since every apparent conflict between ordinary and special morality can, by reflection, be resolved into a conflict within ordinary morality itself, the professional faces no greater moral difficulties than anybody else.[4]

However, this reduction of special professional to ordinary morality may seem to professionals themselves to distort their moral conflicts. Lawyers, for example, who defend the interests of clients whose interests are morally indefensible might think they are doing their duty *as lawyers*; and that in so doing they act in the face of ordinary morality, not with the ultimate sanction of ordinary morality. Doctors might believe that as doctors they have a special allegiance to the norm of health; a norm which they must respect even to the extent of sacrificing other moral interests a patient might have. It is such conflicts which make professionals even more morally uncomfortable than the rest of us. Since their obligations are derived from a certain conception of their profession, there may well be cases in which a conflict between two norms would be resolvable, were it simply a matter of resolving conflicting norms within ordinary morality; yet this does not settle the conflict between the professional and the ordinary norm.[5]

This gives us our second theory of special professional morality, according to which there are moral obligations which derive not from ordinary morality but from the nature of the professions. We may call this the parallel view, because according to it, professional morality is parallel with, not subordinate to, ordinary morality. The profession itself is a source of special moral obligations; hence fundamental conflicts with ordinary morality are possible, dilemmas of professional morality are not dissolvable into dilemmas of ordinary morality, and professionals are faced, at least potentially, with moral perplexities which are different than those faced by ordinary people.

THE ORDINARY DUTY OF VERACITY

...My main point is that ordinary morality provides reasons not only for condemning lying and deception, but also for considering deception a lesser wrong then lying. When we turn to the fiduciary relationship between professional and client, however, we find the "moral gap" between lying and deception much greater than in ordinary morality: Professional morality considers lying a more serious wrong than does ordinary morality, yet does not consider deception morally wrong at all. Hence, there might be situations in which, from the point of view of ordinary morality, it would be justifiable to lie, but not from the point of view of professional morality; there are also situations in which ordinary morality would, but professional morality would not, prohibit deception.

The distinction between lying and deception is fairly obvious, although the definition of lying is a question of some philosophical complexity.[6] We may consider a lie to be a statement which the speaker believes to be false.[7] What I call a deception, on the other hand, consists either in true statements which are nonetheless misleading, or in actions which convey a false impression, or in the deliberate withholding of information where the person not informed is misled into drawing a false conclusion. Deception can be inadvertent, but where it is deliberate, the agent must want someone to draw a false conclusion. Now most of us see a clear moral difference between lying and deception: Where we think it necessary to plant false beliefs, most of us would prefer to do so without actually lying, if we can.[8] Nonetheless this interesting moral distinction is commonly overlooked by philosophers, who seem to think that the duty of veracity is simply the duty not to deceive.[9] When, however, philosophers do acknowledge the distinction, they are apt to think that it is morally invalid; or else they accept its moral force but fail to explain it in any very satisfactory way. For example, Benjamin and Curtis, in their book *Ethics in Nursing*,[10] citing a case in which a nurse conveys a false impression about a patient's medication without actually lying to the patient, assert that the nurse would be "compounding deception with self-deception if she were to believe that there is a significant ethical difference." The authors leave the impression that in their view there can never be a "significant ethical difference" between deceiving and lying, although the example shows no more than that in the given case, in which the patient is assumed to have a clear right to the information, the wrong to the patient is so great as to make insignificant any difference in the way in which the deception is accomplished. But this does not show that in cases where deception is justified, there is no significant difference between deceiving by lying and deceiving by evasion or by withholding information; nor does it show that there are no cases in which it might be justified to deceive by evasive or misleading statements but *not* justified to deceive by telling a lie.

What would be an argument *against* the distinction between lying and deception? There might be many. It might be pointed out that lying and deception are equally harmful to the person deceived, since they deprive him of information rightfully his. It might be argued that whether one plants false beliefs by means of lying, or by means of evasive or misleading statements (or actions), is a question of means, whereas morality judges by intentions and consequences, and lying and deception are done with the same intention and (if successful) have the same consequence, namely, that someone is wrongfully made to have a false belief. Or it could be said that to deceive someone is to show that you do not respect that person, for you claim for yourself the right to give him false beliefs and thus to manipulate him: Hence deception is a form of contempt for others.

Thus deception, no less than lying, harms a person's interest in having true beliefs, in having the information necessary to make intelligent decisions, in not being manipulated, and in being regarded with respect. What these arguments show, however, is that there are very good reasons why we should object to deception, and that some of them are the same reasons we have for objecting to lying. What they do not show is that there are no additional reasons for objecting to lying, which are not reasons for objecting to deception.

Let us consider some philosophers who acknowledge the distinction between lying and deception. Peter Geach, for instance, who counsels "total abstinence from lying,"[11] tells the amusing story of one St. Athanasius, who "was rowing on a river when the persecutors came rowing in the opposite direction: 'Where is the traitor Athanasius?' 'Not far away,' the Saint gaily replied." Here we have the concurrence of a contemporary moral philosopher with the opinion of a Christian Saint that when deception is justified, the gain in producing it without actually lying is great enough to be a cause for gaiety. No less a moralist than Kant, who even in the *Lectures on Ethics*[12] seems to take a position absolutely prohibiting lying (or what Kant calls lying), gives the following example: 'It is possible to deceive without making any statement whatever. I can make believe, make a demonstration from which others will draw the conclusion I want, though they have no right to expect that my action will express my real mind. In that case, I have not lied to them.... I may, for instance, wish people to think that I am off on a journey, and so I pack my luggage....'[13] This is a case in which deception, at least in Kant's view, is not even morally problematic, although lying (suppose I told my neighbors, "I will soon be off on a journey") would be excluded.

The philosophers Chisholm and Feehan offer an explanation for the distinction. They write:

> *Why* is it thought wrong to lie? And why is lying thought to be *worse*, other things being equal, than other types of intended deception?
>
> The answer would seem to be this. It is assumed that, if a person L *asserts* a proposition p to another person D, then D has the *right to expect* that L

himself believes p. And it is assumed that L knows, or at least that he ought to know that, if he asserts p to D, while believing himself that p is not true, then he violates this right of D's. But analogous assumptions are not made with respect to all other types of intended deception. When the man of Kant's example packs his luggage, he does not thereby give his friends the right to assume that he is about to make a journey. Lying, unlike the other types of intended deception, is essentially a breach of faith.[14]

What this explanation fails to tell us is both why D *has* such a right against L when L asserts a proposition, and why D does *not* have an equivalent right when L does something without asserting a proposition. (Why do I not have a right to assume that if you pack your bags, then you are going on a journey?) Clearly Chisholm and Feehan, like Kant himself, are far too tolerant of "other forms of intended deception." Kant's neighbors would complain that they had been deceived, and there would be some merit in their complaint; though we might indeed concede that there is some merit in their friends' defense that he had not given them "the right to assume" that his action of packing his bags would in this case have its natural and expected consequence.

These authors fail to explain what is wrong with deception, and why deception, though wrong, is not as wrong as lying. They leave the impression that if deception is wrong, it must be wrong for some other reason altogether than the reason (breach of faith, according to Chisholm and Feehan) that makes lying wrong. But we must not defend the distinction in such a way that deception turns out either to be not wrong at all, or wrong for entirely different reasons than the wrong of lying. Ordinary morality holds that lying is worse than deception, not that it has another moral character altogether. Fortunately, we have already seen excellent reasons why deception should be considered morally wrong, and analogous to lying. I will now give three arguments to show why lying is a greater wrong. The first two distinguish between lying and deception by degree only: Lying is a greater violation of a principle which deception also violates. The third argument, drawn from Kant, does, however, introduce a new idea: that lying violates the social contract in a way that deception does not.

The first argument is that the liar takes advantage of weakness more than does the deceiver. Consider a typical case of deception in the professions: The surgeon, who smilingly enters the patient's room and reports that the operation went very well, but fails to mention that the findings were devastating. The deception occurs (the false belief is formed) only if the patient assumes that when the surgeon said the operation went well, he meant well from the patient's point of view rather than from the surgeon's (i.e., there were no complications or unexpected difficulties). This may be a natural inference, but it is an inference: If deception harms the victim's interest in the truth, this harm can occur only if the victim draws an inference grounded on what he has been told (or has observed, in Kant's example). We can defend ourselves against this harm by adopting the following maxim of prudence governing belief: "Believe everything you are told but draw no inferences unless supported by independent evidence." If we followed such a rule no one would ever be harmed by deception. Such a rule would impose far fewer burdens on life than a rule which protected against lying, to wit, "Believe nothing you hear unless it is supported by independent evidence." Most of us find the cost of following either rule excessive, hence we are vulnerable to the deceiver as well as to the liar. But the costs are not equal. Each rule may be regarded as a defense, where the cost of the defense against lying is greater than the cost of the defense against deception. Since weakness may be measured by the costs of defense (the more it costs to protect yourself against something, the weaker you are with respect to that thing), and since we are therefore weaker with respect to lying than we are with respect to deception, we can say that the liar takes advantage of our weakness to a greater degree than the deceiver, and is consequently morally worse, even though the harm produced by each is the same.

The second argument follows easily from the first. The liar is more responsible for the harm caused than is the mere deceiver. The reason for this is that in mere deception, the person deceived participates in his own deception, hence is in part responsible for causing it. This is usually obvious: In the case of the surgeon, the patient could have unmasked the deception simply by asking the surgeon a direct question about the findings. The patient is at fault for failing to ask. Even where there is a lie, of course, the victim must bear some responsibility for being deceived, since he has imprudently trusted the liar and failed to verify the statement made to him. But usually it is unreasonable for the victim to seek such verification: In the absence of reason to think otherwise, it is unreasonable not to accept for truth direct statements made to you. But the victim of deception does not simply believe what is said: He draws an inference which is based on, but not verified by, the evidence offered, and then fails to ask the speaker to confirm the inference. The victim of the lie fails to verify a direct statement, but the victim of deception fails to verify a conclusion of his own *and* fails to seek confirmation from the speaker, and hence is more responsible for the ensuing harm (his coming to hold a false belief).

We now come to the third difference between lying and deception. Suppose we adopted a social contract point of view and postulated that the duty of veracity depends on an original undertaking not to deceive. A lie would then be a violation of this implicit agreement. Such a view was held by Ross, who, however, confined the duty of veracity to the duty to use language truthfully: "Yet the peculiar stringency of the duty of veracity seems to spring from an implicit understanding that language shall be used to convey the real opinions of the speakers ..."[15] We could even make the strong claim that unless there were such an implicit understanding, speech itself would be frustrated (and society as we know it impossible), since words establish their meaning only by being applied in standard situations, that is, by being spoken when they truly apply. Now the social contract point itself does not establish a difference with deception, since the undertaking is not to deceive, not merely not to lie. To establish a difference we would have to make one or both of two further points. The first is that the promise to speak the truth is more important than the promise not to deceive, since speech is necessary to *any* human society, whereas non-deception is necessary only for a tolerable or decent society. Truth we might say is an enabling condition for society, whereas non-deception is but an enhancing condition. This point, though powerful, rests on the assumptions above

connecting meaningful speech with truth telling and with human society, assumptions clearly beyond our present scope.

The second point depends on our interpretation of the social contract, that is, how we affirm and reaffirm the promise to be truthful. Suppose we held that in addition to the underlying "implicit understanding," there is also a more explicit promise made every time we speak, so that to speak at all is virtually to warrant that our words are true. A lie would then amount to a violation of the very promise made by the speech act in which the lie is stated. If we further supposed that it would be implausible to make a parallel claim about deception, then a clear moral difference would emerge: A lie violates a warrant given by the very act of speech, whereas deception violates at most only the underlying "implicit understanding." Such a view would explain our feeling that a liar is less trustworthy than a mere deceiver, since the liar violates his promise in the very act of making it, whereas the deceiver violates only the remote understanding of the original agreement.

VERACITY AND THE PROFESSIONAL–CLIENT RELATIONSHIP

I now consider that I have both elucidated and defended what ordinary reflective morality has to say about veracity. According to it, lying and deception are both wrong for a number of basically similar reasons; but there are also good reasons for considering lying morally worse than deception. I now propose to argue that the situation is different with respect to professional morality. But first we must resolve a difficulty: What is professional morality? From what does it come, given that we are prevented by our previous rejection of the "priority" approach from simply deriving its precepts from ordinary morality. We have already indicated that some "conception" of the profession is needed, a conception according to which it might be possible to hold, for example, that the overriding obligation of the doctor is to the patient's health, or of the lawyer to the client's strictly legal rights. I propose to solve this problem by presenting models of a profession, or more precisely, models of the professional–client relationship. Modelling is a frequently used device, which enables us to understand basic relationships within the subject matter being modelled, by representing these relationships as something else, presumably more easily understood.

A number of interesting modelling proposals have been put forward in professional ethics, notably with respect to the doctor–patient relationship. I shall just note one, that of Szasz and Hollender.[16] They distinguish three models, which they call activity-passivity, guidance-cooperation, and mutual participation. Although they do not state explicitly what principle governs the derivation of the models, the idea seems to be the location of the control of the relationship: In the first two models the doctor controls, in the third, doctor and patient "mutually participate." (They do not consider the possibility that the patient might control the relationship.) The difference between the first and second models seems to be the kind of control exercised: The "cooperative" patient "is expected to . . . 'obey' his doctor . . . he is neither to question nor to argue or disagree with the orders he receives."[17]

Szasz and Hollender's principle, to distinguish models according to the location of the control of the relationship, is provocative, and I follow it in my own proposals. If we consider the ability to control the relationship, then we have the following possibilities. Either the position of the parties is one of equal power and control, or it is not. If the position is one of equality, then we have two possibilities: Either the relationship is competitive or it is cooperative. If competitive, then we have an adversary model characterized by arm's-length bargaining and contractual agreements; that is what both Veatch and May, in their analysis of doctor–patient relationships, call contract, but with explicit recognition that contract involves mutual wariness based on the need to compromise conflicting interests.[18] A cooperative relationship, on the other hand, also based on equality, is characterized by partnership, mutual trust and other-reliance; this is equivalent to the models of mutual participation which Szasz and Hollender advocate.[19]

If the position is not one of equality, then again we have two possibilities: either the professional is superior to the client, or the client to the professional. In the latter case, we have an agency model: The professional merely carries out the wishes of the client. The client determines the ends to be attained, and the professional acts to achieve these ends, being an instrument of the client's will. But if the professional is superior, then we have two further possibilities: Either the professional uses the client for his or her ends, which we call exploitation (this arises, for example, where the patient is an "interesting case" potentially suitable for write-up in the journals; or where the legal client has a novel problem which the lawyer may use to achieve a landmark legal victory); or the professional works for the client's ends, in which case we have a fiduciary model. Hence our principle gives us five models: adversary, cooperative, agency, exploitation, and fiduciary.

It is not my intention to discuss these models in detail, since I am primarily interested in the fiduciary.[20] The important distinction is that between the fiduciary model and the agency model. In each case the professional works entirely for the client, so it may seem that there is no difference. But there are two senses of "for the client." In the agency model, the agent works at the direction of the principal, that is, he does only those things the principal himself would do, if he had the ability, knowledge or inclination. When the agent acts, it is as if the principal were acting. In the fiduciary model, however, the fiduciary acts in the interests of the beneficiary. Here the fiduciary does not necessarily act as if he were the beneficiary nor does he do only those things which the beneficiary would do, were he in a position to act for himself. Hence the fiduciary has an independent responsibility for his acts on behalf of the beneficiary. He is not a mere instrument of the will of another, confined only to judgments about means and methods but never allowed to determine ends and principles. In a fiduciary relationship, the professional services the true interests of the client, not the client's immediate wishes or desires.[21]

When we reflect on the duties a fiduciary relationship might entail, we are struck with a paradox. On the one hand, a fiduciary relationship rests on trust. On the other hand, a fiduciary relationship encourages deception. I propose to resolve this paradox by widening the moral gap between deception and lying.

That professional–client relationships rest on trust is an oft-noted platitude; but it is in fact not true of any of our models but the fiduciary. It is only in this model that the professional uses his or her superior position to serve the client's interests, possibly contrary to the client's wishes or desires and possibly beyond the client's ability to understand the procedures the professional recommends.[22] If the professional merely carries out the client's wishes (agency) there is no need of trust, since the client can determine for himself whether the professional acts as desired. A contract model involves arm's-length bargaining between equals, which enables adversaries to reach agreements fair to each; trust is unnecessary. Partnerships indeed generate trust, but do not rest on it: If each partner is an equal, respectful of the other's knowledge and abilities, trust will naturally develop, but the partnership can carry on without it. Exploitation perhaps requires that the victim-client be trusting, but not that the professional-exploiter be trustworthy. Only in the fiduciary relationship must the professional act to protect the beneficiary's interests as he alone understands them. In the absence of trust, the client is unlikely to submit to the professional's authority, and will prefer an agency or contract model, in which the client may make use of the professional's services without the necessity of submitting to the professional's control. If the professional is not trustworthy, the relationship cannot be said to be fiduciary at all. It is not my intention to debate the merits of the models, but only to draw conclusions about one professional duty, that of veracity, within the fiduciary model.

VERACITY IN THE FIDUCIARY RELATIONSHIP

But why should the fiduciary relationship condone deception? The reason is that the relationship is governed by certain strictly defined ends. People enter into relations with professionals for specific and limited purposes: to improve their health, to protect their legal rights, to enhance their financial condition. If the relationship is fiduciary, the professional pledges to use his or her superior position to protect only those interests for the protection of which the relationship exists. One consults a doctor to protect one's health, not one's finances: It is not within the professional competence of a doctor to make judgments about financial matters. (This is not to say the doctor should not provide information about costs, but that he is not obligated to make judgments about them. The doctor tells me what, in this opinion, is the medically desirable treatment; my financial advisor tells me whether he thinks I can afford it.)

If we take this strict view of the fiduciary context, then we find a significant difference between ordinary morality and the special (professional) morality which governs the fiduciary relationship. Ordinary morality is designed to protect people's total package of interests which, as interests, are considered equally worthy of protection; but professional morality protects only those interests for which the professional relationship exists. Professional morality is thus spared the necessity of assigning weights to various interests in order to balance them in cases of conflict. Deception is thus not a violation of professional morality, since professionals are not mandated to protect the client's interest in having true beliefs, in not being manipulated or in being treated with respect. Nor can there be said to be any underlying contract beyond the pledge by the professional to use his or her superior position to further the goals of the relationship: health, legal rights, and so on. A patient's interest in the truth, for example, is exactly as relevant to the doctor's professional concern as the patient's interest in friends or enjoyable leisure: That is, all these interests are relevant to the physician's responsibility only as they might affect the patient's health. It is a medical judgment whether a person's health might be affected by the possession of certain information, and therefore, within the doctor's responsibility; but it is not a medical judgment, and so not within his responsibility whether a person's other interests ought to be respected at the price of some risk to the person's health. Insofar as information might affect a patient's health, what to tell the patient, whether to tell the patient, and how to tell the patient become purely medical questions, to be answered on medical grounds. Since the interests which deception harms are not otherwise relevant to the fiduciary medical context, there is no reason within that context to prohibit deception. To say this is at bottom only to say that a physician, acting as such, should make medical judgments, not financial judgments, not legal judgments, and not moral judgments either. . . .

It is important to be clear about what I am advocating. My point is that professional morality as it emerges from a certain conception of the professional–client relationship does not prohibit deception; but this is not to say that the professional may deceive for whatever reason he or she chooses. Ordinary morality governs all human relationships, and ordinary morality does not normally condone deception. Professional morality, however, as I understand it, allows deception where necessary to protect the client's relevant interests, but these interests only. It is at the point where, in the professional's best judgment, possession of certain information might harm the client's relevant interests, that professional and ordinary morality may conflict.

Let us consider two examples. Suppose a patient who has been in a serious accident has undergone surgery to restore mobility in an injured leg. After some days, the surgeon concludes that the operation has failed, and that chances of recovered mobility are slight. It is unlikely the patient will ever walk again. This news may be expected to depress the patient badly. Should the patient be informed? Assuming that the depression will not affect the patient's physical condition in a negative way, then ordinary morality must govern. It is not the doctor's professional duty to protect patients from depressing news, even if health-related. (It may, however, be his, that is anyone's, *moral* duty in these circumstances.)

Suppose another patient has undergone major heart surgery, from which he is recovering. While the patient is in the hospital, the patient's business suffers serious reverses. The patient's doctors fear this news will sufficiently upset the patient so as to impede or perhaps preclude complete recovery. Should they advise the family not to inform the patient? Although the information in question is not itself medical, the judgment about its effects is a medical judgment, and their duty is to so advise. Now suppose (implausibly, in my opinion)) ordinary morality might hold that the patient's right

to know and to make all decisions concerning his own life, including his business affairs, outweighs the patient's interest in health, as Goldman seems to think.[23] If so, there is a conflict between ordinary and professional morality and professional morality must rule.

But given that professional morality has a significantly greater tolerance for deception than has ordinary morality, how can we resolve the paradox that the professional relationship depends on trust? My answer is to require a significantly greater preclusion of lying. Indeed, it is probably best if professional morality excluded lying altogether. We have already seen some reasons why lying should be considered a greater violation of trust than deception. First, deception cannot occur without some blame, even complicity, on the part of the person deceived. In the case of deception, we might say, trust has not been pushed to the limit, since the direct question which would prevent the deception has not been asked. To this we may add (second), that lying vitiates, but deception does not, what may be called the maxim of trust, "You may believe what you are told." Where this maxim is respected, then it, together with the prudent maxim, "Draw no inferences unless supported by independent evidence," will protect anyone from any kind of deliberate deception. Third, as we have seen, lying violates a promise made in the very act of speech, and so is a greater breach of trust than deception, which violates only the original understanding. And fourth, we may consider that the fiduciary relationship depends on a pledge, by the professional, to protect the interests of the client. But if the professional is capable of lying, how can the client expect that this pledge will be respected? If the professional will lie to the client in order to protect the client's interests, perhaps he will also lie to the client about whether he will protect his interests.

Finally, since lying is a great violation of trust, there is a strong reason for requiring a greater prohibition of lying in a relationship governed by trust, than in ordinary morality. The reason is that trust is not as important in the ordinary relationships of life for which ordinary morality is designed, first, because to a large extent ordinary relationships depend on the recognition by the parties that everyone's self-interest is served best in the long run if everyone obeys the rules of morality (this is the contract element underlying ordinary morality); and second because in ordinary life we do not consign our interests to the care of another. What distinguishes the fiduciary situation from ordinary life is that the client-beneficiary, being unable to control the relationship, must trust the fiduciary-professional to act in his, the beneficiary's, best interest, even where this contradicts the beneficiary's own judgment. This significant difference between ordinary life and the fiduciary relationship is sufficient to explain why the fiduciary relationship must impose a more stringent prohibition against lying than does ordinary morality.

There will, therefore, be situations in which a professional should tell the truth when ordinary morality would condone lying. A woman has been seriously injured in an automobile accident in which one of her children was killed, the others badly crippled.[24] She regains consciousness in the hospital and immediately inquires after her children. The nurses on duty are afraid that evasion will only arouse her suspicions and cause mounting anxiety. Ordinary morality might surely condone a lie in this situation. But if the woman insists on a straight answer, the nurses will be placed in a dilemma arising from their fiduciary responsibility not to lie. Only in an extreme case—for example, where they are certain beyond reasonable doubt that severe medical consequences would follow full disclosure—can a lie be justified. In a less clear case—where, for example, they are unable to judge how detrimental to the patient's subsequent recovery full disclosure would be—they are obligated to answer questions truthfully, even if ordinary morality might counsel lying. To do otherwise would jeopardize the fiduciary relationship which underlies the provision of future care of the patient.

NOTES

1. Alan Goldman, *The Moral Foundations of Professional Ethics* ([Totowa, NJ: Rowman and Littlefield] 1980), p. 1.

2. By ordinary morality, it is well to point out, we do not mean man-in-the-street morality, but rather the morality which governs us simply in virtue of the fact that we are moral agents. Ordinary morality is reflective or critical morality, that is, the views ordinary people should or would hold, were they properly reflective. Special morality, on the other hand, governs only those who have special status or engage in special relationships.

3. [Goldman, op. cit.], p. 22. It is our reflective moral consciousness which determines what consequences are "morally better."

4. Goldman's book [op. cit.] is the best sustained treatment incorporating this theory of professional morality. But the priority view seems to be widespread (if implicit) in the literature of professional ethics. Discussions of "medical paternalism" generally assume it; see inter alia [Allen E.] Buchanan, "Medical Paternalism," *Philosophy and Public Affairs*, vol. 7, no. 4 (1978), pp. 370–90; and the first two essays in [Michael S.] Pritchard and [Wade L.] Robison (eds.), *Medical Responsibility: Paternalism, Informed Consent, and Euthanasia* [Clifton, NJ: Humana Press] (1979), "The Justification of Paternalism" by [Bernard] Gert and [Charles] Culver and "Paternalism and Health Care" by [James F.] Childress.

5. A very fine discussion of this dual allegiance, and of the moral conflicts it generates, is offered by Gerald Postema, "Moral Responsibility in Professional Ethics," in *New York University Law Review*, vol. 55 (Apr. 1980), pp. 63–89. This essay appears as a chapter in Robison, Pritchard and Ellin (eds.), *Profits and Professions* [: *Essays in Business and Professional Ethics* (1983)].

6. For important contemporary discussions of the concept of lying, see Frederick Siegler, "Lying," *American Philosophical Quarterly*, vol. 3, no. 2 (Apr. 1966) [pp. 128–36]; and Roderick Chisholm and Thomas D. Feehan, "The Intent to Deceive" [(see note 14 below)]. Many passages from classical philosophers (Augustine, Aquinas, Kant, etc.) are conveniently reprinted in Bok, *Lying* (see note 9 [below]).

7. Two important conceptual questions which cannot be discussed here are whether the statement made by the liar must *be* false, or whether it is enough for the liar to believe it is false; and whether the liar must tell the lie with the intent to deceive the hearer. For discussion, see essays in note 6 above.

8. A recent article in the *New York Times* (Jan. 26, 1982) presents a nice illustration: "[President Franklin Delano] Roosevelt was not a liar," said Warren Moscow, who covered him for the Hearst papers and then for the *New York Times*, "He was a dissimulator. He had this habit

of nodding and saying. 'Yes, yes, yes,' as if he was agreeing with you, and all he was doing was saying he heard you." Reporter Moscow expects the reader to object to lying but to find "dissimulation" merely amusing.

9. One philosopher who does not see any distinction between lying and deception is Sissela Bok, *Lying* [*: Moral Choice in Public and Private Life* (New York: Pantheon)] (1978), especially chaps. 2 and 3, whose discussion moves back and forth between lying and deception as if there were no difference between them....

10. [Martin] Benjamin and [Joy] Curtis, *Ethics in Nursing* [New York: Oxford University Press] (1981), p. 65.

11. [Peter] Geach, *The Virtues* [*: The Stanton Lectures, 1973–74*, New York: Cambridge University Press] (1977), p. 114.

12. [Immanuel Kant, *Lectures on Ethics*, Louis] Infield translation [Harper and Row] (1963), pp. 147–54. Reprinted in [Samuel] Gorovitz et al., eds., *Moral Problems in Medicine* [Englewood Cliffs, NJ: Prentice-Hall] (1976), pp. 94–97. Doubts on the attribution to Kant of the views expressed in the *Lectures* are discussed by Bok [op. cit.], pp. 315–16.

13. [Kant, op. cit.], p. 95.

14. [Roderick Chisholm and Thomas D. Feehan], "The Intent to Deceive," *Journal of Philosophy*, vol. 74, no. 3 (Mar. 1977), pp. 143–59; [quote] at p. 153.

15. Sir David [W. D.] Ross, *The Right and the Good* [Oxford: Clarendon] (1930), appendix i. Reprinted in [Wilfrid] Sellars and [John] Hospers. *Readings in Ethical Theory* [Englewood Cliffs, NJ: Prentice-Hall] (1952), p. 196.

16. Thomas S. Szasz and Marc H. Hollender, "The Basic Models of the Doctor-Patient Relationship," *American Medical Association Archives of Internal Medicine* 97 (1956), pp. 585–92. Reprinted in Gorovitz et al. [op. cit.], pp. 64–69.

17. Ibid., p. 66.

18. See Robert M. Veatch, "Models for Ethical Medicine in a Revolutionary Age," *Hastings Center Report* vol. 2, no. 3 (June 1972), pp. 5–7 [rpt. chap. 4, sel. 10, *EIPL*—ED.]; and William F. May, "Code and Covenant or Philanthropy and Contract," in *A Poynter Reader*, ed. David H. Smith (Bloomington, IN: Poynter Center, 1979). This is an extended version of an essay that appeared in *Hastings Center Report*, vol. 5, no. 2 (Dec. 1975), pp. 19–38. [Excerpted in chap. 4, sel. 11. *EIPL*—ED.]

19. The partnership idea also, of course, underlies so-called holistic medicine....

20. Perhaps it is worth noting that the fiduciary relationship is popular in the law as well as in medicine....

21. The distinction between serving true needs or interests and merely appealing to taste and pleasure goes back at least as far as Plato....

22. William May has also recognized the peculiar significance of trust in a fiduciary relationship....

23. Goldman's view is that the right to know is based on the right to make important life choices and decisions, and this right can never be violated for reasons of health....

24. I take this example from Gert and Culver, op. cit., note 4 above, p. 7....

Paul Ekman and Mark G. Frank

Lies That Fail

Paul Ekman is one of the preeminent researchers on emotions and their expression and an expert on lying who has worked widely with police, federal agencies, and the Department of Homeland security. Until recently he taught in the Psychiatry Department of the University of California, San Francisco.

Lies fail for many reasons. Some of these reasons have to do with the circumstances surrounding the

From Michael Lewis and Carolya Saami, eds., *Lying and Deception in Everyday Life* (New York: Guilford Press, 1993). References were deleted from this text.

lie, and not with the liar's behavior. For example, a confidant may betray a lie; or, private information made public can expose a liar's claims as false. These reasons do not concern us in this chapter. What concerns us are those mistakes made during the act of lying, mistakes liars make despite themselves; in other words, lies that fail because of the liars' behaviors. Deception clues or leakage may be shown in a change in the expression on the face, a movement of the body, an inflection to the voice, a swallowing in the throat, a very deep or shallow breath, long pauses between words, a slip of the tongue, a microfacial expression, or a gestural slip.

There are two basic reasons why lies fail—one that involves thinking, and one that involves emotions. Lies fail due to a failure of the liar to prepare his or her line, or due to the interference of emotions. These reasons have different implications for the potential behavioral clues that betray a lie.

LIES BETRAYED BY THINKING CLUES

Liars do not always anticipate when they will need to lie. There is not always time to prepare the line to be taken, to rehearse and memorize it. Even when there has been ample advance notice, and a false line has been carefully devised, the liar may not be clever enough to anticipate all the questions that may be asked, and to have thought through what his answers must be. Even cleverness may not be enough, for unseen changes in circumstances can betray an otherwise effective line. And, even when a liar is not forced by circumstances to change lines, some liars have trouble recalling the line they have previously committed themselves to, so that new questions cannot be consistently answered quickly.

Any of these failures—in anticipating when it will be necessary to lie, in inventing a line which is adequate to changing circumstances, in remembering the line one has adopted—produce easily spotted clues to deceit. What the person says is either internally inconsistent, or at odds with other incontrovertible facts, known at the time or later revealed. Such obvious clues to deceit are not always

as reliable and straight-forward as they seem. Too smooth a line may be the sign of a well rehearsed con man. To make matters worse, some con men knowing this purposely make slight mistakes in order not to seem too smooth! This was the case with Clifford Irving, who claimed he was authorized by Howard Hughes to write Hughes' biography. While on trial, Irving deliberately contradicted himself (albeit minor contradictions) because he knew that only liars tell perfectly planned accounts. The psychological evidence supports Irving's notion that planned responses are judged as more deceptive than unplanned ones. However, we believe in general that people who fabricate without having prepared their line are more likely to make blatant contradictions, to give evasive and indirect accounts—all of which will ultimately betray their lies.

Lack of preparation or a failure to remember the line one has adopted may produce clues to deceit in *how* a line is spoken, even when there are no inconsistencies in *what* is said. The need to think about each word before it is spoken—weighing possibilities, searching for a word or idea—may be obvious in pauses during speech, speech disfluencies, flattened voice intonation, gaze aversion, or more subtly in a tightening of the lower eyelid or eye brow, certain changes in gesture, and a decrease in the use of the hands to illustrate speech. Not that carefully considering each word before it is spoken is always a sign of deceit, but in some circumstances it is—particularly in contexts in which responses should be known without thought.

LYING ABOUT FEELINGS

A failure to think ahead, plan fully, and rehearse the false line is only one of the reasons why mistakes are made when lying, which then furnish clues to the deceit. Mistakes are also made because of difficulty in concealing or falsely portraying emotion. Not every lie involves emotions, but those that do cause special problems for the liar. An attempt to conceal an emotion at the moment it is felt could be betrayed in words, but except for a slip of the tongue, it usually is not. Unless there is a wish to confess what is felt, the liar does not have to put into words the feelings being concealed. One has less choice in concealing a facial expression, or rapid breathing, or a tightening in the voice.

When emotions are aroused changes occur automatically without choice or deliberation. These changes begin in a split second; this is a fundamental characteristic of emotional experience. People do not actively decide to feel an emotion; instead, they usually experience emotions as happening to them. Negative emotions, such as fear, anger, or sadness, may occur despite either efforts to avoid them or efforts to hide them.

These are what we will call "reliable" behavioral signs of emotion, reliable in the sense that few people can mimic them at all or correctly. Narrowing the red margins of the lips in anger is an example of such a reliable sign of anger, typically missing when anger is feigned, because most people can not voluntarily make that movement. Likewise, when people experience enjoyment they not only move their lip corners upward and back (in a prototypical smile), but they also show a simultaneous contraction of the muscles that surround the eye socket (which raises the cheek, lowers the brow, and creates a "crows feet" appearance). This eye muscle contraction is typically missing from the smile when enjoyment is feigned or not felt. And, as in the case of the involuntary movement of the red margins of the lips in anger, most people cannot voluntarily make this eye muscle movement when they are not truly feeling enjoyment.

Falsifying an experienced emotion is more difficult when one is also attempting to conceal another emotion. Trying to look angry is not easy, but if fear is felt when the person tries to look angry, conflicting forces occur. One set of impulses, arising from fear, pulls in one direction, while the deliberate attempt to appear angry pulls in the other direction. For example, the brows are involuntarily pulled upward and together in fear, but to falsify anger the person must pull them down. Often the signs of this internal struggle between the felt and the false emotion betray the deceit.

Usually, lies about emotions involve more than just fabricating an emotion which is not felt. They also require concealing an emotion which is being experienced. Concealment often goes hand in hand with fabrication. The liar feigns emotion to mask signs of the emotion to be concealed. Such concealment attempts may be betrayed in either of two ways: (1) some signs of the concealed emotion may escape efforts to inhibit or mask it, providing what Ekman and Friesen termed *leakage*; or (2) what they called a *deception clue* does not leak the concealed emotion but betrays the likelihood that a lie is being perpetrated. Deception clues occur when only a fragment leaks which is not decipherable, but which does not jibe with the verbal line being maintained by the liar, or when the very effort of having to conceal produces alterations in behavior, and those behavioral alterations do not fit the liar's line.

FEELINGS ABOUT LYING

Not all deceits involve concealing or falsifying emotions. The embezzler conceals that she is stealing money. The plagiarizer conceals that he has taken the words of another and pretends they are his own. The vain middle-aged man conceals his real age, dying his gray hair and claiming he is seven years younger than he is. Yet even when the lie is about something other than emotion, emotions may become involved. The vain man might be embarrassed about his vanity. To succeed in his deceit he must conceal not only his age but his embarrassment as well. The plagiarizer might feel contempt toward those he misleads. He would thus have to conceal not only the source of his work and pretend an ability that is not his, but also conceal his contempt. The embezzler might feel surprise when someone else is accused of her crime. She would have to conceal her surprise or at least conceal the reason why she is surprised.

Thus, emotions often become involved in lies that were not undertaken for the purpose of concealing emotions. Once involved, the emotions must be concealed if the lie is not to be betrayed. Any emotion may be the culprit, but three emotions are so often intertwined with deceit to merit separate explanation: fear of being caught, guilt about lying, and delight in having duped someone.

Fear of Being Caught

In its milder forms, fear of being caught is not disruptive and may even help the deceiver to avoid mistakes by maintaining alertness. Moderate levels of fear can produce behavioral signs that are noticeable by the skilled lie catcher, and high levels of fear produce just what the liar dreads, namely, evidence of his or her fear or apprehension. The research literature on deception detection suggests that the behavior of highly motivated liars is different from that of less motivated ones. In other words, the behavior of liars who fear being caught is different from the behaviors of liars who do not fear being caught.

Many factors influence how the fear of being caught in a lie (or, *detection apprehension*) will be felt. The first determinant to consider is the liar's beliefs about his target's skill as a lie catcher. If the target (i.e., the person being lied to) is known to be gullible, there usually will not be much detection apprehension. On the other hand, a target known to be tough to fool, who has a reputation as an expert lie catcher, will increase the detection apprehension.

The second determinant of detection apprehension is the liar's amount of practice and previous success in lying. A job applicant who has lied about qualifications successfully in the past should not be overly concerned about an additional deception. Practice in deceit enables the liar to anticipate problems. Success in deceit gives confidence and thus reduces the fear of being caught.

The third determinant of detection apprehension is fear of punishment. The fear of being caught can be reduced if the target suggests that the punishment may be less if the liar confesses. Although they usually cannot offer total amnesty, targets may also offer a psychological amnesty, hoping to induce a confession by implying that the liar need not feel ashamed nor even responsible for committing the crime. A target many sympathetically suggest that the acts are understandable and might have been committed by anyone in the same situation. Another variation might be to offer the target a face-saving explanation of the motive for the behavior in which the lie was designed to conceal.

A fourth factor influencing fear of being caught is the personality of the liar. While some people find it easy to lie, others find it difficult to lie; certainly more is known about the former group than the latter. One group, called *natural liars*, lie easily and with great success—even though they do not differ from other people on their scores on objective personality tests. Natural liars are people who have been getting away with lies since childhood, fooling their parents, teachers, and friends when they wanted to. This instills a sense of confidence in their abilities to deceive such that they have no detection apprehension when they lie. Although this sounds as if natural liars are like psychopaths, they are not; unlike natural liars, psychopaths show poor judgment, no remorse or shame, superficial charm, antisocial behavior without apparent compunction, and pathological egocentricity and incapacity for love.

Such natural liars may need to have two very different skills—the skill needed to plan a deceptive strategy, and the skill needed to mislead a target in a face-to-face meeting. A liar might have both skills, but presumably one could excel at one skill and not the other. Regretably, there has been little study of the characteristics of successful deceivers; no research has asked whether the personality characteristics of successful deceivers differ depending on the arena in which the deceit is practiced.

So far we have described several determinants of detection apprehension: the personality of the liar and, before that, the reputation and character of the lie catcher. Equally important are the *stakes*—the perceived consequences for successful and unsuccessful attempts at deception. Although there is no direct empirical evidence for this assertion, research on the role of appraisal in the experience of emotion is consistent with our thinking. There is a simple rule: the greater the stakes, the more the detection apprehension. Applying this simple rule can be complicated because it is not always so easy to figure out what is at stake; for example, to some people winning is everything, so the stakes are always high. It is reasonable to presume that what is at stake in any deception situation may be so idiosyncratic that no outside observer would readily know.

Detection apprehension should be greater when the stakes involve avoiding punishment, not just earning a reward. When the decision to deceive is first made, the stakes usually involve obtaining rewards. The liar thinks primarily about what might be gained. An embezzler may think only about the monetary gain when he or she first chooses to lie. Once deceit has been underway for some time the rewards may no longer be available. The company may become aware of its losses and suspicious enough that the embezzler is prevented from taking more. At this point, the deceit might be maintained in order to avoid being caught, and avoiding punishment becomes the only stake. On the other hand, avoiding punishment may be the motive from the outset, if the target is suspicious or the liar has little confidence.

There are two kinds of punishment which are at stake in deceit: the punishment that lies in store if the lie fails; and the punishment for the very act of engaging in deception. Detection apprehension should be greater if both kinds of punishment are at stake. Sometimes the punishment for being caught deceiving can even be far worse than the punishment the lie was designed to avoid.

Even if the transgressor knows that the damage done if caught lying will be greater than the loss from admitting the transgression, the lie may be very tempting. Telling the truth brings immediate and certain losses, while telling a lie promises the possibility of avoiding all losses. The prospect of being spared immediate punishment may be so attractive that the liar may underestimate the likelihood that he or she will be caught in the lie. Recognition that confession would have been a better policy comes too late, when the lie has been maintained so long and with such elaboration that confession may no longer win a lesser punishment.

Sometimes there is little ambiguity about the relative costs of confession versus continued concealment. There are actions which are themselves so bad that confessing them wins little approval for having come forward, and concealing them adds little to the punishment which awaits the offender. Such is the case if the lie conceals child abuse, incest, murder, treason, or terrorism. Unlike the rewards possible for some repentant philanderers, forgiveness is not to be expected by those who confess these heinous crimes—although confession with contrition may lessen the punishment.

A final factor to consider about how the stakes influence detection apprehension is what is gained or lost by the target, not just by the liar. Usually the liar's gains are at the expense of the target. The embezzler gains what the employer loses. Stakes are not always equal; moreover, the stakes for the liar and the target can differ not just in amount but in kind. A philanderer may gain a little adventure, while the cuckolded spouse may lose tremendous self-respect. When the stakes differ for the liar and target, the stakes for either may determine the liar's detection apprehension. It depends upon whether the liar recognizes the difference and how it is evaluated.

Deception Guilt

Deception guilt refers to a feeling about lying, not the legal issue of whether someone is guilty or innocent. Deception guilt must also be distinguished from feelings of guilt about the content of a lie. Thus, a child may feel excitement about stealing the loose change off his parents' dresser, but feel guilt over lying to his or her parents to conceal the theft. This situation can be reversed as well—no guilt about lying to the parents, but guilt about stealing the money. Of course, some people feel guilt about both the act and the lie, and some people will not feel guilt about either. What is important is that it is not necessary to feel guilty about the content of a lie in order to feel guilty about lying.

Like the fear of being caught, deception guilt can vary in strength. It may be very mild, or so strong that the lie will fail because the deception guilt produces leakage or deception clues. When it becomes extreme, deception guilt is a torturing experience, undermining the sufferer's most fundamental feelings of self-worth. Relief from such severe deception guilt may motivate a confession despite the likelihood of punishment for misdeeds admitted. In fact the punishment may be sought by the person who confesses in order to alleviate the tortured feelings of guilt.

When the decision to lie is first made, people do not always accurately anticipate how much they may later suffer from deception guilt. Liars may not realize the impact of being thanked by their victims for their seeming helpfulness, or how they will feel when they see someone else blamed for their misdeeds—as in the recent case of the "gentleman bandit" who felt so guilty about someone else being prosecuted for his robberies that he turned himself in to the police. Another reason why liars underestimate how much deception guilt they will feel is that it is only with the passage of time that a liar may learn that one lie will not suffice, that the lie has to be repeated again and again, often with expanding fabrications in order to protect the original deceit.

Shame is closely related to guilt, but there is a key qualitative difference. No audience is needed for feelings of guilt, no one else need know for the guilty person is his own judge. Not so for shame. The humiliation of shame requires disapproval or ridicule by others. If no one ever learns of a misdeed there will be no shame, but there still might be guilt. Of course there may be both. The distinction between shame and guilt is very important because these two emotions may tear a person in opposite directions. The wish to relieve guilt may motivate a confession, but the wish to avoid the humiliation of shame may prevent it.

There exists a group of individuals who fail to feel any guilt or shame about their misdeeds; these people have been referred to as sociopaths or psychopaths. For these individuals, the lack of guilt or shame pervades all or most aspects of their lives. Experts disagree about whether the lack of guilt and shame is due to upbringing or some biological determinants. There is agreement that the psychopath's lack of guilt about lying and lack of fear of being caught will make it more difficult for a target to detect a psychopath's lies.

Conversely, some people are especially vulnerable to shame about lying and deception guilt; for example people who have been very strictly brought up to believe lying is one of the most terrible sins. Those with less strict upbringing, that did not particularly condemn lying, could more generally have been instilled with strong, pervasive guilt feelings. Such guilty people appear to seek experiences in which they can intensify their guilt, and stand shamefully exposed to others; this appears to be the case for psychiatric patients suffering from generalized anxiety disorders. Unfortunately, unlike the psychopathic personality, there has been very little research about guilt-prone individuals.

Whenever the deceiver does not share social values with the victim, odds are there will not be much deception guilt. People feel less guilty about lying to those they think are wrongdoers. A philanderer whose marital partner is cold and unwilling in bed might not feel guilty in lying about an affair. A similar principle is at work to explain why a diplomat or spy does not feel guilty about misleading the other side. In all these situations, the liar and the target do not share common goals or values.

Lying is authorized in most of these examples—each of these individuals appeals to a well-defined social norm which legitimizes deceiving an opponent. There is little guilt about such authorized deceits when the targets are from opposing sides, and hold different values. There also may be authorization to deceive targets who are not opponents, who share values with the deceiver. Physicians may not feel guilty about deceiving their patients if they think it is for the patient's own good. Giving a patient a placebo, a sugar pill identified as a useful drug, is an old, time-honored, medical deceit. If the patient feels better, or at least stops hassling the doctor for an unneeded drug which might actually be harmful, many physicians believe that the lie is justified. In this case, the patient benefits from the lie, and not the doctor. If a liar thinks he is not gaining from the lie he probably will not feel any deception guilt.

Even selfish deceits may not produce deception guilt when the lie is authorized. Poker players do not feel deception guilt about bluffing (but they do feel detection apprehension). The same is true about bargaining whether in a Middle East bazaar, Wall Street, or in the local real estate agent's office. The home owner who asks more for his house than he will actually sell it for will not feel guilty if he gets his asking price. This lie is authorized. Because the participants expect misinformation, and not the truth, bargaining and poker are not necessarily lies. These situations by their nature provide prior notification that no one will be entirely truthful.

Deception guilt is most likely when lying is not authorized. Deception guilt should be most severe when the target is trusting, not expecting to be misled because honesty is expected between liar and target. In such opportunistic deceits, guilt about lying will be greater if the target suffers at least as much as the liar gains. Even then there will not be much, if any, deception guilt unless there are at least some shared values between target and liar. A student turning in a late assignment may not feel guilty about lying to the professor if the student feels the professor sets unreachable standards and assigns undoable workloads. This student may feel fear of being caught in a lie, but he or she may not feel deception guilt. Even though the student disagrees with the professor about the workload and other matters, if the student still cares about the professor he or she may feel shame if the lie is discovered. Shame requires some respect for those who disapprove; otherwise disapproval brings forth anger or contempt, not shame.

Liars feel less guilty when their targets are impersonal or totally anonymous. A customer who conceals from the check-out clerk that he or she was undercharged for an expensive item will feel less guilty if he or she does not know the clerk. If the clerk is the owner, or if it is a small family owned store, the lying customer will feel more guilty than he or she will if it is one of a large chain of supermarkets. It is easier to indulge the guilt-reducing fantasy that the target is not really hurt, does not really care, will not even notice the lie, or even deserves or wants to be misled, if the target is anonymous.

Often there will be an inverse relationship between deception guilt and detection apprehension. What lessens guilt about the lie increases fear of being caught. When deceits are authorized there should be less deception guilt, yet the authorization usually increases the stakes, thus making detection apprehension high. In a high stakes poker game there is high detection apprehension and low deception guilt. The employer who lies to his employee whom he has come to suspect of embezzling, concealing his suspicions to catch him in the crime, also is likely to feel high detection apprehension but low deception guilt.

While there are exceptions, most people find the experience of guilt so toxic that they seek ways to diminish it. There are many ways to justify deceit. It can be considered retaliation for injustice. A nasty or mean target can be said not to deserve honesty. "The boss was so stingy, he didn't reward me for all the work I did, so I took some myself." Or the liar can blame the victim of his or her lies; for example, Machiavellian personality types tend to see their victims as so gullible that they bring lies upon themselves.

| Sissela Bok | # Lying and Lies to the Sick and Dying |

Sissela Bok is a Professor at Harvard University.

TRUTH AND TRUTHFULNESS

... "Truth"—no concept intimidates and yet draws thinkers so powerfully. From the beginnings of human speculation about the world, the questions of what truth is and whether we can attain it have loomed large. Every philosopher has had to grapple with them. Every religion seeks to answer them. ...

In all such speculation, there is great risk of a conceptual muddle, of not seeing the crucial differences between two domains: the *moral* domain of intended

From *Lying: Moral Choice in Public and Private Life* (New York: Pantheon, 1978), selections from chapters 1, 2, 6, 14, and 15.

truthfulness and deception, and the much vaster domain of truth and falsity in general. The moral question of whether you are lying or not is not *settled* by establishing the truth or falsity of what you say. In order to settle this question, we must know whether you *intend your statement to mislead....*

Any number of appearances and words can mislead us; but only a fraction of them are *intended* to do so. A mirage may deceive us, through no one's fault. Our eyes deceive us all the time. We are beset by self-delusion and bias of every kind. Yet we often know when we mean to be honest or dishonest. Whatever the essence of truth and falsity, and whatever the sources of error in our lives, *one* such source is surely the human agent, receiving and giving out information, intentionally deflecting, withholding, even distorting it at times....

We must single out, therefore, from the countless ways in which we blunder misinformed through life, that which is done with the *intention to mislead*: and from the countless partial stabs at truth, those which are intended to be truthful. Only if this distinction is clear will it be possible to ask the moral question with rigor. And it is to this question alone—the intentional manipulation of information—that the court addresses itself in its request for "the truth, the whole truth, and nothing but the truth."

DEFINING INTENTIONAL DECEPTION AND LYING

When we undertake to deceive others intentionally, we communicate messages meant to mislead them, meant to make them believe what we ourselves do not believe. We can do so through gesture, through disguise, by means of action or inaction, even through silence. Which of these innumerable deceptive messages are also lies? I shall define as a lie any intentionally deceptive message which is *stated*. Such statements are most often made verbally or in writing, but can of course also be conveyed via smoke signals, Morse code, sign language, and the like. Deception, then, is the larger category, and lying forms part of it....

LYING AND CHOICE

Deceit and violence—these are the two forms of deliberate assault on human beings. Both can coerce people into acting against their will. Most harm that can befall victims through violence can come to them also through deceit. But deceit controls more subtly, for it works on belief as well as action. Even Othello, whom few would have dared to try to subdue by force, could be brought to destroy himself and Desdemona through falsehood. The knowledge of this coercive element in deception, and of our vulnerability to it, underlies our sense of the *centrality* of truthfulness....

All our choices depend on our estimates of what is the case; these estimates must in turn often rely on information from others. Lies distort this information and therefore our situation as we perceive it, as well as our choices.

THE PERSPECTIVE OF THE DECEIVED

Those who learn that they have been lied to in an important matter—say, the identity of their parents, the affection of their spouse, or the integrity of their government—are resentful, disappointed, and suspicious. They feel wronged; they are wary of new overtures. And they look back on their past beliefs and actions in the new light of the discovered lies. They see that they were manipulated, that the deceit made them unable to make choices for themselves according to the most adequate information available, unable to act as they would have wanted to act had they known all along.

It is true, of course, that personal, informed choice is not the only kind available to them. They may *decide* to abandon choosing for themselves and let others decide for them—as guardians, financial advisors, or political representatives. They may even decide to abandon choice based upon information of a conventional nature altogether and trust instead to the stars or to throws of the dice or to soothsayers.

But such alternatives ought to be personally chosen and not surreptitiously imposed by lies or other forms of manipulation. Most of us would resist loss of control over which choices we want to delegate to others and which ones we want to make ourselves, aided by the best information we can obtain. We resist because experience has taught us the consequences when others choose to deceive us, even "for our own good." Of course, we know that many lies are trivial. But since we, when lied to, have no way to judge which lies are the trivial ones, and since we have no confidence that liars will restrict themselves to just such trivial lies, the perspective of the deceived leads us to be wary of *all* deception. . . .

Deception, then, can be coercive. When it succeeds, it can give power to the deceiver—power that all who suffer the consequences of lies would not wish to abdicate. . . .

THE PRINCIPLE OF VERACITY

. . .I believe that we must at the very least accept as an initial premise Aristotle's view that lying is "mean and culpable" and that truthful statements are preferable to lies in the absence of special considerations. This premise gives an initial negative weight to lies. It holds that they are not neutral from the point of view of our choices; that lying requires explanation, whereas truth ordinarily does not. It provides a counterbalance to the crude evaluation by liars of their own motives and of the consequences of their lies. And it places the burden of proof squarely on those who assume the liar's perspective.

This presumption against lying can also be stated so as to stress the positive worth of truthfulness or veracity. I would like . . . to refer to the "principle of veracity" as an expression of this initial imbalance in our weighing of truthfulness and lying. . . .

TYPES OF EXCUSES

What is it, then, that can conflict with the requirement for truthfulness so as to make lies permissible at times? Say you are caught in a compromising lie. What excuses might you offer? What kinds of excuses?

An excuse seeks to extenuate, sometimes to remove the blame entirely from something which would otherwise be a fault. It can seek to extenuate in three ways. First, it can suggest that what is seen as a fault is not really one. Secondly, it can suggest that, though there has been a fault, the agent is not really blameworthy, because he is not responsible. And finally, it can suggest that, though there has been a fault, and though the agent is responsible, he is not really to blame because he has good reasons to do as he did.

(a) Excuses of the first type may claim that the supposed lie is not really a lie, but a joke, perhaps, or an evasion, an exaggeration, a flight of fancy. Or else such an excuse may argue that since it is impossible to give objective distinctions between truth and falsehood, the supposed lie cannot be proved to be one.

(b) The second type of excuse holds that, though there may have been deception, the agent is not really or not completely responsible. The liar may claim he never meant to mislead, or was incompetent, perhaps drunk, or talking in his sleep, or coerced into deceiving. Or else he may take refuge in arguing that no one can ever be held responsible for lies, that free choice in that respect is a myth.

Both these types of excuses obviously cover a vast territory and are in constant use by liars. But it is the third type which will be the focus of [our] attention . . .—the type of excuse which is most fundamental for the process of evaluating deliberate lies. In this third type of excuse, the liar admits the lie, accepts responsibility for it, but offers reasons to show that he should be partially or even wholly cleared of blame. All three kinds of excuses are often present in the same effort to extenuate any one lie. . . .

(c) The third type of excuse, then, offers moral reasons for a lie, reasons to show that a lie ought, under the circumstances, to be allowed.

PATERNALISM

...To act paternalistically is to guide and even coerce people in order to protect them and serve their best interests, as a father might his children....

The need for some paternalistic restraints is obvious. We survive only if protected from harm as children. Even as adults, we tolerate a number of regulations designed to reduce dangers such as those of infection or accidents. But it is equally obvious that the intention of guarding from harm has led, both through mistake and through abuse, to great suffering. The "protection" can suffocate; it can also exploit. Throughout history, men, women, and children have been compelled to accept degrading work, alien religious practices, institutionalization, and even wars alleged to "free" them, all in the name of what someone has declared to be their own best interest. And deception may well have outranked force as a means of subjection: duping people to conform, to embrace ideologies and cults—never more zealously perpetrated than by those who believe that the welfare of those deceived is at issue.

Apart from guidance and persuasion, the paternalist can manipulate in two ways: through force and through deception.

———————

One reason for the appeal of paternalistic lies is that they, unlike so much deception, are felt to be without bias and told in a disinterested wish to be helpful to fellow human beings in need. On closer examination, however, this objectivity and disinterest are often found to be spurious. The benevolent motives claimed by liars are then seen to be mixed with many others much less altruistic—the fear of confrontation which would accompany a more outspoken acknowledgment of the liar's feelings and intentions; the desire to avoid setting in motion great pressures to change, as where addiction or infidelity are no longer concealed; the urge to maintain the power that comes with duping others (never greater than when those lied to are defenseless or in need of care). These are motives of self-protection and of manipulation, of wanting to retain control over a situation and to remain a free agent. So long as the liar does not see them clearly, his judgment that his lies are altruistic and thus excused is itself biased and unreliable.

The perspective of the deceived, then, challenges the "helpfulness" of many paternalistic lies. It questions, moreover, even the benefits that are thought to accrue to the liar. The effects of deception on the liars themselves—the need to shore up lies, keep them in good repair, the anxieties relating to possible discovery, the entanglements and threats to integrity—are greatest in a close relationship where it is rare that one lie will suffice. It can be very hard to maintain the deceit when one is in close contact with those one lies to. The price of "living a lie" often turns out not even to have been worth the gains for the liars themselves.

JUSTIFICATION?

The two simplest approaches to paternalistic lying, then, have to be ruled out. It is not all right to lie to people just because they are children, or unable to judge what one says, or indeed because they belong to any category of persons at all. And the simple conviction voiced by Luther and so many others that the "helpful lie" is excused by its own altruism is much too uncritical. It allows far too many lies to go unquestioned. Both of these views fail to take into consideration the harm that comes from lying, not only to the deceived but to the liars and to the bonds they share.

———————

DECEPTION AS THERAPY

A forty-six-year-old man, coming to a clinic for a routine physical check-up needed for insurance purposes, is diagnosed as having a form of cancer likely to cause him to die within six months. No known cure exists for it. Chemotherapy may prolong life by a few extra months, but will have side effects the physician does not think warranted in this case. In addition, he believes that such therapy should be reserved for patients with a chance for recovery or remission. The patient has no symptoms giving him any reason to believe that he is not perfectly healthy. He expects to take a short vacation in a week.

For the physician, there are now several choices involving truthfulness. Ought he to tell the patient what he has learned, or conceal it? If asked, should he deny it? If he decides to reveal the diagnosis, should he delay doing so until after the patient returns from his vacation? Finally, even if he does reveal the serious nature of the diagnosis, should he mention the possibility of chemotherapy and his reasons for not recommending it in this case? Or should he encourage every last effort to postpone death?

In this particular case, the physician chose to inform the patient of his diagnosis right away. He did not, however, mention the possibility of chemotherapy. A medical student working under him disagreed; several nurses also thought that the patient should have been informed of this possibility. They tried, unsuccessfully, to persuade the physician that this was the patient's right. When persuasion had failed, the student elected to disobey the doctor by informing the patient of the alternative of chemotherapy. After consultation with family members, the patient chose to ask for the treatment.

Doctors confront such choices often and urgently. What they reveal, hold back, or distort will matter profoundly to their patients. Doctors stress with corresponding vehemence their reasons for the distortion or concealment: not to confuse a sick person needlessly, or cause what may well be unnecessary pain or discomfort, as in the case of the cancer patient; not to leave a patient without hope, as in those many cases where the dying are not told the truth about their condition; or to improve the chances of cure, as where unwarranted optimism is expressed about some form of therapy. Doctors use information as part of the therapeutic regimen; it is given out in amounts, in admixtures, and according to timing believed best for patients. Accuracy, by comparison, matters far less.

Lying to patients has, therefore, seemed an especially excusable act. Some would argue that doctors, and *only* doctors, should be granted the right to manipulate the truth in ways so undesirable for politicians, lawyers, and others.[1] Doctors are trained to help patients; their relationship to patients carries special obligations, and they know much more than laymen about what helps and hinder recovery and survival.

Even the most conscientious doctors, then, who hold themselves at a distance from the quacks and the purveyors of false remedies, hesitate to for swear all lying. Lying is usually wrong, they argue, but less so than allowing the truth to harm patients. B. C. Meyer echoes this very common view:

> [O]urs is a profession which traditionally has been guided by a precept that transcends the virtue of uttering truth for truth's sake, and that is, "so far as possible, do no harm."[2]

Truth, for Meyer, may be important, but not when it endangers the health and well-being of patients. This has seemed self-evident to many physicians in the past—so much so that we find very few mentions of veracity in the codes and oaths and writings by physicians through the centuries. This absence is all the more striking as other principles of ethics have been consistently and movingly expressed in the same documents.

The two fundamental principles of doing good and not doing harm—of beneficence and nonmaleficence—are the most immediately relevant to medical practitioners, and the more frequently stressed. To preserve life and good health, to ward off illness, pain, and death—these are the perennial tasks of medicine and nursing. These principles have found powerful expression at all times in the history of medicine. In the Hippocratic oath physicians promise to:

> use treatment to help the sick . . . but never with a view to injury and wrong-doing.[3]

And a Hindu oath of initiation says:

> Day and night, however thou mayest be engaged, thou shalt endeavor for the relief of patients with all thy heart and soul. Thou shalt not desert or injure the patient even for the sake of thy living.[4]

But there is no similar stress on veracity. It is absent from virtually all oaths, codes, and prayers.

The Hippocratic Oath makes no mention of truthfulness to patients about their condition, prognosis, or treatment. Other early codes and prayers are equally silent on the subject. To be sure, they often refer to the confidentiality with which doctors should treat all that patients tell them; but there is no corresponding reference to honesty toward the patient. One of the few who appealed to such a principle was Amatus Lusitanus, a Jewish physician widely known for his skill, who, persecuted, died of the plague in 1568. He published an oath which reads in part:

> If I lie, may I incur the eternal wrath of God and of His angel Raphael, and may nothing in the medical art succeed for me according to my desires.[5]

Later codes continue to avoid the subject. Not even the Declaration of Geneva, adopted in 1948 by the World Medical Association, makes any reference to it. And the Principles of Medical Ethics of the American Medical Association[6] still leave the matter of informing patients up to the physician.

Given such freedom, a physician can decide to tell as much or as little as he wants the patient to know, so long as he breaks no law. In the case of the man mentioned at the beginning ... some physicians might feel justified in lying for the good of the patient, others might be truthful. Some may conceal alternatives to the treatment they recommend; others not. In each case, they could appeal to the AMA Principles of Ethics. A great many would choose to be able to lie. They would claim that not only can a lie avoid harm for the patient, but that it is also hard to know whether they have been right in the first place in making their pessimistic diagnosis; a "truthful" statement could therefore turn out to hurt patients unnecessarily. The concern for curing and for supporting those who cannot be cured then runs counter to the desire to be completely open. This concern is especially strong where the prognosis is bleak; even more so when patients are so affected by their illness or their medication that they are more dependent than usual, perhaps more easily depressed or irrational.

Physicians know only too well how uncertain a diagnosis or prognosis can be. They know how hard it is to give meaningful and correct answers regarding health and illness. They also know that disclosing their own uncertainty or fears can reduce those benefits that depend upon faith in recovery. They fear, too, that revealing grave risks, no matter how unlikely it is that these will come about, may exercise the pull of the "self-fulfilling prophecy." They dislike being the bearers of uncertain or bad news as much as anyone else. And last, but not least, sitting down to discuss an illness truthfully and sensitively may take much-needed time away from other patients.

These reasons help explain why nurses and physicians and relatives of the sick and dying prefer not to be bound by rules that might limit their ability to suppress, delay, or distort information. This is not to say that they necessarily plan to lie much of the time. They merely want to have the freedom to do so when they believe it wise. And the reluctance to see lying prohibited explains, in turn, the failure of the codes and oaths to come to grips with the problems of truth telling and lying.

But sharp conflicts are now arising. Doctors no longer work alone with patients. They have to consult with others much more than before; if they choose to lie, the choice may not be met with approval by all who take part in the care of the patient. A nurse expresses the difficulty which results as follows:

> From personal experience I would say that the patients who aren't told about their terminal illness have so many verbal and mental questions unanswered that many will begin to realize that their illness is more serious than they're being told. ...
>
> Nurses care for these patients twenty-four hours a day compared to a doctor's daily brief visit, and it is the nurse many times that the patient will relate to, once his underlying fears become overwhelming. ... This is difficult for us nurses because being in constant contact with patients we can see the events leading up to this. The patient continually asks you, "Why isn't my pain decreasing?" or "Why isn't the radiation treatment easing the pain?" ... We cannot legally give these patients an honest answer as a nurse (and I'm sure I wouldn't want to) yet the problem is still not resolved and the circle grows larger and larger with the patient alone in the middle.[7]

The doctor's choice to lie increasingly involves co-workers in acting a part they find neither humane nor wise. The fact that these problems have not been carefully thought through within the medical profession, nor seriously addressed in medical education, merely serves to intensify the conflicts.[8] Different doctors then respond very differently to patients in exactly similar predicaments. The friction is increased by the fact that relatives often disagree even where those giving medical care to a patient are in accord on how to approach the patient. Here again, because physicians have not worked out to common satisfaction the question of whether relatives have the right to make such requests, the problems are allowed to be haphazardly resolved by each physician as he sees fit.

THE PATIENT'S PERSPECTIVE

The turmoil in the medical profession regarding truth telling is further augmented by the pressures that patients themselves now bring to bear and by empirical data coming to light. Challenges are growing to three major arguments for lying to patients: that truthfulness is impossible; that patients do not want bad news; and that truthful information harms them. . . .

The second argument for deceiving patients refers specifically to giving them news of a frightening or depressing kind. It holds that patients do not, in fact, generally want such information, that they prefer not to have to face up to serious illness and death. On the basis of such a belief, most doctors in a number of surveys stated that they do not, as a rule, inform patients that they have an illness such as cancer.

When studies are made of what patients desire to know, on the other hand, a large majority say that they *would* like to be told of such a diagnosis.[9] All these studies need updating and should be done with large numbers of patients and non-patients. But they do show that there is generally a dramatic divergence between physicians and patients on the factual question of whether patients want to know what ails them in cases of serious illness such as cancer. In most of the studies, over 80 percent of the persons asked indicated that they would want to be told.

Sometimes this discrepancy is set aside by doctors who want to retain the view that patients do not want unhappy news. In reality, they claim, the fact that patients say they want it has to be discounted. The more someone asks to know, the more he suffers from fear which will lead to the denial of the information even if it is given. Informing patients is, therefore, useless; they resist and deny having been told what they cannot assimilate. According to this view, empirical studies of what patients say they want are worthless since they do not probe deeply enough to uncover this universal resistance to the contemplation of one's own death.

This view is only partially correct. For some patients, denial is indeed well established in medical experience. A number of patients (estimated at between 15 percent and 25 percent) will give evidence of denial of having been told about their illness, even when they repeatedly ask and are repeatedly informed. And nearly everyone experiences a period of denial at some point in the course of approaching death.[10] Elisabeth Kübler-Ross sees denial as resulting often from premature and abrupt information by a stranger who goes through the process quickly to "get it over with." She holds that denial functions as a buffer after unexpected shocking news, permitting individuals to collect themselves and to mobilize other defenses. She described prolonged denial in one patient as follows:

> She was convinced that the X-rays were "mixed up": she asked for reassurance that her pathology report could not possibly be back so soon and that another patient's report must have been marked with her name. When none of this could be confirmed, she quickly asked to leave the hospital, looking for another physician in the vain hope "to get a better explanation for my troubles." This patient went "shopping around" for many doctors, some of whom gave her reassuring answers, others of whom confirmed the previous suspicion. Whether confirmed or not, she reacted in the same manner; she asked for examination and reexamination.[11]

But to say that denial is universal flies in the face of all evidence. And to take any claim to the contrary as "symptomatic" of deeper denial leaves no room for reasoned discourse. There is no way that such universal denial can be proved true or false. To believe in it is a metaphysical belief about man's condition, not a statement about what patients do and do not want. It is true that we can never completely understand the possibility of our own death, any more than being alive in the first place. But people certainly differ in the degree to which they can approach such knowledge, take it into account in their plans, and make their peace with it.

Montaigne claimed that in order to learn both to live and to die, men have to think about death and be prepared to accept it.[12] To stick one's head in the sand, or to be prevented by lies from trying to discern what is to come, hampers freedom—freedom to consider one's life as a whole, with a beginning, a duration, an end. Some may request to be deceived rather than to see their lives as thus finite; others reject the information which would require them to do so; but most say that they want to know. Their concern for knowing about their condition goes far beyond mere curiosity or the wish to make isolated personal choices in the short time left to them; their stance toward the entire life they have lived, and their ability to give it meaning and completion, are at stake.[13] In lying or withholding the facts which permit such discernment, doctors may reflect their own fears (which, according to one study,[14] are much stronger than those of laymen) of facing questions about the meaning of one's life and the inevitability of death.

Beyond the fundamental deprivation that can result from deception, we are also becoming increasingly aware of all that can befall patients in the course of their illness when information is denied or distorted. Lies place them in a position where they no longer participate in choices concerning their own health, including the choice of whether to be a "patient" in the first place. A terminally ill person who is not informed that his illness is incurable and that he is near death cannot make decisions about the end of his life: about whether or not to enter a hospital, or to have surgery; where and with whom

to spend his last days; how to put his affairs in order—these most personal choices cannot be made if he is kept in the dark, or given contradictory hints and clues.

It has always been especially easy to keep knowledge from terminally ill patients. They are most vulnerable, least able to take action to learn what they need to know, or to protect their autonomy. The very fact of being so ill greatly increases the likelihood of control by others. And the fear of being helpless in the face of such control is growing. At the same time, the period of dependency and slow deterioration of health and strength that people undergo has lengthened. There has been a dramatic shift toward institutionalization of the aged and those near death. (Over 80 percent of Americans now die in a hospital or other institution.)

Patients who are severely ill often suffer a further distancing and loss of control over their most basic functions. Electrical wiring, machines, intravenous administration of liquids, all create new dependency and at the same time new distance between the patient and all who come near. Curable patients are often willing to undergo such procedures; but when no cure is possible, these procedures merely intensify the sense of distance and uncertainty and can even become a substitute for comforting human acts. Yet those who suffer in this way often fear to seem troublesome by complaining. Lying to them, perhaps for the most charitable of purposes, can then cause them to slip unwittingly into subjection to new procedures, perhaps new surgery, where death is held at bay through transfusions, respirators, even resuscitation far beyond what most would wish.

Seeing relatives in such predicaments has caused a great upsurge of worrying about death and dying. At the root of this fear is not a growing terror of the *moment* of death, or even the instants before it. Nor is there greater fear of *being* dead. In contrast to the centuries of lives lived in dread of the punishments to be inflicted after death, many would now accept the view expressed by Epicurus, who died in 270 B.C.:

> Death, therefore, the most awful of evils, is nothing to us, seeing that, when we are, death is not come, and when death is come, we are not.[15]

The growing fear, if it is not of the moment of dying nor of being dead, is of all that which now precedes dying for so many: the possibility of prolonged pain, the increasing weakness, the uncertainty, the loss of powers and chance of senility, the sense of being a burden. This fear is further nourished by the loss of trust in health professionals. In part, the loss of trust results from the abuses which have been exposed—the Medicaid scandals, the old-age home profiteering, the commercial exploitation of those who seek remedies for their ailments;[16] in part also because of the deceptive practices patients suspect, having seen how friends and relatives were kept in the dark; in part, finally, because of the sheer numbers of persons, often strangers, participating in the care of any one patient. Trust which might have gone to a doctor long known to the patient goes less easily to a team of strangers, no matter how expert or well-meaning.

It is with the working out of all that *informed consent*[17] implies and the information it presupposes that truth telling is coming to be discussed in a serious way for the first time in the health professions. Informed consent is a farce if the information provided is distorted or withheld. And even complete information regarding surgical procedures or medication is obviously useless unless the patient also knows what the condition is that these are supposed to correct.

Bills of rights for patients, similarly stressing the right to be informed, are now gaining acceptance.[18] This right is not new, but the effort to implement it is. Nevertheless, even where patients are handed the most elegantly phrased Bill of Rights, their right to a truthful diagnosis and prognosis is by no means always respected.

The reason why even doctors who recognize a patient's right to have information might still not provide it brings us to the third argument against telling all patients the truth. It holds that the information given might hurt the patient and that the concern for the right to such information is therefore a threat to proper health care. A patient, these doctors argue, may wish to commit suicide after being given discouraging news, or suffer a cardiac arrest, or simply cease to struggle, and thus not grasp the small remaining chance for recovery. And even where the outlook for a patient is very good, the disclosure of a minute risk can shock some patients or cause them to reject needed protection such as a vaccination or antibiotics.

The factual basis for this argument has been challenged from two points of view. The damages associated with the disclosure of sad news or risks are rarer than physicians believe; and the *benefits* which result from being informed are more substantial, even measurably so. Pain is tolerated more easily, recovery from surgery is quicker, and co-operation with therapy is greatly improved. The attitude that "what you don't know won't hurt you" is proving unrealistic; it is what patients do not know but vaguely suspect that causes them corrosive worry.

It is certain that no answers to this question of harm from information are the same for all patients. If we look, first, at the fear expressed by physicians that informing patients of even remote or unlikely risks connected with a drug prescription or operation might shock some and make others refuse the treatment that would have been best for them, it appears to be unfounded for the great majority of patients. Studies show that very few patients respond to being told of such risks by withdrawing their consent to the procedure and that those who do withdraw are the very ones who might well have been upset enough to sue the physician had they not been asked to consent beforehand.[19] It is possible that on even rarer occasions especially susceptible persons might manifest physical deterioration from shock; some physicians have even asked whether patients who die after giving informed consent to an operation, but before it actually takes place, somehow expire because of the information given to them.[20] While such questions are unanswerable in any one case, they certainly argue in favor of caution, a real concern for the person to whom one is recounting the risks he or she will face, and sensitivity to all signs of stress.

The situation is quite different when persons who are already ill, perhaps already quite weak and discouraged, are told of a very serious prognosis. Physicians fear that such knowledge may cause the patients to commit suicide, or to be frightened or depressed to the point that their illness takes a downward turn. The fear that great numbers of patients will commit suicide appears to be unfounded.[21] And if some do, is that a response so unreasonable, so much against the patient's best interest that physicians ought to make it a reason for concealment or lies? Many societies have allowed suicide in the past; our own has decriminalized it; and some are coming to make distinctions among the many suicides which ought to be prevented if at all possible, and those which ought to be respected.[22]

Another possible response to very bleak news is the triggering of physiological mechanisms which allow death to come more quickly—a form of giving up or of preparing for the inevitable, depending on one's outlook. Lewis Thomas, studying responses in humans and animals, holds it not unlikely that:

> There is a pivotal movement at some stage in the body's reaction to injury or disease, maybe in aging as well, when the organism concedes that it is finished and the time for dying is at hand, and at this moment the events that lead to death are launched, as a coordinated mechanism. Functions are then shut off, in sequence, irreversibly, and, while this is going on, a neural mechanism, held ready for this occasion, is switched on.[23]

Such a response may be appropriate, in which case it makes the moments of dying as peaceful as those who have died and been resuscitated so often testify. But it may also be brought on inappropriately, when the organism could have lived on, perhaps even induced malevolently, by external acts intended to kill. Thomas speculates that some of the deaths resulting from "hexing" are due to such responses. Lévi-Strauss describes deaths from exorcism and the casting of spells in ways which suggest that the same process may then be brought on by the community.[24]

It is not inconceivable that unhappy news abruptly conveyed, or a great shock given to someone unable to tolerate it, could also bring on such a "dying response," quite unintended by the speaker. There is every reason to be cautious and to try to know ahead of time how susceptible a patient might be to the accidental triggering—however rare—of such a response. One has to assume, however, that most of those who have survived long enough to be in a

situation where their informed consent is asked have a very robust resistance to such accidental triggering of processes leading to death.

When, on the other hand, one considers those who are already near death, the "dying response" may be much less inappropriate, much less accidental, much less unreasonable. In most societies, long before the advent of modern medicine, human beings have made themselves ready for death once they felt its approach. Philippe Ariès describes how many in the Middle Ages prepared themselves for death when they "felt the end approach." They awaited death lying down, surrounded by friends and relatives. They recollected all they had lived through and done, pardoning all who stood near their deathbed, calling on God to bless them, and finally praying. "After the final prayer all that remained was to wait for death, and there was no reason for death to tarry."[25]

Modern medicine, in its valiant efforts to defeat disease and to save lives, may be dislocating the conscious as well as the purely organic responses allowing death to come when it is inevitable, thus denying those who are dying the benefits of the traditional approach to death. In lying to them, and in pressing medical efforts to cure them long past the point of possible recovery, physicians may thus rob individuals of an autonomy few would choose to give up.

Sometimes, then, the "dying response" is a natural organic reaction at the time when the body has no further defense. Sometimes it is inappropriately brought on by news too shocking or given in too abrupt a manner. We need to learn a great deal more about this last category, no matter how small. But there is no evidence that patients in general will be debilitated by truthful information about their condition.

Apart from possible harm from information, we are coming to learn much more about the benefits it can bring patients. People follow instructions more carefully if they know what their disease is and why they are asked to take medication; any benefits from those procedures are therefore much more likely to come about.[26] Similarly, people recover faster from surgery and tolerate pain with less medication if they understand what ails them and what can be done for them.[27]

NOTES

1. Plato, *The Republic*, 389b.

2. B. C. Meyer, "Truth and the Physician," *Bulletin of the New York Academy of Medicine* 45 (1969): 59–71.

3. W.H.S. Jones, trans., *Hippocrates*, Loeb Classical Library (Cambridge, MA: Harvard University Press, 1923), p. 164.

4. Reprinted in M. B. Etziony, *The Physician's Creed: An Anthology of Medical Prayers, Oaths and Codes of Ethics* (Springfield, IL: Charles C. Thomas, 1973), pp. 15–18.

5. See Harry Friedenwald, "The Ethics of the Practice of Medicine from the Jewish Point of View," *Johns Hopkins Hospital Bulletin*, no. 318 (Aug. 1917), pp. 256–61.

6. "Ten Principles of Medical Ethics," *Journal of the American Medical Association* 164 (1957): 1119–20.

7. Mary Barrett, Letter [to the Editor], *Boston Globe*, 16 November 1976, p. 1.

8. Though a minority of physicians have struggled to bring them to our attention. See Thomas Percival, *Medical Ethics*, 3d ed. (Oxford: John Henry Parker, 1849), pp. 132–41; Worthington Hooker, *Physician and Patient* (New York: Baker and Scribner, 1849), pp. 357–82; Richard C. Cabot, "Teamwork of Doctor and Patient Through the Annihilation of Lying," in *Social Service and the Art of Healing* (New York: Moffat, Yard and Co., 1909), pp. 116–70; Charles C. Lund, "The Doctor, the Patient, and the Truth." *Annals of Internal Medicine* 24 (1946): 955; Edmund Davies, "The Patient's Right to Know the Truth." *Proceedings of the Royal Society of Medicine* 66 (1973): 533–36.

9. For the views of physicians, see Donald Oken, "What to Tell Cancer Patients." *Journal of the American Medical Association* 175 (1961): 1120–28; and tabulations in Robert [M.] Veatch. *Death, Dying, and the Biological Revolution* (New Haven and London: Yale University Press, 1976), pp. 229–38. For the view of patients, see Veatch, ibid.: Jean Aitken-Swan and E. C. Easson, "Reactions of Cancer Patients on Being Told Their Diagnosis." *British Medical Journal* (1959), pp. 779–83; Jim McIntosh, "Patients' Awareness and Desire for Information About Diagnosed but Undisclosed Malignant Disease," *Lancet* 7 (1976): 300–303; William D. Kelly and Stanley R. Friesen, "Do Cancer Patients Want to Be Told?." *Surgery* 27 (1950): 822–26.

10. See Avery Weisman, *On Dying and Denying* (New York: Behavioral Publications, 1972); Elisabeth Kübler-Ross, *On Death and Dying* (New York: Macmillan, 1969); Ernest Becker, *The Denial of Death* (New York: Free Press, 1973): Philippe Ariès, *Western Attitudes Toward Death*, trans. Patricia M. Ranum (Baltimore and London: Johns Hopkins University Press, 1974); and Sigmund Freud, "Negation," *Collected Papers*, ed. James Strachey (London: Hogarth, 1950), 5: 181–85.

11. Kübler-Ross, *On Death and Dying*, p. 34.

12. Michel de Montaigne, *Essays*, bk. 1, chap. 20.

13. It is in literature that these questions are most directly raised. Two recent works where they are taken up with striking beauty and simplicity are May Sarton, *As We Are Now* (New York: Norton, 1973); and Freya Stark, *A Peak in Darien* (London: John Murray, 1976).

14. Herman Feifel et al., "Physicians Consider Death," *Proceedings of the American Psychoanalytical Association*, 1967, pp. 201–2.

15. See Diogenes Laertius, *Lives of Eminent Philosophers*, p. 651. Epicurus willed his garden to his friends and descendants, and wrote on the eve of dying: "On this blissful day, which is also the last of my life, I write to you. My continual sufferings from strangury and dysentery are so great that nothing could augment them; but over against them all I set gladness of mind at the remembrance of our past conversation." (Letter to Idomeneus, Ibid, p. 549).

16. See Ivan Illich, *Medical Nemesis* (New York: Pantheon, 1976), for a critique of the iatrogenic tendencies of contemporary medical care in industrialized societies.

17. The law requires that inroads made upon a person's body take place only with the informed voluntary consent of that person. The term "informed consent" came into common use only after 1960, when it was used by the Kansas Supreme Court in *Nathanson* v. *Kline*, 186 Kan. 393, 350, p.2d, 1093 (1960). The patient is now entitled to full disclosure of risks, benefits, and alternative treatments to any proposed procedure, both in therapy and in medical experimentation, except in emergencies or when the patient is incompetent, in which case proxy consent is required.

18. See, for example, "Statement on a Patient's Bill of Rights," reprinted in Stanley Joel Reiser, Arthur J. Dyck, and William J. Curran, [eds.] *Ethics in Medicine* (Cambridge, MA, and London: MIT Press, 1977), p. 148.

19. See Ralph Alfidi. "Informed Consent: A Study of Patient Reaction," *Journal of the American Medical Association* 216 (1971): 1325–29.

20. See Steven R. Kaplan, Richard A. Greenwald, and Arvey I. Rogers, Letter to the Editor, *New England Journal of Medicine* 296 (1977): 1127.

21. Oken, "What to Tell Cancer Patients"; Veatch, *Death, Dying, and the Biological Revolution*; Weisman, *On Dying and Denying*.

22. Norman L. Cantor, "A Patient's Decision to Decline Life-Saving Treatment: Bodily Integrity Versus the Preservation of Life," *Rulgers Law Review* 26 (1973): 228–64; Danielle Gourevitch, "Suicide Among the Sick in Classical Antiquity," *Bulletin of the History of Medicine* 18 (1969): 501–18....

23. Lewis Thomas, "A Meliorist View of Disease and Dying," *Journal of Medicine and Philosophy*, 1 (1976): 212–21.

24. Claude Lévi-Strauss, *Structural Anthropology* (New York: Basic Books 1963), p. 167. See also Eric Cassell, "Permission to Die," in John Behnke and Sissela Bok, eds., *The Dilemmas of Euthanasia* (Garden City, NY: Doubleday, Anchor Books, 1975). pp. 121–31.

25. Aries, *Western Attitudes Toward Death*, p. 11.

26. Barbara S. Hulka, J. C. Cassel, et al. "Communication. Compliance, and Concordance between Physicians and Patients with Prescribed Medications," *American Journal of Public Health* (Sept. 1976), pp. 847–53. The study shows that of the nearly half of all patients who do not follow the prescriptions of the doctors (thus foregoing the intended effect of these prescriptions), many will follow them if adequately informed about the nature of their illness and what the proposed medication will do.

27. See Lawrence D. Egbert, George E. Batitt, et al., "Reduction of Postoperative Pain by Encouragement and Instruction of Patients," *New England Journal of Medicine* 270 (1964). pp. 825–27. See also Howard Waitzskin and John D. Stoeckle, "The Communication of Information About Illness." *Advances in Psychosomatic Medicine* 8 (1972), pp. 185–215.

Joseph Collins | # Should Doctors Tell the Truth?

Joseph Collins was a physician who wrote this now-classic article on physicians and truthfulness.

This is not a homily on lying. It is a presentation of one of the most difficult questions that confront the physician. Should doctors tell patients the truth? Were I on the witness stand and obliged to answer the question with "yes" or "no," I should answer in the negative and appeal to the judge for permission to qualify my answer. The substance of this article is what that qualification would be.

Though few are willing to make the test, it is widely held that if the truth were more generally told, it would make for world-welfare and human betterment. We shall probably never know. To tell the whole truth is often to perpetrate a cruelty of which many are incapable. This is particularly true of physicians. Those of them who are not compassionate by nature are made so by experience. They come to realize that they owe their fellow-men justice, and graciousness, and benignity, and it becomes one of the real satisfactions of life to discharge that obligation. To do so successfully they must frequently withhold the truth from their patients, which is tantamount to telling them a lie. Moreover, the physician soon learns that the art of medicine consists largely in skillfully mixing falsehood and truth in order to provide the patient with an amalgam which will make the metal of life wear and keep men from being poor shrunken things, full of melancholy and indisposition, unpleasing to themselves and to those

From the August 1927 issue by special permission of *Harper's Monthly Magazine*, vol. 155 (1927), pp. 320–6.

who love them. I propose therefore to deal with the question from a pragmatic, not a moral standpoint.

"Now you may tell me the truth," is one of the things patients have frequently said to me. Four types of individuals have said it: those who honestly and courageously want to know so that they may make as ready as possible to face the wages of sin while there is still time; those who do not want to know, and who if they were told would be injured by it; those who are wholly incapable of receiving the truth. Finally, those whose health is neither seriously disordered nor threatened. It may seem an exaggeration to say that in forty years of contact with the sick, the patients I have met who are in the first category could be counted on the fingers of one hand. The vast majority who demand the truth really belong in the fourth category, but there are sufficient in the second—with whom my concern chiefly is—to justify considering their case.

One of the astonishing things about patients is that the more serious the disease, the more silent they are about its portents and manifestations. The man who is constantly seeking assurance that the vague abdominal pains indicative of hyperacidity are not symptoms of cancer often buries family and friends, some of whom have welcomed death as an escape from his burdensome iterations. On the other hand, there is the man whose first warning of serious disease is lumbago who cannot be persuaded to consult a physician until the disease, of which the lumbago is only a symptom, has so far progressed that it is beyond surgery. The seriousness of disease may be said to stand in direct relation to the reticence of its possessor. The more silent the patient, the more serious the disorder.

The patient with a note-book, or the one who is eager to tell his story in great detail, is rarely very ill. They are forever asking, "Am I going to get well?" and though they crave assistance they are often unable to accept it. On the other hand, patients with organic disease are very chary about asking point blank either the nature or the outcome of their ailment. They sense its gravity, and the last thing in the world they wish to know is the truth about it; and to learn it would be the worst thing that could happen to them.

This was borne in upon me early in my professional life. I was summoned one night to assuage the pain of a man who informed me that he had been for some time under treatment for rheumatism—that cloak for so many diagnostic errors. His "rheumatism" was due to a disease of the spinal cord called locomotor ataxia. When he was told that he should submit himself to treatment wholly different from that which he had been receiving, the import of which any intelligent layman would have divined, he asked neither the nature nor the probable outcome of the disease. He did as he was counselled. He is now approaching seventy and, though not active in business, it still engrosses him.

Had he been told that he had a disease which was then universally believed to be progressive, apprehension would have depressed him so heavily that he would not have been able to offer the resistance to its encroachment which has stood him in such good stead. He was told the truth only in part. That is, he was told his "rheumatism" was "different"; that it was dependent upon an organism quite unlike the one that causes ordinary rheumatism; that we have preparations of mercury and arsenic which kill the parasite responsible for this disease, and that if he would submit himself to their use, his life would not be materially shortened, or his efficiency seriously impaired.

Many experiences show that patients do not want the truth about their maladies, and that it is prejudicial to their well-being to know it, but none that I know is more apposite than that of a lawyer, noted for his urbanity and resourcefulness in Court. When he entered my consulting room, he greeted me with a bonhornie that bespoke intimacy but I had met him only twice—once on the golf links many years before, and once in Court where I was appearing as expert witness, prejudicial to his case.

He apologized for engaging my attention with such a triviality, but he had had pain in one shoulder and arm for the past few months, and though he was perfectly well—and had been assured of it by physicians in Paris, London, and Brooklyn—this pain was annoying and he had made up his mind to get rid of it. That I should not get a wrong slant on his condition, he submitted a number of laboratory reports furnished him by an osteopath to show that secretions and excretions susceptible of chemical examinations were quite normal. His determination seemed to be to prevent me from taking a view of his health which might lead me to counsel his retirement. He was quite sure that anything like a thorough examination was unnecessary but he submitted to it. It revealed intense and extensive disease of the kidneys. The pain in the network of nerves of the left upper-arm was a manifestation of the resulting autointoxication.

I felt it incumbent upon me to tell him that his condition was such that he should make a radical change in his mode of life. I told him if he would stop work, spend the winter in Honolulu, go on a diet suitable to a child of three years, and give up exercise, he could look forward confidently to a recovery that would permit of a life of usefulness and activity in his profession. He assured me he could not believe that one who felt no worse than he did should have to make such a radical change in his mode of life. He impressed upon me that I should realize he was the kind of person who had to know the truth. His affairs were so diversified and his commitments so important that he *must* know. Completely taken in, I explained to him the relationship between the pain from which he sought relief and the disease, the degeneration that was going on in the excretory mechanisms of his body, how these were struggling to repair themselves, the procedure of recovery and how it could be facilitated. The light of life began to flicker from the fear that my words engendered, and within two months it sputtered and died out. He was the last person in the world to whom the truth should have been told. Had I lied to him, and then intrigued with his family and friends, he might be alive today.

———————

The longer I practice medicine the more I am convinced that every physician should cultivate lying as a fine art. But there are many varieties of lying. Some are most prejudicial to the physician's usefulness. Such are: pretending to recognize the disease and understand its nature when one is really ignorant; asserting that one has effected the cure which

nature has accomplished, or claiming that one can effect cure of a disease which is universally held to be beyond the power of nature or medical skill; pronouncing disease incurable which one cannot rightfully declare to be beyond cessation or relief.

There are other lies, however, which contribute enormously to the success of the physician's mission of mercy and salvation. There are a great number of instances in support of this but none more convincing than that of a man of fifty who, after twenty-five years of devotion to painting, decided that penury and old age were incompatible for him. Some of his friends had forsaken art for advertising. He followed their lead and in five years he was ready to gather the first ripe fruit of his labor. When he attempted to do so he was so immobilized by pain and rigidity that he had to forgo work. One of those many persons who assume responsibility lightly assured him that if he would put himself in the hands of a certain osteopath he would soon be quite fit. The assurance was without foundation. He then consulted a physician who without examining him proceeded to treat him for what is considered a minor ailment.

Within two months his appearance gave such concern to his family that he was persuaded to go to a hospital, where the disease was quickly detected, and he was at once submitted to surgery. When he had recovered from the operation, learning that I was in the country of his adoption, he asked to see me. He had not been able, he said, to get satisfactory information from the surgeon or the physician; all that he could gather from them was that he would have to have supplementary X-ray or radium treatment. What he desired was to get back to his business which was on the verge of success, and he wanted assurance that he could soon do so.

He got it. And more than that, he got elaborate explanation of what surgical intervention had accomplished, but not a word of what it had failed to accomplish. A year of activity was vouchsafed him, and during that time he put his business in such shape that its eventual sale provided a modest competency for his family. It was not until the last few weeks that he knew the nature of his malady. Months of apprehension had been spared him by the deception, and he had been the better able to do his work, for he was buoyed by the hope that his health was not beyond recovery. Had he been told the truth, black despair would have been thrown over the world in which he moved, and he would have carried on with corresponding ineffectiveness.

The more extensive our field of observation and the more intimate our contact with human activity, the more we realize the finiteness of the human mind. Every follower of Hippocrates will agree that "judgment is difficult and experience fallacious." A disease may have only a fatal ending, but one does not know; one may know that certain diseases, such as general paresis, invariably cause death, but one does not know that tomorrow it may no longer be true. The victim may be reprieved by accidental or studied discovery or by the intervention of something that still must be called divine grace.

A few years ago physicians were agreed that diabetes occurring in children was incurable; recently they held that the disease known as pernicious anemia always ended fatally; but now, armed with an extract from the pancreas and the liver, they go out to attack these diseases with the kind of confidence that David had when he saw the Philistine approach.

We have had enough experience to justify the hope that soon we shall be able to induce a little devil who is manageable to cast out a big devil who is wholly out of hand—to cure general paresis by inoculating the victim with malaria, and to shape the course of some varieties of sleeping sickness by the same means.

I am thankful for many valuable lessons learned from my early teachers. One of them was an ophthalmologist of great distinction. I worked for three years in his clinic. He was the most brutally frank doctor I have known. He could say to a woman, without the slightest show of emotion, that she was developing a cataract and would eventually be blind. I asked a colleague who was a coworker in the clinic at that time and who has since become an eminent specialist, if all these patients developed complete opacity of the crystalline lens.

"Not one half of them," said he. "In many instances the process is so slow that the patient dies before the cataract arrives; in others it ceases to progress. It is time enough for the patient to know

he has cataract when he knows for himself that he is going blind. Then I can always explain it to him in such a way that he does not have days of apprehension and nights of sleeplessness for months while awaiting operation. I have made it a practice not to tell a patient he has cataract."

"Yes, but what do you tell them when they say they have been to Doctor Smith who tells them they have cataract and they have come to you for denial or corroboration?"

"I say to them, 'You have a beginning cloudiness of the lens of one eye. I have seen many cases in which the opacity progressed no farther than it has in your case; I have seen others which did not reach blindness in twenty years. I shall change your glasses, and I think you will find that your vision will be improved.'"

And then he added, "In my experience there are two things patients cannot stand being told: that they have cataract or cancer."

There is far less reason for telling them of the former than the latter. The hope for victims of the latter is bound up wholly in early detection and surgical interference. That is one of the most cogent reasons for bi-yearly thorough physical examination after the age of forty-five. Should we ever feel the need of a new law in this country, the one I suggest would exact such examination. The physician who detects malignant disease in its early stages is never justified in telling the patient the real nature of the disease. In fact, he does not know himself until he gets the pathologist's report. Should that indicate grave malignancy no possible good can flow from sharing that knowledge with the patient.

It is frequently to a patient's great advantage to know the truth in part, for it offers him the reason for making a radical change in his mode of life, sometimes a burdensome change. But not once in a hundred instances is a physician justified in telling a patient point blank that he has epilepsy, or the family that he has dementia præcox, until after he has been under observation a long time, unless these are so obvious that even a layman can make the diagnosis. We do not know the real significance of either disease, or from what they flow—we know that so many of them terminate in dementia that the outlook for all of them is bad. But we also know that many cases so diagnosticated end in complete recovery; and that knowledge justifies us in with-holding from a patient the name and nature of his disorder until we are beyond all shadow of doubt.

Patients who are seriously ill are greedy for assurance even when it is offered half-heartedly. But those who have ailments which give the physician no real concern often cannot accept assurance. Not infrequently I have been unable to convince patients with nervous indigestion that their fears and concern were without foundation, and yet, years later when they developed organic disease, and I became really concerned about them, they assured me that I was taking their ailments too seriously.

There was a young professor whose acquaintance I made while at a German university. When he returned he took a position as professor in one of the well-known colleges for women. After several years he consulted me for the relief of symptoms which are oftentimes associated with gastric ulcer. It required no elaborate investigation to show that in this instance the symptoms were indicative of an imbalance of his nervous system. He refused to be assured and took umbrage that he was not given a more thorough examination each time that he visited me. Finally he told me that he would no longer attempt to conceal from me that he understood fully my reasons for making light of the matter. It was to throw him off the track, as it were. No good was to be accomplished from trying to deceive him; he realized the gravity of the situation and he was man enough to confront it. He would not show the white feather, and he was entitled to know the truth.

But the more it was proffered him, the greater was his resistance to it. He gave up his work and convinced his family and friends that he was seriously ill. They came to see me in relays; they also refused to accept the truth. They could understand why I told the patient the matter was not serious, but to them I could tell the facts. It was their right to know, and I could depend upon them to keep the knowledge from the patient and to work harmoniously with me.

My failure with my patient's friends was as great as with the patient himself. Fully convinced his back was to the wall, he refused to be looked upon as a lunatic or a hypochondriac and he decided to seek other counsel. He went from specialist to naturopath, from electrotherapist to Christian Scientist, from sanatorium to watering place and, had there been gland doctors and chiropractors in those days, he would have included them as well. Finally, he migrated to the mountains of Tennessee, and wooed nature. Soon I heard of him as the head of a school which was being run on novel pedagogic lines; character-building and health were the chief aims for his pupils; scholastic education was incidental. He began writing and lecturing about his work and his accomplishments, and soon achieved considerable notoriety. I saw him occasionally when he came north and sometimes referred to his long siege of ill-health and how happily it had terminated. He always made light of it, and declared that in one way it had been a very good thing: had it not been for that illness he would never have found himself, never have initiated the work which was giving him repute, happiness, and competency.

One summer I asked him to join me for a canoe trip down the Allegash River. Some of the "carrys" in those days were rather stiff. After one of them I saw that my friend was semi-prostrated and flustered. On questioning him, I learned that he had several times before experienced disagreeable sensations in the chest and in the head after hard manual labor, such as chopping trees or prying out rocks. He protested against examination but finally yielded. I reminded myself how different it was fifteen years before when he clamored for examination and seemed to get both pleasure and satisfaction from it, particularly when it was elaborate and protracted. He had organic disease of the heart, both of the valve-mechanism and of the muscle. His tenure of life depended largely on the way he lived. To counsel him successfully it was necessary to tell him that his heart had become somewhat damaged. He would not have it. "When I was really ill you made light of it, and I could not get you interested. But now, when I am well, you want me to live the life of a dodo. I won't do it. My heart is quite all right, a little upset no doubt by the fare we have had for the past two weeks, but as soon as I get back to normal I shall be as fit as you are, perhaps more so."

We returned to New York and I persuaded him to see a specialist, who was no more successful in impressing him with the necessity of careful living than I was. In despair, I wrote to his wife. She who had been so solicitous, so apprehensive, and so deaf to assurance during the illness that was of no consequence wrote, "I am touched by your affectionate interest, but Jerome seems so well that I have not the heart to begin nagging him again, and it fills me with terror lest he should once more become introspective and self-solicitous. I am afraid if I do what you say that it might start him off again on the old tack, and the memory of those two years frightens me still."

He died about four years later without the benefit of physician.

No one can stand the whole truth about himself; why should we think he can tolerate it about his health, and even though he could, who knows the truth? Physicians have opinions based upon their own and others' experience. They should be chary of expressing those opinions to sick persons until they have studied their psychology and are familiar with their personality. Even then it should always be an opinion, not a sentence. Doctors should be detectives and counsellors, not juries and judges.

Though often it seems a cruelty, the family of the patient to whom the truth is not and should not be told are entitled to the facts or what the physician believes to be the facts. At times, they must conspire with him to keep the truth from the patient, who will learn it too soon no matter what skill they display in deception. On the other hand, it is frequently to the patient's great advantage that the family should not know the depth of the physician's concern, lest their unconcealable apprehension be conveyed to the patient and then transformed into the medium in which disease waxes strong—fear. Now and then the good doctor keeps his own counsel. It does not profit the family of the man whose coronary arteries are under suspicion to be told that he has angina pectoris. If the patient can be induced to live decorously, the physician has discharged his obligation.

I recall so many instances when the truth served me badly that I find it difficult to select the best example. On reflection, I have decided to cite the case of a young man who consulted me shortly after his marriage.

He was sane in judgment, cheerful in disposition, full of the desire to attract those who attracted him. Anything touching on the morbid or "unnatural" was obviously repellent to him. His youth had been a pleasant one, surrounded by affection, culture, understanding, and wealth. When he graduated he had not made up his mind what he wanted to do in the world. After a year of loafing and traveling he decided to become an engineer. He matriculated at one of the technical schools, and his work there was satisfactory to himself and to his professors.

He astonished his intimates shortly after obtaining a promising post by marrying a woman a few years older than himself who was known to some of them as a devotee of bohemian life that did not tally with the position in society to which she was entitled by family and wealth. She had been a favorite with men but she had a reputation of not being the "marrying kind."

My friend fell violently in love with her, and her resistance went down before it. His former haunts knew him no more, and I did not see him for several months. Then, late one evening, he telephoned to say that it was of the greatest importance to him to consult me. He arrived in a state of repressed excitement. He wanted it distinctly understood that he came to me as a client, not as a friend. I knew, of course, that he had married. This, he confessed, had proved a complete failure, and now his wife had gone away and with another woman, one whom he had met constantly at her home during his brief and tempestuous courtship.

I attempted to explain to him that she had probably acted on impulse; that the squabbles of early matrimony which often appeared to be tragedies, were adjustable and, fortunately, nearly always adjusted.

"Yes," said he, "but you don't understand. There hasn't been any row. My wife told me shortly after marrying me that she had made a mistake, and she has told me so many times since. I thought at first it was caprice. Perhaps I should still have thought so were it not for this letter." He then handed me a letter.

I did not have to read between the lines to get the full significance of its content. It set forth briefly, concretely, and explicitly her reasons for leaving. Life without her former friend was intolerable, and she did not propose to attempt it longer.

He knew there were such persons in the world, but what he wanted to know from me was, Could they not, if properly and prudently handled, be brought to feel and love like those the world calls normal? Was it not possible that her conduct and confession were the result of a temporary derangement and that indulgent handling of her would make her see things in the right light? She had not alienated his love even though she had forfeited his respect; and he did not attempt to conceal from me that if the tangle could not be straightened out he felt that his life had been a failure.

I told him the truth about this enigmatic gesture of nature, that the victims of this strange abnormality are often of great brilliancy and charm, and most companionable; that it is not a disease and, therefore, cannot be cured.

In this instance, basing my opinion upon what his wife had told him both in speech and in writing, I was bound to believe that she was one of the strange sisterhood, and that it was her birthright as well as her misfortune. Such being the case, I could only advise what I thought might be best for their mutual and individual happiness. I suggested that divorce offered the safest way out for both. He replied that he felt competent to decide that for himself; all that he sought from me was enlightenment about her unnatural infatuation. This I had only too frankly given him.

Two days later his body with a pistol wound in the right temple was found in a field above Weehawken.

That day I regretted that I had not lied to him. It is a day that has had frequent anniversaries.

Ronald H. Stein

Lying and Deception for Counselors and Clients

Ronald H. Stein writes widely on the ethics of counseling.

One of the most fundamental ethical principles of an effective counselor–client relationship is veracity; the relationship builds upon an ethical bond of honesty, integrity, candor, and truthfulness. As a general rule, the relationship is seriously undermined when either of the parties engages in deception or lying.

Bok (1978) defines a lie as "any intentionally deceptive message which is stated" (p. 13). A lie may be either spoken or written. Regardless of the form it takes, there must be a clear intent by the author to deceive the person receiving the information. This form of lying is termed a "lie of commission" because an affirmative act has been committed. I will argue that there is another form of lying called the "lie of omission." This lie occurs when the counselor deliberately allows another person to believe that information is true when in fact the counselor knows it to be false. Intentionally allowing a client to believe something that the counselor knows to be false, and not bringing this fact to the client's attention, is as much a deliberate act of deception as a lie of commission.

Deception is a much broader category because it involves both intentionally deceptive statements and deceptive acts. Synonyms for deception include double-dealing, trickery, subterfuge, and fraud.

From *Ethical Issues in Counseling*, Prometheus, 1990.

Why do people lie and practice deception? The most common reason given is that those who lie are really performing an act of kindness. Consider the following case: You are a seventeen-year veteran counselor in an agency that serves infants and children who suffer from severe multiple physical handicaps. Two months ago the Smedleys registered their nine-month-old son, Bobby, on the advice and recommendation of a pediatrician. Bobby is the Smedleys' only child. You have had numerous occasions during the past two months to observe Bobby as well as discuss his case, on a regular basis with his physical therapist and the agency's consulting pediatrician. All who have observed Bobby conclude that not only is he severely physically handicapped but severely mentally retarded as well.

One day the Smedleys come to you and, during casual conversation, they remark that "it is tough to have a handicapped child." They have struggled at great length with the problem, not only between themselves but also with members of their family. The Smedleys have finally come to accept the fact that Bobby is severely physically handicapped. But the one thing they know they could never accept, and "thank God, will never have to accept," is the fact that he would be mentally retarded. They then turn to you in a questioning fashion and say, "Thank God, isn't it wonderful that he is not also mentally retarded."

How do you respond? You appear to have two options. First, confirm the parents' statement that, "yes, it is wonderful that he is not mentally retarded," or second, you could, with great skill, say to them that "we need to talk about this because, based upon our observations and our experience, your son appears to be mentally retarded, though it is too early to tell the extent of it."

You decide to lie to the Smedleys because you think it would be an act of kindness and, in your opinion, in the best interests of your clients. You reached this conclusion for the followings reasons: There is probably very little that the Smedleys can do to change the reality that their son is mentally retarded; therefore, living a little longer with this myth would not do any harm and certainly would not affect the development of the child. In fact, it may be good for the Smedleys to have a little longer to adjust to the situation that their baby is not normal and to have an opportunity to develop additional support systems to deal with this fact as well as to address the grief of the family members, which many times develops in situations such as this.

Also, perhaps it is not your job to tell them. Certainly, as the child gets older, it should become more obvious to the parents that their child is mentally retarded and, therefore, the best approach is for them to discover this for themselves. So, with a little luck, you should probably be able to dodge the problem altogether.

It might be argued that this case is similar to the act of kindness that causes one not to tell a dying patient that she is dying. Using similar reasoning, a counselor might decide not to tell a patient she is dying because it would not change the circumstances of her death. Also, it might be in the patient's best interest to let her enjoy her remaining time without being needlessly confused or caused unnecessary pain and suffering (Bok, 1978).

Letters of recommendation written on behalf of students and employees by counselors are often cited as another act of lying out of kindness (Bok, 1978). The reasoning runs something like the following: In this day and age there are only two types of recommendations—good recommendations and great recommendations. Since the system has become so inflated, the counselor feels obligated to compensate by supplying the client with an exaggerated recommendation. The counselor reasons that the lie is justified because he is only acting on the best interests of the student by "leveling the playing field."

Another explanation offered for why people lie is that it prevents harm. The best example of this is lying to an enemy in war. In this instance, the lie is justified because it saves lives and saves the country from some evil, in this case the enemy. For the counselor, there may be an occasion to lie to save a life. For example, a crisis intervention counselor or hotline operator may stretch the bounds of truth when a person calls and threatens suicide. The caller says he will carry out the act unless the counselor gets hold of the individual's parent. The counselor may deceive the caller into believing that the parent is being summoned while stealing precious moments necessary for the police to respond.

Another, less magnanimous reason for lying is to achieve personal gain. The counselor may exaggerate his credentials in a brochure soliciting clients for his consulting business. It is important to note that many times what is represented as a lie for the public good is, in reality, a lie for private gain. In the words of Bok (1978), "We cannot take for granted either the altruism or the good judgment of those who lie to us, no matter how much they intend to benefit us. We have learned that much deceit for private gain masquerades as being in the public interest" (p. 169).

Finally, fear is often given as a justification for lying. For example, a person may lie because he is afraid of what other people may think of him if he told the truth. This explanation is often used to justify exaggerations. Lies are often perpetrated out of fear; the consequences of telling the truth may be too great. We may lie to escape punishment for doing something wrong, or we may lie to escape involvement in an awkward or unpleasant situation.

Some counselors claim that it is not wrong to lie because they possess a certain professional license that frees them from ordinary moral constraints when they are in the service of clients. In essence, it is all right to lie if it improves the counseling relationship. In the words of a colleague who wished to remain anonymous, "Other professionals regard fabricated disclosures as merely a synthesis of life experiences tailored to a particular situation and, therefore, not deception but a method of enhancing communication in the counseling relationship."

One interesting point about lying and deception is that when the counselor chooses to lie rather than tell the truth, he feels morally obligated to defend his action to himself and/or to others. While the truth needs no defense (Bok, 1978), a lie always needs to be defended as just, right, or proper by providing adequate reasons. The reasons counselors offer for choosing to lie or use deception rather than telling

the truth are many and varied. First, since it is the job of the counselor to help the client, the counselor may decide to lie because the falsehood is in the best interest of the client. This is a "means/ends" argument, where the lie (the means) becomes justified by the result (the end) it creates. For example, a counselor might argue that he was justified in lying to a client if to do so helped the client deal with a problem or was in keeping with the counselor's higher obligation to protect the client's rights; for example, in protecting the client's right to confidentiality. Certainly we can think of cases where such justification is valid, such as in instances where a lie saves a life.

However, all too often this justification is used in cases where it is not clear that the end would not have resulted without the lie, or where the lie actually created more harm than good. Nonetheless, this justification is the most common rationale offered by counselors when confronted with having lied.

Other justifications offered in defense of lying include the argument that the agency or individual would not understand the information or would misuse it if provided; therefore, the counselor is justified in lying or withholding information. A parallel argument offered by counselors is that clients or parents really cannot handle the truth; therefore, the counselor is acting in their best interest (albeit paternalistically) by feeding them information that the counselor believes they can handle, i.e., a lie. Sometimes telling the truth is dismissed by the counselor on the grounds that it really will not do any good; therefore, it does not really matter. Conversely, counselors may justify lying because it does not cause harm. As Bok (1978) points out, it is naive and foolish to believe that lying does not cause harm.

Sometimes a justification for lying is offered on the grounds that the counselor has been forced into the situation. In this instance, we might hear such statements as, "Sure, I lied. What do you expect from me? I didn't want to get involved in the first place." Or, "Sure, I lied, but only because you made me do something that wasn't in my job description." In this justification, the counselor shifts the blame or guilt to the supervisor or colleague since, the counselor argues, it is permissible to lie when one has been mistreated or has had one's rights violated—i.e., as a result of coercion.

Finally, a justification may be offered in the form of using a lie to educate the victim or to get revenge: "It's all right to lie to a liar because he's only getting what he deserves."

The counselor may in fact lie or deceive on behalf of the client. These acts of deception usually take the form of letters of recommendation, reports to other agencies, parents, or reports to students. A counselor may also lie to or deceive his supervisor or employer regarding absenteeism, lack of productivity, or personal problems that affect job performance. Supervisors may lie to or deceive counselors when doing evaluations and in telling the counselors why the supervisor is upset.

THE HARM IN LYING AND DECEPTION

As we have seen, one of the justifications given by a person who lies or deceives is that the lie or deception has not caused any harm. Bok (1978) has identified a number of harms that result from lies and deceit. A lie hurts the liar by reducing the confidence of clients and peers. The counselor who lies fears getting caught. This fear produces vulnerability and could even lead to treachery or blackmail. Lies hurt, then, because they isolate the liar. A lie biases the counselor's judgment by making it appear as though lying is a viable option for extricating oneself from a tight spot. Eventually, greater risks are taken on the naïve assumption that one more lie will remove the danger.

Perhaps the most insidious effect of lying is the freedom it robs from the person on whom the lie is perpetrated. The liar's victims are unable to make choices for themselves according to the most accurate information available. They are unable to act as they would have wanted to act had they known the truth (Bok, 1978). In fact, the lie may cause a client to choose some detrimental course of action, which most probably would not have been chosen had the truth been known (Steininger et al., 1984).

Besides reducing one's range of choices, lying is coercive. It takes power away from the victim and gives it to the liar. Lying enables the perpetrator to manipulate the behavior of his victim. This is an excellent example of the old adage "Knowledge is power."

Finally, lying can undermine and destroy the counseling relationship and ultimately undermine the credibility of the profession of counseling in the public's eye.

It is not my intention to suggest that there are no circumstances in which it would be appropriate for the counselor to lie. Such a statement would be naïve and foolish. In fact, Bok (1978) offers a test to determine the circumstances in which it would be appropriate to lie rather than tell the truth.

When considering deception, counselors should ask themselves two questions: (1) Could a truthful alternative to lying be chosen? If so, then counselors should choose to tell the truth rather than lie. Engaging in a lie should be done only as a last resort (Bok, 1978). (2) What moral arguments can be made for and against the choice to lie in the specific situation? Counselors need to consider carefully the justifications put forth in defense of lying. They should ask themselves several important questions: Are these justifications adequate? Are they defensible? Do the arguments in favor of the lie clearly and convincingly outweigh those against the lie?

Finally, the decision to lie should only be made after applying Bok's "Test of Publicity," which requires that counselors ask what the public's reaction would be if society knew that counselors had chosen to lie over telling the truth, given the specific circumstances of some case. In a sense, Bok has suggested a reasonable-man standard to guide counselors in assessing the appropriateness of choosing to lie over telling the truth. If the public would accept and understand the choice to lie rather than tell the truth, then the counselor's decision to lie would be justified. "We must share the perspective of those affected by our choices, and ask how we would react if the lies we are contemplating were told to us. We must, then, adopt the perspective not only of liars but of those lied to; and not only of particular persons but of all those affected by lies—the collective perspective of reasonable persons seen as potentially deceived. We must formulate the excuses and the moral arguments used to defend the lies and ask how they would stand up under the public scrutiny of these reasonable persons" (Bok, 1978, p. 93).

REFERENCES

Bok, S. 1978. *Lying: Moral Choice in Public and Private Life*, New York: Pantheon Books.
Steininger M.: Newell, J. D.: and Garcia, L. T. 1984. *Ethical Issues in Psychology*, Homewood, Ill.: Dorsey Press.

Benjamin Freedman

Offering Truth: One Ethical Approach to the Uninformed Cancer Patient

Benjamin Freedman was a bioethicist at McGill University.

Medical and social attitudes toward cancer have evolved rapidly during the last 20 years, particularly in North America.[1,2] Most physicians, most of the time, in most hospitals, accept the ethical proposition that patients are entitled to know their diagnosis. However, there remains in my experience a significant minority of cases in which patients are never informed that they have cancer or, although informed of the diagnosis, are not informed when disease progresses toward a terminal phase. Although concealment of diagnosis can certainly occur in cases of other terminal or even nonterminal serious illnesses, it seems to occur more frequently and in more exacerbated form with cancer because of the traditional and cultural resonances of dread associated with cancer.

These cases challenge our understanding of and commitment to an ethical physician–patient relationship. In addition, they are observably a significant source of tension between health-care providers. When the responsible physician persists

in efforts to conceal the truth from patients, consultant physicians, nurses, social workers, or others may believe that they cannot discharge their functions responsibly until the patient has been told. Alternatively, when a treating physician decides to inform the patient of his or her diagnosis, strong resistance from family members who have instigated a conspiracy of silence may be anticipated.

This article outlines one approach, employed in my own ethical consultations and at some palliative care services or specialized oncology units. This approach, offering truth to patients with cancer, affords a means of satisfying legal and ethical norms of patient autonomy, ameliorating conflicts between families and physicians, and acknowledging the cultural norms that underlie family desires.

COMMON FEATURES OF CASES

Mrs A is a woman in her 60s with colon cancer, with metastatic liver involvement and a mass in the abdomen. She is not expected to survive longer than weeks. Other than a course of antibiotics, which she was just about to complete, no active treatment is indicated or intended. She is alert. She knows that she has an infection; her family refuses to inform her that she has cancer. The precipitating cause of the ethical consultation, requested by the newly assigned treating physician (Dr H), is his ethical discomfort with treating Mrs A in this manner.

When one is confronted with a case of concealment, it is worth wondering how it came about that everyone but the patient has been told of the diagnosis, so that similar situations may be avoided in the future. Often, a diagnosis is defined in the course of surgery and disclosed to waiting relatives; this may most appropriately be handled by a prior understanding with the patient, communicated to the family, as to whether and how much they will be told before the patient awakens. But there are at least two other major ways in which a situation of concealment might develop.

A patient might be admitted in medical crisis, at a time when he or she is obtunded and incapable of being informed of his or her condition and treatment options. Law and ethics alike require that the medical team inform and otherwise deal with the person who is most qualified to speak on the patient's behalf (usually, the next of kin), until the patient has recovered enough to speak for himself or herself. Unfortunately for this plan, though, a patient will often fail to cross, at one moment, the bright line from incompetent to competent. Consequently, patterns of communicating with the relative instead of with the patient may persist beyond the intended period. Such situations have their own momentum. Later disclosure to the patient will need to deal both with the burden of providing bad news and with the fact that this information has been concealed from the patient up to that point.

A second typical way in which concealment develops is the following. A patient with close family ties is always attended by a relative (commonly, spouse or child) at medical appointments. Before a firm diagnosis is established, that relative manages to elicit a promise from the physician not to tell the patient should the tests show that the patient has cancer. Faced with a distraught and deeply caring relative, the physician goes along, at least as a temporizing tactic, only to discover, as described above, how the situation develops its own inertia. The cycle may be broken in a number of ways. Sometimes the physician simply decides to call a halt to concealment; often the patient's care is transferred to another physician who has not been a party to the conspiracy, as had happened with Mrs A.

As clinical ethicist, I met with Dr H and the relevant family members (husband, daughter, and son). Most of the discussion was held with the son; the husband, a first-generation Greek-Canadian immigrant, knows little English and was at any rate somewhat withdrawn. As expected, they are a close family, deeply solicitous of the patient, and convinced that she will suffer horribly were she to be told she has cancer. They confirmed my sense that the Greek cultural significance of cancer equals death—something that in this case is in all likelihood true.

At this time the family was willing to sign any document we wanted them to, assuming all responsibility for the decision to conceal the truth from Mrs A. "Do us this one favor" was a plea that punctuated the discussion.

Although other factors, such as the context of treatment and the patient's own idiosyncratic personality, may cause the same kind of problem in communication, my experience suggests the situation is often, as here, mediated by cultural factors. As one text on ethnic factors in family counseling puts it, "Greek Americans do not believe that the truth shall make you free, and the therapist should not attempt to impose the love of truth upon them."[3] (And compare Dalla-Vorgia et al.[4]) I often find other immigrant families of Mediterranean or Near Eastern origin reacting similarly, for example, Italian families and those of Sephardic Jews who have immigrated from Morocco. In all cases, in my experience, there is a special plea on the part of families to respect their cultural pattern and tradition. Health-care providers often feel the force of this claim and its corollary: informing the patient would be an act of ethical and cultural imperialism. Moreover, the family not uncommonly feels strongly enough that legal action is threatened unless their wishes are respected. Mrs A's family, in fact, threatened to sue at one point when they were told that Mrs A's diagnosis would be revealed.

TELLING FAMILIES WHY THE PATIENT SHOULD BE INFORMED

By the time a clinical ethical consultation is requested, the situation has often become highly charged emotionally. In addition to the unpleasantness of threats of legal action, there may have been some physical confrontation.

> Mrs S was a Sephardic woman in her 70s with widespread metastatic seedings in the pleura and pericardium from an unknown primary tumor. Her family insisted that she not be informed of her diagnosis and prognosis. Suffering from a subjective experience of apnea, she was to have a morphine drip begun to alleviate her symptoms. The family physically expelled the nurse from the room. If their mother were to learn she was getting morphine, they said, she would deduce that her situation was grave.

Such aberrant behavior cannot fairly be understood without realizing that these families may be acting out of uncommonly deep concern for the well-being of the patient, as they (perhaps misguidedly) understand it. The health-care team shares the same ultimate goal, to care for the patient in a humane, decent, caring manner. This commonality can serve as the basis for continuing discussion, as in the above case of Mrs A, the Greek patient.

> Discussion with the family was long and meandering. The usual position of the health-care team was explained in some detail: patients in our institution are generally told their diagnosis; we are accustomed to telling patients that they have cancer, and we know how to handle the varied normal patient reactions to this bad news; patients do not (generally) kill themselves immediately on being told, or die a voodoo death, in spite of the family's fears and cultural beliefs about patient reaction to this diagnosis. Patients have a right to this information and may have the need to attend to any number of tasks pending death: to say goodbye, to make arrangements, to complete unfinished business. As her illness progresses, decisions will likely need to be made about further treatment, for example, of

infections or blockages that develop. Already, one of Mrs A's kidneys is blocked and her urine is backing up. If the mass should obstruct her other kidney, for example, should a catheter be placed directly into the kidney or not? These decisions of treatment management for dying patients are dreadful and should if possible be made by the patient, with awareness of her choices and prospects. In addition, Mrs A is very likely already suspicious that she is gravely ill, and we have no means of dealing with her fears without the ability to speak to her openly. Finally, the fears that the family expresses about the manner of informing her—"How can we tell our mother, 'You have cancer, it will kill you in weeks'"—are groundless: she must be told that she is very ill, but we would never advise telling her she has a period of x weeks to live—a statement that is never wise or medically sound—nor will we try to remove her hope.

The physician or other health-care provider may be primarily motivated by the ethical principle of respect for patient autonomy, grounding a patient's right to know of his or her situation, choices, and likely fate. Connected with this may be the correct belief that any consent to treatment that the patient provides without having an opportunity to learn the reason for that treatment is legally invalid. To be properly informed, consent must be predicated on information about the nature and consequences of treatment, which must in turn be understood in the context of the patient's illness. A patient cannot validly consent to the passing of a tube into the kidney without being informed that her urinary tract is blocked, or of the reason for that blockage.

These reasons, so determinative for the physician, often carry no weight with the family. In Mrs A's case, for example, the family pledged to sign anything we would like to free us of liability. Our response, that their willingness cannot affect either our moral or legal obligation, which vests in the patient directly, was similarly unpersuasive; nonetheless, it was a fact and had to be said.

The direct negative impact on the patient's care and comfort that results from her being left in the dark represents more in the way of common ground between family and health-care provider. It is often quite clear that failure to reveal the truth causes a variety of unfortunate psychosocial results. As in all such cases, we highlighted for Mrs A's family the strong possibility that she already suspects she is ill and dying of cancer but is unable to speak about this with them because all of us, in our concealment and evasions, had not given her "permission" to broach the topic. Mrs A is dying, but there are things worse than dying, for example, dying in silence when one needs to speak.

It is also important to emphasize to families that the patient may have "unfinished business" that the or she would like to complete. For example, after one of my earliest consultations of this nature, the patient in question chose to leave the hospital for several weeks to revisit his birthplace in Greece.

Finally, it is sometimes the case that the failure to discuss with the patient his or her diagnosis can directly result in inadequate or inappropriate medical care. Mrs S, above, was denied adequate comfort measures because the institution of morphine might tip her off to her condition. In another case, the son and daughter-in-law of a patient insisted that she not receive chemotherapy for an advanced but treatable blood cancer so that she would be spared the knowledge of her disease and the side effects of treatment. In such cases, great injury is added to the insult of withholding the truth from a patient. Often, it is this prospect that serves as the trigger to mobilize the health-care team to seek an ethical consultation.

OFFERING TRUTH TO THE UNINFORMED PATIENT WITH CANCER

A patient's knowledge of diagnosis and prognosis is not all-or-nothing. It exists along a continuum, anchored at one end by the purely theoretical "absolute ignorance" and at the other by the unattainable "total enlightenment." Actual patients are to be found along this continuum at locations that vary in response to external factors (verbal information, nonverbal clues, etc.) as well as internal dynamics, such as denial.

The approach called here "offering truth" represents a brief dance between patient and health-care provider, a pas de deux, that takes place within that continuum. When offering truth to the patient with cancer, rather than simply ascertaining that the patient is for the moment lucid, and then proceeding to explain all aspects of his or her condition and treatment, both the physician(s) and I attempt repeatedly to ascertain from the patient how much he or she wants to know. In dealing with families who insist that the patient remain uninformed, I explain this approach, a kind of compromise between the polar stances. I also explain that sometimes the results are surprising, as indeed happened with Mrs A.

In spite of all the explanations we provided to Mrs A's family of the many reasons why it might be best to speak with her of her illness, they continued to resist. Mrs A, the son insisted, would want all the decisions that arise to be made by the physicians, whom they all trusted, and the family itself.

If their assessment of Mrs A is correct, I pointed out, we have no problem. Dr H agrees with me that while Mrs A has a *right* to know, she does not have a *duty* to know. We would not force this information on her—indeed, we cannot. Patients who do not want to know will sometimes deny ever having been told, however forthrightly they have been spoken to. So Mrs A will be offered this information, not have it thrust on her—and if they are right about what she wants, and her personality, she will not wish to know.

Mrs A was awake and reasonably alert, although not altogether free of discomfort (nausea). She was told that she had had an infection that was now under control, but that she remains very ill, as she herself can tell from her weakness. Does she have any questions she wants to ask; does she want to talk? She did not. We repeated that she remains very ill and asked if she understands that—she did. Some patients, it was explained to her, want to know all about their disease—its name, prognosis, treatment choices, famous people who have had the disease, etc—while others do not want to know so much, and some want to leave all of the decisions in the hands of their family and physicians. What would she like? What kind of patient is she? She whispered to her daughter that she wants to leave it alone for now.

That seemed to be her final word. We repeated to her that treatment choices would need to be made shortly. She was told that we would respect her desire, but that if she changed her mind we could talk at any time; and that, in any event, she must understand that we would stay by her and see to her comfort in all possible ways. She signified that she understood and said that we should deal with her children. Both Dr H and I understood this as explicitly authorizing her children to speak for her with respect to treatment decisions.

The above approach relies on one simple tactic: a patient will be offered the opportunity to learn the truth, at whatever level of detail that patient desires. The most important step in these attempts is to ask questions of the patient and then listen closely to the patient's responses. Since the discussion at hand concerns how much information the patient would like to receive, here, unlike most physician-patient interchanges, the important decisions will need to be made by the patient.

Initiating discussion is relatively easy if the patient is only recently conscious and responsive; it is more difficult if a conspiracy of silence has already taken effect. The conversation with the patient might be initiated by telling him or her that at this time the medical team has arrived at a fairly clear understanding of the situation and treatment options. New test results may be alluded to; this is a fairly safe statement, since new tests are always being done on all patients. These conversational gambits signal that a fresh start in communication can now be attempted. (At the same time it avoids the awkwardness of a patient's asking. "Why haven't you spoken to me before?")

The patient might then be told that, before we talk about our current understanding of the medical situation, it is important to hear from the patient himself or herself, so that we can confirm what he or she knows or clear up any misunderstanding that

may have arisen. The patient sometimes, with more than a little logic, responds, "Why are you asking me what is wrong? You're the doctor, you tell me what's wrong." A variety of answers are possible. A patient might be told that we have found that things work better if we start with the patient's understanding of the illness; or that time might be saved if we know what the patient understands, and go from there; or that whenever you try to teach someone, you have to start with what they know. Different approaches may suggest themselves as more fitting to the particular patient in question. The important thing is to begin to generate a dynamic within which the patient is speaking and the physician responding, rather than vice versa. Only then can the pace of conversation and level of information be controlled by the patient. The structure of the discussion, as well as the content of what the physician says, must reinforce the message: We are now establishing a new opportunity to talk and question, but you as the patient will have to tell us how much you want to know about your illness.

The chief ethical principle underlying the idea that patients should be offered the truth is, of course, respect for the patient's personal autonomy. By holding the conversation, the patient is given the opportunity to express autonomy in its most robust, direct fashion: the clear expression of preference. Legal systems that value autonomy will similarly protect a physician who chooses to offer truth and to respect the patient's response to that offer; "a medical doctor need not make disclosure of risks when the patient requests that he not be so informed."[5] A patient's right to information vests in that patient, to exercise as he or she desires; so that a patient's right to information is respected no less when the patient chooses to be relatively uninformed as when full information is demanded.[6] This stance is entirely consistent with the recent adoption of the widely noted (and even more widely misconstrued) Patient Self-Determination Act.[7] The major innovation this entails has been to involve institutions in the process of informing patients of their rights. However, the Patient Self-Determination Act has not changed state laws about informed consent to treatment in any way,[8] and as such the basic question here addressed—a physician's responsibility to inform patients of their diagnoses—remains entirely unaffected.

When offering truth, we are forced to recognize that patients' choices should be respected not because we or others agree with those choices (still less, respected *only* when we agree with those choices), but simply because those are the patient's choices. Indeed, the test of autonomy comes precisely when we personally disagree with the path the patient had chosen. If, for example, patient choice is respected only when the patient chooses the most effective treatment, when respecting those choices we would be respecting only effective therapeutics, not the person who has chosen them.

Many physicians hold to the ideal of an informed, alert, cooperative, and intelligent patient. But the point of offering truth—rather than inflicting it—is to allow the patient to choose his or her own path. As a practical matter, of course, it could scarcely be otherwise. A physician with fanatic devotion to informing patients can lecture, explain, even harangue, but cannot force the patient to attend to what the physician is saying, or think about it, or remember it.

Families need to confront the same point. Ambivalence and conflict are often observed among family members concerning whether the patient who has not been informed "really" knows (or suspects, etc.), and by offering the patient the opportunity to speak, this issue may be settled. More fundamentally, though, the concealing family—which is after all characterized by deep concern for the patient's well-being—will rarely (has never, in my experience to date) maintain that even if the patient demands to know the truth, the secret should still be kept. The family rather relies on the patient's failure to make this explicit demand as his or her tacit agreement to remain ignorant. Families can be helped to see that there may be many reasons for the patient's failure to demand the truth (including the fact that the patient may believe the lies that have been offered). If the patient wishes to remain in a state of relative ignorance, he or she will tell us that when asked; and if the patient states an explicit desire to be informed,

families will find it hard to deny his or her right to have that desire respected.

Some families, naturally enough, suspect chicanery, that this approach is rigged to get the patient to ask for the truth. To them I respond that my experience proves otherwise: to my surprise and that of the physicians, some patients ask to leave this in the family's hands; to the surprise of families, some patients who seemed quietistic in fact strongly wish to be told the truth (which many of them had already suspected). We cannot know what the patient wants until we ask, I tell them, and we all want to do what the patient wants.

Having held the discussion, it is important to move on to its resolution as soon as possible.

> I met with Mrs S's children, together with a nurse, medical resident, and medical student, for about an hour and a half; the treating oncologist also made a brief appearance. The discussion featured a lengthy and eloquent exposition by the resident of why Mrs S needs to be spoken to, and a passionate and equally eloquent appeal by one son to respect the different culture from which they come. Finally, I introduced the idea that we offer her the truth, and then follow her lead. This was agreed to by the family, and I left.

The medical student thanked me some days later and told me the rest of the story. The tension that had existed between health-care team and family had largely dissipated; as the student put it, "People were able to look each other in the eye again." Mrs S was lucid but fatigued that evening; for that reason, and probably because they had already spent so much time talking at our meeting, the family delayed the agreed-on discussion. Unexpectedly, Mrs S did not survive the night.

CONCLUSION

The problem of the uninformed patient with cancer can be described in many different ways, for example, as faulty physician-patient communication; as an obstacle to good medical care; as a cause of stress among hospital staff; and as a failure to respect patient autonomy. A dimension at least as important as these, but rarely acknowledged, is the clash it may represent between diverse cultures and their basic moral commitments.

The approach presented above reflects an effort to maintain accepted standards of the physician-patient relationship while respecting the cultural background and requirements of families. This form of respect involves reasonable accommodation to these cultural expectations but should not be confused with uncritical acquiescence. The critical question is, perhaps, this: How should we react to a family that refuses to allow the patient an offering of truth, that maintains that discussion itself to be contrary to cultural norms? Under those circumstances, I believe the offering must be made notwithstanding family demands. My reasons have as much to do with my beliefs about the nature of ethnic and religious moral norms themselves as with the view that in cases of conflict, our public morality (as concretized in law) should prevail.

First, I believe that members of a cultural community are as prone to mistaking what their own norms require of them as we within the broader culture are to mistaking our own moral obligations. The norm of protecting the patient clearly requires rather than prohibits disclosure in some cases, including some described above, to prevent physical or psychological damage or to enable some final task to be consummated. All of the factors that we recognize sometimes to derange our own moral judgment—inertia, ill-grounded prejudices and generalizations, lack of the courage to confront unpleasant situations, and many more—may operate as powerfully in deranging the views of those from another culture. Their initial sense of what ethics require may, that is, be mistaken, from the point of view of their own norms as well as those of modern, Western, secular culture.

Second, even if a family's judgment of what their culture requires is accurate, we must not presume that a patient like Mrs A will choose, in extremis, to abide by her own cultural norms. Like any immigrant, she may have adopted the norms of broad society, or, acculturated to some lesser degree, she may act according to some hybrid set of values. Concretely, the offering of truth is about her diagnosis; symbolically, it is a process that allows her to declare her own preference regarding which norms shall be respected and how.

A last word is in order about the view implicit in this approach regarding the nature of a bioethical consultation. As these cases illustrate, patients, families, and health-care professionals come to a meeting from different moral worlds, as well as different backgrounds and biographies; and these worlds involve not simply rights and privileges, but duties as well. A successful consultation attempts to clarify on behalf of the different parties their own moral principles and associated moral commitments. It needs to proceed from the premise that all present ultimately share a common goal: the well-being of the patient.

REFERENCES

1. Oken D. What to tell cancer patients: a study of medical attitudes. *JAMA.* 1961;175:1120–1128.
2. Novack DH, Plumer R. Smith RL. Ochitil H, Morrow GR, Bennett JM. Changes in physicians' attitudes toward telling the cancer patient. *JAMA.* 1979;241:897–900.
3. Welts EP. The Greek family. In: McGoldrick MM, Pearce JK, Giordano J. *Ethnicity and Family Therapy.* New York, NY: Guilford Press; 1982:269–288.
4. Dalla-Vorgia P, Katsouyanni K, Garanis TN, et al. Attitudes of a Mediterranean population to the truth-telling issue. *J. Med. Ethics.* 1992;18:67–74.
5. *Cobbs v Grant*, 502 P2d 1 (Cal 1972) (a similar provision for a patient's right to waive being informed was established by the Supreme Court of Canada in *Reibl v Hughes* 2SCR 880 [1980]).
6. Freedman B. The validity of ignorant consent to medical research. *IRB Rev Hum Subjects Res.* 1982;4(2):1–5.
7. The Patient Self Determination Act, sections 4206 and 4751 of the Omnibus Reconciliation Act of 1990, Pub L 101–508.
8. McCloskey E. Between isolation and intrusion: the Patient Self Determination Act. *Law Med Health Care.* 1991;19:80–82.

Sue De Wine

Giving Feedback: The Truthful Consultant

Sue De Wine's book on consulting contains lots of helpful hints and strategies.

We all like to receive feedback but are afraid to ask for it. If I asked you "How am I doing?" you may really tell me and I may not like the answer! Feedback requires active listening and careful description of observed behavior. These two skills are the cornerstones to effective feedback and impactful interventions into human behaviors.

... Most of what the process consultant does when he or she intervenes with individuals or groups is to manage the feedback process. The consultant makes observations that provide information, asks questions that direct the client's attention to the consequences of the individual's behavior, and provides suggestions that have implicit evaluations built into them (i.e., any given suggestion implies that other things that have not been suggested are less appropriate than what has been suggested).

Feedback comes in two forms: information on a person's behavior, and information on what impact that behavior can have on others. Remember that the overall purpose of feedback is to help, not attack. When giving feedback, make sure you can answer *yes* to these questions:

Timing: Have I checked with the receiver to determine the best time and place to give feedback?

Motivation: Am I being supportive while giving the feedback rather than ridiculing and hurting the receiver?

Language: Am I using positive or neutral rather than derogatory statements?

Tone: Am I using a friendly and caring tone of voice?

Value: Is the feedback useful to the receiver rather than an outlet for my feelings, frustrations, or anger?

Focus: Am I focusing on actions rather than attitudes or personalities?

Specificity: Am I using specific examples of observed behavior?

Information: Am I giving a manageable amount of helpful information rather than overloading the receiver with more information than is necessary?

Questions: Have I asked the receiver questions to ensure that my feedback was clear and helpful?

When receiving feedback, check for *yes* answers to these questions:

Timing: Have I agreed to the time and place for receiving feedback?

Trust: Do I trust the giver to accurately present information concerning my behavior?

Nondefensiveness: Am I prepared to listen to the feedback, rather than argue, refute, or justify my actions?

Specificity: If feedback is vague, am I requesting specific behavioral examples?

Tone: Am I using a neutral rather than a defensive tone of voice?

Questions: Have I asked questions that clarify the feedback?

From Sue de Wine, *The Consultant's Craft* (Boston: Bedford/St. Martin's, 2001), pp. 307–314.

Feedback is best when it is asked for and when there is a need for impartial knowledge. The client has to understand the difference between wisdom, which is a personal attribute of an individual, and knowledge, which is gained from books and facts. It is the consultant's job to be honest, direct, and non-threatening.

Sometimes I am surprised at how willingly organizational members receive feedback. Just when I would expect defensiveness and denial, they admit the picture I am painting is on target.

One illustration of this occurred with a colleague, Elizabeth Bernett, when we worked with a healthcare organization. We conducted interviews and asked for written statements about what was preventing this group from moving forward and cooperating with each other.

Participants told Elizabeth and me some very negative examples of how this group was dysfunctional. Some of the traits attributed to the group included being distrustful, deceitful, uncompromising, and overly critical of each other. We decided we would take the plunge and list all of the statements made by the group. We expected resistance and defensiveness. When we finished describing the list of attributes there was a long pause, and then someone spoke up and said, "Yep, that's us." Another said, "Sure sounds like us, doesn't it?" Nods of heads and general agreement indicated they accepted this feedback. Now our task was to find out if they were ready to change some of these behaviors or would they resist change because somehow these behaviors suited their individual agendas.

TYPES OF FEEDBACK

There are a variety of methods to provide feedback, many of which cause defensiveness. The function of feedback is to describe another person's observable behavior, disclose your thoughts and feelings about that behavior, interpret motives, and prescribe specific remedies. These may be our objectives; however, my experience has been that when people are evaluated they often feel attacked and begin to defend themselves.

Feedback is a way of helping another person to consider changing his or her behavior. It is communication to a person (or group) that gives that person information about how she or he affects others. As in a guided missile system, feedback helps an individual keep his or her behavior "on target" and thus achieve individual goals.

People give three kinds of feedback to others:

Evaluative: observing the other's behavior and responding with one's critique of it. "You are always late for everything. You are undependable."

Interpretive: observing the behavior and trying to analyze why the person is behaving that way. "You are late to meetings. I think you are spreading yourself too thin—trying to do too many things at the same time, and consequently you don't do anything really well."

Descriptive: observing the behavior and simply feeding back to the person specific observations without evaluating them, but sharing with the person how her or his behavior affects the speaker. "At the meeting last week you were 30 minutes late, on Monday you came when the meeting was half over, and today you missed the first 45 minutes of the meeting. I am concerned about the information you are missing by not being here."

In the first example, *always* and *undependable* are evaluative terms and create a climate of defensiveness on the part of the receiver. Chances are the person isn't *always* late, and using an all-inclusive term like *always* serves only to make the person angry. The receiver then naturally looks for ways to refute the statement. "I wasn't late to the staff meeting on Friday! You're being unfair."

In the second example the observer is playing dime-store psychologist and trying to figure out why someone is behaving a certain way. Unless you are a trained psychologist, your business is not to analyze and interpret someone else's behavior. You don't know why someone acts a particular way. All you can observe is behavior. You can't observe attitudes, nor should you be critiquing them.

In descriptive feedback we are describing, as specifically as possible, what we have actually observed the individual doing. We present that factual information, without judging the rightness or wrongness of the behavior and without trying to figure out why the person may have behaved that way.

EFFECTIVE FEEDBACK

Feedback should describe problematic behavior that the receiver can correct. Ideally, it is offered in response to the receiver's request, but whether or not it is solicited, effective feedback should be timely, clear, and accurate.

Useful Content

We have already discussed why feedback is more useful if it is descriptive rather than judgmental. Describing one's reaction to problematic behavior leaves the individual free to use the feedback or not, as the individual sees fit. Avoiding judgmental language reduces the need for the receiver to react defensively. Specific observations are more convincing than general ones. To be told that one is inattentive will probably not be as useful as to be told that: "Just now when we were deciding how to assimilate new employees, you were reading your mail. It made me feel that you were not interested or involved in the discussion."

Effective feedback takes into account the needs of both the receiver and the giver of the feedback. Feedback can be destructive when it serves only the giver's needs and fails to consider the needs of the person on the receiving end. For example, I may need to complain about the lateness of a report. The report writer may not need to hear my complaints because she is already aware of the deadline and cannot change the fact that some missing data from another department prevented her from finishing it earlier. It may make me feel better to "blow off steam" but in this instance it may actually impede the other person's ability to complete the task.

Effective feedback is directed toward behavior that the receiver can change. Frustration is only increased when a person is reminded of some shortcoming over which she or he has no control. One receptionist was criticized for her high-pitched voice over the phone. She had actually worked with a speech therapist and had improved it as much as possible. To continue to criticize her for something she could not change was not helpful; in fact, it was harmful. If the problem was severe enough, then her supervisor should have discussed other career options, but simply to continue to provide feedback that the problem existed could do nothing to bring about change.

Feedback is most useful when it is solicited rather than imposed and when the receiver has formulated the kinds of questions that people observing can answer. Unfortunately, people don't ask for feedback often enough. Therefore, we should take advantage of those rare opportunities when someone does ask us to take the time to provide it. It is easy to miss opportunities because one may dismiss a request as superficial.

For example, someone recently asked me, "How are things going?" (referring to a project she was working on). I said, "Oh, just fine." Her response was, "No, I really mean, *how do you think things are going?*" Then I said, "Oh, you *really* want some feedback about your performance?" If the person had not persisted, I would have missed a very good opportunity to provide feedback about her work performance at a time when she was actually requesting it!

Timeliness

In general, feedback is most useful at the earliest opportunity after the given behavior has occurred (depending, of course, on the person's readiness to hear it and the support that is available from others). One of the most delayed examples of feedback I have witnessed occurred with two female trainers with whom I was working. We were designing a seminar and the two began discussing their earlier work together. Finally, one said, "Let's be sure we get straight what each person's role will be throughout the course of this seminar because we aren't always clear about how much we want someone to be involved." When she was asked to explain her point further, she described a workshop the two of them had designed in which she felt her talents were not fully used. In fact, she was unclear about the role she should take. I ended up being the mediator in this discussion, and I asked when this workshop had occurred only to discover it had been eight years earlier! Feedback that delayed is useless and unfair. It is unfair because the person who chose not to provide the feedback closer to the time the behavior occurred had been harboring resentment for a long time. Indirectly she may have been acting on that resentment in her behavior toward the other person, who could do nothing about it.

Another example of poor timing would be if I asked my husband, during a formal banquet, how he liked my new outfit. To actually give me straightforward feedback, which may have been negative, at that time would have been inappropriate. What I really wanted him to say was, "You look great" whether I did or not! Why? Because there was nothing I could do to correct my appearance at that moment. The next time I was selecting an outfit to wear or buying a new one, when I could make a reasonable decision about how to use this information, would be a more appropriate time to tell me the outfit makes me look unattractive (if he dares to tell me that at all!). To provide such criticism in the middle of a social event could make both of us miserable!

Clarity and Accuracy

One way of checking to ensure clear communication is to ask the receiver to rephrase the feedback to see if it corresponds to what the sender had in mind. In this way too, the sender is training the other person to provide descriptive feedback.

Both giver and receiver should have an opportunity to check with others about the accuracy of the feedback. Is this one person's impression or an impression shared by others? A teacher knows that an entire classroom of students will not always be happy with the way in which the class is structured. The teacher must therefore check for themes that exist among most of the students. When you get disturbing or confusing feedback, be sure to check it with co-workers and colleagues. "Have you ever noticed me behaving in this way…?"

Feedback, then, is a way of giving help; it is a corrective mechanism for the individual who wants to learn how well his or her behavior and intentions match and a means for establishing one's identity—for answering "Who am I?" Feedback can be informal or a formal evaluation process, like performance appraisal.

TIPS ON PROVIDING FEEDBACK

Negative feedback is misunderstood much more readily than positive feedback. Consequently, go slowly and be descriptive. I prefer never to put negative feedback in a memo. There are too many opportunities to misinterpret the language. I use memos for good news and face-to-face meetings for bad news. I want to be sure people have a chance to ask any questions they might have when I am telling them something they may not want to hear. However, once the negative information has been communicated face-to-face, follow-up written documents are absolutely necessary to maintain a "paper trail."

Positive feedback that is too general has little impact. We shouldn't assume when we tell employees that they're doing a "good job" that the information will positively affect their performance. If they don't know exactly what it is they did well, it is unlikely they will know what to continue doing! In fact, if the feedback is perceived as too general, it might also be interpreted as insincere.

Keep feedback impersonal. It is important that the person and the person's actions be separated in discussions. I can like the person, respect the person, but find a particular behavior unacceptable. I love my children deeply, but I dislike intensely their tendency to squabble with each other. It is their behavior I find distasteful, not their person. Thus, when you provide feedback, make it impersonal and attach it to a specific behavior, not to the personality of the individual with whom you are talking.

Tailor the feedback to fit the person. Some people appreciate receiving straightforward, direct feedback about their efforts. Others cannot tolerate such directness and need positive reinforcement before they are prepared to handle negative information. Others learn best by example. Still others must hear new information several times before they really listen.

Use humor when appropriate. Sometimes it is easier to tease someone and indirectly provide feedback. This works when the relationship is a good one: The humorous memo in the beginning of this chapter was sent anonymously to the president of a company. It would be great if the president had a sense of humor, recognized the criticism as valid, and responded with his own humorous memo (I can imagine a variety of scenarios!). However, many top-level executives might not be able to handle such forms of feedback. In another organization, a short story written about the head of the unit satirized a recent series of decisions (or lack of them!). The story was never mentioned by the unit head in public. In private he

expressed his inability to accept the feedback in that form.

Sometimes subtlety works best. There are times when direct confrontation over an issue is not the best approach. You may be calling too much attention to a problem others can then trivialize. For example, one woman who was constantly asked to take the minutes at executive meetings simply placed the memo pad in front of the senior member's chair at the next meeting, and then offered to provide him with a pen so he could take the minutes at that meeting. He got the message without her having to make a big deal out of the issue and began rotating this secretarial function among all present.

We know who we are by "bumping up against" other people. Their feedback helps shape our identity, self-esteem, and self-concept. The more feedback we provide for others, the better they are able to perform. The more we *ask* for feedback from others about ourselves, the clearer image we have of how others see us.

Burton M. Leiser

Truth in the Marketplace

Burton M. Leiser was a philosophy professor at Pace University.

FALSE CLAIMS OF EFFECTIVENESS

An ad in a magazine directed at the teenage market carries a picture of a young girl whose tears are streaming down her cheeks. "Cry Baby!" the ad proclaims.

> That's right, cry if you like. Or giggle. You can even pout. Some things you can do just because you're a woman. And, also because you're a woman, you lose iron every month. The question is, are you

putting that iron back? You may be among the 2 out of 3 American women who don't get enough iron from the food they eat to meet their recommended iron intake. ... But One-A-Day Brand Multiple Vitamins Plus Iron does. ... One-A-Day Plus Iron. One of the things you should know about, because you're a woman.

Two claims, at least, are made or implied by this advertisement. The first is that most American women do not get enough iron in their diets to make up for the "deficiency" that results from menstruation. The second is that One-A-Day tablets will fill the gap. As for the first claim, the American Medical

From *Liberty, Justice, and Morals: Contemporary Value Conflicts*, 2nd ed. (New York: MacMillan, 1979). pp. 279–97.

Association pointed out long ago that "the average diet of Americans is rich in iron." This statement was made during the AMA's campaign against Ironized Yeast, which also claimed to offer beneficial results from the Vitamin B that was included in its compound. The AMA showed that Vitamin B was found in sufficient quantities in the average American diet to require no special supplement.[1] Now, if there is no significant lack of iron in the average person's diet (and this includes the average woman), there is no deficiency for One-A-Day tablets to fill. To be sure, some Americans do suffer from a lack of certain vitamins and minerals because they do not have an adequate diet. But the answer to this is not for them to take One-A-Day pills, but to eat more nutritious food.

Prior to 1922, Listerine had been advertised as "the best antiseptic for both internal and external use." It was recommended for treating gonorrhea and for "filling the cavity, during ovariotomy." During the years that followed, it was also touted as a safe antiseptic that would ward off cold germs and sore throat, and guard its users against pneumonia. Mothers were urged to rinse their hands in Listerine before touching their babies, and, after prayers, to "send those youngsters of yours into the bathroom for a goodnight gargle with Listerine." During the Depression the promoters of Listerine warned those who had jobs to hold on to them. To do that it was necessary to "fight colds as never before. Use Listerine."[2] Gerald B. Lambert, a member of the family that manufactured the product, told how Listerine came to be advertised as a mouthwash. He was deeply in debt, and, needing some cash to bail himself out, he decided to move into the family business. In discussing the advertising of the mixture, his brother asked whether it might be good for bad breath. Lambert was shocked at the suggestion that "bad breath" be used in advertising a respectable product. In the discussion that followed, the word *halitosis*, which had been found in a clipping from the British medical journal *Lancet*, was used. The word was unfamiliar to everyone at the meeting, but immediately struck Lambert as a suitable term to use in a new advertising campaign.

The campaign caught on, Lambert paid off his debt, and in eight years made $25 million for his company.[3]

Now, how effective is Listerine for the ailments it claimed to cure? The AMA pointed out that the manufacturers of these antiseptics exaggerated the germ-killing powers of their products, that they did not tell of the hazardous germs that were not affected by Listerine, and that they failed to mention that the ability of a compound to kill germs in a test tube or on a glass plate in the laboratory is no indication of its capability of killing them in the mouth, the teeth, the gums, or the throat, let alone in other parts of the body.[4]

When a false claim of effectiveness is made, it is claimed that a product (treatment, remedy, or whatever) does X, when in fact that product does not do X. This is true of all false claims of effectiveness. But if a product does not do X, it does not follow that it does nothing else. Some products may do nothing: they may give the consumer no benefit, but at the same time do him no harm, other than the financial loss that he has suffered by buying the product. But some products may have *harmful* effects that are ignored in the promotional literature or advertisements that prompt people to buy them. Listerine may be harmless, though it will not prevent colds. Hoxsey's pastes[5] and many other preparations were (and are) harmful. Clearly, though the promoters of both Listerine and Hoxsey's treatments are guilty of false and misleading advertising, there is a further element of guilt in Hoxsey's kind of operation.

Still, the abuses go on, by some of the most respected firms in the food and drug line. In one recent year, the Food and Drug Administration seized shipments of Peritrate SA, a drug prescribed for the massive chest pain of the heart condition known as angina pectoris (Warner-Chilcott Laboratories); Serax, a tranquillizer (Wyeth Laboratories); Lincocin, an antibiotic (Upjohn); Lasix, a diuretic (Hoechst Pharmaceuticals); and Indoklon, an alternative to electroshock in some cases of depression (Ohio Chemical and Surgical Equipment Company)—all for false and deceptive promotion directed to the medical profession. Ayerst Laboratories was required by the FDA to send a "corrective letter" to some 280,000 doctors, retracting a claim that Atromid-S had a "beneficial effect" on heart disease, and the FDA ruled that Searle, Mead-Johnson, and Syntex had sent literature to physicians that misleadingly minimized the hazards of their birth control pills (Ovulen-21, Oracon, Norquen, and Norinyl-1).[6]

Unfortunately, moral suasion is not enough. Many persons, whatever their line of work, are not sufficiently resistant to the temptation to profit at the expense of others, and they are not touched by the moral arguments that might be brought to bear against their practices. One of the state's principal functions is the protection of its citizens against harm that might be done to them by others, even when they are unwitting collaborators in doing harm to themselves. It is the government's duty to require all hazardous substances to be labeled as such, so that everyone can see for himself what dangers he might expose himself to by ingesting them. It is no infringement on the citizen's freedom for the government to require of manufacturers of poisons that they clearly label their products with a warning that everyone may recognize. And the government is not interfering unreasonably with drug manufacturers when it demands that they print only scientifically verifiable facts in the literature that they distribute to the physicians who may be prescribing those products for their patients' use. Nor is it an unconscionable denial of freedom for the government to prevent persons who claim to cure diseases from practicing upon others unless they can offer some proof that the "cures" they offer are efficacious. For the government's right to protect its citizens against physical assault has never been questioned, and the purveyors of false and misleading information about harmful substances are as surely guilty of assault (if not in the legal sense, then at least in the moral sense) as they would have been had they poured their poisons into their victims' morning coffee. To argue that because the consumer has a choice and does not have to buy the product or use it, he is responsible for whatever happens to him, is like arguing that the poison victim had the choice of not drinking his coffee, and that by lifting the cup to his lips, he absolved the poisoner of all responsibility. The law has long maintained that a person who harms another is responsible for the harm that he does, even if he did so at the victim's request and with his active assistance. When a man is seeking relief from pain or illness and in that search relies upon the statements and claims made by drug salesmen, he is certainly entitled to no less protection than is offered to one who is determined to commit suicide.

THE PROMOTION OF DANGEROUS PRODUCTS

Any person who urges another to purchase and use a product or service assumes a responsibility toward him. The advertiser is not merely an innocent middleman who conveys a message from one person to another. He helps to create the message, using all the specialized skills of his art to persuade the potential consumer to act favorably upon his appeal. He shares in the rewards of successful advertising campaigns. He therefore assumes a responsibility for the product he induces the customer to purchase. In particular, if the product is dangerous or harmful, the advertiser who has persuaded the consumer to use it shares responsibility with the manufacturer for any harm that may result. This responsibility ought to be enforced by law, both with penal sanctions when the harm is particularly great and with appropriate remedies in tort. It is in any case a moral responsibility, for were it not for the advertiser's intervention, the consumer might never have suffered the damage done to him by the product he purchased.

By the same token, the advertiser has a right to feel . . . that he has contributed to the well-being of those who have been well served by the products and services he has helped to market. For every potential moral wrong that a person might commit, there must be an equivalent moral good that he might perform.

Those advertising agencies who have worked with the American Cancer Society to produce messages that have helped to persuade people to give up smoking or to refrain from becoming smokers have performed an important public service. Any utilitarian assessment of their performance would almost surely conclude that they had contributed to human happiness and significantly reduced the amount of pain and suffering in the world. Other advertising campaigns have assisted humanitarian organizations to raise funds for their operations and to further their causes. The government has employed advertising to discourage harmful behavior and to encourage beneficial activities. For example, during World War II, numerous ads reminded workers of the dangers inherent in talking about matters that might have helped the enemy and discouraged absenteeism at a time when the nation needed a steady supply of war matériel to carry its war effort to a successful conclusion. Similarly, advertising campaigns mounted by heavily overpopulated nations have had some effect in encouraging their citizens to employ contraceptive devices so as to bring population growth down to a manageable level. The agencies that have helped to mount such campaigns can justly take pride in their work, for it is reasonable to believe that they have contributed to the sum of human happiness through their efforts.

On the other hand, some products that are heavily advertised are known—or ought to be known by those who market them—to be dangerous and capable of inflicting grave injuries upon those who use them. For example, Ultra Sheen Permanent Creme Relaxer is an emulsion used by consumers and professional beauticians to straighten curly hair. Ads represented it as "gentle" and "easy" to use. A woman in a television commercial for the product said that it "goes on cool while it really relaxes my hair. And the Conditioner and Hair Dress protects against moisture, so my hair doesn't go back." But the FTC found that Ultra Sheen's active ingredient was sodium hydroxide—lye—which straightens hair "by breaking down the cells of the hair shaft.... In some instances, [it] makes it brittle and causes partial or total hair loss." Moreover, the FTC found that

it was neither cool nor gentle, but is "a primary skin irritant. It is caustic to skin and breaks down the cells which form the epidermis. Ultra Sheen relaxer in some instances causes skin and scalp irritation and burns, which may produce scars and permanent follicle damage. It also causes eye irritation and may impair vision." Because direct contact with eyes, scalp, or skin could cause irritation or injury, the FTC found that the product was not easy to use, contrary to the claims expressed in the ads. The FTC accordingly ordered the respondents to warn their customers of the product's dangers, to inform them of the presence of lye in it, to stop misrepresenting it, and to give clear instructions as to procedures to be followed in the event of injury to the customer.[7]

The law has for a long time recognized the duty a manufacturer owes to the purchaser of his product, particularly when the product is inherently dangerous. This duty has gradually been extended to others involved in the distribution and marketing of inherently dangerous products, so that persons and firms who retail automobiles, firearms, explosives, and poisons (for example) can be held liable in tort for damage caused by products that result from defects or negligence in the way they are labeled or handled.[8] At the very least, one would expect a warning to appear on the label of any product whose use might result in serious physical injury. The advertising and mass marketing of products that are prone to cause grave injury is a questionable practice.

This is not to say that dangerous products, including poisons, should not be sold. In the fifth chapter of *On Liberty*, John Stuart Mill argued that people ought to be permitted to purchase poisons, but that merchants who sold such substances were under a moral obligation (which should be a legal obligation as well) to label such substances clearly so that those who purchase them will know what they are buying. Mill's label rule should be extended to advertisements, because the decision to purchase a product is often made soon after an advertisement is seen. The product's hazards should be prominently displayed in advertisements so that the potential consumer may know what he or she is buying before the purchase is made....

MISLEADING STATEMENTS OR CONTEXTS

Campbell Soup Company sponsored a television commercial that showed a thick creamy mixture that the announcer suggested was Campbell's vegetable soup. Federal investigators discovered that the bowl shown in the commercial had been filled with marbles to make it appear thicker than it really was and to make it seem to contain more vegetables than it did. Max Factor promoted a wave-setting lotion, Natural Wave, by showing how a drinking straw soaked in the lotion curled up. The FTC pointed out, however, that it did not logically follow that human hair would react as drinking straws did. The implication left in the viewer's mind, therefore, was false, because, in fact, straight hair did not curl after being soaked in Natural Wave. Such visual trickery is quite common in television commercials, in newspaper and magazine advertisements, in direct mail advertisements, and on package labels.

Misleading statements are also very common. Some agencies have advertised for talented men and women, and especially for children, who would be given an "excellent chance" of being put to work doing television commercials "at no fee." The agencies seldom placed anyone, and, though they charged no fees, they sent their clients to photographers who charged them substantial fees for taking their publicity pictures, or referred them to a firm that took "screen tests," also for lots of money. The photographers were always closely allied with the agencies, and the latter always shared a very healthy proportion of the fees charged.[9]

In none of these cases could one say that false statements were made. Strictly speaking the advertisers were not guilty of lying to the public, if lying is defined as the deliberate utterance of an untrue statement. For, taken literally, none of the statements made in these advertisements is untrue. But the messages of the ads are misleading. Because of the pictorial matter in them, the reader or viewer makes inferences that are false, and the advertiser juxtaposes those pictures with the narrative in such a way that

false inferences *will* be made. It is through those false inferences that he expects to earn enough money to pay for the ad and to have something left over for himself.

The land promoter who sends a glossy pamphlet advertising his "retirement city" in Arizona may not make a single false statement in the entire pamphlet. But by filling it with beautiful color photographs of swimming pools, golf links, and lush vegetation, none of which exists within 100 miles of the land he is selling, he leads his prospects to believe that certain features exist within that area which do *not* exist. Thus, without uttering or printing a single false statement, he is able to lead his prospects to believe what he knows is not true.

CONCEALMENT OF THE TRUTH

Merchants and producers have many ways of concealing truth from the customers—not by lying to them, but simply by not telling them facts that are relevant to the question of whether they ought to purchase a particular product or whether they are receiving full value for their money. An example that occurred a few years ago involved ham. Major packers, including Swift, Armour, and others, were selling ham that was advertised as being particularly juicy. The consumer was not told, however, that the hams were specially salted and that hypodermic syringes were used to inject large quantities of water into them. The "juice" was nothing but water that evaporated during cooking, leaving a ham some 40 percent smaller than the one that had been put into the oven. The housewife purchasing such a ham had no advance warning that she was purchasing water for the price of ham, unless she knew that the words *artificial ham* that were printed in small letters on the seal of the package meant that that was the case. Even that small warning was added only because of pressure brought to bear against the packers by the FTC. And there was no publicity to arouse the consumer to the special meaning of the term *artificial ham*.[10] . . .

A burglar or a thief may be heavily fined or sent to jail for many months for stealing a relatively small amount of money or valuables from a single person. But a salesman who cheats hundreds of people out of equal sums of money that total, in the aggregate, hundreds of thousands of dollars, is immune to prosecution, and may, in fact, be one of the community's most respected citizens. If Armour and Swift and other large corporations can bilk their customers out of enormous sums of money and do it with impunity, why, one might ask, should the petty thief be subjected to such severe penalties?

THE DUTY TO TELL THE WHOLE TRUTH

The advertising agency is hired by a firm to sell that firm's products. By signing a contract, it undertakes an obligation to do its utmost to fulfill that goal. Acceptance of that charge does not, however, relieve employees of the agency of their duties as citizens or as human beings. Their immediate goal as advertising men may be to obtain accounts and to keep them by increasing the customer's sales, but that goal should never be achieved at the expense of harm to unsuspecting persons. The duty not to direct advertising to children is related to this moral obligation, as is the duty to label hazardous substances with clear and unmistakable warnings. Such moral obligations may not be enforced by the law. Persons who are concerned with doing what is right need not set the limits of their conduct at the bounds delineated by the law, for the law does not always conform with standards of moral right. To be more specific, if the law permits an advertiser to refrain from mentioning a particular hazard that his product poses to his customer, it does not follow that he has a moral right to withold that information from them. If the law provides no sanctions against deceptive advertising, an ethical advertiser will nevertheless not engaged in willful deception of those who place their trust in him.

In a broad view of advertising, the small leaflets that are enclosed in the boxes in which drugs are packed may be regarded as advertisements of a sort. They contain technical information for the doctor's reference and are designed to prevent improper use of the drug. But they are also designed to influence physicians to use drugs for certain medical conditions, and may therefore be regarded as at least partially intended to serve as marketing devices.

A recent study revealed that certain drugs are advertised and packaged in Latin America in ways that the FDA would condemn (or has condemned) as unacceptable in the United States. Winstrol, a synthetic derivative of testosterone, is considered too toxic in the United States for all but the narrowest use. The AMA warns that such drugs "should not be used to stimulate growth in children who are small but otherwise normal and healthy." But in Latin America, Winstrol is widely promoted as an appetite stimulant for underweight children. A spokesman from the Winthrop Drug Company complained that the advertising was quoted out of context and that the company complied with the laws and medical practices of each country in which it did business.

Another Winthrop product, Commel (dipyrone), is a painkiller that may cause fatal blood diseases and may not be sold in the United States as a routine treatment for pain, arthritis, or fever. According to the AMA, the "only justifiable use [of dipyrone] is as a last resort to reduce fever when safer measures have failed." But a packet of the drug purchased in Brazil recommends that the drug be used for "migraine headaches, neuralgia, muscular or articular rheumatism, hepatic and renal colic, pain and fever which usually accompany grippe, angina, otitis, and sinusitis, toothache, and pain after dental extractions." The company's comments about the matter were as evasive as they were about Winstrol.

E. R. Squibb & Sons' Raudixin, which is occasionally used in this country to treat high blood pressure, was found to induce such deep depressions that hospitalization was often necessary, and suicide sometimes followed. But in Brazil, the package insert says it is the "ideal medicine for the treatment of emotional disturbances such as states of tension and anxiety, and in states characterized by nervousness, irritability, excitability and insomnia. . . . Raudixin is the drug of choice in daily practice." A company spokesman acknowledged that the insert had been written 20 years ago, conceded that the insert had not been rewritten in 20 years, but insisted that it complied with Brazilian drug regulations.

The aim of drug companies' ads, and even of their package inserts, is not so much to inform physicians of the uses and potential hazards of their products as to persuade them to prescribe them. When forced to do so by government regulations, they will write truthful and informative inserts, but when government regulations are lax, they will subject the public to needless hazards and rationalize their conduct by claiming that they are doing nothing unlawful. This not only is morally unacceptable but should be legally proscribed. Those who believe in minimal government interference in private affairs would prefer to see government regulations of all industries, including the drug industry, reduced as much as possible. But so long as an industry behaves irresponsibly and endangers the lives and health of the persons it is supposed to serve, the public has no alternative but to rely upon government for protection.

THE FORM OF THE ADVERTISEMENT

. . . Some firms advertise a product as if it were on sale at a reduced price when, in fact, the product never sold at the so-called regular price. A paint manufacturer, for example, advertised: "Buy I gallon for $6.98 and get a second gallon free." But it *never* sold its paint at $6.98 per gallon.

Encyclopedia salesmen sometimes misrepresent themselves as agents for school boards or as public opinion pollsters. They offer "free" sets of encyclopedias, allegedly as a public relations "service," but ask for a small monthly charge for a ten-year research service that will presumably guarantee the worried customer's children their places in medical school or law school.

Record clubs and book clubs falsely advertise "free" books which are not free at all but are consideration for a binding contract to purchase a number of books at a supposedly reduced price which, after postage and handling charges are added, is often higher than the retail price of the same books. The "club" members are customers and the "clubs" are profit-making businesses.

Insurance companies and other firms use photographs or drawings of impressive buildings in their ads and on their stationery to suggest that they are large, long-established firms, even though they may occupy no more than a single office. One firm recently hung its own sign on a large, modern municipal government building and filmed its commercials in front of the disguised structure, leaving the impression that its own offices were housed there.

Small-size type may be used to obscure limitations on insurance coverage, and bold type may emphasize irrelevant facts, such as coverage that is common to all policies of a given class.

Misleading words and phrases—particularly those having special technical meanings that are unfamiliar to the uninitiated—are used to create false impressions in the minds of laymen. Ordinary language may be used in such a way as to suggest to the uninitiated that certain conditions apply when they do not apply at all. For example, an ad saying, "This policy will pay your hospital and surgical bills" suggests (though it does not literally say) that *all* of the hospital and surgical bills of the insured will be paid; and "This policy will replace your income" suggests that *all* of the insured's income will be replaced if he becomes disabled—when, in fact, only a small portion of his bills or his income will be paid or replaced.

Some companies don't hesitate to make inconsistent claims for competing products that they manufacture or distribute. The Sterling Drug Company, for example, distributes Bayer aspirin in the United States and also manufactures Vanquish. In 1970, the company was simultaneously running ads that made the following claims:

> For Bayer: "Aspirin is already the strongest pain reliever you can buy." Combining Bayer with other drugs or buffering it would not improve it. "No one has ever found a way to improve Bayer Aspirin, because Bayer Aspirin is 100% Aspirin. None is faster or more effective than Bayer Aspirin. Even WE can't improve it though we keep trying."
>
> For Vanquish:.It has "a unique way" of relieving headache "with extra strength and gentle buffers.... It's the only leading pain reliever you can buy that does."

Thus, Sterling Drug is both unable and able to produce a pain reliever that is more effective than Bayer. Buffering doesn't and does add to the strength or gentleness of aspirin.[11]

Another device is the half-truth which becomes an outright lie because it creates a completely false impression. Excedrin, for example, ran an ad reporting that a "major hospital study" showed that "it took more than twice as many aspirin tablets to give the same pain relief as two Excedrin." But the ad failed to point out that the Excedrin tablets contained twice as much aspirin as plain aspirin tablets and that another study had demonstrated that Excedrin had caused more intestinal upset than two brands of aspirin when given in equal doses.[12]

Although most of these examples have been derived from studies of the drug industry, that industry has no monopoly on deceptive advertising practices. Similar examples can be cited from industries as diverse as automobiles, lumber, oil, household cleaning products, and real estate. Unscrupulous and deceptive practices in many industries have caused severe financial losses to unsuspecting individuals. Even when the individual's loss is relatively small, collectively the damage may amount to hundreds of millions of dollars. With these financial losses there are inevitably other costs that are more difficult to assess, not the least of which is the emotional damage, the anger, and the resentment that must follow when the loss represents a major portion of an individual's earnings or savings. Some of this undoubtedly spills over into resentment against a system that permits what the victims perceive to be grave injustices against themselves and the classes or groups to which they belong. Advertising alone cannot be held responsible for any social dislocations that might result from such resentments, but the advertising industry cannot wholly escape responsibility for its contributions to the sense of injustice that prevails in so many quarters today....

A FINAL WORD ON ADVERTISING

Advertising has an important and constructive role to play in the life of the nation. It is not true that all advertising men are unscrupulous or that all businessmen are concerned only with selling, no matter what the cost to their customers. Nor is it true that advertisements are necessarily misleading or fraudulent....

...But even when the message is not distorted, those who use the mass media to disseminate it should do so with some sense of social and public responsibility. It is far worse, though, when the message is distorted. And even David Ogilvy, for all his insistence on honesty in advertising, admits that he is "continuously guilty of *suppressio veri* [the suppression of the truth]. Surely it is asking too much to expect the advertiser to describe the shortcomings of his product? One must be forgiven for putting one's best foot foward."[13] So the consumer is *not* to be told all the relevant information; he is *not* to be given all the facts that would be of assistance in making a reasonable decision about a given purchase. In particular, he will *not* be told about the weaknesses of a product, about its shock hazards, for example, if it is an electrical appliance; about the danger it poses to the consumer's health if it is a cleaning fluid; about the danger it poses to his life if it is an automobile tire that is not built to sustain the heavy loads of today's automobile at turnpike speeds; or, if one carries the doctrine to its final conclusion, about the possibly harmful side effects of a new drug that is advertised to the medical profession. Telling the truth combined with "*suppressio veri*" is *not* telling the truth. It is *not* asking too much of the advertiser to reveal such facts when they are known to him, and he should *not* be forgiven for "putting his best foot forward" at his customer's expense.... All aspirin is the same, for example, whether it is stamped *Bayer* and sells for $1.95 per hundred or whether it is an unadvertised brand of U.S.P. aspirin that sells for 35 cents per hundred. But the advertiser will try to convince you that what is true of Bayer aspirin is not true of the other product. This is unfair to the consumer, whether he is rich or poor; but it is particularly unfair to the poor consumer, who could use in other ways the money he spends paying for Bayer's advertising.

Advertising has an important role to fill in our society. It is not likely to disappear. But it is not always carried on in the most ethical manner. Its supporters tend to exaggerate the benefits that have flowed from it, and they are not at all shy about boasting about its effectiveness in their trade meetings and in their efforts to win new business. But they often shrug off any suggestion that their efforts may have harmful effects upon some segments of society by denying that they are all *that* effective. They cannot have it both ways. If advertising is as effective as its practitioners claim it to be, then it possesses enormous potential for harm as well as for good. Because many, though not all, advertisers are concerned primarily about selling their products and only secondarily, if at all, about telling the truth, it is reasonable to suggest that some government regulation be exercised over this industry; and in particular, that advertisers—both producers and agencies—be held liable for harm or damage that results to consumers from misleading or false claims in advertisements, and that they be required to make good any financial loss that consumers may suffer as a result of reliance upon any misleading advertisement, whether the advertisement was "fraudulent" in the criminal sense or not. If laws were passed, both on the federal level and at the state or provincial level, making agencies and producers responsible for restitution of damages suffered by customers who relied upon their "messages," there would be a great incentive for those concerned to confine their claims to those that could be substantiated and to resort to fewer misleading gimmicks. Though such legislation would not eliminate all abuses, it would go a long way toward assuring the public that the advertising messages to which it was exposed respected the truth.

NOTES

1. See James G. Burrow, *AMA: Voice of American Medicine* (Baltimore: Johns Hopkins [University] Press, 1963), p. 268; and Arthur J. Cramp. *Nostrums and Quackery and Pseudo-medicine* (Chicago: University of Chicago Press, 1936), vol. 3, pp. 29–31.

2. James H. Young, *The Medical Messiahs* (Princeton, NJ: Princeton University Press, 1967), pp. 147f.

3. See David Ogilvy, *Confessions of an Advertising Man* (New York: Atheneum, 1963), p. 86. Also Gerald B. Lambert, "How I Sold Listerine," in *The Amazing Advertising Business*, ed. the Editors of *Fortune* (New York: Simon and Schuster, 1957), chap. 5.

4. Young, op. cit., p. 155.

5. [A paste. promoted as a cure for cancer, which was both ineffective and potentially deadly.—ED.]

6. Mortin Mintz, "Drugs: Deceptive Advertising," in David Sanford (ed.), *Hot War on the Consumer* (New York: Pitman, 1969), pp. 91ff.

7. *FTC in the Matter of Johnson Products Company, Inc., and Bozell & Jacobs, Inc.*, Docket no. C-2788 (February 10, 1976).

8. Cf. John G. Fleming, *The Law of Torts*, 4th ed. (Sydney, Austl.: Law Book Company, 1971), pp. 452ff.

9. *Consumer Reports*, [op. cit.] p. 560.

10. Cf. *Consumer Reports*, March and August, 1961; follow-up reports, April and August, 1962.

11. Select Committee Hearings, Pt. 1, *Analgesics* (Washington [DC]: U.S. Government Printing Office, 1971), p. 230.

12. Ibid.

13. Ogilvy. [op. cit.], pp. 158f.

CASES

CASE 4.1
Lying (for Journalists)

Stephen Hess

"JOURNALISTS, who are in the business of telling the truth, should not lie," says Marvin Kalb, former correspondent for CBS and NBC, now Harvard's Edward R. Murrow Professor of Press and Public Policy. Why is a proposition so simple so controversial in journalism circles?

The "right to lie" has been heatedly debated in recent years because of two TV newsmagazine stories aired in 1992. NBC's *Dateline* was caught in multiple lies when it created a flaming crash to try to prove that GM trucks with the gasoline tank mounted outside the frame are unsafe. ABC's *Prime Time Live* lied when its producers faked employment records and job references while trying to expose Food Lion supermarkets for allegedly selling tainted meats.

Exposing unsafe vehicles and unhealthy food is good. Lying is bad. What's a journalist to do? According to the Society of Professional Journalists' handbook on ethics, as summarized by Susan Paterno, lying or deception may be used only when all other means have been exhausted, when the story illustrates an extremely serious social problem or prevents profound harm to individuals, when the journalists reveal their deception to the public, and when the harm prevented by the information outweighs the damage caused by the deception.

———————

Questions

1. Regardless of the intention of a journalist who lies to uncover a story, does the fact that the journalist did indeed *lie* undermine their credibility?

2. Do you agree with Susan Paterno and her position that lying "may be used when all other means have been exhausted"? Taking into account the positions of previous authors in this chapter, why or why not?

From Stephen Hess, "Lying (for Journalists)," *The Little Book of Campaign Etiquette* (Washington D.C.: Brookings Institution Press, 1998), 86.

CASE 4.2

Revisiting the Truth-Telling Debate: A Study of Disclosure Practices at a Major Cancer Center

Mary R. Anderlik, Rebecca D. Pentz, and Kenneth R. Hess

... At M.D. Anderson Cancer Center, requests from families to withhold information from patients are not uncommon. On the other hand, most physicians do not encounter this situation on a daily basis, nor is this situation encountered at least once a year by every physician practicing at the institution. A substantial minority of respondents reported that they never abide by a family's request to withhold a diagnosis or information concerning prognosis. The majority of respondents indicated a degree of flexibility in responding to family requests. In their comments on the questionnaire, some of these physicians indicated that they resolve the situation by tacitly placing the decision concerning disclosure with the patient (that is, by making the patient's assertiveness in asking questions the test of the patient's desire for and ability to cope with information). If the patient asks a question, the physician answers it truthfully, but the physician does not initiate the discussion of diagnosis or prognosis. Other studies document the same approach among oncologists practicing at hospitals affiliated with Harvard Medical School and surgeons treating cancer patients at several hospitals in the United Kingdom. This approach has been criticized as an inappropriate shifting of responsibility.

Respondents appear to be more willing to abide by a family's request to withhold information related to prognosis than diagnosis. Greater receptivity to family requests in the area of prognosis may reflect medical uncertainty about prognosis, a belief that prognostic information is less important than other kinds of information in motivating patients to comply with a therapeutic regimen, or the lack of clear legal requirements in this area. If physicians' greater reticence to communicate prognosis rests on a belief that patients do not want this information, it may be time for physicians to reconsider this belief. In surveys conducted over the last two decades, most people indicate that they would want their physician to give them a realistic survival estimate if they were to develop a life-threatening disease. A lively debate concerning the desirability of a consistent policy of truth-telling in the area of prognosis continues.

Families identified by respondents as Arab or Middle Eastern made the most requests for withholding of information, followed by families identified as Spanish or Hispanic. The distribution of requests according to racial/ethnic group does not match the distribution of patients at M.D. Anderson, suggesting a true cultural effect (although the relatively low number of requests from Asian families and the absence of requests from Native American families likely reflects the small numbers of these ethnic groups in the M.D. Anderson patient population). On the other hand, family requests to withhold information from the patient were reported from every ethnic group except Native Americans, suggesting that this is not purely a "minority culture" or "international patient" concern.

When we asked about reasons for withholding information from patients, using a list of factors adapted from Oken's questionnaire, sensitivity to cultural norms was the factor most frequently selected. The patient's fragile emotional state and respect for the patient's expressed wishes vied for second place (family wishes were ranked fifth). Maintenance of hope, which has occupied such a prominent place in the ethos of oncology, ranked

From Mary R. Anderlik, Rebecca D. Pentz, and Kenneth R. Hess, "Revisiting the Truth-Telling Debate: A Study of Disclosure Practices at a Major Cancer Center," *Journal of Clinical Ethics* 11.3 (Fall 2000) 251–59.

fourth. Respondents' comments provided nuanced illustrations of these reasons. Some of the comments that affirmed truth telling also emphasized the importance of a positive, hope-affirming presentation. Others suggested that truth should be tailored to the wishes of the individual in a manner reminiscent of the approach of "offering truth" advanced by Benjamin Freedman, among others. Not surprisingly, and array of somewhat disparate contextual factors appear to influence physicians' decision making concerning disclosure.

Respondents' comments indicate that a number of physicians at M.D. Anderson resolve the cultural conflict by telling family members that physicians in the United States are required to disclose information to patients. Note that these physicians do not challenge the cultural norm of the family or patient; rather, they assert that the cultural norm of the United States, truth-telling, applies because the family and patient have, as it were, brought themselves within U.S. jurisdiction by seeking treatment here. Resorting to law may be attractive because it preserves the integrity of U.S. healthcare professionals by according victory to the current professional norm of truth-telling, without requiring the kind of strong justification necessary for an assertion that the norm applies universally.

Economic as well as ethical imperatives may compel heightened sensitivity to cultural factors in general and to the wishes of family members of international patients in particular. International patients are usually full-pay patients, and therefore an important healthcare market. The resulting interest in pursuing international patients suggests that physicians at M.D. Anderson and other institutions like it will be confronted with family requests to withhold information with increasing frequency.

Questions

1. Is deception necessary to coerce patients to comply with a therapeutic regimen when the prognosis isn't optimistic?
2. In dealing with the duty of a doctor to disclose information, the right of patients to make a competent decision regarding their treatment and the rights, if any, of the families of the patient's, what considerations can you think of to justify each position?
3. Is deception for the common good always a good thing? If so, define the common good.

CASE 4.3
Flying or Lying in Business Class
Robert C. Solomon

A few months ago, you graduated from business school and began working at National Inc. in New York City. It was exciting for you and your spouse to live in New York, but also very expensive, especially since you still have huge loans to pay off from college. Your boss at National is sending you to a conference in Amsterdam. This is a great opportunity for you to display your talents. New hires are watched closely to see if they have the maturity and sophistication to work with foreign clients.

At National employees have the option of getting an advance for their plane tickets, instead of paying for them and being reimbursed later. National also has a policy of sending employees business class on any flight of five hours or more. You were surprised at the amount of the advance for the business-class ticket and realize that you could use it to buy two coach tickets.

Your spouse has not yet found a job in New York and is getting a little depressed. When your spouse hears about the trip and expresses an interest in going with you, you agree that it is a good idea. You can't really afford a vacation, and it would be nice to stay in a good hotel and enjoy the sights in Amsterdam. Since the company is so large, and you submit your receipts to the accounting division, your boss would never know if you bought one or two tickets. Two coach tickets may even cost the company less money.

Questions

1. Should you ask your boss if you can use the money to buy two tickets?
2. Does the fact that the two coach tickets cost less justify not telling your boss?

CASE 4.4
Willful Ignorance? Or Deception?

Robert C. Solomon

Two contract hires have been working in the accounts department at a major bank for eight months. The manager of their section had worked with HR (human resources) in posting the job and had agreed to a starting salary of $29,500, which the two hires had accepted. In a review of the section, the manager received a list of employees and their salaries and noticed that the two were listed as being paid $35,900. The manager assumed that it was a typographical error, but notified HR for a correction HR responded that the two were indeed receiving that amount. Neither employee had informed the manager at any time during his or her employment that the salary was higher than what they had been offered.

As their manager, what would you do?

Questions

1. What would you do if you were being (modestly) overpaid?
2. Should the employees have told? Why? Is it possible that they just didn't notice? If they didn't notice, does their responsibility change? Why?

5

Privacy, Confidentiality, Secrecy, and Trust

Introduction

Hey, can you keep a secret? Since childhood, you have probably been asked to keep thousands of secrets. Secrets do, in fact, play a central role in our everyday lives. Almost everyone has a secret, information that they wish to keep from public view. In some cases, it may be personal information regarding one's health, habits, or associations. In other instances, it may be information that has been shared about another person or, in professional contexts, information related to employment. This chapter explores the ethical concerns that surround the role of privacy, confidentiality, secrecy, and trust in professional life.

When entering almost any professional career, you are going to encounter situations in which you must establish and maintain privacy and confidentiality. The instructors at your college or university, for example, are compelled by federal law to keep your grades and other personal information confidential. Accordingly, they are not permitted to share that information with third parties without your consent. Similarly, doctors, nurses, lawyers, accountants, and engineers face similar situations in which they have a moral, and often a legal, obligation to maintain privacy regarding the information they obtain within the context of their professional relationships.

The nature and scope of these relationships may, however, vary across the professions. The duty to maintain trade secrets, for example, may differ from the duty of a physician not to disclose information from a patient's medical records. Consequently, some professionals may face, on a more regular basis, conflicts that challenge their obligation to protect confidentiality. Take a health care professional, for example, who encounters a patient who is HIV positive but wishes to withhold that information from a spouse. Should the physician protect the patient's confidentiality or share the diagnosis with the spouse? What ethical principles may help to provide guidance in this situation?

While the basic concepts of privacy, secrecy, and confidentiality are related, they differ in significant ways. Privacy refers to the actual state of affairs regarding access to specific information. Information is private when access is limited. Information may be private when it is limited to one person, such as a secret about oneself; to a few people, such as in the development of a new business plan; or even when several people have access to the information, such as access to your health care records. Information is public, on the other hand, when anyone may have access to the information.

Since professionals often must deal with private information, they must understand the extent to which that information can be kept private and establish an appropriate understanding with their clients. As part of that understanding, professionals must strive to create a confidential relationship. Confidentiality involves the establishment of the rules, or agreements, that govern the sharing of private information. Information is confidential when one person agrees not to share the private information offered by one person to a third party without the confider's permission. A breach of confidentiality occurs when there is a failure to uphold that agreement.

Breaches of confidentiality are serious matters for all professionals, as they threaten the foundation of trust that is essential to the relationship between the professional and the client. Yet, not all private information shared between clients and professionals can be kept confidential. In some cases, there are legal restrictions regarding the extent to which a professional can keep information private. A psychologist who discovers that a client is sexually abusing children cannot keep that information confidential. And in some cases, deliberate invasions of privacy may be necessary to achieve a greater good. Is it a breach of trust and an unwarranted invasion of privacy to use covert surveillance to attempt to detect the abuse of children by their caregivers?

The readings in this chapter explore these questions. As you read them, consider how we should best define privacy and confidentiality in professional practice. What is the extent of a professional's obligation regarding the protection of private information? How explicit should a professional be in establishing the boundaries of confidentiality? How, if at all, do the ethical obligations differ from one profession to another?

Mary Beth Armstrong

Confidentiality: A Comparison Across the Professions of Medicine, Engineering, and Accounting

Mary Beth Armstrong is Accounting Professor Emeritus at Orfalea College of Business, California Polytechnic State University.

INTRODUCTION

Professions are organizations of people sharing a certain expertise (e.g., knowledge of medicine, law,

From *Professional Ethics*, Vol. 3, No.1 © Mary Beth Armstrong, 1994.

accounting). The expertise is typically of a theoretical nature and requires extensive education and training. Thus, society restricts practice of the expertise to licensed individuals. But monopoly and special knowledge lead to power; and power in the hands of a few can result in harm to the many. Thus, at the heart of every profession is a service ideal, or promise to use the special knowledge and monopoly to benefit, not harm society. All professions, by their very nature, must be concerned with and must strive to advance the public interest.

Keeping professional secrets or confidences has long been considered to be in the public interest. Arguments defending professional confidentiality are both deontological and utilitarian. Deontological justifications for confidentiality are based on the notions of privacy, autonomy, promise keeping and loyalty, while utilitarian arguments stress the positive benefits to society when professionals can be trusted to keep confidences. As one court stated (1965, *Hammonds v. Aetna*):

> Since the layman is unfamiliar with the road to recovery, he cannot sift through the circumstances of his life, and habits to determine what is information pertinent to his health. As a consequence, he must disclose all information in his consultations with his doctor—even that which is embarrassing, disgraceful, or incriminating. To promote full disclosure, the medical profession extends the promise of secrecy.

Since professional confidentiality is recognized as a *prima facie* duty, it therefore follows that it is morally binding on professionals unless it is in conflict with equal or stronger duties.... Beauchamp and Childress (1989, p. 53) assert four requirements for justified infringements of a *prima facie* principle or rule:

(1) The moral objective justifying the infringement must have a realistic prospect of achievement.
(2) Infringement of a *prima facie* principle must be necessary in the circumstances, in the sense that there are no morally preferable alternative actions that could be substituted.

(3) The form of infringement selected must constitute the least infringement possible, commensurate with achieving the primary goal of the action.
(4) The agent must seek to minimize the effects of the infringement.

When individual decision makers or public policy formulators advocate the breaking of professional confidences, the principles most often evoked are those of "not causing harm" or "preventing harm." Thus, the interests of the client or patient, to whom the professional owes the *prima facie* duty of confidentiality, is pitted against the interests of others in society (or even society itself) who may be harmed if confidentiality is kept.

Not all duties, however, are of equal weight nor do they all impose an equal burden on the professional.... In general, positive duties are obligations to bring about good or be meritorious and generally require some action on the part of the professional. Negative duties, on the other hand, are duties to not harm or not do bad, and most often require inaction or compliance with rules defining ones role. Negative duties are seen as more obligatory than positive duties. Thus, keeping a professional confidence, a negative duty, would be a stronger duty than the positive duty to take action to prevent harm, assuming the magnitude of the potential harm to society is equal to the magnitude of the potential harm done to the client/patient by revealing the confidence.

Ruland and Lindblom ... describe four criteria for policy makers to utilize to determine when professionals should be bound by the negative duty to maintain confidentiality and when they should reveal the confidences to prevent an impending harm: relentlessness, the uncertainty of outcomes, the nature of responsibilities and the magnitude of the consequences.

Relentlessness refers to the dischargability of a duty. Since all positive acts of beneficence cannot be performed, some ethicists see positive duties as relentless and thus never obligatory. However, Ruland and Lindblom would find positive duties obligatory in "circumstances that can be defined as less than relentless" (p. 265). Thus, for example, even though accountants cannot be held to a duty to disclose all information of benefit to the public, they may have a duty to disclose certain limited sets of information.

The uncertainty of outcomes criteria refers to the fact that "the strictness of a positive duty is related to the probability that something bad will occur or that something good will not occur if the duty is not fulfilled" (p. 265). Usually, if a negative duty is violated some bad end will occur. When a positive duty is violated, however, the bad end can be avoided by other means. "There are circumstances, however, in which failure to act on a positive duty will have an almost certain outcome.... When the circumstances do occur they could ... change the relative strictness of a positive duty to act" (p. 265).

The nature of the responsibility for positive duties refers to changing levels of responsibility because of circumstances that create special duties for particular persons. Ruland and Lindblom illustrate the concept by reference to several scenarios involving a drowning person and an individual observing the drowning. The individual's responsibility to save (positive duty) the drowning victim depends on circumstances. Can the rescuer swim? Is s/he a lifeguard? Are others present who could also do the saving? Does the rescuer have other, conflicting duties, such as child care? Thus the strength of a positive duty is affected by who else might share the responsibility and by the nature of the shared duty.

The magnitude of the consequences is self explanatory. As the magnitude of the consequences increases (for a positive duty) and the magnitude decreases (for a negative duty), the positive duty can be seen to outweigh the negative duty.

Beauchamp and Childress (1989, p. 337) employ a similar notion when they state that "it is necessary to consider both the probability and the magnitude of harm and to balance both against the rule of confidentiality":

		Magnitude of Harm	
		Major	Minor
Probability	High	1	2
of Harm	Low	3	4

"As the health professionals' assessment of the situation approaches 1 in the above chart ... the weight of the obligation to breach confidentiality increases. As the situation approaches 4, the weight decreases." Cases 2 and 3 are more difficult to resolve. However, Beauchamp and Childress see no moral obligation to breach confidentiality in case 2 (high probability of a minor harm) and conclude that, in case 3, some form of risk/benefit analysis is called for, since judgement about probabilities and magnitudes are required. They also imply (p. 338) that reasonable doubts ought to be settled in favor of preserving confidentiality.

Unfortunately, Beauchamp and Childress do not give guidance to their readers to help them assess the probability of the risk of harm or its magnitude. Nor do they distinguish between types of harm (e.g., bodily harm, loss of wealth, damage to reputation). Ought all "harms" be treated equally? Presumably these distinctions and difficult assessments are to be made by individual professional practitioners in concrete situations, based upon guidelines by her/his professional organization. Such guidance, presumably, would include rules to be followed in typical and commonly encountered situations within the particular profession. Ideally, these rules would be well conceived and based upon the same concepts described herein.

THE MEDICAL PROFESSION

Confidentiality in the medical profession dates back to the fourth century B.C. and the Hippocratic Oath. "Whatsoever things I see or hear concerning the life of a man, in any attendance on the sick or even apart therefrom, which ought not to be noises about, I will keep silent thereon, counting such things to be holy secrets."

In 1803, Thomas Percival published his Code of Medical Ethics, which was the basis for the American Medical Association's (AMA) code, first promulgated in 1847. Over the next century several major revisions were made to the AMA code, the most dramatic coming in 1957. That year's Principles of Medical Ethics stated the following (section nine):

A physician may not reveal the confidence entrusted to him in the course of medical attendance . . . unless he is required to do so by law or unless it becomes necessary in order to protect the welfare of the individual or the community.

The 1980 revision to the AMA's Principles of Medical Ethics (Preamble, section IV) states:

A physician shall respect the rights of patients, of colleagues, and of other health professionals, and shall safeguard patient confidences within the constraints of the law.

Another section ("5.05 Confidentiality") states:

The obligation to safeguard patient confidences is subject to certain exceptions which are ethically and legally justified because of overriding social considerations. Where a patient threatens to inflict serious bodily harm to another person and there is reasonable probability that the patient may carry out the threat, the physician should take reasonable precautions for the protection of the intended victim, including notification of law enforcement authorities. Also, communicable diseases, gun shot and knife wounds, should be reported as required by applicable statutes or ordinances.

The change in language between the 1957 Code and the 1980 Code reflects a watershed event in the history of medical confidentiality; the *Tarasoff* case [*Tarasoff v. Regents of the University of California*]. This case involved one Prosenjit Poddar, a man obsessed with a student he met at a dance, Tatiana Tarasoff. Poddar revealed to Dr. Moore, the staff psychologist at the University of California, Berkeley student health services, that he thought of harming and maybe killing Tarasoff. When Poddar purchased a gun and discontinued therapy, Dr. Moore notified the campus police, who questioned and then released Poddar. Two months later Poddar killed Tarasoff.

In 1974 the California Supreme Court ruled that Dr. Moore had a duty to warn Tarasoff. In 1976 the same court reheard the case and changed the

ruling from the duty to warn, to the duty to protect, an intended victim through a variety of means, including warning.

Shortly after the *Tarasoff* case, a series of cases followed both within and outside of California. For example, in 1980 in *Liparl v. Sears, Robuck & Co.* the court extended the class of potential victims beyond those identifiable to the therapist to include the general public, since the harm was foreseeable. Also, state legislators have been busy redefining the law as it relates to medical confidentiality. In 1985 the state of California enacted a statute requiring psychotherapists to use reasonable care to protect the identified victim from a potentially dangerous patient by notifying the victim (or by notifying the police if the victim is unknown).

The end is not in sight. The AIDS epidemic is a particularly ripe arena for controversy regarding confidentiality. Some analysts may use a Tarasoff-type approach and argue that doctors have a duty to protect potential victims (including the general public) from the harm inflicted by this deadly disease. Others believe that, since the repercussions of disclosure of AIDS on the patient are so adverse, they outweigh even the potential contraction of the disease by a third party. AIDS patients are often ostracized from society and left to die.

Increasingly creative forms of medical practices in recent years have resulted in additional complexities in doctor–patient relationships. As more and more physicians become employees of HMOs, hospital corporations, and other groups, the previously-described distinction between external professionals (those with professional/client relationships) and internal professionals (those with professional/employer relationships) becomes blurred. Additional conflicts may arise between loyalties to the group/employer and confidentiality commitments to individual patients.

To date the AMA has, in effect, offered the following guidance to physicians relative to appropriate breaches of confidentiality: protect threatened victims and the general public, when required to do so by law. Since courts and legislatures are still busy deciding when a physician should or should not maintain patient confidences, doctors almost need to be lawyers to keep abreast of their professional responsibilities, as delineated by the AMA. Apparently, officials within the medical profession who are charged with the responsibility of making policy for its members have decided that courts and legislatures, rather than themselves, should grapple with issues such as resolving conflicts among *prima facie* duties, prioritizing duties (i.e., positive/negative), defining harm, assessing risks of harm, assessing strengths of loyalties, etc. As Beauchamp and Childress (1989, p. 341) conclude: "rules of medical confidentiality are not at present well delineated and would profit from a thorough restructuring." The medical profession is not unique in its struggle with confidentiality. The next two sections of this paper will discuss the issues from the prospective of engineers, who have traditionally been professional employees (or internal professionals), and accountants, who are more equally divided between internal and external professionals.

THE ENGINEERING PROFESSION

Engineers comprise a large and diverse profession with dozens of professional societies and over 500,000 members. One of the first sources of official ethical guidance for engineers was the 1912 Code of Ethics of American Institute of Electrical Engineers. In that code an engineer was told that he should consider "the protection of a client's or employer's interests his first professional obligation" (Peterson and Farrell, 1986, p. 8). In 1947 the Engineers' Council for Professional Development [ECPD], a model for many engineers' codes, called for the engineer to "discharge his duties with fidelity to the public, his employers and clients, and with fairness and impartiality to all. It is his duty to interest himself in public welfare and to be ready to apply his special knowledge for the benefit of mankind" (Peterson and Farrell, 1986, p. 8).

The 1974 revision of the ECPD Canons of Ethics stated that "Engineers shall hold paramount the safety, health, and welfare of the public in the performance of their professional duties" (Peterson and Farrell, 1986, p. 8). Thus, in 62 years the engineers'

thinking on the issues had evolved from a primary duty to clients and employers to simultaneous (and presumably equal, and sometimes conflicting) duties to clients, employers and public, to a primary duty to the general public.

Currently, the American Society of Civil Engineers, the America Society of Mechanical Engineers, the Institute of Industrial Engineers, and Tau Beta Phi have adopted language similar to the 1974 ECPD Canons. The American Association of Engineering Societies [AAES], an umbrella organization comprised of 22 engineering societies, uses even stronger language: "Engineers perceiving a consequence of their professional duties to adversely affect the present or future public health and safety shall formally advise their employers or clients and, if warranted, consider further disclosure" (Gorlin, 1990, p. 64).

In 1989 the AAES issued "Public Policy Perspectives: Ethical Standards," which stated the following policy, intended to aid engineers who feel they have no choice but to blow the whistle (Gorlin, 1990, p. 65):

> Engineers, in their contributions to technological endeavors, must continually balance creativity and the end effects of their work upon the public welfare. Their contributions may be affected by management and financial decisions which are in conflict with their own ethical standards.
>
> AAES urges that these conflicts be disclosed and resolved with appropriate mechanisms to protect the public safety, and adequate protection for the engineer who jeopardizes his or her career, reputation, and well-being by making such disclosures in the public interest. To this end, AAES is cooperating with various organizations in examining these points and developing measures to enhance ethical approaches wherever technology is present.

> *Action Agenda*
> Encourage disclosure necessary to protect the public safety. Establish active society support of individuals who make disclosures.

The BART case is a good example of engineering "society support of individuals who make disclosures." It involved the faulty design of the automatic train control system of the Bay Area Rapid Transit (BART) system that runs through three counties in northern California. Three engineers became concerned over a period of years with the way the system was being developed. All three expressed concerns to their respective managements, and all three received no significant response. Toward the end of 1971 the three engineers decided that the public safety could be in jeopardy if the system were implemented, so they decided to go over their managers' heads and take their concerns to the BART Board of Directors. The Board ruled in favor of management, who traced the complaints back to the three engineers and fired them.

One of the fired engineers enlisted the support of the California Society of Professional Engineers (CSPE), which began a study of the situation. The study brought to light many engineering and management problems which confirmed the claims of the three engineers. Actual malfunctions, such as an October 1972 incident where the system gave a command to a train to speed up when it should have a slowed down (causing the train to jump the tracks and injure several people), also confirmed the engineers' complaints. Thus, with the help of the CSPE, the three engineers were publicly vindicated, but were still out of work and experiencing difficulty getting hired by *any* company. However, although filing an *amicus curlae* brief may have been a step in the right direction, helping the unemployed engineers secure new employment would have sent an even stronger message to other engineers facing similar circumstances.

———————

In grappling with the confidentiality problem, engineers have concluded that the duty to the public's safety, health and welfare is a higher duty than other, conflicting, *prima facie* duties. Although this conclusion does not satisfy the needed analysis nor does it give much guidance relative to risk assessment, definitions of harm, and the myriad other related questions, it is a foundation upon which to build.

THE ACCOUNTING PROFESSION

Accountants, like engineers, work for a variety of organizations and perform a variety of functions. This paper, however, will examine professional guidance from only two sources: the American Institute of Certified Public Accountants (AICPA), and the Institute of Management Accountants (IMA). AICPA members are licensed by the state (similar to physicians), while IMA members are not (similar to many engineers). The presence of a licensing requirement, or state certification, presumably gives stronger authority to confidentiality rules that are embedded in state business and professional codes than to similar rules promulgated by professional societies. I will return to this point later in this section.

The AICPA membership is almost evenly divided between external, independent accountants who work for CPA firms, and internal accountants who work for large corporations or government as management (internal) accountants or internal auditors. Those CPAs who work as independent, external accountants are almost evenly divided between auditors and tax advisors/management consultants. Originally the AICPA Code of Professional Conduct was applicable only to CPAs performing the audit function as external, independent auditors. In 1988 the Code of Conduct was expanded to include all AICPA members, external and internal, no matter what their function.

The AICPA Code of Professional Conduct is divided into two main sections, Principles and Rules. The former are aspirational in nature, while the latter are mandatory and violators are subject to disciplinary action. In Ruland and Lindblom's terms, the principles are positive duties (unless they suggest refrainment) while the rules are negative duties, and will usually (but not always) trump the positive duties if the two are in conflict.

The Principle entitled "The Public Interest" states: "In discharging their professional responsibilities, members may encounter conflicting pressures from among each of [several] groups [clients, credit grantors, governments, employers, investors, the business and financial community, and others]. In resolving those conflicts, members should act with integrity, guided by the precept that when members fulfill their responsibility to the public, clients' and employers' interests are best served." Thus, the Principles section of the Code seems to establish a positive duty to place the public interest above other interests when there is a conflict.

Rule 301 states "A member in public practice shall not disclose any confidential client information without the specific consent of the client." It goes on to explain: "This rule shall not be construed (1) to relieve a member of his or her professional obligations under rules 202 and 203 [i.e., to follow appropriately established accounting rules]; (2) to affect in any way the member's obligation to comply with a validly issued and enforceable subpoena or summons; (3) to prohibit review of a member's professional practice under AICPA or state CPA society authorization; or (4) to preclude a member from initiating a complaint with or responding to any inquiry made by a recognized investigative or disciplinary body."

The negative duty to maintain client confidentiality does not allow for exceptions other than the following which are explicitly stated: Members have to disclose information if the promulgated accounting rules require it, if the information is subpoenaed, if it is part of a peer or quality review of the CPA firm, or is part of an AICPA or State investigation of the CPA's adherence to professional standards. Notably absent are exceptions for the public interest (e.g., the Savings and Loan crisis, where appropriate accounting rules may have been followed, but they did not tell an accurate story) and exceptions for compliance with the law (as the AMA code provides).

Case law relative to accounting confidentiality has been expanding rapidly, though not as rapidly as in the medical profession. In *Fund of Funds, Ltd. v. Arthur Andersen & Co.* (1982), the auditors were held liable when they did not reveal to one client that it was being defrauded by another client. Since the CPA firm audited both clients, it knew (or should have known) that one client was defrauding the other, and the courts held that it had a duty to warn the defrauded client. In a New York case, *White v. Guarente*, the auditor was held liable for

not revealing to limited partners that they were being defrauded by a general partner (Causey, 1988, p. 30). Liability may even exist where newly discovered information reveals fraudulent client activity *after* the financial statements are issued (for additional discussion of recent case law, see Causey, 1988). Thus the courts do not appear to be persuaded by the argument that CPAs (or medical doctors) who adhere to confidentiality rules promulgated by state business and professional codes are "obeying the law," and the practical effect of such rules may be that they carry no more authority than do similar rules promulgated by professional societies.

Although management (internal) accountants who are members of the AICPA are included in the AICPA Code of Professional Conduct (except where explicitly excluded), the code was, for years, directed toward CPAs in public practice engaged in the auditing function. The *Standards of Ethical Conduct for Management Accountants*, promulgated by the IMA, explicitly address the concerns of internal accountants. The IMA Standards state: "Management accountants have a responsibility to refrain from disclosing confidential information acquired in the course of their work except when authorized, unless legally obligated to do so." The Standards also discuss actions to be taken by management accountants who encounter unethical behavior within their organization:

> If the ethical conflict still exists after exhausting all levels of internal review, the management [i.e. internal] accountant may have no other recourse on significant matters than to resign from the organization and to submit an informative memorandum to an appropriate representative of the organization. Except where legally prescribed, communication of such problems to authorities or individuals not employed or engaged by the organization is not considered appropriate.

REFERENCES

Beauchamp, T. and Childress, J. (1989). *Principles of Biomedical Ethics*, 3rd Edition. Oxford: Oxford U.P.

Causey, Denzil, Jr. (August, 1988). "The CPA's Guide to Whistleblowing," *The CPA Journal*, pp. 26–37.

Gorlin, Rena, ed. (1990). *Codes of Professional Responsibility*. Washington, D.C.: Bureau of National Affairs.

Peterson, James and Farrell, Dan. (1986). *Whistleblowing: Ethical and Legal Issues in Expressing Dissent*. Dubuque: Kendall/Hunt.

Fund of Funds, Ltd. v. Arthur Andersen & Co., 545 F. Supp. 1314 (SDNY 1982).

Hammonds v. Aetna. Sur. Co., 243 F. Supp. 793, 801 (N.D. Ohio 1965).

Lipari v. Sears, Roebuck & Co., 497 F. Supp. 185 (D. Neb. 1980).

Tarasoff v. Regents of University of California. 17C, 3d 425; 131 Cal. Rpt. 14, 551 p. 2d 334 (1976).

Robert C. Solomon and Fernando Flores | # Building Trust

Fernando Flores is a senator in Chile and formerly ran a successful consulting firm in Berkeley, California. Robert C. Solomon taught philosophy and business at the University of Texas at Austin.

In our experience, business people feel uncomfortable talking about trust, except, perhaps, in the most abstract terms of approbation. When the topic of trust comes up, they heartily nod their approval, but then they nervously turn to other topics. Executives are talking a great deal about trust these days, perhaps because they rightly suspect that trust in many corporations seems to be at an all-time low. One of our associates, who also consults for major corporations, recently gave a lecture on the importance of trusting your employees to several hundred executives of one of America's largest corporations. There was an appreciative but stunned silence, and then one of them—asking for all of them—queried, "but how do we control them?" It is a telling question that indicates that they did not understand the main point of the lecture, that trust is the very opposite of control. Or, perhaps, they understood well enough, but suffered a lack of nerve when it came time to think through its implications. Like the first-time skydiver who had eagerly read all of the promotional literature about the thrills of the sport and had listened carefully to instructions, he asked, incredulously, "but now you want us to *jump out of the plane!?*" We all know the importance of trust, the advantages of trust, and we all know how terrible life can be without it. But when it comes time to put that knowledge into practice, we are all like the novice skydiver. Creating trust is taking a risk. Trust entails lack of control, in that some power is transferred or given up to the person who is trusted. It is leaping from the dark, claustrophobic fuselage of our ordinary cynicism into what seems like the unsupported free-fall of dependency. And yet, unlike skydiving, nothing is more necessary.

Today, there is a danger that trust is being oversold. There is such a thing as too much trust, and then there is "blind trust," trust without warrant, foolish trust. Trust alone will not, as some of our pundits promise, solve the problems that our society now faces. Thus we think there is good reason to listen to doubters like Daryl Koehn, who rightly asks, "should we trust trust?"[1] But the urgency remains,

This essay is one of two based on a talk given at the DePaul University Conference on Trust in Business, in Chicago, February 20–21, 1997. Special thanks to George Brenkert, Daryl Koehn, Ken Alpern and, especially, the terrific anonymous reviewers for *BEQ* and to Business Design Associates in Alameda, CA. A companion piece appears in the *Journal for Professional and Business Ethics*, edited by Daryl Koehn, and both are part of a book now published by Oxford University Press, *Building Trust*, 2001.

we believe, on the side of encouraging and understanding trust. There is a lot of encouraging going on today. What is lacking, we want to suggest, is understanding. The problem is not just lack of an adequate analysis. The problem is an aggressive *mis*understanding of trust that pervades most of our discussions. The problem, if we can summarize it in a metaphor or two, is that trust is treated as if it were a "medium" in which human transactions take place, alternatively, as "ground," as "atmosphere" or, even more vaguely, as "climate." Benjamin Barber, for instance, who is one of the early writers on trust and often appealed to by the current crop of commentators, says that trust is "the basic stuff or ingredient of social interaction." But as "stuff" or "ingredient," as a "resource" (Fukuyama[2]), as "medium," "ground," "atmosphere" or "climate," trust all too easily tends to seem inert, simply "there" or "not there," rather than a dynamic aspect of human interaction and human relationships.

This is our thesis: Trust is a *dynamic aspect of human relationships.* It is an ongoing process that must be initiated, maintained, sometimes restored and continuously authenticated. Trust isn't a social substance or a mysterious entity; trust is a social practice, defined by choices. It is always relational: A trusts B (to do C, D, E). We can say that A is "trusting," but by that we mean that he or she has a disposition to readily trust people. Indeed, the very word "trust" is misleading, insofar as it seems to point to an entity, a thing, some social "stuff." Although we will continue to use the word, it might better be thought of as "trusting," an activity, a decision, a transitive verb, not a noun. Accordingly, the discussion of trust, in other words, is shot through with what French existentialist Jean-Paul Sartre called "bad faith," the distancing of our own actions and choices and the refusal to take responsibility for them. The not very subtle message of too much of the talk about trust today is, *The problem isn't me/us, it's them,* as if WE are perfectly willing to trust others—if they are trustworthy, that is, but, unfortunately, they are not or have not proven themselves so. Thus say the Bosnians and the Serbs, the Israelis and the Palestinians, many parents and their teenage kids, and all too many managers and their employees.

The misunderstanding of trust, accordingly, takes the form of a dangerous rationalization. Trust(ing) presupposes trustworthiness. Either one is trustworthy or one is not. So trusting takes the form of a kind of knowledge, the recognition (which may, of course, be fallible) that someone is trustworthy. So, if one trust, so the rationalization goes, then nothing need be said, and it is much better that nothing be said. That is the core of our problem. Trust is rendered inarticulate, unpresentable. According to this view, to even raise the question, "do you trust me?" or "Can I trust you?" is to already instigate, not only indicate, distrust. (Blaze Starr's mother warns her, "never trust a man who says, 'Trust me.'"[3]) If one does not trust, then nothing much is accomplished by saying so, except, perhaps, as an insult, a way of escalating an already existing conflict or, perhaps, as a confirming test ("If you tell me that I should trust you, then you are doubly a liar"). When a politician or a business leader says, "trust me," he takes a considerable risk. Those who support him may well wonder why he needs to say that, and become suspicious. For those who are already suspicious of him, such an intrusive imperative confirms their suspicions.[4] On the other hand, when someone says "I trust you," there is always the possibility of some sense of manipulation, even the unwanted imposition of a psychological burden, one of whose consequences may be guilt.

The reason for talking about trust is not just to "understand" the concept philosophically but to put the issue of trust "on the table" in order to be able to talk it through in concrete, practical situations. By talking through trust, trust can be created, distrust mitigated. Not talking about trust, on the other hand, can result in continuing distrust, and lack of trust is calamitous to one's flourishing as a business and as individuals.

Economic approaches to trust, while well-intended and pointing us in the right direction, are dangerously incomplete and misleading. Trust in business is not merely a tool for efficiency, although it does have important implications for dealing with complexity and therefore efficiency.[5] Moreover, it would hardly be honest to guarantee (as many authors do these days), that more trust will make business more efficient and improve the bottom line. Usually, of course, trust has this effect, but there is no necessary connection between trust and efficiency, and this is neither the aim nor the intention of trust. Indeed, trust as a mere efficiency-booster may be a paradigm of *inauthentic* or phony trust, trust that is merely a manipulative tool, a facade of trust that, over the long run, increases *dis*trust, and for good reason. Employees can usually tell when the "empowerment" they receive like a gift is actually a noose with which to hang themselves, a set-up for blame for situations which they cannot really control. Managers know what it is like when they are awarded more responsibility ("I trust you to take care of that") without the requisite authority. Like many virtues, trust is most virtuous when it is pursued for its own sake, even if there is benefit or advantage in view. (Generosity and courage both have their pay-offs, but to act generously or courageously *merely* in order obtain the pay-offs is of dubious virtue.) To think of trust as a business tool, as a mere means, as a lubricant to make an operation more efficient, is to not understand trust at all. Trust is, first of all, a central concept of ethics. And because of that, it turns out to be a valuable tool in business as well.

TRUST AS AN EMOTIONAL SKILL: SIMPLE TRUST, BLIND TRUST, AUTHENTIC TRUST

Trust is an emotional phenomenon. This is not to say that its significance is first of all "felt," or that it is merely transient. Trust, like love and indignation, finds its significance in the bonds it creates (or, better, in the bonds we create through such emotions), and it is the very essence of trust, like love (but unlike indignation), that it is enduring. Nevertheless (as with love) it may be cut short, betrayed, interrupted, and, on occasion, it may be all too fleeting, usually because it has been foolish. But trust, like all emotions, is dynamic. It defines our relationships and our relationship—our "being tuned"—to the world.

The importance of understanding emotion as a dynamic is essential to our view of emotion in general and trust in particular.[6] The contrast is the usual passivity picture of emotions as physiological interruptions of our lives that *happen to* us. Trust, in particular, is not something that simply happens, or is found or intuited. It is rather created through interaction and in the making of relationships. This is not to deny that there is an innate predisposition to trust, as evidenced so obviously in most babies, and it is compatible with the fact that trust may (tentatively) be established very quickly, within the first few minutes, of a relationship. But what this means is that we will have to be very careful how we talk about trust, careful that we do not collapse and confuse several very different phenomena.

Trust comes in various forms and degrees of sophistication and articulation. We can and ought to distinguish, just to begin with: *simple trust*, naive trust, trust as yet unchallenged, unquestioned (the faith of a well brought up child), *blind trust*, which is not actually naive but stubborn, obstinate, possibly even self-deluding, *basic trust*, which consists in the sense of physical and emotional security which most of us happily take for granted, which is most blatantly violated in war and in acts of random violence, and *authentic trust*, which is trust reflected upon, its risks and vulnerabilities understood, with *distrust* held in balance. (Distrust admits of similar distinctions and levels of sophistication.) Authentic trust, as opposed to simple trust, does not exclude or deny distrust but rather accepts it, even embraces it, but transcends it, absorbs it, overcomes it. With simple trust, one can always be surprised. The reasons for distrust are not even considered, much less taken seriously. Authentic trust can be betrayed, of course, but it is a betrayal that was foreseen as a possibility. There is no denial or self-deception, as in blind trust. There is no naivete, as in simple trust. Authentic trust need not be opposed to basic trust, but when basic trust is violated authentic trust sees clearly what trust remains. Once trust is spelled out, all sorts of new possibilities arise. It can be examined. It can be specified. It can be turned into explicit agreements and contracts. The mistake is to think that such agreements and contracts *precede* or *establish* trust. There can, of course, be agreements and contracts in the absence of trust, typically with elaborate enforcement mechanisms. But it is just as much of a mistake to conflate all trust with articulated trust as it is to conflate all trust with simple or basic (inarticulate) trust. The emotional life of trusting relationships is much more intricate and humanly complex than either contracts and cognitive interactive strategies or "non-cognitive security about motives" would alone allow.

Trust is created (and damaged) through dialogue, in conversation, by way of promises, commitments, offers, demands, expectations, explicit and tacit understandings. It is through such dialogue and conversation, including the rather one-way conversation of advertising, that producers make the nature and quality of their products known, that professionals and companies make their services and the abilities known, that expectations get initiated and intensified. This is not to say that trust is entirely linguistic, the product of promises and expectations verbally created. There is a good deal of trust embodied in our mere physical presence to one another, in our gestures, looks, smiles, handshakes and touches. Animals (especially "social" animals) have enormously complex trust relationships, often highly competitive at the same time, as any casual observation of two or more dogs (or wolves) together will confirm. Nor is the emphasis on dialogue and conversation suggested to imply—as so many social analyses too quickly conclude—that trust is an "agreement" or a "contract" (formal or informal). Contracts, too, are too static (although the negotiation of them, and negotiation out of them, may be dynamic indeed). Nor should trust be understood *primarily* in terms of limited or momentary interactions or transaction—or any number of them. Analyses of trust too often take as their paradigm either the most intimate of relationships—mother and child, husband and wife or lovers—or the most casual of them—notably, the one-shot business deal (for example, buying gas on

the Interstate), or, the repeated one-shot business deal (buying gas at the same station on the way back down the Interstate). An interaction—even repeated interaction—is not yet a relationship, although, obviously, such repeated exchanges—and, occasionally, even a single one, can easily turn into one. A relationship is by its very nature on-going and dynamic, in which one of the central concerns of the relationship is the relationship itself, its status and identity and, consequently, the status and identity of each and all of its members. Trust is and essential and "existential" dimension of that dynamic relationship.

With this in mind, we can understand why lying betrays trust and is so damaging. Even just one lie—or a serious exaggeration or attempt to "spin" the truth can undermine the accumulated trust and good will with which most of us approach new relationships and come to take for granted in established ones. Betrayal from a friend or neighbor may, with great difficulty, be overcome and eventually forgiven (though rarely forgotten), if only because these people are not easily eliminated from our lives. But betrayals in business, where associations are voluntary and there are always other possibilities, are typically fatal. Why work with or work a deal with someone you can no longer trust when there are so many others available?

REFERENCES

1. Daryl Koehn, "Should We Trust Trust?" *American Business Law Journal*, vol. 34(2), 1996: 184–203.
2. Francis Fukuyama, *Trust: The Social Virtues and the Creation of Prosperity* (New York: Free Press, 1996).
3. Blaze Starr was the long-time mistress of Louisana governor Earl Long. The line occurs in the movie, starring Paul Newman and Lolita Davidovich, *Blaze* (1989).
4. E.g., Dick Morris on Bill Clinton's campaign strategy, *Behind the Oval Office* (New York: Knopf. 1997)
5. Nicholas Luhmann, "Trust: A Mechanism for the Reduction of Social Complexity," in his *Trust and Power* (New York: Wiley, 1980) pp. 4–103.
6. Martin Heidegger, *Being and Time (Sein und Zeit)*, trans. Joan Stambaugh (S.U.N.Y., 1996), esp. pp. 134–9.

Terry Pinkard

Invasions of Privacy in Social Science Research

Terry Pinkard is University Professor in the Philosophy Department at Georgetown University.

THE RIGHT TO PRIVACY

... Although it is a substantial good, privacy is only one good among many. Moreover, not all aspects of privacy are equally important. Rational people can agree (and have agreed) to sacrifice some dimension of privacy for other goods. In this respect, privacy is somewhat like liberty: liberty is not unrestricted, and particular liberties are commonly surrendered in order to secure other goods. The claim that not all aspects of privacy are equally important amounts, then, to little more than the view now accepted almost everywhere that rights are not absolute; the right to privacy can legitimately be exercised and can create duties for others only when the right has an overriding status. While there is disagreement concerning the conditions sufficient to justify intruding upon privacy, ... it is widely and properly recognized that some conditions are specifiable. I shall attempt such a specification for social science research in the concluding section. ...

THE JUSTIFICATION OF INVASIONS OF PRIVACY

A moral right to privacy must be derived from some set of moral principles or rules that require persons to leave others alone. However, we have not addressed either the problem of valid restrictions on this right or the problem of its theoretical justification. This section explores these two problems in order, with particular emphasis on whether certain privacy-invading activities of social science investigators can be justified.

C_1: Social scientists unjustifiably invade their subjects' privacy whenever they manipulate subjects into doing something embarrassing or, disclosing private embarrassing facts, and, thereby place their subjects in a false public light or intrude into their private domains.

This criterion will strike many social scientists as indefensibly strong, for some methodologies *necessarily* involve deception or manipulation leading to embarrassment and intrusion into private domains. Without the use of such techniques the validity of their research would be imperiled. If Stanley Milgram had been forced to tell his subjects that his experiment was about obedience and that investigators actually were not shocking people, the experiment would have been lost. Likewise, the element of deception is crucial in most participant-observer experiments that invade privacy—such as those in which people feigned heart attacks on Philadelphia subways to study "helping behavior." Social scientists who study cults and fringe groups by posing as believing members rely on deception that can involve revelations of private information. It would seem from the investigator's point of view, then, that criterion C_1 is too stringent and would, as the cliché goes, throw the baby out with the bathwater. Surely, one can hear the social scientist insisting, it cannot be *much* of a justification for prohibiting

From *Ethical Issues in Social Science Research*, edited by Tom L. Beauchamp, Ruth R. Faden, R. Jay Wallace, Jr., and LeRoy Walters (Baltimore: Johns Hopkins University Press, 1982), pp. 257–73.

social science research involving human subjects if the only grounds are that it violates some loosely formulated idea of a right to . . . privacy, with no history of case law behind the formulation presented. But is the social scientist justified in this complaint about strong criterion C_1?

In order to address the question, let us first consider reformulating our "strong criterion," substituting the phrase "under certain conditions when" at the very beginning of the criterion for the word "whenever," so as to make the criterion weaker. Let us call this criterion C_2.

> C_2: Social scientists unjustifiably invade their subjects' privacy under certain conditions when they manipulate subjects into doing something embarrassing or disclosing private embarrassing facts, and thereby place their subjects in a false public light or intrude into their private domains.

This formulation would make the proposed criterion far more acceptable to social scientists, though specification of the actual exceptive conditions would then of course make all the difference. This strategy will naturally seem to offer a more promising criterion than C_1, for no one would claim that *all* deceit or intrusion on privacy is wrong or that deceit or manipulation are *always* wrong when they lead to invasions of privacy. One may justifiably deceive one's opponents in poker, the enemy in wartime, even sometimes deceive and invade the privacy of one's spouse—as when one plans a surprise party. Journalists are often regarded as justified in and admired for disclosing private embarrassing facts (under certain conditions, as in C_2). If deceit and invasion of privacy are not always wrong in these contexts, perhaps they are sometimes permissible in similar contexts of social science research, and for similar reasons. Still, the question remains: Can justifying conditions be added to C_2 that improve it over C_1—so as to permit enough social science research without permitting too much in the way of invasions of privacy?

One general answer has been given to these problems of justification by Justice William H. Rehnquist,

who argues for a utilitarian approach to problems of privacy. His argument does not uniquely apply to the social sciences, but it provides a perspective on the present issues that may be generalized to the social sciences. Rehnquist argues as follows: Government cannot escape certain conflicts between freedom and order. Both are respectable goods, and on some occasions we cannot have both. Efficient, intelligent law enforcement, which is necessary for the achievement of both goods, requires some sacrifice of privacy—for example, in dissemination of arrest records. So, Rehnquist argues, one must *balance* the goods of privacy and efficient law enforcement when rights to privacy conflict with rights to be protected. If damage to the individual in the dissemination of criminal and arrest records to relevant authorities is slight (with strictures on the use to which the information may be put so as to avoid abuse), while the gain in social utility is great, then even those whose privacy has been invaded ought not to object.

Rehnquist supports this position with the following example. If a police officer parks in front of a tavern each evening from 5:30 to 7:30 and records the license numbers of cars coming and going into the tavern's parking lot during that time, many would consider the action a violation of the right to privacy, an unwarranted invasion. But suppose that on the previous two evenings a patron of the tavern had been killed shortly after leaving it, and evidence suggested that the culprit had been present at the bar when the patron left. Suddenly the picture changes; it is no longer so clear that privacy has been invaded, or at least not so clear that it has been wrongly or unjustifiably invaded.

Justice Rehnquist takes these conclusions to be justified on utilitarian grounds. I agree with him that they are justified, and I heartily endorse his example, but I do not think the proper justification is utilitarian, and I do not think the justification supports C_2 over C_1 either. Let me, then, offer a different justification, one that leads to a defense of C_1—a justification also suitable to handle privacy invasions in social research. This justification naturally starts from the conclusion reached in the previous section on the right to privacy. The analysis of rights as valid claims that are presumptive (or prima facie valid) does not mean that rights never have an overriding status. As Ronald Dworkin has pointed out in his *Taking Rights Seriously*, some rights are so basic that ordinary justifications for state interference—such as lessening inconvenience or promoting utility—are insufficient justifications for overriding rights. In Dworkin's terms, the individual rights of citizens "trump" the reasons why we generally permit state control and planning over our lives. Indeed *everything* is trumped by a right *except another right with which it conflicts.* The citizen who bears a right does not hold a privilege and is not subject to the charity or professional etiquette of another. The right can justifiably be demanded as one's due precisely up to that point at which it comes into conflict with another right. There are numerous examples in social science research to illustrate this point. . . .

It is necessary for social justice and the institution of morality that what may be called "safe" areas of social life be carved out that are almost entirely free from intrusion. These are areas strictly protected by "rights," our most demanding moral rules. Within these areas, invasions of privacy, lying, and deception are virtually always wrong, especially where certain intimate relationships with important goods attached are at stake, because there is so seldom a warrant powerful enough to override a right. The "safe" areas are, however, only protected *areas:* they do not encompass the whole of everyday life and so cannot be protected against conflict with *other* areas that are also "safe." Rights, as we earlier remarked, can conflict with other rights. The alternative—that there are no "safe" areas protected by rights—is morally perilous, for it threatens to put morality on a shifting basis where clever legalistic reasoning with exception clauses can justify anything (e.g., on grounds of social utility).

The issues, then, turn out to be the following: no "safe" area has an ironclad safety about it, because someone's rights may always be of sufficient power to override someone else's rights in any given safe area. Social research leading to violations

of rights (protected in a safe area) can *in theory* sometimes be morally justified, even when it involves deception and invasions of privacy. Thus "in theory" C_1 may seem wrong and indefensible, and C_2 therefore preferable. However, "in theory" is not good enough. I prefer C_1 over C_2 because I do not believe social science is actually justified in its practices of deception and invasion of privacy in safe areas where rights are violated. Accordingly, I shall now argue that social science research that invades a safe area is *always* morally unjustified.

APPLICATIONS TO SOCIAL SCIENCE RESEARCH

There are, no doubt, goods intrinsic to the pursuit of social science, knowledge being the obvious one. The *utility* of social science—its being a significant means to some other valued end such as the efficiency of police work sought by some criminologists—is less apparent. Certainly it is difficult to justify the involvement of human subjects where risk and no obvious benefit to the subjects is involved. . . . However, we can address both the invasion of privacy and the deception some social science research involves by placing them in the context of the obligation to respect persons and the right to privacy, as discussed above. First, we can quickly pass beyond the uncontroversial observation that with proper informed consent much research, including research that poses significant risks, would have nothing against it, even if it involved privacy invasions or deceptions. (Our strong criterion, it is to be remembered, exclude[s] activities having the prior consent of subjects.) If an investigator discloses to subjects in advance that there is a possibility of deception or invasion of privacy, then research becomes like a poker game—a structured situation where deception or invasion of privacy not only may occur but is expected. Adequate disclosures, provided to voluntary participants and informing them of the possibility of an invasion of privacy or deception, should satisfy the moral requirements of respect for persons.

Where obtaining such informed consent is impossible, as is often the case in social science research, the problem of justification is correspondingly stickier. Research into "helping behavior" by feigning heart attacks on subway trains is again a case in point. Here reasonable expectations are interfered with by deliberate intrusions. People in subways have their "private sphere" intruded upon much as they would by cavesdroppers or con artists. It is difficult to imagine an agreement among rational agents on this point that would permit such intrusions into their private sphere. Who could agree to conferring rights on people to manipulate others or oneself, where either oneself or the others are unwittingly manipulated, merely on grounds that knowledge of "helping behavior" would be accumulated?

This situation differs from the other situations where consent legitimated deceit and invasion of privacy. In the poker analogy, a socially structured situation is present in which deceit or intrusion into a private sphere is to be *expected* and in which the anticipated manipulation contributed to the value of the enterprise for the participant. Any rational agent would easily agree to such deception or limitation of privacy. Deceit to plan a surprise party for one's spouse is similar and easily endorsed by rational agents. But the subway case is significantly different. It is not a structured, understood and consensual situation like a game of poker. It is not even like an antagonistic international conflict such as war or a structured interpersonal relationship. In the latter contexts, there exist principles—however general—broadly delineating what is permitted and what is not. People studied in deceptive social science research are duped in a situation without familiar rules into revealing something about themselves that very likely they would rather not reveal. Their solitude—even though they are in public—is thus invaded. (The notion of "solitude in public" should not be troublesome. The earlier example of the police noting license plate numbers without any overriding justification is an example.) Such invasions are not covered by even tacit understandings, let alone by governing principles; and of course there is no prior expectation.

Participant-observer research where the researcher pretends to be a member or sympathizer of a group in order to elicit certain responses from the real participants provides another case in point, for here too no favorable analogy exists to the structured and consensual situations where deceit and invasion of privacy are legitimate. Typically, people studied feel both betrayed and invaded.... Structured social roles often carry with them an understanding of the amount of privacy *proper* to each. To have had someone pose as a friend only to extract private information from you is not only to have been deceived; it is to have had the bounds of what can legitimately be known about you overstepped. A gain in knowledge no more justifies this violation of one's rights than it could justify having a person pose as a lover to a member of a corporation so that the board of directors could discover his or her "real" attitude toward a task. One should add: no matter how much that knowledge furthered the aims of the corporation. Our judgments in these cases thus should be set in the context of a model of moral reasoning that focuses on principles that are *shared* between people and to which we can imagine people *contractually* agreeing. It is not the *consequences* (in the utilitarian sense) of adopting a principle that justifies it, but its being (at least hypothetically) *agreed upon*. This idea of hypothetical agreement rests on what we called earlier the principle of respect for persons, for the validity of the contract depends upon the consent of the contracting parties. Moral principles are justified when they are contracted to in order to balance conflicting interests and competing points of view.

Of all people, social scientists do not need to be reminded of the complex ways in which societies are structured so that behavior which in one case is excusable may in another case be reprehensible. Lying to a close friend about a surprise party is among the excusable cases, but there one has already been granted access and privilege beyond those of the social *researcher* by virtue of a nondeceptive ongoing personal relationship. It is worth noting that no favorable analogy with governmental invasion of privacy exists here. The government has a right to collect certain types of potentially embarrassing information such as the information gathered in the census or that needed at IRS. Often there may be conflicts between rights of government and rights of individuals. But the social science researcher has no moral right to his or her investigations corresponding to the rights of government. At best, the researcher can argue that the research will have some great yield (in social utility, e.g.) and should be supported. But he or she cannot validly argue that the investigation should be supported even in face of its violating individual rights to privacy by intruding into our "safe" areas. In Ronald Dworkin's earlier mentioned phrase, rights trump utility, and certainly they trump the needs and interests of social science researchers. One can validly adjust or "balance" matters *only when rights compete*. However, there is no *right* to perform research which competes with the individual's right to privacy, and hence there is nothing to balance. Or, to state the thesis in a somewhat milder form: there may be *thin* constitutional grounds for claiming some form of First Amendment right to perform research . . ., but I know of no moral or legal grounds whatever that would support a right to perform research sufficient to override individual rights to privacy.

Milgram's experiments occupy in the minds of some a deliciously grey area here, which might explain why so many people have conflicting intuitions about these experiments. They certainly did involve manipulation and deceit, and they do prompt people to reveal things about themselves that one would assume they would rather not have revealed. Yet they also took place in a laboratory setting voluntarily consented to by participants—a facility that was outside, so to speak, the normal course of life. In this respect, Milgram's investigations differ from those into helping behavior . . . Does this laboratory setting and the limited consent of subjects

make a morally significant difference? I take it that some of the conflicting intuitions concerning Milgram's works are conflicts about whether or not the laboratory setting is enough like a poker game for the deception in it to be justified. To me, this seems implausible. Had a general warning been available to the participants beforehand that deception might be employed, intuitions about the rightness or wrongness of the experiments would no doubt have been considerably less divided. One would not expect this kind of change in intuition to occur if the laboratory were indeed the kind of "structured situation" in which deceit is to be suspected.

To be sure, giving such a general warning would in some cases hamper or render impossible certain forms of research. But remember that putting restrictions on the admissibility of evidence hampers police work, and putting restrictions on the use of confidential information hampers banks. That restrictions hamper or prevent certain activities from reaching valuable goals efficiently should not be surprising; nor should it be surprising that morality as the regulation and guidance of life puts restrictions on even important constructive activities. We all complain and grouch with some good reason that *our* activities (whether they be law enforcement, social science, legislation, or what not) are restricted to the point of inefficiency or the diminishment of their final goal; and it should not be surprising that this complaint is pervasive. We should not, however, be blind to the cogency of ethical reasons for these restrictions when they exist. That clearly valuable work such as Milgram's might be hampered or rendered impossible by the desiderate introduced here may be unfortunate, but not on that account unjust.

The argument of this paper is in the end a simple one: there is a right to privacy, even if vaguely defined and subject to challenge in *some ways*. Social scientists do not have a right to invade our privacy; they have no *right* to override our rights. And, on the view presented here, there can be no alternative utilitarian or knowledge-based justification for overriding the right to privacy. . . .

Sissela Bok

The Limits of Confidentiality

Sissela Bok is a Professor at Harvard University.

THE PROFESSIONAL SECRET

...Doctors, lawyers, and priests have traditionally recognized the duty of professional secrecy, regarding what individuals confide to them: personal matters such as alcoholism or depression, marital difficulties, corporate or political problems, and indeed most concerns that patients or clients want to share with someone, yet keep from all others.[1] Accountants, bankers, social workers, and growing numbers of professionals now invoke a similar duty to guard confidences. As codes of ethics take form in old and new professions, the duty of confidentiality serves in part to reinforce their claim to professional status, and in part to strengthen their capacity to offer help to clients.

Confidential information may be more or less intimate, more or less discrediting, more or less accurate and complete. No matter how false or trivial the substance of what clients or patients convey, they may ask that it be kept confidential, or assume that it will be even in the absence of such a request, taking it for granted that professionals owe them secrecy. Professionals, in turn, must not only receive and respect such confidences; the very nature of the help they can give may depend on their searching for even the most deeply buried knowledge.

...But the duty of confidentiality is no longer what it was when lawyers or doctors simply kept to themselves the confidences of those who sought their help. How can it be, when office personnel and collaborators and team members must have access to the information as well, and when clients and patients with numerous interdependent needs consult different professionals who must in turn communicate with one another? And how can it be, given the vast increase in information collected, stored, and retrievable that has expanded the opportunities for access by outsiders? How can it be, finally, when employers, school officials, law enforcement agencies, insurance companies, tax inspectors, and credit bureaus all press to see some of this confidential information?

So much confidential information is now being gathered and recorded and requested by so many about so many that confidentiality, though as strenuously invoked as in the past, is turning out to be a weaker reed than ever. Employers, schools, government agencies, and mental health and social service organizations are among the many groups now delving into personal affairs as never before. Those with fewest defenses find their affairs most closely picked over. Schools, for instance, are looking into the home conditions of students with problems, sometimes even requesting psychiatric evaluations of entire families, regardless of objections from health professionals on grounds of confidentiality. And access to public welfare assistance, work training programs, and many forms of employment may depend on the degree to which someone is willing to answer highly personal questions.

At the same time, paradoxically, a growing number of discreditable, often unlawful secrets never even entered into computer banks or medical records have come to burden lawyers, financial advisers, journalists, and many others who take themselves to be professionally bound to silence. Faced with growing demands for both revelation and secrecy, those who have to make decisions about whether or not to uphold confidentiality face numerous difficult moral quandaries. Legislation can sometimes dictate their choice. But the law differs from state to state and from nation to nation, and does not necessarily

From *Secrets: The Ethics of Concealment and Revelation* (New York: Random House, 1983), pp. 116–35.

prescribe what is right from a moral point of view. Even if it did, it could never entirely resolve many of the quandaries that arise, since they often present strong moral arguments on both sides. Consider, for example, the following case:

> A forty-seven-year-old engineer has polycystic kidney disease, in his case a genetic disorder, and must have his blood purified by hemodialysis with an artificial kidney machine. Victims of the disease [at the time of his diagnosis] usually die a few years after symptoms appear, often in their forties, though dialysis and transplants can stave off death for as much as ten years.
>
> The patient has two children: a son, eighteen, just starting college, and a daughter, sixteen. Though the parents know that the disease is genetic—that their children may carry it and might transmit it to their own offspring—the son and daughter are kept in the dark. The parents insist the children should not be told because it would frighten them unnecessarily, would inhibit their social life, and would make them feel hopeless about the future. They are firm in saying that the hospital staff should not tell the children; the knowledge, they believe, is privileged and must be kept secret. Yet the hospital staff worries about the children innocently involving their future spouses and victimizing their own children.[2]

It is not difficult to see the conflicting and, in themselves, quite legitimate claims on each side in this case: the parents' insistence on privacy and on the right to decide when to speak to their children about a matter of such importance to the family; and the staff members' concern for the welfare of the children. But the question of whether the parents are wrong to keep the information from the children must be separated from that of what the staff members should do about what they see as harmful secrecy. Should they reject their obligation of confidentiality in this case? . . .

These questions require us to look more closely at the nature of confidentiality and its powerful hold and to ask what it is that makes so many professionals regard it as the first and most binding of their duties.

Confidentiality refers to the boundaries surrounding shared secrets and to the process of guarding these boundaries. While confidentiality protects much that is not in fact secret, personal secrets lie at its core. The innermost, the vulnerable, often the shameful: these aspects of self-disclosure help explain why one name for professional confidentiality has been "the professional secret." Such secrecy is sometimes mistakenly confused with privacy; yet it can concern many matters in no way private, but that someone wishes to keep from the knowledge of third parties.

Confidentiality must also be distinguished from the testimonial privilege that protects information possessed by spouses or members of the clergy or lawyers against coerced revelations in court. While a great many professional groups invoke confidentiality, the law recognizes the privilege only in limited cases. In some cases, only lawyers can invoke it; in others, physicians and clergy can as well; more recently, psychiatrists and other professionals have been added to their number. Who ought and who ought not to be able to guarantee such a privilege is under ceaseless debate. Every newly established professional group seeks the privileges of existing ones. Established ones, on the other hand, work to exclude those whom they take to be encroaching on their territory.

The principle of confidentiality postulates a duty to protect confidences against third parties under certain circumstances. Professionals appeal to such a principle in keeping secrets from all outsiders and seek to protect even what they would otherwise feel bound to reveal. While few regard the principle as absolute, most see the burden of proof as resting squarely on anyone who claims a reason for overriding it. Why should confidentiality bind thus? And why should it constrain professionals to silence more than, say, close friends?

JUSTIFICATION AND RATIONALE

The first and fundamental premise is that of individual autonomy over personal information. It asks that we respect individuals as capable of having secrets. Without some control over secrecy and openness about themselves, their thoughts and plans, their actions, and in part their property, people could neither maintain privacy nor guard against danger. But of course this control should be only partial. Matters such as contagious disease place individual autonomy in conflict with the rights of others. And a variety of matters cannot easily be concealed. No one can maintain control, for example, over others seeing that they have a broken leg or a perennially vile temper.[3]

The second premise is closely linked to the first. It presupposes the legitimacy not only of having personal secrets but of sharing them, and assumes respect for relationships among human beings and for intimacy. It is rooted in loyalties that precede the formulation of moral justification and that preserve collective survival for one's tribe, one's kin, one's clan. Building on such a sense of loyalty, the premise holds that it is not only natural but often also right to respect the secrets of intimates and associates, and that human relationships could not survive without such respect.

This premise is fundamental to the marital privilege upheld in American law, according to which one spouse cannot be forced to testify against the other; and to the ancient Chinese legal tradition, so strongly attacked in the Maoist period, that forbade relatives to report on one another's misdeeds and penalized such revelations severely.[4] No more than the first premise, however, does this second one suffice to justify all confidentiality. It can conflict with other duties, so that individuals have to choose, say, between betraying country or friend, parents or children; and it can be undercut by the nature of the secret one is asked to keep.

The third premise holds that a pledge of silence creates an obligation beyond the respect due to persons and to existing relationships. Once we promise someone secrecy, we no longer start from scratch in weighing the moral factors of a situation. They matter differently, once the promise is given, so that full impartiality is no longer called for.

In promising one alienates, as Grotius said, either a thing or some portion of one's freedom of action: "To the former category belong promises to give; to the latter, promises to perform."[5] Promises of

secrecy are unusual in both respects. What they promise to give is allegiance; what they promise to perform is some action that will guard the secret—to keep silent, at least, and perhaps to do more. Just what performance is promised, and at what cost it will be carried out, are questions that go to the heart of conflicts over confidentiality.[6] To invoke a promise, therefore, while it is surely to point to a prima facie ground of obligation, is not to close the debate over pledges of secrecy. Rather, one must go on to ask whether it was right to make the pledge in the first place, and right to accept it; whether the promise is a binding one, and even if it is, what circumstances might nevertheless justify overriding it.[7]

Individuals vary with respect to the seriousness with which they make a promise and the consequent weight of the reasons they see as sufficient to override it. Consider the CIA agents who take an oath of secrecy before gaining access to classified information; the White House butler who pledges never to publish confidential memoirs; the relatives who give their word to a dying author never to publish her diaries; the religious initiate who swears on all he holds sacred not to divulge the mysteries he is about to share; the engineer who signs a pledge not to give away company trade secrets as a condition of employment. Some of these individuals take the pledge casually, others in utter seriousness. If the latter still break their pledge, they may argue that they were coerced into making their promise, or that they did not understand how it bound them. Or else they may claim that something is important enough to override their promise—as when the relatives publish the author's diaries after her death for a sum of money they cannot resist, or in the belief that the reading public would be deprived without such documents.

For many, a promise involves their integrity and can create a bond that is closer than kinship, as the ceremonies by which people become blood brothers indicate. The strength of promising is conveyed in such early practices as those in which promisors might offer as a pledge their wife, their child, or a part of their body.[8] And promises of *secrecy* have been invested with special meaning, in part because of the respect for persons and for relationships called for by the first two premises.

Taken together, the three premises give strong prima facie reasons to support confidentiality. With certain limitations, I accept each one as binding on those who have accepted information in confidence. But of course there are reasons sufficient to override the force of all these premises, as when secrecy would allow violence to be done to innocent persons, or turn someone into an unwitting accomplice in crime. At such times, autonomy and relationship no longer provide sufficient legitimacy. And the promise of silence should never be given, or if given, can be breached.

It is here that the fourth premise enters in to add strength to the particular pledges of silence given by professionals.[9] This premise assigns weight beyond ordinary loyalty to professional confidentiality, because of its utility to persons and to society. As a result, professionals grant their clients secrecy even when they would otherwise have reason to speak out: thus lawyers feel justified in concealing past crimes of their clients, bankers the suspect provenance of investors' funds, and priests the sins they hear in confession.

According to this premise, individuals benefit from such confidentiality because it allows them to seek help they might otherwise fear to ask for; those most vulnerable or at risk might otherwise not go for help to doctors or lawyers or others trained to provide it. In this way, innocent persons might end up convicted of crimes for lack of competent legal defense, and disease could take a greater toll among those ashamed of the nature of their ailment. Society therefore gains in turn from allowing such professional refuge, the argument holds, in spite of the undoubted risks of not learning about certain dangers to the community; and everyone is better off when professionals can probe for the secrets that will make them more capable of providing the needed help.

The nature of the helpfulness thought to override the importance of revealing some confidences differs from one profession to another. The social worker can offer support, counsel, sometimes therapy; physicians provide means of relieving suffering and of curing disease; lawyers give assistance in self-protection against the state or other individuals. These efforts may conflict, as for army psychiatrists whenever their mission is both to receive the confidences of troubled military personnel and to serve as agents of the state, obligated to report on the condition of their patients. And the help held to justify confidentiality about informants by police and journalists is not directed to individuals in need of relief at all, but rather to society by encouraging disclosures of abuses and crime.

Such claims to individual and social utility touch on the *raison d' être* of the professions themselves; but they are also potentially treacherous. For if it were found that a professional group or subspecialty not only did not help but actually hurt individuals, and increased the social burden of, say, illness or crime, then there would be a strong case for not allowing it to promise professional confidentiality. To question its special reason for being able to promise confidentiality of unusual strength is therefore seen as an attack on its special purposes, and on the power it acquires in being able to give assurances beyond those which nonprofessionals can offer.

A purely strategic reason for stressing professional confidentiality is that, while needed by clients, it is so easily breached and under such strong pressures to begin with. In schools and in offices, at hospitals and in social gatherings, confidential information may be casually passed around. Other items are conveyed "off the record" or leaked in secret. The prohibition against breaching confidentiality must be especially strong in order to combat the pressures on insiders to do so, especially in view of the case and frequency with which it is done.

Together with the first three premises for confidentiality, the defense of the fourth helps explain the ritualistic tone in which the duty of preserving secrets is repeatedly set forth in professional oaths and codes of ethics. Still more is needed, however, to explain the sacrosanct nature often ascribed to this duty. The ritualistic nature of confidentiality in certain religious traditions has surely had an effect on its role in law and medicine. A powerful esoteric rationale for secrecy linked the earliest practices of medicine and religion. Thus Henry Sigerist points out that in Mesopotamia medicine, like other sacred knowledge, was kept secret and not divulged to the profane; conversely, many religious texts ended with a warning that "he who does not keep the secret will not remain in health. His days will be shortened."[10]

However strong, these historical links between faith and professional practice give *no* added justification to professional confidentiality. The sacramental nature of religious confession is a matter of faith for believers. It may be respected even in secular law on grounds of religious freedom; but it adds no legitimacy to that of the four premises when it comes to what professionals conceal for clients.[11]

The four premises are not usually separated and evaluated in the context of individual cases or practices. Rather, they blend with the ritualistic nature attributed to confidentiality to support a rigid stance that I shall call the rationale of confidentiality. Not only does this rationale point to links with the most fundamental grounds of autonomy and relationship and trust and help; it also serves as a rationalization that helps deflect ethical inquiry. The very self-evidence that it claims can then expand beyond its legitimate applications. Confidentiality, like all secrecy, can then cover up for and in turn lead to a great deal of error, injury, pathology, and abuse.

When professionals advance confidentiality as a shield, their action is, to be sure, in part intentional and manipulative, but in part it also results from a failure to examine the roots of confidentiality and to spell out the limits of its application. It can lead them to sweeping claims such as that made by the World Medical Association in its 1949 International Code of Medical Ethics: "A doctor shall preserve absolute secrecy on all he knows about his patient because of the confidence entrusted in him."[12]

INDIVIDUAL CLIENTS AND THEIR SECRETS

Among the most difficult choices for physicians and others are those which arise with respect to confidences by children, mentally incompetent persons, and those who are temporarily not fully capable of guiding their affairs. While some such confidences— as about fear or hopes—can be kept secret without difficulty, others are more troubling. Consider the following case:

> Janet M., a thirteen-year-old girl in the seventh grade of a small-town junior high school, comes to the office of a family physician. She has known him from childhood, and he has cared for all the members of her family. She tells him that she is pregnant, and that she has had a labtest performed at an out-of-town clinic. She wants to have an abortion. She is afraid that her family, already burdened by unemployment and illness, would be thrown into a crisis by the news. Her boyfriend, fifteen, would probably be opposed to the abortion. She asks the doctor for help in securing the abortion, and for assurance that he will not reveal her condition to anyone.

Cases such as Janet's are no longer rare. In small towns as in large cities, teen-age pregnancy is on the rise, teen-age abortion commonplace. Many families do provide the guidance and understanding so desperately needed at such times; but when girls request confidentiality, it is often out of fear of their families' reaction. Health professionals should clearly make every effort to help these girls communicate with their families. But sometimes there is no functioning family. Or else family members may have been so brutal or so unable to cope with crisis in the past that it is legitimate to be concerned about the risks in informing them. At times, it is even the case that a member of the girl's own family has abused her sexually.[13]

Health professionals are then caught in a conflict between their traditional obligation of confidentiality and the normal procedure of consulting with a child's parents before an irreversible step is taken. In this conflict, the premises supporting confidentiality are themselves in doubt. Just how autonomous should thirteen-year-olds be with respect to decisions about pregnancy? They are children still, but with an adult's choice to make. And what about even younger girls? In what relation does a physician stand to them, and to their parents, regarding such secrets?

Because the premises of autonomy and of relationship do not necessarily mandate secrecy at such times, deciding whether or not to pledge silence is much harder. Even the professional help that confidentiality allows is then in doubt. Pregnant young girls are in need of advice and assistance more than most others; confidentiality too routinely extended may lock them into an attitude of frightened concealment that can do permanent damage. Health professionals owe it to these patients, therefore, to encourage and help them to communicate with their families or others responsible for their support. But to *mandate*, as some seek to do, consultation with family members, no matter how brutal or psychologically abusive, would be to take a shortsighted view. Not only would it injure those pregnant girls forced into family confrontations; many others would end by not seeking professional help at all, at a time when they need it most.

Childhood and adolescent pregnancies are far from the only conditions that present professionals with conflicts over confidentiality. Veneral disease, drug and alcohol addiction among the young, as well as a great many problems of incompetent and disturbed individuals past childhood, render confidentiality similarly problematic.

If, on the other hand, the act has been carefully thought through, breaches of confidentiality are much less justified, no matter how irrational the project might at first seem to outsiders. Say the person planning to give his money away wants to live the rest of his life as a contemplative, or that the patient planning to abandon medical treatment has decided to cease delaying death in view of his progressively debilitating and painful disease; it is harder to see the basis for a breach of professional confidentiality in such cases, since it is more difficult to prove that the person's act is necessarily self-destructive from his point of view. Professionals are constantly at risk of assuming too readily that the purposes they take to be overriding and to which they have dedicated their careers—financial prudence, for instance—are necessarily more rational

for all others than conflicting aims. This professional bias has to be taken into account in any decision to override confidentiality on grounds of irrationality and self-harm.

Sometimes, however, a patient's insistence on confidentiality can bring quite unintended risks. Because people live longer, and often suffer from multiple chronic diseases, their records have to be accessible to many different health professionals. Their reluctance to have certain facts on their medical records may then be dangerous. One physician has pointed to some of the possible consequences of such concealment:

> The man who insists that no record be made of a psychiatric history, or the drugs that would suggest that there is one, and wants no record of his syphilis and penicillin injections and subsequent recovery, is the same man who must face squarely the risk of future syphilitic disease of the nervous system or even lethal penicillin reactions because future medical personnel never followed through in the right manner. They do not even know that the problem existed; they and the patient stumbled blindly into trouble.[14]

Do patients have the same claims to confidentiality about personal information when persons from whom it is kept run serious risks? Consider again the family mentioned earlier in which the father wishes to conceal from his children that he suffers from polycystic kidney disease. It is now two years later. The father, much closer to death, has told his two children about the genetic nature of his disease. He was prompted to do so, in part, by his daughter's plans to many. She, however, fears disclosing to her future husband that the same disease may strike her and affect their children. Now it is her turn to insist on confidentiality, not only from her father but from all others who know the facts, including the health professionals involved.

Does a professional owe confidentiality to clients who reveal plans or acts that endanger others directly? Such a question arises for the lawyer whose client lets slip that he plans a bank robbery, or that he has committed an assault for which an innocent man is standing trial; for the pediatrician who suspects that a mother drugs her children to keep them quiet; and for the psychiatrist whose patient discloses that he is obsessed by jealousy and thoughts of violence to his wife....

The autonomy we grant individuals over personal secrets, first of all, cannot reasonably be thought to extend to plans of violence against innocent persons; at such times, on the contrary, someone who knows of plans that endanger others owes it to them to counteract those plans, and, if he is not sure he can forestall them, to warn the potential victims. Nor, in the second place, can patients who voice serious threats against innocent persons invoke confidentiality on the basis of their relationship with therapists or anyone else without asking them to be partially complicitous. The third premise, basing confidentiality in part on a promise, is likewise overridden, since in the absence of legitimacy for the first two, it ought to be clearly understood that no one, whether professionally trained or not, should give such a pledge. The benefits invoked in the fourth premise, finally, are not only not demonstrated in these cases; even if they were, they could not override the injustice done to those unwittingly placed at risk.

...What should a doctor do if he has a patient who suffers from an incurable and highly contagious veneral disease and who plans to marry without disclosing this fact to his fiancée? According to many theologians, the doctor's obligation of secrecy would then cease: the young man forfeits such consideration through his intent to act in a way that might gravely injure his fiancée. The doctor is therefore free to speak, but with certain limitations: he must reveal only so much of the secret as is necessary to avert the harm, and only to the person threatened, who has a right to this information, rather than to family members, neighbors, or the curious or gossip-hungry at large.

These commentators also discussed a subject that still divides the contemporary debate: Should the breach of secrecy to avert grave harm be obligatory, or merely permitted? Should the professional feel free to choose whether or not to warn the endangered person, or acknowledge a duty to do so? It is one thing to say that he no longer owes the client confidentiality; but does he also *owe* the endangered person the information? Do lawyers, for example, owe any information to persons who may be injured by their clients' unlawful tax schemes, plans for extortion, or threats of violence? And if they do recognize some such obligation, how does it weight against that of confidentiality?

The duty of confidentiality clearly has some weight; as a result, the obligation to warn potential victims is not as great for professionals as it might be for others who happen to hear of the danger. Yet it is a strong one nevertheless, especially where serious harm is likely to occur. In such cases, the duty to warm ought to be overriding. Professionals should not then be free to promise confidentiality, nor should a client expect to be able to entrust them with such projects, any more than with stolen goods or lethal weapons.

The same is true for confidences regarding past crimes. Here, too, confidentiality counts; but it must be weighted against other aims—of social justice and restitution. It is therefore hard to agree with those lawyers who argue as a matter of course that they owe clients silence about past, unsolved murders; it is equally hard to agree with Swiss bankers claiming that confidentiality suffices to legitimate the secret bank accounts that attract so many depositors enriched through crime, conspiracy, and political exploitation.

SECRECY AS A SHIELD

The greatest burden of secrecy imposed by confidentiality, however, is that of the secrets professionals keep to protect themselves rather than patients and clients. Confidentiality can be used, here as elsewhere, as a shield for activities that could ill afford to see the light of day. An example of how dangerous such shielding can be is afforded by the story of the death in 1976 of Anneliese Michel, a young German student, after ten months of exorcism.

Anneliese Michel had been under periodic medical care since she was sixteen years old. She had been diagnosed as suffering both from recurrent epileptic seizures and from anorexia nervosa. When she was twenty-two, her parents persuaded her to withdraw from university studies. Ernst Alt, the local parish priest, suspected that she might be possessed by devils and that exorcism might cure her. He saw the seizures as evidence of such possession rather than of epilepsy, and decided to consult Germany's leading "satanologist," the eighty-three-year-old Adolf Rodewyk, S.J. Father Rodewyk concluded that the convulsions were trancelike states of possession in which, among other manifestations, a devil calling himself Judas made no secret of his identity.

Father Rodewyk recommended exorcism. The *Rituale Romanum* of 1614, still followed in cases of exorcism, prescribes that a bishop must agree to the procedure before it can be undertaken, and that the person thus treated must be beyond medical help. Father Rodewyk assured Bishop Joseph Stangl of Würzburg that Anneliese's case was one for exorcists, not for doctors; and the bishop authorized the rites, ordering "strictest secrecy and total discretion."

For ten months, the young woman took part in lengthy sessions with the parish priest and Father Wilhelm Renz, an expert called in for the exorcism. The two prayed with her and tried, by means of holy water, adjurations, and commands, to drive out the devils—by then thought to number at least six and calling themselves, in addition to Judas, by such names as Lucifer, Nero, and Hitler. Anneliese was convinced that she was thus possessed and that the powers of good and of evil were fighting over her soul. She wrote in her diary that the Savior had told her she was a great saint. Fearing that doctors might diagnose her voices and seizures as psychiatric symptoms and send her to a mental hospital, she avoided health professionals. As the months wore on, she grew weaker, eating and drinking next

to nothing. During one particularly stormy session of exorcism, she rushed head first against the wall facing her bed, then lay back exhausted. The devils were finally declared to have left. The next morning, she was found dead in her bed.

In April 1978, her parents and the two priests who had conducted the exorcism were brought to trial. They were convicted of negligent homicide for having failed to seek medical help up to the very end. Physicians testified that, even as late as a few days before Anneliese died, her life could have been saved had she had medical attention. The four accused were sentenced to six months imprisonment.

The priests sincerely believed that they were doing their best to save Anneliese Michel. Insofar as they believed Father Rodewyk's attesting to the presence of devils, they could hardly think medical treatment appropriate. But they knew their belief that Anneliese was possessed by devils would be shared by few, and so they conspired with her parents to keep the sessions of exorcism secret to the very end. Two kinds of confidentiality come together here: that between priest and penitent, and that between caretaker and patient. But neither one should have been honored in this case, for while they protect much that is spoken by penitents and by patients, they were never intended to protect all that is done by priests or caretakers in response, least of all when it constitutes treatment of very sick persons by dangerous methods without medical assistance.

The case is an extreme one. Strict adherence to the stipulation in the *Rituale Romanum* of 1614 that someone must be beyond medical help would have required much more careful consultation with physicians, before leaping to the conclusion that exorcism was called for. When publicity about the case arose, Catholics and non-Catholics alike were distressed at how the young woman had been treated. What is worth nothing, however, is that her need for medical help went unnoticed because of the secrecy in which the exorcism was conducted. The case illustrates, therefore, what can happen in almost any system of advising and helping those in need whenever secrecy shields what is done to them. And it raises broader questions about confidentiality: Exactly whose secret should it protect? The patient's or client's alone? Or the professional's? Or all that transpires between them?

In principle, confidentiality should protect only the first. But in practice, it can expand, like all other practices of secrecy, to cover much more. It may even be stretched so far as to include what professionals hide *from* patients, clients, and the public at large.

The sick, the poor, the mentally ill, the aged, and the very young are in a paradoxical situation in this respect. While their right to confidentiality is often breached and their most intimate problems openly bandied about, the poor care they may receive is just as often covered up under the same name of confidentiality. That is the shield held forth to prevent outsiders from finding out about negligence, overcharging, unnecessary surgery, or institutionalization. And far more than individual mistakes and misdeeds are thus covered up, for confidentiality is also the shield that professionals invoke to protect incompetent colleagues and negligence and unexpected accidents in, for instance, hospitals, factories, or entire industries.

The word "confidentiality" has by now become a means of covering up a multitude of questionable and often dangerous practices. When lawyers use it to justify keeping secret their client's plan to construct housing so shoddy as to be life-threatening, or when government officials invoke it in concealing the risks of nuclear weapons, confidentiality no longer serves the purpose for which it was intended; it has become, rather, a means for deflecting legitimate public attention.

———

Government agencies sometimes request confidentiality, not so much to deflect inquiry as to be able to conduct it in the manner most likely to resolve difficult problems. Thus the U.S. Center for Disease Control argued, in 1980, that it needed to be able to promise confidentiality to hospitals seeking its help for nosocomial, or hospital-induced, infections. Such infection is a major health risk, conservatively estimated as killing twenty thousand persons a year in the United States alone, and contributing to the deaths of over forty thousand others in a substantial manner. When a hospital experiences an outbreak of nosocomial infection, it can call on the expert advice of the Center for Disease Control in order to find the cause of the infection and to reverse its course; but to do so under conditions of publicity is to invite rumor, lawsuits, and patient anxiety, according to those who argued in favor of extending confidentiality to the hospitals. The center saw a need to promise such confidentiality to a hospital in order to help it combat infection, much as a doctor might promise silence to an individual patient with a similar affliction.

The center's request for an exemption from the Freedom of Information Act on such grounds was turned down. No proof had been advanced that the dangers the hospitals feared were realistic. Patients did not appear to be staying away from hospitals that had experienced outbreaks of nosocomial infection; and no suit had been won on the basis of information provided by the center.

The step from patient confidentiality to hospital confidentiality is a large one, but it is often lightly taken in arguments that ignore the differences between the two. The first two premises underlying confidentiality, of autonomy regarding personal information and the respect for intimacy and human bonds, are obviously applicable, if at all, in a different manner when it comes to institutions. And the fourth premise, concerning the benefit to individuals from having somewhere to turn when vulnerable and in need of help, and the indirect benefit to society from allowing professionals to give counsel in strict confidence, must be scrutinized with care whenever the claim is made that it applies to government agencies, law firms, or corporations. We ask of them a much higher degree of accountability.

To be sure, these institutions should be able to invoke confidentiality for legitimate activities such as internal memoranda and personnel files; but it is a different matter altogether to claim confidentiality for plans that endanger others. Such protection attracts all who seek surreptitious assistance with bribery, tax evasion, and similar schemes. And because corporate or consulting law is so lucrative, the power to exercise confidentiality for such secrets then shields not merely the company and the client but the lawyer's own links to, and rewards from, highly questionable practices.

The premises supporting confidentiality are strong, but they cannot support practices of secrecy—whether by individual clients, institutions, or professionals themselves—that undermine and contradict the very respect for persons and for human bonds that confidentiality was meant to protect.

NOTES

1. See Robert E. Regan, *Professional Secrecy in the Light of Moral Principles* (Washington, DC: Augustinian Press. 1943); Alan H. Goldman, *The Moral Foundations of Professional Ethics* (Totowa, NJ: Rowman and Little-field, 1980); LeRoy Walters, "Ethical Aspects of Medical Confidentiality," in Tom L. Beauchamp and LeRoy Walters. eds., *Contemporary Issues in Bioethics* (Encino, CA: Dickenson, 1978), pp. 169–75; Susanna J. Wilson, *Confidentiality in Social Work* (New York: Free Press, 1978); William Harold Tiemann, *The Right to Silence: Privileged Communication and the Pastor* (Richmond, VA: John Knox Press, 1964); William W. Meissner, "Threats to Confidentiality," *Psychiatric Annals* 2 (1979):54–71.

2. From the newsletter *Hard Choices*, Office for Radio and Television for Learning (Boston: 1980), p. 9.

3. For a discussion on whether this partial autonomy over personal information should be defended in terms of property, see Arthur R. Miller *The Assault on Privacy* (Ann, Arbor: University of Michigan Press, 1971), pp. 211–16.

4. For the marital privilege, see Sanford Levinson. *The State and Structures of Intimacy* (New York: Basic Books, forthcoming). For the Chinese tradition, see Derk Bodde and Clarence Morris, *Law in Imperial China* (Cambridge, MA: Harvard University Press, 1967), p. 40.

5. Hugo Grotius. *The Law of War and Peace*, trans. Francis Kelsey (Indianapolis, IN: Bobbs-Merrill, 1925), bk. 2, chap. 11. p. 331.

6. I discussed the question of lying to protect confidences in *Lying* [: *Moral Choice in Public and Private Life* (New York: Pantheon, 1978)], chap. 11.

7. For different views on the binding forces of promises, see William Godwin, *Enquiry Concerning Political Justice* (1793; 3rd ed. 1798), bk. 3. chap. 3; Richard Price, *A Review of the Principal Questions in Morals* (1758; 3rd ed. 1787), chap. 7 (both in D. H. Munro, ed., *A Guide to the British Moralists* [London: William Collins, 1972], pp. 187–97, 180–86). For more general treatments of promising, see Grotius, *Law of War and Peace*, bk. 2, chap. 11, pp. 328–42; John Searle, *Speech Acts* (Cambridge: Cambridge University Press, 1969); Charles Fried, *Contract as Promise* (Cambridge, MA: Harvard University Press, 1981).

8. Nietzsche, in *Ecce Homo*, trans. Kaufmann, p. 64, relates such pledges to the bond between debtor and creditor; he argues that the memory necessary for people to keep promises only developed through such painful, often cruel experiences.

9. For discussions of whether some or all of these premises should be accepted, and whether they are grounded on utilitarian or deontological considerations, see Goldman, *Moral Foundations of Professional Ethics*, Leo J. Cass and William J. Curran, "Rights of Privacy in Medical Practice," partially reprinted in Samuel Gorovitz et al., *Moral Problems in Medicine* (Englewood Cliffs, NJ: Prentice-Hall, 1976), pp. 82–85; Benjamin Freedman, "A Meta-Ethics for Professional Morality," *Ethics* 89:1 (1978):1–19; Benjamin Freedman, "What Really Makes Professional Morality Different: Response to Martin," *Ethics* 91:4 (1981):626–30; Mike W. Martin, "Rights and the Meta-Ethics of Professional Morality," *Ethics* 91:4 (1981):619–25.

10. Henry E. Sigerist, *A History of Medicine*, vol. 1 *Primitive and Archaic Medicine* (New York: Oxford University Press, 1951), p. 433.

11. Jeremy Bentham, otherwise opposed to testimonial privileges for professionals, argues in favor of "excluding the evidence of a Catholic priest respecting the confessions intrusted to him," holding that freedom of religion outweighs the social costs of such practices. See *Works of Jeremy Bentham* [ed. John Bowring (Edinburgh: W. Tait, 1843)], 7:366–68.

12. [International] Code of [Medical] Ethics, 1949 World Medical Association, in *Encyclopedia of Bioethics* (New York: Free Press, 1978), pp. 1749–50.

13. I have discussed abortion in "Ethical Problems of Abortion," *Hastings Center Studies* 2 (1974):33–52.

14. Lawrence Weed, *Your Health Care and How to Manage it* (Arlington, VT: Essex, 1978), p. 79.

Alan Donagan

Justifying Legal Practice in the Adversary System: A Look at Confidentiality

Alan Donagan was the Phyllis Fay Professor of humanities at the University of Chicago.

———————

There can be no doubt that the adversary system imposes upon lawyers a strong duty of confidentiality with respect to their clients' affairs. According to Canon 4 of the American Bar Association's Code of Professional Responsibility (1970), "*A lawyer should preserve the confidences and secrets of a client*."[1] And in the first of the "ethical considerations" in which this canon is explained, it adds:

> A client must feel free to discuss whatever he wishes with a lawyer and a lawyer must be equally free to obtain information beyond that volunteered by his client. A lawyer should be fully informed of all the facts of the matter he is handling in order for his client to obtain the full advantage of our legal system.... The observance of the ethical obligation of a lawyer to hold inviolate the confidences and secrets of his client not only facilitates the full development of facts essential to proper representation of the client but also encourages laymen to seek early legal assistance.[2]

To anybody who accepts the adversary system because of the standard justification, this must seem loose in the extreme. The right of clients, by virtue of their human dignity, to get a hearing for their views both about their rightful due and about the facts of their case has been replaced by something quite different, the right of clients, *irrespective of anything they can possibly claim as their rightful due, and of what they confess in confidence to their lawyer*

the facts are, "to obtain full advantage of our legal system." If the American Bar Association seriously asserts such a right as this, it has an obligation to make a public case for it. The standard justification of the adversary system is not such a case, nor is anything else. I have encountered in the voluminous literature on the subject.

In answering general questions it is well to keep particular examples in mind; an example it is well to keep in mind in thinking about this general question has already given rise to a ruling by the New York Bar Association's Committee on Professional Ethics. It has become generally known as "the Lake Pleasant [bodies] case."[3] In presenting the pertinent facts of it, I substitute letters of the alphabet for the names of those who took part.

> In the summer of 1973, *C* stood charged in _____ County with the crime of murder. The defendant was assigned two attorneys, *A* and *B*. A defense of insanity had been interposed by counsel for *C*. During the course of the discussions between *C* and his two counsel, three other murders were admitted by *C*.... On or about September 1973, *B* conducted his own investigation based upon what his client had told him and with the assistance of a friend the body of *D* was found.... *B* personally inspected the body and was satisfied, presumably, that this was the body of *D* that his client had told him that he murdered.
>
> This discovery was not disclosed to the authorities, but became public during the trial of *C* in June of 1974, when to...establish the defense of insanity, these three other murders were brought before the jury by the defense.... Public indignation reached the fever pitch.... *A* was No Billed by the Grand Jury, but [an indictment] was returned as

From *The Good Lawyer: Lawyers' Roles and Lawyers' Ethics*, edited by David Luban (Totowa, NJ: Rowman and Allanheld, 1984), pp. 123–49.

against *B*, accusing him of having violated § 4200 (1) of the Public Health Law, which, in essence, requires that a decent burial be accorded the dead, and § 4143 of the Public Health Law, which, in essence, requires anyone knowing of the death of a person without medical attendance, to report the same to the proper authorities. Defense counsel move[d] for dismissal of the Indictment on the grounds that a confidential, privileged communication existed between him and *C*.[4]

In a subsequent colloquy on the case, *B* divulged the following further information:

> As we spoke to *C*, we knew of the particular murder he was charged with, but he was reluctant, very reluctant, to talk about the others in which *A* had indicated he was possibly involved. There were two known murders, because those bodies had been found.... [W]ith the suspicion we had of other murders, we knew that the only defense that we could have with this man was insanity.... I finally convinced *C* that the more murders we could reveal if necessary would show the jury that in fact he was insane. We gained his confidence, and after drawing a map we went up to the mountains...we finally found the body.... After taking some pictures, we went back to the car and *A* said, "What shall we do?" My answer was to go back and question *C* now on the second body.... There was never any question in our minds about keeping the secret. It was assumed from our training in law school.[5]

From tragedy to farce. The charges against *B* were dismissed in the county court, the judge virtually transcribing his judgment from an Amicus Curiae Memorandum of Law submitted by the National Association of Criminal Defense Lawyers.[6] The judge declared that

> [t]here must always be a conflict between... obstruction of...justice and the preservation of the right against self-incrimination which permeates the mind of the attorney as the alter ego of his client. But that is not the situation before this court. We have the Fifth Amendment right, derived from the Constitution, on the one hand, as against the trivia of a pseudocriminal statute on the other, which has seldom been brought into play.[7]

Yet, if the court's finding was narrowly technical, the judge's parting compliments to *B* were not: "It is the decision of this Court *B* conducted himself as an officer of the Court with all the zeal at his command to protect the constitutional rights of his client."[8] The Appellate Division's judgment, upholding the trial judge, was more circumspect:

> In view of the fact that the claim of absolute privilege is not all-encompassing...we believe that an attorney must protect his client's interests, but also must observe basic human standards of decency.
>
> We write to emphasize our serious concern regarding the consequences which emanate from a claim of an absolute attorney-client privilege. Because the only question...on this appeal was a legal one with respect to the sufficiency of the indictments, we limit our determination to that issue and do not reach the ethical questions underlying the case.[9]

The courts having washed their hands, the New York State Bar Association's Committee on Professional Ethics applauded their inaction as morally right:

> A lawyer should not reveal a client's confidences or secrets learned during the course of representation, even though they include the revelation by the client of his prior commission of serious undiscovered crimes.[10]

And finally, as its chairman, Robert J. Kutak, has proudly announced, in May 1981 the American Bar Association's Commission on the Evaluation of Professional Standards in the final draft of its proposed Model Rules went further than any representative body of lawyers until then in strengthening the principle of confidentiality "by expanding [it] to encompass all information relating to representation, and by narrowing the exceptions for disclosure."[11] If the proposed Model Rules become law by judicial legislation, honest lawyers will be forbidden on pain of such sanctions as disbarment to disclose any information whatever acquired from a client about completed crimes or frauds, except where their services were used in committing them, or any about crimes or frauds in progress or contemplation when their consequences are "insubstantial."

In this way, almost unnoticeably, the principle of confidentiality, already distorted to protect unjust lawyers in wronging their neighbors to serve unjust clients, will be transformed into an instrument for punishing just lawyers who refuse to commit such wrongs. If, as is probable, the public is helpless, protest is futile. Nevertheless, there is an intellectual duty to expose the shoddiness of the reasons offered not only for the final transformation but also for the original distortion.

Nobody denies that apart from special professional duties of confidentiality, information may be acquired by a member of the community of such a nature that it is his or her duty to communicate it either to some public authority or to other private individuals. Such information is of at least two kinds. The first is information for want of which public authorities are likely, by commission or omission, to act contrary to the common good: for example, information about crimes in progress or contemplation, or about matters the law requires to be publicly investigated, such as deaths or some personal injuries, or the whereabouts of illegal weapons, drugs, or property apparently lost or stolen. The second is information the withholding of which would wrong a private individual: for example, information about the whereabouts of the individual's lost or stolen property, and, more important still, about harm to members of his or her family or friends, whether suffered or in prospect. The duty to disclose such information is in some cases a legal one and in others not. In most jurisdictions, for example, it is not a legal duty to inform the public authorities that, while jogging in the park, you encountered a human body with its throat cut. Presumably it has not been made a legal duty because your duty as a human being and citizen—your moral duty—is evident, and the possibility that anybody with pretensions to moral decency would fail to discharge it has been thought negligible.

Nor is it seriously asserted that ordinary assurances of confidentiality could justify failure to communicate such information. Since it is wrong to promise to keep secret what you have no right to keep secret, it is wrong to give anyone expressly unlimited assurances of confidentiality and ordinary assurances are given with a tacit understanding as to their limits. Suppose that you ask one neighbor whether he knows where another is and he replies, "I'll tell you, if you promise to keep it secret." Were you to promise and were he then to tell you that the neighbor about whom you inquired was lying dead in her basement, would it be reasonable to consider that your promise of confidentiality obliged you to keep that information secret? There is a tacit understanding when such confidences are made that the information you are to be given is not such that it would be your duty to divulge it. And even if you had wrongly given an unlimited assurance, it would not bind you... promises to do wrong are invalid.

What reasons, then, can be given for maintaining that the professional relation of attorney to client justifies an attorney in keeping secrets confided by the client, even though no ordinary duty of confidentiality could justify it? Prima facie, the standard justification for the adversary system yields none. A client's dignity is violated if he or she is unable to be professionally represented in putting forward his or her view of the facts of any case to which he or she is a party and of its rights and wrongs. In representing a client, an attorney has a strict duty to keep secret any information the client may reveal about his or her doings, provided the client furnishes an innocent interpretation of them that can be accepted as possibly true. But there is no apparent reason why that should oblige an attorney to withhold information it would otherwise be one's moral duty to disclose. Nothing it might be one's duty as a citizen or as a human being to disclose would be about doings of a client that permit an innocent interpretation.

In the mountain of fervid special pleading on behalf of extending the lawyer's professional duty of confidentiality beyond what the standard justification of the adversary system plainly allows, I have found only two arguments of any weight. The first is set out in the Amicus Curiae brief of the National Association of Criminal Defense Lawyers in the Lake Pleasant case:

> The Attorney is the alter ego of the client.... The client's Fifth Amendment rights cannot be violated

by his attorney.... Because the discovery of the body of *D* would have presented "*a significant link in the chain of evidence tending to establish his guilt*," *C* was constitutionally exempt from any statutory requirement to disclose the location of the body. And *B*, as *C*'s attorney, was not only equally exempt, but under a positive stricture precluding such disclosure. *C*, although constitutionally privileged.... was free to make such a revelation.... *B* was affirmatively required to withhold disclosure.[12]

In this argument, the right not to incriminate oneself is correctly taken to be a legal one. I do not question that a just and decent society must accord that legal right to all human beings, although I am acquainted with no theory of why it must that satisfies me.[13] But a legal right, even one that society is morally obliged to grant, is not necessarily a moral right. A murderer has no moral right whatever to escape incrimination by concealing the victim's body, although it would be wrong to compel him or her to reveal where it is. To the extreme wickedness of the original crime there has been added the wickedness of obstructing justice, of calculated cruelty to the victim's family and friends, and of desecrating a human body. That the legal right against self-incrimination should entitle the murderer to enlist professional associates in that obstruction, cruelty, and desecration is monstrous as moral theory. A morally decent attorney can be the client's alter ego only in actions that he or she believes the client may possibly have a moral right to do. That there are good moral reasons why a client should not be coerced into refraining from a wrong does not exculpate his attorney in also committing that wrong.

That the argument from an extended right against self-incrimination is confused and sophistical is shown by its acknowledged exceptions. Not even the Commission on the Evaluation of Professional Standards has had the effrontery to maintain that it is a lawyer's duty to withhold information about continuing crimes in which a client is implicated. Yet no such exception could be made if it were a true principle that a lawyer as the client's alter ego has a duty to withhold all incriminating information that the client has a legal right to withhold. Nor does it appear that the false principle can be amended in a morally

coherent way to yield the exceptions the commission desires. Obviously a consequentialist solution will not do. More harm is sometimes caused by withholding information about past crimes than about continuing ones: for example, the parents of the murdered girl in the Lake Pleasant case may be presumed to have suffered more than would the multimillionaire victim of a continuing scheme for embezzling a few thousand dollars. And if a nonconsequentialist solution has been proposed, I do not know of it.

The second of the two serious arguments for extending lawyers' professional duty of confidentiality has been most clearly expressed by Monroe H. Freedman. It can be reduced to three steps:

1. The dignity of human individuals is not respected if lawyers, in defending their clients, cannot ascertain from them all they know about the facts of their cases.[14]
2. "The client can not be expected to reveal to the lawyer all information that is potentially relevant, including that which may well be incriminating, unless the client can be assured that the lawyer will maintain all such information in the strictest confidence."[15]
3. Therefore, the dignity of human individuals is not respected if they are denied the services of lawyers who will maintain even incriminating information in the strictest confidence.

The conclusion of this argument unquestionably follows from its premises. But are those premises, namely 1 and 2, true?

As they stand, neither is plausible, and I doubt whether Freedman himself would maintain either in its full generality. Consider 1: no intelligent client will disclose to his or her lawyer information revealing complicity in a continuing major crime, even though that information may ensure an acquittal on a lesser charge. However, it would be absurd to contend that the client's dignity is thereby violated. It is true that a client is disadvantaged if deterred from confiding to the lawyer all that he or she knows about the case; it is also true that some things that may deter the client would violate his or her dignity. But it does not follow that any client's dignity would be violated if he or she were deterred from confiding information to the lawyer by the normal moral limitations on the duty of confidentiality.

Yet would it not be in some cases? This question takes us to premise 2 and to a class of examples by which Freedman defends it. Clients who are in fact completely innocent may withhold information from their lawyers because, owing to misunderstandings of the law, they mistakenly believe it to establish that they are guilty of a crime. For example, a battered wife who has shot her brutal husband in self-defense may deny that she has shot him at all because, not knowing that killing in self-defense is lawful, she falsely believes herself guilty of murder. In such cases, Freedman contends,

> the lawyer must seek the truth from the client, not shun it. That means that [he] will have to dig and pry and cajole, and, even then, [he] will never be successful without convincing the client that full disclosure to the lawyer will never result in prejudice to the client by any word or action of the attorney.[16]

This seems reckless. It need not be denied that sometimes even the most adroit lawyer may be unable to persuade a timid and ignorant innocent to give information without promising strict confidentiality with respect to past crimes; but is there the slightest reason to suppose that this will be generally the case? It seems more probable that a lawyer of ordinary competence would be able to discern the nature of the fears that might prompt a client to lie or to conceal the truth, and that it would be enough to explain what the law in fact is. If that is so, premise 2 is not true as it stands and cannot bear the burden Freedman's argument places on it.

In sum, given the limited duty of professional confidentiality that can indisputably be derived from the standard justification of the adversary system, there is no reason to believe that, with reasonably competent lawyers, innocent clients will be deterred from confiding in them unless they are unreasonably timid and suspicious or unless they have reasons, independent of their beliefs about the legal system, for preferring to suffer a miscarriage of justice rather than to allow certain things they know to be used

in their defense. In that case, no reason has been given why the respect owed to the dignity of clients who are in fact innocent requires that the duty of professional confidentiality be extended beyond any ordinary, morally bounded duty. *A fortiori*, no reason has been offered why it is required by the respect owed to the dignity of clients who are in fact guilty.

THE DUTY TO EXPOSE A CLIENT'S PERJURY

Those who maintain that it is a lawyer's professional duty to elicit from clients, by faithful promises of strict confidentiality, everything they know pertaining to their cases must also assert that the lawyer is restrained by those promises from exposing them should they then choose to offer perjured evidence. To others, this consequence is a *reductio ad absurdum*. The considerations that generate this conflict have been authoritatively expressed by Freedman as a "trilemma."[17] There are persuasive reasons for each of the following principles:

1. In criminal trials, counsel for the defense must ascertain all relevant facts known to the accused, because the lawyer cannot effectively defend the client if he or she is ignorant of anything that may affect the course of the trial.
2. Counsel must hold in strict confidence disclosures made by the client, because otherwise the client would not feel free to confide fully, and counsel would then be unable to ascertain all relevant facts.
3. The lawyer is an officer of the court, and his or her conduct before the court should be candid.

"As soon as one begins to think about these responsibilities," Freedman justly observes, "it becomes apparent that the conscientious attorney is faced with what we may call a trilemma—that is, the lawyer is required to know everything, to keep it in confidence, and to reveal it to the court."[18]

It is evident that such a conflict of obligations can be resolved only by weakening one or more of the principles that generate it, and which is to be weakened can be determined only by recourse to the foundations of the adversary system itself. Accordingly, Freedman reasons as follows. As an officer of the court, the task of counsel for the defense is to defend the client competently and zealously. Principle 1 lays down a fundamental condition for a competent defense, that the lawyer ascertain all relevant facts; principle 2 states a necessary condition for ascertaining them, that the lawyer reliably assure the client that all disclosures will be held in strict confidence. It follows that the lawyer's function as an officer of the court restricts an obligation of candor. Hence the principle that must be weakened is 3: the candor that counsel for the defense owes to the court must not be interpreted as requiring any breach of assurances to the client of confidentiality.

The defect of this reasoning has already been identified in analyzing Freedman's views about the duty of confidentiality. The assumption that lawyers cannot be expected to ascertain all the pertinent facts of a case unless they can assure their clients of unlimited confidentiality, although a dogma cherished by the National Association of Criminal Defense Lawyers, is unfounded with respect to clients who are in fact innocent. As for clients who are in fact guilty, while they have a legal right not to incriminate themselves, they have no moral right to enlist informed professional help in concealing their guilt. It is not a defect in the adversary system, properly understood, that it allows the guilty to plead innocence only under the disadvantage that their lawyers cannot be fully informed about the pertinent facts.

Once principles 1 and 2 have been independently weakened, there is no need to weaken 3. It is to the credit of the Canadian Bar Association that it has perceived this. Its Code of Professional Conduct requires a lawyer to warn clients that if, having disclosed incriminating information (for which, of course, they furnish innocent explanations), they proceed to deny it at trial, the lawyer cannot argue their untrue testimony to the jury and must explain to the court why he or she cannot.[19] In doing so, it has correctly deduced what the requirements of the adversary system, as founded on the fundamental principle of respect for human dignity, in fact are.

To this Freedman objects that "the inevitable result of the position taken by the Canadian Bar Association would be to caution the client not to be completely candid with the attorney. That, of course, returns us to resolving the trilemma by maintaining confidentiality and candor, but sacrificing complete knowledge."[20] Yes, but only in the case of guilty clients or of unreasonably timid ones, and that, I have argued, does not infringe the principle on which the adversary system rests. Freedman's remark that this solution "is denounced by the [ABA] Standards as 'unscrupulous,' 'most egregious,' and as 'professional impropriety,' "[21] savors of leg-pulling. The Canadian Bar Association lays it down that Canadian lawyers must warn clients that the information they vouchsafe cannot be kept confidential if it shows that evidence subsequently presented on their behalf is perjured. What the American Bar Association denounces is what moral theologians call "affected ignorance";[22] the description of it in the ABA Standards is: "the tactic . . . of advising the client at the outset not to admit anything to the lawyer which might handicap the lawyer's freedom in calling witnesses or in otherwise making a defense."[23] An intelligent scoundrelly client may well adopt the tactic on hearing a Canadian lawyer's warning, but the warning is not advice to adopt it. Freedman's observations about the perils of constructing a defense in ignorance of pertinent facts show that he or she would have cause to be apprehensive in doing so.

NOTES

1. The full text of the code is reprinted in Monroe H. Freedman, *Lawyers' Ethics in an Adversary System* (Indianapolis, IN: Bobbs-Merrill, 1975), pp. 132–238. Canon 4 may be found at p. 178.

2. Ibid., p. 4. Quoting *American Bar Association Standards Relating to the Defense Function* (1971), pp. 145–46.

3. All information about this case is derived from Patrick A. Keenan, Stuart C. Goldberg, and G. Griffith Dick, eds., *Teaching Professional Responsibility: Materials and Proceedings from the National Conference* (Detroit: University of Detroit School of Law, 1979), pp. 237–325.

4. Keenan et al., *Teaching Professional Responsibility*, p. 277, quoting from Judge Ormand N. Gale in 83 Misc. 2d 186, 372 N.Y.S. 2d 798.

5. Ibid., pp. 316–18.

6. Ibid., pp. 279–81; cf. 265–75.

7. Ibid., p. 281.

8. Ibid.

9. Ibid., p. 285 (from a report in *New York Law Journal*, March 7, 1978).

10. Ibid., p. 282 (from N.Y. Appellate Division, Fourth Department, decisions filed December 17, 1975).

11. Robert J. Kutak, "The Adversary System and the Practice of Law," in David Luban, ed., *The Good Lawyer: Lawyers' Roles and Lawyers' Ethics* (Totowa, NJ: Rowman and Allanheld, 1984), pp. 172–187. That the discussion draft of the proposed Model Rules which the commission published in January 1980 was arguably in certain respects *weaker* than the present code had already been remarked by David Luban, "Professional Ethics: A New Code for Lawyers," *Hastings Center Report* 10:3 (1980), p. 14. [For the Model Rules, see appendix 1, sample code 1, *EIPL.*—ED.]

12. Keenan et al., *Teaching Professional Responsibility*, pp. 267–68.

13. David Luban, in "Corporate Counsel and Confidentiality," in *Ethics and the Legal Profession*, ed.

by [Michael Davis and] Frederick A. Elliston (Buffalo, NY: Prometheus, 1986), perceives the difficulty of the problem and opens a promising line for investigation.

14. Freedman, *Lawyers' Ethics in an Adversary System*, p. 5.

15. Ibid.

16. Ibid., p. 30.

17. Ibid., pp. 27–42, esp. pp. 27–28. [See chap. 3, sel. 5, *EIPL.*—ED.]

18. Ibid., p. 28.

19. Ibid., p. 38; referring to *Canadian Bar Association, Code of Professional Conduct*, chap. 8, sect. 9, at 59–60, 62–64. Special Committee on Legal Ethics, Preliminary Report, June 1973.

20. Ibid.

21. Ibid.

22. Cf. St. Thomas Aquinas. *Summa Theologiae*, I–II, 6, 8.

23. *ABA Standards Relating to the Defense Function*, Commentary b to Sec. 3.2, at 205; quoted in Freedman, *Lawyers' Ethics in an Adversary System*, p. 36 note.

Parents, Lies, and Videotape: Covert Video Surveillance in Pediatric Care

Wayne Vaught

Wayne Vaught, Ph.D., is associate Professor of Philosophy and Medicine at the University of Missouri-Kansas City.

INTRODUCTION

In the United States, the use of covert video surveillance (CVS) is becoming increasingly common. Hidden video cameras are virtually everywhere, secretly recording our dialy lives. They are located in banks, supermarkets, and malls. They are on street corners monitoring traffic. They are in parking lots, office buildings, and hospitals. Several companies now offer small and inexpensive hidden camera surveillance systems, making CVS available to virtually anyone....

Some health professionals now advocate for the use of CVS to detect cases of child abuse, such as in Munchausen syndrome by proxy (MSBP). MSBP is a form of abuse whereby caregivers either fabricate symptoms or induce illness in those, under their care. Often, this abuse is inflicted by parents on their very young children.... Foreman and Far-sides define MSBP as "an especially malignant form of child abuse in which the carer (usually the mother) fabricates or exacerbates illness in the child to obtain medical attention."[1] According to Donna Rosenberg, "the children are injected, suffocated, poisoned, phlebotomized, lied to and lied about, usually by their mothers."[2] While such abuse may seem outlandish and rare, the American Professional Society on the Abuse of Children estimates that there are approximately 600 new cases of MSBP per year in the United States.[3] This is significant given that mortality rates for abused children have been reported at around 10 percent.[4]

Two recent studies... found CVS to be an effective diagnostic tool for either documenting or ruling out suspected cases of MSBP. In these cases, hospital staff placed video equipment in patient rooms to record the interactions between parents and their hospitalized children. Southall and colleagues conducted their study at North Staffordshire Hospital in the United Kingdom. In this study, CVS confirmed 33 out of 39 suspected cases of parental abuse. Intentional suffocation occurred in 30 of those cases....

Proponents of CVS believe that the difficulty of confirming suspected cases of MSBP necessitates its use. The perpetrators are often unlikely suspects. They are usually the biological mothers.... Unfortunately, the deceptive nature of the abuse makes it difficult to identify. Furthermore, the common "indicators" of MSBP are often too vague to allow for a definitive diagnosis. According to Hall and colleagues, the stereotypical indicators of MSBP perpetrators (a female caretaker who has a history of healthcare work, does not have a good relationship with the father, is unusually friendly with hospital staff, and is unconcerned or sympathetic when a doctor cannot make a diagnosis) are not sensitive enough to allow health professionals to make accurate diagnoses. In fact, many of these indicators may be consistent with caring, non-abusive parents.

Given the nature of the abuse, discussing the issue with suspected parents is not an option.... If confronted, parents would likely deny such allegations. Whether true or not, such an allegation would strain the relationship between parents and health professionals and would likely prevent an accurate diagnosis from being made. An accurate diagnosis is necessary to eliminate parental abuse and to prevent health professionals from becoming unwitting accomplices by continuing to subject these children to unnecessary, and potentially harmful, tests and treatments while seeking to diagnose an illness these children do not have.... When MSBP is suspected, CVS may provide the only effective means of accurately diagnosing and eliminating the abuse.

Although the goal of CVS is admirable (protecting innocent children from abuse), critics challenge that it constitutes a morally questionable invasion of personal privacy and thus a breach of trust.... Proponents counter that while CVS does threaten privacy and trust, the need to protect innocent children is of greater concern and is justified when necessary to eliminate abuse....

Does CVS constitute a breach of trust?...

CVS, TRUST, AND FIDUCIARY OBLIGATIONS

A *fiduciary* is defined as one who is entrusted with the care of another. Typically, a fiduciary relationship arises between patients and health professionals when patients seek and health professionals agree to provide medical services. When patients are minors, their parents most often initiate the fiduciary relationship. Health professionals have knowledge and skills that their patients, or their patient's parents, lack. Patients' medical needs, combined with a lack of knowledge and skills, make them vulnerable to health professionals. Vulnerability gives rise to the need for trust....

Yet vulnerability alone does not give rise to trust. We are also vulnerable to criminals, but we do not trust them. What, then, is necessary to establish a trusting relationship? Current scholarship tends to emphasize the importance of two factors essential to establishing and maintaining trust relationships: competence and good will.... Robert Solomon and Fernando Flores similarly contend that "one of the obvious conditions of trust is the competence of the person trusted. It makes no sense to trust someone to do something that he or she probably cannot do." But competence alone does not engender trust. Highly competent professionals have been known to manipulate and abuse their patients. In addition to competence, trust will develop only when parents believe that healthcare professionals are motivated properly....

PARENTAL TRUST AND HEALTH PROFESSIONALS

Because parents usually initiate their child's relationship with health professionals, it is useful to begin by considering CVS within the context of the pediatric health professional's fiduciary obligations to parents. First, we must ask what it is that parents entrust to health professionals. In a pediatric setting, parents entrust health professionals with their child's health and well-being. In so doing, they trust health professionals to provide accurate diagnoses and competent medical treatment. In this role, healthcare professionals are trusted not to cause harm to either children or parents. Professional competence and good will is essential when considering the use of CVS, since a lack of either could result in inappropriate applications of the technology. Without proper consideration and motivation, innocent parents could be subjected to unnecessary limitations on their privacy, possibly resulting in considerable harm....

Professional competence is necessary to perform this assessment properly. Thus, to avoid breaches of parental trust, health professionals must be able to make an accurate assessment of the need for CVS and use it appropriately.

...First and foremost, health professionals must have good reasons, based on sound judgment, to believe that the child's medical condition might be related to MSBP....

In addition to competent care, parents trust health professionals to act in their child's best interest....When health professionals suspect parental abuse, the use of CVS to accurately diagnose the abuse would be consistent with their fiduciary obligation to properly care for the children entrusted to them....

However, trust in health professionals depends on more than a positive assessment of their competence and motivation. In fact, most concerns about the use of CVS do not focus on questions regarding a health professional's competence or good will. Rather, it tends to focus on the extent of the professional's discretionary powers....

Entrusting someone to care for something of value requires some discretionary latitude, but seldom is that discretion absolute. Most patients want to maintain control over the range of decisions a health professional may make on their behalf....People who say to their physician, "oh, do whatever you think is best...you're the doctor," have limited claims to a breach of trust on the grounds that the professional exceeded her discretionary powers. However, in most cases parents are unwilling to grant unlimited discretionary power to health professionals. Thus, even in cases where health professionals provide competent care with the child's best interests in mind, they may still breach parental trust by exceeding their discretionary powers.

In the United States, the emphasis on individualism, self determination, and patient autonomy has changed the expectations related to a professional's discretionary powers. Physicians are no longer endowed with the authority to do "whatever they think is best." The prevailing interest in informed consent and advance directives attests to the primacy of the patient's wishes in medical decision making. The patient's right to be an informed decision maker limits a health professional's discretionary powers. In the case of children, parents generally serve as surrogate decision makers and seek to protect their children's best interest. Accordingly, parents trust physicians to consult with them regarding diagnostic tests and treatment options. By usurping this parental role, health professionals would generally exceed their discretionary powers and risk a breach of parental trust.

Do health professionals exceed their discretionary powers when they use CVS to detect MSBP, thereby constituting a breach of trust? CVS might at first appear to breach the parents' trust in that it requires health professionals to engage in sensitive diagnostic monitoring without first obtaining parental consent. On the one hand, use of CVS limits the parents' decisional authority. On the other hand, it limits parental privacy. Not realizing that their child is being monitored, parents may inadvertently disclose, and have recorded, sensitive information not related to the patient's medical condition. Such disclosures could cause embarrassment or significant harm. To protect parents from such harm, parental consent appears to be essential.

The difficulty with informed consent, especially in MSBP, is that the parents are the suspected cause of the child's "illness." We could not reasonably require health professionals to obtain parental consent for CVS and then expect them to document parental abuse. Informed consent would render CVS useless. Parents would simply refrain from abusing their children while in the hospital. This is problematic given that the abuse may continue when the child returns home or is admitted to a different hospital, and could increase the likelihood of significant morbidity or mortality.

Given this difficulty, we must consider whether health professionals may ever legitimately abandon parental consent when treating children. In some cases, such as medical emergencies or the treatment of adolescents for sexually transmitted diseases, health professionals can provide treatment without parental consent. However, parental consent is generally sought prior to providing most medical services.... In cases of suspected abuse, the parents' ability to serve as effective surrogates is brought into question. Here, health professionals no longer believe parental consent to be capable of achieving its desired goal of safeguarding patient interests. Consequently, it may be necessary and appropriate to usurp parental consent to protect those interests.... Health professionals who abandon informed consent to protect children from parental abuse are fulfilling their fiduciary obligations. In this way, their actions would not constitute a breach of parental trust.

The unauthorized limitation on personal privacy is another way in which the use of CVS may exceed a health professional's discretionary powers and result in a breach of parental trust. The use of CVS does limit parental privacy. In fact, critics argue that the invasion of privacy resulting from CVS in itself constitutes a breach of trust....

Does CVS constitute an unreasonable limitation on parental privacy, and hence a breach of trust?

By entrusting their child's care to health professionals, parents begin to limit their own personal privacy. In part, such limitations arise from information they explicitly provide. Since they provide the information, the subsequent limitation on their privacy is not a breach of trust. In other cases, health professionals may limit parental privacy in unexpected, yet necessary, ways. For example, health professionals are trained to observe the child's overall appearance, not simply to focus on areas of parental concern. So, for instance, while a parent may seek medical attention for an ear infection, conscientious health professionals would also take notice of signs of abuse or neglect. Should their physical findings lead them to suspect parental abuse, they are required, ethically and legally, to investigate their concerns. Because such "undesired" observations are essential to care for the child properly, they would not constitute an unwarranted invasion of privacy or a breach of trust. This is true even if the parents were to claim, "We brought our daughter here for you to look in her ears, not at the bruises on her back." Here, the limitation on privacy follows from the health professional's fiduciary obligations. Such limitations must be expected and cannot be construed as an over extension of discretionary powers or a breach of parental trust.

Personal privacy is even more limited in hospital settings. Although CVS has been compared to spying on parents in their homes, hospital rooms should not be equated with private bedrooms. Patient rooms are certainly not "public" areas, and efforts are often made to protect patient privacy, but they are designed to be used for observation, diagnosis, and treatment. To accomplish these tasks, hospital staff (including physicians, nurses, and technicians, in addition to medical and nursing students), enter patient rooms at times, and with greater frequency, than we would ever expect in a private bedroom. Parents should expect, by admitting their children to the hospital, that health professionals will be using diagnostic tools to determine the underlying cause of their child's illness. Furthermore, they should expect that anything said or done in a hospital room could be heard or observed by hospital staff. If it is relevant to patient care, it will be documented in the patient's chart. If parents are engaging in harmful or illegal activities, they will be reported. Given the limited expectation of privacy in patient rooms, the use of CVS merely serves as an extension of health professionals' legitimate investigational tools should they begin to suspect parental abuse.

Critics might challenge that while we do limit our personal privacy when seeking care from health professionals, in most cases people are, or should be, aware of those limitations and can actively seek to control them. CVS, on the other hand, is problematic because parents are completely unaware of its presence. It thus creates an unexpected limitation on parental privacy, which may result in a breach of trust. . . .

Yet, the justification for limiting parental privacy through the use of CVS ultimately depends not on whether parents are aware of its use, but rather on whether they have a reasonable expectation of personal privacy in their child's hospital room. Consider, for example, a related scenario in which a series of thefts prompts an office manager to place a hidden camera in her office. The subsequent taping of an employee rummaging through her desk drawers would not constitute an unwarranted limitation on personal privacy, even though the employee was not aware that the room was being recorded. This is because the thief has no reasonable expectation of privacy in the manager's office. If, on the other hand, the manager placed a camera above a restroom stall, an area where privacy is expected, the subsequent taping would most certainly constitute an unwarranted invasion of privacy and a breach of trust. While there is a lack of awareness of CVS in both cases, they are differentiated by the expectation of personal privacy in the respective areas. When there is no reasonable expectation of privacy, CVS does not constitute an unwarranted limitation of privacy.

A child's hospital room is considerably different from a parent's private bedroom. In a hospital room the reasonable expectation of privacy is much lower. To avoid breaches of trust, some attention should be given to helping parents understand those expectations. On the one hand, this may include

placing signs in public areas. In addition, hospital staff should avoid attempting to persuade suspected abusers that the patent's room is a private area. On the other hand, hospital staff need not be overly descriptive in explaining the limitations of parental privacy. The constant interaction with hospital staff should be enough to suggest that privacy is limited. Additionally, too much disclosure would ultimately undermine the effectiveness of CVS in detecting MSBP. Ultimately, the risks to the parent stemming from unauthorized limitations to their privacy must be weighed against the benefits of protecting a defenseless child from abuse. Since CVS may be the only effective way of confirming and eliminating such abuse, it may outweigh the parental claims to privacy. Additionally, the implementation of strict guidelines to protect parental confidentiality will minimize the potential for serious harms to parents resulting from this limitation on their privacy. In this way, health professionals can fulfill their fiduciary obligations to both parents and children.

Although some limitations on our privacy are necessary whenever we seek assistance from health professionals, we nevertheless expect that private information will be kept confidential. Confidentiality involves a trust relationship regarding the boundaries of privacy. Breaches of confidentiality are breaches of trust. To avoid such breaches in the case of CVS, health professionals must show due diligence in protecting the identity of and information about individuals monitored by such technology. By implementing CVS to detect MSBP, health professionals accept the responsibility of protecting parental privacy and confidentiality. Policies must be in place to protect the information obtained by CVS and to punish those responsible for inappropriate disclosures. Health professionals must also be sure that the tapes are properly secured to prevent unauthorized access and potential misuse.

Should abuse be observed, it would be necessary to turn the tapes over to the proper authorities so that the child can be removed from an abusive environment. The limits to parental confidentiality that result from turning tapes over to child protective services are justified on the grounds that it is necessary to protect a child's life and is required by law. In this way, health professionals are acting to protect what has been entrusted to them. Nevertheless, steps should be taken to provide the appropriate agencies with only that information necessary to diagnose MSBP accurately. Even in cases where CVS is appropriate and the ensuing limitations on parental privacy and confidentiality justified, the failure to protect sensitive information from "non-essential" personnel would constitute an unwarranted limitation on patient privacy and thus a breach of trust.

———————

Health professionals may be reluctant to inform parents about the use of CVS. Their reluctance may stem from embarrassment or fear of parental response. They may fear that non-abusive parents will no longer trust them as care providers or will seek legal action for an invasion of privacy. When CVS exonerates suspected parents, healthcare professionals should explain that MSBP was a legitimate consideration and that the use of CVS was meant only to protect their child from possible harm. Health professionals could explain that most perpetrators of MSBP appear to be loving parents. They could then emphasize that the suspicion of abuse should not be taken to imply that the parents appear to be child abusers. Not only does this discussion follow from a health professional's fiduciary obligations, but it will likely allow for the preservation of a trusting relationship.

TRUST, CHILDREN, AND HEALTHCARE PROFESSIONALS

Thus far, I have focused on trust and the professional's role as fiduciary as it relates to the relationship between parents and health professionals. This is because most concerns about CVS in pediatric care tend to concentrate on breaches of trust within this relationship. But this focus is too limited. Although pediatric health professionals do have fiduciary obligations to parents, most pediatricians view their primary fiduciary relationship as being with the child. The justification for the use of CVS in patient care stems largely from the fiduciary obligations that health professionals have to their pediatric patients.

Unfortunately, there has been unsettling silence on the issues of trust relationships between health professionals and their pediatric patients. One reason for the focus on parents is that trust relationships have traditionally been construed in terms of contractual relations between consenting adults. Since children cannot enter into such contracts, we tend to ignore them in terms of breaches of trust. . . .

———————

Accordingly, we must consider trust outside of the usual contractual framework and consider the trust relationship between children and health professionals as it relates to the issue of CVS in patient care.

. . . Infants typically develop a trusting relationship with their parents. By providing comfort, shelter, and food to meet the child's basic needs, parents help to instill trust in their children. By encouraging such trust with a vulnerable, non consenting individual, parents accept a moral obligation not to violate that trust and cause harm to their children. Abuses of this trusting relationship are particularly disturbing in cases of MSBP.

Consider the following case: . . .

> 16:14 PM: the child walks past her mother, who deliberately trips her up with her leg and kicks her in the abdomen and back on three occasions. The child cries and reaches for her mother who initially ignores her and then, suddenly, picks her up and cuddles her.

The mother has encouraged a trusting relationship. The child expects to be comforted by her mother, and reaches for her when hurt. Yet it is the mother who intentionally inflicts the injury. She then continues to nurture her child's trust by picking her up and cuddling her, contributing to the child's misguided trust in her mother. The mother's actions constitute a clear breach of trust even though it does not violate any contractual agreements between parent and child.

Similarly, health professionals, in conjunction with parents, seek to instill a trusting relationship with their pediatric patients. We encourage children to "trust" their healthcare providers. Consequently, we can speak meaningfully about a child's trust in health professionals and the ensuing professional obligations to that child. When health professionals encouraged a trusting relationship with a vulnerable child, they incur a direct moral obligation to the child. It is for this reason that we must still consider the implications of trust for the use of CVS in cases where the parents are untrustworthy.

While children may be unable to articulate their expectations in relation to trust, we can reasonably argue that by encouraging a trust relationship, health professionals incur many of the same moral obligations that they would have with consenting adult patients. Namely, they ought to act with professional competence and should seek to promote their patients' welfare. I have already considered some of these dimensions in the previous section. The failure to fulfill these obligations would breach the trust of both parents and children.

One concern, however, directly related to the trust relationship between children and health professionals stems from possible harms to children that may result from the use of CVS. In fact, some critics argue that in using CVS health professionals jeopardize the child's safety in their effort to catch parents engaging in abusive behavior....

...By knowingly permitting abuse to occur, which is the case with CVS, health professionals assume some moral responsibility for the subsequent harm. In fact, critics challenge CVS based on the fact that it requires health professionals to allow parental abuse to continue long enough to confirm parental intent....

Although health professionals must allow child abuse to occur long enough to guarantee proper documentation, which could result in harm to the child, it is nevertheless consistent with their fiduciary obligations to the child. First, while abuse is being permitted, it occurs for a much shorter period than would be allowed if CVS were not in place. Without CVS, parents would be able to inflict abuse

repeatedly, and for extended periods of time, completely undetected. This would allow for even greater harm than would likely occur with the use of CVS.

Second, without adequate documentation, there would be no way of effectively removing these children from abusive situations once they leave the hospital. Without proof of parental abuse, these children would remain with their parents, who could then subject them to ongoing and increasingly harmful abuse....

Accordingly, abused children can be assisted quicker and more effectively with the use of CVS than without it. This, it seems, does promote the child's overall well-being.

Furthermore, the risks associated with CVS as a diagnostic tool may be similar to the risks associated with other diagnostic tests, some of which may cause harm to children. Since CVS is being done in a hospital, where health professionals can respond quickly to harms inflicted by parents, this potential risk is minimized. As with other tests, the potential risks have to be weighed against the potential benefits. On balance, health professionals can more readily fulfill their fiduciary obligations to their pediatric patients by minimizing the overall risk of harm with CVS than without it. On these grounds, CVS appears to be consistent with health professionals' fiduciary obligations to their pediatric patients.

We must also consider CVS in relation to the professional's discretionary powers. As suggested earlier, health professionals may betray trust by exceeding these powers. One difficulty, however, with non-contractual trust relationships is that it becomes difficult to determine the exact parameters of those discretionary powers. In the parent–child relationship, parents exercise broad discretionary powers relating to the proper care of their children. While children may develop a trust relationship with a health professional, the professional's discretionary power is nowhere near as extensive as that of the parents. Nevertheless, some discretionary power must be afforded to health professionals so that they may fulfill their obligation to protect the child's health and well-being. If a health professional suspects parents of child abuse, the professional has an obligation to the child to determine the accuracy of the suspicion and to protect the child's interests by removing the source of the abuse. Such discretionary powers seem necessary if we are to speak of professionals as having any real moral obligation to protect a child. We cannot claim that a child's trust in health professionals entails an obligation to protect the child's interests and then deny those professionals the discretionary powers necessary to fulfill this obligation. Where CVS provides the only method for health professionals to protect an abused child from harm, it is an essential component of their discretionary powers and is consistent with their fiduciary obligations to pediatric patients.

NOTES

1. D.M. Foreman and C. Farsides, "Ethical Use of Covert Videoing Techniques in Detecting Munchausen Syndrome by Proxy," *British Medical Journal 307* (1993): 611.

2. D. Rosenberg, "Web of Deceit: A Literature Review of Munchausen Syndrome by Proxy," *Child Abuse and Neglect* 11 (1987): 548.

3. C. Ayoub and R. Alexander, "Definitional Issues in Munchausen by Proxy," *American Professional Society on the Abuse of Children* 11, no. 1 (1998): 7.

4. See note 3 above, p. 1305.

Sissela Bok | # Defining Secrecy—Some Crucial Distinctions

Sissela Bok wrote one of the most popular books on the subject of lying. She followed it up with this book on secrets.

Lying and secrecy intertwine and overlap. Lies are part of the arsenal used to guard and to invade secrecy; and secrecy allows lies to go undiscovered and to build up. Lying and secrecy differ, however, in one important respect. Whereas I take lying to be prima facie wrong, with a negative presumption against it from the outset, secrecy need not be. Whereas every lie stands in need of justification, all secrets do not. Secrecy may accompany the most innocent as well as the most lethal acts; it is needed for human survival, yet it enhances every form of abuse. The same is true of efforts to uncover or invade secrets.

A path, a riddle, a jewel, an oath—anything can be secret so long as it is kept intentionally hidden, set apart in the mind of its keeper as requiring concealment. It may be shared with no one or confided on condition that it go no farther; at times it may be known to all but one or two from whom it is kept. To keep a secret from someone, then, is to block information about it or evidence of it from reaching that person, and to do so intentionally; to prevent him from learning it, and thus from possessing it, making use of it, or revealing it. The word "secrecy" refers to the resulting concealment. It also denotes the methods used to conceal, such as codes or disguises or camouflage, and the practices of concealment, as in trade secrecy or professional confidentiality. Accordingly I shall take concealment, or hiding, to be the defining trait of secrecy. It presupposes separation, a setting apart of the secret from the non-secret, and of keepers of a secret from those excluded. The Latin *secretum* carries this meaning of something hidden, set apart. It derives from *secernere*, which originally meant to sift apart, to separate, as with a sieve. It bespeaks discernment, the ability to make distinctions, to sort out and draw lines: a capacity that underlies not only secrecy but all thinking, all intention and choice. The separation between insider and outsider is inherent in secrecy; and to think

From Sissela Bok, *Secrets* (New York: Vintage Books, 1989). Notes were deleted from this text.

something secret is already to envisage potential conflict between what insiders conceal and outsiders want to inspect and lay bare.

Several other strands have joined with this defining trait to form our concept of secrecy. Although they are not always present in every secret or every practice of secrecy, the concepts of sacredness, intimacy, privacy, silence, prohibition, furtiveness, and deception influence the way we think about secrecy. They intertwine and sometimes conflict, yet they come together in our experience of secrecy and give it depth.

Too exclusive an emphasis on the links between the secret and the sacred can lead one to see all secrecy as inherently valuable. And those who think primarily of the links between secrecy and privacy or intimacy, and of secrets as personal confidences, have regarded them as something one has a duty to conceal. Negative views of secrecy are even more common. Why should you conceal something, many ask, if you are not afraid to have it known? The aspects of secrecy that have to do with stealth and furtiveness, lying and denial, predominate in such a view. We must retain a neutral definition of secrecy, rather than one that assumes from the outset that secrets are guilty or threatening, or on the contrary, awesome and worthy of respect. A degree of concealment or openness accompanies all that human beings do or say. We must determine what is and is not discreditable by examining particular practices of secrecy, rather than by assuming an initial evaluative stance.

It is equally important to keep the distinction between secrecy and privacy from being engulfed at the definitional stage. The two are closely linked, and their relationship is central. In order to maintain the distinction, however, it is important first to ask how they are related and wherein they differ. Having defined secrecy as intentional concealment, I obviously cannot take it as identical with privacy. I shall define privacy as the condition of being protected from unwanted access by others— either physical access, attention, or access to personal information. Claims to privacy are claims to control access to what one takes to be one's personal domain.

Privacy and secrecy overlap whenever the efforts at such control rely on hiding. But privacy need not hide; and secrecy hides far more than what is private. A private garden need not be a secret garden; a private life is rarely a secret life. Conversely, secret diplomacy rarely concerns what is private, any more than do arrangements for a surprise party or for choosing prize winners.

Why then are privacy and secrecy so often equated? In part, this is so because privacy is such a central part of what secrecy protects that it can easily be seen as the whole. People claim privacy for differing amounts of what they are and do and own; if need be, they seek the added protection of secrecy. In each case, their purpose is to become less vulnerable, more in control. When do secrecy and privacy most clearly overlap? They do so most immediately in the private lives of individuals, where secrecy guards against unwanted access by others—against their coming too near, learning too much, observing too closely. Secrecy guards, then, the central aspects of identity, and if necessary, also plans and property. It serves as an additional shield in case the protection of privacy should fail or be broken down. Thus you may assume that no one will read your diary; but you can also hide it, or write it in code, as did William Blake, or lock it up. Secret codes, bank accounts, and retreats, secret thoughts never voiced aloud, personal objects hidden against intruders: all testify to the felt need for additional protection.

Similarly, groups can create a joint space within which they keep secrets, surrounded by an aura of mystery. Perhaps the most complete overlap of privacy and secrecy in groups is that exemplified in certain secret societies. The members of some of these societies undergo such experiences that their own sense of privacy blends with an enlarged private space of the group. The societies then have identities and boundaries of their own. They come into being like living organisms, vulnerable; they undergo growth and transformation, and eventually pass away.

It is harder to say whether privacy and secrecy overlap in practices of large-scale collective secrecy, such as trade or military secrecy. Claims of privacy are often made for such practices, and the metaphors of personal space are stretched to apply to them. To be sure, such practices are automatically private in one sense so long as they are not public. But the use of the language of privacy, with its metaphors of personal space, spheres, sanctuaries, and boundaries, to personalize collective enterprises should not go unchallenged. Such usage can be sentimental, and distort our understanding of the role of these enterprises.

The obsessive, conflict-ridden invocation of privacy in Western society has increased the occasions for such expanded uses of the metaphors of privacy; so has the corresponding formalization of the professional practices of secrecy and openness. At times the shield of privacy is held up to protect abuses, such as corporate tax fraud or legislative corruption, that are in no manner personal.

While secrecy often guards what is private, therefore, it need not be so, and it has many uses outside the private sphere. To see all secrecy as privacy is as limiting as to assume that it is invariably deceptive or that it conceals primarily what is discreditable. We must retain the definition of secrecy as intentional concealment, and resist the pressure to force the concept into a narrower definitional mold by insisting that privacy, deceit, or shame always accompanies it. But at the same time we must strive to keep in mind these aspects of our underlying experience of secrecy, along with the others—the sacred, the silent, the forbidden, and the stealthy.

Secrecy is as indispensable to human beings as fire, and as greatly feared. Both enhance and protect life, yet both can stifle, lay waste, spread out of all control. Both may be used to guard intimacy or to invade it, to nurture or to consume. And each can be turned against itself; barriers of secrecy are set up to guard against secret plots and surreptitious prying, just as fire is used to fight fire.

Conflicts over secrecy—between state and citizen, or parent and child, or in journalism or business or law—are conflicts over power: the power that comes through controlling the flow of information. To be able to hold back some information about oneself or to channel it and thus influence how one is seen by others gives power; so does the capacity to penetrate similar defenses and strategies when used by others. To have no capacity for secrecy is to be

out of control over how others see one; it leaves one open to coercion. To have no insight into what others conceal is to lack power as well.

In seeking some control over secrecy and openness, and the power it makes possible, human beings attempt to guard and to promote not only their autonomy but ultimately their sanity and survival itself. The claims in defense of this control, however, are not always articulated. Some take them to be so self-evident as to need no articulation; others subsume them under more general arguments about liberty or privacy. But it is important for the purposes of considering the ethics of secrecy to set forth these claims. The claims in defense of some control over secrecy and openness invoke four different, though in practice inseparable, elements of human autonomy: identity, plans, action, and property. They concern protection of what we are, what we intend, what we do, and what we own. Some capacity for keeping secrets and for choosing when to reveal them, and some access to the underlying experience of secrecy and depth, are indispensable for an enduring sense of identity, for the ability to plan and to act, and for essential belongings. With no control over secrecy and openness, human beings could not remain either sane or free.

Against every claim to secrecy stands, however, the awareness of its dangers. Secrecy can harm those who make use of it in several ways. It can debilitate judgment, first of all, whenever it shuts out criticism and feedback. The danger of secrecy goes far beyond risks to those who keep secrets. Because it bypasses inspection and eludes interference, secrecy is central to the planning of every form of injury to human beings. It cloaks the execution of these plans and wipes out all traces afterward. It enters into all prying and intrusion that cannot be carried out openly. While not all that is secret is meant to deceive—as jury deliberations, for instance are not—all deceit does rely on keeping something secret. And while not all secrets are discreditable, all that is discreditable and all wrongdoing seek out secrecy (unless they can be carried out openly without interference).

Given both the legitimacy of some control over secrecy and openness, and the dangers this control carries for all involved, there can be no presumption either for or against secrecy in general. Secrecy differs in this respect from lying, promise breaking, violence, and other practices for which the burden of proof rests on those who would defend them. Conversely, secrecy differs from truthfulness, friendship, and other practices carrying a favorable presumption. The resulting challenge for ethical inquiry into the aims and methods of secrecy is great. Not only must we reject definitions of secrecy that invite approval or disapproval; we cannot even begin with a moral presumption in either direction. This is not to say, however, that there can be none for particular practices, nor that these practices are usually morally neutral.

I shall rely on two presumptions that flow from the needs and dangers of secrecy that I have set forth. The first is one of *equality*. Whatever control over secrecy and openness we conclude is legitimate for some individuals should, in the absence of special considerations, be legitimate for all. My second presumption is in favor of *partial individual control* over the degree of secrecy or openness about personal matters—those most indisputably in the private realm. Without a premise supporting a measure of individual control over personal matters, it would be impossible to preserve the indispensable respect for identity, plans, action, and belongings that all of us need and should legitimately be able to claim. Such individual control should extend, moreover, to what people choose to share with one another about themselves—in families, for example, or with friends and colleagues. Without the intimacy that such sharing makes possible, human relationships would be impossible. At the same time, however, it is important to avoid any presumption in favor of *full* control over such matters for individuals. Such full control is not necessary for the needs that I have discussed, and would aggravate the dangers. It would force us to disregard the legitimate claims of those persons who might be injured, betrayed, or ignored as a result of secrets inappropriately kept or revealed.

Deborah G. Johnson | # Hacker Ethics

Deborah G. Johnson is Ann Shirley Carter Olsson Professor of Applied Ethics Technology, Culture, and Communication at the University of Virginia.

I am going to use the term *hacker* to refer to a person who engages in behavior that attacks the Internet and *hacking* to refer to the activity.... When hacker and hacking were first coined, hacker referred to a computer enthusiast and hacking referred to the feats such enthusiasts were able to accomplish. Hackers were individuals who loved computers and would spend hours and hours figuring out how to do clever things with them. Usually hackers were young men who had acquired a good deal of knowledge about computers, and they shared this knowledge with one another through the first electronic bulletin boards. Often hackers organized computer clubs and user groups, circulated newsletters, and even had conventions.

Only later did the term *hacker* acquire negative connotations. Hacker began to be used to refer to those who used computers for illegal actions, especially gaining unauthorized access to computer systems, and stealing (and then sharing) proprietary software. Resisting this change in usage, many oldline computer enthusiasts pushed for a distinction between *crackers* and *hackers*. Hacker, they hoped, would continue to have its original, heroic meaning, while cracker would refer to those who engage in illegal activities—cracking into systems.

From Deborah G. Johnson, *Computer Ethics*, Prentice Hall © 2001, pp. 97–102.

This distinction has not, however, taken hold. Hacker and hacking are now routinely used to refer to those who gain unauthorized access and accomplish other disruptive feats. Still, such a wide variety of illegal activities now occur on the Internet that it seems most useful to reserve the term hacking for only a subset of these. I propose to use the term hacking to refer to the subset of illegal behaviors that involve unauthorized access and aim at disruption and damage. Such acts undermine the security and the integrity of the Internet. On this definition, such acts as intentionally sending viruses or worms that damage computer systems, denial of service attacks, and unauthorized taking control of a Web site all count as hacking.

. . . . In most cases, hacking is illegal and the harmfulness of the activity is apparent. Most Internet users want a system that is reliable; works without interruption; has privacy and integrity; and doesn't require a lot of effort or resources to make secure. Thus, from the perspective of most Internet users, hackers are a nuisance or worse. They snoop around trying to get access to systems they are not authorized to access; they plant viruses and worms bringing systems down and making them unreliable; they copy and distribute proprietary software; they cause expensive denial of service delays. They force everyone to invest more and more effort and resources in security.

There are interesting sociological and psychological questions to be asked about hackers and why they hack. For example, why is it mostly male teenagers who hack? Why do they believe they can get away without being detected even though the technology is now highly traceable? Why is it that individuals who probably wouldn't break into a store on the street are willing to try to break into a computer system? While these are fascinating questions, from an ethical perspective the behavior is transparently undesirable and, therefore, not at all controversial or difficult. Hacking behavior generally doesn't pose difficult or complicated ethical challenges or dilemmas.

The situation was not always like this. In the early days of computing, the situation was different. Computers were just beginning to be used more and more, and the technology to connect computers to one another via telecommunications lines had just become available. At this time, there were no laws specifying what could or couldn't be done via remote access. There weren't laws specifically prohibiting unauthorized access; the idea of designing a worm or virus to infect a computer system had not yet occurred, let alone been prohibited. . . . [T]here were a multitude of policy vacuums.

In those days, the ethical questions were pressing because the policy vacuums had to be filled and there were substantial ethical questions about what rules would be fair and would lead to the best consequences. Perhaps the most pressing issue had to do with the ownership of software. . . . [M]any of the first computer enthusiasts had an alternative vision of the potential of computers. They saw in the reproducibility of computer information and software, the enormous potential to spread information and knowledge across the globe. They saw the parallel between computing and the printing press and envisioned how computing could exponentially extend the spread of knowledge. The fact that electronic information could be reproduced without loss to the original and without loss to the original holder of the information meant the availability of information at essentially no cost. This was a vision of *sharing* of knowledge, not one of property and commercialization. Many enthusiasts resisted the idea of making software into intellectual property. They argued that information should be free (i.e., un-ownable).

Unfortunately, this vision of the potential of computer and information technology has largely been lost. Instead, it is now taken for granted that most information is (or could be or should be) proprietary. Acts of accessing, replicating, and distributing information without permission are immediately seen as privacy- or property-rights violations. Compared to the early days of computing, a good deal of legislation—specifying what is and is not allowed on the Internet—now exists. Most of the policy vacuums have been filled. Thus, the arguments that hackers used to give in their defense now seem somewhat anachronistic. Still, the arguments in defense of hacking are enlightening and for this reason, I will discuss several of them briefly.

The arguments that hackers gave in their defense in the early days of computing can be sorted into four arguments. I have already suggested the first argument; it is the argument to the effect that all information should be free. . . .

The second argument is that break-ins illustrate security problems to those who can do something about them. Remember the Robert Morris case at the beginning of this chapter. Morris claimed that he was trying to expose a flaw in the system. He had tried other means to get the problem fixed but system administrators had not listened to him. Hence, he defended his action on grounds that he was doing a service to computer system administrators and users by demonstrating the seriousness of the problem. In fact, he confessed that he didn't mean to do as much damage as he had done; the worm got out of control.

The argument, in effect, claims that hacking does some good. Hacking illustrates the weaknesses—the vulnerabilities—of computer systems to those who can repair them, before more serious damage is done.

Under careful scrutiny, this argument falters. It suggests that hacking into a system should be understood as an act of whistle-blowing. Individuals "blow the whistle" on illegal or dangerous activities so as to draw attention to a situation, to prevent harm and get the situation fixed. The literature on whistle-blowing suggests that whistle-blowers should always try first to fix the problem through internal channels because it is better to get a bad situation fixed with the least risk or danger (to those who are in danger as well as to the whistle-blower). Yes, we can imagine cases in which an individual is frustrated in her attempts to get a flaw fixed and we can imagine cases in which the flaw is serious enough for severe action. . . . Still, such cases are going to be rare, not the typical motive for hacking in or using a virus.

Arguing by analogy, Spafford gives a convincing counter to the whistle-blowing argument. Spafford suggests that the hacker defense amounts to saying that "vigilantes have the right to attempt to break into the homes in my neighborhood on a continuing basis to demonstrate that they are susceptible to burglars" (Spafford, 1992). Since we would never accept this argument made in defense of burglars,

we should not accept it for hacking. Spafford also points out that online break-ins, even when done to call attention to flaws in security, wastes time and money, and pressures individuals and companies to invest in security. Many do not have the resources to fix systems or implement tighter security, yet the "vigilante behavior" forces upgrades.

An analogy with automobile security seems relevant here. Thirty years ago, depending on where you lived, many individuals were able to leave their automobiles on city streets without locking them and without fear of the car being stolen. Now, in many parts of the world, owners not only must lock their automobiles, they must invest in elaborate security devices to protect against stealing. Indeed, automobile manufacturers now routinely include such devices on cars. All the resources put into automobile security (the owner's money, the police force's time, automobile manufacturers' expertise) could have been invested elsewhere, if so many individuals were not trying to steal automobiles.

Analogously, those who attempt to gain unauthorized access, plant viruses, make denial of service attacks, and so on, compel the investment of time, energy, and other resources into making the Internet secure, when these resources could be used to improve the Internet in other ways. It is important to see that this applies as much to the energies and resources of the designers and manufacturers of computer and information technology as to service providers and individual users.

This defense of hacking does not, then, seem to have force. It is unquestionably a good thing for those who become aware of flaws in the security of computer systems to inform computer administrators and urge them to fix these flaws. We can even imagine cases in which the flaws in security are extremely serious and an individual's reports of the threat to security fall on deaf ears. It is difficult, nevertheless, to imagine a case that justifies using viruses, denial of service attacks, or accessing private files as a means to get the problem fixed.

Another argument, used in defense of gaining unauthorized access to computer systems, is that breaking into a computer system does no harm as long as the hacker changes nothing. And, if the hacker learns something about how computer systems operate, then, something is gained at no loss to anyone.

A little thought reveals the weakness of the first part of this argument, for individuals can be harmed simply by the unauthorized entry. After all, nonphysical harm is harm nonetheless. If individuals have proprietary rights and rights to privacy, then they are harmed when these rights are violated, just as individuals are harmed when they are deprived of their right to vote or their right to due process. Moreover, hackers can do physical harm. For example, hackers could gain access to computer systems used in hospitals where patients are at risk or systems running industrial processes where workers are at physical risk from dangerous chemicals or explosions. Suppose a hacker were to access and tamper with the computer system used to match donated organs with those in need of organs. Here time is absolutely critical. A slow down in the system caused by tampering could make the difference between life and death.

So, the hacker defense that they are doing no harm and actually learning about computer systems is not convincing. Hacking can be dangerous and can put people at unnecessary risk.

To be sure, hackers may learn about computing and computer systems from their hacking activities. It may be argued in particular that hacking is a good way to learn about how to design computer systems to make them more secure. This argument is complex and tricky. The fact that one learns from an activity does not justify it. Giving electric shocks to learners when they make mistakes may promote learning, but this does not make it a good teaching method. Allowing children to stick things in electric outlets might result in their learning the dangers of the outlets, but there are less dangerous ways to teach this lesson. So, just because hackers learn from hacking does not make it a good thing.

Hacking is not the only way to learn about computing or computer security. Aside from the standard ways one learns in the classroom (by reading, listening to a teacher, doing problems), one can imagine a variety of creative ways to teach people about computers and computer security. These might include challenging games or tournaments that encourage learners to be creative and clever.

To justify hacking as a means to learning about computing and computer security, an argument would have to show not just that hackers learn but that hacking is the only way or the best way to learn. Showing that hacking is the "best way" would have to show that the improvement in knowledge and skill was so great as to counterbalance the risks and dangers to those who might be harmed by the hacking. In other words, if hacking promotes learning, the good of the learning would have to be weighed against the negative consequences of this method of learning. So, this defense of hacking is also not convincing.

Finally, hackers used to argue that they would help keep Big Brother at bay. This argument may be more understandable after . . . comprehending the threats to privacy that have arisen because of the use of computer and information technology. The thrust of the argument is that computers and information technology are being used to collect information about individuals and to do things to individuals that they don't want done. Hackers have the computer savvy to find out what is going on and tell us about it. They can assure us that covert illegalities and abuse will not go undetected. In short, the argument suggests that hackers are good vigilantes. Imagine government agencies gathering information they are not authorized or justified in gathering. Imagine companies maintaining secret databases of information that is prohibited by law from being collected or used. Hackers provide protection against this. By gaining unauthorized access to government and commercial systems, they can see when abuse is occurring and alert the public.

The argument is correct in suggesting that the public needs protection against abuses of information and Big Brother. Still, are hackers the best agents for this kind of protection? Would the cost of tolerating hackers be worth what we gain in protection? Do hackers solve the problem or make it worse?

We have many options to monitor for such things as information abuse and government surveillance. We could create a national data protection commission that would have the authority to monitor information practices, propose legislation, and prosecute violators. Commission or no commission, we could develop better laws and clearer guidelines for information practices. We could assign special obligations to computer professionals calling upon them to report any information they acquire about data abuse and/or illegal surveillance. We could encourage users to report suspicious behavior. In short, there are a variety of strategies that could be adopted to protect the public from Big Brother.

While toleration of hackers is one such strategy, it is not the most attractive. The problem is that the public would get rid of one problem by creating another. We might reduce the threat of data abuse and covert surveillance by government and by commercial interests, but in exchange we would be at the mercy of vigilantes. The vigilantes might decide to take a look at our files or explore our computer systems, in the name of protection. Suffice it to say that we would have exchanged the rule of law and protection by formal authorities, for rule by vigilantes.

So, hacking is not justified. It causes harm; it violates legitimate privacy and property rights; it often deprives users of access to their own computer systems and to the Internet; and, it compels investment in security when the invested resources might have been used for other activities. The arguments in defense of hacking are not convincing. Hacking is unethical and has rightly been made illegal.

Nevertheless, a note of caution is in order lest some of the arguments made by hackers be too quickly dismissed. Several of the arguments point to potentials of the Internet that are being neglected—to the detriment of the Internet. Implicit in the hacker arguments is a concern to take advantage of the enormous potential of the Internet for spreading and sharing information. The reproducibility of the Internet makes it possible for information to be reproduced at negligible cost; in theory this means information and knowledge could be spread across the globe at little cost. On the other hand, this potential is undermined by extensive property rights that restrict distribution of information. Hackers seem aware of this, as well as of the vulnerability of computer systems to attack and failure. This vulnerability is often under-appreciated when important information and activities are put online without adequate security. Finally, hackers' concerns about Big Brother are worthy of consideration. . . . [P]rivacy on the Internet is rapidly shrinking.

So, while hacking is disruptive, dangerous, and unjustified, discussion provoked by hackers and hacking—of what should be allowed and not allowed on the Internet—should not be squelched too quickly. Hacking represents a countercurrent in the development of the Internet, and to take advantage of the enormous potential of the Internet, it behooves us to listen to countercurrents.

Newshour | # The Princess and the Press

HAYNES JOHNSON, Journalist/Author: Obviously, there's a larger problem here. I mean, there's always going to be a symbiosis between glamour, fame, success, great money, and the press. The public loves it. The Bible loved it. You go back and look at the stories from the beginning. What's happened, though, is it's gone beyond that. We're now in an age of excess, where the big money takes over.

From a transcript of *Newshour with Jim Lehrer*, September 2, 1997, after the death of Princess Diana in a high-speed automobile accident in Paris.

The paparazzis are part of a larger problem. And I think we've all got to be honest about that. I think we have the paradox here. We have the best-trained, most professional news business in our history—Americans. We're serious, solid, and all that. That's—for us. At the same time we're also so wrapped up in celebrity and scandal that it's like the O. J. trial drives everything else out, so all you see is another O. J. or a Tonya Harding, or some sort of endless spectacle, and, of course, Diana is a part of that process.

———

JIM LEHRER: What did you do when you heard Tom Bearden report a moment ago that there are pictures being circulated around the world now of the death scene—these people in the car dying—with an asking price of $6 million?

JIM GAINES: I sighed. It's hard to believe. But there it is. I mean, I think Haynes is right. It's a different day, and this stuff will happen. I mean, it would be wrong for us to say we're shocked, shocked to find out that the press is a business—maybe not like every other business but a business nevertheless—it is. And here's capitalism at work. This stuff will happen, and the irony is that the more you try to tighten up on it, the more press agents try to tighten up in behalf of their clients, probably the rarer and more valuable these pictures will become and the worse the situation would get.

JIM LEHRER: Do you agree with *New York Times* columnist Abe Rosenthal and others, and Haynes Johnson included, that people who have had jobs like you have had bear whatever responsibility there is for this, along with the photographers.

JIM GAINES: Yes. I would say it's definitely true. There's no question about it. I think, as Margaret Carlson pointed out in this week's *Time*, even *Time* magazine has printed pictures of pictures. I mean, we wouldn't buy those pictures, but we would print the front page of the *Sun* or the *Globe* or something if there was something newsworthy. And I don't think we certainly wouldn't have

done it of pictures of this scene, but, you know, that's been done in the past.

———

JIM LEHRER: . . . I think we could probably sit here for a few minutes and work out a scenario where these $6 million photographs become a huge story in and of themselves in say a week or ten days, we might be talking about those photographs on this program, and you might be running stories on them in the *Hartford Courant*. How are we going to do that without running those photographs?

JOHN LONG: Just don't run them. We just have to draw the line. I mean, we've reached a point here—this is like a watershed. This thing hit. This thing is going to change attitudes. We have to draw the line and say, no, we will not run these things.

JIM LEHRER: Who's got to draw the line and who's got to make those kinds of decisions?

JOHN LONG: We do; the photographers who shoot the stuff, the editors who put it in the paper, and the public who buys the papers.

JIM LEHRER: Sally Quinn, is that going to happen?

SALLY QUINN, Author/Journalist: I don't think so. I think we'll all for the next week or two, while everyone is in mourning, everyone will sort of be much more responsible, and then I think it'll go back the way it was before. And, you know, I was saying to Haynes earlier, it sort of puts you in a difficult position to say there are other people responsible, besides the photographers who were chasing them. And I don't really want to come across as a pro-paparazzi, who's out to kill people. But I think that, you know, there's sort of a chain of responsibility that goes all the way up. And if includes not only the driver, who was drunk, and perhaps someone in the car who said, hurry up and get away, but the people who were demanding the publicity, the readers, the editors, readers like me, the editors, and also the owners. I mean, you know, Rupert Murdoch owns a lot of these newspapers and periodicals. Where are the owners and the publishers who put the pressure on the editors to get the circulation, who then put the pressure on the photographers, who—to get the story?

JIM LEHRER: The French actress, Catherine Deneuve, said today, in fact, she said, these photographers are dogs of war, unleashed by unscrupulous editors and publishers and they should not be treated like criminals.

———————

SALLY QUINN: They should not be treated like criminals.

———————

If you're in a public place and a person's walking across a public street, you take their picture, and that's fine, but I think when you start invading their territory or when you start stalking or harassing, then regardless of whether you're a journalist or photographer or paparazzi or just an ordinary crazy person—(laughing)—

JIM LEHRER: Just an ordinary crazy person, right.

SALLY QUINN: —it shouldn't be allowed.

———————

HAYNES JOHNSON: … There's clearly a line has been crossed, as Sally says. If you're talking or following or pushing, pursuing, even maybe causing a crash, it's a complicated question. That's one thing. They have a right to photograph the celebrity people who are public figures; they don't have a right to go in your house; they don't have a right to break the law; they don't have a right to invade your privacy, stick cameras in your face, the way we saw those thing of Di, having to come out of a car like this—

———————

JIM GAINES: … I think the line is clear. It's harassment, physical intimidation, and things that are civilly, you know, recoverable.

JIM LEHRER: I read your piece that you wrote in this week's *Time*, where you talked about when you were the managing editor of *People Magazine*, your job was to chronicle everything that Princess Diana did. Why? Why was that your job?

JIM GAINES: Because she was an immensely interesting, fascinating character, the stuff of dreams and hopes and fantasies. She was a wonderful story.

———————

JIM LEHRER: Did you feel at any time that you were invading her privacy, or did you feel like she was a willing participant, and she'd made a deal?

JIM GAINES: We never got close to invading her privacy. She was very, very public, very easy to photograph. She photographed wonderfully, and she was very, very good to the press. I think she paid perhaps for some of that ease with the press.

JIM LEHRER: John Long, does your profession, the press photographers, through your association, plan to do anything now? Do you feel under siege? Do you feel you've been tarred? Do you feel you have got a problem because of this?

JOHN LONG: Yes. We do feel we have a problem. We've had a problem for a long time. The growing tabloid culture, the tabloid TV, the tabloid newspapers have been—the increased awareness of this kind of activity has been something that we've been fighting for a long, long time. It's part of our bylaws that we don't invade privacy; that we don't intimidate people.

JIM LEHRER: Who defines that? How do you define that—when you're invading somebody's privacy and when you're intimidating somebody?

JOHN LONG: You have to hit it with a journalistic principle of does the public need this information to make informed choices. That's the whole purpose of the news industry, is to bring information to people so they can make informed choices. If they need that information, then we will take the pictures, and we will publish the pictures. … It's a line drawn in the sand. How do you—every time you think you grab it, it's moved someplace else. It's a very difficult thing to do, and it changes over time. But that's the principle we tried to work under, and will we be doing anything in the future, yes, we will. We haven't had a chance to really put any new—I don't—we probably won't be creating any new guidelines. We've got the guidelines in place. What we'll be doing is emphasizing them to our members.

———

SALLY QUINN: And, you know, I really do think that if you were walking down the street today and there were five newspapers for sale and one of them had pictures, you may be hesitant to buy it, but you'd certainly be sort of fascinated and curious to stop and look at those pictures. I mean, it's really like looking at an accident. I mean, when people drive down the highway and suddenly an accident occurs and there are 25 people around it, this is human nature. Those pictures

will come out, and everybody in the world will have a chance to see them.

———

JIM LEHRER: Yes, but you're saying, Sally Quinn, that the public is saying, hey, I want to see those photographs, and I will pay to see those photographs of these people dying in the backseat of a car.

SALLY QUINN: I'm not saying this is the way I think it should be. I just—I'm saying this is the way I think it is. And I mean, I think that the very reason that you have these tabloids is a perfect example of why this is going to happen and why it will continue to happen. I don't think that—I really—I know we are all saying it's a watershed—I don't think it really is a watershed. I think that things will go back exactly the way they are, maybe there will be rules made against stalking or whatever, but I think that as long as the money is there, this is going to continue.

CASES

CASE 5.1

Should Doctors Talk to Relatives Without a Competent Patient's Consent?

O Mytton

I began clinical school over two years ago. It was a memorable time: finally setting out to become a doctor—there was a mixture of excitement and uncertainty. I was conscious of the image of a naive, well intentioned medical student, who becomes worn

down by "the system" and ultimately ends up compromising his original ethical standpoint. For this reason I approached ethics with much interest.

One of the first principles we learnt concerned confidentiality. This appeared simple: do not tell

From *J Med Ethics* 2005;31:266. doi: 10.1136/jme.2004.006957.

others who are not involved in the patient's care, information gleaned from a consultation. It also appeared reasonable and an important part of the doctor/patient relationship. During a group discussion, however, we found it more complicated. How does one hold a confidential consultation on a ward? Which discussions are appropriate with colleagues, friends, or someone on the end of a telephone?

From an early stage one area that vexed me was the issue of doctors talking to the relatives of competent patients. The General Medical Council (GMC) guidelines do not discuss sharing information with relatives of competent patients.[1] Despite this they state that protection of confidence is important, and that consent for disclosure outside the health care team should be sought. This would imply that consent should always be sought from a patient before talking to relatives when the patient is not present. This seemed difficult. Surely relatives would want and expect information?

During my clinical attachments, however, I routinely saw doctors talking to relatives without any apparent attempt to seek permission from the patient first. I, and others, found this at odds with what we were taught.

A typical scenario would be this. An elderly patient presents with chest pain. She is diagnosed with and treated for a myocardial infarction (MI). Later the ward round takes place. Surrounded by the family, granny (as she has now become) is doing well—a little tired, perhaps bemused by all the fuss. The medical firm descends. Clever words are exchanged. Chins are rubbed. The consultant asks a few pertinent questions. He then explains his diagnosis and its significance. The family rush in with their questions—they are young and sharp. Consultant and firm turn and leave Fine.

Sometimes though they seem to drag the family with them, and then a second dialogue develops—a more earnest, serious affair, away from granny. "Just what is granny's prognosis?"

I talked to clinicians about this. They acknowledged that it was important to involve relatives and share information with them, agreeing also that consent for disclosure should first be sought. It was, however, clear that clinicians did think carefully about exactly what was said to whom.

I was unsure what I thought. I had agreed with the guidelines. Yet I was seeing a practice that was inconsistent with the guidelines, but which functioned well. Was this poor practice or were the guidelines, the basis for our teaching, too simple? I had two concerns about this "rule bending." First, that the patient's autonomy may be weakened when left out of a conversation. Second, that information may be shared with relatives that the patient does not wish to be shared.

On further reflection and observation I saw how the involvement of relatives tended to act to promote exchange of information and evaluation of choices. In this way autonomy can be enhanced, particularly if one holds a view of autonomy that stresses the importance of evaluation and rational choices.[2,3]

Regarding the second concern, the sharing of information with relatives that a patient wants to remain confidential: this does give rise to a few complaints. Mistakes will happen and every area of medicine has risks; our response is to balance potential benefits against risk. Here I judged the benefits of talking to relatives to be greater than the rare but significant distress caused by sharing information.

During my first year I tried to reconcile the two approaches, the one taught in the classrooms and the other learnt on the wards. I favoured the latter, not because it is theoretically better but because in practice it works well. This reflects my experience of classroom ethical teaching which is that it is limited when based on the guidelines alone, and so needs to be grounded in clinical situations. The BMA called for more teaching of ethics.[4]...

REFERENCES

1. General Medical Council. *Confidentiality: protecting and providing information*. London: General Medical Council, 2000.
2. Hope T. Savulescu J. Hendrick J. *Medical ethics and law: the core curriculum*. Edinburgh: Churchill Livingstone, 2003.
3. Dworkin G. *The theory and practice of autonomy*. Cambridge: Cambridge University Press, 1988.
4. Eaton L. Medical ethics teaching should be overhouled, says BMA *BMJ* 2003;327:1306.

Questions

1. Regarding medical disclosure, should patient autonomy be the primary concern of a physician? How can one determine a patient's autonomy or competency?

2. Can disclosure to relatives provide more autonomy for the patient by discussing and promoting more choices?

3. Discuss the limits of confidentiality. How can a greater awareness of medical ethics promote a greater understanding of this controversial issue?

CASE 5.2

DeLay PAC Is Indicted for Illegal Donations: Corporate Gifts Aided GOP in Texas Races

R. Jeffrey Smith

A grand jury in Texas indicted yesterday a state political action committee organized by House Majority Leader Tom DeLay (R-Tex.) for accepting $120,000 in allegedly illegal corporate campaign contributions shortly before and after the 2002 elections that helped Republicans cement their control of the House of Representatives.

The indictment follows a lengthy investigation in Austin that previously had targeted the defunct political action committee's executive director, John Colyandro. He was indicted last year for accepting illegal corporate donations and for illegally laundering $190,000 in corporate funds through the Republican National State Elections Committee that later wound up in the hands of Texas Republican candidates.

The criminal charges are based on a Texas election law, akin to rules in 17 other states, that strictly bars political contributions from corporations for election purposes. But according to evidence submitted in a related civil trial, the committee, Texans for a Republican Majority (TRMPAC), raised and spent at least $523,000 in corporate funds—most of which were not reported to state election officials.

The funds paid for surveys, mailings, receptions, candidate investigations and probes of Democratic candidates that helped Republicans gain control of the Texas House for the first time in 130 years, and enabled them to redraw the state's congressional districts in 2003 in such a way that Texas voters elected five more Republicans to Congress in 2004.

DeLay, who was a member of the committee's advisory board, signed fundraising solicitations and participated in at least one conference call to discuss the committee's plans, was not named in the indictment. He also has not been publicly identified as a target of the continuing investigation by Travis County District Attorney Ronald Earle.

DeLay spokesman Kevin Madden responded to the indictment with a written statement saying that it "is limited to a political organization and does not affect Mr. DeLay."

From the *Washington Post*, Sept. 9, 2005.

Madden also disclosed for the first time that DeLay had "voluntarily" talked to Earle's office about the investigation last month, and that DeLay said then that his involvement in the committee's activities was "limited to serving on the political action committee's advisory board along with other elected Texas officials and ... appearing at fundraising events."

Madden said DeLay "assured the district attorney's office that he was not involved in the day-to-day operations of TRMPAC, and to his knowledge all activities were properly reviewed and approved by lawyers" for the committee.

When asked yesterday about DeLay, however, Earle said at a news conference that he was hampered in bringing charges by a provision of the election law that gives him direct authority only over residents of Travis County. He has separately said he does not face that limitation with respect to bringing new charges under the state money-laundering statute.

DeLay's residence is in Fort Bend County, where the prosecutor is an elected Republican, John F. Healey Jr. If Earle found evidence of criminal wrongdoing by DeLay under the election statute, he could only pass on the information to Healey with a recommendation that he pursue the matter.

Earle has not done so, several sources said yesterday, but has until the end of this month to decide the matter under a three-year statute of limitations.

The grand jury singled out two contributions that it said the committee illegally accepted—a $20,000 contribution from AT&T Corp. on Nov. 18, 2002, and a $100,000 contribution from the Alliance for Quality Nursing Home Care Inc. on Oct. 24, 2002. The latter donation generated considerable controversy in Texas political circles after local newspapers reported that state Rep. Tom Craddick accepted it in a white envelope from the head of a large Texas nursing home chain during a meeting at a Houston restaurant.

Craddick's attorney, Roy Q. Minton, said that Craddick—who was later elected speaker of the House and in that role oversaw the redrawing of congressional districts—immediately passed the check along to TRMPAC. "Just because the guy happens to be speaker of the House does not mean it's against the law," Minton said.

Terry Scarborough, an attorney for TRMPAC before it formally went out of business this summer, declined to comment on the committee's indictment. Four additional indictments by the grand jury separately accused the Texas Association of Business with accepting additional illegal corporate funds and coordinating its expenditure with TRMPAC. Attorneys for the association have denied wrongdoing.

Questions

1. Most of the funds of TRMPAC were not reported to state election officials, but were used to heavily influence elections. What ethical dilemmas are the basis for the laws prohibiting this practice?

2. The provision of jurisdiction doesn't allow the district attorney of Travis County to prosecute DeLay directly. Regardless of this legal loophole, should DeLay have been named in the indictment as the organizer of the committee?

CASE 5.3
You're a Voyeur, I'm a Voyeur
Dwight Garner

That's what I remember thinking, in the days after Diana's death, when a paparazzo with the improbably Dickensian name of Romualdo Rat was among the Gang of Seven picked up by the Paris police for tailing the princess's Mercedes. In the stiffly egalitarian *New York Times*, which bestows honorifics on serial killers and Nobel Prize-winners alike, the photographer picked up an apt title of his own: Mr. Rat.

Perversely, I couldn't help but cheer him. I was tired already of the saccharine banalities about Diana; further, I saw her senseless death as a fairly straightforward case of drunk driving—or, in the British usage, "drink driving," which always makes me envision a martini glass at the wheel of a sporty roadster. You can convince me that paparazzi are bottom feeders and bad customers, and that they make life hell for some celebrities. (If you need proof, rent a copy of "Blast 'Em," Joseph Blasioli's stomach-turning 1993 documentary about "stalkerazzi." Watching how these men work is nearly as shocking and revealing as watching how meat is made.) But you cannot convince me that they are guilty of murder. If Di's addled driver thought he was trying to shake armed terrorists, he was very badly mistaken.

In an uncanny coincidence, an exhibit of paparazzi photographs—planned long before Diana's death—opened last week at New York's tony Robert Miller Gallery. The show, a glance back at the work of several decade's worth of photographers like Mr. Rat, has a good deal to say about our fascination with star wattage, and with the informal and unposed "stolen" image. The show also chronicles (if not quite as dramatically as Blasioli's documentary) the often uneasy relationship between celebrity

photographers and their frequently unwilling prey. Like paparazzi pix themselves, the show is a guilty pleasure.

The photographs in "Paparazzi," virtually all of them in black-and-white, date from the mid-1950s to the present. (The show's final image is one of Diana, seen from behind, walking arm-in-arm with Ralph Lauren.) But the bulk of these images are from the late '50s and early '60s, surely the golden age of glamour in America. These weren't just the Camelot years but the dawn of the jet set; indeed, many of the photographs depict celebrities stepping smartly off airplanes. The Italian photographer Luigi Leoni's silvery images (all from 1960) of Eva Peron, Maurice Chevalier and actress Anna Magnani arriving at the Rome airport feel almost like formal portraits; the scenes are as ritualized as press conferences.

This was an era before zoom lenses and rat-a-tat-tat speed drives, when a huge pop of light from an outsized flashbulb cast itself over a subject as if the moment were a baptism. A photograph like Marcello Geppetti's "Anita Ekberg in Her Convertible Mercedes With a Friend, Via Veneto," taken one night in Rome in 1960, is an ample reminder of how moving true glamour, against all of our better instincts, can be. It helps to contrast this photo with a more recent image, a few feet away from the Ekberg shot, of singer Mariah Carey with her boss and former husband Tony Mottola; the pair look like they've been smuggled in from a Holiday Inn lounge act.

It's no surprise that this show leans heavily on Italian photographers. The term *paparazzi* itself derives from a character in Fellini's 1960 movie "La Dolce Vita," a celebrity chaser named Paparazzo. One of the shocking things about this show, however, is how composed and artful many of these

From *Salon Magazine*, Sept. 15, 1997.

snapshots seem to us now. Partly this is nostalgia at work; partly it is simple talent. Geppetti's 1962 photograph of director Michelangelo Antonioni and actress Monica Vitti fighting off a young photographer, for example, or Tazio Secchiarolli's image, from the same year, of Fellini on the set of "8 ½," resonate like works by artists who have received far more acclaim. The photos feel like art, and they are priced like it. Secchiarolli's Fellini shot is offered, in the show's catalog, for $2,400.

Geppetti's image of an angry Antonioni isn't the only photograph here that depicts celebrities tangling, Sean Penn-style, with paparazzi. There's a wonderful series of images by Secchiarolli in which Anita Ekberg's James Bond-ish boy-pal Anthony Steel chases the photographer down the street. (Secchiarolli evidently kept shooting away.) Another series of Ekberg photos, these by Geppetti, shows the actress confronting paparazzi with a bow and arrows. A small notation in the gallery's catalog reads: "Original arrows available for sale upon request."

Writers and intellectuals have rarely been targeted by paparazzi—never mind the fact that both Susan Sontag and Philip Roth made the *cover* of Vanity Fair in the pre-Tina Brown early '80s—and this is probably good for all of us. So it's a bit of shock to stumble across photographer Dino Pedriali's three very nude, very intrusive photos of the late writer Pier Paolo Pasolini taken through a large picture window in 1975. In the first, a hunky Pasolini reclines nude on a bed reading a book—his pose resembles that of a Playgirl centerfold—his manhood quite in evidence. In the second, he's spotted the photographer and is leaping up in alarm. In the third he stands, defiantly naked, glaring out of the window with his face pressed against the glass. I walked past shaking my head and counting my blessings; at least it wasn't a dangling Dean Koontz.

The spookiest and most resonant photo in the exhibition is without a doubt a 1960 Marcello Geppetti picture of Jayne Mansfield, taken near Rome. The image is titled, poignantly, "Jayne Mansfield Lying on the Ground After Having Been Assaulted by a Woman Jealous of Her Beauty," and it shows a dazed, hurt-looking Mansfield on the street, in a white dress, surrounded by men who are about to help her to her feet. It's a shot that resembles the famous photograph of Robert Kennedy following his assassination in 1968, and it's the one that sticks with you and makes you uneasy as you leave this exhibit.

It wasn't a photographer who physically assaulted Mansfield—yet she, like Diana, was attacked in a different manner almost daily because of her beauty and fame, caught in a crush of attention. It's possible to believe that Mr. Rat didn't kill Diana and still recognize that, for the photographers—and, by extension, for all of us—the line between love and hate doesn't really exist any longer.

Questions

1. Although celebrities have chosen a career in the limelight, are there still basic privacy rights that should be respected?

2. What are the limits of privacy? The "pursuit of happiness"? A celebrity lifestyle?

3. Do the photographers (paparazzi) have a right to "get the picture" by any means possible, as it is a tenant of their chosen profession?

4. Since most of the celebrities exposed in the art show have since passed away, and this time of "stalkerazzi" is regarded as historically "quaint," should these pictures fetch a price upwards of $2,500?

CASE 5.4

Trade Secrets: It's Not Who You Know

Philip H. Albert

If knowledge is power, then Google and Yahoo are much stronger as a result of their recent acquisitions of notable search experts from their competitors.

Several months ago, Google hired Kai-Fu Lee, an expert in search technology and the China market, away from Microsoft. Yahoo recently hired Andrei Broder away from IBM. Despite the relative timing, it looks like Broder will start real work before Lee, which provides a lesson for the rest of us on the right way and the wrong way to acquire talent.

For those who don't follow the search business, Broder was part of the team at Digital Equipment Corporation that developed what was once the largest Internet search engine by far: AltaVista. Even those that do follow the search business might have trouble keeping up with what comes next.

Compaq acquired DEC and spun off AltaVista, which was in turn acquired by Overture Services, which was in turn acquired by Yahoo. So it might feel like a homecoming for Broder. Not the typical scenario that would lead to litigation.

Now, on the other side of Moffett Field, Google hires Kai-Fu Lee away from Microsoft. The paper trail, at least according to Microsoft, shows that Lee introduced himself to Google via an e-mail asking about opportunities in China, and mentioning that he was working on areas very related to Google's business.

Other tidbits were obtained from Microsoft computers used by Lee. A document Microsoft claims is from the "recycle bin" on one of those computers

discussed employment conditions, including that Google would pay Lee even if Microsoft could prevent him from working at Google for a year. Ouch.

TRADE SECRETS AND HIRING

The mysterious case of Google, Microsoft, and Lee focuses on trade secrets. A trade secret is anything you don't want your competition to know and has value because it is kept a secret. Every organization is entitled to keep its trade secrets to itself, even to the point of having employees agree that they will not use or disclose the trade secrets once they leave.

One way to do this is to obtain a signed noncompete agreement. This says an employee agrees not to work for competitors for a certain time period after leaving. It also precludes the employee from using noncompany-specific knowledge as well as trade secrets, and is generally a more accepted way to protect your property than, say, using a blunt instrument.

Inherently, it is also a way to keep employees from leaving because they might have to take a year or more off before starting their new jobs.

Trade secrets and employment agreements vary from state to state, and state law sometimes can override the terms of the noncompete agreement. This causes problems in the Google-Microsoft-Lee case. Google claims California law applies because Google is in California, while Microsoft says Washington law applies because the noncompete says so.

Question

1. Think about the ethical questions regarding noncompete agreements. Trade secrets are an integral part to the success of a business, but they inherently bind employees from making autonomous decisions about their careers. Weigh the arguments for and against for both sides.

From Newsfactor.com, Dec. 7, 2005.

6

Integrity and Loyalty

Whistle-Blowing and Self-Regulation

Introduction

With luck, you will never be asked to do anything unethical in your professional life. Many of us, working with ethical people in (morally) healthy, happy environments, never have to face the awful choice confronted by the whistleblower. We never have to stand up to our bosses or our coworkers and insist, often at the price of our own careers, that we will not allow an immoral practice to continue.

We hope that this book has helped you how to recognize morally questionable situations and practices and to understand what is at stake when important values are compromised. But that intellectual process is importantly different from the real courage that is required to act when you witness—or, still worse, are asked to tolerate or even participate in—immoral actions. Sadly, many professionals find themselves in such tough situations. Nurses see doctors with addiction problems coming to the hospital to treat the sick or even to operate. Lawyers are asked to help corporations perform morally dubious sales and transactions. Accountants are asked to "look the other way" about slipshod or dishonest earnings reports (think of the Arthur Andersen accountants who audited Enron).

This chapter considers two tough questions. When should you blow the whistle on your employer or fellow professional? And what does it take, as a person, to do so?

The fundamental moral tension in whistle-blowing is between loyalty and a sense of what is right and wrong. Whistle-blowers often feel that the "insider information" they possess about a morally questionable practice comes to them only because they were welcomed into a company or a profession, and so they should not betray that trust by exposing the wrongdoing. Whistle-blowers also worry about the harm they will do to others and the harms they will likely suffer themselves. Most whistle-blowers report real personal damage from their action—including the loss of financial security, career, even family. We are taught from a young age not to be "a tattletale." You may have seen the movie *Scent of a Woman*, in which the hero is asked to report evidence of wrongdoing by some fellow classmates. He refuses to do so, even though it means he will be kicked out of school—and he refuses to do so, we are to understand, because of his moral fiber. He doesn't want to be a rat. And indeed, loyalty is a tremendously important moral good, without which our professional lives—and indeed, our personal lives—would be much the worse.

So why would anyone ever blow the whistle? The second half of this chapter is especially concerned with moral courage. It is true that, at least sometimes, the morally appropriate thing to do is to keep a secret. It is usually a bad idea to betray a confidence. But sometimes a morally courageous person identifies a practice that is clearly immoral. He or she recognizes a great harm that is being done or that may occur if someone doesn't speak up, if everyone fails to say "No." At times like this, moral courage—and what we think of as moral character or integrity—is required. Sometimes we have to stand up for what we believe is right, or against what we think is wrong, no matter what the cost.

| Sissela Bok | # Whistleblowing and Professional Responsibility |

Sissela Bok is a member of the American Academy of Political and Social Science and is an Eleanor Roosevelt Fellow. She is a professor at Harvard University.

"Whistleblowing" is a new label generated by our increased awareness of the ethical conflicts encountered at work. Whistleblowers sound an alarm from within the very organization in which they work, aiming to spotlight neglect or abuses that threaten the public interest.

The stakes in whistleblowing are high. Take the nurse who alleges that physicians enrich themselves in her hospital through unnecessary surgery; the engineer who discloses safety defects in the braking systems of a fleet of new rapid-transit vehicles; the Defense Department official who alerts Congress to military graft and overspending: all know that they pose a threat to those whom they denounce and that their own careers may be at risk. . . .

NATURE OF WHISTLEBLOWING

Three elements, each jarring, and triply jarring when conjoined, lend acts of whistleblowing special urgency and bitterness: dissent, breach of loyalty, and accusation.

Like all dissent, whistleblowing makes public a disagreement with an authority or a majority view. But whereas dissent can concern all forms of disagreement with, for instance, religious dogma or government policy or court decisions, whistleblowing has the narrower aim of shedding light on negligence or abuse, or alerting to a risk, and assigning responsibility for this risk.

Would-be whistleblowers confront the conflict inherent in all dissent: between conforming and sticking their necks out. The more repressive the authority they challenge, the greater the personal risk they take in speaking out. At exceptional times, as in times of war, even ordinarily tolerant authorities

From Sissela Bok, "Whistleblowing and Professional Responsibility," *New York University Education Quarterly*, 11 (Summer 1980): 2–7. Reprinted with permission. Notes were deleted from the text.

may come to regard dissent as unacceptable and even disloyal.

Furthermore, the whistleblower hopes to stop the game; but since he is neither referee nor coach, and since he blows the whistle on his own team, his act is seen as a violation of loyalty. In holding his position, he has assumed certain obligations to his colleagues and clients. He may even have subscribed to a loyalty oath or a promise of confidentiality. Loyalty to colleagues and to clients comes to be pitted against loyalty to the public interest, to those who may be injured unless the revelation is made.

Not only is loyalty violated in whistleblowing, hierarchy as well is often opposed, since the whistleblower is not only a colleague but a subordinate. Though aware of the risks inherent in such disobedience, he often hopes to keep his job. At times, however, he plans his alarm to coincide with leaving the institution. If he is highly placed, or joined by others, resigning in protest may effectively direct public attention to the wrongdoing at issue. Still another alternative, often chosen by those who wish to be safe from retaliation, is to leave the institution quietly, to secure another post, then to blow the whistle. In this way, it is possible to speak with the authority and knowledge of an insider without having the vulnerability of that position.

It is the element of accusation, of calling a "foul," that arouses the strongest reactions on the part of the hierarchy. The accusation may be of neglect, of willfully concealed dangers, or of outright abuse on the part of colleagues or superiors. It singles out specific persons or groups as responsible for threats to the public interest. If no one could be held responsible—as in the case of an impending avalanche—the warning would not constitute whistleblowing.

The accusation of the whistleblower, moreover, concerns a present or an imminent threat. Past errors or misdeeds occasion such an alarm only if they still affect current practices. And risks far in the future lack the immediacy needed to make the alarm a compelling one, as well as the close connection to particular individuals that would justify actual accusations. Thus an alarm can be sounded about safety defects in a rapid-transit system that threaten or will shortly threaten passengers, but the revelation of

safety defects in a system no longer in use, while of historical interest, would not constitute whistleblowing. Nor would the revelation of potential problems in a system not yet fully designed and far from implemented.

Not only immediacy, but also specificity, is needed for there to be an alarm capable of pinpointing responsibility. A concrete risk must be at issue rather than a vague foreboding or a somber prediction. The act of whistle-blowing differs in this respect from the lamentation or the dire prophecy. An immediate and specific threat would normally be acted upon by those at risk. The whistleblower assumes that his message will alert listeners to something they do not know, or whose significance they have not grasped because it has been kept secret.

The desire for openness inheres in the temptation to reveal any secret, sometimes joined to an urge for self-aggrandizement and publicity and the hope for revenge for past slights or injustices. There can be pleasure, too—righteous or malicious—in laying bare the secrets of co-workers and in setting the record straight at last. Colleagues of the whistleblower often suspect his motives: they may regard him as a crank, as publicity-hungry, wrong about the facts, eager for scandal and discord, and driven to indiscretion by his personal biases and shortcomings.

For whistleblowing to be effective, it must arouse its audience. Inarticulate whistleblowers are likely to fail from the outset. When they are greeted by apathy, their message dissipates. When they are greeted by disbelief, they elicit no response at all. And when the audience is not free to receive or to act on the information—when censorship or fear of retribution stifles response—then the message rebounds to injure the whistleblower. Whistleblowing also requires the possibility of concerted public response: the idea of whistleblowing in an anarchy is therefore merely quixotic.

Such characteristics of whistleblowing and strategic considerations for achieving an impact are common to the noblest warnings, the most vicious personal attacks, and the delusions of the paranoid. How can one distinguish the many acts of sounding an alarm that are genuinely in the public interest from all the petty, biased, or lurid revelations that pervade our querulous and gossip-ridden society? Can we draw distinctions between different whistleblowers, different messages, different methods?

We clearly can, in a number of cases. Whistleblowing may be starkly inappropriate when in malice or error, or when it lays bare legitimately private matters having to do, for instance, with political belief or sexual life. It can, just as clearly, be the only way to shed light on an ongoing unjust practice such as drugging political prisoners or subjecting them to electroshock treatment. It can be the last resort for alerting the public to an impending disaster. Taking such clear-cut cases as benchmarks, and reflecting on what it is about them that weighs so heavily for or against speaking out, we can work our way toward the admittedly more complex cases in which whistleblowing is not so clearly the right or wrong choice, or where different points of view exist regarding its legitimacy—cases where there are moral reasons both for concealment and for disclosure and where judgments conflict. Consider the following cases:[1]

A. As a construction inspector for a federal agency, John Samuels (not his real name) had personal knowledge of shoddy and deficient construction practices by private contractors. He knew his superiors received free vacations and entertainment, had their homes remodeled and found jobs for their relatives—all courtesy of a private contractor. These superiors later approved a multimillion no-bid contract with the same "generous" firm.

Samuels also had evidence that other firms were hiring nonunion laborers at a low wage while receiving substantially higher payments from the government for labor costs. A former superior, unaware of an office dictaphone, had incautiously instructed Samuels on how to accept bribes for overlooking sub-par performance.

As he prepared to volunteer this information to various members of Congress, he became tense and uneasy. His family was scared and the fears were valid. It might cost Samuels thousands of dollars to protect his job. Those who had freely provided Samuels with information would probably recant or withdraw their friendship. A number of people might object to his using a dictaphone to gather information. His agency would start covering up and vent its collective wrath upon him. As for reporters and writers, they would gather for a few days, then move on to the next story. He would be left without a job, with fewer friends, with massive battles looming, and without the financial means of fighting them. Samuels decided to remain silent.

B. Engineers of Company "A" prepared plans and specifications for machinery to be used in a manufacturing process and Company "A" turned them over to Company "B" for production. The engineers of Company "B," in reviewing the plans and specifications, came to the conclusion that they included certain miscalculations and technical deficiencies of a nature that the final product might be unsuitable for the purposes of the ultimate users, and that the equipment, if built according to the original plans and specifications, might endanger the lives of persons in proximity to it. The engineers of Company "B" called the matter to the attention of appropriate officials of their employer who, in turn, advised Company "A." Company "A" replied that its engineers felt that the design and specifications for the equipment were adequate and safe and that Company "B" should proceed to build the equipment as designed and specified. The officials of Company "B" instructed its engineers to proceed with the work.

C. A recently hired assistant director of admissions in a state university begins to wonder whether transcripts of some applicants accurately reflect their accomplishments. He knows that it matters to many in the university community, including alumni, that the football team continue its winning tradition. He has heard rumors that surrogates may be available to take tests for a fee, signing the names of designated applicants for admission, and that some of the transcripts may have been altered. But he has no hard facts. When he brings the question up with the director of admissions, he is told that the rumors are unfounded and asked not to inquire further into the matter.

INDIVIDUAL MORAL CHOICE

What questions might those who consider sounding an alarm in public ask themselves? How might they articulate the problem they see and weigh its injustice before deciding whether or not to reveal it? How can they best try to make sure their choice is the right one? In thinking about these questions it helps to keep in mind the three elements mentioned earlier: dissent, breach of loyalty, and accusation. They impose certain requirements—of accuracy and judgment in dissent; of exploring alternative ways to cope with improprieties that minimize the breach of loyalty; and of fairness in accusation. For each, careful articulation and testing of arguments are needed to limit error and bias.

Dissent by whistleblowers, first of all, is expressly claimed to be intended to benefit the public. It carries with it, as a result, an obligation to consider the nature of this benefit and to consider also the possible harm that may come from speaking out: harm to persons or institutions and, ultimately, to the public interest itself. Whistleblowers must, therefore, begin by making every effort to consider the effects of speaking out versus those of remaining silent. They must assure themselves of the accuracy of their reports, checking and rechecking the facts before speaking out; specify the degree to which there is genuine impropriety; consider how imminent is the threat they see, how serious, and how closely linked to those accused of neglect and abuse.

If the facts warrant whistleblowing, how can the second element—breach of loyalty—be minimized? The most important question here is whether the existing avenues for change within the organization have been explored. It is a waste of time for the public as well as harmful to the institution to sound the loudest alarm first. Whistleblowing has to remain a last alternative because of its destructive side effects: it must be chosen only when other alternatives have been considered and rejected. They may be rejected if they simply do not apply to the problem at hand, or when there is not time to go through routine channels or when the institution is so corrupt or coercive that steps will be taken to silence the whistleblower should he try the regular channels first.

What weight should an oath or a promise of silence have in the conflict of loyalties? One sworn to silence is doubtless under a stronger obligation because of the oath he has taken. He has bound himself, assumed specific obligations beyond those assumed in merely taking a new position. But even such promises can be overridden when the public interest at issue is strong enough. They can be overridden if they were obtained under duress or through deceit. They can be overridden, too, if they promise something that is in itself wrong or unlawful. The fact that one has promised silence is no excuse for complicity in covering up a crime or a violation of the public's trust.

The third element in whistleblowing—accusation—raises equally serious ethical concerns. They are concerns of fairness to the persons accused of impropriety. Is the message one to which the public is entitled in the first place? Or does it infringe on personal and private matters that one has no right to invade? Here, the very notion of what is in the public's best "interest" is at issue: "accusations" regarding an official's unusual sexual or religious experiences may well appeal to the public's interest without being information relevant to "the public interest."

Great conflicts arise here. We have witnessed excessive claims to executive privilege and to secrecy by government officials during the Watergate scandal in order to cover up for abuses the public had every right to discover. Conversely, those hoping to profit from prying into private matters have become adept at invoking "the public's right to know." Some even regard such private matters as threats to the public: they voice their own religious and political prejudices in the language of accusation. Such a danger is never stronger than when the accusation is delivered surreptitiously. The anonymous accusations made during the McCarthy period regarding political beliefs and associations often injured persons who did not even know their accusers or the exact nature of the accusations.

From the public's point of view, accusations that are openly made by identifiable individuals are more likely to be taken seriously. And in fairness to those criticized, openly accepted responsibility for blowing the whistle should be preferred to the denunciation or the leaked rumor. What is openly stated can more easily be checked, its source's motives challenged, and the underlying information examined. Those under attack may otherwise be hard put to defend themselves against nameless adversaries. Often they do not even know that they are threatened until it is too late to respond. The anonymous denunciation, moreover, common to so many regimes, places the burden of investigation on government agencies that may thereby gain the power of a secret police.

From the point of view of the whistleblower, on the other hand, the anonymous message is safer in situations where retaliation is likely. But it is also often less likely to be taken seriously. Unless the message is accompanied by indications of how the evidence can be checked, its anonymity, however safe for the source, speaks against it.

During the process of weighing the legitimacy of speaking out, the method used, and the degree of fairness needed, whistleblowers must try to compensate for the strong possibility of bias on their part. They should be scrupulously aware of any motive that might skew their message: a desire for self-defense in a difficult bureaucratic situation, perhaps, or the urge to seek revenge, or inflated expectations regarding the effect their message will have on the situation. (Needless to say, bias affects the silent as well as the outspoken. The motive for holding back important information about abuses and injustice ought to give similar cause for soul-searching.)

Likewise, the possibility of personal gain from sounding the alarm ought to give pause. Once again there is then greater risk of a biased message. Even if the whistleblower regards himself as incorruptible, his profiting from revelations of neglect or abuse will lead others to question his motives and to put less credence in his charges. If, for example, a government employee stands to make large profits from a book exposing the iniquities in his agency, there is danger that he will, perhaps even unconsciously, slant his report in order to cause more of a sensation.

A special problem arises when there is a high risk that the civil servant who speaks out will have to go through costly litigation. Might he not justifiably try

to make enough money on his public revelations—say, through books or public speaking—to offset his losses? In so doing he will not strictly speaking have *profited* from his revelations: he merely avoids being financially crushed by their sequels. He will nevertheless still be suspected at the time of revelation, and his message will therefore seem more questionable.

Reducing bias and error in moral choice often requires consultation, even open debate: methods that force articulation of the moral arguments at stake and challenge privately held assumptions. But acts of whistleblowing present special problems when it comes to open consultation. On the one hand, once the whistleblower sounds his alarm publicly, his arguments will be subjected to open scrutiny; he will have to articulate his reasons for speaking out and substantiate his charges. On the other hand, it will then be too late to retract the alarm or to combat its harmful effects, should his choice to speak out have been ill-advised.

For this reason, the whistleblower owes it to all involved to make sure of two things: that he has sought as much and as objective advice regarding his choice as he can *before* going public; and that he is aware of the arguments for and against the practice of whistleblowing in general, so that he can see his own choice against as richly detailed and coherently structured a background as possible. Satisfying these two requirements once again has special problems because of the very nature of whistleblowing: the more corrupt the circumstances, the more dangerous it may be to seek consultation before speaking out. And yet, since the whistleblower himself may have a biased view of the state of affairs, he may choose not to consult others when in fact it would be not only safe but advantageous to do so; he may see corruption and conspiracy where none exists.

NOTE

1. Case A is adapted from Louis Clark, "The Sound of Professional Suicide," *Barrister*, Summer 1978, p. 10; Case B is Case 5 in Robert J. Baum and Albert Flores, eds., *Ethical Problems of Engineering* (Troy, N. Y.: Rensselaer Polytechnic Institute, 1978), p. 186.

Michael Davis

Some Paradoxes of Whistleblowing

Michael Davis is a Senior Fellow at the Illinois Institute of Technology Center for the Study of Ethics in the Professions and a professor of philosophy.

Most acts, though permitted or required by morality, need no justification. There is no reason to think them wrong. Their justification is too plain for words. Why then is whistleblowing so problematic that we need *theories* of its justification? What reason do we have to think whistleblowing might be morally wrong?

Whistleblowing always involves revealing information that would not ordinarily be revealed. But there is nothing morally problematic about that; after all, revealing information not ordinarily revealed is one function of science. Whistleblowing always involves, in addition, an actual (or at least declared) intention to prevent something bad that would otherwise occur. There is nothing morally problematic in that either. That may well be the chief use of information.

What seems to make whistleblowing morally problematic is its organizational context. A mere individual cannot blow the whistle (in any interesting sense); only a member of an organization, whether a current or a former member, can do so. Indeed, he can only blow the whistle on his own organization (or some part of it). . . .

The whistleblower cannot blow the whistle using just any information obtained in virtue of membership in the organization. A clerk in Accounts who, happening upon evidence of serious wrongdoing while visiting a friend in Quality Control, is not a whistleblower just because she passes the information to a friend at the *Tribune*. She is more like a self-appointed spy. She seems to differ from the whistleblower, or at least from clear cases of the whistleblower, precisely in her relation to the information in question. To be a whistleblower is to reveal information with which one is *entrusted*.

But it is more than that. The whistleblower does not reveal the information to save his own skin (for example, to avoid perjury under oath). He has no excuse for revealing what his organization does not want revealed. Instead, he claims to be doing what he should be doing. If he cannot honestly make that claim—if, that is, he does not have that intention—his revelation is not whistleblowing (and so, not justified as whistleblowing), but something analogous, much as pulling a child from the water is not a rescue, even if it saves the child's life, when the "rescuer" merely believes herself to be salvaging old clothes. What makes whistleblowing morally problematic, if anything does, is this high-minded but unexcused misuse of one's position in a generally law-abiding, morally decent organization, an organization that *prima facie* deserves the whistleblower's loyalty (as a burglary ring does not).

The whistleblower must reveal information the organization does not want revealed. But, in any actual organization, "what the organization wants" will be contested, with various individuals or groups asking to be taken as speaking for the organization. Who, for example, did what Thiokol wanted the night before the *Challenger* exploded? In retrospect, it is obvious that the three vice presidents, Lund, Kilminster, and Mason, did not do what Thiokol wanted—or, at least, what it would have wanted. At the time, however, they had authority to speak for the company—the conglomerate Morton-Thiokol head-quartered in Chicago—while

From *Business and Professional Ethics Journal* 15 (Spring 1996). Reprinted by permission of the author. Notes were deleted from the text.

the protesting engineers, including Boisjoly, did not. Yet, even before the explosion, was it obvious that the three were doing what the company wanted? To be a whistleblower, one must, I think, at least temporarily lose an argument about what the organization wants. The whistleblower is disloyal only in a sense—the sense the winners of the internal argument get to dictate. What can justify such disloyalty?

THE STANDARD THEORY

According to the theory now more or less standard,[1] such disloyalty is morally permissible when:

(S1) The organization to which the would-be whistleblower belongs will, through its product or policy, do serious considerable harm to the public (whether to users of its product, to innocent bystanders, or to the public at large);

(S2) The would-be whistleblower has identified that threat of harm, reported it to her immediate superior, making clear both the threat itself and the objection to it, and concluded that the superior will do nothing effective; and

(S3) The would-be whistleblower has exhausted other internal procedures within the organization (for example, by going up the organizational ladder as far as allowed)—or at least made use of as many internal procedures as the danger to others and her own safety make reasonable.

Whistleblowing is morally required (according to the standard theory) when, in addition:

(S4) The would-be whistleblower has (or has accessible) evidence that would convince a reasonable, impartial observer that her view of the threat is correct; and

(S5) The would-be whistleblower has good reason to believe that revealing the threat will (probably) prevent the harm at reasonable cost (all things considered).

Why is whistleblowing morally required when these five conditions are met? According to the standard theory, whistleblowing is morally required, when it is required at all, because "people have a moral obligation to prevent serious harm to others if they can do so with little cost to themselves."[2] In other words, whistleblowing meeting all five conditions is a form of "minimally decent Samaritanism" (a doing of what morality requires) rather than "good Samaritanism" (going well beyond the moral minimum). . . .

THREE PARADOXES

That's the standard theory—where are the paradoxes? The first paradox I want to call attention to concerns a commonplace of the whistleblowing literature. Whistleblowers are not minimally decent Samaritans. If they are Samaritans at all, they are good Samaritans. They always act at considerable risk to career, and generally, at considerable risk to their financial security and personal relations.

In this respect, as in many others, Roger Boisjoly is typical. Boisjoly blew the whistle on his employer, Thiokol; he volunteered information, in public testimony before the Rogers Commission, that Thiokol did not want him to volunteer. As often happens, both his employer and many who relied on it for employment reacted hostilely. Boisjoly had to say goodbye to the company town, to old friends and neighbors, and to building rockets; he had to start a new career at an age when most people are preparing for retirement.

Since whistleblowing is generally costly to the whistleblower in some large way as this, the standard theory's minimally decent Samaritanism provides *no* justification for the central cases of whistleblowing. That is the first paradox, what we might call "the paradox of burden."

The second paradox concerns the prevention of "harm." On the standard theory, the would-be whistleblower must seek to prevent "serious and considerable harm" in order for the whistleblowing to be even morally permissible. There seems to be a good deal of play in the term *harm*. The harm in question can be physical (such as death or disease), financial (such as loss of or damage to property), and perhaps even psychological (such as fear or mental illness). But there is a limit to how much the standard theory can stretch "harm." Beyond that limit are "harms" like injustice, deception, and waste. As morally important as injustice, deception, and waste can be, they do not seem to constitute the "serious and considerable harm" that can require someone to become even a minimally decent Samaritan.

Yet, many cases of whistleblowing, perhaps most, are not about preventing serious and considerable physical, financial, or psychological harm. For example, when Boisjoly spoke up the evening before the *Challenger* exploded, the lives of seven astronauts sat in the balance. Speaking up then was about preventing serious and considerable physical, financial, and psychological harm—but it was not whistleblowing. Boisjoly was then serving his employer, not betraying a trust (even on the employer's understanding of that trust); he was calling his superiors' attention to what he thought they should take into account in their decision and not publicly revealing confidential information. The whistleblowing came after the explosion, in testimony before the Rogers Commission. By then, the seven astronauts were beyond help, the shuttle program was suspended, and any further threat of physical, financial, or psychological harm to the "public" was—after discounting for time—negligible. Boisjoly had little reason to believe his testimony would make a significant difference in the booster's redesign, in safety procedures in the shuttle program, or even in reawakening concern for safety among NASA employees and contractors. The *Challenger*'s explosion was much more likely to do that than anything Boisjoly could do. What Boisjoly could do in his testimony, what I think he tried to do, was prevent falsification of the record.

Falsification of the record is, of course, harm in a sense, especially a record as historically important as that which the Rogers Commission was to produce. But falsification is harm only in a sense that almost empties "harm" of its distinctive meaning, leaving it more or less equivalent to "moral wrong." The proponents of the standard theory mean more by "harm" than that. De George, for example, explicitly says that a threat justifying whistleblowing must be to "life or health."[3] The standard theory is strikingly more narrow in its grounds of justification than many examples of justified whistleblowing suggest it should be. That is the second paradox, the "paradox of missing harm."

The third paradox is related to the second. Insofar as whistleblowers are understood as people out to prevent harm, not just to prevent moral wrong, their chances of success are not good. Whistleblowers generally do not prevent much harm. In this too, Boisjoly is typical. As he has said many times, the situation at Thiokol is now much as it was before the disaster. Insofar as we can identify cause and effect, even now we have little reason to believe that—whatever his actual intention—Boisjoly's testimony actually prevented any harm (beyond the moral harm of falsification). So, if whistleblowers must have, as the standard theory says (S5), (beyond the moral wrong of falsification) "good reason to believe that revealing the threat will (probably) prevent the harm," then the history of whistleblowing virtually rules out the moral justification of whistleblowing. That is certainly paradoxical in a theory purporting to state sufficient conditions for the central cases of justified whistleblowing. Let us call this "the paradox of failure."

A COMPLICITY THEORY

As I look down the roll of whistleblowers, I do not see anyone who, like the clerk from Accounts, just happened upon key documents in a cover-up. Few, if any, whistleblowers are mere third-parties like the good Samaritan. They are generally deeply involved in the activity they reveal. This involvement suggests that we might better understand what justifies (most) whistleblowing if we understand the whistleblower's obligation to derive from *complicity* in wrongdoing rather than from the ability to prevent harm.

Any complicity theory of justified whistleblowing has two obvious advantages over the standard theory. One is that (moral) complicity itself presupposes (moral) wrongdoing, not harm. So, a complicity justification automatically avoids the paradox of missing harm, fitting the facts of whistleblowing better than a theory which, like the standard one, emphasizes prevention of harm.

That is one obvious advantage of a complicity theory. The second advantage is that complicity invokes a more demanding obligation than the ability to prevent harm does. We are morally obliged to avoid doing moral wrongs. When, despite our best efforts, we nonetheless find ourselves engaged in some wrong, we have an obligation to do what we reasonably can to set things right. If, for example, I cause a traffic accident. I have a moral (and legal) obligation to call help, stay at the scene until help arrives, and render first aid (if I know how), even at substantial cost to myself and those to whom I owe my time, and even with little likelihood that anything I do will help much. Just as a complicity theory avoids the paradox of missing harm, it also avoids the paradox of burden.

What about the third paradox, the paradox of failure? I shall come to that, but only after remedying one disadvantage of the complicity theory. That disadvantage is obvious—we do not yet have such a theory, not even a sketch. Here, then, is the place to offer a sketch of such a theory.

Complicity Theory

You are morally required to reveal what you know to the public (or to a suitable agent or representative of it) when:

(C1) what you will reveal derives from your work for an organization;

(C2) you are a voluntary member of that organization;

(C3) you believe that the organization, though legitimate, is engaged in serious moral wrongdoing;

(C4) you believe that your work for that organization will contribute (more or less directly) to the wrong if (but *not* only if) you do not publicly reveal what you know;

(C5) you are justified in beliefs C3 and C4; and

(C6) beliefs C3 and C4 are true.

The complicity theory differs from the standard theory in several ways worth pointing out here. The first is that, according to C1, what the whistleblower reveals must derive from his work for the organization. This condition distinguishes the whistleblower from the spy (and the clerk in Accounts). The spy seeks out information in order to reveal it: the whistleblower learns it as a proper part of doing the job the organization has assigned him. The standard theory, in contrast, has nothing to say about how the whistleblower comes to know of the threat she reveals (S2). For the standard theory, spies are just another kind of whistleblower.

A second way in which the complicity theory differs from the standard theory is that the complicity theory (C2) explicitly requires the whistleblower to be a *voluntary* participant in the organization in question. Whistleblowing is not—according to the complicity theory—an activity in which slaves, prisoners, or other involuntary participants in an organization engage. . . .

A third way in which the complicity theory differs from the standard theory is that the complicity theory (C3) requires moral wrong, not harm, for justification. The wrong need not be a new event (as a harm must be if it is to be *prevented*). It might, for example, consist in no more than silence about facts necessary to correct a serious injustice.

The complicity theory (C3) does, however, follow the standard theory in requiring that the predicate of whistleblowing be "serious." Under the complicity theory, minor wrongdoing can no more justify whistleblowing than can minor harm under the standard theory. While organizational loyalty cannot forbid whistleblowing, it does forbid "tattling," that is, revealing minor wrongdoing.

A fourth way in which the complicity theory differs from the standard theory, the most important, is that the complicity theory (C4) requires that the whistleblower believe that her work will have contributed to the wrong in question if she does nothing, but it does *not* require that she believe that her revelation will prevent (or undo) the wrong. The complicity theory does not require any belief about what the whistleblowing can accomplish (beyond ending complicity in the wrong in question). The whistleblower reveals what she knows in order to prevent complicity in the wrong, not to prevent the wrong as such. She can prevent complicity (if there is any to prevent) simply by publicly revealing what she knows. The revelation itself breaks the bond of complicity, the secret partnership in wrongdoing, that makes her an accomplice in her organization's wrongdoing. The complicity theory thus avoids the third paradox, the paradox of failure, just as it avoided the other two.

The fifth difference between the complicity theory and the standard theory is closely related to the fourth. Because publicly revealing what one knows breaks the bond of complicity, the complicity theory does not require the whistleblower to have enough evidence to convince others of the wrong in question. Convincing others, or just being able to convince them, is not, as such, an element in the justification of whistleblowing.

The complicity theory does, however, require (C5) that the whistleblower be (epistemically) justified in believing both that his organization is engaged in wrongdoing and that he will contribute to that wrong unless he blows the whistle. Such (epistemic) justification may require substantial physical evidence (as the standard theory says) or just a good sense of how things work. The complicity theory does not share the standard theory's substantial evidential demand (S4).

In one respect, however, the complicity theory clearly requires more of the whistleblower than the standard theory does. The complicity theory's C6—combined with C5—requires not only that the whistleblower be *justified* in her beliefs about the organization's wrongdoing and her part in it, but also that she be *right* about them. If she is wrong about either the wrongdoing or her complicity, her revelation will not be justified whistleblowing....

The complicity theory says nothing on at least one matter about which the standard theory says much—going through channels before publicly revealing what one knows. But the two theories do not differ as much as this difference in emphasis suggests. If going through channels would suffice to prevent (or undo) the wrong, then it cannot be true (as C4 and C6 together require) that the would-be whistleblower's work will contribute to the wrong if she

does not publicly reveal what she knows. Where, however, going through channels would *not* prevent (or undo) the wrong, there is no need to go through channels. Condition C4's if-clause will be satisfied. For the complicity theory, going through channels is a way of finding out what the organization will do, not an independent requirement of justification. That, I think, is also how the standard theory understands it.

TESTING THE THEORY

Let us now test the theory against Boisjoly's testimony before the Rogers Commission. Recall that under the standard theory any justification of that testimony seemed to fail for at least three reasons: First, Boisjoly could not testify without substantial cost to himself and Thiokol (to whom he owned loyalty). Second, there was no serious and substantial harm his testimony could prevent. And, third, he had little reason to believe that, even if he could identify a serious and considerable harm to prevent, his testimony had a significant chance of preventing it.

Since few doubt that Boisjoly's testimony before the Rogers Commission constitutes justified whistleblowing, if anything does, we should welcome a theory that—unlike the standard one—justifies that testimony as whistleblowing. The complicity theory sketched above does that:

(C1) Boisjoly's testimony consisted almost entirely of information derived from his work on booster rockets at Thiokol.

(C2) Boisjoly was a voluntary member of Thiokol.

(C3) Boisjoly believed Thiokol, a legitimate organization, was attempting to mislead its client, the government, about the causes of a deadly accident. Attempting to do that certainly seems a serious moral wrong.

(C4) On the evening before the *Challenger* exploded, Boisjoly gave up objecting to the launch once his superiors, including the three Thiokol vice presidents, had made it clear that they were no longer willing to listen to him. He also had a part in preparing those superiors to testify intelligently before the Rogers Commission concerning the booster's fatal field joint. Boisjoly believed that Thiokol would use his failure to offer his own interpretation of his retreat into silence the night before the launch, and the knowledge that he had imparted to his superiors, to contribute to the attempt to mislead Thiokol's client.

(C5)   The evidence justifying beliefs C3 and C4 consisted of comments of various officers of Thiokol, what Boisjoly had seen at Thiokol over the years, and what he learned about the rocket business over a long career. I find this evidence sufficient to justify his belief both that his organization was engaged in wrong-doing and that his work was implicated.

(C6)   Here we reach a paradox of *knowledge*. Since belief is knowledge if, but only if, it is *both* justified *and* true, we cannot *show* that we know anything. All we can show is that a belief is now justified and that we have no reason to expect anything to turn up later to prove it false. The evidence now available still justifies Boisjoly's belief both about what Thiokol was attempting and about what would have been his part in the attempt. Since new evidence is unlikely, his testimony seems to satisfy C6 just as it satisfied the complicity theory's other five conditions.

Since the complicity theory explains why Boisjoly's testimony before the Rogers Commission was morally required whistleblowing, it has passed its first test, a test the standard theory failed.

NOTES

1. Throughout this essay. I take the standard theory to be Richard T. De George's version in *Business Ethics*, 3rd Edition (New York: Macmillan, 1990), pp. 200–214 (amended only insofar as necessary to include non-businesses as well as businesses). Why treat De George's theory as standard? There are two reasons: first, it seems the most commonly cited; and second, people offering alternatives generally treat it as the one to be replaced. The only obvious competitor, Norman Bowie's account, is distinguishable from De George's on no point relevant here. See Bowie's *Business Ethics* (Englewood Cliffs, NJ: Prentice Hall, 1982), p. 143.

2. De George, op. cit.

3. De George, p. 210: "The notion of *serious* harm might be expanded to include serious financial harm, and kinds of harm other than death and serious threats to health and body. But as we noted earlier, we shall restrict ourselves here to products and practices that produce or threaten serious harm or danger to life and health."

Ronald Duska

Whistleblowing and Employee Loyalty

Ronald Duska is Charles F. Lamont Post Chair of Ethics and the Professions Professor of Ethics at the American College.

There are proponents on both sides of the issue—those who praise whistleblowers as civic heroes and those who condemn them as "finks." Maxwell Glen

---

From Tom L. Beauchamp and Norman E. Bowie, *Ethical Theory and Business* (Englewood Cliffs, NJ: Prentice Hall, 2001). Reprinted by permission of the author.

and Cody Shearer, who wrote about the whistleblowers at Three Mile Island say, "Without the *courageous* breed of assorted company insiders known as whistleblowers—workers who often risk their livelihoods to disclose information about construction and design flaws—the Nuclear Regulatory Commission itself would be nearly as idle as Three Mile Island. . . . That whistle-blowers deserve both gratitude and protection is beyond disagreement."[1]

Still, while Glen and Shearer praise whistleblowers, others vociferously condemn them. For example, in a now infamous quote, James Roche, the former president of General Motors said:

> Some critics are now busy eroding another support of free enterprise—the loyalty of a management team, with its unifying values and cooperative work. Some of the enemies of business now encourage an employee to be *disloyal* to the enterprise. They want to create suspicion and disharmony, and pry into the proprietary interests of the business. However this is labeled—industrial espionage, whistle blowing, or professional responsibility—it is another tactic for spreading disunity and creating conflict.[2]

From Roche's point of view, not only is whistleblowing not "courageous" and not deserving of "gratitude and protection" as Glen and Shearer would have it, it is corrosive and impermissible.

Discussions of whistleblowing generally revolve around three topics: (1) attempts to define whistleblowing more precisely, (2) debates about whether and when whistleblowing is permissible, and (3) debates about whether and when one has an obligation to blow the whistle.

In this paper I want to focus on the second problem, because I find it somewhat disconcerting that there is a problem at all. When I first looked into the ethics of whistleblowing it seemed to me that whistleblowing was a good thing, and yet I found in the literature claim after claim that it was in need of defense, that there was something wrong with it, namely that it was an act of disloyalty.

If whistleblowing is a disloyal act, it deserves disapproval, and ultimately any action of whistleblowing needs justification. This disturbs me. It is as if the act of a good Samaritan is being condemned as

an act of interference, as if the prevention of a suicide needs to be justified.

In his book *Business Ethics*, Norman Bowie claims that "whistleblowing . . . violate(s) a *prima facie* duty of loyalty to one's employer." According to Bowie, there is a duty of loyalty that prohibits one from reporting his employer or company. Bowie, of course, recognizes that this is only a *prima facie* duty, that is, one that can be overridden by a higher duty to the public good. Nevertheless, the axiom that whistleblowing is disloyal is Bowie's starting point.[3]

Bowie is not alone. Sissela Bok sees "whistleblowing" as an instance of disloyalty:

> The whistleblower hopes to stop the game; but since he is neither referee nor coach, and since he blows the whistle on his own team, his act is seen as a *violation of loyalty*. In holding his position, he has assumed certain obligations to his colleagues and clients. He may even have subscribed to a loyalty oath or a promise of confidentiality. . . . Loyalty to colleagues and to clients comes to be pitted against loyalty to the public interest, to those who may be injured unless the revelation is made.[4]

Bowie and Bok end up defending whistleblowing in certain contexts, so I don't necessarily disagree with their conclusions. However, I fail to see how one has an obligation of loyalty to one's company, so I disagree with their perception of the problem and their starting point. I want to argue that one does not have an obligation of loyalty to a company, even a prima facie one, because companies are not the kind of things that are properly objects of loyalty. To make them objects of loyalty gives them a moral status they do not deserve and in raising their status, one lowers the status of the individuals who work for the companies. Thus, the difference in perception is important because those who think employees have an obligation of loyalty to a company fail to take into account a relevant moral difference between persons and corporations.

But why aren't companies the kind of things that can be objects of loyalty? To answer that we have to ask what are proper objects of loyalty. John Ladd states the problem this way, "Granted that loyalty is the wholehearted devotion to an object of some kind, what kind of thing is the object? Is it an abstract entity, such as an idea or a collective being? Or is it a person or group of persons?"[5] Philosophers fall into three camps on the question. On one side are the idealists who hold that loyalty is devotion to something more than persons, to some cause or abstract entity. On the other side are what Ladd calls "social atomists," and these include empiricists and utilitarians, who think that at most one can only be loyal to individuals and that loyalty can ultimately be explained away as some other obligation that holds between two people. Finally, there is a moderate position that holds that although idealists go too far in postulating some super-personal entity as an object of loyalty, loyalty is still an important and real relation that holds between people, one that cannot be dismissed by reducing it to some other relation.

There does seem to be a view of loyalty that is not extreme. According to Ladd, "'loyalty' is taken to refer to a relationship between persons—for instance, between a lord and his vassal, between a parent and his children, or between friends. Thus the object of loyalty is ordinarily taken to be a person or a group of persons."[6]

But this raises a problem that Ladd glosses over. There is a difference between a person or a group of persons, and aside from instances of loyalty that relate two people such as lord/vassal, parent/child, or friend/friend, there are instances of loyalty relating a person to a group, such as a person to his family, a person to this team, and a person to his country. Families, countries, and teams are presumably groups of persons. They are certainly ordinarily construed as objects of loyalty.

But to what am I loyal in such a group? In being loyal to the group am I being loyal to the whole group or to its members? It is easy to see the object of loyalty in the case of an individual person. It is simply the individual. But to whom am I loyal in a group? To whom am I loyal in a family? Am I loyal to each and every individual or to something larger, and if to something larger, what is it? We are tempted to think of a group as an entity of its own, an individual in its own right, having an identity of its own.

To avoid the problem of individuals existing for the sake of the group, the atomists insist that a group is nothing more than the individuals who comprise it, nothing other than a mental fiction by which we refer to a group of individuals. It is certainly not a reality or entity over and above the sum of its parts, and consequently is not a proper object of loyalty. Under such a position, of course, no loyalty would be owed to a company because a company is a mere mental fiction, since it is a group. One would have obligations to the individual members of the company, but one could never be justified in overriding those obligations for the sake of the "group" taken collectively. A company has no moral status except in terms of the individual members who comprise it. It is not a proper object of loyalty. But the atomists go too far. Some groups, such as a family, do have a reality of their own, whereas groups of people walking down the street do not. From Ladd's point of view the social atomist is wrong because he fails to recognize the kinds of groups that are held together by "the ties that bind." The atomist tries to reduce these groups to simple sets of individuals bound together by some externally imposed criteria. This seems wrong.

There do seem to be groups in which the relationship and interactions create a new force or entity. A group takes on an identity and a reality of its own that is determined by its purpose, and this purpose defines the various relationships and roles set up within the group. There is a division of labor into roles necessary for the fulfillment of the purposes of the group. The membership, then, is not of individuals who are the same but of individuals who have specific relationships to one another determined by the aim of the group. Thus we get specific relationships like parent/child, coach/player, and so on, that don't occur in other groups. It seems then that an atomist account of loyalty that restricts loyalty merely to individuals and does not include loyalty to groups might be inadequate.

But once I have admitted that we can have loyalty to a group, do I not open myself up to criticism from the proponent of loyalty to the company? Might not the proponent of loyalty to business say: "Very well. I agree with you. The atomists are short-sighted. Groups have some sort of reality and they can be proper objects of loyalty. But companies are groups. Therefore companies are proper objects of loyalty."

The point seems well taken, except for the fact that the kinds of relationships that loyalty requires are just the kind that one does not find in business. As Ladd says, "The ties that bind the persons together provide the basis of loyalty." But all sorts of ties bind people together. I am a member of a group of fans if I go to a ball game. I am a member of a group if I merely walk down the street. What binds people together in a business is not sufficient to require loyalty.

A business or corporation does two things in the free enterprise system: It produces a good or service and it makes a profit. The making of a profit, however, is the primary function of a business as a business, for if the production of the good or service is not profitable, the business would be out of business. Thus nonprofitable goods or services are a means to an end. People bound together in a business are bound together not for mutual fulfillment and support, but to divide labor or make a profit. Thus, while we can jokingly refer to a family as a place where "they have to take you in no matter what," we cannot refer to a company in that way. If a worker does not produce in a company or if cheaper laborers are available, the company—in order to fulfill its purpose—should get rid of the worker. A company feels no obligation of loyalty. The saying "You can't buy loyalty" is true. Loyalty depends on ties that demand self-sacrifice with no expectation of reward. Business functions on the basis of enlightened self-interest. I am devoted to a company not because it is like a parent to me; it is not. Attempts of some companies to create "one big happy family" ought to be looked on with suspicion. I am not devoted to it at all, nor should I be. I work for it because it pays me. I am not in a family to get paid, I am in a company to get paid.

The cold hard truth is that the goal of profit is what gives birth to a company and forms that particular group. Money is what ties the group together. But in such a commercialized venture, with such a goal, there is no loyalty, or at least none need be expected. An employer will release an employee and an employee will walk away from an employer when it is profitable for either one to do so.

Not only is loyalty to a corporation not required, it more than likely is misguided. There is nothing as pathetic as the story of the loyal employee who, having given above and beyond the call of duty, is let go in the restructuring of the company. He feels betrayed because he mistakenly viewed the company as an object of his loyalty. Getting rid of such foolish romanticism and coming to grips with this hard but accurate assessment should ultimately benefit everyone.

To think we owe a company or corporation loyalty requires us to think of that company as a person or as a group with a goal of human fulfillment. If we think of it in this way we can be loyal. But this is the wrong way to think. A company is not a person. A company is an instrument, and an instrument with a specific purpose, the making of profit. To treat an instrument as an end in itself, like a person, may not be as bad as treating an end as an instrument, but it does give the instrument a moral status it does not deserve; and by elevating the instrument we lower the end. All things, instruments and ends, become alike.

Remember that Roche refers to the "management team" and Bok sees the name "whistleblowing" coming from the instance of a referee blowing a whistle in the presence of a foul. What is perceived as bad about whistleblowing in business from this perspective is that one blows the whistle on one's own team, thereby violating team loyalty. If the company can get its employees to view it as a team they belong to, it is easier to demand loyalty. Then the rules governing teamwork and team loyalty will apply. One reason the appeal to a team and team loyalty works so well in business is that businesses are in competition with one another. Effective motivation turns business practices into a game and instills teamwork.

But businesses differ from teams in very important respects, which makes the analogy between business and a team dangerous. Loyalty to a team is loyalty within the context of sport or a competition. Teamwork and team loyalty require that in the circumscribed activity of the game I cooperate with my fellow players, so that pulling all together, we may win. The object of (most) sports is victory. But winning in sports is a social convention, divorced from the usual goings on of society. Such a winning is most times a harmless, morally neutral diversion.

But the fact that this victory in sports, within the rules enforced by a referee (whistleblower), is a socially developed convention taking place within a larger social context makes it quite different from competition in business, which, rather than being defined by a context, permeates the whole of society in its influence. Competition leads not only to victory but to losers. One can lose at sport with precious few consequences. The consequences of losing at business are much larger. Further, the losers in business can be those who are not in the game voluntarily (we are all forced to participate) but who are still affected by business decisions. People cannot choose to participate in business. It permeates everyone's lives.

The team model, then, fits very well with the model of the free market system, because there competition is said to be the name of the game. Rival companies compete and their object is to win. To call a foul on one's own teammate is to jeopardize one's chances of winning and is viewed as disloyalty.

But isn't it time to stop viewing corporate machinations as games? These games are not controlled and are not ended after a specific time. The activities of business affect the lives of everyone, not just the game players. The analogy of the corporation to a team and the consequent appeal to team loyalty, although understandable, is seriously misleading, at least in the moral sphere where competition is not the prevailing virtue.

If my analysis is correct, the issue of the permissibility of whistleblowing is not a real issue since there is no obligation of loyalty to a company. Whistleblowing is not only permissible but expected when a company is harming society. The issue is not one of disloyalty to the company, but of whether the whistleblower has an obligation to society if blowing the whistle will bring him retaliation.

NOTES

1. Maxwell Glen and Cody Shearer, "Going After the Whistle-blowers," *Philadelphia Inquirer*, Tuesday, August 2, 1983, Op-ed page, p. 11A.

2. James M. Roche, "The Competitive System, to Work, to Preserve, and to Protect," *Vital Speeches of the Day* (May 1971): 445.

3. Norman Bowie, *Business Ethics* (Englewood Cliffs, N.J.: Prentice Hall, 1982), pp. 140–143.

4. Sissela Bok, "Whistleblowing and Professional Responsibilities," *New York University Education Quarterly* 2(1980): 3.

5. John Ladd, "Loyalty," *The Encyclopedia of Philosophy* 5: 97.

6. Ibid.

Lynne McFall | # Integrity

Lynne McFall has a Ph.D. in philosophy and is a novelist. She is author of *The One True Story of the World.*

Olaf (upon what were once knees).
does almost ceaselessly repeat
"there is some shit I will not eat"

— *e. e. cummings*

From *Ethics* 9: (Oct 1987), pp. 11–16. Reprinted with permission.

COHERENCE

Integrity is the state of being "undivided; an integral whole." What sort of coherence is at issue here? I think there are several.

One kind of coherence is simple consistency: consistency within one's set of principles or commitments. One cannot maintain one's integrity if one has unconditional commitments that conflict, for example, justice and personal happiness, or conditional commitments that cannot be ranked, for example, truth telling and kindness.

Another kind of coherence is coherence between principle and action. Integrity requires "sticking to one's principles," moral or otherwise, in the face of temptation, including the temptation to redescription.

Take the case of a woman with a commitment to marital fidelity. She is attracted to a man who is not her husband, and she is tempted. Suppose, for the purity of the example, that he wants her too but will do nothing to further the affair; the choice is hers. Now imagine your own favorite scene of seduction.

After the fact, she has two options. (There are always these two options, which makes the distinction between changing one's mind and weakness of the will problematic, but assume that this is a clear case.) She can (1) admit to having lost the courage of her convictions (retaining the courage of her mistakes) or (2) rewrite her principles in various ways (e.g., by making fidelity a general principle, with exceptions, or by retroactively canceling her "subscription"). Suppose she chooses the latter. Whatever she may have gained, she has lost some integrity. Weakness of the will is one contrary of integrity. Self-deception is another. A person who admits to having succumbed to temptation has more integrity than the person who sells out, then fixes the books, but both suffer its loss.

A different sort of incoherence is exhibited in the case where someone does the right thing for (what he takes to be) the wrong reason. For example, in Dostoevsky's *The Devils*, Stepan Verkhovensky says, "All my life I've been lying. Even when I spoke the truth. I never spoke for the sake of the truth, but for my own sake." Coherence between principle and action is necessary but not sufficient. One's action might *correspond* with one's principle, at some general level of description, but be inconsistent with that principle more fully specified. If one values not just honesty but honesty for its own sake, then honesty motivated by self-interest is not enough for integrity.

So the requirement of coherence is fairly complicated. In addition to simple consistency, it puts constraints on the way in which one's principles may be held (the "first-person" requirement), on how one may act given one's principles (coherence between principle and action), and on how one may be motivated in acting on them (coherence between principle and motivation). Call this *internal coherence*. . . .

To summarize the argument so far: personal integrity requires that an agent (1) subscribe to some consistent set of principles or commitments and (2), in the face of temptation or challenge, (3) uphold these principles or commitments, (4) for what the agent takes to be the right reasons.

These conditions are rather formal. Are there no constraints on the *content* of the principles or commitments a person of integrity may hold?

INTEGRITY AND IMPORTANCE

Consider the following statements.

> Sally is a person of principle: pleasure.
>
> Harold demonstrates great integrity in his single-minded pursuit of approval.
>
> John was a man of uncommon integrity. He let nothing—not friendship, not justice, not truth—stand in the way of his amassment of wealth.

That none of these claims can be made with a straight face suggests that integrity is inconsistent with such principles.

A person of integrity is willing to bear the consequences of her convictions, even when this is difficult, that is, when the consequences are unpleasant. A person whose only principle is "Seek my own pleasure" is not a candidate for integrity because there is no possibility of conflict—between pleasure and principle—in which integrity could be lost. Where there is no possibility of its loss, integrity cannot exist.

Similarly in the case of the approval seeker. The single-minded pursuit of approval is inconsistent with integrity. Someone who is describable as an egg sucker, brownnose, fawning flatterer cannot have integrity, whatever he may think of the merits of such behavior. A commitment to spinelessness does not vitiate its spinelessness—another of integrity's contraries.

The same may be said for the ruthless seeker of wealth. A person whose only aim is to increase his bank balance is a person for whom nothing is ruled out: duplicity, theft, murder. Expedience is *contrasted* to a life of principle, so an ascription of integrity is out of place. Like the pleasure seeker and the approval seeker, he lacks a "core," the kind of commitments that give a person character and that makes a loss of integrity possible. In order to sell one's soul, one must have something to sell. . . .

Most of us, when tempted to "sell out," are tempted by pleasure, approval, money, status, or personal gain of some other sort. The political prisoner under the thumbscrew wants relief, however committed he may be to the revolution. Less dramatically, most of us want the good opinion of others and a decent standard of living. Self-interest in these forms is a legitimate aim against which we weigh our other concerns. But most of us have other "higher," commitments, and so those who honor most what we would resist are especially liable to scorn.

This tendency to objectify our own values in the name of personal integrity can best be seen, I think, in a more neutral case. Consider the following claim:

> The connoisseur showed real integrity in preferring the Montrachet to the Mountain Dew.

Even if he was sorely tempted to guzzle the Mountain Dew and forbore only with the greatest difficulty, the connoisseur, we would say, did not show integrity in preferring the better wine. Why? Resisting temptation is not the only test of integrity; the challenge must be to something *important*. . . .

One may die for beauty, truth, justice, the objection might continue, but not for Montracher. Wine is not that important. . . .

When we grant integrity to a person, we need not *approve* of his or her principles or commitments, but we must at least recognize them as ones a reasonable person might take to be of great importance and ones that a reasonable person might be tempted to sacrifice to some lesser yet still recognizable goods. It may not be possible to spell out

these conditions without circularity, but that this is what underlies our judgments of integrity seems clear enough. Integrity is a personal virtue granted with social strings attached. By definition, it precludes "expediency, artificiality, or shallowness of any kind." The pleasure seeker is guilty of shallowness, the approval seeker of artificiality, and the profit seeker of expedience of the worst sort. . . .

INTEGRITY, FRIENDSHIP, AND THE OLAF PRINCIPLE

An attitude essential to the notion of integrity is that there are some things that one is not prepared to do, or some things one *must* do. I shall call this the "Olaf Principle," in honor of e. e. cummings's poem about Olaf, the "conscientious objector." This principle requires that some of one's commitments be unconditional.

In what sense?

There are, in ordinary moral thought, expressions of the necessity or impossibility of certain actions or types of actions that do not neatly correspond to the notions of necessity and impossibility most often catalogued by moral theorists. "I *must* stand by my friend" (or "I *cannot* let him down") may have no claim to logical, psychological, rational, or moral necessity in any familiar sense. There is nothing logically inconsistent in the betrayal of friendship, or one could never be guilty of it. It is not psychologically impossible, since many have in fact done it and survived to do it again. Rationality does not require unconditional allegiance, without some additional assumptions, for one may have better reason to do a conflicting action, for example, where the choice is between betraying a friend and betraying one's country (although I am sympathetic to E. M. Forster's famous statement to the contrary). Nor is the necessity expressed one that has a claim to universality, for different persons may have different unconditional commitments. Impartiality and absoluteness are not what is at stake, for the choice may be between a friend and ten innocent strangers, and one person may have different unconditional commitments at different times. It is not clear, then, what sense of *unconditional commitment* is at issue.

Unless corrupted by philosophy, we all have things we think we would never do, under any imaginable circumstances, whatever we may give to survival or pleasure, power and the approval of strangers; some part of ourselves beyond which we will not retreat, some weakness however prevalent in others that we will not tolerate in ourselves. And if we do that thing, betray that weakness, we are not the persons we thought; there is nothing left that we may even in spite refer to as *I*.

I think it is in this sense that some commitments must be unconditional: they are conditions of continuing as ourselves.

Suppose, for example, that I take both friendship and professional advancement to be great goods, and my best friend and I are candidates for a promotion. Suppose, too, that I know the person who has the final decision has an unreasoned hatred of people who drink more than is socially required, as my friend does. I let this be known, not directly of course, with the predictable result that I am given the promotion.

Now in one sense I have not done anything dishonest. My friend may be the first to admit the pleasure he takes in alcohol. It may even be one of the reasons I value his friendship. (Loyal drinking companions are not easy to come by.) But this is clearly a betrayal of friendship. Is it so obviously a failure of integrity?

In *any* conflict between two great goods, I may argue, one must be "betrayed." And between you and me, I choose me.

What is wrong with this defense?

To beat someone out of a job by spreading vicious truths is proof that I am no friend. It is in the nature of friendship that one cannot intentionally hurt a friend in order to further one's own interests. So if I claim to be this person's friend, then I am guilty of incoherence, and therefore lack integrity.

Why does incoherence seem the wrong charge to make? The answer, I think, is that it is much too weak.

Some of our principles or commitments are more important to us than others. Those that can be sacrificed without remorse may be called *defeasible* commitments. For many of us, professional success is an important but defeasible commitment. I would like to be a successful philosopher, esteemed by my colleagues and widely published, but neither success nor failure will change my sense of personal worth.

Contrasted to defeasible commitments are *identity-conferring* commitments: they reflect what we take to be most important and so determine, to large extent, our (moral) identities. . . .

For many of us, friendship is an identity-conferring commitment. If we betrayed a friend in order to advance our careers, we could not "live with" ourselves; we would not be the persons we thought we were. This is what it means to have a "core": a set of principles or commitments that makes us who we are. Such principles cannot be justified by reference to other values, because they are the most fundamental commitments we have; they determine what, for us, it to *count* as a reason. . . .

| Cheshire Calhoun | Standing for Something |

Cheshire Calhoun teaches women's studies and philosophy at Arizona State University.

We admire and trust those who have integrity, take pride in our own, rue its absence in politics, and

From *Journal of Philosophy* XCII 5 (May) 1995, pp. 17–22.

regret our own failures to act with integrity. Clearly, integrity is a virtue, but it is less clear what it is a virtue *of* or why we might prize it.

PERSONAL AND SOCIAL VIRTUES

...Some virtues are personal, others are social, yet others are both. A personal virtue, like temperance, consists in having the proper relation to oneself—in this case, to one's desires. Social virtues consist in having the proper relation to others. Civility, for instance, is a social virtue, a desirable mode of conducting oneself among others. Some virtues are both personal and social. Self-respect, for instance, might be thought to involve having both a proper regard for one's own moral status (and thus the right relation to oneself) and a proper regard for one's place among other moral beings (and thus the right relation to others); it is a virtue exercised both by holding oneself to standards and by demanding rightful treatment from others....

Characterizing integrity as a purely personal virtue does not imply that there is anything self-indulgent about striving to have integrity. But it does imply that integrity is not essentially connected to how we conduct ourselves among others and that its fitting us for proper social relations is not what makes it a virtue. Is there any reason to think that integrity is less like temperance, a purely personal virtue, and more like self-respect, a personal and social virtue? Taking the notion of "standing for something" and the self-indulgence criticism of integrity in turn, I want to suggest two reasons for not confining the analysis of integrity to understanding its nature as a personal virtue. First, doing so fails to provide us with an adequate explication of what it means to stand for something. Second, although such analyses can counter the self-indulgence charge, they cannot make the person of integrity's relation to other persons central to that defense.

Standing For

I take it that the notion of standing for something is central to the meaning of integrity. Indeed, part of the intuitive appeal of the integrated-self, identity, and clean-hands pictures lay in their articulating part of what is meant by standing for something. When, however, the analysis of integrity is confined to understanding it as a personal virtue, "standing *for*" something ultimately reduces to "standing *by*" the line that demarcates self from not-self. On the integrated-self, identity, and clean-hands pictures, the adoption of principles and values as one's own establishes the line between self and not-self. Acting with integrity, that is, on one's own judgment, is thus intimately tied to protecting the boundaries of the self—to protecting it against disintegration, against loss of self-identity, and against pollution by evil. Acting without integrity undermines the boundaries of the self, whether that be accomplished through the abandonment of one's autonomy, the betrayal of one's deepest commitments, or the contamination of one's agency through association with evil. On all three views, loss of integrity signals loss of some important dimension of selfhood.

To the extent that integrity is, indeed, a personal virtue, this account of the significance of standing by one's principles and values rings true. What drops out of these accounts, however, is the centrality of standing *for* principles and values that, in one's own best judgment, are worthy of defense because they concern how *we*, as beings interested in living justly and well, can do so.

...I am strongly inclined to think that integrity is a *social* trait and that its fitting us for community membership is precisely what makes it a social *virtue*. Looking at integrity as a social virtue enables us to see persons of integrity as insisting that it is in some important sense for us, for the sake of what ought to be our project or character as a people, to preserve what ought to be the purity of our agency that they stick by their best judgment. It is to a picture of integrity as a social virtue that I now turn.

STANDING FOR SOMETHING

What then is the social virtue of integrity? I begin with this picture: I am one person among many persons, and we are all in the same boat. None of us can answer the question—"What is worth doing?"—except from within our own deliberative points of view. This "What is worth doing?" question can take many specific forms. What evils, if any, ought one morally to refuse doing no matter the consequences? What, for philosophers, is worth writing about? What is worth keeping, what worth reforming in the social identity "Black" or "woman" or "gay"? What principles take precedence over what others? What is one, if not the only, worthwhile way of conducting a good life? That they are answerable only from within each person's deliberative viewpoint means that all of our answers will have a peculiar character. As one among many deliberators, each can offer only her own judgment. Although each aims to do more than this—to render a judgment endorsable by all—nothing guarantees success. The thought, "It is just my judgment and it may be wrong," cannot be banished no matter how carefully deliberation proceeds. But given that the only way of answering the "What is worth doing" question is to plunge ahead using one's own deliberate viewpoint, one's best judgment becomes important. As one among many deliberators who may themselves go astray, the individual's judgment acquires gravity. It is, after all, not *just* her judgment about what it would be wrong or not worthwhile to do. It is also her *best* judgment. Something now hangs for all of us, as co-deliberators trying to answer correctly the "What is worth doing?" question, on her sticking by her best judgment. Her standing for something is not just something she does for herself. She takes a stand for, and before, all deliberators who share the goal of determining what is worth doing.

To have integrity is to understand that one's own judgment matters because it is only within individual persons' deliberative viewpoints, including one's own, that what is worth our doing can be decided. Thus, one's own judgment serves a common interest of co-deliberators. Persons of integrity treat their own endorsements as ones that matter, or ought to matter, to fellow deliberators. Absent a special sort of story, lying about one's views, concealing them, recanting them under pressure, selling them out for rewards or to avoid penalties, and pandering to what one regards as the bad views of others, all indicate a failure to regard one's own judgment as one that

should matter to others. The artist who alters his work of genius, making it saleable to a tasteless public, lacks integrity because he does not regard his best aesthetic judgment as important to anyone but himself. He abandons the co-deliberative perspective. And those who act for the sake of preserving their identity without asking whether it is worth preserving lack integrity, because they do not even raise the "What is worth doing?" question. "Whatever sells" and "whatever is me" cannot ground action with integrity because these reasons do not address the co-deliberative question of what is worth doing.

That hypocrites lack integrity is a common observation. Analyses of integrity as a personal virtue, however, do not plausibly explain why. On the integrated-self and identity pictures of integrity, one would have to say that hypocrites lack integrity because their actions are not integrated with their endorsements; or because in the course of pretending commitment, they are untrue to their real, identity-conferring commitments; or because sustained pretense undermines the agent's ability to be clear and un-self-deceived about what she really does endorse. Although hypocrisy may be bad in these ways for the hypocrite, this is not typically why we charge hypocrites with lacking integrity. Hypocrites mislead. And it is because they deliberately mislead us or others about what is worth doing that they lack integrity. Jim Bakker, for instance, persuaded a lot of people to invest money in his doing God's work. His embezzling revealed that he had misled them either about the value of doing God's work or the value of his doing it. Neither the integrated-self nor the identity picture of integrity can explain why misleading others, by itself and not because of its deleterious effects on the hypocrite, has anything to do with lacking integrity. If, however, integrity is not a merely personal virtue, but the social virtue of acting on one's own judgment because doing so matters to deliberators' common interest in determining what is worth doing, then hypocritical misrepresentation of one's own best judgment clearly conflicts with integrity.

This view of integrity also helps to explain the shame at failure to abide by one's own judgment as something more than mere shame at the unsturdiness of one's will or the guilty awareness of violating a standard. If an agent passes herself off as someone who insists on the importance of private spaces and then secretly indulges in reading another's private letters, the thoughts, "I have no self-control" and "This is wrong," are different from the thought, "I have no integrity." Neither the weakness nor the wrongness of the act immediately reveals lack of integrity. Rather, the thought, "I have no integrity," accompanies the revelation of one's inability to stand for something before others.

Finally, looking at integrity not as the personal virtue of keeping oneself intact but as the social virtue of standing for something before fellow deliberators helps explain why we care that persons have the courage of their convictions. The courageous provide spectacular displays of integrity by withstanding social incredulity, ostracism, contempt, and physical assault when most of us would be inclined to give in, compromise, or retreat into silence. Social circumstances that erect powerful deterrents to speaking and acting on one's own best judgment and undermine the possibilities for deliberating

about what is worth doing. We thus have reason to be thankful when persons of integrity refuse to be cowed.

CONCLUDING REMARK

What I have had to say about integrity suggests that integrity may be a master virtue, that is, less a virtue in its own right than a pressing into service of a host of other virtues—self-knowledge, strength of will, courage, honesty, loyalty, humility, civility, respect, and self-respect. My aim was to understand that service. What is a person who tries to have integrity trying to do? I have not rejected (though I have revised) the ideas that she is trying to be autonomous, or loyal to deep commitments, or uncontaminated by evils. But I have tried to argue that this is not the whole story. She is also trying to stand for what, in her best judgment, is worth persons' doing.

Amy Gutmann | # Can Virtue Be Taught to Lawyers?

Amy Gutmann is president of the University of Pennsylvania and the Christopher H. Brawne Distinguished Professor of Political Science, Communications, and Philosophy.

"Can virtue be taught?" Plato rightly thought this a most challenging question. But our question—Can virtue be taught to lawyers?—presents a still greater challenge. We can begin to meet the challenge, as Socrates might suggest, by addressing the prior question: What is virtue for lawyers? For without figuring out what legal virtue is, we can only pretend to know whether lawyers can be taught virtue, or learn it.

What virtues are fitting for lawyers in their most common activities as advocates and counselors in a constitutional democracy?

Consider the view of legal virtue offered by the standard conception of lawyering. "When acting as an advocate, a lawyer must, within the established constraints upon professional behavior, maximize the likelihood that the client will prevail."[1] To maximize the likelihood that your client prevails, you must be not just an advocate of your client's preferences or interests, but a zealous advocate.

The obligation of zealous advocacy has been amply criticized by David Luban, among others,

From *Stanford Law Review*, Vol. 45, No.6 (Jul., 1993), pp. 1759–1771.

for losing sight of the larger aim of the law in furthering social justice.[2] The standard conception makes most sense in the context of the adversary process of criminal law, which does not of course comprehend most of what lawyers do. Even zealous advocates of their clients' preferences or interests may be held responsible—legally, professionally, and morally—for their actions. Authorization by clients does not immunize lawyers from responsibility for doing wrong any more than authorization by military officers exonerates soldiers from wrongdoing. What constitutes legal wrongdoing is often a tricky question, but the principle of responsibility does not stand or fall on hard cases.

A partial truth of the standard conception remains, and I want to pursue its implications here. Far worse than being a zealous lawyer is being a lazy or incompetent one, unwilling or unable to take on someone else's cause as your own. Lawyers who represent their clients simply for the sake of making a living, and therefore do not represent them well as long as they can get away with it, use their clients merely as means to their own self-interested ends. In criticizing the standard conception, we should not lose sight of the virtue of ardent (and perhaps at times zealous) advocacy. This is a virtue entailed in the legal obligation to argue other people's causes, not one's own. The advocacy virtues are necessary to safeguarding the basic interests of citizens in the face of threats to their civil and political rights.

... What constitutes adequate representation? Ardent legal advocates, like good doctors, need to know not just the preferences of their clients, but their informed preferences. Like good friends, good lawyers do not take every and any preference of their clients as dispositive of what they should do in their clients' defense.[3] Unlike good friends, good lawyers know, or should know, a lot more than their clients about the probable consequences for their clients' lives of various legal strategies. Proponents of the standard conception and critics alike can grant that ardent advocacy is sometimes a great virtue of lawyers. But we also should recognize that lawyers are not in a position to know what their obligation of ardent advocacy entails unless they understand their clients' informed preferences. ...

———

Clients are typically not experts in the law, or at least not in the part of the law for which they seek legal counsel. We need to rely upon legal counsel to develop informed preferences regarding legal services. Whether we know it or not, we are dependent on lawyers for becoming informed about the nature of legal processes and outcomes, and their likely impact on our lives. But the process of legal understanding is not one-way. Lawyers also depend, or should depend, upon their clients for understanding whether and what legal strategies would best serve their clients' interests. And clients depend on lawyers for advising us on whether and how to proceed with our cases. The decision in the end is ours, not theirs. But lawyers have a responsibility for helping us make an informed decision by engaging with us in a deliberative process which entails the give-and-take of information, understanding, and even argument about our alternatives. Whenever ardent advocacy is a legal virtue, so is the willingness and ability of lawyers to deliberate with clients, explaining the aims and likely consequences of alternate strategies, listening to the clients' concerns, reacting to them, and arriving at an understanding of their clients' informed preferences after mutual evaluation of the possibilities. The deliberative virtues include the disposition to discuss various legal strategies with clients, and to understand clients' goals and their informed reaction to relevant legal strategies to the extent feasible. These deliberative virtues are a precondition of good advocacy.

A mundane example illustrates this internal criticism of the standard conception. Suppose a group of divorce lawyers are excellent at arguing court cases for their clients but spend little or no time trying to understand their clients' informed preferences with regard to marriage and divorce. The vast majority of their clients do not start out with anything close to an expert knowledge of legal possibilities, let alone of the probable consequences and experiences attached to arguing their cases in court or settling them out of court. The lawyers take their clients' preferences at face value. When a client comes into their office saying that he does not want to pay his spouse a penny if he can get away with it, they tell him they will do whatever they can within the limits of the law to help him. They can threaten his spouse with litigation over custody and scare her into settling for a minimum amount of child support.[4] And the lawyers often succeed in this strategy or in others that are also well-designed to satisfy their clients' expressed preferences. Their clients, on the other hand, typically fail miserably. They are never encouraged to consider the bad consequences of their desire to punish their spouses, and by extension, their children, who may never forgive them for the excessive misery wrought on their family for the sake of selfishness or revenge.

This group of successful divorce lawyers could practice their profession differently and still be successful as zealous advocates, far more successful in one important sense. They could help their clients examine the broader implications of their initial preferences, and explore with them the pros and cons of alternative strategies. The initial preferences of clients are sometimes, perhaps often, contrary to what their informed preferences would be. It is not reasonable to expect clients to inform themselves, even to know the questions they need to ask, independently of the guidance of legal counsel. These divorce lawyers, therefore, may seem like ardent advocates but in one critical sense they fail to fulfill the responsibilities of ardent advocates. They have not tried to understand, and to help their clients understand, their informed preferences. These lawyers bear some responsibility (not necessarily "full" responsibility) for their clients' uninformed preferences, because clients typically have no reasonable alternative but to depend on lawyers for informing them about the pitfalls and possibilities of the legal strategies available to them.... On its own terms, the standard conception is incomplete if it does not ally the virtues of deliberation with clients with those of ardent advocacy.

But this defense of deliberative virtues is incomplete, and we can expose its incompleteness by considering a more compelling conception of law: the justice conception. Ardent advocacy may be a necessary virtue for lawyers in their roles as advocates, but lawyers cannot know if and when they should be advocates without thinking about the larger social purposes of law, in particular about the central place of law in serving social justice in a constitutional democracy. (Of course, this is not to say that legal practices as we know them consistently serve the cause of social justice, but rather that the social justification of some legal services rests critically on their doing so.) The core of the justice conception is captured by the Model Rule's characterization of a lawyer as a "public citizen having special responsibility for the quality of justice."[5]

The justice conception, as one might infer from its label, shifts the primary virtue of lawyering from advocacy to justice. Advocacy, even zealous advocacy, may still be an important virtue for (some) lawyers, but only insofar as justice demands. It would be surprising, moreover, especially in a society where some people are economically disadvantaged and socially stigmatized, to find that justice always, or even generally, demands zealous advocacy of lawyers, regardless of the nature of their clients' cause. The justice conception does not demand that lawyers aim directly at what they deem just, even if that means arguing against their clients' cause. Where the adversary system is justified, so are lawyers justified in ardently arguing their clients' cases. But the adversary system is not justified in all legal contexts, and even where it is, it may not justify zealous advocacy, meaning maximizing the likelihood that one's client cause will prevail (which is what the standard conception requires). The virtue of justice, to follow David Luban's "fourfold root of sufficient reasoning," requires that lawyers be able to justify (1) the legal institution within which they act (e.g., the adversary system of criminal justice), (2) their legal role (e.g., advocate for clients) as necessary to that institution, (3) their role obligation (e.g., zealousness in advocacy) as necessary to the role, and (4) their role acts (e.g., cross-examining an alleged victim of rape about her irrelevant sexual history) as necessary to the role obligation.[6] If the justification fails at any stage, as it does in stages three and four of the parenthetical example, then lawyers are not justified in acting as zealous advocates.

Whereas the standard conception defends zealous advocacy as the primary legal virtue, the justice conception views as virtuous only those dispositions and acts required by the legal pursuit of social justice. The justice conception highlights an important legal virtue that the standard conception neglects, or even denies: the willingness and capacity of lawyers to act according to the demands of justice, rather than the preferences (even the informed preferences) of their clients when the two conflict. Partisan advocacy is not justified for all legal roles. Even when advocacy is justified, zealous advocacy may not be. And zealous advocacy does not justify certain tactics on behalf of one's clients (such as discrediting a plaintiff by raising irrelevant facts about her sexual history).

Louis Brandeis is sometimes cited as the paradigm of a virtuous lawyer on the justice conception—someone who put justice first in the practice of law. When he was acting as legal counsel to William McElwain, the owner of a large shoe factory embroiled in a labor dispute, Brandeis told McElwain in front of John Tobin, who was representing the striking workers, that Tobin was "absolutely right."[7] Brandeis proceeded to convince McElwain to end the seasonality of employment that was troubling his labor force. McElwain's company flourished. What should we make of the Brandeis example? I think that it demonstrates that the demands of justice on lawyers are both greater and less than what proponents of the justice conception commonly convey.

What more could the justice conception demand than that lawyers follow Luban's fourfold root of sufficient legal reasoning? We need not question whether the fourfold root is sufficient to reasoning to wonder whether legal reasoning of this sort is sufficient to acting justly as a lawyer. In focusing on the steps of legal reasoning that must be satisfied by justified legal action, proponents of the justice conception take something critical for granted concerning the lawyer–client relation that some questioning of the Brandeis example may reveal. Suppose Brandeis told McElwain in front of Tobin that Tobin

was "absolutely right" and left it at that. Brandeis still would have represented the right position to his client, but McElwain would have been far less likely to abide by it. He might well have fired Brandeis and gotten himself a lawyer more sympathetic to his cause. Or he might have gone along with Brandeis out of deference to Brandeis's legal expertise even though Brandeis's moral position on this matter was largely, if not entirely, independent of his legal expertise. Or suppose Brandeis had deceived McElwain into doing the right thing, thereby pursuing the cause of justice with morally suspect means. For lawyers to work effectively in bringing both the means and ends of law into conformity with social justice, they must be disposed not to deceive their clients into doing the right thing, but rather to aid their clients in deliberating about the demands of social justice.

Proponents of the justice conception conflate the idea that lawyers have a greater responsibility to pursue justice (by virtue of their role and/or their having more power to do so) with the idea that they are more likely to subscribe to the correct conception of justice (by virtue of their practical judgment). The practical judgment of lawyers, their capacity for "logical thinking, a nose for facts, good judgment of people, toleration"[8] does not translate into a comparative advantage over other thoughtful people in discerning what constitutes just social policy or the most justifiable of competing principles of social justice . . . Justice is not well-served by authorizing lawyers to pursue just ends independently of their clients' authorization, because the unauthorized means are morally suspect, and the ends lawyers choose to pursue may be worse than those that would be chosen by well-informed clients.

Had Brandeis deceived McElwain or simply quit as his legal counsel because he deemed McElwain's cause unjust, the story would illustrate a weakness of the justice conception as commonly articulated, rather than its potential strength. The commitment of lawyers to pursuing (what they believe are) just causes is only half the conception, the most commonly articulated half. The neglected half is a disposition to deliberate with their clients with the aim of arriving at a mutual understanding of what justice in a constitutional democracy permits or demands. By its very nature, deliberation is subverted by deceptive means.

If their cause is just, why be so concerned with the means that lawyers use to pursue justice? Why recommend deliberation between lawyers and clients, a sharing of information and understanding on relevant matters, rather than that lawyers use their legal expertise and authority simply to convince clients to do what they, the expert lawyers, believe is just? Luban uses the Brandeis model to illustrate the noblesse oblige tradition of law, where lawyers use their authority and expertise to pursue that understanding of social justice they think best.[9] This is not the deliberative model even if it eschews deception. Deliberation demands far more. It requires an active engagement with clients that aims at a better understanding of the value of legal action and its alternatives than either party to the deliberation probably had at the outset. The value of the best legal action on behalf of a client may often be its contribution to the pursuit of social justice, but social justice cannot routinely be pursued by a legal counsel independently of the client's informed consent.

The demand for deliberative virtues has two distinct sources internal to the justice conception of law, and one external to it.... The first internal source has to do with the distribution of the virtue of justice, the second with its content. Regarding the distribution of justice as a virtue, it is not in practice reasonable to rely upon lawyers as a group for a firmer commitment to social justice (beyond the rule of law) or just social policies than their clients. Lawyers are more expert in navigating the law than their clients, but they are also, by virtue of their expertise and professional autonomy, politically more powerful and therefore potentially more likely to subvert social justice in pursuit of their own professional or personal interests. Legal expertise does not make lawyers more committed to the cause of social justice than their clients, and it is hard to see why it would. The justice conception therefore cannot credibly claim that the disposition to pursue just ends is a virtue more distinctive to lawyers than their clients. Nor can it authorize lawyers to act upon their substantive conception of justice independently of

deliberating with their clients about its content. Were the justice conception to recommend such independent action beyond upholding the rule of law, it would be justifying a form of tyranny.

It does not follow that lawyers must defer to their clients' preferences as required by the standard conception, but rather that deliberation with clients places an important internal constraint on (and opportunity for) the legal pursuit of justice. This constraint is important both because it respects the principle of informed consent, and because it increases the chances that justice will actually be pursued and the virtue of justice will be as widely distributed among citizens as constitutional democracies require. . . .

The recommendation that lawyers deliberate with their clients follows also from an understanding of the content of social justice in a constitutional democracy. Constitutional democracies are created to cope with reasonable disagreements, including disagreements over the content of social justice and just social policy. At the same time, constitutional democracies must be constituted by, and authorize public officials to act upon, a public conception of social justice which itself is not universally accepted. Ongoing deliberation over its contents is one requirement of a conception of social justice suitable to constitutional democracy. Saying that lawyers should deliberate with their clients about justice is another way of saying that they should act justly, where the conception of justice now includes consideration of the social process of reasoning, not just its content. Reasoning by lawyers themselves is not enough, however logical, cognizant of the facts, tolerant and understanding of human nature legal reasoning is. Neither is deliberation a sufficient condition of legal justice, although it is both necessary and neglected.

What can motivate good people to enter a profession where advocacy is more often better rewarded than the pursuit of social justice and where the pursuit of social justice is often not a realistic aim of legal counsel? Law can be an attractive career not only because people make good money in it or pursue social justice by its means, but also because lawyers can live a good life in the law by helping other people live good lives. The character conception of legal virtue builds upon this understanding of legal purposes, which is potentially more inclusive than advocacy in an adversary process or the pursuit of social justice.

The character conception, as articulated by Anthony Kronman, runs roughly as follows. Law is a habit-forming profession. The good habit that it can cultivate is practical judgment, *phronesis*. Living a good life in the law means living a life characterized primarily by practical judgment, not by client advocacy or the pursuit of social justice by means of the law. Both client advocacy and the pursuit of social justice are too instrumental to serve as adequate motivations for good people to become lawyers. Kronman worries that "the lawyer who chooses his career for public-spirited reasons alone, may see himself merely as the instrument by which some communal good is to be achieved. He may even hate his work, find it dull and unrewarding in itself, but still consider it the most economical route to whatever political arrangements he values for their own sake."[10]

This particular worry is not warranted for two reasons. One relates to Kronman's overly restrictive understanding of the public-spirited reasons for becoming a lawyer, and the other relates to a narrow notion of the nature of practical judgment in law. The insight of the character conception is that law at its best requires the virtue of practical judgment. But the conception, as Kronman proposes it, unnecessarily separates public-spirited reasons for becoming a lawyer from the exercise of practical judgment. Suppose you have public-spirited reasons for becoming a lawyer. You want to contribute in some small way to defending people's legal rights and obligations. Another element of your public-spiritedness is that you believe that the equal defense of every citizens' legal rights and obligations constitutes an essential element of the public good in a constitutional democracy. You correctly believe that by the very process of competently defending people's rights and obligations, you are contributing to social justice. In

being motivated by social justice, you therefore need not have anything resembling a purely instrumental relation to your work.

Even if your attitude toward legal work is not purely instrumental, could it be, as Kronman also suggests, that the legal practice of defending citizens' rights and obligations is dull and unrewarding, especially by contrast to the practice of practical judgment? Even this more qualified claim rests on a misunderstanding of how lawyers can best defend citizens' rights and obligations. Lawyers should not simply enlist what they consider the best legal means to pursue what they consider the most justified ends for their clients. In the service of social justice, law at its best enlists the practical judgment of lawyers, and (as we have seen) the exercise of practical judgment by lawyers requires deliberation with clients, the mutual interchange of relevant information, and understanding. If a life dedicated to the exercise of practical judgment is rewarding in itself, as the character conception rightly suggests it can be, then legal practice in defense of social justice may also be rewarding in itself, because it too enlists the virtue of practical judgment.

Practical judgment is a generally valuable virtue. The character conception is therefore correct in recommending practical judgment as a constitutive part of a good life. But the demands of practical judgment differ importantly from one realm of life to another. In private life, practical judgment often does not require the disposition and skills of deliberation. In many matters of private life, we need not engage in the mutual exchange of reasons, empirical and moral understandings with other people in order to arrive at a decision. The distinctive demands of practical judgment do not divide neatly between private and public realms. In some matters of law, for example, clients may know precisely what they want, and know enough about the law to be confident that their preferences are informed and therefore in need of nothing but technical input from legal counsel. This is the attractively unsanctimonious view of lawyers that Anthony Trollope attributes to John Bold, the political reformer:

> Bold was not very fond of his attorney but, as he said, merely wanted a man who knew the forms of law, and who would do what he was told for his money. He had no idea of putting himself in the hands of a lawyer. He wanted law from a lawyer as he did a coat from a tailor, because he could not make it so well himself.[11]

Because our options for legally pursuing even mundane matters these days are so complex in their implications for our own and other people's lives, this view of lawyers as hired hands is unrealistic at best and dangerous at worst.

Complex professional decisions typically require deliberation between professional and client, if only (but not only) to figure out what a client wants, and how a professional can best help the client without making things worse (by using means, for example, that are incompatible with some other valued end that only deliberation brings to light). Deliberation is a constitutive part of practical judgment with regard to complex professional decisions that affect the interests of other people, and practical judgment is, as the character conception correctly suggests, an indispensable virtue of good lawyering. If lawyers do not deliberate with their clients, if they pursue their own independently-arrived-at conception of their clients' interests or social justice, then they act paternalistically, treating their clients as children, and even unjustly, using them as mere means rather than ends in themselves, as constitutional democracy demands. If lawyers deliberate with their clients not only, or even primarily, about social justice, but about the ways in which the law can contribute to their well-being, then many kinds of legal practices can be motivated for public-spirited reasons and because they are conducive to living a good life as a lawyer. Living a good life in the law is dependent upon doing good with the law, but lawyers can do good even when they are not self-consciously serving the cause of social justice. This is an important insight of the character conception of law. Another public-spirited reason for being a lawyer is to help people by deliberating with them about how the law

can (and cannot) help them live a good life. Helping people in this way requires lawyers to have the virtue of practical judgment, and a necessary element of practical judgment in the legal realm is the disposition to deliberate with clients.

To summarize: The standard conception of law, the justice conception, and the character conception, as commonly articulated, neglect the virtue of deliberation in legal practice. Yet consistently pursued, all three point to the moral importance for lawyers of the disposition to deliberate. Whether the law aims at ardent advocacy of clients' informed preferences, the pursuit of social justice, or the ability of lawyers to live a good life in the law, deliberation becomes a necessary (but not sufficient) virtue for lawyers. Each of these three conceptions of the law is incomplete. The law actually and ideally aims at elements of all three conceptions which have yet to be synthesized into a more comprehensive view.

We need not choose among the three conceptions, or arrive at a more comprehensive conception to acknowledge the importance of legal deliberation. Can lawyers be taught the disposition to deliberate with clients, and the skills of deliberation? Yes, if legal education is self-consciously aimed at teaching the deliberative virtues, and if legal practices are better designed to encourage lawyers to deliberate. These are of course two big "ifs," which I now must leave largely in the hypothetical.

In conclusion, I can only mention, briefly and tentatively, two ways of moving legal education further in the direction of teaching the deliberative virtues. The first is a change in law school education that would parallel what has been happening in many medical schools and for related reasons: the expansion of clinical practice for the purpose of teaching future lawyers how better to communicate with their clients. Clinical practice is perhaps more often viewed as a means of encouraging law students to pursue public-interest law, but clinical work need not be motivated only or even primarily by this purpose. Clinical practice can also be designed and directed to cultivate the skills and dispositions of deliberation, which should characterize good lawyers, whether they enter the world of corporate, private, prosecutorial, or public defense law.

A second way of moving legal education further in the direction of teaching deliberation is for regular law school courses to teach more of the knowledge and understanding that is necessary to make informed judgments about alternative legal strategies. This entails teaching students to think in philosophically and empirically rigorous ways about the value and consequences of pursuing alternate legal strategies and defending different legal doctrines. Learning to think like a lawyer would mean learning to think rigorously not only about legal doctrine but also about the consequences and moral values of alternate legal (and nonlegal) decisions. And also to understand the different evaluations people may place on various legal alternatives in light of their own distinctive conceptions of the good life. The Socratic method employed for the sake of deliberation would have students engaging in the give-and-take of argument about the value of various legal strategies in light of considerations of social justice and conceptions of the good life in a constitutional democracy.

NOTES

1. Murray L. Schwartz, *The Professionalism and Accountability of Lawyers*, 66 CAL. L. REV. 673 (1978).

2. *David Luban, Lawyers and Justice: An Ethical Study* 3–147, 393–403 (1988).

3. *See* Charles Fried, *The Lawyer as Friend: The Moral Foundations of the Lawyer-Client Relationship*, 85 YALE L.J. 1060, 1060-69 (1975).

4. I am grateful to Andrew Koppelman for this example.

5. Model Rules of Professional Conduct Preamble (1989).

6. For a detailed description and defense of this conception of legal ethics, see Luban, *supra* note 2.

7. *Philippa Strum, Louis D. Brandeis: Justice for the People* 96–97 (1984).

8. David Luban, *The Noblesse Oblige Tradition in the Practice of Law*, 41 Vand. L. Rev. 717, 725 (1988).

9. *Id.* at 720–27.

10. Anthony T. Kronman, *Living in the Law*, 54 U. Chi. L. Rev. 835, 843–44 (1987).

11. Anthony Trollope, The Warden 25 (David Skilton ed., Oxford University Press 1980) (1855).

Thomas Nagel | # Ruthlessness in Public Life

Thomas Nagel is a Professor of Philosophy and Law at New York University.

I

The great modern crimes are public crimes. To a degree the same can be said of the past, but the growth of political power has introduced a scale of massacre and despoliation that makes the efforts of private criminals, pirates, and bandits seem truly modest.

Public crimes are committed by individuals who play roles in political, military, and economic institutions. (Because religions are politically weak, crimes committed on their behalf are now rare.) Yet unless the offender has the originality of Hitler, Stalin, or Amin, the crimes don't seem to be fully attributable to the individual himself. Famous political monsters have moral personalities large enough to transcend the boundaries of their public roles; they take on the full weight of their deeds as personal moral property. But they are exceptional. Not only are ordinary soldiers, executioners, secret policemen, and bombardiers morally encapsulated in their roles, but so are most secretaries of defense or state, and even many presidents and prime ministers. They

From *Public and Private Morality*, edited by Stuart Hampshire (New York: Cambridge University Press, 1978), pp. 75–91.

act as officeholders or functionaries, and thereby as individuals they are insulated in a puzzling way from what they do: insulated both in their own view and in the view of most observers. Even if one is in no doubt about the merits of the acts in question, the agents seem to have a slippery moral surface produced by their roles or offices.

———————

There is, I think, a problem about the moral effects of public roles and offices. Certainly they have a profound effect on the behavior of the individuals who fill them, an effect partly restrictive but significantly liberating. Sometimes they confer great power, but even where they do not, as in the case of an infantryman or police interrogator, they can produce a feeling of moral insulation that has strong attractions. The combination of special requirements and release from some of the usual restrictions, the ability to say that one is only following orders or doing one's job or meeting one's responsibilities, the sense that one is the agent of vast impersonal forces or the servant of institutions larger than any individual—all these ideas form a heady and sometimes corrupting brew.

But this would not be so unless there were something to the special status of action in a role. If roles encourage illegitimate release from moral restraints it is because their moral effect has been distorted. It will help to understand the distortion if we consider another curiosity of current moral discourse about public life: the emphasis placed on those personal restrictions that complement the lack of official restraint—the other side of the coin of public responsibility and irresponsibility. Public figures are not supposed to use their power openly to enrich themselves and their families, or to obtain sexual favors. Such primitive indulgences are generally hidden or denied, and stress is laid on the personal probity and disinterest of public figures. This kind of personal detachment in the exercise of official functions is thought to guarantee their good moral standing, and it leaves them remarkably free in the public arena. No doubt private transgressions are widespread, but when they are inescapably exposed the penalty can be severe, for a delicate boundary of moral restraint

that sets off the great body of public power and freedom has been breached. . . .

The exchange seems fairly straightforward. The exercise of public power is to be liberated from certain constraints by the imposition of others, which are primarily personal. Because the office is supposedly shielded from the personal interests of the one who fills it, what he does in his official capacity seems also to be depersonalized. This nourishes the illusion that personal morality does not apply to it with any force, and that it cannot be strictly assigned to his moral account. The office he occupies gets between him and his depersonalized acts.

Among other things, such a picture disguises the fact that the exercise of power, in whatever role, is one of the most personal forms of individual self-expression, and a rich source of purely personal pleasure. The pleasure of power is not easily acknowledged, but it is one of the most primitive human feelings—probably one with infantile roots. Those who have had it for years sometimes realize its importance only when they have to retire. Despite their grave demeanor, impersonal diction, and limited physical expression, holders of public power are personally involved to an intense degree and probably enjoying it immensely. But whether or not it is consciously enjoyed, the exercise of power is a primary form of individual expression, not diminished but enhanced by the institutions and offices on which it depends.

When we try, therefore, to say what is morally special about public roles and public action, we must concentrate on how they alter the demands on the individual. The actions are his, whether they consist of planning to obliterate a city or only firing in response to an order. So if the moral situation is different from the case where he acts in no official capacity, it must be because the requirements are different.

II

Some of the moral peculiarity of official roles can be explained by the theory of obligation. Whoever takes on a public or official role assumes the obligation to serve a special function and often the interests of a special group. Like more personal obligations, this limits the claim that other sorts of reasons can make on him. Recall E. M. Forster's remark: "I hate the idea of causes, and if I had to choose between betraying my country and betraying my friend, I hope I should have the courage to betray my country." He was not talking about public office, but similar problems can arise there. In a rigidly defined role like that of a soldier or judge or prison guard, only a very restricted set of considerations is supposed to bear on what one decides to do, and nearly all general considerations are excluded. With less definition, other public offices limit their occupants to certain considerations and free them from others, such as the good of mankind. Public figures sometimes even say and believe that they are obliged to consider only the national or state interest in arriving at their decisions as if it would be a breach of responsibility for them to consider anything else.

This apparent restriction on choice is easy to accept partly because, looked at from the other direction, it lifts restraints that might otherwise be burdensome. But any view as absolute as this is mistaken: there are no such extreme obligations, or offices to which they attach. One cannot, by joining the army, undertake an obligation to obey any order whatever from one's commanding officer. It is not possible to acquire an obligation to kill indebted gamblers by signing a contract as a Mafia hit man. It is not even possible to undertake a commitment to serve the interests of one's children in complete disregard of the interests of everyone else. Obligations to the state also have limits, which derive from their moral context.

Every obligation or commitment reserves some portion of the general pool of motivated action for a special purpose. Life being what it is, each person's supply of time, power, and energy is limited. The kinds of obligations one may undertake, and their limits, depend on how it is reasonable to allocate this pool, and how much liberty individuals should have to allocate it in radically uneven ways. This is true for personal obligations. It applies to public ones as well.

In private life some exclusivity is necessary if we are to allow people to form special relations and attachments, and to make special arrangements with each other on which they can rely. For similar reasons larger groups should be able to cooperate for mutual benefit, or to form social units that may have a geographical definition. And it is natural that the organization of such cooperative units will include institutions, roles, and offices and that the individuals in them will undertake obligations to serve the interests of the group in special ways—by promoting its prosperity, defending it against enemies, etc. To a degree, large-scale social arrangements can be seen as extensions of more individual obligations and commitments.

It may be that the added power conferred by an institutional role should be used primarily for the benefit of that institution and its constituents. The interests of mankind in general have a lesser claim on it. But this does not mean that prohibitions against harming others, directly or indirectly, are correspondingly relaxed. Just because the power to kill thousands of people is yours only because you are the secretary of defense of a certain country, it does not follow that you should be under no restrictions on the use of that power which do not derive specifically from your obligations to serve that country. The same reasoning that challenges private obligations that imply too much of a free hand in carrying them out, will also disallow public commitments with inadequate restraints on their greater power. Insofar as public obligations work like private ones, there is no reason to think that individuals in public roles are released from traditional moral requirements on the treatment of others, or that in public life, the end justifies the means.

III

Morality is complicated at every level. My basic claim is that its impersonal aspects are more prominent in the assessment of institutions than in the assessment of individual actions, and that as a result, the design of institutions may include roles whose occupants must determine what to do by principles different from those that govern private individuals. This will be morally justified, however, by ultimate considerations that underlie individual morality as well. . . . My main contention is that the degree to which ruthlessness is acceptable in public life—the ways in which public actors may have to get their hands dirty—depends on moral features of the institutions through which public action is carried out.

Two types of concern determine the content of morality: concern with what will happen and concern with what one is doing. Insofar as principles of conduct are determined by the first concern, they will be outcome-centered or consequentialist, requiring that we promote the best overall results. Insofar as they are determined by the second, the influence of consequences will be limited by certain restrictions on the means to be used, and also by a loosening of the requirement that one always pursue the best results. The action-centered aspects of morality include bars against treating others in certain ways which violate their rights, as well as the space allotted to each person for a life of his own, without the perpetual need to contribute to the general good in everything he does. Such provisions are described as action-centered because, while they apply to everyone, what they require of each person depends on his particular standpoint rather than on the impersonal consequentialist standpoint that surveys the best overall state of affairs and prescribes for each person whatever he can do to contribute to it.

The interaction and conflict between these two aspects of morality are familiar in private life. They result in a certain balance that emphasizes restrictions against harming or interfering with others, rather than requirements to benefit them, except in cases of serious distress. For the most part it leaves us free to pursue our lives and form particular attachments to some people, so long as we do not harm others.

When we apply the same dual conception to public institutions and activities, the results are different. There are several reasons for this. Institutions are not persons and do not have private lives, nor do institutional roles usually absorb completely the lives of their occupants. Public institutions are designed to serve purposes larger than those of particular individuals or families. They tend to pursue the interests of masses of people (a limiting case would be that of a would government, but most actual institutions have a less than universal constituency). In addition, public acts are diffused over many actors and sub-institutions; there is a division of labor both in execution and in decision. All this results in a different balance between the morality of outcomes and the morality of actions. These two types of moral constraint are differently expressed in public life, and both of them take more impersonal forms.

Some of the same agent-centered restrictions on means will apply to public action as to private. But some of them will be weaker, permitting the public employment of coercive, manipulative, or obstructive methods that would not be allowable for individuals. There is some public analogue to the individual's right to lead his own life free of the constant demand to promote the best overall results, but it appears in the relations of states to one another rather than in their relations to their citizens: States can remain neutral in external disputes, and can legitimately favor their own populations—though not at any cost whatever to the rest of the world.

There is no comparable right of self-indulgence or favoritism for public officials or institutions vis-á-vis the individuals with whom they deal. Perhaps the most significant action-centered feature of public morality is a special requirement to treat people in the relevant population equally. Public policies and actions have to be much more impartial than private ones, since they usually employ a monopoly of certain kinds of power and since there is no reason in their case to leave room for the personal attachments and inclinations that shape individual lives.

In respect to outcomes, public morality will differ from private in according them greater weight. This is a consequence of the weakening of certain action-centered constraints and permissions already described, which otherwise would have restrictive effects. The greater latitude about means in turn makes it legitimate to design institutions whose aim is to produce certain desirable results on a large scale, and to define roles in those institutions whose responsibility is mainly to further those results. Within the appropriate limits, public decisions will be justifiably more consequentialist than private ones. They will also have larger consequences to take into account.

I have simply adapted a point made by Rawls in "Two Concepts of Rules." He argued that utilitarianism could justify practices that exclude utilitarian reasoning in some circumstances. I am arguing that a more complex morality than utilitarianism will likewise have different implications for human conduct when applied to its assessment directly and when applied indirectly via the assessment of institutions through which action occurs. The details of this morality cannot be explained here, but many of its features depend on an idea of moral universality different from that which underlies utilitarianism. Utilitarian assessment decides, basically, whether something is acceptable from a general point of view that combines those of *all* individuals. The method of combination is basically majoritarian. The alternative is to ask whether something is acceptable from a schematic point of view that represents in essentials the standpoint of each individual. The method of combination here is a form of unanimity, since acceptability from the schematic point of view represents acceptability to each person. Both of these moral conceptions can claim to count everyone equally, yet they are very different. My own opinion is that morality should be based on acceptability to each rather than on acceptability to all. . . .

IV

Because they are specialized, not all public institutions are equally sensitive to overall consequences. An important exception is the judiciary, at least in a society where the courts are designed to protect individual rights against both public and private encroachment. Neither the institution itself nor the roles it defines—judge, juror, prosecutor—are dominated by a concern with overall results. They act on narrower grounds. To some extent this narrowing of grounds is itself justified by consequentialist reasoning about the overall effects of such an institution. However the courts also embody the state's action-centered moral constraints—impersonal but not consequentialist. Very importantly, they are supposed to enforce its impartiality in serious dealings with individual citizens. And by setting limits to the means that can be employed by other public institutions, they leave those institutions free to concentrate more fully on achieving results within those limits.

To illustrate the positive claim that these limits differ from those that operate in private life, let me consider two familiar examples of public action: taxation and conscription. Both are imposed by the legislature in our society, and it may be thought that they are therefore indirectly consented to by the population. I believe it is a desperate measure to impute consent to everyone who is drafted or pays income taxes on the ground that he votes or accepts certain public services. Consent is not needed to justify such legislative action, because the legislature is an institution whose authority to make such decisions on consequentialist grounds is morally justified in other ways. Its periodic answerability to the electorate is one feature of the institution (another being the constitutional protection of rights) that contributes to its legitimacy—but not by implying each citizen's consent to its actions. Particularly when those actions are coercive the defense of consent is not credible.

Some would describe taxation as a form of theft and conscription as a form of slavery—in fact some would prefer to describe taxation as slavery too, or at least as forced labor. Much might be said against these descriptions, but that is beside the point. For within proper limits, such practices when engaged in by governments are acceptable whatever they are called. . . . The results achieved by taxation in an egalitarian welfare state would not be produced either by a right of individual expropriation or by a duty of charity. Taxation therefore provides a case in which public morality is derived not from private morality, but from impersonal consequentialist considerations applied directly to public institutions, and secondarily to action within those institutions. There is no way of analyzing a system of redistributive taxation into the sum of a large number of individual acts all of which satisfy the requirements of private morality.

In the case of conscription, the coercion is extreme, and so is what one is forced to do. You are told to try to kill people who are trying to kill you, the alternative being imprisonment. Quite apart from fighting, military service involves unusual restrictions of liberty. Even assuming agreement about when conscription is acceptable and what exemptions should be allowed, this is a kind of coercion that it would be unthinkable to impose privately. *A* can't force *B* to help him fight a gang of hoodlums who are robbing them both, if *B* would rather give his money. Again, the more impersonal viewpoint of public morality gives a different result.

But not everything is permitted. Restrictions on the treatment of individuals continue to operate from a public point of view, and they cannot be implemented entirely by the courts. One of the hardest lines to draw in public policy is the one that defines where the end stops justifying the means. If results were the only basis for public morality then it would be possible to justify anything, including torture and massacre, in the service of sufficiently large interests. Whether the limits are drawn by specific constitutional protections or not, the strongest constraints of individual morality will continue to limit what can be publicly justified even by extremely powerful consequentialist reasons.

———————

Josiah Royce | # Loyalty

…In loyalty, when loyalty is properly defined, is the fulfilment of the whole moral law. You can truthfully centre your entire moral world about a rational conception of loyalty. Justice, charity, industry, wisdom, spirituality, are all definable in terms of enlightened loyalty.

III

Loyalty shall mean, according to this preliminary definition: *The willing and practical and thoroughgoing devotion of a person to a cause.* A man is loyal when, first, he has some cause to which he is loyal; when, secondly, he *willingly* and *thoroughly* devotes himself to this cause; and when, thirdly, he expresses his devotion in some *sustained and practical way,* by acting steadily in the service of his cause. Instances of loyalty are: The devotion of a patriot to

his country, when this devotion leads him actually to live and perhaps to die for his country; the devotion of a martyr to his religion; the devotion of a ship's caption to the requirements of his office when, after a disaster, he works steadily for his ship and for the saving of his ship's company until the last possible service is accomplished, so that he is the last man to leave the ship, and is ready if need be to go down with his ship.

Such cases of loyalty are typical. They involve, I have said, the willingness of the loyal man to do his service. The loyal man's cause is his cause by virtue of the assent of his own will. His devotion is his own. He chooses it, or, at all events, approves it. Moreover, his devotion is a practical one. He does something. This something serves his cause. Loyalty is never mere emotion. Adoration and affection may go with loyalty, but can never alone constitute loyalty.

From *The Philosophy of Loyalty* (New York, Macmillan, 1908).

Furthermore, the devotion of the loyal man involves a sort of restraint or submission of his natural desires to his cause. Loyalty without self-control is impossible. The loyal man serves. That is, he does not merely follow his own impulses. He looks to his cause for guidance. This cause tells him what to do, and he does it. His devotion, furthermore, is entire. He is ready to live or to die as the cause directs.

And now for a further word about the hardest part of this preliminary definition of loyalty: A loyal man, I have said, has a cause. I do not yet say that he has a good cause. He might have a bad one. I do not say, as yet, what makes a cause a good one, and worthy of loyalty. All that is to be considered hereafter. But this I now premise: If one is loyal, he has a cause which he indeed personally values. Otherwise, how could he be devoted to it? He therefore takes interest in the cause, loves it, is well pleased with it. On the other hand, loyalty never means the mere emotion of love for your cause, and never means merely following your own pleasure, viewed *as* your private pleasure and interest. For if you are loyal, your cause is viewed by you as something outside of you. Or if, like your country, your cause includes yourself, it is still much larger than your private self. It has its own value, so you as a loyal person believe. This essential value it would keep (so you believe) even if your private interest were left out of account. Your cause you take, then, to be something objective— something that is not your private self. It does not get its value merely from your being pleased with it. You believe, on the contrary, that you love it just because of its own value, which it has by itself, even if you die. That is just why one may be ready to die for his cause. In any case, when the loyal man serves his cause, he is not seeking his own private advantage.

Moreover, the cause to which a loyal man is devoted is never something *wholly* impersonal. It concerns other men. Loyalty is social. If one is a loyal servant of a cause, one has at least possible fellow-servants. On the other hand, since a cause, in general, tends to unite the many fellow-servants in one service, it consequently seems to the loyal man to have a sort of impersonal or superpersonal quality about it. You can love an individual. But you can be loyal only to a tie that binds you and others into some sort of unity, and loyal to individuals only through the tie. The cause to which loyalty devotes itself has always this union of the personal and the seemingly superindividual about it. It binds many individuals into one service. Loyal lovers, for instance, are loyal not merely to one another as separate individuals, but to their love, to their union, which is something more than either of them, or even than both of them viewed as distinct individuals.

So much for a preliminary view of what loyalty is. Our definition is not complete. It raises rather than solves problems about the nature of loyalty. But thus indeed we get a first notion of the general nature of loyalty.

IV

But now for a next step. Many people find that they have a need of loyalty. Loyalty is a good thing for them. If you ask, however, why loyalty may be needed by a given man, the answer may be very complex. A patriot may, in your opinion, need loyalty, first because his country needs his service, and, as you add, he actually owes this service, and so needs to do his duty, viz. to be loyal. This first way of stating a given man's need of a given loyalty, turns upon asserting that a specific cause rightly requires of a certain man a certain service. The cause, as one holds, is good and worthy. This man actually ought to serve just that cause. Hence he stands in need of loyalty, and of just this loyalty.

But in order thus to define this man's need of loyalty, you have to determine what causes are worthy of loyalty, and why this man ought to serve his own cause. To answer such questions would apparently presuppose a whole system of morals,—a system which at this stage of our argument we have not yet in sight.

But there is another,—a simpler, and, at the outset, a lower way of estimating the value of loyalty. One may, for the time, abstract from all questions as to the value of causes. Whether a man is loyal to a good cause or to a bad cause, his own personal attitude, when he is loyal, has a certain general quality. Whoever is loyal, whatever be his cause, is devoted, is active, surrenders his private self-will, controls himself, is in love with his cause, and believes in it. The loyal man is thus in a certain state of mind which has its own value for himself. To live a loyal life, whatever be one's cause, is to live in a way which is certainly free from many well-known sources of inner dissatisfaction. Thus hesitancy is often corrected by loyalty; for the cause plainly tells the loyal man what to do. Loyalty, again, tends to unify life, to give it centre, fixity, stability.

Well, these aspects of loyalty are, so far as they go, good for the loyal man. We may therefore define our need of loyalty in a certain preliminary way. We may take what is indeed a lower view of loyalty, regarding it, for the moment, in deliberate abstraction from the cause to which one is loyal. We may thus regard loyalty, for the moment, just as a personal attitude, which is good for the loyal man himself.

Bernard Williams | # Politics and Moral Character

Bernard Williams was Knightbridge chair of Philosophy at the University of Cambridge.

What sorts of persons do we want and need to be politicians? This question, and the broader question of what we morally want from politics, are importantly different from the question of what the correct answers are to moral problems which present themselves within political activity. We may want—we may *morally* want—politicians who on some occasions ignore these problems. Moreover, even in cases where what we want the politician to do is to consider, and give the right answer to, such a problem, it is not enough to say that we want him to be the sort of person who can do that. Since some of the correct answers involve actions which are nonetheless very disagreeable, further questions arise about the sorts of persons who will give—in particular, who may find it too easy to give—those right answers.

It is cases where the politician does something morally disagreeable, that I am concerned with: the problem that has been called that of *dirty hands*. The central question is: how are we to think about the involvement of politicians in such actions, and about the dispositions that such involvement requires? This is not in the first place a question about what is permissible and defensible in such connections; though something, obviously, will have to be said about

what it means to claim that a politician has adequate reason to do something which is, as I put it, "morally disagreeable."

It is widely believed that the practice of politics selects at least for cynicism and perhaps for brutality in its practitioners. This belief, and our whole subject, notoriously elicit an uncertain tone from academics, who tend to be either over-embarrassed or under-embarrassed by moralizing in the face of power. Excited, in either direction, by the subject, they often take rather large-scale or epic examples, such as the conduct of international relations by hostile powers, or ruthless policies which may or may not be justified by history. I will touch marginally on those kinds of issue at the end, but my first concern is more with the simply squalid end of the subject, and with the politician not so much as national leader or maker of history, but as professional. I shall defer the more heady question of politicians being criminals in favor of the more banal notion that they are crooks.

There is of course one totally banal sense of the claim that they are crooks, namely that some break the law for their own advantage, take bribes, do shady things which are not actually illegal for personal gain. This dimension of effort is for the

From *Public and Private Morality*, edited by Stuart Hampshire (New York: Cambridge University Press, 1978), pp. 55–73.

purpose of the present discussion beside the point. It does raise one or two interesting questions, for instance the absence from politics of any very robust notion of professional ethics. Some professions, such as [law and medicine], have elaborate codes of professional ethics: I take it that this is not because their vocation rises nobly above any thoughts of personal gain, but because their clients need to be protected, and be seen to be protected, in what are particularly sensitive areas of their interests. Some areas of business have similar provisions, but in general the concept of a professional business ethic is less developed than that of a professional medical or legal ethic. One might think that politics was concerned quite generally with sensitive areas of the clients' interests, yet even in places where it is recognized that these restrictions govern the activities of doctors and lawyers, the politician's professional conduct is perceived as more like that of the businessman. The explanation of this fact I take not to be very mysterious: roughly, there are several reasons why it is in the interest of most in these professions to belong to a respectable cartel, but in the case of politicians, the circumstances in which they are able to run a cartel are circumstances in which they have little motive to keep it respectable.

How are the morally dubious activities which belong to this irrelevant class, distinguished from those which concern our enquiry? Certainly not by the first sort being *secret*. For the first sort are often not secret, and in some cultures are barely meant to be so, it being an achievement calling for admiration that one has stolen extensively and conspicuously from the public funds. Even more obviously, many dubious acts of the more strictly political kind are themselves secret. The point rather is that not all acts done by politicians are political acts, and we are concerned with those that are. Relative to some appropriate account of what the politician is supposed to be up to as a politician, stealing from public funds is likely to count as a diversion of effort. However, it is to be recognized that not all classifications which would be made on these principles by the most respectable northwest European or North American opinion would come out the same elsewhere: thus bribery can be an integral and functional part of a political system. What must count as a

political activity anywhere, however, is *trying to stay in office*. There are, needless to say, unacceptable ways of staying in office, and there are among them ways of staying in office which defeat the purposes of the methods for acquiring office (rigging the ballot). But this is a matter of means—the *objective* of staying in office, though it cannot by every means or in every circumstance by decently attained, is itself highly relevant to the business of politics, whereas the objectives of enriching oneself or of securing sinecures for one's family are not.

We shall leave aside the dubious activities of politicians which are not primarily political activities. But since the question we shall be concerned with is primarily what dispositions we want in politicians, we should not at the same time forget the platitude that the psychological distance between the two sorts of activity may be very small indeed. Not every politically ruthless or devious ruler is disposed to enrich himself or improperly advance his friends: the ones who are not are usually morally and psychologically more interesting. But the two sorts of tendency go together often enough, and cries for "clean government" are usually demands for the suppression of both.

––––––––––

Among political acts are some for which there are good political reasons, as that important and worthy political projects would fail without these acts, but which are acts which honorable, scrupulous, etc. people might, prima facie at least, be disinclined to do. Besides those, there are more, and more insidious, cases in which the unpalatable act seems necessary not to achieve any such clear-cut and noble objective, but just to keep going, or to preempt opposition to a worthy project, or more generally to prevent a worthy project becoming impossible later. What the unpalatable acts may be depends on the political environment; at present we are concerned with a relatively ordered situation where political activity involves at least bargaining and the expression of conflicting interests and ideals. In such a situation a politician might find himself involved in, or invited to, such things as: lying, or at least concealment and the making of misleading statements; breaking promises; special pleading; temporary coalition with the distasteful; sacrifice of the interests of worthy persons to those of unworthy persons; and (at least if in a sufficiently important position) coercion up to blackmail. We are not at this point considering more drastic situations in which there is a question, for instance, of having opponents killed. (I mean by that, that *there is no question of it*, and it would be thought outrageous or insane to mention it as an option. The situation is not one of those in which such options are mentioned and then, all things considered, laid aside.)

The less drastic, but still morally distasteful, activities are in no way confined to politics. That they should seem necessary follows just from there being large interests involved, in a context of partly unstructured bargaining. It is the same, for instance, with a lot of business of the more active variety. But it attracts more obloquy in politics than elsewhere: the use of such means is thought more appropriate to the pursuit of professedly self-interested ends than where larger moral pretensions are entertained. But the fact that there are larger moral pretensions is itself not an accident. Besides the point that some objectives other than the self-interest of the professional participants are necessary—at the limit, are necessary for the activity even to be politics—there is the point that democracy has a tendency to impose higher expectations with regard even to the means, since under democracy control of politicians is precisely supposed to be a function of the expectations of the electorate.

I have mentioned acts, done in pursuit of worthy political ends, which "honorable, scrupulous, etc. people might, prima facie at least, be disinclined to do." But, it will be said, if it is for some worthy political objective and the greater good, does not that merely show that it is an act which these honorable people should *not* be disinclined to do? At most, the characteristic which the act possesses is that it is of a type which these people would be disinclined to do if it were not in this interest; and that, it may be said, is irrelevant. But this Utilitarian response either does not get to the question which concerns us, or else gives an inadequate answer to it. It does not get to the question if it merely insists that the otherwise

discreditable act is the one, in these circumstances, to be done, and says nothing about the dispositions of the agent, and how his dispositions express themselves in a view of this act. It gives an inadequate answer if it says that the only disposition such an agent needs is the disposition to do what is Utilitarianly right. Even Utilitarians have found that answer inadequate: it is not self-evident, and many Utilitarians agree that it is not even true, that the best way to secure their objective of the greatest happiness all round is to have agents each of whom is pursuing, as such, the greatest happiness all round. Beyond that level of discussion, again, there is the deeper point that moral dispositions other than Utilitarian benevolence may themselves figure in people's conceptions of "happiness."

In any case, it is not enough to say that these are situations in which the right thing to do is an act which would *normally* be morally objectionable. That description best fits the case in which an act and its situation constitute an *exception*. We may recall the repertoire, familiar from Ross and other writers, of obligations properly overridden in emergencies. There, the decision is often easy—of course we break the routine promise to save the drowning child, and to doubt it, or to feel uneasy about having done it, would be utterly unreasonable. It is a clear overriding circumstance. While it is not as though the promise or other defeated obligation had never existed (one still has the obligation at least to explain), nevertheless it is quite clearly and unanswerably overridden, and complaints from the disadvantaged party would, once things had been explained, be unacceptable. Of course, not all cases of the straight overriding kind are clear cases of that kind. One can be in doubt what to do, and here there is room for unease. But the unease, within this structure, is directly related to the doubt or unclarity: the question will be "did I really do the right thing?" If one has an uneasy sense that one may have done wrong to the victim, it is because one has an uneasy sense that one may have done the wrong thing.

Some situations in politics are no doubt of that structure. But the situations I have in mind (of course, as I have said, they are not confined to politics) are of a different structure. In these, the sense that a discreditable thing has been done is not the product of uncertainty, nor again of a recognition that one has made the wrong choice. A sense that something discreditable has been done will, moreover, be properly shared by the victims, and they will have a complaint that they have been wronged. The politician who just could not see that they had a complaint, and who, after he had explained the situation to them, genuinely thought that their complaint was based on a misunderstanding and that they were unreasonable to make it (as one might properly think in the first kind of case) is a politician whose dispositions are already such as to raise our questions in a very pressing form.

———————

It may be said that the victims do not have a right to complain because their relation to the action is not the same in the political context as it would be outside it: perhaps it is not even the same action. There is some truth, sometimes, in this claim. It does apply to some victims themselves involved in politics: a certain level of roughness is to be expected by anyone who understands the nature of the activity, and it is merely a misunderstanding to go on about it in a way which might be appropriate to more sheltered activities. But this consideration—which might be called *Truman's kitchen-heat principle*—does not go all the way. There are victims outside politics, and there are victims inside it who get worst than they could reasonably expect; and in general there are political acts which no considerations about appropriate expectations or the going currency of the trade can in themselves adequately excuse.

I mentioned the "moral claims" of politics. In some cases, the claims of the political reasons are proximate enough, and enough of the moral kind, to enable one to say that there is a moral justification for that particular political act, a justification which has outweighed the moral reasons against it. Even so, that can still leave the moral remainder, the uncancelled moral disagreeableness I have referred to. The possibility of such a remainder is not peculiar to political action, but there are features of politics which make it specially liable to produce it. It particularly arises in cases where the moral justification

of the action is of a consequentialist or maximizing kind, while what has gone to the wall is a right: there is a larger moral cost attached to letting a right be overridden by consequences, than to letting one consequence be overridden by another, since it is part of the point of rights that they cannot just be overridden by consequences. In politics the justifying consideration will characteristically be of the consequentialist kind. Moreover, an important aspect of consequentialist reasoning lies in maximizing *expectation,* the product of the size of the payoff and its probability. Since in the political sphere of action the payoffs are, or can readily be thought to be, very large, the probabilities can be quite small, and the victims may find that their rights have been violated for the sake of an outside chance.

Where the political reasons are of the less proximate kind, for instance defensive, or preemptive, or concerned with securing an opportunity, we may speak, not of the moral claims of politics, but merely of the claims of politics against morality. While an anxious politician may hope still to find some moral considerations bearing the situation, he may discover that they have retreated merely to the overall justification of the pursuit of his, or his party's, worthwhile objectives, or some similar overarching concern. The Olympian point of retreat is notoriously so distant and invulnerable that the rationale of seriously carrying on the business of politics ceases to be disturbed by any moral qualms or any sense of non-political costs at all. Decent political existence lies somewhere between that—or its totally cynical successor, from which even the distant view of Olympus has disappeared—and an absurd failure to recognize that if politics is to exist as an activity at all, some moral considerations must be expected to get out of its way.

If that space is to have any hope of being occupied, we need to hold on to the idea, and to find some politicians who will hold on to the idea, that there are actions which remain morally disagreeable even when politically justified. The point of this is not at all that it is edifying to have politicians who, while as ruthless in action as others, are unhappy about it. Sackcloth is not suitable dress for politicians, least of all successful ones. The point—and this is basic to my argument—is that only those who are reluctant or disinclined to do the morally disagreeable when it is really necessary have much chance of not doing it when it is not necessary.

There are two different reasons for this. First, there is no disposition which just consists in getting it right every time, whether in politics or in anything else. Whether judgment is well exercised, whether immediate moral objections are given the right weight, or any, against large long-term issues, is, on any sensible view of those processes, something that involves patterns of sentiment and reaction. In a body of persons considering a practical question, it essentially involves their shared dispositions and their mutual expectations—what considerations can be heard, what kinds of hesitation or qualification or obstacle it is appropriate or effective to mention. (There is a remark attributed to Keynes, about an American official: "a man who has his ear so close to the ground that he cannot hear what an upright man says.") That is the first, and main, reason, and one which any reasonable view of deliberation must accept: a habit of reluctance is an essential obstacle against the happy acceptance of the intolerable.

The second reason, which I have already included in my account, is something less widely acceptable: that reluctance in the necessary case, is not only a useful habit, but a correct reaction *to that case*, because that case does involve a genuine moral cost. The fact that reluctance is justified even in the necessary case—and in speaking of "reluctance," I mean not just initial hesitation in reaching for the answer, but genuine disquiet when one arrives at it—is in fact something that helps to explain the nature, and the value, of the habit of reluctance which was appealed to in the first reason. It embodies a sensibility to moral costs. Utilitarianism, which hopes (in some of its indirect forms) to appeal to habits of reluctance, cannot in fact make any sense of them at this level, because it lacks any sense of *moral* cost, as opposed to costs of some other kind (such as utility) which have to be considered in arriving at the moral decision. Utilitarianism has its special reasons for not understanding the notion of a moral cost, which are connected with its maximizing conceptions; but much other moral philosophy shares that incapacity.

Yet it is a notion deeply entrenched in many people's moral consciousness. Why so many moral philosophers learn to forget it is a harder question, and perhaps a deeper one, than why some politicians do.

––––––––––

Another reason for concern in the political case lies in the professional (and in itself perfectly proper) commitment to staying in power. I have already suggested that it involves an essential ambivalence: it is impossible to tell, at the limit, where it merges into simple ambition, and into that particular deformation of political life, under all systems, which consists in the inability to consider a question on its merits because one's attention is directed to the consequences of giving (to one's colleagues, in the first instance) a particular answer. Where that has widely taken over, the citizens have reason to fear their politicians' judgment.

The dispositions of politicians are differently related to their tasks and to their public than are those of a profession such as the legal profession for which partly analogous questions arise. Those differences all give greater reason for concern, and make more pressing the question: what features of the political system are likely to select for those dispositions in politicians which are at once morally welcome and compatible with their being effective politicians? What features of the system can help to bring it about that fairly decent people can dispose of a fair degree of power? How does one ensure a reasonable succession of colonists of the space between cynicism and political idiocy?

It is a vast, old, and in good part empirical question. If one adapts Plato's question, *how can the good rule?*, to Machiavelli's, *how to rule the world as it is?*, the simplest conflation—*how can the good rule the world as it is?*—is merely discouraging. It is also, however, excessively pious: the conception of the good that it inherits from Plato invites the question of how the good could do anything at all, which the Machiavellian conception of the world as it is raises the question of how anyone could do anything with it. (A popular sense of "realism" gets its strength from the fact that the second of those questions has some answers, while the first has none.) But if one modifies from both ends, allowing both that the good need not be as pure as all that, so long as they retain some active sense of moral costs and moral limits; and that the society has some genuinely settled politics and some expectations of civic respectability: then there is some place for discussing what properties we should like the system, in these respects, to have. There are many: I will mention, only in barest outline, four dimensions of a political system which seem to bear closely on this issue.

(a) There is the question, already touched on, of the balance of publicity, and the relations of politician and public, particularly of course in a democracy. The assumption is widespread, particularly in the USA, that public government and a great deal of public scrutiny must encourage honest government, and apply controls to the cynicism of politicians. There is, however, no reason to suppose that the influence of such practices and institutions will be uniformly in one direction. The requirements of instant publicity in a context which is, as we are supposing, to some mild degree moralized, has an evident potential for hypocrisy, while, even apart from that, the instant identification of particular political acts, as they are represented at the degree of resolution achievable in the media, is a recipe for competition in preemptive press releases.

(b) A similar question is that of the relations of politicians to one another; and there is another approved belief, that it is in the interest of good government that politicians should basically be related to one another only functionally, that they should not share a set of understandings which too markedly differentiate them from people who are not politicians. Yet it is not clear how far this is true, either. For it is an important function of the relations of politicians to one another, what courses of action are even discussible, and that is a basic dimension of a moral culture. Very obviously, a ruthless clique is worse than a clique checked by less ruthless outsiders, but that is not the only option. Another is that of a less ruthless clique resisting more ruthless outsiders.

(c) A very well-known point is that of the relation of potential politicians to actual ones, the question of political recruitment. Notoriously, systems where succession is problematic or discontinuous have the property of selecting for the ruthless. No sensible critic will suggest that if that is so, it is at all easy to change, but it is nevertheless an important dimension of assessment of a political system.

(d) A slightly less obvious variant of the same sort of issue concerns the promotion-pattern within a political organization; in particular, the position of the bottleneck between very top jobs and rather less top jobs. Except in very favored circumstances, it is likely to be the case that getting to the top of a political system will require properties which, while they need not at all necessarily be spectacularly undesirable or even regrettable, may nevertheless perhaps lean in the direction of the kind of ambition and professionalism which does not always make for the best judgment, moral or practical. It is desirable that the system should not put too heavy stress on those properties too soon in the business; there can then be an honorable and successful role, below the final bottleneck, for persons without the elbow-power to get into or through the bottleneck. Government concentrated on a few personalities of course tends to weaken this possibility. Related is the question of the prestige of jobs below the top one....

———

Last, I should like to make just one point about the further dimension of the subject, in which one is concerned not just with the disagreeable or distasteful but with crimes, or what otherwise would be crimes. This is a different level from the last; here we are concerned not just with business but, so to speak, with the Mafia. My question, rather as before, is not directly whether actions of a certain kind—in this case such things as murders, torture, etc.—are ever justified, but rather, if they are justified, how we should think of those who politically bring them about. I shall call the actions in question, for short, *violence*. It might be worth distinguishing, among official acts of violence, what could be called *structured* and *unstructured* violence; the former related to such processes as executions under law, application of legal force by the police, etc., while the latter include acts (it may be, more abroad than at home) pursued in what is regarded as the national interest.

I shall set out a list of four propositions which some would regard as all true, and which, if they were all true, would make the hope of finding politicians of honorable character, except in minor roles and in favorable circumstances, very slim.

(i) There are violent acts which the state is justified in doing which no private citizen as such would be justified in doing.

(ii) Anything the state is justified in doing, some official such as, often, a politician is justified in ordering to be done.

(iii) You are not morally justified in ordering to be done anything which you would not be prepared to do yourself.

(iv) Official violence is enough like unofficial violence for the preparedness referred to in (iii) to amount to a criminal tendency.

I take it that no one except anarchists will deny (i), at least so far as structured violence is concerned (it is admitted that the distinction between structured and unstructured violence is imprecise). It may be said that structured violence constitutes acts which none but the state could even logically perform; thus nothing done by a private citizen as such could constitute a judicial execution. But I take it that while this is true, it does not cut very deep into the essential issues; thus there is another description of the act which is a judicial execution under which that act could logically, but ought not to be, performed by a private citizen. A more substantial issue is whether the only violence that is legitimate for the state is structured violence. This I doubt, too. Even if regular military operations are counted as structured violence, there may be other acts, bordering on the military or of an irregular character, which a state may be lucky if it is in a position to do without altogether.

An important issue connected with this is the extent to which a political leader's task, particularly in a democracy, is defined in terms of defending the interests of the state; and whether, if the interests of some other, rival, state will be advanced unless some act of violence is authorized, he can be justified

in refusing to authorize that act. A similar problem arises in the case where he thinks that the interests of another state should, in justice, prevail. He certainly has a right to that opinion; to what extent has he the right to act on it while still performing that role?

The (imprecise) distinction between structured and unstructured violence also bears on (iv); (iv) is perhaps more plausible with unstructured than with structured violence. It is very widely agreed that the distinction between the official and the unofficial can make a moral difference to the estimation of acts of violence; there are similarly psychological differences in the dispositions underlying the two kinds of acts, even if it is unclear how deep those differences may, in many cases, go (an unclarity which itself makes some people unduly nervous about the legitimacy of official violence). If that is right, then (iv) will fail, and the disobliging conclusion will not follow from the argument, even granted the truth of (i) and the platitudinous truth of (ii). At least, it will be enough to prevent its following with full generality. But while we may certainly agree that (iv) is not exceptionlessly true, it is quite plausible to claim that there are acts, particularly perhaps of unstructured violence, for which (iv) really does hold true, but which nevertheless would be justified under (i). To suppose that there could be no such acts, to suppose in particular that if an act is such that (iv) applies to it, then it must follow that it could not be justified, would be, it seems to me, to take a highly unrealistic view either of politics, or of the possible psychology of agents who will do that act.

In this case, attention turns to (iii); (iii) seems to me false, and more interestingly so than (iv). If so, then there is perhaps a larger class of arguments which have some currency in moral discussion which will have to be abandoned or given extra help; as that one should be a vegetarian unless one would be prepared to work in an abattoir, or that one should not accept experimentation on animals unless one were prepared to conduct it (assuming that one had the skills) oneself. However it may be with those cases, at any rate our understanding of honesty and decency in politicians should be modified by reflection on (iii). The consideration that they should not order something unless they were prepared to do it themselves should be counterweighted with the consideration that if they were prepared to do it themselves, they might be far too willing to order it.

NOTES

1. I have said something about such cases in "Ethical Consistency," reprinted in *Problems of the Self* (Cambridge 1973), chap. 11.

2. I assume that rights can sometimes be overridden. to define "rights" so that this should not ever be possible would have wider consequences—since one must say something about possible conflicts of rights among themselves—and is anyway undesirable: if all rights have

to be *absolute* rights, then it is possible to conclude that there are no rights at all.

3. I have known a politician, now dead, who used to say "that is not a *serious* political argument" to mean, more or less, "that is an argument about what to do in politics which mentions a non-political consideration"—in particular, a moral consideration. This posture was to some degree bluff.

4. "Lawyers as Professionals: Some Moral Issues," 5:1 *Human Rights* (1975), pp. 1–24. [See chap. 3, sel. 5, *EILP.—Ed.*] I am grateful for discussion of these issues to Dick Wasserstrom, Andy Kaufman, and other participants in the Council for Philosophical Studies Institute on Law and Ethics, Williams College, MA, 1977.

CASES

CASE 6.1
Is It Ethical to Criticize Other Dentists' Work?
Charles F. Squire

Q I see patients who have had poor-quality treatment (such as open contacts and poor margins), particularly often when posterior composites are used. The patients complain of food impaction, sensitivity and cost (the latter is especially a problem, considering that many of the restorations are only a few years old). I know what to do clinically, but how do I respond when the patients ask me if their previous dentists did a poor job?

A Whew! There is not an easy solution to resolve the ethical aspect of your question. There are whole chapters in dental ethics textbooks devoted to working through this ethical dilemma. The American Dental Association's Principles of Ethics and Code of Professional Conduct ("the Code") addresses the issue with Code Section 4.C, Justifiable Criticism, and its accompanying Advisory Opinion 4.C.1.

From the *Journal of the American Dental Assoc.*, June 2005, Vol. 136.

4.C. Justifiable Criticism. Dentists shall be obliged to report to the appropriate reviewing agency as determined by the local component or constituent society instances of gross or continual faulty treatment by other dentists. Patients should be informed of their present oral health status without disparaging comment about prior services. Dentists issuing a public statement with respect to the profession shall have a reasonable basis to believe that the comments made are true.

Advisory Opinion. 4.C.1. Meaning of "Justifiable." Patients are dependent on the expertise of dentists to know their oral health status. Therefore, when informing a patient of the status of his or her oral health, the dentist should exercise care that the comments made are truthful, informed and justifiable. This may involve consultation with the previous treating dentist(s), in accordance with applicable law, to determine under what circumstances and conditions the treatment was performed. A difference of opinion as to preferred treatment should not be communicated to the patient in a manner which would unjustly imply mistreatment. There will necessarily be cases where it will be difficult to determine whether the comments made are justifiable. Therefore, this section is phrased to address the discretion of dentists and advises against unknowing or unjustifiable disparaging statements against another dentist. However, it should be noted that, where comments are made which are not supportable and therefore unjustified, such comments can be the basis for the institution of a disciplinary proceeding against the dentist making such statements.

Our reader acknowledges awareness of the need to honor his or her patient's autonomy by accurately informing the patients of their present oral health status without making disparaging comments about prior services.

It is important to draw the distinction between bad outcomes of appropriate therapy and bad outcomes attributable to bad work (therapy). We all know that bad outcomes can occur with our therapy even when all proper methods are followed. Bad outcomes can be caused by occasional lapses of professional judgment and skill (human fallibility) and that of "gross or continual faulty treatment."

When a dentist makes a statement to a patient regarding the efficacy and quality of treatment rendered by a previous dentist, it is important to keep in mind that the patient has no obligation to treat that statement or opinion as confidential. Patients may waive any confidentiality protections they are afforded under state law. Therefore, the statement deserves the same deference given to any public statement, since it potentially can be communicated or shared by the patient with others. It is ethically wise to apply a strong burden of proof requirement to ensure that the statement is informed and totally justifiable. There is also the individual dentist's obligation to the self-governing dental profession and the public at large to report to appropriate agencies and professional societies any "gross or continual" faulty treatment by other dentists.

In a perfect world, Dentist B always would be able and willing to communicate with previous treating Dentist A about the outcomes of previous questionable treatment and resolve differences of opinion and know the circumstances of the rendered therapy.

As clinical dentists, our first obligation is to place the well-being of patients ahead of our own interests (with certain limits). First and foremost, we must give patients complete and truthful information regarding their current oral health status. When patients ask about the efficacy of another dentist's therapy, it is not unethical or unprofessional to remember that the burden of proof regarding faulty or bad treatment—not just the outcome of that therapy—is demanding and a prudent dentist must exercise great caution before making comments about another dentist's treatment.

Uninformed or unjustifiable criticism is disparaging and can lead to unpleasant consequences for the unwary professional. It may be best to let state dental boards and the ethics committee of local and state dental societies determine the true competency of our peers who perform gross or consistently poor clinical work.

Questions

1. Think about the concept of professional loyalty. Although patients are a top priority (according to "The Code"), can disparaging comments about another dentist's work provide the care for which "The Code" calls?

2. What are some of the roadblocks you can determine by thinking about "Justifiable Criticism"? How can a dentist be sure of the patient's interpretation of her or his diagnosis?

CASE 6.2

Blowing the Whistle in Iraq

Megan Rickel

In January 2004, Spc. Joe Darby blew the whistle on his military colleagues involved in the Abu Ghraib prisoner abuse scandal. Seven members of the 372nd military police company have since been indicted and tried after Spc. Darby made public the now-infamous pictures. While Darby was officially commended for reporting the abuse, some feared that he would suffer repercussions (social or career-wise) for his actions, as he wasn't specifically following orders to report the abuse.

Spc. Jeremy Sivits was the first soldier to be tried following the whistle blowing. His defense attorneys insisted that Sivits was merely following orders, as he had been trained, to photograph the abuse. For Sivits, following orders was the right thing to do.

Questions

1. What ethical issues skirt the fine line between right and wrong, as outlined by this case?

2. Should the fear of repercussions of disobeying military orders, as in the defense of Jeremy Sivits, be an allowable excuse for not whistle-blowing? How should such experiences be accounted for in determining ultimate responsibility?

3. Should whistle-blowing be praised? Why or why not?

CASE 6.3

Ten Whistleblowers and How They Fared

Myron Glazer

In 1959, Frank Serpico joined the New York City police force. For Serpico, the police had always represented the meshing of authority and service. His early days on the force propelled him into the conflict between the norms governing police behavior set by department regulations and the actual "code" generated by the police. Formal regulations precluded the taking of any items from neighorhood stores and sanctioned the acceptance of bribes. In the station house and out on patrol a different set of rules applied. "Shopping" for items of food at local stores was clearly acceptable and taking money to pardon a lawbreaker became standard fare. Serpico was caught in a dilemma that faces many rookie police. Which set of norms should he uphold?[1]

Like many other whistleblowers in industry, government, and the academic world, initially Serpico was caught between his desire to follow his moral beliefs, and the organizational pressures to conform. How do workers handle such a conflict? And what happens to their personal lives and their careers once they have blown the whistle? In an effort to understand the dynamics of the process, I have interviewed or exchanged letters with nine prominent whistleblowers and have corresponded with the wife of a tenth, who is deceased.[2] Their cases portray three distinct paths through which individuals move toward public disclosure:

Unbending resisters protest within the organization about unethical or illegal behavior that they have observed. They maintain a strict commitment to their principles, despite efforts to cajole or coerce them. Ultimately, as a consequence of neglect and retaliation within the organization, they take a public stand.

From *The Hastings Center Report*, Dec. 1983.

Implicated protestors speak out within their organizations, but acquiesce when they are ordered to conform. They find themselves drawn into illegal or unethical behavior, which they expose when they fear legal liability.

Reluctant collaborators become deeply involved in acts they privately condemn. They seek public remedy and personal expiation only when they leave the organization.

Once an employee has blown the whistle, the responses of his or her superiors can take two broad forms. There are "degradation ceremonies" to punish and alienate resisters and protesters; and "ceremonies of status elevation," which reinforce the whistleblower's feeling that what he or she is doing is right. Whether and when someone will blow the whistle will depend on the peculiar mixture of sustenance and punishment, as well as the person's courage and the circumstances of his or her life. My observations also reveal that the whistleblower's fate need not be grim.

BLOWING THE WHISTLE

Like Serpico, Bob Leuci, the protagonist of *The Prince of the City*, was also caught in a net of conflicting loyalties. He has aptly described to me the "erosion process" by which young police officers became "bent":

I remember the first time I was in a situation that scared me. We were in a police car and there was a fight in the street. I was working with this big, strong guy. I was nervous when I got out of the car and approached the fight. "Am I good enough to handle this kind of thing?" Two guys were going at each other with knives. I backed off a bit, but one guy came at me. My partner pushed me aside. "You move toward my partner again, and I'll kill you." And all of a sudden I got this feeling. He didn't say "You move toward me," but he said, "You move toward my partner." Whether he would have killed this guy or not, had the guy come at him, I don't know. But he would have killed him if the guy came at me. When hearing that, in that sort of context, you have this feeling of something very, very special about working with someone when your life may be in danger. So I was with a guy who was fifteen years my senior and a wonderful policeman. The first time he went in to get dinner, and came out with a sandwich I asked, "Did you pay for it?" He answered, "No, it's okay." It was in fact okay coming from him. It *was* okay. This man would not do anything wrong; he would not do anything criminal certainly, and what was so terrible about this? But what happens is that emotionally things are going on that you don't realize. There is an erosion process that is taking place, and it is changing you. That is something that I certainly didn't notice for many years. But it was happening to me—happening to a lot of people around me.[3]

Serpico felt similar pulls of loyalty born of comparable experiences. Yet he began to drift from the others on the force as he tired of the endless shoptalk. In a search for outside interests he took courses for a degree in sociology and moved to Greenwich Village where he spent time with aspiring women artists and dancers. Serpico's disenchantment peaked when, as a plainclothes officer, he accidentally received a $300 payoff, which he immediately took to one of the top men in the New York City Department of Investigation. The captain told Serpico that he could go before the grand jury, but that word would get out that he had been the chief witness and he might end "face down in the East River." Or, the captain continued, Serpico could forget the whole thing.

This is a crucial decision for the whistleblower. The organization counts on the threat of punishment to exercise control. But this can often backfire. Serpico's alienation toward the police force intensified. He felt powerless to require others to live up to their responsibilities. Doubting his own belief in the honesty of his comrades and leaders and knowing that serious rule-breaking was endemic at all levels of the department, he felt increasingly isolated from those whose trust was essential for his survival. He refused, however, to complete the cycle of self-alienation by turning his back on his own beliefs of proper police conduct. Serpico resisted the temptation to go along with the group, even though the pressure increased markedly when he transferred to the South Bronx with assurances by high-level police officials that it was free of corruption.

The combination of blatant police wrongdoing and the extreme poverty of the neighborhood aggravated his dilemma. In desperation, he bluffed to a superior that he had gone to "outside sources" about police payoffs. This threat generated an investigation and eight of his peers were eventually tried. But no higher-ups were indicted, despite promises from the district attorney. Ostracized by most police after testifying and feeling increasingly vulnerable, Serpico convinced his immediate superior to accompany him to *The New York Times*. This led to a series of front-page articles on police corruption and ultimately to the establishment of the Knapp Commission. Its lengthy, independent investigation verified all of Serpico's charges and led to important changes in the New York City Police Department. Serpico would leave his mark.[4]

Several months later, Serpico was shot and seriously wounded during a drug raid. Had he been set up by his comrades? He retired, received a pension, and left the country for a time. Serpico still maintains that a principled officer must resist. Serpico reappeared in 1981 and reported on a television news program that he was writing a book. Since Serpico's experiences, another police officer, detective Robert Ellis, has assisted investigators in the apprehension of corrupt fellow police. He reports the difficulty of his activities and the subsequent threats made upon his wife and daughter. "I don't want my friends in other commands to think that for eight years they were dealing with a spy," he said. "I want it simply to be said that I am an honest cop" (*The New York Times*, July 3, 1977; p. 1).

The experience of other unbending resisters shows similar links between initial protest, retaliation against the whistleblower from one's superiors, and a continuing search for affirmation of professional ideals. In 1973 Joseph Rose, an experienced lawyer, joined the Associated Milk Producers Incorporated (AMPI) as an in-house attorney. Rose quickly became aware of illegal political payments to the Nixon reelection campaign, which were part of the Watergate investigation. In a phone interview in 1982, he told me:

> My assignment in the corporation included fiduciary responsibilities. When I found out that so much money had gone under the table, I might have been able to take a moral posture of "All right—that's a past offense that I can indeed defend." But the criminal conspiracy was ongoing, and the law concerning criminal conspirators states that you don't have to participate in the original crime to be indicted as a coconspirator later. All you need is to know about it and take steps to cover it up or otherwise further the conspiracy. Second, money was misused. The Watergate televised proceedings had started. An airline retrieved money that it had paid for similar purposes. When that broke, I went to the law books and became convinced of the duty to recover these assets. A whole chain of events led me more and more to believe that the current executives were in very deep themselves. I talked to a lawyer and former judge here in San Antonio named Joe Frazier Brown. He urged me to start keeping notes on everything I did. He also urged me to gather all of the documents that supported my position, to bypass the general manager, and to take the evidence to the board of directors. I was never allowed to do that. My attempt [to talk to the board] happened on a weekend during their convention in Minneapolis. Labor Day followed, and then Tuesday I went into work. I found a guard posted at my door; locks had been changed. The general manager demanded to see me. My services had become very, very unsatisfactory. When I was fired, I felt virtually a sense of relief. I was glad to be out of it, and I planned to keep my mouth shut. Then I had a call from one of the lawyers involved in an antitrust case against AMPI. He said, "They are really slandering you—making some very vicious attacks on you." I had indicated to AMPI executives that if the board would not listen to me, I would go right to the dairy farmers and they obviously felt my career and credibility had to be completely destroyed to protect

their own tails. After I was terminated, I had a call both from the Watergate Special Prosecutor's office and from the Congressional Committee's Subcommittee, wanting to know if they could fly down and talk to me. My answer was absolutely, unequivocally not. They both said they had subpoena power, and I said, "You have it. I suggest you use it if you want to talk to me." Of course, I was subpoenaed, first to Congress and then to Mr. Cox's grand jury.

Unlike Serpico who came forth on his own, Joseph Rose correctly feared he would be charged with breaking attorney–client privilege if he testified voluntarily. For Rose the path to public disclosure had been triggered by a series of events—his refusal to engage in illegal and unethical actions, corporate retaliation, and the government requirement that he testify against his former associates. Afterwards Rose was forced to confront the shame of being disreputable in the eyes of others, for as a result of his testimony he remained underemployed for eight years. Potential employers, who accepted AMPI's explanation that Rose had been disloyal, were unwilling to hire him. His father died believing that his son had irrevocably lost his ability to earn a living. A once-successful attorney and his family were forced to live on food stamps.

Rose's career opportunities began to improve appreciably only after *The Wall Street Journal* publicized his case. In the meantime, the AMPI was found guilty and heavily fined, and two of its officers were convicted and sentenced to prison terms. Its finance officers sought and received immunity from prosecution to testify against others.

Rose now looks at American society with cold cynicism.

> ...I believe I can make a contribution to the young people in this country by continuing to respond with a strong warning that all of the public utterances of corporations and indeed our own government concerning "courage, integrity, loyalty, honesty, and duty" are nothing but the sheerest hogwash that disappear very rapidly when it comes to the practical application of these concepts by strict definition. The reason that there are very few Serpicos or Roses is that the message is too clearly out in this society that white-collar crime, or nonviolent crime, should

be tolerated by the public at large, so long as the conduct brings a profit or a profitable result to the institution committing it....

Public disclosure can also come about in an effort to clear one's personal reputation and establish the legitimacy of professionals to resist what they see as their superiors' unethical directives. Dr. Grace Pierce joined the Ortho Pharmaceutical Corporation, a division of Johnson & Johnson, in 1971 after eleven years in private medical practice, service in the Food and Drug Administration, and experience with another drug firm. In 1975 she was assigned to direct a research team attempting to develop Loperamide, a drug for the relief of acute and chronic diarrhea. The liquid Loperamide formulation originated with Janssen, a Johnson & Johnson company in Belgium, and had a very high saccharin content to hide the bitter taste. Dr. Pierce and all the Ortho team members agreed that there was a need to reformulate the drug to diminish the saccharin concentration, particularly with the ongoing controversy over its carcinogenic potential. While her colleagues ultimately acceded to management pressures to accept the high saccharin formulation, Dr. Pierce refused. As the only medical person on the team, she would not agree to begin clinical trials with what she considered a questionable formulation.

After her refusal, Dr. Pierce charged that her immediate superior questioned her judgment, loyalty, and competence. Later, he accused her of misusing company funds on a research trip and of taking an unauthorized vacation. Although she rejected and refuted the accusations, the critique was a clear signal of her diminished prospects.

> When the situation came up and I couldn't get the other people to go along with me, I asked my superior whether we could get three objective consultants outside the company. If they say its okay, I'll do it. Or if you'll permit me to go to the FDA and put the situation to them openly and they say okay, I'll do it. I think I offered alternatives for a reasonable compromise. He refused. Use of saccharin remains a question yet. Nobody knows where this problem of carcinogens is heading. It probably won't be resolved soon, if ever. I was on the spot. I had to get with it or get out. I hated that. I

was cornered. There was no compromise. Nobody from higher up came and said, "Why don't we do that or do this." They were just riding roughshod all over me. I always like to feel I'm a person, not a cog in a machine.... One of my colleagues said, "Grace, you're nuts. Why not write a lengthy memo for the files, make sure you're on record. They're responsible." If I do the research, I'm responsible. I feel responsibility as a physician first. My responsibility to the corporation is second. I think my colleagues' attitude is commonplace. People salve their conscience. They keep the benefits of the job. This memo gives them an escape hatch.

Pierce resigned. Unlike Joseph Rose, she was quickly approached by a colleague to affiliate in a group medical practice, which she joined on a part-time basis. Later the vice president of Personal Products, another subsidiary of Johnson & Johnson, invited her to join his research staff although she alerted him that she might sue Ortho. Within six months she had become director of research. While Dr. Pierce felt vindicated of charges against her integrity and competence, her work situation changed dramatically when she actually filed her suit for "damage to her professional reputation, dissipation of her career, loss of salary, as well as seniority and retirement benefits...."[5]

Despite their excellent relationship, the vice president's attitude cooled. Not unexpectedly, he summoned her at the end of one work day.

> I was fired. He said it was unconscionable that any one working for Personal Products would sue a sister company. I said I didn't think so. He had been aware of the legal thing with Ortho. He was dejected and hurt by the whole thing. The next morning he seemed very sad about seeing me go... I haven't seen him since.

Dr. Pierce carried her suit to the New Jersey Supreme Court, which broke constitutional ground by affirming a professional's right to challenge superiors where professional ethics are at stake. In Grace Pierce's case, however, five of the six judges for the New Jersey Supreme Court ruled that her judgment and Ortho's were simply at variance. Professional ethics were not the issue, according to the court, which sustained Ortho's actions.

POSTPONING THE WHISTLE

Some professionals delay taking a path of direct confrontation and, as a result, they become involved in unethical or illegal behavior. Implicated protesters include those who have spoken up within their organizations, have capitulated and gone along with the policies of their superiors, and have subsequently publicized inappropriate actions when they have become fearful of the consequences of their own involvement.

In the late 1960s, Kermit Vandivier, a technician, assisted in the production of an airplane brake whose faulty design could have endangered Air Force test pilots. He asserted that, despite his repeated pleas and those of several engineers including his supervisor, other engineers and managers in the Goodrich Corporation pushed a false report. When Air Force pilots tested the brakes with near fatal results, Vandivier approached a lawyer who advised him to go to the FBI.

Though Vandivier's account has been reprinted many times in the last decade,[6] he recently provided additional insight. Note how—as a relatively uneducated technician—he felt alienated and powerless. Note also his sense of anomie as people he trusted simply backed off, and his anxiety over his isolation.

At the time of the Goodrich fiasco I had six children of school age at home. My salary, if I remember correctly, was around $125-$135 per week. My only outside source of income was the pay I received from the *Troy Daily News* [TDN]—$15 for the three columns per week I wrote. High principles notwithstanding, I couldn't—at that time—subject myself and my family to "retaliation." Please note I said "at that time," because I think there is one factor which I perhaps have not made entirely clear in the Goodrich story. I don't think anyone within the Goodrich organization really believed—until the moment it actually happened—that the report was going to be issued to the Air Force. Until such time as it was published and delivered to the Air Force, none of us who actually had a part in preparing the phony report was guilty of any criminal act. True, my attorney offered his opinion that we might be guilty of conspiracy to defraud, but qualified that opinion by adding there would have to

be proof we knew at the outset a fraud would ultimately be committed. I can't describe the sense of incredulity I (and I'm sure others) experienced when I learned the report had really been issued, that Goodrich was actually going to try and pull this thing off.... Naturally, my editors at TDN knew what was going on right from the start. When the situation had developed sufficiently we considered whistleblowing in the TDN, but TDN attorneys were concerned that there was simply not enough proof of any wrongdoing at that time and felt that a libel suit could be certain. Meanwhile, I was gathering incriminating data, photographs, charts, movie film, notes of meetings and telephone conversations. I smuggled them out of the plant each day, copied them at night, and returned the originals the following day. Altogether, I amassed more than 1,000 documents and other items (I still have them), which were invaluable evidence at the Senate hearing. When I finally was ready to blow the whistle I had all the evidence necessary to make a strong case. No one was indicted or charged in connection with the hearing, but the day following the hearing the Department of Defense quietly initiated sweeping changes in its inspection and procurement procedures. A DOD official later confirmed the changes were made as a direct result of the hearing....

Vandivier's testimony underscores that the ties of loyalty can be broken and public criticism undertaken when the dangers of continued inaction appear more serious than the fears of retaliation. Under such circumstances, those who contemplate blowing the whistle have a potentially powerful and omnipresent ally in the weight of the law, which holds companies and individuals responsible for the production of faulty products.[7] Many implicated protesters might resist the orders of their superiors were there greater likelihood of apprehension, conviction, and severe punishment for white-collar crimes.[8]

In the early 1970s another serious breach of professional and managerial ethics unfolded. Frank Camps, a senior principal design engineer, was directly involved in the development of the Ford Pinto, which proved to have an unsafe windshield and a gas tank that might explode on impact. He questioned the design and testing procedure and later charged publicly that his superiors who knew of this danger were so anxious to produce a lightweight and cheap car to compete with the imports that they were determined to overlook serious design problems. Camps's level of anxiety grew as he contemplated the consequences of his own involvement.

> We were still in the development stage. I had a certain degree of resentment; these people were not listening although we were having problems with the car. I can remember I went into my manager's office. He said, "Look, we're in the business of selling cars and every time we barrier crash a car and it causes problems, then we have one failure. If we get another car to crash, to see how the first failure happened, we may have two failures. This could compound itself until my bonus would be reduced." Now this was the kind of thinking— the corporate attitude—that my immediate superior had. He didn't say anything about crashing for occupant safety. He just didn't want his bonus to be cut down. I said to my wife, "This guy is a bad actor. This guy is going to get me in trouble if I don't start documenting and protecting myself." This was colossal arrogance, callous indifference toward the safety of people. It bothered me even if only one person should die or be disfigured because of something that I was responsible for.

Camps was a respected and longtime member of Ford's engineering staff and thus not totally without influence. Yet he felt powerless to affect company policy. To avoid complete absorption into a system of relationships and definitions that calibrated human life on a scale of company costs and to protect himself against legal liability, he sued the company.

Camps described the response of fellow engineers, a response that mitigated his sense of isolation.

> Most of the working engineers were very supportive of me at that time. They are still supportive of me. I can recall, right after I filed the suit, other engineers said—"Go get 'em, we wish we could do it, there goes a man with brass balls." While I had tacit support, I was looking for an honest man to stand with me. I found that these guys were suddenly given promotions, nice increases in salary. Next thing I knew, I did not have the support any more.

Camps wasn't alone in his agony over the Pinto. From 1971 to 1978 fifty lawsuits were filed against Ford because of gas-tank explosions in rear-end accidents. In 1980 Ford was brought to trial on a criminal charge in the death of three Indiana girls. The case created national headlines and featured the testimony of a former high-ranking Ford engineer whose statements were similar to those made by Frank Camps within the company.[9] While Ford was found innocent in this trial, the Pinto has come to symbolize management's drive for profits over customer safety. Had Camps been treated as a voice to be heeded rather than a protester to be ignored and punished, Ford might have avoided fatalities and serious injuries, years of litigation, and the stigma of corporate irresponsibility.

WHISTLING LATE IN THE GAME

Many professionals who participate in illegal or unethical acts only blow the whistle once they have left the organization and have reestablished their careers in other companies or fields of work. They seek to make up for their past timidity and to ease their consciences.

The late Arthur Dale Console studied at Cornell Medical College and later practiced neurosurgery. In search of less strenuous work after a serious illness, he joined the E.R. Squibb and Sons pharmaceutical company in 1949 as associate director of research. He found Squibb an ethical company, still run by its founder and maintaining an orientation in which the physician in charge of research was defined as a "physician's physician." During the ensuing years, according to Dr. Console, much changed in the pharmaceutical industry. Larger companies bought out the smaller ones and the search for profit became more intense. The transformation affected all members of the company staff including the director of research, a position that Dr. Console had by then assumed. As he worked, he experienced an increasing tension between his sense of what was appropriate medical decision making and what was required by his more business-oriented superiors. He was particularly disturbed by those instances in which he had pressured physicians to certify drugs that they had not sufficiently tested. He resigned from his position in 1956 after six and a half years in the drug industry, and soon after began to train for a new career as a psychiatrist.

During the 1960s, Console's continuing sense of self-estrangement led him to take the initiative and testify several times before congressional committees. At one hearing he was asked why he had left Squibb. His answer captures the process of capitulating to the pressures of multi-national corporations and the disillusionment that follows.

> I believe that the best answer can be found in my unfinished essay of *The Good Life of A Drug Company Doctor*. Toward the end I said: "These are only some of the things a drug company doctor must learn if he is to be happy in the industry. After all, *it is a business*, and there are many more things he must learn to rationalize. He must learn the many ways to deceive the FDA and, failing in this, how to seduce, manipulate or threaten the physician assigned to the New Drug Application into approving it even if it is incomplete. He must learn that anything that helps to sell a drug is valid even if it is supported by the crudest testimonial, while anything that decreases sales must be suppressed, distorted and rejected because it is not absolutely conclusive proof. He will find himself squeezed between businessmen who will sell anything and justify it on the basis that doctors ask for it and doctors who demand products they have been taught to want through the advertising and promotion schemes contrived by businessmen. If he can absorb all this, and more, and still maintain any sensibilities he will learn the true meaning of loneliness and alienation." During my tenure as medical director I learned the meaning of loneliness and alienation. I reached a point where I could no longer live with myself. I had compromised to the point where my back was against a wall and I had to choose between resigning myself to total capitulation, or resigning as medical director. I chose the latter course.[10]

After he left the pharmaceutical industry, Dr. Console received a grant from Squibb to train for a career in psychiatry, which placed him outside the authority of all corporate structures. Console's widow, a respected psychiatrist in her own right, has provided additional insight into Dr. Console's background, his commitment to Squibb, and his ultimate decision to blow the whistle several years after entering private practice.

> He was one of two surviving brothers who both carried out their father's ambitions to complete medical school. Arthur did so with great distinction.... In spite of two bouts of tuberculosis during this period he went on and completed a neurosurgical residency—the first resident chosen in this separate specialty considered the most prestigious in surgery. Trouble really began when, in attempting to establish a practice, he fell ill a third time, necessitating complete bed rest at home. We had an infant son with club feet requiring frequent surgical intervention and casts, absolutely no income except mine from an also newly established practice and the resulting pressure on me from multiple conflicting responsibilities was overwhelming. It was apparent that he had to find a less physically demanding and an economically sound alternative. It was at this time he accepted the offer to join Squibb as an associate medical director. The decision to give up neurosurgery as a career was a bitter and lasting defeat. The coincidence of Dr. Console's tenure as medical director of Squibb with its changeover from an ethical drug house to a competitive business-oriented company could not have been foreseen, but his sense of having been condemned to second-class medicine then became more and more intolerable. Because of Dr. Console's increasing and outspoken alienation from the drug industry it was clear that an open break was pending. It was imperative for him to look elsewhere for the future. The choice of psychiatry was made after considerable discussion together.... When the opportunity arose to testify in the Kefauver hearings, Dr. Console had already distanced himself from almost all his former colleagues;... The real problem was one of conflict from some sense of loyalty to Squibb, which had been very generous to him, and the pressure of his need to speak out. I did not share this intensity and had some misgivings but felt that he had to follow his own conviction. His moments of "speaking out" appeared then to be an opportunity to vindicate himself in his own eyes before the world.

Dr. Console *chose* to reveal his own complicity in a large-scale effort to profit from unethical marketing procedures. Whistleblowing of this kind can result when people believe deeply that they should have acted earlier to resist illegitimate authority.[11] Although Dr. Console testified over a decade ago, recent scholarship reveals that many of the problems be highlighted continue to characterize the drug industry, particularly in its relationship with Third World countries.[12]

TABOOS AND DEGRADATION CEREMONIES

Those willing to breach the taboo against informing face potent challenges.[13] Their superiors have the power to harass them by questioning their competence and judgment, to terminate their employment, and to blacklist them from other positions. Attorney Joseph Rose learned that the extensive influence of the Associated Milk Producers could bring his career to a standstill.

After I left AMPI, they weren't content with the firing, they wanted to call my ex-employers and completely ruin me. There was an attorney up in New York and I answered one of his ads. It turned out that he was a friend of an executive of AMPI, and indeed his secretary was one of the executive's nieces. I accepted the job and he and I went out on one case. He said right in front of a client. "He doesn't know it yet, but at Christmas time, I am going to fire him." I thought he was kidding, and I didn't pay any attention to it, and then lo and behold, right at Christmas time, right on target before Christmas, he fired me. After he dismissed me, I had been under fire so long that I was about to have a damned nervous breakdown. I did a very peculiar thing. President Ford was in office, and I wrote Ford and said, "This is happening to me, because I wouldn't be a crook." The next thing I knew, John Sales of the Watergate prosecutor's office called me and he said, "How are you?" and the clear implication was "Are you keeping your sanity?" And I said, "John, I'm holding on, but it sure as hell isn't easy." And he said, "Well, we've got an interview for you with the Department of Labor in Dallas." I thought, all of a sudden, there is justice in the world, maybe somebody does care.

So I drove to Dallas, and I interviewed with the guy who was the head of the Department of Labor there, and I'll be damned if he didn't know some of the AMPI people. He made the comment, "I didn't request to interview you, as far as I am concerned, I can throw your resume up to the ceiling and hope it sticks there."

AMPI's influence seemed also to extend into religious organizations. Rose, a devout man, was particularly hurt by this.

My wife and I were attending Castle Hills First Baptist Church in town. I was in very bad emotional shape. I mean *very* bad and one of the high guys at AMPI attended the same church. I went to talk to the leader of the church. I guess I just wanted somebody to talk to, to get this thing out of my system. The man literally turned his back on me and started talking to other people. I felt that I certainly was not abandoning Jesus Christ by abandoning the specific church building.

As Joseph Rose learned through bitter experience, those who break the taboo will experience degradation, which recasts the social identity of whistleblowers, labeling them as unreliable, of poor judgment, and of dangerous character.

Joseph Rose worked in private industry. What of the government employees? A prime example is Ernest A. Fitzgerald, a staff analyst in the Pentagon. In 1969, he appeared before Proxmire's Senate subcommittee investigating the production of the C5A air transport. Fitzgerald "committed truth" by answering affirmatively that there had been a two-billion-dollar overrun in the plane's development.[14] He could have sidestepped the question or lied to the Senator. Had he done so, Fitzgerald would have avoided being labeled as someone who no longer had a future at the Pentagon. Such a designation came from the highest levels of government, including the Secretary of the Air Force and the President of the United States, Richard M. Nixon.

A statement by Alexander Butterfield, White House aide (and the man who later revealed the existence of the secret Nixon tapes) best summed up the official view toward Fitzgerald.

Fitzgerald is no doubt a top-notch cost expert, but he must be given very low marks in loyalty, and after all loyalty is the name of the game. Only a basic "nogoodnik" would take his official grievances so far from normal channels. We should let him bleed for a while at least.[15]

While such retaliation did not break Fitzgerald, it extracted a heavy price from him and his family. In a recent conversation he has spoken of the impact on his children as comparable to radiation—difficult to measure but potentially very damaging.

Butterfield's statement implicitly highlights some of the central characteristics of "successful degradation ceremonies" that Harold Garfinkel has identified: the whistleblower's actions are "out of the ordinary" and in contrast to those of a loyal employee or peer, the actions are not accidental and reflect on the entire person of the whistleblower; the denunciation reinforces the values of the group, which stress silence and loyalty.[16] The message is clear. Whether in industry or government or academia, the whistleblower who is determined to reject self-estrangement despite the attacks of superiors must be able to withstand the charge of being labeled incompetent and disloyal.

CEREMONIES OF STATUS ELEVATION

New York City detective Bob Leuci received crucial encouragement from government prosecutors Scoppetta and Shaw in his decision to do undercover work against racketeers and corrupt police. Note how Leuci's sense of self is directly tied to his identification with these two men.

I undertook this investigation because of the support that I received from Scoppetta and Shaw, incredible support. It was the same kind of support that I received from my partners when I was working out on the street. You have a sense that there is somebody who truly cares about you.

The experiences of James Boyd and Marjorie Carpenter offer a sharp example of the way in which efforts toward status elevation can alleviate the pressures toward self-estrangement. Boyd and Carpenter are credited with exposing and bringing down the powerful Senator Thomas Dodd of Connecticut in the late 1960s. Boyd, Dodd's assistant for twelve years, and Carpenter, Dodd's secretary, suspected that the Senator was pocketing large amounts of campaign funds.[17] According to Boyd, Dodd sensed their suspicions, fired them both, and spread the word that they were disreputable employees who were dismissed when he discovered that they were engaged in a sordid love affair. Boyd suspected that the Senator also intended to blacklist him from employment in Washington.

I didn't come to the decision to really go at it, tooth and nail, until I saw him trying to keep me from getting a job. I didn't want to go back with him. I was trying to get away from him for some time, but he tried to use the power to keep me from getting a job, and then, in a roundabout way, boasting to me what he was doing, toying with me as if I were some kind of a creature, instead of a partner as we had started out.

Boyd had decided to expose Senator Dodd but could not act until he was approached by Drew Pearson and Jack Anderson.[18] The two journalists assessed his suspicion, and encouraged him to act against Dodd with their explicit promise that they would define the case as their highest priority, would never back off no matter how great the heat, and would continue to demand an investigation by the Senate and other legal authorities.

After this careful agreement, Boyd and Carpenter obtained keys to Dodd's office, and removed and copied thousands of documents that contained evidence of Dodd's financial dealings with major corporations and others who sought his intervention on their behalf. Boyd and Carpenter had taken bold and controversial action, which resulted in Dodd's eventual censure by the Senate.

HEALING THE WOUNDS

The available literature on whistleblowers often emphasizes the dead end that awaits those who break with peers and superiors. My evidence provides a more intricate mosaic. Virtually all the individuals discussed here have been able to rebuild their careers and belief in their competence and integrity. They found an escape hatch in private practice, consulting, and the media. Ironically perhaps the diversity of American economic and social institutions provides opportunities to those who have dared defy the authority of the established ones.

Although Frank Serpico never sought to develop a new career, he is a national figure who continues to be respected for his courageous stand. His name is synonymous with police integrity. Bob Leuci completed his twenty years in the New York City Police Department, is a popular speaker on college campuses, and is currently writing a novel about police work.

Joseph Rose is a successful attorney in San Antonio. Former colleagues who avoided him and believed the accusation that he had betrayed AMPI now treat him with respect. Some clients seek him out expressly because they know of his past difficulties and admire his toughness. When we spoke in the winter of 1983 his practice was flourishing.

Grace Pierce works exclusively in clinical medicine. She has expanded her work in the group clinic by opening an office in her home, believes she provides an important service to local patients, and has time to enjoy her garden.

"I really lucked out," she says. Her skills, the support of the medical community, and the receptiveness of her patients have provided an up-beat continuity to her work and personal life. She does, however, harbor many troubling questions about whistleblowing and its effectiveness in changing organizational policies. A few months ago she wrote:

And now that the "whistleblowers" have been re-established or re-settled into other pursuits of living what has happened to the persons, institutions or corporations that created these dilemmas? Have there been corrective steps taken to avoid similar episodes of employee disenchantment? Have those offenders to the whistleblowers changed in any way—have there been any recriminations? Is there less deception or corruption or is it better concealed? Have the pathways of whistleblowers been kept open, or even broadened for other employees who may be confronted with similar ethical issues? Are the courts any more or less supportive? Were these struggles really worth it? Have our little pieces of this world actually improved because of these actions? Are there other ways and means available to resolve the whistleblower's conflicts—perhaps more effectively and perhaps less painfully with less personal sacrifice? Is there still a place for "idealists" in a world quite full of "realists"?

Unique opportunities arose for both Kermit Vandivier and Frank Camps after their break with former superiors. Vandivier has built a new career at the *Troy Daily News*:

Looking back, I would say probably the best thing that ever happened to me was the Goodrich thing. That gave me the push I probably wouldn't have had otherwise. When you have six kids and you've got a job that looks fairly secure, and you like it—which I did—I liked the Goodrich job—and you feel like you're accomplishing something—you don't feel like quitting or starting a new career. I went into a different field. I would never have gotten a job at Goodyear or Bendix, the other two brake manufacturers. I don't think anyone in private industry would touch me. I am a troublemaker, you know. I went to work for the *Troy Daily News* the day following my abrupt departure from BFG. I have served as a general assignment reporter and have covered a variety of beats, including the police, city hall and political beats.... Two years ago the TDN became involved in cable television. I was named cable news director and given the responsibility of organizing and implementing the project.

Like Vandivier, Frank Camps found that others were interested in his skills and eager to hire him. Camps now serves as a consultant to attorneys involved in product liability litigations. He underscores how important those relationships have become in recreating his career and his sense of himself.

When I filed my suit, six months before I left Ford, it gained wide publicity, not only in the Detroit papers but in many papers and in many television outlets in the cities where the Ford plants were located. It also got into *The Wall Street Journal*. I began getting calls from attorneys all over the country, and I couldn't quite comprehend what they were driving at until one of the attorneys said he would like me to help him on a case. He came up with an hourly figure and a retainer that was absolutely staggering, based on what I was making at Ford. He became my mentor.... All of those feelings I had—the anxiety, resentment, anger, helplessness, that's all gone, because of what I now accomplish. I am doing what I want to do, when I want to do it. I can speak my mind truthfully and openly in a court of law. There is nothing more gratifying than to know that you are now involved in due process. Incidentally, in all of the cases I have been involved in, I have not been on the losing side even one time.

Ernest Fitzgerald has spent more than a decade in litigation to secure his former position. He has defeated a bureaucracy committed to his expulsion and banishment. An out-of-court settlement with former President Richard Nixon, the return to previous duties, and the court-directed government payment of his legal fees have all provided clear evidence for his complete and public vindication. Fitzgerald has survived as the nation's best-known whistleblower.

Finally, James Boyd has taken a more circuitous route. He has published a book about his experiences in the Dodd case, has directed the Fund for Investigation Journalism, has written for *The New York Times Magazine*, and has completed several projects with Jack Anderson. He and Marjorie Carpenter Boyd live with their two children in a rural area far from Washington. She continues to believe that they acted appropriately and were guided by their need for a sense of inner satisfaction, which she finds characteristic of many whistleblowers. As Boyd reflects on the last fifteen years, he can count some of the costs and gains of his decision to take on a United States Senator.

I have friends from that period of my life who are now retired. If I had done that, I would have been retired now for three years, and I would have been getting $35,000 a year. I realize that there is a tremendous material loss involved. Also you lose something—there's something in an institution, various supports—professional, friendship, life-support type things—that you lose when you are separated from that institution. What I have gained is a whole new outlook on life—a feeling of

independence—of "being my own man"—working at my own hours—and all that sort of thing, which I find enormously attractive....

In a recent note Rose aptly summarized his views.

Gandhi said that noncooperation with evil is as much a duty as cooperation with good; Burke said the only thing necessary for the triumph of evil is for good men to do nothing. Both concepts are still viable ... although expensive.

For each of these whistleblowers there was no going back. Yet there was a future.[19] That message is as vital as the severe price they paid.

NOTES

An early version of this paper was presented as the keynote address at Speaker's Day ceremonies, Western New England College, April 1, 1981. It is part of a larger work in progress.

1. Peter Maas, *Serpico* (New York: The Viking Press, 1973). For a participant observation account of police training see Richard Harris, *The Police Academy: An Inside View* (New York: John Wiley, 1973). Other studies of the police support Serpico's experiences and observations. See Lawrence W. Sherman, *Police Corruption* (New York: Anchor, 1974).

2. In those instances where the whistleblowers lived beyond driving distance, I exchanged letters with them and did a lengthy, taped, telephone interview during the summer of 1982. Unless otherwise noted all quoted material is from the interviews or letters. Since I was interested in the whistleblowers' perceptions of their experience, I did not interview other people involved in the cases. The material on Frank Serpico derives from published sources.

Three of the whistleblowers discussed in this article—Joseph Rose, Grace Pierce, and Frank Camps—also described their experiences in Alan Westin, ed. *Whistle Blowing? Loyalty and Dissent in the Corporation* (New York: McGraw-Hill, 1981).

For a study that reports on 51 cases of whistleblowers, see Lea P. Stuart, "'Whistle Blowing' Implications for Organizational Communication," *Journal of Communication* 30:4 (Autumn 1980), 90–101. For an intensive case study read Robert M. Anderson, Robert Perrucci, Dan D. Schendel, and Leon E. Tractman, *Divided Loyalties: Whistle-Blowing at BART* (West Lafayette, IN: Purdue University, 1980).

3. Bob Leuci's experiences are recounted by Robert Daly, *Prince of the City* (Boston: Houghton Mifflin, 1978). This statement is taken from a class visit to Smith College, March 12, 1981. Since then, I have had numerous other discussions with Leuci.

4. David Burnham, "Graft Paid to Police Said to Run into Millions," *The New York Times*, April 25, 1970. New York City, *The Knapp Commission Report on Police Corruption* (New York: George Braziller, 1973).

5. Alfred G. Feliu, "Discharge of Professional Employees: Protecting Against Dismissal for Acts Within a Professional Code of Ethics," *Columbia Human Rights Law Review*, 11 (1979–1980). See especially pp. 186–87.

6. Kermit Vandivier, "The Aircraft Brake Scandal," *Harper's*, April 1972, pp. 45–52.

7. For a discussion of the recent legislation to protect and encourage whistleblowing see Westin, *Whistle Blowing?*, pp. 131–167.

8. For a pertinent instance, see Eberhard Faber, "How I Lost our Great Debate about Corporate Ethics," *Fortune*, November 1976, pp. 180–88.

9. Richard T. DeGeorge, "Ethical Responsibilities of Engineers in Large Organizations: The Pinto Case," *Business Professional Ethics Journal* I (Fall 1981), 1–17.

10. "A. Dale Console" in Ralph Nader, Peter J. Petkas, and Kate Blackwell, eds. *Whistle Blowing* (New York: Bantam, 1972), pp. 122–23. Also see, Hearings before the Subcommittee on Monopoly of the Select Committee on Small Business. United States Senate, Ninety-first Congress, First Session on Present Status of Competition in the Pharmaceutical Industry, Part II, March 13, 1959, pp. 4484.

11. Other reluctant collaborators now have become international figures. See Philip Agee, *Inside the Company* (New York: Bantam Books, 1976). His decision to identify publicly CIA agents makes him the country's most controversial whistleblower. For a debate on his actions, see "On Naming C.I.A. Agents," *The Nation* (March 14, 1981), pp. 295–301.

12. See Ray H., Elling, "The Political Economy of International Health With a Focus on the Capitalist World-System," in Michael Lewis, ed. *Social Problems and Public Policy, Vol. II* (Stanford, CT: Jai Press, 1982).

13. For a recent and illuminating study of the role of the informer, see Victor Navasky, *Naming Names* (New York: Viking, 1980).

14. A. Ernest Fitzgerald, *The High Priests of Waste* (New York: W.W. Norton, 1972). For a pertinent study, see Mark Ryter, *A Whistle-blower's Guide to the Federal Bureaucracy* (Washington: Institute for Policy Studies, 1977).

15. Media Transcripts Incorporated Program 20/20. December 18, 1980, p. 14.

16. Harold Garfinkel, "Conditions of Successful Degradation Ceremonies," *The American Journal of Sociology* 61 (January 1956), 420–24; Victor W. Turner, *The Ritual Process* (Chicago: Aldine, 1969), pp. 168–203.

17. James Boyd, *Above the Law* (New York: New American Library, (1968).

18. Drew Pearson and Jack Anderson, *The Case Against Congress* (New York: Simon and Schuster, (1968). Part 1: Portraits of a Senator. The Dodd case was one among other factors leading to the Senate's ultimate reconsideration of its principles of behavior and the revision of its own code of ethics. See the special section entitled "Revising the U.S. Senate Code of Ethics," *Hastings Center Report* (February 1981), pp. 1–28.

19. These findings are confirmed by a recent government report. The U.S. Merit Systems Protection Board, *Whistle Blowing and the Federal Employee* (Washington, D.C.: U.S. Government Printing Office, October 1981), particularly p. 41.

Questions

1. How do, or should, workers handle the conflict between conformity and personal ethical duty?

2. Many times hindsight allows companies and the public to praise whistle-blowers, because of their personal ethical code, as in the case of Camps and the Ford Pinto. Should there be more allowances for whistle-blowers who suspect wrongdoing on the part of a company, in order to prevent the disastrous effects?

CASE 6.4
Winners and Losers
Mimi Swants and Sherron Watkins

Dear Mr. Lay,

Has Enron become a risky place to work? For those of us who didn't get rich over the last few years, can we afford to stay?

Skilling's abrupt departure will raise suspicions of accounting improprieties and valuation issues. Enron has been very aggressive in its accounting—most notably the Raptor transactions and the Condor vehicle. We do have valuation issues with our international assets and possibly some of our EES MTM positions.

The spotlight will be on us, the market just can't accept that Skilling is leaving his dream job. I think that the valuation issues can be fixed and reported with other goodwill write-downs to occur in 2002. How do we fix the Raptor and Condor deals? They unwind in 2002 and 2003, we will have to pony up Enron stock and that won't go unnoticed.

To the layman on the street, it will look like we recognized funds flow of $800 mm from merchant asset sales in 1999 by selling to a vehicle (Condor) that we capitalized with a promise of Enron stock in later years. Is that really funds flow or is it cash from equity issuance?

We have recognized over $550 million of fair value gains on stocks via our swaps with Raptor, much of that stock has declined significantly—Avici by 98%, from $178 mm to $5 mm, The New Power Co by 70%, from $20/share to $6/share. The value in the swaps won't be there for Raptor, so once again Enron will issue stock to offset these losses. Raptor is an LJM entity. It sure looks to the layman on the street that we are hiding losses in a related company and will compensate that company with Enron stock in the future.

I am incredibly nervous that we will implode in a wave of accounting scandals. My 8 years of Enron work history will be worth nothing on my resume, the business world will consider the past successes as nothing but an elaborate accounting hoax. Skilling is resigning now for "personal reasons" but I think he wasn't having fun, looked down the road and knew this stuff was unfixable and would rather abandon ship now than resign in shame in 2 years.

Is there a way our accounting gurus can unwind these deals now? I have thought and thought about how to do this, but I keep bumping into one big problem—we booked the Condor and Raptor deals in 1999 and 2000, we enjoyed a wonderfully high stock price, many executives sold stock, we then try and reverse or fix the deals in 2001 and it's a bit like robbing the bank in one year and trying to pay it back 2 years later. Nice try, but investors were hurt, they bought at $70 and $80/share looking for $120/share and now they're at $38 or worse. We are under too much scrutiny and there are probably one or two disgruntled "redeployed" employees who know enough about the "funny" accounting to get us in trouble.

What do we do? I know this question cannot be addressed in the all employee meeting, but can you give some assurances that you and Causey will sit down and take a good hard objective look at what is going to happen to Condor and Raptor in 2002 and 2003?

From *Power failure: The Inside story of the Collapse of Euron Broadway Business*, 2004.

Questions

1. What loyalty should a company have to its employees, especially when those employees are stockholders?
2. At what point do employees overthrow their loyalty to their place of work to blow the whistle?

CASE 6.5
Chatty Doctors
Megan Rickel

You are in your doctor's office for your yearly checkup. After the nurse comes in and records your vitals, there is a short wait until the doctor comes in to examine you.

DOCTOR: Hello, how are you doing today?

YOU: Great, I have really been eating better since last time and I've really . . .

DOCTOR: You know, my wife and I just went to this great place by the pier, Pont's, have you heard of it?

YOU: Well, no, but I've been exerc . . .

DOCTOR: It is fantastic, a bit on the pricey side, but it was our anniversary

YOU: Congratulations.

DOCTOR: Thanks (ruffles through your chart). I see nothing our of the ordinary here, see you next year!

With that, he closes the door behind him.

Later that evening, you meet with your book club, and after the meeting, you mention this experience to your friend who also has recently been to the doctor.

FRIEND: I would be thrilled if my doctor treated me like a human being, instead I feel like I'm nothing but a collection of symptoms and test results.

You think to yourself: I wish there was a happy medium.

Questions

1. As a patient, should one expect some personal discourse with one's doctor or only speak about relevant medical issues?
2. How can doctors self-regulate a potential desire to be "chatty"? What ethical issues should be at the forefront of this self-regulation?
3. Does the patient have an ethical duty to request a specific type of treatment?

7

Professionalism, Justice, and Social Welfare

Introduction

Questions of justice inevitably arise within professional practice. In some cases, we may consider justice in terms of how an individual is treated as a professional. Did you get the raise or promotion that you "deserved" because of your hard work and dedication to your employer? Is your workload comparable to others of similar rank and salary, or is it distributed unevenly? If so, is that unfair? Other considerations of justice go beyond the individual and concern the professional's obligations to society more generally. What, if any, obligations do professionals have to use their skills to ensure social justice more broadly construed? Do professionals, because of their special skills and training, have a greater responsibility to ensure social welfare than nonprofessionals?

The articles in this chapter explore the concept of justice and consider the obligations of professionals when confronting a wide range of societal inequities. The parable of the Sadhu, for example, raises the question of whether an individual has an obligation to care for other human beings, even when doing so may threaten one's ability to achieve personal goals and ambitions. Does a person have an obligation to care for dying parents, even when it may create economic hardships or cost you a long-sought-after professional advancement? How do you balance professional goals and social responsibilities?

What obligations do those of means have to contribute to correcting economic inequalities more generally? It is unfair that such a small percentage of the population possesses such a large portion of the overall wealth? Does justice demand the establishment of a structured system of redistribution of wealth so as to correct the gross, and growing, disparity between the income of the rich and that of the poor? Or, would such a structured system itself prove to be unjust to those who have worked hard to achieve their wealth? Do those of means, quite literally, *owe* nothing to those without?

Rawls considers some of the theoretical and conceptual issue related to questions of justice and disparities between the rich and the poor. He defines justice as involving the choices that would be made by intelligent hypothetical agents behind a veil of ignorance. As such, they know everything that an average person would know about how social circumstances affect the quality of life, but they do not know where they would fit in the social order. That is, they do not know if they will be healthy, wealthy, or wise. According to Rawls, such agents would choose two principles of justice: that each person would have an equal right to the most extensive basic liberty compatible with a similar liberty for others, and that social and economic inequalities are to be arranged so that they are both (a) reasonably expected to be to everyone's advantage and (b) attached to positions and offices open to all.

The other essays in the chapter consider practical applications of questions of justice in professional practice. What obligations do the rich have to assist the poor? What obligations to health professionals have to provide their services during times or war or to promote universal coverage in health care? While Singer claims that he, as a professor, would have a duty to pull a drowning child out of a pool of water on his way to class, do journalists have a duty to help those when reporting on a natural disaster, or should they simply report on the disaster and not intervene?

Do you feel that professionals have a special obligation to help combat social injustice?

Bowen H. McCoy

The Parable of the Sadhu

Bowen H. McCoy retired from Morgan Stanley in 1990 after 28 years of service. He is now a real estate and business counselor, a teacher, and a philanthropist.

Last year, as the first participant in the new six-month sabbatical program that Morgan Stanley has adopted, I enjoyed a rare opportunity to collect my thoughts as well as do some traveling. I spent the first three months in Nepal, walking 600 miles through 200 villages in the Himalayas and climbing some 120,000 vertical feet. My sole Western companion on the trip was an anthropologist who shed light on the cultural patterns of the villages that we passed through.

During the Nepal hike, something occurred that has had a powerful impact on my thinking about corporate ethics. Although some might argue that the experience has no relevance to business, it was a situation in which a basic ethical dilemma suddenly intruded into the lives of a group of individuals.

How the group responded holds a lesson for all organizations, no matter how defined.

THE SADHU

The Nepal experience was more rugged than I had anticipated. Most commercial treks last two or three weeks and cover a quarter of the distance we traveled.

My friend Stephen, the anthropologist, and I were halfway through the 60-day Himalayan part of the trip when we reached the high point, an 18,000-foot pass over a crest that we'd have to traverse to reach the village of Muklinath, an ancient holy place for pilgrims.

Six years earlier, I had suffered pulmonary edema, an acute form of altitude sickness, at 16,500 feet in the vicinity of Everest base camp—so we were understandably concerned about what would happen at 18,000 feet. Moreover, the Himalayas

This article was originally published in the September–October 1983 issue of HBR.

were having their wettest spring in 20 years; hip-deep powder and ice had already driven us off one ridge. If we failed to cross the pass, I feared that the last half of our once-in-a-lifetime trip would be ruined.

The night before we would try the pass, we camped in a hut at 14,500 feet. In the photos taken at that camp, my face appears wan. The last village we'd passed through was a sturdy two-day walk below us, and I was tired.

During the late afternoon, four backpackers from New Zealand joined us, and we spent most of the night awake, anticipating the climb. Below, we could see the fires of two other parties, which turned out to be two Swiss couples and a Japanese hiking club.

To get over the steep part of the climb before the sun melted the steps cut in the ice, we departed at 3:30 A.M. The New Zealanders left first, followed by Stephen and myself, our porters and Sherpas, and then the Swiss. The Japanese lingered in their camp. The sky was clear, and we were confident that no spring storm would erupt that day to close the pass.

At 15,500 feet, it looked to me as if Stephen were shuffling and staggering a bit, which are symptoms of altitude sickness. (The initial stage of altitude sickness brings a headache and nausea. As the condition worsens, a climber may encounter difficult breathing, disorientation, aphasia, and paralysis.) I felt strong—my adrenaline was flowing—but I was very concerned about my ultimate ability to get across. A couple of our porters were also suffering from the height, and Pasang, our Sherpa sirdar (leader), was worried.

Just after daybreak, while we rested at 15,500 feet, one of the New Zealanders, who had gone ahead, came staggering down toward us with a body slung across his shoulders. He dumped the almost naked, barefoot body of an Indian holy man—a sadhu—at my feet. He had found the pilgrim lying on the ice, shivering and suffering from hypothermia. I cradled the sadhu's head and laid him out on the rocks. The New Zealander was angry. He wanted to get across the pass before the bright sun melted the snow. He said, "Look, I've done what I can. You have porters and Sherpa guides. You care for him.

We're going on!" He turned and went back up the mountain to join his friends.

I took a carotid pulse and found that the sadhu was still alive. We figured he had probably visited the holy shrines at Muklinath and was on his way home. It was fruitless to question why he had chosen this desperately high route instead of the safe, heavily traveled caravan route through the Kali Gandaki gorge. Or why he was shoeless and almost naked, or how long he had been lying in the pass. The answers weren't going to solve our problem.

Stephen and the four Swiss began stripping off their outer clothing and opening their packs. The sadhu was soon clothed from head to foot. He was not able to walk, but he was very much alive. I looked down the mountain and spotted the Japanese climbers, marching up with a horse.

Without a great deal of thought, I told Stephen and Pasang that I was concerned about withstanding the heights to come and wanted to get over the pass. I took off after several of our porters who had gone ahead.

On the steep part of the ascent where, if the ice steps had given way, I would have slid down about 3,000 feet, I felt vertigo. I stopped for a breather, allowing the Swiss to catch up with me. I inquired about the sadhu and Stephen. They said that the sadhu was fine and that Stephen was just behind them. I set off again for the summit.

Stephen arrived at the summit an hour after I did. Still exhilarated by victory, I ran down the slope to congratulate him. He was suffering from altitude sickness—walking 15 steps, then stopping, walking 15 steps, then stopping. Pasang accompanied him all the way up. When I reached them, Stephen glared at me and said: "How do you feel about contributing to the death of a fellow man?"

I did not completely comprehend what he meant. "Is the sadhu dead?" I inquired.

"No," replied Stephen, "but he surely will be!"

After I had gone, followed not long after by the Swiss, Stephen had remained with the sadhu. When the Japanese had arrived, Stephen had asked to use their horse to transport the sadhu down to the hut. They had refused. He had then asked Pasang to have a group of our porters carry the sadhu. Pasang had resisted the idea, saying that the porters would have to exert all their energy to get themselves over the pass. He believed they could not carry a man down 1,000 feet to the hut, reclimb the slope, and get across safely before the snow melted. Pasang had pressed Stephen not to delay any longer.

The Sherpas had carried the sadhu down to a rock in the sun at about 15,000 feet and pointed out the hut another 500 feet below. The Japanese had given him food and drink. When they had last seen him, he was listlessly throwing rocks at the Japanese party's dog, which had frightened him.

We do not know if the sadhu lived or died.

For many of the following days and evenings, Stephen and I discussed and debated our behavior toward the sadhu. Stephen is a committed Quaker with deep moral vision. He said, "I feel that what happened with the sadhu is a good example of the breakdown between the individual ethic and the corporate ethic. No one person was willing to assume ultimate responsibility for the sadhu. Each was willing to do his bit just so long as it was not too inconvenient. When it got to be a bother, everyone just passed the buck to someone else and took off. Jesus was relevant to a more individualistic stage of society, but how do we interpret his teaching today in a world filled with large, impersonal organizations and groups?"

I defended the larger group, saying "Look, we all cared. We all gave aid and comfort. Everyone did his bit. The New Zealander carried him down below the snow line. I took his pulse and suggested we treat him for hypothermia. You and the Swiss gave him clothing and got him warmed up. The Japanese gave him food and water. The Sherpas carried him down to the sun and pointed out the easy trail toward the hut. He was well enough to throw rocks at a dog. What more could we do?"

"You have just described the typical affluent Westerner's response to a problem. Throwing money—in this case, food and sweaters—at it, but not solving the fundamentals!" Stephen retorted.

"What would satisfy you?" I said. "Here we are, a group of New Zealanders, Swiss, Americans, and Japanese who have never met before and who are at the apex of one of the most powerful experiences of our lives. Some years the pass is so bad no one gets over it. What right does an almost naked pilgrim who chooses the wrong trail have to disrupt our lives? Even the Sherpas had no interest in risking the trip to help him beyond a certain point."

Stephen calmly rebutted, "I wonder what the Sherpas would have done if the sadhu had been a well-dressed Nepali, or what the Japanese would have done if the sadhu had been a well-dressed Asian, or what you would have done, Buzz, if the sadhu had been a well-dressed Western woman?"

"Where, in your opinion," I asked, "is the limit of our responsibility in a situation like this? We had our own well-being to worry about. Our Sherpa guides were unwilling to jeopardize us or the porters for the sadhu. No one else on the mountain was willing to commit himself beyond certain self-imposed limits."

Stephen said, "As individual Christians or people with a Western ethical tradition, we can fulfill our obligations in such a situation only if one, the sadhu dies in our care; two, the sadhu demonstrates to us that he can undertake the two-day walk down to the village; or three, we carry the sadhu for two days down to the village and persuade someone there to care for him."

"Leaving the sadhu in the sun with food and clothing—where he demonstrated hand-eye coordination by throwing a rock at a dog—comes close to fulfilling items one and two," I answered. "And it wouldn't have made sense to take him to the village where the people appeared to be far less caring than the Sherpas, so the third condition is impractical. Are you really saying that, no matter what the implications, we should, at the drop of a hat, have changed our entire plan?"

THE INDIVIDUAL VERSUS THE GROUP ETHIC

Despite my arguments, I felt and continue to feel guilt about the sadhu. I had literally walked through a classic moral dilemma without fully thinking through the consequences. My excuses for my actions include a high adrenaline flow, a superordinate goal, and a once-in-a-lifetime opportunity—common factors in corporate situations, especially stressful ones.

Real moral dilemmas are ambiguous, and many of us hike right through them, unaware that they exist. When, usually after the fact, someone makes an issue of one, we tend to resent his or her bringing it up. Often, when the full import of what we have done (or not done) hits us, we dig into a defensive position from which it is very difficult to emerge. In rare circumstances, we may contemplate what we have done from inside a prison.

Had we mountaineers been free of stress caused by the effort and the high altitude, we might have treated the sadhu differently. Yet isn't stress the real test of personal and corporate values? The instant decisions that executives make under pressure reveal the most about personal and corporate character.

Among the many questions that occur to me when I ponder my experience with the sadhu are: What are the practical limits of moral imagination and vision? Is there a collective or institutional ethic that differs from the ethics of the individual? At what level of effort or commitment can one discharge one's ethical responsibilities?

———

The word *ethics* turns off many and confuses more. Yet the notions of shared values and an agreed-upon process for dealing with adversity and change—what many people mean when they talk about corporate culture—seem to be at the heart of the ethical issue. People who are in touch with their own core beliefs and the beliefs of others and who are sustained by them can be more comfortable living on the cutting edge. At times, taking a tough line or a decisive stand in a muddle of ambiguity is the only ethical thing to do. If a manager is indecisive about a problem and spends time trying to figure out the "good" thing to do, the enterprise may be lost.

Business ethics, then, has to do with the authenticity and integrity of the enterprise. To be ethical is to follow the business as well as the cultural goals of the corporation, its owners, its employees, and its customers. Those who cannot serve the corporate vision are not authentic businesspeople and, therefore, are not ethical in the business sense.

———

...I wonder about the role of the professional manager who moves from company to company. How can he or she quickly absorb the values and culture of different organizations? Or is there, indeed, an art of management that is totally transportable? Assuming that such fungible managers do exist, is it proper for them to manipulate the values of others?

What would have happened had Stephen and I carried the sadhu for two days back to the village and become involved with the villagers in his care? In four trips to Nepal, my most interesting experience occurred in 1975 when I lived in a Sherpa home in the Khumbu for five days while recovering from altitude sickness. The high point of Stephen's trip was an invitation to participate in a family funeral ceremony in Manang. Neither experience had to do with climbing the high passes of the Himalayas. Why were we so reluctant to try the lower path, the ambiguous trail? Perhaps because we did not have a leader who could reveal the greater purpose of the trip to us.

Why didn't Stephen, with his moral vision, opt to take the sadhu under his personal care? The answer is partly because Stephen was hard-stressed physically himself and partly because, without some support system that encompassed our involuntary and episodic community on the mountain, it was beyond his individual capacity to do so.

I see the current interest in corporate culture and corporate value systems as a positive response to pessimism such as Stephen's about the decline of the role of the individual in large organizations. Individuals who operate from a thoughtful set of personal values provide the foundation for a corporate culture. A corporate tradition that encourages freedom of inquiry, supports personal values, and reinforces a focused sense of direction can fulfill the need to combine individuality with the prosperity and success of the group. Without such corporate support, the individual is lost.

That is the lesson of the sadhu. In a complex corporate situation, the individual requires and deserves the support of the group. When people cannot find such support in their organizations, they don't know how to act. If such support is forthcoming, a person has a stake in the success of the group and can add much to the process of establishing and maintaining a corporate culture. Management's challenge is to be sensitive to individual needs, to shape them, and to direct and focus them for the benefit of the group as a whole.

For each of us the sadhu lives. Should we stop what we are doing and comfort him; or should we keep trudging up toward the high pass? Should I pause to help the derelict I pass on the street each night as I walk by the Yale Club en route to Grand Central Station? Am I his brother? What is the nature of our responsibility if we consider ourselves to be ethical persons? Perhaps it is to change the values of the group so that it can, with all its resources, take the other road.

John Rawls	# Justice as Fairness

John Rawls was the premier American political philosopher of the twentieth century. This is from his groundbreaking book, A *Theory of Justice.*

My aim is to present a conception of justice which generalizes and carries to a higher level of abstraction the familiar theory of the social contract as found, say, in Locke, Rousseau, and Kant. In order to do this we are not to think of the original contract as one to enter a particular society or to set up a particular form of government. Rather, the guiding idea is that the principles of justice for the basic structure of society are the object of the original agreement. They are the principles that free and rational persons concerned to further their own interests would accept in an initial position of equality as defining the fundamental terms of their association. These principles are to regulate all further agreements: they specify the kinds of social cooperation that can be entered into and the forms of government that can be established. This way of regarding the principles of justice I shall call justice as fairness.

Thus we are to imagine that those who engage in social cooperation choose together, in one joint act, the principles which are to assign basic rights and duties and to determine the division of social benefits. Men are to decide in advance how they are to regulate their claims against one another and what is to be the foundation charter of their society. Just as each person must decide by rational reflection what constitutes his good, that is, the system of ends which it is rational for him to pursue, so a group of persons must decide once and for all what is to count among them as just and unjust. The choice which rational men would make in this hypothetical situation of equal liberty, assuming for the present that this choice problem has a solution, determines the principles of justice.

In justice as fairness the original position of equality corresponds to the state of nature in the traditional theory of the social contract. This original position is not, of course, thought of as an actual historical state of affairs, much less as a primitive condition of culture. It is understood as a purely hypothetical situation characterized so as to lead to a certain conception of justice. Among the essential

From A *Theory of Justice* (Cambridge, Mass.: Harward University Press, 1971).

features of this situation is that no one knows his place in society, his class position or social status, nor does any one know his fortune in the distribution of natural assets and abilities, his intelligence, strength, and the like. I shall even assume that the parties do not know their conceptions of the good or their special psychological propensities. The principles of justice are chosen behind a veil of ignorance. This ensures that no one is advantaged or disadvantaged in the choice of principles by the outcome of natural chance or the contingency of social circumstances. Since all are similarly situated and no one is able to design principles to favor his particular condition, the principles of justice are the result of a fair agreement or bargain. For given the circumstances of the original position, the symmetry of everyone's relations to each other, this initial situation is fair between individuals as moral persons, that is, as rational beings with their own ends and capable, I shall assume, of a sense of justice. . . .

I shall maintain instead that the persons in the initial situation would choose two . . . principles: the first requires equality in the assignment of basic rights and duties, while the second holds that social and economic inequalities, for example inequalities of wealth and authority, are just only if they result in compensating benefits for everyone, and in particular for the least advantaged members of society. These principles rule out justifying institutions on the grounds that the hardships of some are offset by a greater good in the aggregate. It may be expedient but it is not just that some should have less in order that others may prosper. But there is no injustice in the greater benefits earned by a few provided that the situation of persons not so fortunate is thereby improved. The intuitive idea is that since everyone's well-being depends upon a scheme of cooperation without which no one could have a satisfactory life, the division of advantages should be such as to draw forth the willing cooperation of everyone taking part in it, including those less well situated. Yet this can be expected only if reasonable terms are proposed. The two principles mentioned seem to be a fair agreement on the basis of which those better endowed, or more fortunate in their social position, neither of which we can be said to deserve,

could expect the willing cooperation of others when some workable scheme is a necessary condition of the welfare of all. Once we decide to look for a conception of justice that nullifies the accidents of natural endowment and the contingencies of social circumstance as counters in quest for political and economic advantage, we are led to these principles. They express the result of leaving aside those aspects of the social world that seem arbitrary from a moral point of view.

––––––––––––––

I shall now state in a provisional form the two principles of justice that I believe would be chosen in the original position. The first statement of the two principles reads as follows.

- First: each person is to have an equal right to the most extensive basic liberty compatible with a similar liberty for others.
- Second: social and economic inequalities are to be arranged so that they are both (a) reasonably expected to be to everyone's advantage, and (b) attached to positions and offices open to all.

By way of general comment, these principles primarily apply, as I have said, to the basic structure of society. They are to govern the assignment of rights and duties and to regulate the distribution of social and economic advantages. As their formulation suggests, these principles presuppose that the social structure can be divided into two more or less distinct parts, the first principle applying to the one, the second to the other. They distinguish between those aspects of the social system that define and secure the equal liberties of citizenship and those that specify and establish social and economic inequalities. The basic liberties of citizens are, roughly speaking, political liberty (the right to vote and to be eligible for public office) together with freedom of speech and assembly; liberty of conscience and freedom of thought; freedom of the person along with the right to hold (personal) property; and freedom from arbitrary arrest and seizure as defined by the concept of the rule of law. These liberties are all required to be equal by the first principle, since citizens of a just society are to have the same basic rights.

The second principle applies, in the first approximation, to the distribution of income and wealth and to the design of organizations that makes use of differences in authority and responsibility, or chains of command. While the distribution of wealth and income need not be equal, it must be to everyone's advantage, and at the same time, positions of authority and offices of command must be accessible to all. One applies the second principle by holding positions open, and then, subject to this constraint, arranges social and economic inequalities so that everyone benefits.

These principles are to be arranged in a serial order with the first principle prior to the second. This ordering means that a departure from the institutions of equal liberty required by the first principle cannot be justified by, or compensated for, by greater social and economic advantages. The distribution of wealth and income, and the hierarchies of authority, must be consistent with both the liberties of equal citizenship and equality of opportunity.

Peter Singer | # Rich and Poor

Peter Singer is an Australian philosopher who teaches at Princeton University Institute for Values and is most famous for his defense of "animal liberation."

SOME FACTS ABOUT POVERTY

... Consider these facts: by the most cautious estimates, 400 million people lack the calories, protein, vitamins and minerals needed to sustain their bodies and minds in a healthy state. Millions are constantly hungry; others suffer from deficiency diseases and from infections they would be able to resist on a better diet. Children are the worst affected. According to one study, 14 million children under five die every year from the combined effects of malnutrition and infection. In some districts half the children born can be expected to die before their fifth birthday.

Nor is lack of food the only hardship of the poor. To give a broader picture, Robert McNamara, when president of the World Bank, suggested the term "absolute poverty." The poverty we are familiar with in industrialised nations is relative poverty—meaning that some citizens are poor, relative to the wealth enjoyed by their neighbours. People living in relative poverty in Australia might be quite comfortably off by comparison with pensioners in Britain, and British pensioners are not poor in comparison with the poverty that exists in Mali or Ethiopia. Absolute poverty, on the other hand, is poverty by any standard. In McNamara's words:

> Poverty at the absolute level ... is life at the very margin of existence. The absolute poor are severely deprived human beings struggling to survive in a set of squalid and degraded circumstances almost beyond the power of our sophisticated imaginations and privileged circumstances to conceive.

Compared to those fortunate enough to live in developed countries, individuals in the poorest nations have:

- An infant mortality rate eight times higher
- A life expectancy one-third lower

- An adult literacy rate 60 per cent less
- A nutritional level, for one out of every two the population, below acceptable standards;
- And for millions of infants, less protein than is sufficient to permit optimum development of the brain.

McNamara has summed up absolute poverty as "a condition of life so characterised by malnutrition, illiteracy, disease, squalid surroundings, high infant mortality and low life expectancy as to bo beneath any reasonable definition of human decency." ...

Death and disease apart, absolute poverty remains a miserable condition of life, with inadequate food, shelter, clothing, sanitation, health services and education. The Worldwatch Institute estimates that as many as 1.2 billion people—or 23 per cent of the world's population—live in absolute poverty. For the purpose of this estimate, absolute poverty is defined as "the lack of sufficient income in cash or kind to meet the most basic biological needs for food, clothing, and shelter." Absolute poverty is probably the principal cause of human misery today....

The problem is not that the world cannot produce enough to feed and shelter its people. People in the poor countries consume, on average, 180 kilos of grain a year, while North Americans average around 900 kilos. The difference is caused by the fact that in the rich countries we feed most of our grain to animals, converting it into meat, milk, and eggs. Because this is a highly inefficient process, people in rich countries are responsible for the consumption of far more food than those in poor countries who eat few animal products. If we stopped feeding animals on grains and soybeans, the amount of food saved would—if distributed to those who need it—be more than enough to end hunger throughout the world.

These facts about animal food do not mean that we can easily solve the world food problem by cutting down on animal products, but they show that the problem is essentially one of distribution rather than production. The world does produce enough food. Moreover, the poorer nations themselves could produce far more if they made more use of improved agricultural techniques.

So why are people hungry? Poor people cannot afford to buy grain grown by farmers in the richer nations. Poor farmers cannot afford to buy improved seeds, or fertilisers, or the machinery needed for drilling wells and pumping water. Only by transferring some of the wealth of the rich nations to the poor can the situation be changed.

That this wealth exists is clear. Against the picture of absolute poverty that McNamara has painted, one might pose a picture of "absolute affluence." Those who are absolutely affluent are not necessarily affluent by comparison with their neighbours, but they are affluent by any reasonable definition of human needs. This means that they have more income than they need to provide themselves adequately with all the basic necessities of life. After buying (either directly or through their taxes) food, shelter, clothing, basic health services, and education, the absolutely affluent are still able to spend money on luxuries. The absolutely affluent choose their food for the pleasures of the palate, not to stop hunger; they buy new clothes to look good, not to keep warm; they move house to be in a better neighborhood or have a playroom for the children, not to keep out the rain; and after all this there is still money to spend on stereo systems, video-cameras, and overseas holidays.

At this stage I am making no ethical judgments about absolute affluence, merely pointing out that it exists. Its defining characteristic is a significant amount of income above the level necessary to provide for the basic human needs of oneself and one's dependents. By this standard, the majority of citizens of Western Europe, North America, Japan, Australia, New Zealand, and the oil-rich Middle Eastern states are all absolutely affluent. To quote McNamara once more:

> The average citizen of a developed country enjoys wealth beyond the wildest dreams of the one billion people in countries with per capita incomes under $200.

These, therefore, are the countries—and individuals—who have wealth that they could, without threatening their own basic welfare, transfer to the absolutely poor.

At present, very little is being transferred. Only Sweden, the Netherlands, Norway, and some of the oil-exporting Arab states have reached the modest target, set by the United Nations, of 0.7 per cent of gross national product (GNP). Britain gives 0.31 per cent of its GNP in official development assistance and a small additional amount in unofficial aid from voluntary organisations. The total comes to about £2 per month per person, and compares with 5.5 per cent of GNP spent on alcohol, and 3 per cent on tobacco. Other, even wealthier nations, give little more: Germany gives 0.41 per cent and Japan 0.32 per cent. The United States gives a mere 0.15 per cent of its GNP. . . .

THE OBLIGATION TO ASSIST

The Argument for an Obligation to Assist

The path from the library at my university to the humanities lecture theatre passes a shallow ornamental pond. Suppose that on my way to give a lecture I notice that a small child has fallen in and is in danger of drowning. Would anyone deny that I ought to wade in and pull the child out? This will mean getting my clothes muddy and either cancelling my lecture or delaying it until I can find something dry to change into; but compared with the avoidable death of a child this is insignificant.

A plausible principle that would support the judgment that I ought to pull the child out is this: if it is in our power to prevent something very bad from happening, without thereby sacrificing anything of comparable moral significance, we ought to do it. This principle seems uncontroversial. It will obviously win the assent of consequentialists; but non-consequentialists should accept it too, because the injunction to prevent what is bad applies only when nothing comparably significant is at stake. Thus the principle cannot lead to the kinds of actions of which non-consequentialists strongly disapprove—serious violations of individual rights, injustice, broken promises, and so on. If non-consequentialists regard any of these as comparable in moral significance to the bad thing that is to be prevented, they will automatically regard the principle as not applying in those cases in which the bad thing can only be prevented by violating rights, doing injustice, breaking promises, or whatever else is at stake. Most non-consequentialists hold that we ought to prevent what is bad and promote what is good. Their dispute with consequentialists lies in their insistence that this is not the sole ultimate ethical principle: that it is an ethical principle is not denied by any plausible ethical theory.

Nevertheless the uncontroversial appearance of the principle that we ought to prevent what is bad when we can do so without sacrificing anything of comparable moral significance is deceptive. If it were taken seriously and acted upon, our lives and our world would be fundamentally changed. For the principle applies, not just to rare situations in which one can save a child from a pond, but to the everyday situation in which we can assist those living in absolute poverty. In saying this I assume that absolute poverty, with its hunger and malnutrition, lack of shelter, illiteracy, disease, high infant mortality, and low life expectancy, is a bad thing. And I assume that it is within the power of the affluent to reduce absolute poverty, without sacrificing anything of comparable moral significance. If these two assumptions and the principle we have been discussing are correct, we have an obligation to help those in absolute poverty that is no less strong than our obligation to rescue a drowning child from a pond. Not to help would be wrong, whether or not it is intrinsically equivalent to killing. Helping is not, as conventionally thought, a charitable act that it is praise-worthy to do, but not wrong to omit; it is something that everyone ought to do.

Peter Singer

What Should a Billionaire Give—And What Should You?

Peter Singer is the Ira W. DeCamp professor of bioethics at the Center for Human Values at Princeton University. He is the author of many books, including most recently *The Way We Eat: Why Our Food Choices Matter.*

With Christmas approaching, and Americans writing checks to their favorite charities, it's a good time to ask how these two beliefs—that a human life, if it can be priced at all, is worth millions, and that the factors I have mentioned do not alter the value of a human life—square with our actions. Perhaps this year such questions lurk beneath the surface of more family discussions than usual, for it has been an extraordinary year for philanthropy, especially philanthropy to fight global poverty.

For Bill Gates, the founder of Microsoft, the ideal of valuing all human life equally began to jar against reality some years ago, when he read an article about diseases in the developing world and came across the statistic that half a million children die every year from rotavirus, the most common cause of severe diarrhea in children. He had never heard of rotavirus. "How could I never have heard of something that kills half a million children every year?" he asked himself. He then learned that in developing countries, millions of children die from diseases that have been eliminated, or virtually eliminated, in the United States. That shocked him because he assumed that, if there are vaccines and treatments that could save lives, governments would be doing everything possible to get them to the people who need them. As Gates told a meeting of the World Health Assembly in Geneva last year, he and his wife, Melinda, "couldn't escape the brutal conclusion that—in our world today—some lives are seen as worth saving and others are not." They said to themselves, "This can't be true." But they knew it was.

Gates's speech to the World Health Assembly concluded on an optimistic note, looking forward to the next decade when "people will finally accept that the death of a child in the developing world is just as tragic as the death of a child in the developed world." That belief in the equal value of all human life is also prominent on the Web site of the Bill and Melinda Gates Foundation, where under Our Values we read: "All lives—no matter where they are being led—have equal value."

We are very far from acting in accordance with that belief. In the same world in which more than a billion people live at a level of affluence never previously known, roughly a billion other people struggle to survive on the purchasing power equivalent of less than one U.S. dollar per day. Most of the world's poorest people are undernourished, lack access to safe drinking water or even the most basic health services and cannot send their children to school. According to Unicef, more than 10 million children die every year—about 30,000 per day—from avoidable, poverty-related causes.

Last June the investor Warren Buffett took a significant step toward reducing those deaths when he pledged $31 billion to the Gates Foundation, and another $6 billion to other charitable foundations. Buffett's pledge, set alongside the nearly $30 billion given by Bill and Melinda Gates to their foundation, has made it clear that the first decade of the 21st century is a new "golden age of philanthropy." On an inflation-adjusted basis, Buffett has pledged to give more than double the lifetime total given away by two of the philanthropic giants of the past, Andrew Carnegie and John D. Rockefeller, put

From the *New York Times*, Dec. 17, 2006.

together. Bill and Melinda Gates's gifts are not far behind.

Gates's and Buffett's donations will now be put to work primarily to reduce poverty, disease, and premature death in the developing world. According to the Global Forum for Health Research, less than 10 percent of the world's health research budget is spent on combating conditions that account for 90 percent of the global burden of disease. In the past, diseases that affect only the poor have been of no commercial interest to pharmaceutical manufacturers, because the poor cannot afford to buy their products. The Global Alliance for Vaccines and Immunization (GAVI), heavily supported by the Gates Foundation, seeks to change this by guaranteeing to purchase millions of doses of vaccines, when they are developed, that can prevent diseases like malaria. GAVI has also assisted developing countries to immunize more people with existing vaccines: 99 million additional children have been reached to date. By doing this, GAVI claims to have already averted nearly 1.7 million future deaths.

Philanthropy on this scale raises many ethical questions: Why are the people who are giving doing so? Does it do any good? Should we praise them for giving so much or criticize them for not giving still more? Is it troubling that such momentous decisions are made by a few extremely wealthy individuals? And how do our judgments about them reflect on our own way of living?

Let's start with the question of motives. The rich must—or so some of us with less money like to assume—suffer sleepless nights because of their ruthlessness in squeezing out competitors, firing workers, shutting down plants or whatever else they have to do to acquire their wealth. When wealthy people give away money, we can always say that they are doing it to ease their consciences or generate favorable publicity. It has been suggested—by, for example, David Kirkpatrick, a senior editor at Fortune magazine—that Bill Gates's turn to philanthropy was linked to the antitrust problems Microsoft had in the U.S. and the European Union. Was Gates, consciously or subconsciously, trying to improve his own image and that of his company?

This kind of sniping tells us more about the attackers than the attacked. Giving away large sums, rather than spending the money on corporate advertising or developing new products, is not a sensible strategy for increasing personal wealth. When we read that someone has given away a lot of their money, or time, to help others, it challenges us to think about our own behavior. Should we be following their example, in our own modest way? But if the rich just give their money away to improve their image, or to make up for past misdeeds— misdeeds quite unlike any we have committed, of course—then, conveniently, what they are doing has no relevance to what we ought to do.

A famous story is told about Thomas Hobbes, the 17th-century English philosopher, who argued that we all act in our own interests. On seeing him give alms to a beggar, a cleric asked Hobbes if he would have done this if Christ had not commanded us to do so. Yes, Hobbes replied, he was in pain to see the miserable condition of the old man, and his gift, by providing the man with some relief from that misery, also eased Hobbes's pain. That reply reconciles Hobbes's charity with his egoistic theory of human motivation, but at the cost of emptying egoism of much of its bite. If egoists suffer when they see a stranger in distress, they are capable of being as charitable as any altruist.

Followers of the 18th-century German philosopher Immanuel Kant would disagree. They think an act has moral worth only if it is done out of a sense of duty. Doing something merely because you enjoy doing it, or enjoy seeing its consequences, they say, has no moral worth, because if you happened not to enjoy doing it, then you wouldn't do it, and you are not responsible for your likes and dislikes, whereas you are responsible for your obedience to the demands of duty.

Perhaps some philanthropists are motivated by their sense of duty. Apart from the equal value of all human life, the other "simple value" that lies at the core of the work of the Gates Foundation, according to its Web site, is "To whom much has been given, much is expected." That suggests the view that those who have great wealth have a duty to use it for a larger purpose than their own interests. But while such questions of motive may be relevant to our assessment of Gates's or Buffett's character, they pale into insignificance when we consider the effect of what Gates and Buffett are doing. The parents whose children could die from rotavirus care more about getting the help that will save their children's lives than about the motivations of those who make that possible.

Interestingly, neither Gates nor Buffett seems motivated by the possibility of being rewarded in heaven for his good deeds on earth. Gates told a Time interviewer, "There's a lot more I could be doing on a Sunday morning" than going to church. Put them together with Andrew Carnegie, famous for his freethinking, and three of the four greatest American philanthropists have been atheists or agnostics. (The exception is John D. Rockefeller.) In a country in which 96 percent of the population say they believe in a supreme being, that's a striking fact. It means that in one sense, Gates and Buffett are probably less self-interested in their charity than someone like Mother Teresa, who as a pious Roman Catholic believed in reward and punishment in the afterlife.

More important than questions about motives are questions about whether there is an obligation for the rich to give, and if so, how much they should give. A few years ago, an African-American cabdriver taking me to the Inter-American Development Bank in Washington asked me if I worked at the bank. I told him I did not but was speaking at a conference on development and aid. He then assumed that I was an economist, but when I said no, my training was in philosophy, he asked me if I thought the U.S. should give foreign aid. When I answered affirmatively, he replied that the government shouldn't tax people in order to give their money to others. That, he thought, was robbery. When I asked if he believed that the rich should voluntarily donate some of what they earn to the poor, he said that if someone had worked for his money, he wasn't going to tell him what to do with it.

At that point we reached our destination. Had the journey continued, I might have tried to persuade him that people can earn large amounts only when they live under favorable social circumstances, and that they don't create those circumstances by themselves. I could have quoted Warren Buffett's acknowledgment that society is responsible for much of his wealth. "If you stick me down in the middle of Bangladesh or Peru," he said, "you'll find out how much this talent is going to produce in the wrong kind of soil." The Nobel Prize-winning economist and social scientist Herbert Simon estimated that "social capital" is responsible for at least 90 percent of what people earn in wealthy societies like those of the United States or northwestern Europe. By social capital Simon meant not only natural resources but, more important, the technology and organizational skills in the community, and the presence of good government. These are the foundation on which the rich can begin their work. "On moral grounds," Simon added, "we could argue for a flat income tax of 90 percent." Simon was not, of course, advocating so steep a rate of tax, for he was well aware of disincentive effects. But his estimate does undermine the argument that the rich are entitled to keep their wealth because it is all a result of their hard work. If Simon is right, that is true of at most 10 percent of it.

In any case, even if we were to grant that people deserve every dollar they earn, that doesn't answer the question of what they should do with it. We might say that they have a right to spend it on lavish parties, private jets and luxury yachts, or, for that matter, to flush it down the toilet. But we could still think that for them to do these things while others die from easily preventable diseases is wrong. In an article I wrote more than three decades ago, at the time of a humanitarian emergency in what is now Bangladesh, I used the example of walking by a shallow pond and seeing a small child who has fallen in and appears to be in danger of drowning. Even though we did nothing to cause the child to fall into the pond, almost everyone agrees that if we can save the child at minimal inconvenience or trouble to ourselves, we ought to do so. Anything else would be callous, indecent and, in a word, wrong. The fact that in rescuing the child we may, for example, ruin a new pair of shoes is not a good reason for allowing the child to drown. Similarly if for the cost of a pair of shoes we can contribute to a health program in a developing country that stands a good chance of saving the life of a child, we ought to do so.

Perhaps, though, our obligation to help the poor is even stronger than this example implies, for we are less innocent than the passer-by who did nothing to cause the child to fall into the pond. Thomas Pogge, a philosopher at Columbia University, has argued that at least some of our affluence comes at the expense of the poor. He bases this claim not simply on the usual critique of the barriers that Europe and the United States maintain against agricultural imports from developing countries but also on less familiar aspects of our trade with developing countries. For example, he points out that international corporations are willing to make deals to buy natural resources from any government, no matter how it has come to power. This provides a huge financial incentive for groups to try to overthrow the existing government. Successful rebels are rewarded by being able to sell off the nation's oil, minerals or timber.

In their dealings with corrupt dictators in developing countries, Pogge asserts, international corporations are morally no better than someone who knowingly buys stolen goods—with the difference that the international legal and political order recognizes the corporations, not as criminals in possession of stolen goods but as the legal owners of the goods they have bought. This situation is, of course, beneficial for the industrial nations, because it enables us to obtain the raw materials we need to maintain our prosperity, but it is a disaster for resource-rich developing countries, turning the wealth that should benefit them into a curse that leads to a cycle of coups, civil wars, and corruption and is of little benefit to the people as a whole.

In this light, our obligation to the poor is not just one of providing assistance to strangers but one of compensation for harms that we have caused and are still causing them. It might be argued that we do not owe the poor compensation, because our affluence actually benefits them. Living luxuriously, it is said, provides employment, and so wealth trickles down, helping the poor more effectively than aid does. But the rich in industrialized nations buy virtually nothing that is made by the very poor. During the past 20 years of economic globalization, although expanding trade has helped lift many of the world's poor out of

poverty, it has failed to benefit the poorest 10 percent of the world's population. Some of the extremely poor, most of whom live in sub-Saharan Africa, have nothing to sell that rich people want, while others lack the infrastructure to get their goods to market. If they can get their crops to a port, European and U.S. subsidies often mean that they cannot sell them, despite—as for example in the case of West African cotton growers who compete with vastly larger and richer U.S. cotton producers—having a lower production cost than the subsidized producers in the rich nations.

The remedy to these problems, it might reasonably be suggested, should come from the state, not from private philanthropy. When aid comes through the government, everyone who earns above the tax-free threshold contributes something, with more collected from those with greater ability to pay. Much as we may applaud what Gates and Buffett are doing, we can also be troubled by a system that leaves the fate of hundreds of millions of people hanging on the decisions of two or three private citizens. But the amount of foreign development aid given by the U.S. government is, at 22 cents for every $100 the nation earns, about the same, as a percentage of gross national income, as Portugal gives and about half that of the U.K. Worse still, much of it is directed where it best suits U.S. strategic interests—Iraq is now by far the largest recipient of U.S. development aid, and Egypt, Jordan, Pakistan and Afghanistan all rank in the Top 10. Less than a quarter of official U.S. development aid—barely a nickel in every $100 of our G.N.I.—goes to the world's poorest nations.

Adding private philanthropy to U.S. government aid improves this picture, because Americans privately give more per capita to international philanthropic causes than the citizens of almost any other nation. Even when private donations are included, however, countries like Norway, Denmark, Sweden and the Netherlands give three or four times as much foreign aid, in proportion to the size of their economies, as the U.S. gives – with a much larger percentage going to the poorest nations. At least as things now stand, the case for philanthropic efforts to relieve global poverty is not susceptible to the argument that the government has taken care of the problem. And even if official U.S. aid were better-directed and comparable, relative to our gross domestic product, with that of the most generous nations, there would still be a role for private philanthropy. Unconstrained by diplomatic considerations or the desire to swing votes at the United Nations, private donors can more easily avoid dealing with corrupt or wasteful governments. They can go directly into the field, working with local villages and grass-roots organizations.

Nor are philanthropists beholden to lobbyists. As The New York Times reported recently, billions of dollars of U.S. aid is tied to domestic goods. Wheat for Africa must be grown in America, although aid experts say this often depresses local African markets, reducing the incentive for farmers there to produce more. In a decision that surely costs lives, hundreds of millions of condoms intended to stop the spread of AIDS in Africa and around the world must be manufactured in the U.S., although they cost twice as much as similar products made in Asia.

In other ways, too, private philanthropists are free to venture where governments fear to tread. Through a foundation named for his wife, Susan Thompson Buffett, Warren Buffett has supported reproductive rights, including family planning and pro-choice organizations. In another unusual initiative, he has pledged $50 million for the International Atomic Energy Agency's plan to establish a "fuel bank" to supply nuclear-reactor fuel to countries that meet their nuclear-nonproliferation commitments. The idea, which has been talked about for many years, is widely agreed to be a useful step toward discouraging countries from building their own facilities for producing nuclear fuel, which could then be diverted to weapons production. It is, Buffett said, "an investment in a safer world." Though it is something that governments could and should be doing, no government had taken the first step.

Aid has always had its critics. Carefully planned and intelligently directed private philanthropy may be the best answer to the claim that aid doesn't work. Of course, as in any large-scale human enterprise, some aid can be ineffective. But provided that aid isn't actually counterproductive, even relatively inefficient assistance is likely to do more to advance human wellbeing than luxury spending by the wealthy.

The rich, then, should give. But how much should they give? Gates may have given away nearly $30 billion, but that still leaves him sitting at the top of the Forbes list of the richest Americans, with $53 billion. His 66,000-square-foot high-tech lakeside estate near Seattle is reportedly worth more than $100 million. Property taxes are about $1 million. Among his possessions is the Leicester Codex, the only handwritten book by Leonardo da Vinci still in private hands, for which he paid $30.8 million in 1994. Has Bill Gates done enough? More pointedly, you might ask: if he really believes that all lives have equal value, what is he doing living in such an expensive house and owning a Leonardo Codex? Are there no more lives that could be saved by living more modestly and adding the money thus saved to the amount he has already given?

Yet we should recognize that, if judged by the proportion of his wealth that he has given away, Gates compares very well with most of the other people on the Forbes 400 list, including his former colleague and Microsoft co-founder, Paul Allen. Allen, who left the company in 1983, has given, over his lifetime, more than $800 million to philanthropic causes. That is far more than nearly any of us will ever be able to give. But Forbes lists Allen as the fifth-richest American, with a net worth of $16 billion. He owns the Seattle Seahawks, the Portland Trailblazers, a 413-foot oceangoing yacht that carries two helicopters and a 60-foot submarine. He has given only about 5 percent of his total wealth.

Is there a line of moral adequacy that falls between the 5 percent that Allen has given away and the roughly 35 percent that Gates has donated? Few people have set a personal example that would allow them to tell Gates that he has not given enough, but one who could is Zell Kravinsky. A few years ago, when he was in his mid-40s, Kravinsky gave almost all of his $45 million real estate fortune to health-related charities, retaining only his modest family home in Jenkintown, near Philadelphia, and enough to meet his family's ordinary expenses. After learning that thousands of people with failing kidneys die each year while waiting for a transplant, he contacted a Philadelphia hospital and donated one of his kidneys to a complete stranger.

After reading about Kravinsky in The New Yorker, I invited him to speak to my classes at Princeton. He comes across as anguished by the failure of others to see the simple logic that lies behind his altruism. Kravinsky has a mathematical mind—a talent that obviously helped him in deciding what investments would prove profitable—and he says that the chances of dying as a result of donating a kidney are about 1 in 4,000. For him this implies that to withhold a kidney from someone who would otherwise die means valuing one's own life at 4,000 times that of a stranger, a ratio Kravinsky considers "obscene."

What marks Kravinsky from the rest of us is that he takes the equal value of all human life as a guide to life, not just as a nice piece of rhetoric. He acknowledges that some people think he is crazy, and even his wife says she believes that he goes too far. One of her arguments against the kidney donation was that one of their children may one day need a kidney, and Zell could be the only compatible donor. Kravinsky's love for his children is, as far as I can tell, as strong as that of any normal parent. Such attachments are part of our nature, no doubt the product of our evolution as mammals who give birth to children, who for an unusually long time require our assistance in order to survive. But that does not, in Kravinsky's view, justify our placing a value on the lives of our children that is thousands of times greater than the value we place on the lives of the children of strangers. Asked if he would allow his child to die if it would enable a thousand children to live, Kravinsky said yes. Indeed, he has said he would permit his child to die even if this enabled only two other children to live. Nevertheless, to appease his wife, he recently went back into real estate, made some money and bought the family a larger home. But he still remains committed to giving away as much as possible, subject only to keeping his domestic life reasonably tranquil.

Buffett says he believes in giving his children "enough so they feel they could do anything, but not so much that they could do nothing." That means,

in his judgment, "a few hundred thousand" each. In absolute terms, that is far more than most Americans are able to leave their children and, by Kravinsky's standard, certainly too much. (Kravinsky says that the hard part is not giving away the first $45 million but the last $10,000, when you have to live so cheaply that you can't function in the business world.) But even if Buffett left each of his three children a million dollars each, he would still have given away more than 99.99 percent of his wealth. When someone does that much—especially in a society in which the norm is to leave most of your wealth to your children—it is better to praise them than to cavil about the extra few hundred thousand dollars they might have given.

Philosophers like Liam Murphy of New York University and my colleague Kwame Anthony Appiah at Princeton contend that our obligations are limited to carrying our fair share of the burden of relieving global poverty. They would have us calculate how much would be required to ensure that the world's poorest people have a chance at a decent life, and then divide this sum among the affluent. That would give us each an amount to donate, and having given that, we would have fulfilled our obligations to the poor.

What might that fair amount be? One way of calculating it would be to take as our target, at least for the next nine years, the Millennium Development Goals, set by the United Nations Millennium Summit in 2000. On that occasion, the largest gathering of world leaders in history jointly pledged to meet, by 2015, a list of goals that include:

Reducing by half the proportion of the world's people in extreme poverty (defined as living on less than the purchasing-power equivalent of one U.S. dollar per day).

Reducing by half the proportion of people who suffer from hunger.

Ensuring that children everywhere are able to take a full course of primary schooling.

Ending sex disparity in education.

Reducing by two-thirds the mortality rate among children under 5.

Reducing by three-quarters the rate of maternal mortality.

Halting and beginning to reverse the spread of H.I.V./AIDS and halting and beginning to reduce the incidence of malaria and other major diseases.

Reducing by half the proportion of people without sustainable access to safe drinking water.

Last year a United Nations task force, led by the Columbia University economist Jeffrey Sachs, estimated the annual cost of meeting these goals to be $121 billion in 2006, rising to $189 billion by 2015. When we take account of existing official development aid promises, the additional amount needed each year to meet the goals is only $48 billion for 2006 and $74 billion for 2015.

Now let's look at the incomes of America's rich and superrich, and ask how much they could reasonably give. The task is made easier by statistics recently provided by Thomas Piketty and Emmanuel Saez, economists at the Ecole Normale Superieure, Paris-Jourdan, and the University of California, Berkeley, respectively, based on U.S. tax data for 2004. Their figures are for pretax income, excluding income from capital gains, which for the very rich are nearly always substantial. For simplicity I have rounded the figures, generally downward. Note too that the numbers refer to "tax units," that is, in many cases, families rather than individuals.

Piketty and Saez's top bracket comprises 0.01 percent of U.S. taxpayers. There are 14,400 of them, earning an average of $12,775,000, with total earnings of $184 billion. The minimum annual income in this group is more than $5 million, so it seems reasonable to suppose that they could, without much hardship, give away a third of their annual income, an average of $4.3 million each, for a total of around $61 billion. That would still leave each of them with an annual income of at least $3.3 million.

Next comes the rest of the top 0.1 percent (excluding the category just described, as I shall do henceforth). There are 129,600 in this group, with an average income of just over $2 million and a minimum income of $1.1 million. If they were each to give a quarter of their income, that would yield about $65 billion, and leave each of them with at least $846,000 annually.

The top 0.5 percent consists of 575,900 taxpayers, with an average income of $623,000 and a minimum of $407,000. If they were to give one-fifth of their income, they would still have at least $325,000 each, and they would be giving a total of $72 billion.

Coming down to the level of those in the top 1 percent, we find 719,900 taxpayers with an average income of $327,000 and a minimum of $276,000. They could comfortably afford to give 15 percent of their income. That would yield $35 billion and leave them with at least $234,000.

Finally, the remainder of the nation's top 10 percent earn at least $92,000 annually, with an average of $132,000. There are nearly 13 million in this group. If they gave the traditional tithe—10 percent of their income, or an average of $13,200 each—this would yield about $171 billion and leave them a minimum of $83,000.

You could spend a long time debating whether the fractions of income I have suggested for donation constitute the fairest possible scheme. Perhaps the sliding scale should be steeper, so that the superrich give more and the merely comfortable give less. And it could be extended beyond the Top 10 percent of American families, so that everyone able to afford more than the basic necessities of life gives something, even if it is as little as 1 percent. Be that as it may, the remarkable thing about these calculations is that a scale of donations that is unlikely to impose significant hardship on anyone yields a total of $404 billion—from just 10 percent of American families.

Obviously, the rich in other nations should share the burden of relieving global poverty. The U.S. is responsible for 36 percent of the gross domestic product of all Organization for Economic Cooperation and Development nations. Arguably, because the U.S. is richer than all other major nations, and its wealth is more unevenly distributed than wealth in almost any other industrialized country, the rich in the U.S. should contribute more than 36 percent of total global donations. So somewhat more than 36 percent of all aid to relieve global poverty should come from the U.S. For simplicity, let's take half as a fair share for the U.S. On that basis, extending the scheme I have suggested worldwide would provide $808 billion annually for development aid. That's more than six times what the task force chaired by Sachs estimated would be required for 2006 in order to be on track to meet the Millennium Development Goals, and more than 16 times the shortfall between that sum and existing official development aid commitments.

If we are obliged to do no more than our fair share of eliminating global poverty, the burden will not be great. But is that really all we ought to do? Since we all agree that fairness is a good thing, and none of us like doing more because others don't pull their weight, the fair-share view is attractive. In the end, however, I think we should reject it. Let's return to the drowning child in the shallow pond. Imagine it is not 1 small child who has fallen in, but 50 children. We are among 50 adults, unrelated to the children, picnicking on the lawn around the pond. We can easily wade into the pond and rescue the children, and the fact that we would find it cold and unpleasant sloshing around in the knee-deep muddy water is no justification for failing to do so. The "fair share" theorists would say that if we each rescue one child, all the children will be saved, and so none of us have an obligation to save more than one. But what if half the picnickers prefer staying clean and dry to rescuing any children at all? Is it acceptable if the rest of us stop after we have rescued just one child, knowing that we have done our fair share, but that half the children will drown? We might justifiably be furious with those who are not doing their fair share, but our anger with them is not a reason for letting the children die. In terms of praise and blame, we are clearly right to condemn, in the strongest terms, those who do nothing. In contrast, we may withhold such condemnation from those who stop when they have done their fair share. Even so, they have let children drown when they could easily have saved them, and that is wrong.

Similarly, in the real world, it should be seen as a serious moral failure when those with ample income do not do their fair share toward relieving global poverty. It isn't so easy, however, to decide on the proper approach to take to those who limit their contribution to their fair share when they could easily do more and when, because others are not playing their part, a further donation would assist many in desperate need. In the privacy of our own judgment, we should believe that it is wrong not to do more. But whether we should actually criticize people who are doing their fair share, but no more than that, depends on the psychological impact that such criticism will have on them, and on others. This in turn may depend on social practices. If the majority are doing little or nothing, setting a standard higher than the fair-share level may seem so demanding that it discourages people who are willing to make an equitable contribution from doing even that. So it may be best to refrain from criticizing those who achieve the fair-share level. In moving our society's standards forward, we may have to progress one step at a time.

For more than 30 years, I've been reading, writing, and teaching about the ethical issue posed by the juxtaposition, on our planet, of great abundance and life-threatening poverty. Yet it was not until, in preparing this article, I calculated how much America's Top 10 percent of income earners actually make that I fully understood how easy it would be for the world's rich to eliminate, or virtually eliminate, global poverty. (It has actually become much easier over the last 30 years, as the rich have grown significantly richer.) I found the result astonishing. I double-checked the figures and asked a research assistant to check them as well. But they were right. Measured against our capacity, the Millennium Development Goals are indecently, shockingly modest. If we fail to achieve them—as on present indications we well might—we have no excuses. The target we should be setting for ourselves is not halving the proportion of people living in extreme poverty, and without enough to eat, but ensuring that no one, or virtually no one, needs to live in such degrading conditions. That is a worthy goal, and it is well within our reach.

Should Physicians Prepare for War?

INTRODUCTION

Joyce Bermel

Joyce Bermel was Managing Editor at the Hastings Center.

In October 1981, sixty physicians at Contra Costa Hospital in San Francisco refused a request from the Defense Department to pledge at least fifty civilian beds for the care of military casualties who would be airlifted from overseas in the event of a large-scale war. The Defense Department argued, in a letter sent to Contra Costa and other civilian hospitals across the country ... that the extra civilian beds were necessary because "a future large-scale conflict overseas could begin very rapidly and produce casualties at a higher rate than any other war in history." The plan has the support of the American Medical Association and the American Hospitals Association. In refusing to cooperate, the medical staff at Contra Costa responded that participation "would offer tacit approval for the planning of a nuclear war." The controversy raises ethical issues far beyond the question of whether to participate in this plan. What ought to be the moral role of the physician in preparations for a war that the Defense Department acknowledges will result in unprecedented injury, disease, and death? And should that role change depending on whether the conflict is conventional warfare, a limited nuclear conflict, or a total nuclear war?

The proliferation of nuclear weapons, the failure of arms limitation talks, deteriorating relationships between the United States and the Soviet Union, the growth in American and Soviet weapons arsenals—all these have raised anxiety levels about the possibilities of a nuclear war. The medical profession has responded strongly to what it perceives as this overwhelming threat to the public health. In December 1981, the American Medical Association passed a resolution calling on doctors to inform President Reagan and members of Congress about the medical consequences of nuclear war. The Harvard Medical School, among other medical schools, has introduced an elective course on the health effects of nuclear war. Physicians for Social Responsibility (PSR), an organization founded in 1961 to inform the public about the medical consequences of nuclear testing and nuclear war, holds seminars around the country for physicians....

But eager as physicians are to inform politicians and the public about the catastrophic medical consequences of a nuclear war, many would stop short of refusing to participate in a plan to care for the wounded of a future conflict whose scope we cannot predict....

THE OBLIGATION TO CARE FOR CASUALTIES

Jay C. Bisgard, M.D.

Bisgard was Acting Deputy Assistant Secretary for Medical Readiness in the Office of the Assistant Secretary of Defense for Health Affairs.

... Given the sophisticated technology of modern conventional weapons and our ability to move forces quickly, we could very well see a high casualty rate applied to a sizable force at risk. From the Revolutionary War through the Vietnam conflict this country has always recognized a moral obligation to provide medical care for those we send into battle.

From *Hastings Center Report* 12:2 (1982): 15–21.

Today the 15,000 beds in the military hospitals in the United States are no longer adequate to care for the numbers of servicemen and women who could easily become casualties in any large conventional conflict overseas. Recognizing our moral obligation to be able to care for these casualties should the need arise, we must then ask how to overcome a projected shortage of 50,000 acute care beds in the military health care system.

Obviously, we could build more military hospitals.... In 1980, it cost about $180,000 per bed to build civilian hospitals in the United States. To this expense must be added the cost of equipping and manning military hospitals. A somewhat less costly alternative would be to "mothball" these hospitals against the wartime need. Since they would have to be manned quickly, we would have to staff them from the reserves. We could not draft people fast enough. But if this were done and we did not need these hospitals for ten to fifteen years, we would be providing less than optimal care....

There is a third alternative—one that costs the taxpayer virtually nothing unless it is actually needed for casualty care and that also assures the best quality care. We have approximately one million acute care beds in the civilian private sector; 50,000 beds represents only five percent of this capability. Therefore, if civilian hospitals would agree to a totally voluntary partnership with the Department of Defense and the Veterans Administration to plan how we might most effectively cooperate, we could assure contingency care for military casualties, save the taxpayers an unnecessary burden, and make the most efficient use of the nation's health care manpower resources without increasing the size of the reserves or resorting to a draft. The logic of this approach readily won the enthusiastic support of key civil sector health care organizations, such as the American Medical Association and the American Hospital Association. It also won the blessing of the General Accounting Office, Congress, and other federal agencies, including the Department of Health and Human Services. Even more important, it was welcomed by civilian hospitals. Within a few months, over two hundred hospitals across the country had offered to provide more than 20,000 beds.

Then an organization called Physicians for Social Responsibility (or PSR) erroneously concluded that there was an association between this plan, called the Civilian-Military Contingency Hospital System (CMCHS), and nuclear war. PSR has, for many years, advocated nuclear arms limitation, and its members include many illustrious names in American medicine. I don't believe that any rational person, especially a physician, could oppose the concept of reducing the threat of nuclear war. That is not the issue. The ethical dilemma arose in October when PSR began to urge hospitals to refuse to participate in the CMCHS because participation would offer tacit approval to the concept of nuclear warfare.

Let us take a close look at the ethics of this situation. First, we must eliminate the "red herring" of nuclear war. The alleged association between CMCHS and planning for nuclear war was fabricated by PSR with absolutely no basis in fact. Even if there were some association, which there definitely is not, the medical ethical issue at hand is that of care for sick and injured young servicemen and women—not the morality of nuclear war.

I will not debate the morality of nuclear war. To me, the results of moral or immoral war are the same—sick and injured human beings. My sacred vow as a physician was to use my skills to save life and alleviate suffering. It would be a moral outrage for a physician to withhold care from any human being in need because of personal dislike of the victim's sex, color, religion, nationality, or mechanism of injury. If we don't hold that concept sacred, we could refuse care to the drunk driver or the person injured needlessly in an automobile accident because he didn't use his seat belt. Surely, no one would advocate closing emergency rooms to force people to be more responsible in their driving habits. This ethical principle is well founded in military medicine and is symbolized by the caduceus on the lapel of every army medical service officer. The caduceus is the wand of Hermes, the symbol of international neutrality. It is further symbolized by the presence of the Red Cross on the battlefield. Physicians are recognized under the Geneva Convention as neutral noncombatants. We care for anyone in need; ours, theirs, or the innocent civilian caught in a crossfire.

The single most important consideration, and what we must always remember, is our dedication to preserving human life. Regardless of our outside beliefs, we are always concerned primarily with humanity. The Oath of Geneva states that the physician: "Will not permit considerations of religion, nationality, race, party politics, or social standing to intervene between our duty and our patient." The daily prayer of Rabbi Moses ben Maimon, the twelfth-century physician better known as Maimonides, asks God to "preserve the strength of my body and soul so that they may be ever ready to help the rich and the poor, good and bad, enemy as well as friend. In the sufferer, let me only see the human being." These phrases and others like them from the Bible, the Torah, and other sacred and secular writings, are the only reminders that we need; they form the foundation for all medical ethics.

If the ethical question lies not in the actual delivery of care to patients, is it in the act of preparing to treat the casualties of war—any war? This is a more complex issue that has several facets.

One premise of the PSR is that preparation to receive casualties makes war more likely. History has shown that being ill prepared has never prevented a war from occurring: In fact, it has invited attack. When political leaders through the ages have weighed the prospect of going to war, do you think that the medical capabilities of the other side influenced their decisions? Would the United States have been able to stay neutral in World Wars I and II if we had not been prepared to deal with the resulting casualties? Did the medical readiness of Germany and Japan have any influence on our decisions to bomb Dresden, Hiroshima, and Nagasaki? Physicians have not made the decisions to make war. Those decisions have been made by politicians, who seldom have considered the consequences in suffering and loss of lives. In short, the issue is out of our hands, and the presence or absence of medical preparedness is not going to affect those decisions.

If we cannot prevent war by being medically unprepared, what then would be the result of unpreparedness? You know the answer—increased morbidity and mortality. We take for granted the need to prepare plans to deal with natural disasters and plane crashes, and we know it would be preposterous to suggest that destroying airport medical disaster plans would promote flying safety or prevent aircraft accidents. It would also be against medical ethics to take an action that could only result in increased human suffering. One of the cardinal principles of medical practice today has endured through twenty-two centuries. It was taught by Hippocrates: Above all, do no harm. Which then is the physician's ethical obligation: to prepare or not to prepare? The answer is obvious. Saving lives is the only constructive activity amid the mad destruction of war. The names of hospital ships are appropriate reminders: *The Comfort, The Solace, The Benevolence, The Sanctuary, The Haven.*

In thinking about the ethical issues, the following points are important to bear in mind:

1. The most important ethical consideration of any physician is a duty to the patient. Wartime activation of the CMCHS is consistent with this principle in that it will ensure the access to care for any casualty in need. To deny the availability of such care is unethical, irresponsible, and inconsistent with the precedents set through two hundred years of U.S. history.
2. The moral obligation to do no harm is also consistent with the planning aspect of the CMCHS. To oppose preparations to provide medical care to any in sudden need would clearly do harm if casualties were thereby deprived of necessary care. These preparations themselves lead to no harm, and preclude unnecessary expenditures of tax dollars to build, equip, and staff more military hospitals.

THE MORAL BASES OF CONTINGENCY PLANNING

James T. Johnson

Johnson teaches in the department of Religion at Rutgers University.

... To act morally is above all to exercise an intentionality of control over events in terms of moral perceptions that are regarded as important. If modern warfare has undermined our awareness of the obligation to noncombatants, then the problem before us is twofold: to confront that obligation again and to seek to incorporate it into our actions, including our contingency planning. The CMCHS proposal represents one sort of planning clearly in accord with the fundamental moral obligations owed noncombatants. The fact that the particular noncombatants to be treated in the reserved hospital beds would be wounded military personnel has nothing to do with the matter. The wounded soldier in a hospital bed is no less a noncombatant than the chronically ill civilian down the hall or the clergyman walking the street: No one of them, by lack of capacity or social role, is in direct support of the war.

No one thinks it odd to anticipate natural disasters by contingency planning, training of personnel in specific procedures, and stockpiling of useful supplies. To think of the possibility of war in a similar way should be equally acceptable. Wars, like natural disasters, often have a distinctly accidental character. Who could have ever predicted that the worst war Europe had known up to that time would be precipitated by the assassination of an Austrian nobleman in an obscure Balkan city? That nuclear war might begin accidentally has been a problem confronted in much military and civilian planning since the *Dr. Strangelove* era. Indeed, it is characteristic of war that at least one side is almost always caught by surprise, so that the result is similar to the effect of a natural disaster. The whole matter of whether military preparedness encourages or retards the incidence of war is much debated, but that most certainly is not at issue in the CMCHS proposal. Here the issue is one of providing medical aid to the wounded, and the analogy with contingency civilian disaster planning seems very persuasive to me.

Does it matter whether the war is just or not? Emphatically, no. The justice or injustice of a particular war has nothing at all to do with the obligation to care for the victims of that war, whether they be military or civilians, whether they be our own nationals or not. This element in the moral obligation to persons involved in war follows from the recognition that justice and injustice are almost always inextricably mixed on both sides of a conflict. ...

In the present connection, whatever particular critics of the CMCHS plan may think about the morality of war as such or about U.S. military preparedness in particular is not relevant to the question of contingency planning to care for wounded individuals. This is true whether we are thinking about the possibility of nuclear war or warfare using conventional weapons. In any conflict short of a general nuclear catastrophe, where there would be no hope at all of doing anything for most of the victims, the obligation to care for those who have been hurt would remain, and this implies being ready to provide such care. A limited war under contemporary conditions, even if nonnuclear, could easily cause an extremely high level of casualties over a short period of time, overwhelming purely military medical facilities. (The destructiveness of modern conventional weapons must not be forgotten in our preoccupation with nuclear weaponry.) What is different morally about limited war (nuclear or not) and general nuclear war, so far as treatment of the victims is concerned, is simply that in a limited war resources would remain to fulfill the obligation to care for victims.

THE PHYSICIAN AS MORAL LEADER

Thomas H. Murray

Thomas Murray is President of the Hastings Center.

The refusal of sixty physicians at Contra Costa County Hospital in Martinez, California, to set aside a proportion of their civilian hospital beds in the event of war has conjured up a terrifying image: doctors standing over the bleeding bodies of war victims, arms akimbo, jaws clenched, firmly shaking their heads "No!" An awful vision, but utterly beside the point.

It is one thing for a doctor to care for the casualties of war, quite another to participate in the planning for war. Imagine a community where an incompetent or corrupt political administration has contracted to build a profitable sewage system, knowing that it is insufficient and likely to lead to an increase in diseases of many kinds. Imagine further that you—a physician—have been asked to cooperate in designing a contingency plan to handle the epidemic that will almost certainly come. Should you comply? No, for two reasons. First, the existence of such a plan might make the project—the inadequate sewage system—more acceptable to the public, especially if you lend your public esteem as well as your expertise in health matters to the proposal. Second, you would be violating your principal loyalty, to the health and well-being of your patients and your community in general, to acquiesce in a policy you believe would be a danger to health. If the system is built over your objections, and the epidemic occurs, are you permitted to refuse care to the victims? No. Your commitment to health is overriding. In your social and political activities you may protest as loudly as you want, you may refuse all political help to those who threaten health. But when an individual needs your medical care, you are sworn to give it. The crucial difference is between caring for patients in need, which should always be done, and shaping the decisions that will alter the health of masses of people: that is, between *patients* and *public policies*.

———————

There are several reasons why physicians should take a special interest in the planning for large-scale war. First, the medical profession is not merely a collection of individuals who happen to be doctors; it is an institution vested by society with special prerogatives and vital responsibilities in protecting the public health.

Second, because physicians are experts in detecting the causes of ill health and recommending the means for recovery, communities rely on them to bring to public attention neglected sources of disease and to suggest ways to improve the health of their members.

Finally, physicians are in an especially powerful position to focus public attention on policies that may endanger health. Physicians and clergy remain the most trusted professions in the United States. Whatever disparity exists in public reactions to appeals for godliness, the clamor for "health" remains a political trump card—almost as powerful as "defense" or "national security."

The Pentagon already had promises of 20,000 out of the planned 50,000 beds when the Martinez doctors registered their protest. What did they hope to accomplish? Even if they could have prevented the CMCHS plan from succeeding, did they believe that would lessen the probability of nuclear war? I doubt they were that naive.... The Martinez physicians seized on the plan as an issue on which doctors—acting as doctors—could alert the public to what they saw as the intolerable horrors of nuclear war. The impact is twofold: The public sees that many physicians are opposed to the nation's defense strategy; and the broader question—defense planning around tactical nuclear weapons—is dramatically brought to public attention.

Defense planning has become more and more the province of specialists; in abstract ways, they have learned to think dispassionately about kilotons and megadeaths. But being dispassionate about intensely passionate things, like mass death and suffering, is itself a kind of blindness. Defense planning is too important to be left to defense specialists. If the Martinez doctors succeed in intensifying the public debate over tactical nuclear weapons and international disarmament, they are discharging their special moral obligation born of public trust and their loyalty to health, and they will have done all of us a service.

In any society, values will collide, and institutions charged with those values will conflict. The mistake is to think that that is unfortunate. Just the opposite is true. In a well-functioning (dare I say "healthy"?) society, institutions will battle, and the values in conflict will be displayed to the public who in the end should make the decision about how to weigh and balance them. Any institution, left unchecked, will run wild, and the Defense Department is no exception. As its fortunes continue to rise, it is essential that its hegemony be challenged by some other respected institution. What better candidate do we have than medicine?

If special moral obligations flow from physicians' dedication to health, the public esteem in which they are held, and their institutional strength, then doctors do have a special duty to intervene whenever the health of individuals or the public is threatened by any powerful institution, not merely the military. The AMA has clearly accepted this principle where national health insurance is concerned; they claim to oppose NHI on grounds that it threatens the quality of health care. Is the possibility of a "future large-scale war" any less of a threat to public health? Whether the danger comes from incompetent bureaucracies, corrupt politicians, or ignorance from any source, when health is threatened doctors should act.

| Dalai Lama | # The Ethic of Compassion |

The Dalai Lama is the spiritual leader of all Tibetan Buddhists. He is also a Nobel Laureate.

[A]ll the world's major religions stress the importance of cultivating love and compassion. In the Buddhist philosophical tradition, different levels of attainment are described. At a basic level, compassion (*nying je*) is understood mainly in terms of empathy—our ability to enter into and, to some extent, share others' suffering. But Buddhists—and perhaps others—believe that this can be developed to such a degree that not only does our compassion arise without any effort, but it is unconditional, undifferentiated, and universal in scope. A feeling of intimacy toward all other sentient beings, including of course those who would harm us, is generated, which is likened in the literature to the love a mother has for her only child.

But this sense of equanimity toward all others is not seen as an end in itself. Rather, it is seen as the springboard to a love still greater. Because our capacity for empathy is innate, and because the ability to reason is also an innate faculty, compassion shares the characteristics of consciousness itself. The potential we have to develop it is therefore stable and continuous. It is not a resource which can be used up—as water is used up when we boil it. And though it can be described in terms of activity, it is not like a physical activity which we train for, like jumping, where once we reach a certain height we can go no further. On the contrary, when we enhance our sensitivity toward others' suffering through deliberately opening ourselves up to it, it is believed that we can gradually extend out compassion to the point where the individual feels so moved by even the subtlest suffering of others that they come to have an overwhelming sense of responsibility toward those others. This causes the one who is compassionate to dedicate themselves entirely to helping others overcome both their suffering and the causes of their suffering. In Tibetan, this ultimate level of attainment is called *nying je chenmo*, literally "great compassion."

Now I am not suggesting that each individual must attain these advanced states of spiritual development in order to lead an ethically wholesome life. I have described *nying je chenmo* not because it is a precondition of ethical conduct but rather because I believe that pushing the logic of compassion to the highest level can act as a powerful inspiration.

From Dalai Lama, "The Ethic of Compassion," *Ethics for the New Millennium* (New York: Riverhead Books, 1999). pp. 123–127. Reprinted with permission of Riverhead Books.

If we can just keep the aspiration to develop *nying je chenmo*, or great compassion, as an ideal, it will naturally have a significant impact on our outlook. Based on the simple recognition that, just as I do, so do all others desire to be happy and not to suffer, it will serve as a constant reminder against selfishness and partiality. It will remind us that there is little to be gained from being kind and generous because we hope to win something in return. It will remind us that actions motivated by the desire to create a good name for ourselves are still selfish, however much they may appear to be acts of kindness. It will also remind us that there is nothing exceptional about acts of charity toward those we already feel close to. And it will help us to recognize that the bias we naturally feel toward our families and friends is actually a highly unreliable thing on which to base ethical conduct. If we reserve ethical conduct for those whom we feel close to, the danger is that we will neglect our responsibilities toward those outside this circle.

Why is this? So long as the individuals in question continue to meet our expectations, all is well. But should they fail to do so, someone we consider a dear friend one day can become our sworn enemy the next. As we saw earlier, we have a tendency to react badly to all who threaten fulfillment of our cherished desires, though they may be our closest relations. For this reason, compassion and mutual respect offer a much more solid basis for our relations with others. This is also true of partnerships. If our love for someone is based largely on attraction, whether it be their looks or some other superficial characteristic, our feelings for that person are liable, over time, to evaporate. When they lose the quality we found alluring, or when we find ourselves no longer satisfied by it, the situation can change completely, this despite their being the same person. This is why relationships based purely on attraction are almost always unstable. On the other hand, when we begin to perfect our compassion, neither the other's appearance nor their behavior affects our underlying attitude.

Consider, too, that habitually our feelings toward others depend very much on their circumstances. Most people, when they see someone who is handicapped, feel sympathetic toward that person. But then when they see others who are wealthier, or better educated, or better placed socially, they immediately feel envious and competitive toward them. Our negative feelings prevent us from seeing the sameness of ourselves and all others. We forget that just like us, whether fortunate or unfortunate, distant or near, they desire to be happy and not to suffer.

The struggle is thus to overcome these feelings of partiality. Certainly, developing genuine compassion for our loved ones is the obvious and appropriate place to start. The impact our actions have on our close ones will generally be much greater than on others, and therefore our responsibilities toward them are greater. Yet we need to recognize that, ultimately, there are no grounds for discriminating in their favor. In this sense, we are all in the same position as a doctor confronted by ten patients suffering the same serious illness. They are each equally deserving of treatment. The reader should not suppose that what is being advocated here is a state of detached indifference, however. The further essential challenge, as we begin to extend our compassion toward all others, is to maintain the same level of intimacy as we feel toward those closest to us. In other words, what is being suggested is that we need to strive for even-handedness in our approach toward all others, a level ground into which we can plant the seed of *nying je chenmo*, of great love and compassion.

If we can begin to relate to others on the basis of such equanimity, our compassion will not depend on the fact that so and so is my husband, my wife, my relative, my friend. Rather, a feeling of closeness toward all others can be developed based on the simple recognition that, just like myself, all wish to be happy and to avoid suffering. In other words, we will start to relate to others on the basis of their sentient nature. Again, we can think of this in terms of an ideal, one which it is immensely difficult to attain. But, for myself, I find it one which is profoundly inspiring and helpful.

Let us now consider the role of compassionate love and kind-heartedness in our daily lives. Does the ideal of developing it to the point where it is unconditional mean that we must abandon our own interests entirely? Not at all. In fact, it is the best way of serving them—indeed, it could even be said to constitute the wisest course for fulfilling self-interest. For if it is correct that those qualities such as love, patience, tolerance, and forgiveness are what happiness consists in, and if it is also correct that *nying je*, or compassion, as I have defined it, is both the source and the fruit of these qualities, then the more we are compassionate, the more we provide for our own happiness. Thus, any idea that concern for others, though a noble quality, is a matter for our private lives only, is simply shortsighted. Compassion belongs to every sphere of activity, including, of course, the workplace.

| Amartya Sen | # The Economics of Poverty |

Amartya Sen is based at Trinity College, Cambridge, and won the Nobel Prize for his work on welfare economics and the causes of famine.

PHIL PONCE: Professor, when one thinks of the field in which Nobel winners in economics often work, it's oftentimes something like money, markets, the capital, and yet you seem to be more interested in how events affect people. Why is that?

AMARTYA SEN: Well, economics is a very broad subject, and the money and capital and the operation of the stock market, these are matters of interest to economists, as well as matters of—the way the lives of people go, and I happen to be concerned primarily with the latter and in particular with the down side of the latter, namely the people who seem to have a worse time than others—the poor, the unemployed, the hungry, the starving, and so on. So this has been something I've been concerned with for a long time.

PHIL PONCE: Professor, one of the specific issues that the Nobel citation talks about is your interest in understanding famine, and it says that your best-known work has to do with understanding that famine isn't just caused by a shortage of food but by other things like unemployment, drop in income. Why the specific interest in famine?

AMARTYA SEN: Well, there are many reasons, of course, because famines are unfortunately still a real phenomenon in the world. And lots of people die from it, systematically, in different parts of the world, but in my case the personal interest arose also from the fact that I happened to observe from inside a major famine of the 20th century—the Bengal famine, which occurred in India in 1943—in fact, the last famine that occurred in India, in which close to 3 million people died. And I was a nine-and-a-half-year-old boy at that time. It had very impressionable—certainly very striking memories I have from that period, and the people who starved, they came from a particular group—in this care rural laborers—but that's a characteristic I later found of many famines, indeed, sometimes food supply may fall, sometimes not. Food supply fell in the Irish famine of the 1840's. It did not fall in the Bengal famine of '43, and it was at a peak height in the Bangladesh famine of '74. But a section of the community lose their ability to command food by not having jobs—not having enough wage and then they cannot buy food and that's what happened—not a really large proportion usually—but it can still kill millions of people.

From the *NewsHour with Jim Lehrer* transcript. McNeil NewsHour transcript, Oct. 15, 1998. Reprinted with permission.

PHIL PONCE: According to a report that I read, you personally, when you were a boy, personally fed people who were starving refugees

AMARTYA SEN: Well, my parents—you know—since we [were] relatively prosperous, still not rich, lower middle class family—still not rich—a lower middle class family—but quite committed on social matters and come from an academic background. My father was a professor; my grandfather was a professor—we were quite involved in that so I was committed to give anyone who asked for food, a tin, a cigarette tin of rice. But since there are many people asking, I was also told that that's what I could give to anyone. I obviously felt very moral in trying to give as much as I could. And it's a very harrowing experience. Obviously, this didn't do anything to solve the famine, but it's a question that got even more strongly engrained in my mind because of the small participation that I happened to do in this context.

PHIL PONCE: Professor, what does winning this prize mean to you personally?

AMARTYA SEN: Well, I was particularly pleased that the prize was given with the citation about social—about welfare economics and social choice because these are areas in which very interesting, very important work has occurred, and I'm very proud of what others have done and I've learned from them. I think I was led on to that subject by Kenneth Arrow—a great figure in modern economics. And I had very good students and very good colleagues working in this area. So when they mentioned this area, I took that to be a recognition of the importance of that area, and even though I was lucky enough to get the prize. I did think that it was a much wider recognition and in the way it tried to be more appropriate and fair, if the prize was widely shared. But many people have contributed in this area, and this gives me an opportunity to think about them and to the extent to which my own work has been influenced by and dependent on the work that others have done.

PHIL PONCE: Professor, there is this world economic crisis, a lot of turmoil in the markets, and it's

adding a lot of new people to poverty, millions of people. How much do economists know? How much can economists explain what is happening now?

AMARTYA SEN: I think economists—if they set their mind to it—can explain a lot. You know, I think it's really a question of concentrating, the questions—the inquiries—appropriately. We know the nature of the success that some of these economies—for example, the East Asian economies, which are in turmoil now, had. We know the basis of their success, which included using the market mechanism efficiently but open-mindedly, non-dogmatically, letting the government do its job in expanding educational base, doing land reform, helping with the health care. It's a partnership of the public and market arrangement. Now they did not work out pretty well. The financial regularities and there were a lot of lacunae and some of the economies there like Indonesia it didn't work out, what would happen if the economy were to go into a slump, namely, how to deal with those who've been thrown out of the system and given to the wolves, and the kind of social safety net that you need didn't exist. There's a lot to learn from the experience of these countries, both positively as to what they have achieved, as well as negatively as to what to avoid. So I think economists—if they analyze these issues—will have various things to offer. And, indeed, there are a lot of economists who are interested in it. And I would not accept that economists really don't have very much to say on this question.

PHIL PONCE: Professor, do you think people have lost faith in economists because of the current world financial crisis?

AMARTYA SEN: Well, you know, I think the—economics is not a kind of business whereby you could eliminate these problems. You know, it's—odd thing is that earlier on in late 19th century and early 20th century—one of the subjects people studied was business cycle. From time to time you have slump, and at times you have boom. The job of the economist was meant to be to understand why they are caused, rather than to eliminate them. Now

I think it would be nice to eliminate them and, indeed, it is possible certainly to reduce them and eliminate it to a great extent. But the fact that sometimes these things would happen does not indicate that these times of economics is worth nothing. What it does indicate is that we have to pay much more attention than often happens to some of these problems, and since I've spent most of my life on the side of economics, I'm very sympathetic to the view that the economy should spend more time in dealing with the predicament of people who are thrown into turmoil when things go wrong, and also the fact that while there are successes of market economies, there are also needs for supplementation in other fields in terms of public intervention, in terms of political participation, and so forth. So it's a question of taking an adequately broad view of economics, along with its neighboring discipline, and it's also a question of paying more attention to those who are most likely to lose when a crisis hits.

PHIL PONCE: Professor Sen, thank you very much. And, again, congratulations.

AMARTYA SEN: Thank you very much.

Rachel Smolkin | # Off the Sidelines

Rachel Smolkin writes for the American Journalism Review.

A convoy of trucks delivers food to a crowd of starving, frantic people in a Somali village. A famine-relief coordinator turns to you—the reporter—and a photographer. "I'm afraid there'll be a riot if we don't get these trucks unloaded quickly. Could you two please put down your notebook and camera, and help us? It might save a life." What do you do?

In November 2004, G. D. Gearino, a columnist for the News & Observer in Raleigh, presented this scenario during a journalism ethics symposium at Washington and Lee University in Lexington, Virginia. A group of professionals, myself included, met with journalism professor Edward Wasserman and his students to debate real and hypothetical ethics quandaries.

The students—and as I recall, they were unanimous—looked surprised at such an easy question. Of course they would help. Why wouldn't they, if they could save lives? One enterprising future reporter even proposed telling her cameraman to shoot footage of her handing out food to the needy.

I was appalled. I informed the students that a journalist's job is to bear witness to history, not participate in it. By pitching in to help, the journalists would compromise their objectivity and insert themselves as actors in a situation they should be chronicling as detached observers.

But then Katrina slashed the Gulf Coast, and anarchy gripped New Orleans. Riveting news coverage revealed countless acts of kindness by journalists who handed out food and water to victims, pulled them aboard rescue boats or out of flooded cars, offered them rides to safer ground, lent them cell phones to reassure frantic family members and flagged down doctors and emergency workers to treat them.

These actions humanized reporters and helped give them credibility to challenge the lies and befuddlement of government officials. With a few exceptions, the journalists looked like some of the only responsible adults around.

From *American Journalism Review* 27, No. 6, Dec. 2005/Jan. 2006.

I began to wonder. Was I wrong, and were the students right?

Does pitching in to help compromise an idealistic notion of "objectivity" but bolster credibility with the public? Is it simply the right thing to do, regardless of the professional ramifications? And is one of our profession's most basic tenets—that journalists shouldn't intervene—needlessly strident, making reporters seem inhuman?

"I listened with growing horror as NPR attacked the officials trying to aid New Orleans victims, taking an outraged moral high ground," James Lange of Pompano Beach, Florida, wrote to National Public Radio. "We all can see that communications is the main problem: Why did NPR not use its satellite phones and other such gear to help the police communicate? Why did NPR not send in food and water to the convention center? Please, please don't tell me, that you refused to help because it's not our job."

In an online column, NPR Ombudsman Jeffrey Dvorkin shared Lange's comments and those of Mort Cohen of Milwaukee, who called to ask, "Do you ever feel that journalism is an inadequate response to the tragedies you report on?"

"I think this is an issue worth exploring," Dvorkin wrote. "Some in the news business might undoubtedly express astonishment that listeners could be naive about how journalism sees its obligations. But listeners aren't naive at all."

The NPR listeners have a point. But if it's OK—even advisable—for journalists to give out food, water or rides after a devastating hurricane, then where's the line between permissible help and unacceptable activism? How do you decide when to shed your observer status and get involved? And do you disclose your participation to readers and viewers, or will that be seen as showboating and only fuel public contempt?

Among journalists and ethicists I interviewed for this story no one took an absolutist stance that journalists should never help under any circumstances. Some seemed deeply conflicted about when to intervene. Others were perfectly comfortable rendering any assistance possible after the hurricane noting the suffering was so vast that their small contributions hardly altered the outcome of the story.

One reporter who struggled with the question of intervention was the Washington Post's Anne Hull, who is known for her poignant word portraits and wrote one of the most heartrending stories about Katrina's devastation. . . .

In a telephone conversation and in a subsequent e-mail, Hull both articulated the case against intervention and agonized over that detached role. "I think the human suffering that journalists confronted on Hurricane Katrina was a new experience for many journalists who've not covered wars or foreign countries," she says. "I believe journalists should have an ethical framework to guide them, and in the case of covering catastrophe or hardship, we must try to remember that we are journalists trying to cover a story. That is our role in the world, and if we perform it well, it is an absolutely unique service: helping the world understand something as it happens."

But Hull also felt torn: [a woman named] Adrienne Picou had asked if Hull could take her to Baton Rouge. Hull didn't have a car, but a colleague did. "How can you explain that to somebody, why you can't take them to a shelter?" Hull asks. She told Picou she didn't know when she was going or even where she was sleeping that night.

In Hull's work, intervention would certainly alter the outcome. "The sorts of stories I do are often different than the broader survey stories that involve a [mixture] of official and human reaction. I usually focus on an individual caught up in a situation, and my role is to document how they figure their way out of it and the feelings that accompany them as they do it."

After she interviewed the Picous, she stepped away and called her editor. She wanted to tell him about the story, but she also was troubled. "I'm struggling here," she told him. "Buck me up; give me a talk." And her editor, Bill Hamilton, reminded her, "You're not an aid worker. You're not a rescue worker."

Throughout her stay in New Orleans, Hull gave away water, PowerBars, and wet-naps and let countless people use her cell phone. But she feels that during the course of the reporting "when your notebook is still open and you're still gathering facts, you can't give someone a ride . . . . In terms of taking someone out of New Orleans, rescuing them and taking them to a shelter, that seems to go beyond the line of duty for a journalist."

After Hull had said good-bye to the Picous, she was sitting under the interstate typing her story on her laptop when a medic came over to ask directions. "I don't know," she told him. "But see that woman and child over there? She will know, and she needs your help." The medics gave the Picous their first ride in a journey that would wind from a shelter in Northern Louisiana to a cattle ranch in Texas to a new job in Smyrna, Georgia. Once you've completed your reporting, "if you can be of any help in giving assistance, by all means, do it," Hull says.

Other journalists did participate in rescue missions. "I tried to help and when I wasn't needed I took pictures," freelance photographer Marko Georgiev, who was in New Orleans on assignment for the New York Times, wrote in a piece for the National Press Photographers Association. Georgiev described helping SWAT officers pull trapped Lower 9th Ward residents into a boat as floodwaters rose. "I tried to stay unbiased and to shoot and cover the story the best way possible. I also tried to help as many people as I could."

But Georgiev was haunted by the despair he had witnessed. "We came to take our trophies and left," the New Jersey-based photographer concluded in his piece. "They have to stay. No place to go. This story will become their lives. Or is it the other way around?"

For local journalists, the suffering was inescapable, as were the logistical hurdles. "We didn't have any time to talk about the niceties of ethics; it was just trying to put the damn paper out,"

says Brian Thevenot, a reporter for New Orleans' Times-Picayune who wrote about his experience for AJR (see "Apocalypse in New Orleans," October/November).

But he did have one very brief ethics exchange with a colleague. The day after the storm, Thevenot and photographer Ted Jackson went to the hardest-hit area, the edge of the Lower 9th Ward and St. Bernard Parish. Jackson turned to Thevenot and said he had an ethical question for him: "We may need to rescue people."

The decision to intervene is often made in a matter of seconds, without the luxury of forethought. But ethicists say there is some framework for guiding such choices.

"If journalists becoming a part of the story or an actor in unfolding events gets to be the norm, then the journalistic role is compromised on several levels," says Paul McMasters, the First Amendment ombudsman at the Freedom Forum's First Amendment Center. "One is purely practical. If you are handing out food or engaging in a rescue or that sort of thing, you're not observing: you're not taking notes; you're not seeing the larger picture. Secondly, after a while no matter what your motives, it's going to be interpreted by readers and viewers as grandstanding."

McMasters says that among the factors to consider in deciding whether to intervene is "how natural or instinctive the journalist's impulse is and whether or not there is potential for immediate harm or injury without the journalist's involvement. It is very important that the journalist quickly returns to their professional role as soon as the moment passes." But, he adds, "that's not a very good answer. In the world of journalistic ethics, there are seldom good answers or pat answers."

Michael Josephson, founder and president of the Joseph & Edna Josephson Institute of Ethics in Los Angeles, says the journalist's primary obligation is to act as a human being. "Obviously the more serious it is, if people are in dire straits, the more obligated someone is regardless of who they are to render assistance. The other factor is whether there are others there who can render assistance," he says, noting that simply calling someone over might be sufficient.

"I also think we shouldn't be too finicky about the notion that rendering some simple assistance will compromise objectivity," Josephson adds. "Offering someone a drink of water would be something you'd do if they were in your office." To do otherwise, to withhold simple help in the name of professionalism, "will ultimately discredit the profession in most people's eyes."

Susan E. Tifft, a public policy and journalism professor at Duke University, says standards of detachment help journalists strive for impartiality, but the word "objectivity" may not be the most helpful way to describe the journalist's role. Her students are always shocked to learn that "objectivity" refers to a process of inquiry that requires journalists to publish what they actually find—not what they might prefer to find—and doesn't mean journalists have no opinions of their own.

She says helping during a disaster or life-threatening situation doesn't threaten impartiality, and doing so is absolutely appropriate if it rises organically from the scene.

When NPR Ombudsman Dvorkin posed the helping-out conundrum to newsroom staff, "everybody's first response was; 'No. We don't get involved.' And their second response was, 'Well, may be sometimes we have to,'" he says. "I think you can get involved as a human being when your own conscience tells you to."

If you do help, should you write about it? Should you show it?

Chris Merrifield, a promotions producer for CBS affiliate WWL-TV in New Orleans, was carrying gear for a news crew when he saw a driver who had plunged deep into the floodwaters on Interstate 10. Merrifield rushed into waist-high waters to help the man escape from his car. The dramatic footage captured by the cameraman aired

repeatedly on "Inside Edition," MSNBC, CNN and the BBC.

Among journalists and ethicists I talked to, the question of when to reveal aid produced the largest split, with some urging full disclosure and others arguing that would constitute self-aggrandizement and generally should be avoided.

The ethics institute's Josephson recommends that reporters who render aid "be very direct about that in the reporting" as a matter of transparency and discuss their actions with editors. "You do it, and let someone else decide whether it kills the story. You don't let somebody drown while you're conducting an internal debate."

But NPR's Dvorkin feels broadcasting acts of kindness "ends up looking, sounding self-serving and manipulative" and shouldn't be part of the story unless it changes the outcome. "If the reporter has affected the outcome of the story by his or her direct involvement, the reporter has an obligation to reveal that."

Bob Woodruff, an anchor and correspondent for ABC News who arrived in New Orleans the Wednesday after the storm hit, calls the detached-observer ideal "a very ivory tower notion that's not practiced in the field."

"We all helped out," he says, Like many others, Woodruff handed out food and water if people asked for it and assisted in other small ways. But he warns: "Never do it and roll on it with your cameras. By definition, if you need to do it, then your cameraman should need to do it as well.... The real ones don't shoot it."

John Roberts, the chief White House correspondent for CBS News, also shied away from broadcasting scenes of him and his colleagues dispensing aid. His crew did shoot one instance in which they threw a line from their boat to a man floating on an inflated bed and towed him to safety. "Out here, every boat is a rescue boat, even ours," Roberts reported on September 5.

While he used that incident to illustrate the devastation, other acts of kindness went unreported. On the eastbound ramp of 1–10, he and his crew found a woman in her 70s, horribly dirty, suffering and unable to walk. They took her half a mile up the street so she could seek shade under a broken fire truck. "We weren't into grandstanding," he says. "We didn't want to go on the air and crow about what we were doing."

But some other news organizations "did sort of flaunt what they were doing. It led to some heated e-mail about why didn't we use our helicopters to drop food," Roberts says, noting he and his colleagues didn't receive supplies themselves until five days after the hurricane. "I got e-mail asking, 'How could you be so callous and so cruel as to not help?' The fact is that we were helping; we just weren't telling people."

In Roberts' view, "Our job is to report the news. If we help people along the way, that's out of our own sense of compassion." Asked where the line is between being an impartial observer and helping, he replies, "If you're talking about reporting on a war and being a detached observer, I think that's a line that you can't cross. If it comes to human suffering, I think you can."

––––––––––

For me, the images on television and the newspaper work by journalists such as Ainsworth, Hull and Gold made the agony so much more real than when we had pondered *ethics* in Wasserman's class that fall morning.

Here's what I wish I had told his students:

Follow your conscience. Your humanity—your ability to empathize with pain and suffering, and your desire to prevent it—does not conflict with your professional standards. Those impulses make you a better journalist, more attuned to the stories you are tasked with telling. If you change an outcome through responsible and necessary intervention because there's no one else around to help, so be it. Tell your bosses, and when it's essential to a story, tell your readers and viewers, too.

Remember, though, that your primary—and unique—role as a journalist is to bear witness. If you decide to act, do so quickly, then get out of the way. Leave the rescue work to first responders and relief workers whenever possible.

The journalists covering Katrina showed compassion by offering water, rides, and rescue, but their most enduring service was to expose the suffering of citizens trapped in hellish shelters and on sweltering interstates, and to document the inexcusable government response.

Without journalists fulfilling that essential role, the resources to help on a larger scale might never have arrived.

New England Journal of Medicine

A National Health Program for the United States: A Physicians' Proposal

Our health care system is failing. It denies access to many in need and is expensive, inefficient, and increasingly bureaucratic. The pressures of cost control, competition, and profit threaten the traditional

From the *New England Journal of Medicine* 320:102–108 (January 12), 1989.

tenets of medical practice. For patients, the misfortune of illness is often amplified by the fear of financial ruin. For physicians, the gratifications of healing often give way to anger and alienation. Patchwork reforms succeed only in exchanging old problems for new ones. It is time to change fundamentally the trajectory of American medicine—to develop a comprehensive national health program for the United States.

———————

As physicians, we constantly confront the irrationality of the present health care system. In private practice, we waste countless hours on billing and bureaucracy. For uninsured patients, we avoid procedures, consultations, and costly medications. Diagnosis-related groups (DRGs) have placed us between administrators demanding early discharge and elderly patients with no one to help at home—all the while glancing over our shoulders at the peer-review organization. In HMOs we walk a tightrope between thrift and penuriousness, too often under the pressure of surveillance by bureaucrats more concerned with the bottom line than with other measures of achievement. In public health work we are frustrated in the face of plenty; the world's richest health care system is unable to ensure such basic services as prenatal care and immunizations.

Despite our disparate perspectives, we are united by dismay at the current state of medicine and by the conviction that an alternative must be developed. We hope to spark debate, to transform disaffection with what exists into a vision of what might be. To this end, we submit for public review, comment, and revision a working plan for a rational and humane health care system—a national health program.

We envisage a program that would be federally mandated and ultimately funded by the federal government but administered largely at the state and local level. The proposed system would eliminate financial barriers to care, minimize economic incentives for both excessive and insufficient care discourage administrative interference and expense, improve the distribution of health facilities, and control costs by curtailing bureaucracy and

fostering health planning. Our plan borrows many features from the Canadian national health program and adapts them to the unique circumstances of the United States. We suggest that, as in Canada's provinces, the national health program be tested initially in statewide demonstration projects. Thus, our proposal addresses both the structure of the national health program and the transition process necessary to implement the program in a single state. In each section below, we present a key feature of the proposal, followed by the rationale for our approach. Areas such as long-term care; public, occupational, environmental, and mental health; and medical education need much more development and will be addressed in detail in future proposals.

COVERAGE

Everyone would be included in a single public plan covering all medically necessary services, including acute, rehabilitative, long-term, and home care; mental health services; dental services; occupational health care; prescription drugs and medical supplies; and preventive and public health measures. Boards of experts and community representatives would determine which services were unnecessary or ineffective, and these would be excluded from coverage. As in Canada, alternative insurance coverage for services included under the national health program would be eliminated, as would patient copayments and deductibles.

Universal coverage would solve the gravest problem in health care by eliminating financial barriers to care. A single comprehensive program is necessary both to ensure equal access to care and to minimize the complexity and expense of billing and administration. The public administration of insurance funds would save tens of billions of dollars each year. The more than 1500 private health insurers in the United States now consume about 8 percent of revenues for overhead, whereas both the Medicare program and the Canadian national health program have overhead costs of only 2 to 3 percent. The complexity of our current insurance system, with its multiplicity of payers, forces U.S. hospitals to spend more than twice as much as Canadian hospitals on billing and administration and requires U.S. physicians to spend about 10 percent of their gross incomes on excess billing costs.[1] Eliminating insurance programs that duplicated the national health program coverage, though politically thorny, would clearly be within the prerogative of the Congress.[2] Failure to do so would require the continuation of the costly bureaucracy necessary to administer and deal with such programs.

Copayments and deductibles endanger the health of poor people who are sick,[3] decrease the use of vital inpatient medical services as much as they discourage the use of unnecessary ones,[4] discourage preventive care,[5] and are unwieldy and expensive to administer. Canada has few such charges, yet health costs are lower than in the United States and have risen slowly.[6,7] In the United States, in contrast, increasing copayments and deductibles have failed to slow the escalation of costs.

Instead of the confused and often unjust dictates of insurance companies, a greatly expanded program of technology assessment and cost-effectiveness evaluation would guide decisions about covered services, as well as about the allocation of funds for capital spending, drug formularies, and other issues.

PAYMENT FOR HOSPITAL SERVICES

Each hospital would receive an annual lump-sum payment to cover all operating expenses—a "global" budget. The amount of this payment would be negotiated with the state national health program payment board and would be based on past expenditures, previous financial and clinical performance, projected changes in levels of services, wages and other costs, and proposed new and innovative programs. Hospitals would not bill for services covered by the national health program. No part of the operating budget could be used for hospital expansion, profit, marketing, or major capital purchases or leases. These expenditures would also come from the national health program fund, but monies for them would be appropriated separately.

Global prospective budgeting would simplify hospital administration and virtually eliminate billing, thus freeing up substantial resources for increased clinical care. Before the nationwide implementation of the national health program, hospitals in the states with demonstration programs could bill out-of-state patients on a simple per diem basis. Prohibiting the use of operating funds for capital purchases or profit would eliminate the main financial incentive for both excessive intervention (under fee-for-service payment) and skimping on care (under DRG-type prospective-payment systems), since neither inflating revenues nor limiting care could result in gain for the institution. The separate appropriation of funds explicitly designated for capital expenditures would facilitate rational health planning. In Canada, this method of hospital payment has been successful in containing costs, minimizing bureaucracy, improving the distribution of health resources, and maintaining the quality of care.[6–9] It shifts the focus of hospital administration away from the bottom line and toward the provision of optimal clinical services.

PAYMENT FOR PHYSICIANS' SERVICES, AMBULATORY CARE, AND MEDICAL HOME CARE

To minimize the disruption of existing patterns of care, the national health program would include three payment options for physicians and other practitioners: fee-for-service payment, salaried positions in institutions receiving global budgets, and salaried positions within group practices or HMOs receiving per capita (capitation) payments.

Fee-for-Service Payment

The state national health program payment board and a representative of the fee-for-service practitioners (perhaps the state medical society) would negotiate a simplified, binding fee schedule. Physicians would submit bills to the national health program on a simple form or by computer and would receive extra payment for any bill not paid within 30 days.

Payments to physicians would cover only the services provided by physicians and their support staff and would exclude reimbursement for costly capital purchases of equipment for the office, such as CT scanners. Physicians who accepted payment from the national health program could bill patients directly only for uncovered services (as is done for cosmetic surgery in Canada).

Global Budgets

Institutions such as hospitals, health centers, group practices, clinics serving migrant workers, and medical home care agencies could elect to receive a global budget for the delivery of outpatient, home care, and physicians' services, as well as for preventive health care and patient-education programs. The negotiation process and the regulations covering capital expenditures and profits would be similar to those for inpatient hospital services. Physicians employed in such institutions would be salaried.

Capitation

HMOs, group practices, and other institutions could elect to be paid fees on a per capita basis to cover all outpatient care, physicians' services, and medical home care. The regulations covering the use of such payments for capital expenditures and for profits would be similar to those that would apply to hospitals. The capitation fee would not cover inpatient services (except care provided by a physician), which would be included in hospitals' global budgets. Selective enrollment policies would be prohibited, and patients would be permitted to leave an HMO or other health plan with appropriate notice. Physicians working in HMOs would be salaried, and financial incentives to physicians based on the HMO's financial performance would be prohibited.

The diversity of existing practice arrangements, each with strong proponents, necessitates a pluralistic approach. Under all three proposed options, capital purchases and profits would be uncoupled from payments to physicians and other operating costs—a feature that is essential for minimizing entrepreneurial incentives, containing costs, and facilitating health planning.

Under the fee-for-service option, physicians' office overhead would be reduced by the simplification of billing. The improved coverage would encourage preventive care.[10] In Canada, fee-for-service practice with negotiated fee schedules and mandatory assignment (acceptance of the assigned fee as total payment) has proved to be compatible with cost containment, adequate incomes for physicians, and a high level of access to and satisfaction with care on the part of patients.[6,7] The Canadian provinces have responded to the inflationary potential of fee-for-service payment in various ways: by limiting the number of physicians, by monitoring physicians for outlandish practice patterns, by setting overall limits on a province's spending for physicians' services (thus relying on the profession to police itself), and even by capping the total reimbursement of individual physicians. These regulatory options have been made possible (and have not required an extensive bureaucracy) because all payment comes from a single source. Similar measures might be needed in the United States, although our penchant for bureaucratic hypertrophy might require a concomitant cap on spending for the regulatory apparatus. For example, spending for program administration and reimbursement bureaucracy might be restricted to 3 percent of total costs.

Global budgets for institutional providers would eliminate billing, while providing a predictable and stable source of income. Such funding could also encourage the development of preventive health programs in the community, such as education programs on the acquired immunodeficiency syndrome (AIDS), whose costs are difficult to attribute and bill to individual patients.

Continuity of care would no longer be disrupted when patients' insurance coverage changed as a result of retirement or a job change. Incentives for providers receiving capitation payments to skimp on care would be minimized, since unused operating funds could not be devoted to expansion or profit.

PAYMENT FOR LONG-TERM CARE

A separate proposal for long-term care is under development, guided by three principles. First, access to care should be based on need rather than on age or ability to pay. Second, social and community-based services should be expanded and integrated with institutional care. Third, bureaucracy and entrepreneurial incentives should be minimized through global budgeting with separate funding for capital expenses.

ALLOCATION OF CAPITAL FUNDS, HEALTH PLANNING, AND RETURN ON EQUITY

Funds for the construction or renovation of health facilities and for purchases of major equipment would be appropriated from the national health program budget. The funds would be distributed by state and regional health-planning boards composed of both experts and community representatives. Capital projects funded by private donations would require approval by the health-planning board if they entailed an increase in future operating expenses.

The national health program would pay owners of for-profit hospitals, nursing homes, and clinics a reasonable fixed rate of return on existing equity. Since virtually all new capital investment would be funded by the national health program, it would not be included in calculating the return on equity.

Current capital spending greatly affects future operating costs, as well as the distribution of resources. Effective health planning requires that funds go to high-quality, efficient programs in the areas of greatest need. Under the existing reimbursement system, which combines operating and capital payments, prosperous hospitals can expand and modernize, whereas impoverished ones cannot, regardless of the health needs of the population they serve or the quality of services they provide. The national health program would replace this implicit mechanism for distributing capital with an explicit one, which would facilitate (though not guarantee) allocation on the basis of need and quality. Insulating these crucial decisions from distortion by narrow interests would require the rigorous evaluation of the technology and assessment of needs, as well as the active involvement of providers and patients.

For-profit providers would be compensated for existing investments. Since new for-profit investment would be barred, the proprietary sector would gradually shrink.

PUBLIC, ENVIRONMENTAL, AND OCCUPATIONAL HEALTH SERVICES

Existing arrangements for public, occupational, and environmental health services would be retained in the short term. Funding for preventive health care would be expanded. Additional proposals dealing with these issues are planned.

PRESCRIPTION DRUGS AND SUPPLIES

An expert panel would establish and regularly update a list of all necessary and useful drugs and outpatient equipment. Suppliers would bill the national health program directly for the wholesale cost, plus a reasonable dispensing fee, of any item in the list that was prescribed by a licensed practitioner. The substitution of generic for proprietary drugs would be encouraged.

FUNDING

The national health program would disburse virtually all payments for health services. The total expenditure would be set at the same proportion of the gross national product as health costs represented in the year preceding the establishment of the national health program. Funds for the national health program could be raised through a variety of mechanisms. In the long run, funding based on an income tax or other progressive tax might be the fairest and most efficient solution, since tax-based funding is the least cumbersome and least expensive mechanism for collecting money. During the transition period in states with demonstration programs, the following structure would mimic existing funding patterns and minimize economic disruption.

Medicare and Medicaid

All current federal funds allocated to Medicare and Medicaid would be paid to the national health program. The contribution of each program would be based on the previous year's expenditures, adjusted for inflation. Using Medicare and Medicaid funds in this manner would require a federal waiver.

State and Local Funds

All current state and local funds for health care expenditures, adjusted for inflation, would be paid to the national health program.

Employer Contributions

A tax earmarked for the national health program would be levied on all employers. The tax rate would be set so that total collections equaled the previous year's statewide total of employers' expenditures for health benefits, adjusted for inflation. Employers obligated by preexisting contracts to provide health benefits could credit the cost of those benefits toward their national health program tax liability.

Private Insurance Revenues

Private health insurance plans duplicating the coverage of the national health program would be phased out over three years. During this transition period, all revenues from such plans would be turned over to the national health program, after the deduction of a reasonable fee to cover the costs of collecting premiums.

General Tax Revenues

Additional taxes, equivalent to the amount now spent by individual citizens for insurance premiums and out-of-pocket health costs, would be levied.

It would be critical for all funds for health care to flow through the national health program. Such single-source payment (monopsony) has been the cornerstone of cost containment and health planning in Canada. The mechanism of raising funds for the national health program would be a matter of tax policy, largely separate from the organization of the health care system itself. As in Canada, federal funding could attenuate inequalities among the states in financial and medical resources.

The transitional proposal for demonstration programs in selected states illustrates how monopsony payment could be established with limited disruption of existing patterns of health care funding. The employers' contribution would represent a decrease in costs for most firms that now provide health insurance and an increase for those that do not currently pay for benefits. Some provision might be needed to cushion the impact of the change on financially strapped small businesses. Decreased individual spending for health care would offset the additional tax burden on individual citizens. Private health insurance, with its attendant inefficiency and waste, would be largely eliminated. A program of job placement and retraining for insurance and hospital-billing employees would be an important component of the program during the transition period.

DISCUSSION

The Patient's View

The national health program would establish a right to comprehensive health care. As in Canada, each person would receive a national health program card entitling him or her to all necessary medical care without copayments or deductibles. The card could be used with any fee-for-service practitioner and at any institution receiving a global budget. HMO members could receive nonemergency care only through their HMO, although they could readily transfer to the non-HMO option.

Thus, patients would have a free choice of providers, and the financial threat of illness would be eliminated. Taxes would increase by an amount equivalent to the current total of medical expenditures by individuals. Conversely, individuals' aggregate payments for medical care would decrease by the same amount.

The Practitioner's View

Physicians would have a free choice of practice settings. Treatment would no longer be constrained by the patient's insurance status or by bureaucratic dicta. On the basis of the Canadian experience, we anticipate that the average physician's income would change little, although differences among specialties might be attenuated.

Fee-for-service practitioners would be paid for the care of anyone not enrolled in an HMO. The entrepreneurial aspects of medicine—with the attendant problems as well as the possibilities—would be limited. Physicians could concentrate on medicine; every patient would be fully insured, but physicians could increase their incomes only by providing more care. Billing would involve imprinting the patient's national health program card on a charge slip, checking a box to indicate the complexity of the procedure or service, and sending the slip (or a computer-record) to the physician-payment board. This simplification of billing would save thousands of dollars per practitioner in annual office expenses.[1]

Bureaucratic interference in clinical decision making would sharply diminish. Costs would be contained by controlling overall spending and by limiting entrepreneurial incentives, thus obviating the need for the kind of detailed administrative oversight that is characteristic of the DRG program and similar schemes. Indeed, there is much less administrative intrusion in day-to-day clinical practice in Canada (and most other countries with national health programs) than in the United States.[11,12]

Salaried practitioners would be insulated from the financial consequences of clinical decisions. Because savings on patient care could no longer be used for institutional expansion or profits, the pressure to skimp on care would be minimized.

The Effect on Other Health Workers

Nurses and other health care personnel would enjoy a more humane and efficient clinical milieu. The burdens of paperwork associated with billing would be lightened. The jobs of many administrative and insurance employees would be eliminated, necessitating a major effort at job placement and retraining. We advocate that many of these displaced workers be deployed in expanded programs of public health, health promotion and education, and home care and as support personnel to free nurses for clinical tasks.

The Effect on Hospitals

Hospitals' revenues would become stable and predictable. More than half the current hospital bureaucracy would be eliminated, and the remaining administrators could focus on facilitating clinical care and planning for future health needs.

The capital budget requests of hospitals would be weighed against other priorities for health care investment. Hospitals would neither grow because they were profitable nor fail because of unpaid bills—although regional health planning would undoubtedly mandate that some expand and others close or be put to other uses. Responsiveness to community needs, the quality of care, efficiency, and innovation would replace financial performance as the bottom line. The elimination of new for-profit investment would lead to a gradual conversion of proprietary hospitals to not-for-profit status.

The Effect on the Insurance Industry

The insurance industry would feel the greatest impact of this proposal. Private insurance firms would have no role in health care financing, since the public administration of insurance is more efficient[1,13] and single-source payment is the key to both equal access and cost control. Indeed, most of the extra funds needed to finance the expansion of care would come from eliminating the overhead and profits of insurance companies and abolishing the billing apparatus necessary to apportion costs among the various plans.

The Effect on Corporate America

Firms that now provide generous employee health benefits would realize savings, because their contribution to the national health program would be less than their current health insurance costs. For example, health care expenditures by Chrysler, currently $5,300 annually per employee,[14] would fall to about $1,600, a figure calculated by dividing the total current U.S. spending on health by private employers by the total number of full-time-equivalent, nongovernment employees. Since most firms that compete in international markets would save money, the competitiveness of U.S. products would be enhanced. However, costs would increase for companies that do not now provide health benefits. The average health care costs for employers would be unchanged in the short run. In the long run, overall health costs would rise less steeply because of improved health planning and greater efficiency. The funding mechanism ultimately adopted would determine the corporate share of those costs.

Health Benefits and Financial Costs

There is ample evidence that removing financial barriers to health care encourages timely care and improves health. After Canada instituted a national health program, visits to physicians increased among patients with serious symptoms.[15] Mortality rates, which were higher than U.S. rates through the 1950s and early 1960s, fell below those in the United States.[16] In the Rand Health Insurance Experiment, free care reduced the annual risk of dying by 10 percent among the 25 percent of U.S. adults at highest risk.[3] Conversely, cuts in California's Medicaid program led to worsening health.[17] Strong circumstantial evidence links the poor U.S. record on infant mortality with inadequate access to prenatal care.[18]

We expect that the national health program would cause little change in the total costs of ambulatory and hospital care; savings on administration and billing (about 10 percent of current health spending) would approximately offset the costs of expanded services.[19,20] Indeed, current low hospital-occupancy rates suggest that the additional care could be provided at low cost. Similarly, many physicians with empty appointment slots could take on more patients without added office, secretarial, or other overhead costs. However, the expansion of long-term care (under any system) would increase costs. The experience in Canada suggests that the increased

demand for acute care would be modest after an initial surge[21,22] and that improvements in health planning[8] and cost containment made possible by single-source payment[9] would slow the escalation of health care costs. Vigilance would be needed to stem the regrowth of costly and intrusive bureaucracy.

Unsolved Problems

Our brief proposal leaves many vexing problems unsolved. Much detailed planning would be needed to ease dislocations during the implementation of the program. Neither the encouragement of preventive health care and healthful life styles nor improvements in occupational and environmental health would automatically follow from the institution of a national health program. Similarly, racial, linguistic, geographic, and other nonfinancial barriers to access would persist. The need for quality assurance and continuing medical education would be no less pressing. High medical school tuitions that skew specialty choices and discourage low-income applicants, the underrepresentation of minorities, the role of foreign medical graduates, and other issues in medical education would remain. Some patients would still seek inappropriate emergency care, and some physicians might still succumb to the temptation to increase their incomes by encouraging unneeded services. The malpractice crisis would be only partially ameliorated. The 25 percent of judgments now awarded for future medical costs would be eliminated, but our society would remain litigious, and legal and insurance fees would still consume about two thirds of all malpractice premiums.[23] Establishing research priorities and directing funds to high-quality investigations would be no easier. Much further work in the area of long-term care would be required. Regional health planning and capital allocation would make possible, but not ensure, the fair and efficient allocation of resources. Finally, although insurance coverage for patients with AIDS would be ensured, the need for expanded prevention and research and for new models of care would continue. Although all these problems would not be solved, a national health program would establish a framework for addressing them.

Political Prospects

Our proposal will undoubtedly encounter powerful opponents in the health insurance industry, firms that do not now provide health benefits to employees, and medical entrepreneurs. However, we also have allies. Most physicians (56 percent) support some form of national health program, although 74 percent are convinced that most other doctors oppose it.[24] Many of the largest corporations would enjoy substantial savings if our proposal were adopted. Most significant, the great majority of Americans support a universal, comprehensive, publicly administered national health program, as shown by virtually every opinion poll in the past 30 years.[25,26] Indeed, a 1986 referendum question in Massachusetts calling for a national health program was approved two to one, carrying all 39 cities and 307 of the 312 towns in the commonwealth.[27] If mobilized, such public conviction could override even the most strenuous private opposition.

NOTES

1. Himmelstein DU, Woolhandler S. Cost without benefit: administrative waste in U.S. health care. N Engl J Med 1986; 314:441–5.

2. Advisory opinion regarding House of Representatives Bill 85-H-7748 (No. 86-269-MP, R.I. Sup. Ct. Jan 5, 1987).

3. Brook RH, Ware JE Jr, Rogers WH, et al. Does free care improve adults' health? Results from a randomized controlled trial. N Engl J Med 1983; 309:1426–34.

4. Siu AL, Sonnenberg FA, Manning WG, et al. Inappropriate use of hospitals in a randomized trial of health insurance plans. N Engl J Med 1986; 315:1259–66.

5. Brian EW, Gibbens SF. California's Medi-Cal copayment experiment. Med Care 1974; 12:Suppl 12: 1–303.

6. Iglehart JK. Canada's health care system. N Engl J Med 1986; 315.202–8, 778–84.

7. *Idem.* Canada's health care system: addressing the problem of physician supply. N Engl J Med 1986; 315.1623–8.

8. Detsky AS, Stacey SR, Bombardier C. The effectiveness of a regulatory strategy in containing hospital costs: The Ontario experience. 1967–1981. N Engl J Med 1983; 309:151–9.

9. Evans RG. Health care in Canada: patterns of funding and regulation. In: McLachlan G, Maynard A, eds. The public/private mix for health: the relevance and effects of change. London: Nuffield Provincial Hospitals Trust, 1982:369–424.

10. Woolhandler S, Himmelstein DU. Reverse targeting of preventive care due to lack of health insurance. JAMA 1988; 259:2872–4.

11. Reinhardt UE. Resource allocation in health care: the allocation of lifestyles to providers. Milbank Q 1987; 65:153–76.

12. Hoffenberg R. Clinical freedom. London: Nuffield Provincial Hospitals Trust, 1987.

13. Home JM, Beck RG. Further evidence on public versus private administration of health insurance. J Public Health Policy 1981; 2-274–90.

14. Cronin C. Next Congress to grapple with U.S. health policy, competitiveness abroad. Bus Health 1986; 4(2):55.

15. Enterline PE, Salter V, McDonald AD, McDonald JC. The distribution of medical services before and after "free" medical care—the Quebec experience. N Engl J Med 1973; 289:1174–8.

16. Roemer R, Roemer MI. Health manpower policy under national health insurance: the Canadian experience. Hyattsville, Md.: Health Resources Administration, 1977. (DHEW publication no. (HRA) 77–37.)

17. Lurie N, Ward NB, Shapiro MF, et al. Termination of Medi-Cal benefits: a follow-up study one year later. N Engl J Med 1986; 314:1266–8.

18. Institute of Medicine. Preventing Low birthweight. Washington, D.C.: National Academy Press, 1985.

19. Newhouse JP, Manning WG, Morris CN, et al. Some interim results from a controlled trial of cost sharing in health insurance. N Engl J Med 1981; 305:1501–7.

20. Himmelstein DU, Woolhandler S. Free care: a quantitative analysis of the health and cost effects of a national health program. Int J Health Serv 1988; 18:393–9.

21. LcClair M. The Canadian health care system. In: Andreopoulos S, ed. National health insurance: can we learn from Canada? New York: John Wiley, 1975:11–92.

22. Evans RG. Beyond the medical marketplace: expenditure, utilization and pricing of insured health care in Canada. In: Andreopoulos S, ed. National health insurance: can we learn from Canada? New York: John Wiley, 1975:129–78.

23. Danzon PM. Medical malpractice: theory, evidence, and public policy. Cambridge, Mass.: Harvard University Press, 1985.

24. Colombotas J, Kirchncr C. Physicians and social change. New York. Oxford University Press, 1986.

25. Navarro V. Where is the popular mandate? N Engl J Med 1982; 307-1516-8.

26. Pokorny G. Report card on health care. Health Manage Q 1988; 10(1): 3–7.

27. Danielson DA, Mazer A. Results of the Massachusetts Referendum on a national health program. J Public Health Policy 1987; 8:28–35.

This proposal was drafted by a 30-member Writing Committee, then reviewed and endorsed by 412 other physicians representing virtually every state and medical specialty. A full list of the endorsers is available on request. The members of the Writing Committee were as follows: David U. Himmelstein, M.D., Cambridge, Mass. (cochair); Steffie Woolhandler, M.D., M.P.H., Cambridge, Mass. (cochair); Thomas S. Bodenheimer, M.D., San Francisco; David H. Bor, M.D., Cambridge, Mass.; Christine K. Cassel, M.D., Chicago; Mardge Cohen, M.D., Chicago; David A. Danielson, M.P.H., Newton, Mass.; Alan Drabkin, M.D., Cambridge, Mass.; Paul Epstein, M.D., Brookline, Mass.; Kenneth Frisof, M.D., Cleveland; Howard Frurnkin, M.D., M.P.H., Philadelphia; Martha S. Gerrity, M.D., Chapel Hill, N.C.; Jerome D. Gorman, M.D., Richmond, Va.; Michelle D. Holmes, M.D., Cambridge, Mass.; Henry S. Kahn, M.D., Atlanta; Robert S. Lawrence, M.D., Cambridge, Mass.; Joanne Lukomnik, M.D., Bronx, N.Y.; Arthur Mazer, M.P.H., Cambridge, Mass.; Alan Meyers, M.D., Boston; Pauick Murray, M.D., Cleveland; Vicente Navarro, M.D., Dr. P.H., Baltimore; Peter Orris, M.D., Chicago; David C. Parish, M.D., M.P.H., Macon, Ga.; Richard J. Pels, M.D., Boston; Leonard S. Rodberg, Ph.D., New York City; Jeffrey Scavron, M.D., Springfield, Mass.; Gordon Schiff, M.D., Chicago; Isaac M. Taylor, M.D., Boston; Howard Waitzkin, M.D., Ph.D., Anaheim, Calif.; Paul H. Wise, M.D., M.P.H., Boston; and William Zinn, M.D., Cambridge, Mass.

Kenneth J. Arrow | # Social Responsibility and Economic Efficiency

Kenneth J. Arrow is Professor Emeritus at Stanford University and one of the most prominent economic theorists of the twentieth century.

Let us first consider the case against social responsibility: the assumption that the firms should aim simply to maximize their profits. One strand of that argument is empirical rather than ethical or normative. It simply states that firms *will* maximize their profits. The impulse to gain, it is argued, is very strong and the incentives for selfish behavior are so great that any kind of control is likely to be utterly ineffectual. This argument has some force but is by no means conclusive. Any mechanism for enforcing or urging social responsibility upon firms must of course reckon with a profit motive, with a desire to evade whatever response of controls is imposed. But it does not mean that we cannot expect any degree of responsibility at all.

One finds a rather different argument, frequently stated by some economists. It will probably strike the noneconomist as rather strange, at least at first hearing. The assertion is that firms *ought* to maximize profits; not merely do they like to do so but there is practically a social obligation to do so. Let me briefly sketch the argument:

Firms buy the goods and services they need for production. What they buy they pay for and therefore they are paying for whatever costs they impose

From Kenneth J. Arrow, "Social Responsibility and Economic Efficiency." *Public Policy* 21 (Summer 1973). Reprinted by permission.

upon others. What they receive in payment by selling their goods, they receive because the purchaser considers it worthwhile. This is a world of voluntary contracts: nobody *has* to buy the goods. If he chooses to buy it, it must be that he is getting a benefit measured by the price he pays. Hence, it is argued, profit really represents the net contribution that the firm makes to the social good, and the profits should therefore be made as large as possible. When firms compete with each other, in selling their goods or in buying labor or other services, they may have to lower their selling prices in order to get more of the market for themselves or raise their wages; in either case the benefits which the firm is deriving are in some respects shared with the population at large. The forces of competition prevent the firms from engrossing too large a share of the social benefit. Now, as far as it goes this argument is sound. The problem is that it may not go far enough.

Under the proper assumptions profit maximization is indeed efficient in the sense that it can achieve as high a level of satisfaction as possible for any one consumer without reducing the levels of satisfaction of other consumers or using more resources than society is endowed with. But the limits of the argument must be stressed. I want to mention two well-known points in passing without making them the principal focus of discussion. First of all, the argument assumes that the forces of competition are sufficiently vigorous. But there is no social justification for profit maximization by monopolies. This is an important and well-known qualification. Second, the distribution of income that results from unrestrained profit maximization is very unequal. The competitive maximizing economy is indeed efficient—this shows up in high average incomes—but the high average is accompanied by widespread poverty on the one hand and vast riches, at least for a few, on the other. To many of us this is a very undesirable consequence.

Profit maximization has yet another effect on society. It tends to point away from the expression of altruistic motives. Altruistic motives are motives whose gratification is just as legitimate as selfish motives, and the expression of those motives is something we probably wish to encourage. A profit-maximizing, self-centered form of economic

behavior does not provide any room for the expression of such motives.

————

[Even] if the three problems above were set aside ... there are [still] two categories of effects where the arguments for profit maximization break down: The first is illustrated by pollution or congestion. Here it is no longer true (and this is the key to these issues) that the firm in fact does pay for the harm it imposes on others. When it takes a person's time and uses it at work, the firm is paying for this, and therefore the transaction can be regarded as a beneficial exchange from the point of view of both parties. We have no similar mechanism by which the pollution which a firm imposes upon its neighborhood is paid for. Therefore the firm will have a tendency to pollute more than is desirable. That is, the benefit to it or to its customers from the expanded activity is really not as great, or may not be as great, as the cost it is imposing upon the neighborhood. But since it does not pay that cost, there is no profit incentive to refrain.

The same argument applies to traffic congestion when no charge is made for the addition of cars or trucks on the highway. It makes everybody less comfortable. It delays others and increases the probability of accidents; in short, it imposes a cost upon a large number of members of the society, a cost which is not paid for by the imposer of the cost, at least not in full. The person congesting is also congested, but the costs he is imposing on others are much greater than those he suffers himself. Therefore there will be a tendency to overutilize those goods for which no price is charged, particularly scarce highway space.

There are many other examples of this kind, but these two will serve to illustrate the point in question: some effort must be made to alter the profit-maximizing behavior of firms in those cases where it is imposing costs on others which are not easily compensated through an appropriate set of prices.

The second category of effects where profit maximization is not socially desirable is that in which there are quality effects about which the firm knows more than the buyer. Let me illustrate by considering the sale of a used car. (Similar considerations apply to the sale of new cars.) A used car has potential defects and typically the seller knows more about the defects than the buyer. The buyer is not in a position to distinguish among used cars, and therefore he will be willing to pay the same amount for two used cars of differing quality because he cannot tell the difference between them. As a result, there is an inefficiency in the sale of used cars. If somehow or other the cars were distinguished as to their quality, there would be some buyers who would prefer a cheaper car with more defects because they intend to use it very little or they only want it for a short period, while others will want a better car at a higher price. In fact, however, the two kinds of car are sold indiscriminately to the two groups of buyers at the same price, so that we can argue that there is a distinct loss of consumer satisfaction imposed by the failure to convey information that is available to the seller. The buyers are not necessarily being cheated. They may be, but the problem of inefficiency would remain if they weren't. One can imagine a situation where, from past experience, buyers of used cars are aware that cars that look alike may turn out to be quite different. Without knowing whether a particular car is good or bad, they do know that there are good and bad cars, and of course their willingness to pay for the cars is influenced accordingly. The main loser from a monetary viewpoint may not be the customer, but rather the seller of the good car. The buyer will pay a price which is only appropriate to a lottery that gives him a good car or a bad car with varying probabilities, and therefore the seller of the good car gets less than the value of the car. The seller of the bad car is, of course, the beneficiary. Clearly then, if one could arrange to transmit the truth from the sellers to the buyers, the efficiency of the market would be greatly improved. The used-car illustration is an example of a very general phenomenon. . . .

Defenders of unrestricted profit maximization usually assume that the consumer is well informed or at least that he becomes so by his own experience, in repeated purchases, or by information about what has happened to other people like him. This argument is empirically shaky: even the ability of individuals to analyze the effects of their own past purchases may be limited, particularly with respect to complicated mechanisms. But there are two further defects. The risks, including death, may be so great that even one misleading experience is bad enough, and the opportunity to learn from repeated trials is not of much use. Also, in a world where the products are continually changing, the possibility of learning from experience is greatly reduced. Automobile companies are continually introducing new models which at least purport to differ from what they were in the past, though doubtless the change is more external than internal. New drugs are being introduced all the time; the fact that one has had bad experiences with one drug may provide very little information about the next one.

Thus there are two types of situation in which the simple rule of maximizing profits is socially inefficient: the case in which costs are not paid for, as in pollution, and the case in which the seller has considerably more knowledge about his product than the buyer, particularly with regard to safety. In these situations it is clearly desirable to have some idea of social responsibility, that is, to experience an obligation, whether ethical, moral, or legal. Now we cannot expect such an obligation to be created out of thin air. To be meaningful, any obligation of this kind, any feeling or rule of behavior has to be embodied in some definite social institution. I use that term broadly: a legal code is a social institution in a sense. Exhortation to do good must be made specific in some external form, a steady reminder and perhaps enforcer of desirable values. Part of the need is simply for factual information as a guide to individual behavior. A firm may need to be told what is right and what is wrong when in fact it is polluting, or which safety requirements are reasonable and which are too extreme or too costly to be worth consideration. Institutionalization of the social responsibility of firms also serves another very important function. It provides some assurance to any one firm that the firms with which it is in competition will also accept the same responsibility. If a firm has some code imposed from the outside, there is some expectation that other firms will obey it too and therefore there is some assurance that it need not fear any excessive cost to its good behavior.

Let me turn to some alternative kinds of institutions that can be considered as embodying the possible social responsibilities of firms. First, we have legal regulation, as in the case of pollution where laws are passed about the kind of burning that may take place, and about setting maximum standards for emissions. A second category is that of taxes. Economists, with good reason, like to preach taxation as opposed to regulation. The movement to tax polluting emissions is getting under way and there is a fairly widely backed proposal in Congress to tax sulfur dioxide emissions from industrial smokestacks. That is an example of the second kind of institutionalization of social responsibility. The responsibility is made very clear: the violator pays for violations.

A third very old remedy or institution is that of legal liability—the liability of the civil law. One can be sued for damages. Such cases apparently go back to the Middle Ages. Regulation also extends back very far. There was an ordinance in London about the year 1300 prohibiting the burning of coal, because of the smoke nuisance.

The fourth class of institutions is represented by ethical codes. Restraint is achieved not by appealing to each individual's conscience but rather by having some generally understood definition of appropriate behavior.... [w]hen there is a wide difference in knowledge between the two sides of the market, recognized ethical codes can be a great contribution to economic efficiency. Actually we do have examples of this in our everyday lives, but in very limited areas. The case of medical ethics is the most striking. By its very nature there is a very large difference in knowledge between the buyer and the seller. One is, in fact, buying precisely the service of someone with much more knowledge than you have. To make this relationship a viable one, ethical codes have grown up over the centuries, both to avoid the possibility of exploitation by the physician and to assure the buyer of medical services that he is not being exploited. I am not suggesting that these are universally obeyed, but there is a strong presumption that the doctor is going to perform to a large extent with your welfare in mind. Unnecessary medical expenses or other abuses are perceived as violations of ethics. There is a powerful ethical background against which we make this judgment. Behavior that we would regard

as highly reprehensible in a physician is judged less harshly when found among businessmen. The medical profession is typical of professions in general. All professions involve a situation in which knowledge is unequal on two sides of the market by the very definition of the profession and therefore there have grown up ethical principles that afford some protection to the client. Notice there is a mutual benefit in this. The fact is that if you had sufficient distrust of a doctor's services, you wouldn't buy them. Therefore the physician wants an ethical code to act as assurance to the buyer, and he certainly wants his competitors to obey this same code, partly because any violation may put him at a disadvantage but more especially because the violation will reflect on him, since the buyer of the medical services may not be able to distinguish one doctor from another. A close look reveals that a great deal of economic life depends for its viability on a certain limited degree of ethical commitment. Purely selfish behavior of individuals is really incompatible with any kind of settled economic life. There is almost invariably some element of trust and confidence. Much business is done on the basis of verbal assurance. It would be too elaborate to try to get written commitments on every possible point. Every contract depends for its observance on a mass of unspecified conditions which suggest that the performance will be carried out in good faith without insistence on sticking literally to its wording. To put the matter in its simplest form, in almost every economic transaction, in any exchange of goods for money, somebody gives up his valuable asset before he gets the other's; either the goods are given before the money or the money is given before the goods. Moreover there is a general confidence that there won't be any violation of the implicit agreement. Another example in daily life of this kind of ethics is the observance of queue discipline. People line up; there are people who try to break in ahead of you, but there is an ethic which holds that this is bad. It is clearly an ethic which is in everybody's interest to preserve; one waits at the end of the line this time, and one is protected against somebody's coming in ahead of him.

In the context of product safety, efficiency would be greatly enhanced by accepted ethical rules.

Sometimes it may be enough to have an ethical compulsion to reveal all the information available and let the buyer choose. This is not necessarily always the best. It can be argued that under some circumstances setting minimum safety standards and simply not putting out products that do not meet them would be desirable and should be felt by the businessman to be an obligation.

CASES

CASE 7.1
Pigs on Parade: Power, Perks, and Impunity
Arianna Huffington

Surveying the state of corporate America from his number two perch on *Forbes* magazine's list of the 400 Richest People in America, Warren Buffett, the avuncular sage of American capitalism, opened fire with both barrels. At a Berkshire Hathaway shareholder meeting in May 2002, Buffett told his audience, among other things, that Wall Street loves a crook, investment bankers have contempt for investors, stock-option-engorged CEOs are shameless, and American business is teeming with fraud.

Buffett's blast was a remarkably honest assessment—as rare in the world of high finance as it was necessary. The litany of sins committed by the high priests of profit is a study in venality, deceit, theft, treachery, pride, and most of all, greed, greed, and more greed.

And who do you think is paying the price for all of this greed and corruption? The corporate criminals have made out like bandits while the American public has been robbed. Buffett nailed it when he wrote in a recent letter to his shareholders that he

is "disgusted by the situation, so common in the last few years, in which shareholders have suffered billions in losses while the CEOs, promoters, and other higher-ups who fathered these disasters have walked away with extraordinary wealth. To their shame, these business leaders view shareholders as patsies, not partners."

You know things have really gotten out of hand when the most scathing attacks on corporate greed and Wall Street malfeasance are being launched not by knee-jerk business haters and anti-globalization Jeremiahs but by the country's leading investment guru.

FAMILY PIG: JOHN RIGAS

Rigas, Kozlowski, Waksal, Winnick, Lay, Skilling, Fastow, Ebbers, Sullivan. This rogues' gallery of corporate scoundrels has turned our country's state-of-the-art free enterprise system into a smorgasbord of corruption.

From Arianna Huffington, *Pigs at the Trough.*

The stories of these pigs at the trough are as rich and varied as the personalities of their protagonists.

Take John Rigas, the small-town hero who turned into a big time crook. You couldn't make up a story as incredible as the all-too-true tale of Rigas' rise and fall—or a character as unforgettable.

Rigas is straight out of a Frank Capra movie: a self-made man who turned a $300 investment in a local cable franchise into a $7 billion communications empire; a Greek boy who remained true to his roots, refusing to move his company's headquarters out of the little Pennsylvania town where it got its start; a benevolent billionaire who treated his employees like family, put his home phone number on Adelphia cable bills, offered jobs and loans to those down on their luck, helped finance a medical center in his hometown, and every now and then collected tickets and made popcorn at the local movie theater he has owned for nearly half a century.

He clearly considers himself a very moral man. He steadfastly refused, for instance, to carry X-rated programming on Adelphia, even though it cost the company $10 to $20 million in annual revenue. That's what makes the revelations about Rigas's sleazy business practices all the more shocking. His morality is reminiscent of the 1980s televangelist Jim Bakker who, like Rigas, read from the "Good Book" on Sunday and cooked the books on Monday through Friday. Where Rigas is headed, Bakker has been, having served five years in prison for fleecing his flock out of $158 million. Of course, where both men are *ultimately* headed is up to a higher court than any here on Earth. But I have my suspicions that both are more likely to feel the poke of a pitchfork than try on angels' wings.

The problem is that Rigas, like so many CEOs in the headlines today, began to see himself and the multi-billion-dollar company he led as one and the same, adopting the outlook of France's Louis XIV, who notoriously proclaimed: *L'état c'est moi*—"I am the state."

Now he has been forced to resign from the company he founded and is facing charges that he and his sons engaged in conspiracy and securities, wire, and bank fraud. When Rigas and his two sons realized that they could no longer postpone the inevitable,

they offered to present themselves discreetly to the authorities to be charged. However, the government declined. It needed pictures of CEOs in handcuffs to try to convince the public that there was just one set of laws for both the haves and the have-nots.

The Rigases chose to spend the day before their arrest in an all-American car-switching extravaganza. After renting a Chevy Lumina in New York City (surely a downgrade from what they were used to) and attempting to drive from Manhattan to their home in Coudersport, Pennsylvania, John and Michael Rigas noticed that they were being tailed. They pulled a quick U-ey and returned to the Big Apple. While this bizarre scene was being played out, Timothy Rigas was jumping on a train bound for Greenwich, Connecticut. At his destination he impulsively splurged on a 1997 Audi from a local dealer and drove back to New York. From overhead, they must have looked like rats in a maze.

The Rigas clan was reunited back in New York and rose early the next morning. When five armed postal policemen knocked on the door of their apartment, John and Michael Rigas were dressed in blue suits and white shirts, and ready to go. Tim Rigas, in blue blazer and khaki pants, was heard to joke: "We live on the farm. We get up early."

Anyway, the Rigases had enough spare change on hand to cover their $30 million bail and were back home in plenty of time for a nice family dinner. You know what they say: the family that eats together, cheats together.

Maybe at least one of them will end up in a cell next to Dennis Kozlowski, whose story could be subtitled "Still Life in Prison Stripes."

BOSS PIG: DENNIS KOZLOWSKI

When Kozlowski was arrested in May 2002 on charges of evading $1 million in sales taxes on $13.2 million worth of paintings he bought—wryly described by the *New York Times* as "second-tier work by big-name artists"—the question on everyone's lips was: why?

Why would a man who earned $125 million in 2001, owned planes, yachts, and an assortment of multi-million-dollar homes, and who routinely donated millions to charity risk it all in an effort to save a million bucks—probably about what he spent each year to keep his fleet of Harley-Davidson motorcycles running?

But, after immersing myself in Kozlowski's business history, I came up with an altogether different question: Why was anyone surprised? The behavior that now has him facing the possibility of 30 years in prison is exactly the behavior that was the hallmark of his run as Tyco's swashbuckling, take-no-prisoners CEO.

Why is it so shocking to learn that Kozlowski cooked up a con job to avoid paying his personal taxes? After all, this is the same guy who, in 1997, moved his company's nominal headquarters offshore to Bermuda to avoid paying taxes on billions of dollars in overseas earnings. Apparently, life imitates business when it comes to the art of cutting corners.

According to the scabrous portrait painted by prosecutors, Kozlowski bought his extravagant artwork—which included a $3.95 million Monet and a $4.7 million Renoir—to accessorize his $18-million, 13-room apartment on Fifth Avenue. But he then cleverly had his pricey paintings routed through Tyco's offices in New Hampshire so he wouldn't have to spring for New York City's 8.25% sales tax.

In one case, cooperative art dealers didn't even bother to actually ship the paintings to New Hampshire. Instead, they sent them directly to Kozlowski's apartment, shipping empty crates to Tyco headquarters. Unfortunately for Kozlowski, along with creating a paper trail of phony invoices, his co-conspirators generated a number of other deeply incriminating documents. "Here are the five paintings to go to New Hampshire (wink, wink)," reads one smoking gun memo addressed to an art handler.

Adding to this murky moral landscape, it appears that Kozlowski funded some of his art purchases with no-interest loans drawn from a Tyco program designed to help employees buy company stock. Perhaps if he had made do with a few LeRoy Neiman sports scenes and that perennial classic, *Dogs Playing Poker*, he could have avoided downsizing employees and raiding their stock fund.

Like Rigas, somewhere along the way, Kozlowski, the son of a New Jersey cop, began to see himself and the multi-billion-dollar company he led as one and the same. So why not get Tyco to make charitable donations in his name and buy his Manhattan apartment and $11 million in furniture and knick-knacks, including a $6,300 sewing basket, a $15,000 dog umbrella stand, and $2,900 worth of coat hangers? And why not get Tyco shareholders to fork out nearly $100,000 for flowers or a million bucks for his wife's fortieth birthday party on the island of Sardinia with Jimmy Buffett to serenade her? He viewed all of Tyco's assets as his because, well, without him Tyco was nothing.

Dennis the Public Menace's progress from tax aversion to alleged tax evasion began with his loophole-exploiting business practices and ended with his defrauding the public out of tax money New York desperately needs. With the city digging out from under a post-9/11 budget deficit, what are we to make of a clown like Dennis Kozlowski who steals $1 million from the public to decorate his apartment even after he's engorged himself with hundreds of millions from the company trough?

According to the financial press, we were supposed to admire him—until the scandal broke. Maneuvers like these had for years earned Kozlowski the admiration of Wall Street and a glowing reputation as America's "Most Aggressive CEO"—the title of a 2001 cover story in *Business Week*. The magazine even went so far as to laud Kozlowski—an accountant by trade—for his "willingness to test the limits of acceptable accounting and tax strategies." And yes, I believe that, in the same issue, street corner crack dealers were lauded for their "willingness to test the limits of acceptable commerce strategies."

These accounting strategies allowed the company to report billions of dollars in profits every year, while building up $26 billion in debt. Only after the Enron collapse did Wall Street stop applauding and start scrutinizing Tyco's business more closely. The result? The company's stock lost three-quarters of its value in 2002, costing investors $92 billion.

On September 12, 2002, three months after he was indicted for evading sales taxes, Kozlowski and former Tyco CFO Mark Swartz were charged with "enterprise corruption and grand larceny"—for treating Tyco as their "personal piggy bank," and raiding its coffers to the tune of more than $600 million. Former general counsel Mark Belnick was charged with falsifying business records and hiding more than $14 million in loans he took from the company.

The previous May, three weeks before he resigned, Kozlowski gave the commencement address at New Hampshire's St. Anselm's College. A psychoanalyst would have had a field day with the message he chose to impart to the school's Class of 2002. "You will be confronted," he warned them, "with questions every day that test your morals. Think carefully, and for your sake, do the right thing, not the easy thing." You could almost see his superego and his id duking it out underneath his mortarboard.

DOCTOR PIG: SAM WAKSAL

When it comes to Dr. Sam Waksal, the founder of ImClone who pleaded guilty to bank and securities fraud, conspiracy to obstruct justice, and perjury, it's clear that his id won out a long time ago.

A legendary charmer, Waksal helped turn ImClone, which he started in an old shoe factory with $4 million, into a $5.5 billion juggernaut. Dr. Sam was credited with single-handedly making biotech sexy. Along the way, he developed a reputation as a relentless social climber who collected famous friends—among them Mariel Hemingway, Lorraine Bracco, Carl Icahm, Harvey Weinstein, and Mick Jagger—as hungrily as he acquired the trappings of wealth, including a place in the Hamptons and a 7,000-square-foot SoHo loft festooned with $20 million worth of de Koonings, Rothkos, and Picassos. One acquisition he was less inclined to show off was a world-class—and rapidly appreciating—collection of lawsuits.

He even got an invitation to play golf with President Clinton. Waksal did not play golf, but he rushed out on a mad spending spree, buying every golfing accessory the well-turned-out golfer needs. Unfortunately, he could not buy the ability to play the game. Standing at the first tee, Bubba at his side, Waksal swung at the ball with all his strength, succeeding

Match the CEO to the Mansion

KEN LAY Enron	**Boca Raton, Florida** $13.5 million Mediterranean-style, waterfront estate. 15,000 square feet. Parquet and marble flooring. Complete with elevator, boat dock, pool, cabana, tennis courts, and fountain
JOE NACCHIO Qwest	**Nantucket, Massachusetts** "Sequin," a charming $2.5 million wharf-side cottage
DENNIS KOZLOWSKI Tyco	**Rye, New Hampshire** $2.3 million house in exclusive New Hampshire coastal community
JOHN RIGAS Adelphia	**Bachelor Gulch, Colorado** $8.5 million 7,800-square-foot, eight-bedroom, ten-bathroom house on almost 3 acres of land
GARY WINNICK Global Crossing	**Nantucket, Massachusetts** "Edward Cary," an intimate coastal cottage worth somewhere in the region of $2.5 million
BERNIE EBBERS WorldCom	**New York, New York** $18 million, 13-room apartment on Fifth Avenue, complete with $11 million worth of furnishings, including a $6,000 gold shower curtain and high-end art including works by Monet and Renoir
SAM WAKSAL ImClone	**Nantucket, Massachusetts** $5 million coastal mansion, in-house chef, three-bedroom guest house, and boat dock

(They all belong to former Tyco CEO Dennis Kozlowski.)

only in dislodging a massive divot from the ground. "Maybe you can just ride along in the cart for the rest of the game, Sam," the president suggested.

But even as he became a regular on both the society and the business pages of the New York papers, Waksal began to reveal himself as a pathological liar. At his birthday party at Nobu restaurant in New York a couple of years ago, billionaire financier Carl Icahn told the assembled guests, who included

Satan's Stock Portfolio

COMPANY	HIGH	LOW
Enron	$90.75	$.08
Tyco	62.80	6.98
Global Crossing	61.00	.02
ImClone	169.13	5.85
WorldCom	64.50	.11
Xerox	124.00	4.50
Adelphia	87.00	.12
Martha Stewart Omnimedia	39.75	6.29
Qwest	64.00	1.07
Dynegy	89.00	.49
Sunbeam	52.00	.05

Martha Stewart, a story of walking with Waksal on the beach in East Hampton. Waksal pointed to a house and told Icahn that he had just bought it. A few days later, Icahn passed by the house and decided to say "hi" to his buddy. The person who answered the door had never heard of Waksal. All those at the birthday dinner laughed about their daredevil friend. But I hope there was at least some unease, if not outright consternation, beneath the laughter.

Waksal's shaky relationship with the truth has put the future of Erbitux, and the treatment of millions of cancer sufferers, in jeopardy, and placed his own father and daughter, to say nothing of pal Martha Stewart, in harm's way, facing potential prosecution and jail time.

In a matter of months, Waksal morphed from Jay Gatsby in a lab coat to a snake oil–peddling Ivan Boesky.

This is just a mere glimpse of the gluttonous CEOs who have fattened themselves at America's expense. They and their fellow swine have brought disgrace to themselves and uncertainty to the U.S. economy. What differentiates them from their Old West predecessors like Billy the Kid, Jesse James, and the Dalton Gang are just Armani suits in place of leather chaps, crooked accountants instead of guns, and private planes instead of horses.

Questions

1. In each of the men discussed by Huffington, we see some aspect of tax evasion practices. What responsibility do citizens have to the social welfare of their communities, and how did these men evade that responsibility?

2. What are the reaches of the ethical dilemma posed by using shareholder stock for personal expenses?

3. Each of these men purport to have a high personal moral standard, but they seem to view themselves differently when it comes to professional business practices. How can one's professional life be aligned with their personal morality?

CASE 7.2

Groups Debate Costs of Educating Illegal Immigrant Children

Suzanne Gamboa

WASHINGTON—An anti-immigrant group says in a new report that Texas spends $1.03 billion a year educating school-age children who are illegally in the country, but the Texas Education Agency said it has no way to determine those costs.

The report issued by Federation for American Immigration Reform on Wednesday said the country spent $7.4 billion a year educating school-age illegal immigrant children. Dan Stein, the executive director of Federation for Immigration Reform, said the money could instead be used to address education needs of citizen and legal immigrant children.

"This report shows the victims are our own kids who are in overcrowded classrooms in severely stressed financial conditions," he said.

Suzanne Middlebrook, a TEA spokeswoman, said the state agency doesn't collect information on illegal immigrant children because school districts cannot require children to submit information showing they are legally in the country.

FAIR used an Immigration and Naturalization state-by-state breakdown of the overall illegal immigrant population and assumed the undocumented child population was similarly distributed.

"That assumption really isn't examined" in the report, said Walter Ewing, research associate with the Immigration Policy Center of American Immigration Law Foundation in Washington.

Additionally, he said the report suffers from a "very bad case of tunnel vision."

"They are trying to tie undocumented children to the state budget crises ... Does that mean we can credit immigrant children for the budget surpluses of 2000, if now they are to blame for the budget crisis of 2003?"

Stein said his group did the report because momentum is growing to re-examine U.S. law that guarantees education to all children regardless of their citizenship status. "In our view, the issue is very quickly assuming the trajectory it asserted in 1994–95," Stein said, referring to California's Proposition 187 movement. The California proposition, ultimately ruled unconstitutional, denied benefits to illegal immigrants.

But Steve Camarota, research director of the Center for Immigration Studies, a group that supports immigration limits, agrees that educating illegal immigrant schoolchildren is costing billions. But he disagreed that barring them from public education is the solution.

"Administratively, it requires school districts to identify those kids and that's a huge challenge. It also would require, politically, a willingness to kick these kids out of school or tell their parents you've got to pay. Children are a sympathetic population, so it's not going to happen," Camarota said.

Frank Sharry, National Immigration Forum executive director, agreed that the political climate has changed.

He cited the Arizona 2004 ballot initiative to cut off services to immigrants. Last month, eight Arizona Republicans in Congress issued a statement opposing the measure.

"The fact is these kids are here," Sharry said. "Is it better that they go to school or they be on street corners? The answer is obvious."

Questions

1. Outline the arguments on both sides of this issue: do legal taxpayers have a social responsibility to fund education for children of illegal immigrants? On the other hand, what responsibility does a school district have to educate all children?

CASE 7.3

The Fordasaurus

William H. Shaw and Vincent Barry

Before Ford publicly unveiled the biggest sport-utility vehicle ever, the Sierra Club ran a contest for the best name and marketing slogan for it. Among the entries were "Fordasaurus, powerful enough to pass anything on the highway except a gas station" and "Ford Saddam, the truck that will put America between Iraq and a hard place." But the winner was "Ford Valdez: Have you driven a tanker lately?"

Ford, which decided to name the nine-passenger vehicle the Excursion, was not amused. Sales of sport-utility vehicles (SUVs) exploded in the 1990s, going up nearly sixfold, and the company sees itself as simply responding to consumer demand for ever larger models. Although most SUVs never leave the pavement, their drivers like knowing their vehicles can go anywhere and do anything. They also like their SUVs to be big. The Excursion is now the largest passenger vehicle on the road, putting Ford far ahead of its rivals in the competition to build the biggest and baddest SUV. The Excursion weighs 8,500 pounds, equivalent to two mid-sized sedans or three Honda Civics. It is more than 6½ feet wide, nearly 7 feet high, and almost 19 feet long—too big to fit comfortably into some garages or into a single parking space.

Although the Excursion is expensive ($40,000 to $50,000 when loaded with options), it is, like other SUVs, profitable to build. Because Ford based the Excursion on the chassis of its Super Duty truck, the company was able to develop the vehicle for a relatively modest investment of about $500 million. With sales of 50,000 to 60,000 per year, Ford earns about $20,000 per vehicle.

Most SUVs are classified as light trucks. Under current rules, they are allowed to emit up to several times more smog-causing gases per mile than automobiles. In 1999, the Clinton administration proposed tighter emissions restrictions on new passenger cars, restrictions that new vehicles in the light-truck category would also have to meet by 2009. However, these rules would not affect the Excursion, which is heavy enough to be classified as a medium-duty truck.

Ford says that the Excursion, with its 44-gallon gas tank, gets 10 to 15 miles per gallon, and that its emission of pollutants is 43 percent below the maximum for its class. By weight, about 85 percent of the vehicle is recyclable, and 20 percent of it comes from recycled metals and plastics. The company thus believes that the Excursion is in keeping with the philosophy of William Clay Ford, Jr. When he became chairman in September 1998, he vowed to make Ford "the world's most environmentally friendly auto maker." He added, however, that "what we do to help the environment must succeed as a business proposition. A zero-emission vehicle that sits unsold on a dealer's lot is not reducing pollution."

From William H. Shaw and Vincent Barry, *Moral Issues in Business*, 9th ed. (Belmont, CA: Wadsworth, 2004).

The company, however, has failed to win environmentalists to its side. They believe that with the Excursion, the Ford Company is a long way from producing an environmentally friendly product. Daniel Becker of the Sierra Club points out that in the course of an average lifetime of 120,000 miles, each Excursion will emit 130 tons of carbon dioxide, the principal cause of global warming. "It's just bad for the environment any way you look at it," he says. John DeCicco of the American Council for an Energy-Efficient Economy agrees. He worries further that the Excursion is clearing the way for bigger and bigger vehicles. "This is the antithesis of green leadership."

Stung by criticism of the Excursion, William Clay Ford, Jr., has vowed to make the company a more responsible environmental citizen. Worried that if automobile producers don't clean up their act, they will become as vilified as cigarette companies, in August 2000 Ford promised it would improve the fuel economy of its SUVs by 25 percent over the next five years, smugly inviting other automakers to follow its green leadership. To this GM responded that it was the real green leader and "will still be in five years, or 10 years, or for that matter 20 years. End of story." When they aren't bragging about their greenness, however, both companies continue to lobby Congress to forbid the Department of Transportation from studying fuel economy increases.

Update:

According to media reports, yet to be confirmed by Ford, the company is planning on phasing out the Excursion after 2004.

Questions

1. Are environmentalists right to be concerned about the environmental impact of SUVs? How do you explain the growing demand for ever larger passenger vehicles?

2. In developing and producing the Excursion, is the Ford Motor Company sacrificing the environment to profits, or is it acting in a socially responsible way by making the Excursion relatively energy efficient for its vehicle class? If you had been on the board of directors, would you have voted for the project? Why/why not? Do Ford's stockholders have a right to insist that it produce the most profitable vehicles it legally can, regardless of their environmental impact?

8

Reciprocity, Conflicts of Interest, and Government Regulation

Introduction

Professional life often involves working with multiple constituents. In establishing professional relationships, you will develop unique and varied duties and moral responsibilities to a wide range of people. The relationship you have with your boss and your obligations within that relationship will undoubtedly differ from your relationship with colleagues, clients, and associated business partners. In some situations, relationships you have with family and friends may also become intertwined with professional responsibilities. While the intermingling of these various relationships may often prove beneficial to your professional life, they can also create ethical conflicts when the obligations you have to one person conflict with the obligations you have to another. This chapter explores the nature of these conflicts and the methods, both self-imposed and governmental, of controlling them.

One of the most common types of conflict of interest involves nepotism. Nepotism has a long and well-established history in much of professional life. It refers to the practice of hiring someone based more on a personal than a professional relationship. Have you ever been hired for a summer job by a friend of a parent? Is it appropriate to rely on the personal connections of family and friends to land your first "real" job? If you do so, are you being given an unfair advantage over other job applicants who do not have the same friends or acquaintances? Should you be evaluated solely on the merits of your intellect and skills and not based on who you know?

Conflicts of interest, however, go well beyond the obligations of parents to try to help their children succeed. For many professionals, the more challenging conflicts arise between the competing demands of professional relationships. Should physicians, for example, accept gifts from drug companies? It has been a long-standing practice in medicine for pharmaceutical companies to provide food, pens, writing pads, and sample drugs to individual physicians. Some physicians feel that these "perks" of the trade are inconsequential and do not have a negative effect on patient care. Others express concern that by accepting such "perks," physician prescription practices will be influenced in a way that may negatively impact patients, even if only financially.

As Klein and Fleischman point out, the conflicts of interest for health professionals are not limited to those that are merely self-serving. In some situations, as with the physician-investigator, the conflict can be one of trying to advance knowledge of a given disease and advocating for a patient's best interest. Should a physician recommend that a patient enter a research trial, which she is conducting, knowing that the patient *may* receive treatment that is less effective than the standard treatment? This situation can create a conflict of interest for the health care professional whose primary obligation is to protect the patient's best interest.

Protecting clients from unscrupulous practitioners is not the only conflict in professional practice. On the flip side, conflicts of interest may arise when professionals encounter clients or employers who want them to engage in illegal, or morally dubious, behaviors. The sagas surrounding the collapse of Enron, WorldCom, and Tyco provide examples of accountants who were caught between competing obligations to their employers and professional codes of conduct. What should you do when your employer asks you to lie? Should you simply quit, knowing that doing so may have severe financial consequences for your family? Do obligations to one's employer outweigh obligations to one's profession?

Finally, how can we effectively regulate conflicts of interest in professional life? Should the organizations that license professionals take a more active role in regulating potential conflicts of interest? Should the government, either at the state or federal level, provide regulatory oversight regarding conflicts of interests? If so, what role should they government play and how extensive should its policies be? What are the advantages and limitations of governmental oversight?

Adam Bellow | # Nepotism in American Business

Adam Bellow is the former editorial director of the Free Press and is currently an editor-at-large for Doubleday.

No one can pick up the phone these days and get their kid a job, a record deal, or a spot on the national ticket. But more and more, such intervention isn't necessary. Growing up around a business or vocation—learning how it works, getting to know the people in it—creates a powerful advantage that is tantamount to nepotism, and when exercised unworthily it carries a similar stigma.

If all of this can be called nepotism—and it can—it is clearly a new kind of nepotism, a modern or (if you will) postmodern nepotism that adapts an ancient impulse to contemporary cultural conditions. This new, postmodern nepotism works subtly and invisibly, creating opportunities for those who have connections in a given field, and increasingly excluding those who don't. All that

From Adam Bellow, "Nepotism in American Business," in *In Praise of Nepotism: A Natural History* (New York, Doubleday, 2002), pp. 10–15. Notes were deleted from the text.

is required to profit from this kind of opportunity is a willingness to take advantage of it. Indeed, the New Nepotism differs from the Old in being not so much a matter of parents hiring or getting jobs for children as of children themselves choosing to follow in their parents' footsteps. To that extent, the successor phenomenon looks a lot less like nepotism on the part of mothers and fathers than it does opportunism on the part of sons and daughters.

Dictionaries trace the word "nepotism" to the Latin *nepos*, meaning nephew or grandson. But while technically accurate, this etymology is misleadingly narrow. The word actually derives from the Italian *nepote*, which can refer to any family member, of any generation, male or female. The term *nepotismo* was coined sometime in the fourteenth or fifteenth century to describe the corrupt practice of appointing papal relatives to office—usually illegitimate sons described as "nephews"—and for a long time this ecclesiastical origin continued to be reflected in dictionaries. (Even today, some dictionaries list the subordinate definition of "nephew" as "illegitimate child of an ecclesiastic.") The modern definition of nepotism is "favoritism based on kinship," but over time the word's dictionary meaning and its conventional applications have diverged. Most people today define the term very narrowly to mean not just hiring a relative, but hiring one who is grossly incompetent—though technically one would have to agree that hiring a relative is nepotism whether he or she is qualified or not. But nepotism has also proven to be a highly elastic concept, capable of being applied to a much broader range of relationships than simple consanguinity. Many practices that are in fact nepotistic don't look like nepotism, while practices that seem normal and acceptable to some look like nepotism to others.

To understand the nature of a thing it is best to begin with its critics. Thus, from the workingman's perspective nepotism means hiring or promoting the boss's son-in-law, nephew, or girlfriend over the heads of more qualified candidates. This violates our basic sense of fairness and elicits strong reactions of revulsion, both for those who practice nepotism and (even more perhaps) for those who profit from it. Yet nepotism is often the rule in family businesses, and it is usually accepted as "the way things are" by everyone involved. Such nepotism appears to be a problem only when the beneficiary is manifestly unqualified. Even then, whatever damage may result usually hurts only the nepotist himself.

Economists view nepotism as an obstacle to healthy change in business firms, promoting waste and inefficiency. Yet some acknowledge that nepotism may be a rational practice, since engaging in extensive talent searches is a cost that might well be avoided. Still others argue that hiring family members is the best way to promote important values of trust and solidarity within a business enterprise. And despite official nepotism policies, most large companies admit that they prefer to hire the relatives of existing employees, since the proven conduct of a relative is the best guide to the behavior of a prospective worker.

Most Americans see nepotism as a means for the rich to warehouse their unemployable sons while keeping the lower classes in their place. In this view, nepotism appears as part of a strategy of class and elite domination. There is much to be said for this argument. Historically, most elites that have risen through merit of one kind or another normally seek to keep their gains within the family and contrive various ways to pass on property and status to their children. Yet systematic nepotism has been practiced just as widely by the poor and working classes: there are multigenerational families of cops and firemen, and so-called father-son unions still dominate the building trades. In fact, the Old Nepotism has been practiced more or less continuously by both the upper and lower classes as a rational group strategy. It was the middle class that pushed the merit principle, and this is one of the things that makes the New Nepotism such a surprising development: the fact that it is essentially a middle class phenomenon.

In politics, nepotism has appeared in various forms: that of hereditary family rule under a monarchy, the domination of a landed or commercial oligarchy, and (in democratic societies) as a species of corruption linked to patronage. The American Revolutionaries wanted nothing to do with hereditary rule from abroad and feared the dynastic ambition of rich and powerful men in their own country. Early American politics was obsessed with such fears, and the result has been a long struggle to free our political system from its lingering entanglement with the family. The tension between birth and merit was most famously articulated in the debate between Adams and Jefferson about the prospects for a "natural aristocracy." Both wished to see the nation governed by an elite of talent rather than birth, but disagreed on whether this could be achieved. Though we seem to have gone pretty far toward realizing Jefferson's dream of a true meritocracy, we have not been able to do away with nepotism and patronage completely. While some might object that patronage and nepotism are two different things, there is really a good deal of overlap. Nepotism itself is a species of patronage directed at family members. Wherever patronage exists, moreover, nepotism rarely lags behind. . . .

Proponents of economic globalism decry the role of nepotism in fostering bureaucratic corruption and crony capitalism in Africa, Asia, and Latin America; and everyone rejects the resurgent ethnic nationalism that has led to genocidal violence in India, Rwanda, and the Balkans—a violent form of particularism that ultimately springs from the nepotistic preference for one's own cultural, linguistic, or religious group. Even the Dalai Lama comes down on nepotism in *Ethics for the New Millennium*, where he includes the stubborn preference for our own families, communities, and ethnic groups in a list of man-made evils that we must strive to overcome in the twenty-first century. From this angle, nepotism is not just a legal, moral, or political infraction, but a spiritual one as well.

These perspectives reflect the prevailing negative view of the Old Nepotism: it burdened the economy, corrupted government, reduced women and children to chattels, disadvantaged blacks and other minorities, throttled meritocracy, promoted amoral selfishness, and reinforced the American class system. The New Nepotism is clearly different, and it elicits different reactions. For one thing, the American social environment has become more competitive; the playing field is much more level than it was one hundred, fifty, or even twenty years ago, and it is no longer possible for nepotism to be practiced indiscrimately, or in a way that masks incompetence. Time and again we hear that while a famous name may get you in the door, you have to prove your worth or face the consequences.

It is worth dwelling for a moment on the differences between the Old Nepotism and the New. The Old Nepotism involved parents hiring their children outright or pulling strings on their behalf. It was also highly coercive—obedient daughters married according to their parents' wishes, and dutiful sons allowed their fathers to chart their careers and often to select suitable brides for them as well. Since then there has been a great civil rights revolution that has completed the liberation of women and children from patriarchal control. Coming on the other side of this revolution, the New Nepotism operates not (so to speak) from the top down but from the bottom up: it is voluntary, not coercive; it springs from the motives of children, not the interest of parents; it tends to seem natural rather than planned. It reverses the flow of energies in the nepotistic equation, so that instead of parents holding themselves out as examples for their children, today's children validate their parents by following in their footsteps. While not nepotism in the classic sense, it is rightly called nepotism because it involves exploiting the family name, connections, or wealth. The method may be different, but the result is much the same.

Mainly, however, the new nepotism differs in combining the privileges of birth with the iron rule of merit in a way that is much less offensive to democratic sensibilities. This is what explains the astonishing latitude—in effect, the room to fail—that we seem perfectly willing to grant the new successor generation. Americans increasingly feel that there is nothing wrong with hiring a relative, so long as he or she is qualified. We even say that when we hire a relative or pull strings to help relatives who *are* qualified, that is not really nepotism. But this leaves us in the logically inconsistent position of saying that hiring a relative is or is not nepotism depending on the relative's performance.

The reason we have tied ourselves in knots around this question is really quite simple: there is a missing distinction in our lexicon between *good* nepotism and *bad*. Of course, in order to recognize such a distinction we would have to completely revise our view of nepotism as bad by definition. But this should not be difficult, because our negative view of nepotism is not a natural or God-given law but a cultural artifact, the result of several centuries of social and cultural history.

Europeans in general have a much more relaxed and balanced view of nepotism. Despite the occasional scandal—such as the forced resignation in 1999 of twenty EU commissioners charged with blatant nepotism—they tend to accept it as part of the fabric of things. In contrast, the extreme antipathy to nepotism is an American phenomenon. Moreover, it is an attitude that America has been busily exporting to the rest of the world (with mixed success) for the last fifty years, along with the whole complex of values and practices associated with modern technocratic liberalism.

Richard T. De George | # Ethical Issues for Accountants

Richard T. De George is professor of philosophy at the University of Kansas.

ETHICAL ISSUES FOR ACCOUNTANTS

Accountants face a great many pressures from clients who want them to do what is illegal: underreporting income, falsifying accounts, taking questionable deductions, illegally evading income tax, and engaging in outright fraud. None of these pose difficult conceptual issues from a moral point of view. They are illegal and unethical. This fact does not lessen the pressure to act unethically that many CPAs feel and to which they are subject. But the ethically correct thing to do in these issues is not in question.

Other difficulties involve requests to alter financial statements in order to achieve certain purposes (e.g., so the company will be able to get loans the client could not otherwise get) and requests that accounts deviate from standard accounting practices for any number of reasons. Corporations prefer to have their earnings rise in a gently sloping line. They prefer to avoid spikes in earning charts and to balance out windfall earnings over several quarters or years. Some would prefer to keep some assets in reserve in case of a poor quarter or year. They would prefer, therefore, that sometimes their reports not accurately reflect their actual situation. Sometimes this is legal, as when a company defers receipts or defers shipments so that they fall in another quarter or year. Sometimes it is not, and companies seek creative bookkeeping techniques to achieve their goals. The pressure to supply such techniques or to approve them often falls on the CPAs.

Fee setting, billing clients whom one knows are on the verge of bankruptcy, working for clients who

From Richard T. De George, *Business Ethics*, 4th Edition (Englewood Cliffs, NJ: Prentice-Hall, 1995).

can no longer afford their services, and resisting offers to work on a contingency fee basis form another set of issues with an ethical dimension. Still another set of issues involves deciding how to handle mistakes, especially when some accountants feel they are unable to keep up with the constant changes in regulations, law, and accounting practices and rules. A CPA should undertake only those tasks that he or she is competent to perform; but the knowledge that one is over one's head sometimes emerges only as one is sinking. Similarly, the temptation to overcommit oneself and to allow too little time for carrying out one's tasks with the proper care all possibly lead to unethical behavior and practices.

The American Institute of Certified Public Accountants (AICPA) publishes professional rules to guide and govern certified public accountants. Accountants are governed by three codes: Generally Accepted Accounting Principles (GAAP), Generally Accepted Auditing Standards (GAAS), and a Code of Professional Ethics (COPE). The AICPA Rules require independence of the firm or accountant from the client. This means they cannot hold any financial interest in the company. The intent is clearly to avoid conflict of interest. If the accounting firm is to certify a company's financial statements, it should have no incentive, owing to financial holdings in the company, to make the firm's financial situation look better than it is. The Code demands integrity, objectivity, competence, and compliance with standards set forth in GAAS and GAAP. The Rules guard client confidentiality, prohibit contingency fees (e.g., according to which no fee is charged unless a certain specified finding is attained), and preclude encroachment on the client of another accountant or accounting firm and the payment of commissions to obtain a client.

The client is responsible for the financial statements. The CPA does not guarantee the accuracy of the statements. The accountant is neither required nor expected to investigate in depth the accuracy of the data presented in the reports. A CPA might become suspicious of some entries and question them, and must refuse to certify a statement that is misleading. But the client, not the CPA, is responsible for maintaining accurate records, and it is not the

CPA's job routinely to check those records against all other documents or inventories. The CPA certifies that the financial statements conform with generally accepted accounting principles.

For many practicing accountants, obeying the Rules is the guide to ethical behavior. However, for some critics, it is not the honesty of individual accountants as they try to live up to the Rules that is the problem. They attack the rules and the system itself as ethically deficient.

THE ACCOUNTING RULES

The major issue is the (at least) apparent conflict of interest, to which we already referred, that is built into the American accounting system. Critics claim that, although the purpose of certifying the accounts of a corporation is to assure the general public that the corporation's accounts are correct as reported, the system is not set up to guarantee this result. The major stumbling block is that the accounting firm certifying a company's accounts works for the company whose accounts it is auditing. Although the accounting firm is independent, in the sense that it has no financial holdings in the company it is examining, its client—the one who pays its bills—is the company it is examining. It may be fired by that company and replaced by another accounting firm as the client wishes. There is at least on the surface an unavoidable conflict of interest in the operation of any accounting firm. It has the temptation to do nothing to cause disfavor with the company that hires it. Hence, although it is supposed to strive for objectivity, objectivity is not easy to achieve under the circumstances.

A second complaint stems from the fact that the accounting firm simply certifies that the company's accounts are correctly presented and are in accord with the generally accepted accounting and auditing standards. The accounting firm has no responsibility to verify the information it is given by the company whose accounts it is certifying. Furthermore, it has no responsibility to make public any internal discrepancies, fraud, or other irregularities it may discover, even though it may not, of course, itself engage in any cover-up or falsification of the records it does certify. The CPAs are caught between the requirement of confidentiality with respect to the client and the public's interest. Because this is the case, the system does not really assure those interested in the financial health of the company—shareholders, potential shareholders, and to some extent the general public who do business with the company—that the company's records are accurate and reflect its actual financial situation. Furthermore, there are various acceptable methods of handling debits and credits, and those reading financial reports are not always appraised of which alternative methods might have been used and why the one that is used was chosen over the others. Loans and debt are cases in point. If a loan is not likely to be recoverable in full, it is misleading to carry it at its full value. How and when to reduce it for accounting purposes, however, is open to a good deal of discretion, nor can a CPA always know which loans or investments may turn sour and lead to a company's failing.

The public often wonders when businesses go bankrupt how it is that the financial reports did not indicate the seriousness of their plight. The reply that this is not the obligation of the auditor is formally correct, but it is an indication of the problem, rather than an answer to the problem. If it is not the auditor's job to do this, then whose job is it? Can the public interest be protected if it is no one's job to reveal when a corporation is in financial difficulty? If accountants performing audits were paid by the government and required to report an instance of fraud or financial irregularity to the government rather than to the client, would the public be better served than it currently is? The answer is at least arguably yes.

In 1988, the Financial Accounting Standards Board (FASB), which sets standards that the Securities and Exchange Commission requires corporations to follow, proposed requiring that corporations carry as a liability their exposure in terms of retirees' health care benefits. The proposal was adopted as FAS Standard 106 and took effect for large companies in 1993 and for smaller companies in 1995. This method more accurately reflects the company's financial exposure than does the former practice of simply listing the amount paid for this purpose in the past year. Yet, because the new reporting method would at least initially diminish annual corporate earnings considerably, the proposal generated great opposition. Opponents also claimed that future projections were no better than a guess. What do fairness and accuracy in reporting require in this case? What do they amount to when actual liabilities such as this need not be reported? Should corporate opposition be sufficient to preclude and determine reporting regulations? Are the regulations for the benefit of the firms or of the public? These are legitimate questions, raising ethical concerns that deserve at least discussion. Critics claim that accounting firms would take the lead in changing reporting requirements to better serve the public if the firms were not paid by their clients, whose interests are not always served by such reporting regulations.

If there is a conflict between public interest and the interest of their clients, which interest is an accounting firm to put first? If the point of audits and certification were truly to protect the public interest, then accountants and accounting firms would be ethically obliged to place that interest above the interests of their clients. But they are not clearly required to do that, and hence they are in an ethically ambiguous position.

To the extent that accounting firms have taken on the additional task of consulting firms, they have increased the potential for conflict of interest. If the same company both suggests a policy and then audits the results, it is likely to be tempted to make the results look as favorable as possible. Faced with this temptation, some firms have attempted to construct "Chinese walls" between their auditing departments and their consulting departments, such that neither knows what the other is doing.

Critics would prefer changing the system so as preclude the present built-in conflicts of interest. As yet, no widely acceptable alternative has emerged.

The accounting profession itself has responded to public concern by scrutinizing and revising its own rules, yet the AICPA has not been conspicuous in its ability or desire to police itself, enforce its codes, and take punitive actions against those who violate them. In this respect, it fares no better than other professional associations.

Jason E. Klein
and Alan R.
Fleischman

The Private Practicing Physician-Investigator: Ethical Implications of Clinical Research in the Office Setting

Jason Klein served as a research fellow at the New York Academy of Medicine. Alan Fleischman is Senior Vice President at the New York Academy of Medicine and Clinical Professor at the Albert Einstein College of Medicine.

A new model for performing clinical investigations has emerged in the United States. No longer are academic medical centers the sole or even primary site for cutting edge clinical research. Instead, over the past decade, the pharmaceutical industry has turned to commercially oriented networks of physicians practicing in private offices. In 1991, 80 percent of pharmaceutical industry money for clinical research went to investigators in academic medical centers. In 1998, that figure dropped by half, to only 40 percent.[1]

As a result, thousands of private physicians have become physician-investigators, and their patients have become patient-subjects. In 1997, according to some estimates, the number of private physicians engaged in clinical research reached 11,662, triple what it had been in 1990.[2]

The phenomenon has sparked much controversy because of the potential conflict between the physician's two roles. The physician is a clinician, obligated to serve the well-being and interests of the patient. But the physician is now also an investigator, whose aim is to contribute to the development of generalizable knowledge.[3] The conflict can be exacerbated if the pharmaceutical company is paying the physician directly to recruit and retain research subjects.

CHANGING THE LOCUS OF RESEARCH

Academic medical centers had long been favored for clinical trials of new drugs because of academic physicians' expertise in designing research trials, the need to publish results in prestigious journals in order to market the drug, and the academic hospital's sizable source of potential subjects. Today, pharmaceutical companies effectively bypass the academic medical centers. They employ their own research design experts and find subjects in the offices of private practicing community-based physicians, often organized in commercially oriented networks such as contract-research organizations (CROs) and site-management organizations (SMOs).[4]

The major driving force for this change is the desire to contain the very high cost of developing new drugs.[5] Contemporary clinical trials require large numbers of subjects, far more than drug studies performed only a decade ago.[6] Because of new federal regulations that require better gender and ethnic representation, a trial must meet rigorous statistical criteria both to establish that the drug works and to assure that it is safe. And when conducting trials of medications for common disorders, pharmaceutical companies now often seek "medication naïve" subjects. These demands necessitate large numbers of subjects, and engaging independent private practice-based physicians as clinical investigators provides a way of recruiting them rapidly and efficiently.[7]

The CROs and SMOs have emerged to implement and facilitate clinical trials that have been

From Jason E. Klein and Alan R. Fleischman, "The Private Practicing Physician-Investigator: Ethical Implications of Clinical Research in the Office Setting," *Hastings Center Report* 32, no. 4 (2002): 22–26.

designed by the pharmaceutical company, and in many instances even to provide an institutional review board to review consent practices and protect research subjects. The CRO generally turns to an SMO, a for-profit entity that provides, among other services, networks of privately practicing physicians to actually carry out the protocol. The CRO collects the data from clinical investigators and provides them to the pharmaceutical company, which conducts its own analysis. The result is an extremely efficient and cost-effective means for pharmaceutical companies to perform clinical trials.[8]

Very little is known about what motivates privately practicing physicians to participate in clinical research studies. We can speculate that many of the reasons are rather innocuous and even laudable. For some physicians, serving as an investigator allows them to fulfill personal academic goals. For others it may provide a break from the day-to-day routine of patient care. Still others might choose to participate because it allows them to keep abreast of the most current treatments and offer them to their patients.

Some other possible motivations are more dubious. Consider the practice of providing physicians direct financial incentives to bring patients into the study. Typically, physicians receive a flat fee, which can vary widely depending on the complexity of the study, for each patient they enroll.[9] Additionally, some pharmaceutical companies are reportedly offering bonuses to physician-investigators, nurses, and other members of the study teams to "speed up subject recruitment to meet industry-imposed study completion deadlines" and to retain subjects until the study is completed.[10]

Such incentives may have grown more attractive as changes in health care financing and delivery have reduced physicians' personal income. But sometimes the incentives more than make up for the decline in income. Some physician practices are alleged to net profits as high as one million dollars a year from research trials.[11] Patient recruitment into clinical trials has become so lucrative that entire professional conferences now address it. Among the topics at one conference: "Learning the benefit of social marketing," "Examining creative

and media strategies for a successful recruitment campaign," and "Converting 'interested' subjects to 'enrolled' subjects."[12] This business-like, profit-oriented approach to clinical trials stands in contrast to the claim of many physician-investigators that financial compensation is only "for services rendered for the filling out of reports and handling of other administrative details required for reporting purposes."[13]

Incentives to physicians for patient recruitment and retention are not new. In academic medical centers, physician-investigators have for years accrued substantial secondary gain, for either themselves or their departments, by conducting clinical trials. Income from clinical trials can help support research nurses, fellows, laboratory technicians, and coordinators to enhance the academic work of the investigator. Unlike the private practice setting, however, direct personal financial gain has rarely been possible in academia. We ought not trivialize the potential for conflicts of interest in clinical research in the teaching setting, but the isolation of the private office setting, its lack of oversight and accountability, and the potential for direct financial benefit make the conflict there more worrisome.

PATIENTS AND DOCTORS

Moving clinical research closer to the practice of medicine has always had the potential to affect the care of individual patients. Financial incentives aside, there is an inherent conflict of interest when a physician is both clinician and investigator. This also is not a new problem in clinical research. Previously, however, research was restricted mostly to the academic setting, where it is possible to separate clinical care from research to a far greater extent than is likely in office practice. Placing clinical investigation in the isolated and intimate setting of the private office increases the likelihood of a significant conflict, with serious consequences for patient care.

First, patients may believe that their physician can continue to provide them with what has been called the "good of personal care"—the positive knowledge that the physician is acting solely in the patient's best-interest.[14] In fact, research protocols usually limit individualized decisions about study medications and other ancillary treatments in order to gauge as accurately as possible the therapeutic value of the intervention. Patients rarely understand that physicians participating in a clinical trial may be prevented from tailoring treatments.

Patients may also misunderstand the implication of their own participation in the clinical trial. In the past, participating as a subject in research was seen as a burden, since it put one at some risk and involved merely speculative, if any, benefit. The point of the federal regulation of clinical research was to protect vulnerable subjects.[15] During the last fifteen years, however, the public's growing fascination with "miracle" drugs and devices has changed its view of participating in research. No longer is participation seen as primarily a burden. Instead it has become a potential benefit, a way of gaining access to otherwise unavailable therapies.[16]

This new view of research has been corroborated by several studies. Besides citing altruistic motives for serving as research subjects, respondents have reported that they saw it as a way to obtain superior medical care and solicit second opinions,[17] and that the altruistic intentions of their physician motivated them to participate in research.[18] A recent study commissioned by the U.S. President's Advisory Committee on Human Radiation Experiments confirms these findings. In-depth interviews with patient-subjects revealed that for the subjects, "research experiences, particularly for those patients who reported being in research evaluating potential treatments, were inextricably interwoven with their medical care experiences."[19] Patients appear to be confusing standard treatment, where interventions are generally supported by scientific inquiry, with research, where the therapeutic benefit is uncertain and the goal is to discern whether or not the therapy will eventually become standard.

Subjects' confusion can be compounded by the profound trust that people place in their personal physicians. This trust has prompted some to argue that the potential for coercion in patient recruitment is even greater in the private practice setting than in the academic setting.[20] As reported by the ACHRE-commissioned study, the recommendations of a person's physician were "powerful factors influencing" a patient's decision to enroll as a research subject. In fact, many of the participants surveyed stated that their decision to enroll in the research was made before they were even given the consent form.[21] When asked to explain their physician's influence on their decision to participate, subjects cited the expertise of the physician and a belief that the physician would not recommend participation if it were not in the best interest of the patient.

THE RESEARCH ENTERPRISE

Conducting clinical trials in the private office setting also has troubling implications for the research enterprise itself. Financial incentives can and do influence supposedly unbiased investigators, and therefore can influence the quality of research findings. A number of studies offer empirical evidence that industry funding of clinical research may bias the researchers' conclusions.[22] No great leap of the imagination is required to worry that financial gain may influence physician-investigator's individual patient recruitment practices and data collection.

Again, this worry is not exclusively about private practicing physicians, but it is especially pertinent in this context. Because the research is taking place in a closed office environment, there may be greater potential for private practicing physician-investigators to alter or fabricate data in order to have their patients meet eligibility requirements. An extreme example was chronicled in a 1999 *New York Times* story about a physician who made a significant amount of money by inventing fictitious patients, using falsified X-rays, and even submitting a nurse's urine in place of the actual research subjects' because it met the requirements of a particular study.[23] Although this story is surely the exception rather than the rule, it does demonstrate the potential worst-case abuses of a system that is extremely difficult to monitor.

Plainly the money available in the research can damage the data, which can mean that less than optimally studied pharmaceuticals are approved for general use. If this actually happened, and that fact became general knowledge, public trust in the entire research enterprise might diminish.

PROCEDURAL SAFEGUARDS

Yet we need not altogether reject the practice of conducting clinical trials in private office settings. In fact, there are several significant benefits to the arrangement. Placing clinical research in the private practice setting may add "a level of continuity and personal contact to the process—something unavailable from full-time researchers," and it can provide an enormous pool of potential research subjects, which could facilitate the approval of new and important therapeutic agents.[24] Bringing clinical research into the private office also allows ordinary patients and their physicians access to some of the most current and scientifically advanced therapies.

Even with these benefits, however, we need careful scrutiny of the practice and institution of new safeguards and guidelines to protect research subjects. The following recommendations could be adopted through voluntary initiatives but are likely to require regulatory support.

Research ethics education for all investigators. Academic medical centers require clinical investigators conducting federally funded research to successfully complete an educational curriculum on the ethics of human subjects research.[25] This standard ought to apply to all researchers who interact with human subjects, regardless of the source of funding of the research. Private practice physicians who engage in clinical research (and the support staff who interact with subjects) should be certified as understanding the standards of research ethics, including issues related to patient recruitment, the potential for conflict between clinical care and research, informed consent practices, and the assurance of voluntary

participation. Education about issues in ethics does not ensure ethical practice, of course, but it is likely to create an atmosphere that will decrease inadvertent ethical transgressions.

While such a requirement would be a significant change, it is not unrealistic or unfairly rigorous. Physicians and nurses already participate in mandatory continuing education. Each year, they must successfully complete courses and other educational activities on a variety of topics to obtain state recertification of licensure. There may be scant empirical evidence that such education affects either physician or nurse behavior or clinical outcomes, but professionals nonetheless accept the requirements.

Limiting financial incentives. Physicians report significant profit from participation in clinical research—even though they also claim that fees merely compensate them for the services needed to carry out the trial. It is important to limit profits. Per subject reimbursement should be sufficient to compensate for overhead, labor hours, and other relevant costs, but not so high as to create an undue incentive. The desire to enhance knowledge through clinical research ought to be the primary motivation for physician-investigators.

Additionally, pharmaceutical companies should be prevented from offering incentives and bonuses for rapid recruitment and active retention of patients. Without the prospect of sizable financial gain, the pressure to behave unethically would likely be decreased. Possibly, fewer physicians would participate in clinical research under these circumstances, but the enhanced protection of research subjects ought to outweigh this drawback.

Disclosure of potential conflicts. Research subjects must be apprised during the informed consent process of the physician-investigator's potential conflicts—both that inherent in the dual role of clinician and investigator and all those stemming from the financial arrangements of the clinical trial.

Much has been written in recent months about the importance of disclosing and managing financial conflicts of interest in research.[26] The Association of American Medical Colleges has recommended that investigators and support staff in clinical research at academic medical centers reveal all significant financial interests in companies that may gain or lose financially from the results of the study, and that institutions develop a process to manage these conflicts.[27] This approach seems reasonable in the context of research in the private office setting as well. Although disclosure of financial relationships does not dissolve conflict of interest, it can enhance the patient's ability to understand the consequences of participation.

Independent resources for patient questions and concerns. Some have called for independent consent or procedure monitors in other settings in which research subjects may be vulnerable to coercion.[28] Such a requirement would be extremely expensive and logistically impossible in the private practice setting. Yet some independent resource is needed to answer questions and discuss concerns with patients and their families. Since the private office may offer no such resource, one should be created and subjects should be informed about it.

The resource would be a vehicle for empowering and informing research subjects; it could be as simple as a phone or Internet hotline with independent and appropriately trained counselors. A patient-subject could access the system through a simple phone call or email inquiry. Counselors should be able to address simple concerns and questions directly, and they could refer subjects with less easily resolved concerns to research sponsors or federal agencies.

Maintaining the resource could be part of the responsibilities of CROs and SMOs and could be funded collectively by corporate sponsors of research. However, the counselors should be accountable to the FDA and DHHS Office of Human Research Protections rather than to the industry sponsors.

Distribution of educational materials to all potential research subjects. It is important that potential research subjects understand the difference between clinical research and medical treatment, the advantages and disadvantages of being a research subject, and the issues unique to research in which a personal physician is also an investigator. General information on these topics could be included in an informational brochure distributed to all patients in the practice of a physician-investigator.

Some might argue that asking privately practicing physicians to distribute this material holds them to a higher moral standard than investigators in academia must honor. And in fact, ideally, a similar information brochure could be provided to potential research subjects in academic medical settings. Nonetheless, the unique problems of research in the private setting justify more rigorous protection of subjects there.

Responding to the problem posed by clinical research in the private office is not solely a federal matter. Whatever federal regulation is adopted, professional organizations and clinical societies that represent physicians should develop standards for the conduct of research in the private practice setting. Physicians have historically held that they are bound to respect the professional standards created by their peers. If there were professional standards for clinical research in private settings, honored voluntarily, they might obviate the need for stringent federal regulations.

There is also a need for ongoing empirical research to delineate the ethical problems in clinical research. Studies should gather data concerning the real costs to physicians of implementing research protocols, the extent of financial compensation from pharmaceutical companies, patient attitudes toward these arrangements, and the practices and impact of CROs and SMOs. Until there is empirical evidence to support some other set of recommendations, however, the safeguards we have proposed are needed.

NOTES

1. T. Bodenheimer, "Uneasy Alliance: Clinical Investigators and the Pharmaceutical Industry [see comments]," *NEJM* 342 (2000): 1539–44.

2. K. Eichenwald and G. Kolata, "Drug Trials Hide Conflicts for Doctors," *New York Times*, 16 May 1999.

3. R.J. Levine, "Clinical Trials and Physicians as Double Agents," *Yale Journal of Biology and Medicine* 65, no. 2 (1992): 65–74.

4. Department of Health and Human Services, Office of the Inspector General, *Recruiting Human Subjects, Pressures in Industry-sponsored Clinical Research*, Washington, D.C.: Department of Health and Human Services, June 2000; OEI-01-97-00195.

5. J.F. Niblack, "Why Are Drug Development Programs Growing in Size and Cost? A View from Industry," *Food and Drug Law Journal* 52 (1997): 151–54.

6. Pharmaceutical Research and Manufacturers of America, *PhRMA Industry Profile 1998* (Washington, D.C.: Pharmaceutical Research and Manufacturers of America, 1999), 27.

7. M. Hovde and R. Seskin, "Selecting U.S. Clinical Investigators," *Applied Clinical Trials* [VOL?] (1997): 35.

8. S.G. Stolberg and J. Gerth, "In a Drug's Journey to Market, Discovery Is Just the First of Many Steps," *New York Times* 23 July 2000.

9. Department of Health and Human Services, Office of the Inspector General, *Recruiting human subjects.*

10. E.G. DeRenzo, "Coercion in the Recruitment and Retention of Human Research Subjects, Pharmaceutical Industry Payments to Physician-investigators, and the Moral Courage of the IRB," *IRB: A Review of Human Subjects Research* 22, no. 2 (2000): 1–5.

11. Eichenwald and Kolata, "Drug Trials Hide Conflicts for Doctors."

12. Barnett International Conference Group, Fifth Annual Recruitment Conference (advertisement brochure), 2000.

13. DeRenzo, "Coercion in the Recruitment and Retention of Human Research Subjects."

14. R.J. Levine, "Ethics of Clinical Trials: Do They Help the Patient?" *Cancer* 72, no 9 suppl. (1993): 2805–810.

15. Regulations for Protection of Human Subjects, 45 C.F.R. Sect. 46(1981).

16. Levine, "Clinical Trials and Physicians."

17. B.R. Cassileth et al., "Attitudes toward Clinical Trials among Patients and the Public," *JAMA* 248 (1982): 968–70; M.E. Mattson, J.D. Curb, and R. McArdle, "Participation in a Clinical Trial: The Patients' Point of View," *Controlled Clinical Trials* 6, no. 2 (1985): 156–67.

18. S. Madsen, S. Holm, and P. Riis, "Ethical Aspects of Clinical Trials: The Attitudes of the Public and Outpatients," *Journal of Internal Medicine* 245, no. 6 (1999): 571–79.

19. Advisory Committee on Human Radiation Experiments, *Final Report of the Advisory Committee on Human Radiation Experiments* (Washington, D.C.: U.S. Government Printing Office, 1995), 724–57.

20. H.M. Spiro, "Constraint and Consent—On Being a Patient and a Subject," *NEJM* 293, no. 22 (1975): 1134–35.

21. N.E. Kass et al., "Trust, the Fragile Foundation of Contemporary Biomedical Research," *Hastings Center Report* 26, no. 5 (1996): 25–29.

22. M. Friedberg et al., "Evaluation of Conflict of Interest in Economic Analyses of New Drugs Used in Oncology [see comments]," *JAMA* 282 (1999): 1453–57; H.T. Stelfox, "Conflict of Interest in the Debate over Calcium-channel Antagonists [see comments]," *NEJM* 338 (1998): 101–106; M.K. Cho and L.A. Bero, "The Quality of Drug Studies Published in Symposium Proceedings," *Annals of Internal Medicine* 124, no. 5 (1996): 485–89; R.A. Davidson, "Source of Funding and Outcome of Clinical Trials," *Journal of General Internal Medicine* 1, no. 3 (1986): 155–58.

23. K. Eichenwald and G. Kolata, "A Doctor's Drug Studies Turn into Fraud," *New York Times*, 17 May 1999.

24. Eichenwald and Kolata, "Drug Trials Hide Conflicts for Doctors."

25. Department of Health and Human Services, Office of Research Integrity, *PHS Policy on Instruction in the Responsible Conduct of Research* (Rockville, Md.: Department of Health and Human Services, 1 December 2000).

26. J. Martin and D. Kasper, "In Whose Best Interest? Breaching the Academic-Industrial Wall," *NEJM* 343 (2000): 1646–49; K. Morin et al., "Managing Conflicts of Interest in the Conduct of Clinical Trials," *JAMA* 287 (2002): 78–84.

27. Association of American Medical Colleges, Task Force on Financial Conflicts of Interest in Clinical Research, *Protecting Subjects, Preserving Trust, Promoting Progress—Policy and Guidelines for the Oversight of Individual Financial Interests in Human Subjects Research* (Washington, D.C.: Association of American Medical Colleges, December 2001).

28. New York State Department of Health Advisory Work Group on Human Subjects Research Involving Protected Classes, *Recommendations on the Oversight of Human Subjects Research Involving the Protected Classes* (Albany, N.Y.: State of New York Department of Health, 1998); Office of the Maryland Attorney General, *Final Report of the State of Maryland Attorney General's Working Group on Research Involving Decisionally Incapacitated Subjects*, Baltimore, Md.: State of Maryland, 1998.

Karen Sanders

Ethics and Journalism

Karen Sanders is lecturer in Ethics and Political Communication at the University of Sheffield.

Whose round is it? What are we havin'? Where's the pub? When's it open? Why don't we have another one?

—The 5 Ws of journalism (Ian Hislop and Nick Newman)

The Duke of Wellington's famous phrase, "Publish and be damned" is sometimes taken to be a ringing endorsement of the principle of freedom of speech. In fact, it was an insult hurled at a corrupt reporter attempting to extort money from the Duke for suppression of a scurrilous story about him. "Conflicts of interest" were the order of the day for reporters of earlier times. You paid your money and you got your favourable (or suppression of unfavourable) coverage. Newspapers emerged out of a world of contentious reports of battles, diplomatic relations, and political machinations. They were usually wildly partisan and accepted payments from interested parties. The whole notion of objectivity would have been risible to the reporters of Grub Street....

———

The notion of a "conflict of interest" could only arise in a setting where reporters were expected to tell the truth without fear or favour, their prime duty being to purvey news rather than promote views. In other words, the notion that a "conflict of interest" is a moral problem entails a specific understanding of what journalism is.

The UK print industry's code does not mention the issue except in reference to financial journalism (see below). However, the broadcast industry's codes have extensive guidance about avoiding conflicts of interest and the British National Union of Journalists' Code of Conduct lays down the stern admonition that "A journalist shall not accept bribes nor shall he/she allow other inducements to influence the performance of his/her professional duties." It would be difficult to muster a defence of journalistic bribery. But what does it mean to say that a journalist should not allow their performance to be influenced by other inducements? Is this realistic?

INTENTIONS AND MOTIVES

Intentions and motives are key to evaluating actions as morally good or bad. If I set fire to a chair by accidentally dropping a match on it, this is a very different matter to setting fire to it with the intention of incinerating my younger brother. The accidental incineration of my younger brother is a tragedy; his intentional incineration is murder. I might kill my brother by accident or not manage to kill him when I meant to; I would be considered "bad" (rather than just "unlucky" or "ill-fated"), if it were known that I'd intended to kill him even if I didn't achieve my aim. In other words, motives matter.

Understanding the moral weight of motives and intentions, can help clarify the discussion about conflicts of interests. When we watch a BBC news programme, most of us assume that its intention is to give us the news as accurately and fairly as possible. Its proclamation and tradition of respecting public service principles make this a reasonable expectation. However, if I were to discover that an, albeit accurate, news report had been made with the intention of undermining an opposition political leader, I might find my trust in the BBC's integrity undermined. I would be troubled to find the bastion of public service promoting hidden agendas. This concern would be compounded if I were to find that the programme producer was motivated by personal hatred of the politician. However, if I were to read

From Karen Sanders, *Ethics and Journalism* (London: SAGE, 2003).

such a report in a government supporting newspaper, I'd be unlikely to be concerned. The publication's partisan views are declared and well-known; it makes no claims to impartiality. On the other hand, if I were later to discover that the writer of the piece had secretly received government money to do so, my confidence in the reporter's integrity would be shaken.

In part, the ethical issues about conflicts of interest arise from the set of expectations we have about certain practices. On the one hand, intentions and motives can be found to be at odds with those publicly declared. On the other, the very motives and intentions themselves can be considered dishonourable. Intentions and motives are tricky things to disentangle. We are not always entirely sure ourselves what our motive is for an action, let alone able to judge those of others. However, we can arrive at one clear conclusion: if the public's trust in what they see, hear and read is to be maintained, the motives and interests behind the news should be made as transparent as possible.

In the United States this principle has been taken further. Journalists' codes of conduct prohibit any activity which may be understood to establish an interest that conflicts with professional duties and undermines the reporter's credibility. Thus, many organizations forbid reporters from receiving anything but the most trivial gift (a pen or calendar, for example); others, such as the *Wall Street Journal*, insist on paying their way for everything, including contributing to the rental costs for the government pressrooms they use in Washington; others, such as the *Washington Post*, do not allow their reporters to cover subjects on which they are known to have taken a partisan stance. The issue here is not that a reporter necessarily has been seduced into writing a favourable article about say, a holiday destination because of the all-expenses paid trip, but that it is the *perception* that favours may have been purchased which should be avoided. This strict interpretation of the possibility of conflicts of interests, imports a principle which has come to be applied in public life. In his resignation letter of December 1998 the British Labour politician, Peter Mandelson, wrote:

> I do not believe that I have done anything wrong or improper.... But we came to power promising to uphold the highest standards in public life. We have not just to do so, *but we must be seen to do so.*

His acceptance of an undeclared loan from a fellow minister whose business interests Mandelson's own ministry was investigating gave the appearance of a conflict of interest and he was forced to resign. Journalists are often the fiercest critics of politicians in these circumstances and they increasingly seem to be applying the same standards to themselves.

BRIBES, JUNKETS AND FREEBIES

In its strictest sense, bribery is the act or practice of giving or accepting money or some other payment with the object of corruptly influencing the judgement or action of another. Although commonplace in seventeenth and eighteenth century journalism, it is a practice which would seem to have all but disappeared from modern British journalism. A modest contemporary descendent is the "freebie," that is any goods or service received for which no charge is made, and the "junket," an all-expenses paid trip to promote a product. For many years these were considered to be perks of an often poorly paid job. While many reporters are still badly paid, media organizations have become increasingly squeamish about accepting them....

However, the absolute prohibition on freebies is still not common practice throughout the UK print industry. Journalists accept free books, CDs, film tickets, car loans, foreign trips, etc. Why is this considered wrong? The argument is that such practices can be subtly corrupting, undermining a reporter's detachment and objectivity, or at least giving the appearance that they might. On some American publications policies are very strict:

> Reporters shouldn't accept any gifts from the people they may have to write about—no bottles of Scotch, vacations, fountain pens or dinners. Reporters don't even want to have to be in a position of having to distinguish between a gift and a bribe. Return them all with a polite thank you. (Day, 1997: 186)

Some areas of journalism are more susceptible than others to the seduction of freebies and allied "perks." Any kind of reviewing, for example, where the reporter must sample a range of products and provide what can be a highly influential judgement upon them, makes the reporter's integrity vulnerable on two counts. First, he or she must obtain the goods. Rich media institutions can insulate their reporters from the possibly corrupting effect of freebies by buying them or by having them loaned. This is, for example, the approved practice at the BBC. However, a cash-strapped provincial newspaper may find that if they do not accept free goods and services they have nothing to review. Second, reporters are vulnerable to the determined efforts of PR professionals to win favour and publicity for their particular product....

In general, the trend seems to be towards a more transparent, less venal journalistic world. Expenses-paid trips are today far less common than they used to be and reporters are now even charged for accompanying political leaders on their election battle buses. Even reporters' expenses—"exes"—are not what they used to be. The *Daily Mirror*'s fabled "bank in the sky," its accounts department situated at the top of the now demolished building just off Fleet Street, no longer exists. Even expenses, however, were regulated by an informal code of ethics so that:

> A reporter specializing in religious matters was sacked...after sending all his Christmas cards, including one to the editor, via the *Sunday Express* post room. (Anonymous, 1999: 108)

As wages have improved in the national media, and media institutions have changed from personal fiefdoms to money-making machines in huge corporate empires, freebies, junkets and extravagant expenses seem to be going the same way as the print unions.

FINANCIAL JOURNALISM

On 5 May, 2000 the Press Complaints Commission issued a hard-hitting judgement condemning the actions of *The Mirror* "City Slicker" columnists, Anil Bhoyrul and James Hipwell, and the negligence of the paper's editor, Piers Morgan. The "City Slickers" column first appeared in *The Mirror* in May 1998. At first the column was not taken seriously, but with time its influence became considerable. As Bhoyrul put it, "We had created a monster that was out of control. Every time I tipped a share the price shot up between 30 per cent and 100 per cent the next morning. Suddenly, *The Mirror* was engulfed in the Slickers craze—and it was getting scary. Its Top Ten Tips for 1999 produced a return of 142 per cent in terms of performance over the year" (Report 50, 2000).

Both reporters began to purchase shares which were featured in the column. They would identify a share that would become the next day's "tip of the day"; then purchase a number of those shares, publish the "tip of the day" and sell the shares on the day of the tip. After an internal investigation both journalists were summarily dismissed in February 2000 for gross misconduct. The PCC also censured the *Mirror* editor who bought shares that had been tipped by the "City Slicker" columnists. Morgan justified his behaviour on the grounds that he was doing no more than the paper was suggesting its readers did. However, he was found to be in breach of Clause 14 of the code which deals with financial journalism (see Box 8.1). Its aim is to ensure that readers receive disinterested advice and information and that journalists and those connected with them do not profit as a result of the publication of financial information. The editor was also censured for his failure to take firm action against the reporters beyond giving them a verbal warning. It was pointed out that "editors must ensure that the code is observed rigorously by their staff and others who contribute to their newspapers."...

The *Mirror* incident was the one of the most serious to come to light since press self-regulation was introduced by the creation of the Press Council in July 1963. It provides a paradigm case of a conflict of interest in a way that freebies do not. A reporter whose financial predictions determined how much she or her editor might earn could not be trusted to tell the truth in an instance in which truthful information might adversely affect earnings. And it would no longer be possible to rely upon the truthfulness of a reporter whose motives had been so seriously traduced.

Box 8.1 Financial journalism

PCC code Clause 14

i. Even where the law does not prohibit it, journalists must not use for their own profit financial information they receive in advance of its general publication, nor should they pass such information to others.

ii. They must not write about shares or securities in whose performance they know that they or their close families have a significant financial interest, without disclosing the interest to the editor or the financial editor.

iii. They must not buy or sell, either directly or through nominees or agents, shares or securities about which they have written recently or about which they intend to write in the near future.

PUFFERY AND SUPPRESSION

Advertising has been seen as a source of possible conflict of interest on two counts. First, external advertising pressure to influence editorial content is cited as an area of ethical difficulty for journalists. Second, internal pressures from a media company's own marketing and publicity departments are said to attempt to drive journalistic content in certain directions. An example of the first was the threat and eventual withdrawal of advertising from the *Sunday Times* by the Distillers Company, angry at the paper's campaign against it on behalf of the thalidomide victims.... An example of the second is the apparent "puffery" in which the *Sun* and the *Sunday*

Times engaged to promote the launch of Sky television, a sister company to the two as part of News International.

Evidence for these practices tends to be anecdotal. The first Royal Commission on the Press (1947–49) examined the issue of advertising influence on the press and found that individual attempts were infrequent and unsuccessful. But it would be surprising if corporate self-interest did not dictate certain editorial content. Rupert Murdoch is said to have pulled the BBC from his Star satellite service when it upset Chinese leaders. Former *Observer* editor, Donald Trelford, endured pressure from the publisher, Tiny Rowland, to suppress critical stories of Mugabe's rule in Zimbabwe where Rowland's Lonrho empire had extensive business interests. To his credit he resisted. He was not so successful in resisting his proprietor's interest in campaigning against his great rival, Mohammed al Fayed.

Advertising and marketing departments have often been seen as the Great Satan by reporters, besmirching their journalistic purity in the search for filthy lucre. On American newspapers there is a tradition of maintaining a wall of separation between editors and business departments. As Meyer has pointed out, these attitudes are not always entirely sensible. "An editor who understands the newspaper's financial situation is in a stronger position to fight for the resources needed to produce the kind of newspaper that readers deserve" (1991, 45).

In the main, the issues raised by advertising pressures are clear-cut, if not always easy to resolve. A greyer area is the extent to which a reporter's personal views can pose conflicts of interest.

PERSONAL VIEWS

A survey carried out of American journalists found that most would not object to someone from a farming background writing about agricultural issues or someone with a law degree being assigned to court coverage. However, they strongly objected to an atheist writing about religious affairs or a trade unionist being asked to write about big business (Meyer, 1991: 72). The general principle seemed to be that it would be unfairly prejudicial to ask someone known to be antagonistic to sources or an issue to cover a story. Thus, someone who is a member of the Beaufort Hunt might not be best placed to write about hunt saboteurs....

However, it does seem a little ridiculous to assume that all reporters must have a man from Mars stance of total detachment. Simply by virtue of being involved in the local community—as a school governor, shopper at the local grocery shop, dog walker in the local park, worshipper at the local church—may involve a reporter in what might be considered a conflict of interest: I might be asked, for example, to cover a story about the threatened local shop which I happen to use or the problems at the school my children attend. The easiest way to resolve these possible conflicts of interest in reporting a story is disclosure....

Others go further. Keeble cites those who call for a "new transparency" among journalists, calling upon them "to declare their financial interests" much as public officials must now do (2001: 42). This would certainly help clear up malpractice in financial journalism. But how can reporting for the right reasons be promoted outside this specialist area? In other words, how can the notion be encouraged that reporting is about an "honest search for the truth ... an openminded attempt to find out what really happened, accompanied by a willingness to print that truth, however uncomfortable it may be to our own, or the paper's, cherished beliefs" (Randall, 2000: 134–35)? Someone who is already corrupt—who writes favourable reviews in return for weekly crates of wine, for example—would not, in Aristotle's words "listen to an argument to dissuade him, or understand it if he did" (*Nichomachean Ethics*, 1179b25). If a reporter is in the business *only* for money, fame, power, the thrill of the chase and being first, then why not accept those crates of wine? Without ideals about what journalism is for, all the registers in the world won't ensure that reporters act for the right reasons.

Warren E. Burger

Too Many Lawyers, Too Many Suits

Warren E. Burger was the Chief Justice of the U.S. Supreme Court from 1969 to 1986 and presided over several of the most important cases in twentieth century American history.

In a speech to the American Bar Association convention in 1906, the famous legal philosopher and Harvard Law School Dean, Roscoe Pound, criticized lawyers for making litigation a "sporting contest." The A.B.A. did not like the criticism and at first

refused to publish the speech. In "The Litigation Explosion," Walter K. Olson echoes and amplifies Pound's indictment of the legal profession.

Writing especially for nonlawyers, Mr. Olson, a journalist and a senior fellow at the Manhattan Institute, argues that the decline in ethics and the profession's abandonment of age-old constraints on lawyers has created the "litigation business." Lawyers, he tells us, are moving from a profession to a trade, with a corresponding decline in ethics, and

From the *New York Times*, May 12, 1991. Reprinted with permission.

they are developing many of the attitudes exhibited by used car dealers. Lawyers' behavior, Mr. Olson says, is largely responsible for the alarming increase in the number of lawsuits in the United States in comparison to other countries that share the basic structure of our legal system. Mr. Olson adds that this rise parallels the rise in the number of law schools and lawyers—producing a kind of "chicken and egg" situation. . . .

To demonstrate that our society is drowning in litigation, one only has to look at the overworked system of justice, the delays in trials, the clogs businessmen face in commerce and a medical profession rendered overcautious for fear of malpractice suits. The litigation explosion, which developed in barely more than a decade beginning in the 1970's, has affected us at all levels, including, as Mr. Olson notes, "the most sensitive and profound relationships of human life." The consequences of the explosion have become painfully obvious. Suits against hospitals and doctors, which went up 300-fold since the 1970's, increased doctors' medical insurance premiums more than 30-fold for some. We have more lawyers per 100,000 people than any other society in the world. We have almost three times as many lawyers per capita as Britain, with whom we share the common law system.

Mr. Olson notes that lawyers who got their start advertising on late-night television are moving from automobile cases into commercial litigation— or any litigation that earns fees. Another recent book, "Shark Tank," by Kim Isaac Eisler, tells the dismal tale of a mega-law firm, Finley Kumble, and reveals, among other things, the growing use of public relations consultants to tout a law firm's skills and accomplishments. The United States stands alone as the glorifier of lawyers and litigation. And who pays? All of us! Malpractice insurance (which can cost a doctor upward of $50,000 a year), higher automobile insurance rates and other such expenses are a "sales tax" paid by all of us, but one that goes into lawyers' pockets.

There was a time, Mr. Olson indicates, when litigation was viewed as undesirable and, at best, like war, a necessary evil. Strict professional standards, tough laws, and social stigma discouraged shyster

lawyers from the temptation to stir up litigation. Professional ethics were alive and on the minds of most attorneys. Today, however, success at the bar is measured by salaries and bonuses, while many lawyers, Mr. Olson notes, justify their new role in our litigious society by asserting that they are preserving and protecting people's rights—giving more "access to justice." In short, as he aptly puts it, lawyers want Americans to believe that "the more lawsuits there are . . . the closer to perfect the world will become."

The author says this idea—that lawsuits can be used to deter wrongdoing—is one reason for the litigation explosion. Lawsuits, he argues; have become known as assertions of "rights." Lawyers have justified a wide range of grossly unprofessional actions, like flying off to Bhopal, India, to solicit cases, or to Alaska in a chase for cases on oil spills. To those who have praised litigation as having social value per se, one is tempted to cite Judge Learned Hand: "I must say that as a litigant, I should dread a lawsuit beyond almost anything else short of sickness and death."

One way Mr. Olson documents the disintegration of professional ethics is by examining lawyer advertising on television and in print. In 1977, in Bates v. Arizona, the Supreme Court held 5 to 4 that such advertising was protected by the First Amendment; prior to that time, lawyers were forbidden to advertise or to solicit clients. Apart from a handful of "ambulance chasers," only the shysters went further than sending a business card to a potential client or joining the right clubs. Clearly, the disintegration accelerated after the Bates case. But Mr. Olson's argument that the decision itself changed legal ethics attributes too much to it. The author ignores the difference between a profession, like the law, and a trade or business where advertising is more acceptable.

For centuries, the standards of the legal profession were higher than simply compliance with the law. Yet after the Bates ruling, the American Bar Association quickly relaxed its traditional Canons of Professional Ethics, leading some commentators to wonder whether the A.B.A. had become more interested in a large membership than in traditional ethical standards. Today, the ancient and hallowed concept that lawyers are officers of the court is too often treated with an indulgent smile, not only by shyster advertisers, of course, but unfortunately even by some members of the legal profession who have been entrusted with teaching law students.

Legal academia is one of Mr. Olson's frequent targets. For example, he takes on a law professor who argues that in the "contemporary social context" it may be appropriate for lawyers to sponsor and finance litigation. Mr. Olson also perceptively criticizes the tricky business of champerty, allowing a third party, a bank for instance, to finance litigation, with the attorney often agreeing to pay back that third party, or even putting up collateral. Transactions of this kind reflect what has gone on in the savings and loan and the bank scandals—and in the Ivan Boesky and Michael Milken cases. Champerty, as Mr. Olson explains, developed from another form of legal gambling, the contingency fee.

Mr. Olson would be on even sounder ground if he were to expand his discussion and say that a contingency fee is unethical and dishonest, and ought to be unlawful whenever liability is certain, as it often is, for example, in multiple-victim disasters like plane crashes or railroad collisions. Admittedly, unless the measure of damages is fixed by statute, the *amount* of a recovery can vary, even when liability is certain. A highly experienced litigator is likely to get a larger settlement or verdict than an amateur. But if a lawyer soliciting a case is required to tell a client whenever liability is certain, that should at least rule out unconscionable contingency fees of 33 percent and 50 percent in those certain-recovery cases.

Mr. Olson contrasts lawyers' contingency fees with the ethical prohibition against doctors charging a fee contingent on the success of the treatment of a patient. The American Medical Association, unlike the American Bar Association, has not thought that the constitutional protection of advertising called for a change in medical ethics. The Hippocratic oath still prevails among doctors. Because a doctor may *constitutionally* advertise has not meant that doctors may do so *ethically*. Compare this with the A.B.A.'s tentative standard forbidding only "false and misleading" advertising. Shyster advertisers stimulate

litigation with their advertisements, offering a "free" conference. This kind of advertising is reminiscent of that old poem we recited in our school days: "Come into my parlor,' said the spider to the fly."

There is some hope, Mr. Olson points out, of curbing the litigation explosion through third-party arbitration and other forms of "alternative dispute resolution." In 1976, the Judicial Conference of the United States and the A.B.A. sponsored a conference to celebrate the 70th anniversary of Pound's famous speech. That meeting introduced "alternative dispute resolution" into our vocabulary. With hordes of unneeded lawyers flooding the country, perhaps the surplus could be used as arbitrators and mediators.

Who, finally, is to blame for the current problem? Journalists? Lawyers? Law professors? The A.B.A.? The Supreme Court? Mr. Olson indicts all of us; and while there is much to this, those charged with legal stewardship, pre-eminently the A.B.A., can especially be called to account.

The legal and the medical professions are monopolies. Historically, each has largely regulated itself with codes and creeds. Medicine has the Hippocratic oath. Lawyers have no counterpart, but over centuries they have developed common law ethical standards. Up till now, legislative bodies and courts have left regulation to the organized bar. Will that continue? One can only hope that Mr. Olson's book will stimulate moves to control unethical lawyers.

In an era noted for corruption in business, the clergy, academia, science, the political arena—and even among Federal judges—it should not be surprising that there has been a deterioration in the standards and practices of the legal profession. More Federal judges have been found guilty of bribe-taking and tax fraud in the past decade than in the first 190 years of our history. Mr. Olson need not be totally correct in all his criticisms to make "The Litigation Explosion" a valuable contribution to the public interest. Will the legal profession, especially the A.B.A., do anything to clean its own house? It remains uncertain.

Rebecca Dresser

Plan B: Politics and Values at the FDA, Again

Rebecca Dresser is Daniel Noyes Kirby Professor of Law at Washington University in St. Louis.

Plan B is an emergency contraceptive that the U.S. Food and Drug Administration approved for prescription use in 1999. In 2003, a company called Barr Pharmaceuticals submitted to the FDA an application to switch Plan B from prescription to over-the-counter (OTC) status. At a joint meeting late that year, the FDA's Non-prescription Drugs Advisory Committee and Advisory Committee for Reproductive Health Drugs recommended that the agency approve the application. But in a May 2004 letter, FDA officials notified Barr that the application was "not approvable at this time."

The letter, signed by the acting director of FDA's Center for Drug Evaluation and Research, Steven Galson, said that the company had failed to supply data establishing that Plan B would be safe for younger women using it without professional supervision. A drug can qualify for OTC status only if it confers benefits that outweigh its risks, and the manufacturer tries to show that it does by offering evidence of acceptable product performance in a study of actual consumer use. Label comprehension is also a central concern. Because consumers will take the drug without a clinician's guidance, the label must include clear instructions for safe and effective use.[1]

Barr's application to sell Plan B without a prescription relied primarily on a study of 585 women. Though the data overall met the OTC standards, the sample size for young adolescents was inadequate, Galson asserted: just twenty-nine subjects were under sixteen and none was under fourteen.

Barr had also submitted an alternative (and novel) proposal to assign Plan B a dual status—OTC for women over sixteen and by prescription for younger women. But Galson denied this proposal because it was incomplete.

The FDA letter described what Barr could do to gain approval for OTC status. First, it could furnish more data showing that young adolescents could use Plan B safely without professional assistance. Alternatively, it could submit a more complete application for dual status. The latter option would be more complicated, however. Barr would have to describe a satisfactory labeling, marketing, and education approach that took into account the different age groups and access routes for a dual status product. The FDA would also have to verify its statutory authority to approve a drug as prescription-only for some people and OTC for others.

Although Galson denied that the agency was under political pressure to decide as it did, skeptics charged that Plan B had become a pawn in the presidential campaign. Groups supporting OTC status charged that the decision was actually motivated by the administration's quest to win votes in the November election. Conservative groups and members of Congress had opposed the switch, claiming that an easily available emergency contraceptive could promote unsafe sex among teenagers. They also said that OTC status would conflict with the administration's other policies favoring abstinence for teens.[2]

But pro-choice and medical organizations argued that the data were more than adequate to support the switch. According to the existing data, Plan B reduces the pregnancy rate after unprotected sex

From the *Hastings Center Report*, Nov.–Dec. 2004.

from 8 percent to 1 percent. The drug is most effective when taken within twenty-four hours after intercourse, which is much easier to do if the drug has OTC status. Researchers have detected no serious side effects in women and no harm to children born to women taking the drug. Like several other contraceptives, Plan B fails to protect against sexually transmitted diseases, but OTC supporters cite studies indicating that women with convenient access to emergency contraceptives do not decrease their use of condoms.[3]

Researchers say that Plan B may act in two ways to prevent pregnancy. One is by preventing ovulation and the other is by preventing the fertilized egg from implanting in the uterus. The latter possibility makes the drug objectionable to people who think it is wrong to terminate developing human life after conception. Those favoring OTC status say that the objection can be addressed by product labeling that allows women who hold this moral view to avoid using the drug.

THE HYBRID NATURE OF FDA DECISIONS

Much of the negative reaction to the Plan B ruling labeled the decision "unscientific." For example, an editorial in the *New England Journal of Medicine* stated that: "Until now, [FDA] approval has been based on scientific evidence from well-designed clinical trials with adequate power to establish safety and rule out toxicity with some reasonable level of confidence. Political considerations have wisely been kept out of the decision-making process."[4] Yet the Plan B decision was only the latest of a long line of FDA rulings that were controversial because of disagreements over which values should take priority in drug-approval decisions. Like most other science policy decisions, drug-approval decisions necessarily build on judgments about both science and values. And interest groups often lobby the agency to make choices that will reflect their constituents' values.

The events surrounding RU-486 offer one illustration. By the early 1990s, this drug had been approved for clinical use in several countries, but pro-life and pro-choice forces struggled for more than a decade before the FDA deemed the product safe and effective for U.S. women. Although the debate was presented as hinging on the adequacy of medical evidence concerning safety, it was substantially influenced by abortion politics. Indeed, when RU-486 was linked to a California woman's death in 2003, abortion opponents claimed once again that the product was unsafe and petitioned the FDA to restrict access to the drug.[5]

Silicone-gel breast implants were the focus of another values conflict at the FDA. In 1992, former commissioner David Kessler restricted the availability of implants on the ground that adequate safety data were lacking. According to his ruling, implants could not be provided to women for breast augmentation, but could be available for breast reconstruction to women enrolled in clinical trials evaluating the devices. In Kessler's judgment, the risks of implants were too great to allow their use for enhancement purposes, but acceptable in studies of implants to relieve the effects of disease.

Kessler invoked values in defense of his ruling: "Certainly as a society, we are far from according cosmetic interventions the same importance as a matter of public health that we accord to cancer treatments."[6] In turn, critics said Kessler had inappropriately devalued the benefits of breast augmentation: "In waving aside the benefits of breast implants for most women who had them, Kessler appeared to be introducing an impossibly high standard for the devices: since there were no benefits, there should be no risks."[7]

The values conflict over breast implants continues even today. In 2003, an FDA advisory committee found that trial data collected since Kessler's ruling were sufficient to demonstrate safety and efficacy. A majority of the committee recommended that implants be approved for both augmentation and reconstruction, but critics charged that several committee members were plastic surgeons with financial interests in making implants more widely available. The FDA later denied the application, saying that more data on long-term safety were needed.[8]

VALUES IN FDA DECISIONS

Value judgments are implicit in any FDA approval decision because determinations about a product's safety depend partly on judgments about the importance of the benefit it offers. If a product appears to reduce burdensome symptoms or extend life in many seriously ill patients, the agency is likely to approve the product even if it also presents material risks to some of those patients. The agency is less likely to accept such risks if a product targets only mild symptoms, and even less likely if the benefits are seen as purely cosmetic. Similar judgments affect the agency's evidentiary requirements. The FDA's accelerated approval program exemplifies its willingness to be less demanding about safety and efficacy data when drugs offer significant benefits to seriously ill patients.

It is disingenuous for either side in the Plan B controversy to suggest that the dispute is simply about the amount or quality of scientific data. Like the disagreements over RU-486 and siliconegel breast implants, the disagreement over whether Plan B should become an OTC drug reflects conflicting ethical judgments about the possible consequences of such a situation. People who see unwanted pregnancy as a serious harm are more likely to consider Barr's study data adequate, while those worried about preserving traditional norms surrounding marriage and procreation are more likely to find the data deficient.

Rather than criticizing FDA officials for taking values into account, we should criticize them for failing to disclose which values affected the decision. Certain features of the FDA's "not approvable" ruling suggest that it relied on unarticulated

value preferences. The FDA notification letter said that the data on Plan B use by young teenagers were insufficient, but it did not say which risks warranted further investigation. The letter failed to cite specific physical or other potential harms to girls under seventeen or concerns related to their ability to understand the product label. These omissions left the agency vulnerable to complaints that the decision was based on different, undisclosed considerations.

The Plan B dispute at the FDA, like others before it and others that will follow it, is about what matters to the participants. Rather than attempting to disguise value conflicts as disputes over data, it would be better to recognize them, as Kessler did in his decision about breast implants. Participants in FDA deliberations should be required to explain the values underlying their judgments about the adequacy of research data so that others have the opportunity to examine, and possibly challenge, those judgments. We cannot banish values and politics from FDA decisionmaking, but we can insist that they be brought into the open.

NOTES

1. R. Steinbrook, "Waiting for Plan B—The FDA and Nonprescription Use of Emergency Contraception," *NEJM* 350 (2004): 2327–29.

2. M. Kaufman, "Debate Intensifies over 'Morning After' Pill," *The Washington Post*, February 13, 2004.

3. B. Vastag, "Plan B for 'Plan B'?" *JAMA* 291 (2004): 2805–06.

4. J.M. Drazen, M.F. Greene, and A.J.J. Wood, "The FDA, Politics, and Plan B," *NEJM* 350 (2004): 1561–62.

5. M. Kaufman, "Death after Abortion Pill Reignites Safety Debate," *The Washington Post*, November 3, 2003.

6. D.A. Kessler, "The Basis of the FDA's Decision on Breast Implants," *NEJM* 326 (1992): 1713–15.

7. M. Angell, *Science on Trial: The Clash of Medical Evidence and the Law in the Breast Implant Case* (New York: Norton 1996), 63.

8. L. Neergaard, "FDA Nixes Bid on Silicone Implants," *The Washington Post*, January 8, 2004.

David Orentlicher
and Lois Snyder

Can Assisted Suicide Be Regulated?

David Orentlicher, MD, JD, is Samuel R. Rosen Professor of Law and is the Co-Director in the Center for Law and Health at Indiana University School of Law in Indianapolis.

Lois Snyder, JD, is director of the Center for Ethics and Professionalism at the American College of Physicians, and has been an Adjunct Professor of Bioethics at the Center for Bioethics of the University of Pennsylvania in Philadelphia.

BACKGROUND CONSIDERATIONS

Regulations serve several important goals. Most importantly, they provide guidance as to the line between permissible and impermissible behavior. We permit people to drive at some speeds but not at other speeds. Similarly, assisted suicide regulations typically would limit the practice to *physician*-assisted suicide and to patients who possess decision-making capacity.

Drawing lines between the permissible and impermissible, and implementing mechanisms to enforce those lines, can enhance public trust. Society tolerates potentially dangerous practices only if there are adequate protections against the risk of harm. Moreover, many individuals are willing to conform their behavior to what is morally and legally required only if they are assured that others will do the same. Well-enforced regulations can help provide that assurance.

Regulations also serve an important monitoring function. As new regulations are implemented, data can be collected and analyzed to see if the regulations are working as intended or whether modifications are necessary to ensure more appropriate behavior.

Regulations have drawbacks as well as benefits. They can be cumbersome and administratively inefficient. They can also be counterproductive. For example, procedural requirements for the withdrawal of life-sustaining treatment from incompetent patients prevent premature withdrawal from patients who would want treatment continued. However, they also can interfere with the rights of patients who would want treatment withdrawn. If a state requires clear and convincing evidence of the patient's wishes, and the wishes must have specifically anticipated the patient's current condition, patients may be treated against what would have likely been their preferences. Because regulations have advantages and disadvantages, it is often difficult to decide exactly how much regulation is appropriate. If regulation is too light, serious harms can result. If regulation is too heavy, different harms can result. Too permissive a right to assisted suicide might lead to many premature deaths. Too restrictive a right (or no right) might result in unnecessary suffering.

IS IT POSSIBLE TO LEGALIZE ASSISTED SUICIDE IN SOME CIRCUMSTANCES WITHOUT ULTIMATELY OPENING THE DOOR TO ASSISTED SUICIDE AND/OR EUTHANASIA FOR ALL INDIVIDUALS?

Proposals for assisted suicide typically permit only physicians to assist, and they generally would not permit euthanasia. Proposals also limit the right to patients who are terminally ill and who have the mental capacity to make medical decisions. For

From *The Journal of Clinical Ethics* vol. 11, no. 4, Winter 2000.

example, all four limitations are part of Oregon's Death with Dignity Act, the only law in the United States permitting physician-assisted suicide. Under that law, the patient must be a competent adult and within six months of death to exercise the statutory right to obtain a "prescription for medication to end his or her life in a humane and dignified manner."

…It is difficult in practice—and in principle—to distinguish between patients who are terminally ill and those who are not terminally ill. For patients with solid tumors, predictions of life expectancy are reasonably good. For patients with congestive heart failure, however, it is not possible to predict with much certainty whether they can live for only a few months or another year or two. Moreover, even when we can make reliable determinations of life expectancy, it does not follow that the patient's right to die should hinge on whether the patient is terminally ill. If a patient has an incurable disease and is suffering greatly, should it matter whether the patient has five months or 25 months to live? Indeed, it can be argued that the patient who has 25 months to live will experience much more total suffering than the patient with only five months to live.

Similarly, it may be difficult to hold the line between assisted suicide and euthanasia. Many dying patients will be too disabled to take the lethal dose of medication, but their desire to die may be just as justified as that of patients who retain the ability to commit suicide. Arguably, it is unfair and discriminatory to permit less disabled patients the option to end their lives while denying that option to patients who are more disabled. Finally, some argue, it should not matter whether the patient is competent. If the patient left explicit instructions for euthanasia in the event of incompetence and serious illness, why shouldn't those instructions be carried out as would other instructions left by the patient?

Experience supports concern that a limited right to assisted suicide will lead to an unlimited right to both assisted suicide and euthanasia. The history of the right to refuse life-sustaining treatment is a history of discarded distinctions. Whether the patient is terminally ill, whether the treatment is a ventilator or a feeding tube, or whether the treatment is withheld

or withdrawn are no longer considered conceptual restrictions to the right to refuse treatment.

These arguments are well taken, but there are important counterarguments. First, the concern about expansions beyond a limited right to assisted suicide assumes that such expansions would be wrong. However, good moral reasons may exist to support a right to assisted suicide for some patients who are not terminally ill or a right to euthanasia for some patients who are unable to take medications by themselves. Indeed, it may be more troublesome to withhold life-sustaining treatment from a "pleasantly senile" patient who had never expressed preferences about treatment than to permit euthanasia for a competent patient who is within a few days of death and suffering greatly. But if expansions of a right to assisted suicide would involve practices that are not morally different from assisted suicide for the terminally ill, it is hard to see why expansions of the right would be unacceptable. If society decides that assisted suicide for the terminally ill is morally appropriate, it would not be wrong to also permit assisted suicide for other patients who have the same moral justification for ending their lives as terminally ill patients. If, on the other hand, there are important moral differences between assisted suicide and euthanasia or between suicide for the terminally ill and suicide for those who are not terminally ill, those differences ought to provide sufficient protection against the risk of expansion. The right to abortion has not led to a right to infanticide or to a right to abortion after viability, in large part because there are important moral differences between previable fetuses and viable fetuses or infants.

Second, the expansion of the right to refuse life-sustaining treatment has been greatly overstated by many commentators. Although it is true in theory that the patient's diagnosis and prognosis are no longer relevant for purposes of treatment withdrawal, in practice they matter very much. As illustrated by court decisions in Michigan, New Jersey, and Wisconsin, legal standards make it much more difficult to withdraw treatment from incompetent patients who are neither terminally ill nor permanently unconscious.

Third, in terms of the reasons for the legal distinction between assisted suicide and treatment withdrawal, there is good reason to think that a right to assisted suicide for the terminally ill would remain limited. It has been argued that the distinction between assisted suicide and treatment withdrawal has existed not because of any real moral difference between the two acts, but because the distinction does a generally good job of sorting morally justified from morally unjustified patient deaths. In this view, the morality of a patient's death depends on the patient's condition, not on the mechanism of the death. That is, the right to refuse life-sustaining treatment ultimately rests on the moral sentiment that people should be able to die when they are suffering greatly from an irreversible illness, rather than on the position that patients have an autonomy right to refuse any and all bodily invasions. In this view, we allow treatment withdrawal but deny assisted suicide because the *typical* person who refuses life-sustaining treatment is irreversibly ill and suffering greatly (and therefore morally justified in wanting to die) while the *typical* person who wishes to commit suicide is not irreversibly ill (and therefore not morally justified in wanting to die). Permitting assisted suicide but limiting the right to the terminally ill may allow the law to better sort morally justified from morally unjustified deaths. Accordingly, further expansions of the right would occur only if necessary to better serve the goal of sorting morally justified from morally unjustified patient deaths.

EVEN IF LINES CAN BE DRAWN, ARE THEY LIKELY TO BE OBSERVED?

As mentioned, many proposals would limit physician-assisted suicide to terminally ill patients. But it is not always clear when a patient becomes terminally ill. Similarly, although a law might require that the patient be competent and not suffering from treatable depression, physicians are often not very good at detecting treatable depression in their patients. Requirements of second opinions are not a foolproof safeguard. Physicians can often find sympathetic colleagues who will ratify their opinions.

Without doubt, there will be slippage. Even with the most careful guidelines and the most stringent safeguards, mistakes will be made. However, that is not necessarily the correct measure of success or failure. Rather, it may be more appropriate to ask whether the mistakes would be any more frequent or more serious with assisted suicide than with treatment withdrawal. Patients often refuse life-sustaining treatment because they believe they are terminally ill or irreversibly dependent on life-sustaining treatment. Medical uncertainty means that many of these patients might choose death on the basis of an erroneous assumption about their prognosis, just as patients might choose assisted suicide in the mistaken belief that they are terminally ill. Concerns about treatable depression are also an issue for treatment withdrawal. Patients who refuse a ventilator, dialysis, or other treatments may have an undetected depression.

Commentators often cite the Dutch experience to show that slippage is inevitable. Leading studies have reported that, in about 25 to 30 percent of cases involving euthanasia or assisted suicide, patients did not make an explicit and contemporaneous request to have their life ended, as required under the safeguards developed by the medical profession and the courts in The Netherlands. However, these and other rule violations need not reflect the administration of euthanasia against the patient's wishes or in response to coercion by family members or physicians. Although that does happen, the violations often reflect two types of deviation: (1) failure to adhere to reporting requirements or to obtain outside review and (2) situations in which euthanasia is probably consistent with the patient's wishes but in which the evidence of the patient's wishes but in which the evidence of the patient's wishes does not meet the formal requirement of contemporaneous, consistent, and persistent expressions. In other words, the abuses in The Netherlands often involve violations of the letter but not the spirit of the law.

Still, there may be undetected abuses in The Netherlands. In most cases of physician-assisted suicide or euthanasia, physicians do not meet their legal obligation to report the case to public authorities.

But, even if we accept the most serious charges of abuse regarding The Netherlands' experience, it still does not follow that we can distinguish between physician-assisted suicide and withdrawal of life-sustaining treatment. The Dutch experience may show that legalizing euthanasia or assisted suicide leads to abuse, but the same concerns of abuse arise with the withdrawal of life-sustaining treatment. Studies have consistently shown that physicians do not always follow ethical and legal guidelines when withdrawing life-sustaining treatment. Nevertheless, the slippage is not believed to be serious enough to prohibit the refusal of life-sustaining treatment.

DECISIONS ABOUT PHYSICIAN-ASSISTED SUICIDE WILL TYPICALLY OCCUR IN THE PRIVACY OF THE PATIENT–PHYSICIAN RELATIONSHIP, MAKING ABUSES UNDETECTABLE

Typically, proposals to legalize assisted suicide include a requirement that the suicide be assisted by a physician. Indeed, Oregon's right to assisted suicide is a right to *physician*-assisted suicide. The requirement of a physician's participation serves a few important purposes. First, it is thought to protect against abuse. Proponents of this view believe that physicians will be better able than family members or friends to detect a treatable depression. In addition, although it is not always possible to detect coercion, physicians can intervene if there is reason to suspect that the suicide request is motivated by the coercion of family or friends. Second, physicians can provide what is often the least painful and quickest method of assisted suicide—death by ingestion of prescribed medications. Third, it is important to have a physician confirm the patient's diagnosis and prognosis, to ensure that the patient truly is terminally (or irreversibly) ill.

Still, it is argued, the additional safeguards provided by physicians' participation may not be sufficient. In this view, regulation of assisted suicide must rely too heavily on physicians' self-regulation. Patients, with their physicians, would be able to decide about suicide and commit suicide without outside involvement. Moreover, the confidentiality of discussions between patients and physicians would prevent adequate oversight. In other words, discussions and decisions about assisted suicide are inherently private in nature and therefore ill-suited to public regulation. Either sensitivity to patients' privacy would make it impossible to examine whether a decision to die was reached properly, or the necessary regulations to ensure propriety would be so intrusive that they would too greatly undermine patient confidentiality.... Concerns about patients' privacy and physicians' self-regulation are not as important with treatment withdrawals, it is argued, because they take place in the hospital, where there is a good deal of oversight.

However, there are several responses to the concern about physicians' self-regulation. First, third parties are often privy to decisions about assisted suicide. Timothy Quill's patient Diane had discussed her plans with her husband and children; so, too, did Janet Adkins, as well as many others whose deaths were assisted by Jack Kevorkian. The patient's family can often protect the patient's interests. If a physician coerces a patient to agree to assisted suicide, family members may question the patient's sudden change of heart. Second, cases involving withdrawing and withholding treatment take place outside of a hospital, either in a nursing home, where oversight is poor, or at the patient's home. In these settings, the privacy of the patient-physician and other relationships can hide improper behavior. Nevertheless, we seem to be confident that physicians are not abusing their authority. If we can trust physicians' self-regulation with these treatment withdrawals, why can't we trust physicians' self-regulation with assisted suicide? Third, physicians who bend or ignore the law are subject to legal penalty. If a patient dies and there is reason to suspect an unjustified act of euthanasia or assisted suicide, an autopsy can establish how the patient died. The physician will then need to be able to show that the suicide occurred in accordance with the law. The physician could create fraudulent entries in the patient's medical record, but frauds are difficult to conceal—especially since other evidence is likely to be inconsistent with the altered records. Finally, if the concern about the privacy of the patient–physician relationship rests on the fact that public evidence of a patient's consent does not reflect the subtle coercion that can occur in the privacy of patient–physician communications, that concern also applies just as much to decisions regarding the withdrawal or withholding of life-sustaining treatment.

DEMAND FOR ASSISTED SUICIDE IS PREDICATED ON CONCERNS THAT ARE INHERENTLY SUBJECTIVE, MAKING IT DIFFICULT TO DEVELOP SUFFICIENTLY RIGOROUS LEGAL STANDARDS

...If assisted suicide is justified for the relief of suffering, individuals must decide whether they are appropriate candidates for assisted suicide, for only the individuals themselves can know whether their suffering has become intolerable. Accordingly, if assisted suicide were legalized, physicians or other potential assisters would have no basis for turning down a request for assisted suicide by any competent adult.

This is an important argument, but there is also an important response. Even if one accepts the view that individual autonomy should be the guiding principle for a right to assisted suicide, it does not follow that every competent adult should be allowed to choose assisted suicide....

Consider the following analogy. If a young, otherwise healthy adult refuses antibiotics for a bacterial pneumonia, and offers no plausible reason for the refusal, we are likely to assume that the person is making an incompetent refusal of treatment. Even if the person seems competent, we are likely to conclude otherwise because it is difficult to imagine why a competent person would refuse treatment in such a situation. In short, even if a

theory for assisted suicide is based entirely on self-determination, objective limits on the circumstances under which a person can choose assisted suicide can still be justified.

IS IT POSSIBLE TO PROHIBIT ASSISTED SUICIDE?

Heretofore, we have presented regulatory arguments against legalizing assisted suicide. Under those arguments, even if assisted suicide can be morally acceptable in principle, it cannot be implemented in a moral way in practice. There is also an important regulatory argument in favor of legalization. According to proponents of this argument, even if assisted suicide is morally problematic, it cannot be effectively prohibited in practice, and the costs of prohibition outweigh the costs of legalization.

This argument is made for many morally controversial practices. Regulation is chosen as an alternative to prohibition because the practices will occur in the face of prohibition, and the costs of a "black market" are viewed as too great. For example, the U.S. experiment with a prohibition on the manufacture, importation, or sale of alcoholic beverages lasted 14 years, until the public concluded that it was better to have alcohol available legally than illegally. Similarly, restrictions on gambling have loosened considerably in recent years, with many states joining Nevada in permitting lotteries, casinos, and other games of chance. With legalization, more people engage in the practice. On the other hand, the role of criminal or other undesirable elements is reduced. Thus, legalizing abortions results in more abortions, but it also nearly eliminates deaths of women from septic abortion.

Studies have consistently reported that some physicians assist patients' suicides despite the illegality of their action. In a significant number of these cases, it appears that physicians are not acting in accordance with the kinds of regulations that would be adopted if assisted suicide were permitted. Proponents of assisted suicide argue that, with legalization, we can be more confident that assisted suicide will be employed appropriately. In other words, patients turn to the Jack Kevorkians of the world and physicians fail to follow safeguards (such as consulting with colleagues) only when assisted suicide is illegal. Opponents of assisted suicide respond that legalization will result in more assisted suicides overall, and that this would be worse than having a smaller number of suicides occur illicitly.

There is no obvious answer to this argument....

Lisa Belkin | # Prime Time Pushers

Lisa Belkin is a contributing writer for the *New York Times*.

Wherever you flip on the TV dial nowadays you will find commercials for medications that you cannot actually buy. Not without the permission of your doctor (or the aid of the Internet, but we'll talk more about that later). These are serious drugs, with potentially dangerous consequences, but the mood of the ads is upbeat and cheery. Cholesterol busters battle for market share. Antidepressants come with handy checklists of symptoms. Joan Lunden hawks Claritin. Newman from "Seinfeld" pitches an influenza drug. Pfizer spokesman Bob Dole promotes cures for erectile dysfunction.

No, you are not simply getting old and noticing this more. Television ads for prescription drugs, which were all but outlawed as recently as four years ago, are now taking over your TV set. To wit: Pharmaceutical companies spent an estimated $1.7 billion on TV advertising in 2000, 50 percent more than what they spent in 1999, more than double the 1998 amount. In 1991, only one brand of prescription medication was marketed on network television by the route the industry calls "direct to consumer," or DTC. By the end of 1997, there were 12 drugs on that list, and by 2000, there were at least 50.

The rush to the airwaves was triggered by the U.S. Food and Drug Administration, which, until four years ago, had required that manufactures include nearly all of the consumer warning label in any pitch—something possible in a magazine advertisement, but prohibitive in a 30-second television spot. The sole exceptions were for so-called reminder and help-seeking ads—ones that named either the product or the condition being treated, but not both. The result was some very confusing ads.

For the better part of a decade, advertising agencies, pharmaceutical companies, and the major television networks lobbied for less restrictive rules, and, in August 1997, the FDA issued a "clarification" of its 30-year-old regulations. Television commercials may now name both the product and the disease, as long as viewers are given information about "major" risks of the drug and directed to other sources of information—Web sites, magazine ads, toll-free numbers—for more detail. (And you thought those phone numbers were simply there to be helpful.)

Thus the United States became one of only two countries in the world (New Zealand being the other) where prescription drugs are hawked in prime time. Proponents of the FDA's policy shift say it creates a more informed patient because viewers see the ads, then have an intelligent give-and-take with a doctor. Critics say the shift creates more business for pharmaceutical companies by encouraging patients to seek out expensive, potentially dangerous drugs that they—and too often their doctors—know little about. "It was a sellout," says Larry D. Sasich, a pharmacist with Public Citizen's Health Research

From *Mother Jones*, March/April 2001.

Group in Washington, D.C. "It's nothing more than a response to pressure from Madison Avenue."

Whatever the motivation, the shift has resulted in a quiet but dramatic transformation of the whole of our health care system. Gone is the time when doctors held complete power and prescription medicines were treated as a sacred and separate world. These ads mark the full dawning of an age when our very health is sold to us like soap. So turn on your TV set, relax, and take a pill. It's Prilosec time.

Before we talk about what is wrong (and unseemly and potentially dangerous about all of this), let's look at what's right. Seen through a certain lens, the explosion of DTC drug advertising is a continuation of the patients' rights movement that began in force 30 years ago. Allowing such ads, says Nancy Ostrove, a branch chief within the FDA's Division of Drug Marketing, Advertising, and Communication, is not only a recognition of the unstoppable power of television, but also the best way to inform consumers about available drugs. "There are certain real health benefits that can be achieved," she says.

Talk to any pharmaceutical company and they will tell you how thrilled they are to be educating the public. "From our point of view, one of the main purposes of direct-to-consumer advertising is education," says Emily Denney, a program manger in public affairs at AstraZeneca. Her company makes Prilosec, a drug that treats gastroesophageal reflux disease, a painful condition in which acid leaks from the stomach, causing chronic heartburn and even ulceration of the esophagus. Because of the $79.5 million the company spent on Prilosec ads in 1999, Denney says, "patients have been more easily able to diagnose symptoms that went ignored for many years. Our whole goal is just to encourage a conversation with your health care provider."

It is, to be sure, a self-interested, image-polishing argument, but the fact is that millions of us are sick and do not know it. According to the American Diabetes Association, more than 5 million diabetics in this country are unaware that they have the disease; one-third of Americans with major depression seek no treatment; and millions of Americans are ignorant of the fact that they have high blood pressure.

Now consider this: In the two years since ads for Viagra first began to air, millions of men have visited their doctors specifically to get that drug—and thousands of them were diagnosed with serious underlying conditions. The Pharmaceutical Research and Manufactures of America estimates that for every million men who asked for the medicine, it was discovered that 30,000 had untreated diabetes, 140,000 had untreated high blood pressure, and 50,000 had untreated heart disease.

Let's face it, though, even the drug companies would agree that they are not spending all this money just to be helpful. They are spending all this money to sell their products. "We don't invest in things we don't find valuable to the business," says AstraZeneca's Denney.

Direct-to-consumer advertising has paid off handsomely for the pharmaceutical companies—often turning solid earners into blockbuster drugs. After spending nearly $80 million on Prilosec advertising in 1999 (up from $50 million in 1998), AstraZeneca saw sales rise 27 percent, to $3.8 billion. Pfizer, in turn, upped consumer advertising for its cholesterol drug, Lipitor, by more than $45 million in 1999, and sales of the drug jumped too—56 percent, to $2.7 billion.

Some of the most dramatic ad-and-effect can be seen in the category of allergy drugs. Claritin maker Schering-Plough launched the televised assault against sneezing in 1998 when it spent $185 million on advertising and saw sales more than double to $2.1 billion. Following the leader, Pfizer spent $57 million to promote its drug Zyrtec in 1999 and saw a 32 percent increase in sales; that same year, Aventis spent $43 million to promote Allegra, and sales increased by 50 percent.

There is no reason to believe, however, that there was any increase in the number of allergy sufferers in the United States during this time, and no sudden outpouring of pollen either. There was just an increase in the sale of prescription allergy medications. According to Scott Levin, a pharmaceutical consulting company in Pennsylvania, doctor visits by patients complaining of allergy symptoms were relatively stable between 1990 and 1998, at a rate of 13 to 14 million per year. In 1999, there were

18 million allergy visits. The cause of the spike, critics point out, is clearly the advertising.

The purpose of allergy ads in particular and pharmaceutical ads in general "is to drive patients into doctors' offices and ask for drugs by brand name," says Sasich, of Public Citizen. And once they are in that office, patients often get what they want. "Physicians are more interested in pleasing their patients than you might think," says Steven D. Findlay, an analyst who is director of research and policy at the National Institute for Health Care Management. "It's a subtle interchange and exchange that happens between patient and doctor."

"Patients can be difficult to dissuade," says Dr. Jack Berger, an internist and rheumatologist in private practice in White Plains, New York, and sometimes it is easier for doctors to give in. "It adds an extra source of confusion and frustration to the doctor/patient relationship when the patient starts directing the treatment based on what they learned on TV," he says.

Studies have shown that patients requesting specific drugs often get just what they ask for. A survey by the FDA of people who had recently been to their doctors, for instance, found that 72 percent had seen or heard an ad for prescription drugs in the previous three months, mostly on TV. Close to 25 percent of those respondents had also asked their doctors for the first time about a condition or illness. Of those who asked for a specific drug by name, nearly half were given a prescription for it; 21 percent were recommended a different drug.

"These ads have had a very large impact on a somewhat hypochondriacal public," says Findlay. The ads do, in fact, educate consumers, he says, but what they often teach is how to describe your symptoms so you will be given a certain medication. "The purpose of advertising is not to inform people," Findlay continues. "It never has been and it never will be. The purpose of advertising, as we all know, is to make people buy more product so the company can make more money. It makes you desire that new product, just like that new car or that new gizmo."

Yes, doctors still hold the prescription pad, but parents have long held the credit cards and toys are advertised directly to kids. At a dinner recently, Findlay listened as two other guests "kept going on

and on about Celebrex," a new arthritis drug from Pfizer/Pharmacia. "They were talking about it like you talk about PCs," he says, "and there was a pride in the fact that they both were taking Celebrex, because it's advertised, it's on TV."

Evolution in advertising favors the slick and jazzy, and so it is with DTC television spots. In the old days, when the ads could not mention both the disease and the cure, the industry argued that such rules led to confusion. In the words of the Pharmaceutical Researchers and Manufactures of America, the restrictions "prompted companies to advertise on television in more oblique ways, which, while meeting legal requirements, may have been less helpful to consumers. Consumers were often left to guess what the medicine was for."

Now the rules have changed. What, then, are we to make of new ads like those for Prilosec that feature a lithe woman in a flowing purple gown against the background of a clock with the uninformative slogan "It's Prilosec Time"? Is this a cure for depression? Irregularity? The ad itself gives no clue.

The original Prilosec ads, AstraZeneca's Denney says, described gastroesophageal reflux disease, or GERD, in some detail, showing cartoons of people in obvious distress and quizzing viewers about how often they experience heartburn. But GERD "is not the most pleasing-sounding word," Denney explains, and "you can't describe it perfectly in 60 seconds"— which may be why the company shifted to these more free-form reminder ads, which play up the fact that the pill itself is purple. And it's not just on television. The woman in the purple dress also appears in print ads, on the Web, and in subway stations plastered with purple pills. "The purpleness is a form of branding," Denney says. "People know Prilosec as 'the little purple pill.'"

One can't help but wonder, however, if such branding is having a far more troubling effect— whether occasional heartburn sufferers looking for a silver (or, in this case, purple) bullet might not be pressing their doctors for a powerful drug they don't really need. Americans tend to prefer the easy fix, and the ubiquitousness of direct-to-consumer ads, which dress medicine up in the same telegenic tinsel as perfume or sports cars, make our health seem as simple as we would like it to be. "The ads send a strong signal," says a report from the National Institute for Health Care Management, "that prescription drugs are just like any consumer product—soap, cereal, cars, snack food, etc."

Look more closely at a category of drugs known as statins—sold under such brand names as Lipitor, Pravachol, and Zocor—which have proved so effective at lowering cholesterol that some doctors see advertising them as a public service. "There are countless people who would be better served if they knew these drugs were available," says Dr. Ira S. Nash, associate director of the cardiovascular institute at the Mount Sinai School of Medicine in New York City. Yet other doctors worry about the side effect of those same ads. Statins can cause dangerous liver complications and their use needs to be carefully monitored by a doctor. In most cases, statins should be prescribed only to patients who have tried the lines of first defense—namely, diet and exercise—and who have failed to lower their cholesterol in spite of these lifestyle changes. If the ads make fighting cholesterol look too easy, patients may insist on skipping the hard part and going straight for the pill. "It takes time to speak to a patient about exercise, weight control, and diet. It takes less time to just write a prescription," says Dr. Berger, the private practitioner, and there is a danger that doctors will choose the easier course.

Cholesterol, at least, is a problem that can be measured. What about conditions whose symptoms are far more difficult to evaluate? Last year's ads for Paxil fall into this category. Paxil is an antidepressant approved by the FDA for the secondary purpose of treating social anxiety disorder, which Glaxo-SmithKline's ads describe as "an intense, persistent fear and avoidance of social situations." In its true, clinical form, it is a real and debilitating condition, but by reducing it to an ad—in which the subject experiences dread while giving an office presentation—Paxil can too easily sound like a pill for shyness.

One television ad that I find particularly egregious, bordering on offensive, is for a relatively new drug called Sarafem. The chemical composition of the pill is identical to that of Prozac, but last summer manufacturer Eli Lilly and Company received FDA permission to market it simultaneously for treatment of premenstrual disphoric disorder, or PMDD. The condition differs from PMS in that its symptoms are more emotional than physical and include depression, anxiety, and bursts of anger. And yet a television spot for the drug shows a frustrated woman struggling with a shopping cart in front of a supermarket, and makes Sarafem look like an easy fix for your average bad day.

"They're making everything into a disease," adds Dr. Nash, "and not only is it a disease, but it's a disease that society has a pill for."

Because more is at stake, viewers should bring a higher level of skepticism to pharmaceutical ads. Instead, there is reason to believe they are bringing less. A recent study in the *Journal of General Internal Medicine* found that nearly half of respondents believed that drug ads are prescreened and somehow sanctioned by the FDA. In fact, quite the opposite is true. The FDA's Ostrove explains that the agency is "forbidden by law from requiring preclearance." Although some pharmaceutical companies choose to submit their ads in advance, she says, they do so at their own discretion. All the FDA can require is that a copy of an ad be sent to its office when the ad begins to air.

Once the commercial arrives at the agency's Rockville, Maryland, headquarters, it is reviewed by 1 of the 14 employees who screen 30,000 pieces of promotional material each year. "We allow a certain degree of puffery," Ostrove says, "but we don't allow overstatement of effectiveness or minimization of the risks." Even with such allowances, the FDA found that for the first 37 drugs marketed directly to consumers on television, 20 ads failed to comply with federal regulations, including those requiring "fair balance" and the disclosure of side effects.

Of the estimated 200 television drug spots aired since the 1997 FDA rule change, the agency has cited 32 for noncompliance and has asked the companies to change all or part of the ads. The FDA told Pfizer/Pharmacia, for instance, that an advertisement for the arthritis drug Celebrex was misleading because "various multiple physical activities portrayed by arthritis patients (such as rowing a boat and riding a scooter)," along with "the audio statement 'Powerful 24-hour relief from osteoarthritis pain and stiffness,' collectively suggest that Celebrex is more effective than has been demonstrated by substantial evidence." In other words, the product does not work as advertised. Judith Glova, a spokeswoman for the company, says the ad was pulled and modified slightly—a statement was added, for example, noting that "individual results may vary"—and put back on television.

Similarly, Eli Lilly and Company was told that an ad for the osteoporosis drug Evista was misleading because "it mischaracterizes the nature of osteoporosis, resulting in an overstatement of Evista's benefits." Specifically, the agency said, the ad's description of osteoporosis as "a disease of thin, weak bones that can fracture and take away your independence" exaggerated both the risk and the consequence of a fracture. Eli Lilly spokesman David Marbaugh says the ad has been "suspended" while the company works with the FDA to revise the ad.

Most recently, I was pleased to learn, the FDA sent a letter to Eli Lilly about the ads for Sarafem— the very spots showing a woman struggling with a shopping cart. The ad does not define the condition it is designed to treat, the agency said, and as a result "trivializes the seriousness of PMDD." The company was asked to "immediately cease using this broadcast advertisement."

Eli Lilly decided to honor the agency's request, but, legally, the company could have kept running the ads indefinitely. As Findlay, the health care analyst, notes, "Everybody thinks the agency [the FDA] is this big 900-pound gorilla, but their actual power is limited." Essentially, all the agency can do is request compliance. If a company refuses, the FDA cannot impose fines or other punishments but must instead go through the courts for an injunction. "As a matter of course, most companies do change their ads," Findlay says, "but that is because they are concerned about the public relations implications. The heaviest hammer the FDA has in this department is embarrassing manufacturers."

The guiding rule of medicine is, "First, do no harm." What, then, is the harm of pharmaceutical ads? Yes, they may be misleading, but it can be argued that most consumer ads are misleading. Why should we care? Who is this hurting? The most measurable harm is economic. "There is very strong circumstantial evidence," says Public Citizen's Sasich, "that some patients are getting drugs that may be stronger than they need. A less expensive, more easily obtained drug may be more appropriate."

Celebrex, says Findlay, is one example of potential pharmaceutical overkill. With first-year sales of $1.3 billion in 1999, it was the most successful drug launch in history. Celebrex and similar new arthritis drugs, such as Vioxx, represent an advance because they do not cause the level of gastrointestinal distress that alternative treatments, such as over-the-counter ibuprofen tablets, can. However, Findlay says that "the proportion of people with arthritis at high risk for that side effect is between 10 and 20 percent." But if you extrapolate from the number of prescriptions written for the drug, he says, then Celebrex and similar medications are "being taken by potentially 40 percent of arthritis patients. These medicines are going to people who have no clinically defined need."

A one-year dosage of Celebrex costs $900, says William Pierce, a spokesman for the Blue Cross and Blue Shield Association (BCBSA), while a one-year dosage of generic ibuprofen costs $24. Numbers like these are the major reason why BCBSA expects prescription drug costs to rise at least 15 percent each year through 2004.

"In some plans we are spending more on prescription drugs than on in-patient hospitalization, and one of the major reasons is direct-to-consumer advertising," says Christine Simmon, also of BCBSA, who notes that another reason is the aging of the population. Last year alone, BCBSA saw an estimated "25 percent increase in the cost of prescription drugs compared with 6 to 8 percent for physician and hospital services," she says.

In an effort to curb demand for expensive prescriptions, BCBSA has gone so far as to launch a new corporation, called RxIntelligence, which will attempt to inform the public about why they may not need the newest, flashiest drugs on the market. RxIntelligence, says Simmon, will study such things as the "cost benefit and risk of the drug and whether the existing treatment is just as good"—the sort of information that does not appear in pharmaceutical ads.

The Pharmaceutical Researchers and Manufacturers of America (PHRMA) argues that the increase in prescription drug use "reflects the extraordinary value that medicines provide, to patients and the health care system. Increased utilization of medicines is a good thing—it helps many patients get well quicker." But Findlay reminds us that what we allocate to one slice of the health care pie must be taken from another. "Is this how we want to be spending our money?" he asks. "Do we, want to be spending 25 percent of health care dollars on medication at the expense of home care or PET scans?"

A second harm of rampant pharmaceutical advertising, a harm that is harder to quantify but far more frightening, is to our health. The entire system of direct-to-consumer advertising relies on the assumption that there is an intermediary between the patient and the potentially harmful drug. "While DTC ads prompt patients to consult their doctors about available medicines," says a recent PHRMA report, "the doctor still holds the prescribing pen. Patients cannot get prescription medicines unless their physicians find that the medicines are necessary and appropriate."

But the world is changing in ways that make this statement untrue. Patients are increasingly hearing about new drugs before their doctors do. A recent poll by the American Association of Retired Persons found that 21 percent of consumers had asked their doctors for prescription drugs that the doctors knew little or nothing about. Dr. Berger tells me he knows of doctors who began to prescribe Celebrex before the clinical trials were even published, because patients were asking for it and because initial reports in the press indicated it was effective. Indeed, sales of Celebrex reached $1 billion before the final clinical-trial results were published in a peer-reviewed journal. Many doctors apparently didn't read Celebrex's package insert either. The drug contains sulfa, which can cause an allergic reaction in some patients. "People came in itching with hives," says Berger.

Even when all the known facts about a drug are published, there is no guarantee that new facts might not emerge, especially when the drug is new. One example is the ongoing controversy over the GlaxoSK drug Relenza. Approved in 1999, Relenza is an inhalable powder designed to treat common flu symptoms, reducing the illness's length by about a day. It was introduced with a cheeky television campaign featuring the character Newman from "Seinfeld." The campaign received awards within the advertising industry, but the FDA was not amused. It described the ads as "misleading because they . . . suggest that Relenza is more effective" than has been "demonstrated by substantial evidence."

Soon after Relenza hit the market in October 1999, seven patients using it died. In part because Relenza had been so heavily promoted, the FDA then issued a "public health advisory" saying that while the exact involvement of the drug was unclear, there had been "several reports of deterioration of respiratory function following inhalation of Relenza" in patients with underlying breathing problems. By June 2000, use of Relenza had been linked to 22 deaths; in July, GlaxoSK announced a strengthened warning label for the drug. The FDA has since reaffirmed the safety of Relenza, when it is used as directed, and attributes many of the deaths to its use by patients to whom it should never have been prescribed. Relenza remains on the market, says GlaxoSK spokeswoman Laura Sutton, but the ads are no longer on the air.

It is still possible to buy Relenza over the Internet, however, which adds another variable to consumer access to prescription drugs. In March 1999, 52-year-old Robert McCutcheon, of Lisle, Illinois, died of a heart attack that may have been triggered by Viagra, although there is no definitive way to know. Despite a family history of heart problems, which would have meant he was a poor candidate for the drug, McCutcheon had ordered Viagra online, at one of the growing number of Web sites that sell prescription medications without a doctor visit.

Viagra is hardly the only drug being sold this way. As part of my research for this article, I spent less than five minutes online and purchased a month's supply of Xenical, the Hoffmann-La Roche product for weight loss. It is intended only for patients who are clinically obese, but since no doctor ever saw me, I lied and said I weighed 300 pounds. The site even provided a handy chart telling me the exact weight cutoff for any given height in order to qualify. The pills arrived, as promised, within five business days, charged to my credit card.

Pharmaceutical companies, it should be said, are distressed by this phenomenon. Pfizer, which manufactures Viagra, recently reminded physicians that it is "improper" (though not actually illegal) to prescribe the drug without first examining the patient. And Ostrove calls the availability of drugs online "a separate but serious issue." When the FDA announced in 1997 that it was "clarifying" its regulations to favor television ads, it also announced that it would review the new approach this coming summer. "If we have reason to believe that our policies are creating a public health problem," Ostrove says, "we will reevaluate."

In the meantime, I have this bottle of Xenical sitting on my desk. While I'm not obese, there are those "few extra pounds" I put on over the holidays. What could be the harm? After all, the ads say that this stuff really works.

CASES

CASE 8.1

Drug Company Gifts: Marketing Technique Poses Ethical Questions for Some

Scott J. Turner

Four weeks ago, the Lifespan health system, home base for many of the faculty in the Medical School, proposed strict guidelines to limit interactions with sales representatives, particularly from the pharmaceutical industry.

A month earlier, the federal government warned drug firms against offering financial enticements to healthcare professionals to prescribe or to suggest certain medications, or to switch from one drug to another in treating patients.

From free pens, pads, and drug samples to high-priced meals to underwriting medical education programs, the pharmaceutical industry spends billions annually to market its products. Some members of the medical community call a close link between the healthcare profession and drug industry part of a "golden age" of medicine, helping patients to get the latest and best treatments.

Research has shown that accepting gifts and hospitality from pharmaceutical companies affects

From *George Street* Journal, Nov. 8, 2002 (Brown University).

prescribing patterns to benefit drug companies, often to the deteriment of the patient. To fourth-year medical student Jaya Agarwal, drug company marketing is "bribery" and "bad medicine." She wants doctors, nurses, even fellow medical students, to make their own evidence-based decisions on which medications will best help patients.

Last year, Agrawal was president of the American Medical Student Association (AMSA), the nation's oldest and largest independent medical student group, involving more than 30,000 physicians-in-training.

One of Agrawal's AMSA initiatives was the "PharmFree Campaign." This nationwide effort asks medical students to pledge not to accept industry gifts. It supplements AMSA's "No Free Lunch" movement to persuade students to avoid meals from drug reps. One common marketing strategy for drug reps is to show off new products during the lunch hour while providing free food as compensation to attendees taking time out of their busy routines.

In the next few months, Agrawal hopes to work with Medical School administrators on the issue. She would like to see the school adopt an across-the-board ban of industry gifts. Earlier this semester, she discussed the topic with first-year medical students during an orientation session devoted to professionalism.

"This issue doesn't become reality until your third year of medical school when you go into the clinics and hospitals and start attending drug-sponsored lunches to learn about new products," she said. "It is not a system that puts patients first. One form of professionalism is getting information for patients from non-biased sources. It is a bad habit to rely on drug representatives for information.

"Accepting industry gifts is a dependency developed during the third and fourth years of medical school. I appreciated the opportunity to speak with first-year students before they became indoctrinated in this practice."

Not everyone agrees with Agrawal.

Agrawal "ought to have more faith in the integrity of medical students," said Jeff Trewhitt, spokesman for Pharmaceutical Research and Manufacturers of America (PhRMA). "Medical students will make their own independent judgments. You won't buy a doctor's soul for the price of a pizza pie."

Earlier this year, PhRMA adopted a new marketing code to more tightly govern the industry's relations with healthcare professionals, especially when it comes to meals, travel and other items of substantial value. The code is voluntary.

"What [Agrawal] is suggesting is that medical students and doctors close out a principal source of technical information," said Trewhitt.

To the industry and to some physicians, face-to-face contact is an efficient way to discuss new medications. Accepting a meal or mug in exchange for samples and information on uses and side effects is reasonable, because it translates into getting the best treatments to patients who need them. Funding continuing medical education programs leads to better-educated physicians, Trewhitt said.

Across the healthcare spectrum, the question is asked: To take or not to take from drug companies? Consider the free drug samples offered by drug reps. What better way is there for a company to get a new drug into a physician's repertoire than to hand it over free? Moreover, it is almost standard practice to dispense free drug samples to patients who have the most difficultly affording prescription drugs, said Trewhitt.

"Providing free samples of a new medicine gives a physicians hands-on experience using the new medicine to observe close up how it works so a physician can tell whether or not it is helpful to patients," said Trewhitt.

"Also, when a physician receives free samples, in most cases those are shared with elderly or other patients who have trouble paying for medications."

Hogwash, said Howard Schulman, M.D., clinical assistant professor of medicine. Sooner or later a patient who was given free samples will have to continue treatments by having a prescription for the drug filled. If they have no pharmacy coverage, they will pay dearly.

"It's a myth that free samples help the poor," said Schulman. For an elderly patient, for example, there can be a $1,000 to $2,000 per year difference when you compare a brand-name drug versus a generic.

In a letter late last year to Rhode Island Medical News, Schulman wrote, "For physicians concerned about the potential loss of office samples, I can happily report that for the past three years, since I have had my own practice, I have had a policy that I do not speak with drug reps or accept samples, and it has been great.

"Not only are the reps ill-informed, but they have a habit of getting in your way just when you have a second to breathe.... When patients ask for samples, I tell them that I do not have any. This is not an issue, and I have not lost any patients because I do not give out samples."

Trewhitt defends industry representatives, saying, "There are very rigorous training programs from what I have seen and heard from companies. Salespeople must be able to demonstrate to physicians that they can answer technical questions. You will lose your credibility if you try and blow smoke."

Ed Wing, M.D., has a relationship with drug companies that is both positive and negative. Wing circulated the proposed Lifespan guidelines. He chairs the Department of Medicine, the flagship department in the Medical School. He is physician-in-chief at Rhode Island Hospital and the Miriam Hospital, and executive physician-in-chief at Memorial Hospital of Rhode Island, the VA Medical Center and Women & Infants Hospital.

For the past two years, Wing has stopped drug reps from sponsoring lunches for residents and students. The Department of Medicine spends more than $70,000 per year supplying lunches for residents at Rhode Island Hospital and The Miriam Hospital.

"The pharmaceutical industry is progressive and very important to academic medicine and to physicians, in general," said Wing. "It has put billions of dollars into vital research and into saving lives. I take care of patients with HIV. They now live because of new medications. Before, there were no drugs for treatment, and patients died.

"On the other hand, the industry puts a tremendous amount of money toward marketing drugs to all levels of those in medical training and in practice. Much of what they do in marketing is inappropriate."

As much as possible, Wing says, he tries to restrict medical students and residents from having contact with drug reps. "I think sales people offer biased information. The medical literature says they do influence decision-making. If a person is influenced in training, they will be influenced in their career."

Schulman said the drug industry has sunk "10,000" tentacles into medicine. "I worry that well-respected medical experts, who become industry consultants, may begin to prescribe a new drug in place of one that already is effective, or espouse a new product, which may lead other physicians to follow in their footsteps," he said.

In addition, Schulman is concerned that physicians who depend on industry funding to conduct drug studies may be overly influenced by that dependence. "More often than not, attendees at continuing medical education [CME] programs or hospital grand rounds do not know the extent of industry funding for the session or for associated research," he said.

Industry may help fund a CME program, but it is the accredited medical group that runs it, said Trewhitt. "A company can recommend a speaker, but not choose one. These top physicians have their credibility to maintain. I don't think they will be dictated to by a pharmaceutical company."

Schulman doesn't buy it. "In many ways drug industry tactics unduly influence prescribing patterns of physicians, the studies they conduct and the process of continuing medical education," he said.

Often, an academic researcher who conducts an industry-sponsored study is also a consultant to the funding firm, said Schulman. "The problem is that not enough critical attention, analysis or publicity has been paid to this conflict of interest," he said. "Even worse, the participants are so steeped in this culture that they themselves do not realize how uncritical and biased they have become."

On behalf of the American Medical Association, Herbert Rakatansky, M.D., helped draft guidelines on gifts to physicians from industry. A clinical professor of medicine, Rakatansky is the former chair of the AMA's Council on Ethical and Judicial Affairs.

The guidelines present a middle ground, said Rakatansky. For example, the rules say that any gifts should be of minimal value, and they must come in the context of furthering patient care and medical education. Also, physicians should control the interactions.

"In the real world, I think doctors need to work with industry, such as collaborating on clinical trials," said Rakatansky. "You can't stay away completely. But in those relationships, doctors have a moral obligation to patients. Physicians must always make decisions in a patient's best interest. Industry is obligated to owners and stockholders. We know that."

Many physicians disagree with Wing. "They claim that they can process the information they receive, and that meals won't sway them," he said. "Some argue that restricting drug reps hurts education about new treatments."

Like Agrawal, Wing wants physicians to use bias-free approaches, such as the online Medical Letter, to determine best treatments.

"Giving you samples is a way for a drug rep to get a foot in the door," said Wing. "Once you begin relying on that system, it is hard to stop. It's a system that hurts patient care and drives up costs in the long run."

When it comes to medical students and residents, "it is a problem of trying to influence people in training under the guise of education," said Wing. "It is a situation that is not science based. In fact, it is biased against education."

Agrawal thinks the public opinion is turning against drug companies.

"Voluntary rules, federal warnings, they all add up to public relations strategies," said Agrawal. "They don't have teeth. Some departments in Brown Medical School still provide drug-sponsored lunches. One department even offers professional memberships using funds from drug companies.

"Industry does what it does because it works. I believe that advertising of new and expensive drugs increases their use. Under this system, physicians have no incentives to find their own sources of information. The time has come for federal, state or local rules that create and enforce change."

Before she graduates, Agrawal would like to help the Medical School apply "a tough, consistent position against industry gifts, applied to all departmental faculty and across all educational venues, whether in the Medical School on campus or in the hospitals.

"When asked, most physicians admit they attend drug-sponsored lunches for the food and the same extends to other gifts," she said. "If you are honest with yourself, it's not about learning about new therapies; it's just taking a bribe."

Questions

1. Determine the reciprocal nature between the medical profession and the pharmaceutical industry. Further the arguments between Agrawal and Trewhitt on the basis of the other readings in this chapter.

2. Is the for-profit motivation of the pharmaceutical industry detrimental or complimentary to the care-based medical profession?

CASE 8.2
Moral Conflict in Clinical Trials
Maria Merritt

———————

II. A HARD CASE

Dr. Okero is an investigator conducting a phase 1 clinical trial of a new chemotherapeutic drug for cancer. He is concerned about Ms. Hernandez, a subject in the trial.

Ms. Hernandez is a 49-year-old woman with a diagnosis of metastatic breast cancer. She has three disease sites: her liver, lung, and axilla (underarm area). The liver lesion threatens her liver function, which is crucial to survival. Following her initial diagnosis, she tried a number of clinically available treatments, but none could slow down the growth of her liver lesion. On the advice of her personal physician, she decided to enroll in Dr. Okero's trial.

In this trial, subjects receive the experimental drug by intravenous infusion for up to six twenty-one-day cycles, a standard regimen for clinical cancer treatment. Subjects receive the dose that will be tested for effectiveness in later trials if the drug remains promising after safety testing. The scientific purpose of the trial is to collect data on cumulative toxicity: irreversible effects that may show up in later cycles, such as loss of sensation in the hands and feet. Why does cumulative toxicity matter? Chemotherapy would have little clinical value in cancer treatment if it were limited, by serious irreversible effects, to no more than two or three cycles. Typically, chemotherapy should be given with only reversible toxicities for a total of six cycles. Testing the safety of an experimental form of chemotherapy requires studying the effects of longer-term exposure to it.

Ms. Hernandez has received four cycles of the experimental drug. Two more cycles would complete her participation in the trial. After the fourth cycle, she does not look sick or fatigued, and she has suffered no irreversible impairment in her ability to function normally. Her liver and lung lesions remain stable. The stability of her liver lesion, continuing for twelve weeks now, has been a first in her experience. But her axillary lesion has grown by 22 percent since she first entered the trial. This suggests an increased likelihood of growth at the other two sites in the near future. The prospect of growth in the liver lesion, with consequent decline in liver function, is particularly worrisome.

Dr. Okero has no reason to believe that Ms. Hernandez's trial participation is causing the increased tumor growth. But if she participates through one or two more cycles, she continues to risk cumulative toxicity, and the increased likelihood of tumor growth in the liver undercuts the prospect of direct benefit to her from continued exposure to such risks. Beyond this point it is most likely that the burdens and risks of her participation would be justifiable, if at all, only by the prospect of benefit to others through the trial's scientific results. Dr. Okero's protective duty toward Ms. Hernandez raises the question whether the burdens and risks of her continued participation are excessive.

Yet, he has a scientific duty to collect crucial data of precisely the kind her continuation in the trial promises to provide. Her withdrawal at this point would be a serious scientific loss. Unlike her, all the other subjects in this trial enrolled while already suffering from advanced cancer and had to drop out after only one to three cycles because their health declined so severely. Ms. Hernandez is the first

From *Ethics* 115 (January 2005): 306–330. © 2005 by the University of Chicago. All rights reserved. 0014–1704/2005/11502-0002$10.00.

subject able to provide data on the drug's potential for cumulative toxicity. So far she has suffered no such toxicity. If she remains free from it after another cycle or, better, two more cycles, this will constitute significant evidence that using the drug on the standard treatment regimen does not result in cumulative toxicity.

Without such evidence, it is wrong to pursue the next stage in the drug's development, that is, to test it for effectiveness over the standard number of cycles. The absence of relevant timely data, then, could slow down or even stop the development of an otherwise promising drug, rendering pointless the medical burdens and risks to which subjects in this trial have already been exposed.

Dr. Okero has talked with Ms. Hernandez about the most recent changes in her medical status, and she has in turn discussed them with her personal physician. She has requested a meeting to talk more about how continuation in the trial would compare with her other options. Ms. Hernandez has yet to say "No" to continued participation. (If she had reached a "No" decision, her decision would be final, and this would plainly not be a hard case for Dr. Okero.) The fact that Ms. Hernandez has not decided "No" is what leaves Dr. Okero to carry the full weight of both scientific duty and protective duty regarding the question of her continued participation. The considerations relevant to both are important in this case, and neither duty is obviously overridden by the other. So, even if Ms. Hernandez decides she would like to continue, the problem that remains independently with Dr. Okero, as the principal investigator, is whether to endorse her decision or instead to recommend that she withdraw.

Questions

1. There is a conflict of interest between the research of Dr. Okero and the health of Ms. Hernandez. What are some arguments to justify each case?

2. Taking a utilitarian stance, what would be the outcome of Dr. Okero's decision? Likewise, a Kantian stance?

3. If Dr. Okero receives permission from his patient to go ahead with the study, does that rectify, even a little bit, the conflict of interest posed by this case?

CASE 8.3
Quarantine Ethics
Albert Camus

...The day before Castel called on Rieux, M. Othon's son had fallen ill and all the family had to go into quarantine. Thus the mother, who had only recently come out of it, found herself isolated once again. In deference to the official regulations the magistrate had promptly sent for Dr. Rieux the moment he saw symptoms of the disease in his little boy. Mother and father were standing at the bedside when Rieux entered the room. The boy was in the phase of extreme prostration and submitted without a whimper to the doctor's examination. When Rieux raised his eyes he saw the magistrate's gaze intent on him, and, behind, the mother's pale face. She was holding a handkerchief to her mouth, and her big, dilated eyes followed each of the doctor's movements.

"He has it, I suppose?" the magistrate asked in a toneless voice.

"Yes." Rieux gazed down at the child again.

The mother's eyes widened yet more, but she still said nothing. M. Othon, too, kept silent for a while before saying in an even lower tone:

"Well, doctor, we must do as we are told to do." . . .

In the early days a mere formality, quarantine had now been reorganized by Rieux and Rambert on very strict lines. In particular they insisted on having members of the family of a patient kept apart. If, unawares, one of them had been infected, the risks of an extension of the infection must not be multiplied. Rieux explained this to the magistrate, who signified his approval of the procedure. Nevertheless, he and his wife exchanged a glance that made it clear to Rieux how keenly they both felt the separation thus imposed on them. Mme Othon and her little girl could be given rooms in the quarantine hospital under Rambert's charge. For the magistrate, however, no accommodation was available except in an isolation camp the authorities were now installing in the municipal stadium, using tents supplied by the highway department. When Rieux apologized for the poor accommodation, M. Othon replied that there was one rule for all alike, and it was only proper to abide by it. . . .

. . . By this time no public place or building had escaped conversion into a hospital or quarantine camp with the exception of the Prefect's offices, which were needed for administrative purposes and committee meetings. In a general way, however, owing to the relative stability of the epidemic at this time, Rieux's organizations were still able to cope with the situation. . . .

Meanwhile the authorities had another cause for anxiety in the difficulty of maintaining the food-supply. Profiteers were taking a hand and purveying at enormous prices essential foodstuffs not available in the shops. The result was that poor families were in great straits, while the rich went short of practically nothing. Thus, whereas plague by its impartial ministrations should have promoted equality among our townsfolk, it now had the opposite effect and, thanks to the habitual conflict of cupidities, exacerbated the sense of injustice rankling in men's hearts. They were assured, of course, of the inerrable equality of death, but nobody wanted that kind of equality. Poor people who were feeling the pinch thought still more nostalgically of towns and villages in the nearby countryside, where bread was cheap and life without restrictions. Indeed, they had a natural if illogical feeling that they should have been permitted to move out to these happier places. The feeling was embodied in a slogan shouted in the streets and chalked up on walls: "Bread or fresh air!" This half-ironical battle-cry was the signal for some demonstrations that, though easily repressed, made everyone aware that an ugly mood was developing among us.

The newspapers, needless to say, complied with the instructions given them: optimism at all costs. If one was to believe what one read in them, our populace was giving "a fine example of courage and composure." . . . To form a correct idea about the courage and composure talked about by our journalists you had only to visit one of the quarantine depots or isolation camps established by our authorities. . . .

Tarrou gives an account of a visit he made, accompanied by Rambert, to the camp located in the municipal stadium. . . . It was already surrounded by high concrete walls and all that was needed to make escape practically impossible was to post sentries at the four entrance gates. The walls served another purpose: they screened the unfortunates in quarantine from the view of people on the road. Against this advantage may be set the fact that the inmates could hear all day, though they could not see them, the passing streetcars, and recognize by the increased volume of sound coming from the road the hours when people had knocked off work or were going to it. And this brought home to them that the life from which they were debarred was going on as before, within a few yards of them, and that those high walls parted two worlds as alien to each other as two different planets.

Tarrou and Rambert chose a Sunday afternoon for their visit to the stadium. They were accompanied by Gonzales, the football-player, with whom Rambert had kept in contact and who had let himself be persuaded into undertaking, in rotation with others, the surveillance of the camp. This visit was to enable Rambert to introduce Gonzales to the camp commandant. When they met that afternoon, Gonzales's first remark was that this was exactly the time when, before the plague, he used to start getting into his football togs. Now that the sports fields had been requisitioned, all that was of the past, and Gonzales was feeling—and showed it— at a loose end. This was one of the reasons why he had accepted the post proposed by Rambert, but he made it a condition that he was to be on duty during week-ends only.

On entering the stadium they found the stands full of people. The field was dotted with several hundred red tents, inside which one had glimpses of bedding and bundles of clothes or rugs. The stands had been kept open for the use of the internees in hot or rainy weather. But it was a rule of the camp that everyone must be in his tent at sunset. Shower-baths had been installed under the stands, and what used to be the players' dressing rooms converted into offices and infirmaries. The majority of the inmates of the camp were sitting about on the stands. Some, however, were strolling on the touchlines, and a few, squatting at the entrances of their tents, were listlessly contemplating the scene around them. In the stands many of those slumped on the wooden tiers had a look of vague expectancy.

"What do they do with themselves all day?" Tarrou asked Rambert.

"Nothing."

In his notes Tarrou gives what to his mind would explain this change. He pictures them in the early days bundled together in the tents, listening to the buzz of flies, scratching themselves, and, whenever they found an obliging listener, shrilly voicing their fear or indignation. But when the camp grew overcrowded, fewer and fewer people were inclined to play the part of sympathetic listener. So they had no choice but to hold their peace and nurse their mistrust of everything and everyone. . . .

Yes, there was suspicion in the eyes of all. Obviously, they were thinking, there must be some good reason for the isolation inflicted on them, and they had the air of people who are puzzling over their problem and are afraid. Everyone Tarrou set eyes on had that vacant gaze and was visibly suffering from the complete break with all that life had meant to him. And since they could not be thinking of their death all the time, they thought of nothing. They were on vacation. "But worst of all," Tarrou writes, "is that they're forgotten, and they know it. . . . And that, too, is natural enough. In fact, it comes to this: nobody is capable of really thinking about anyone, even in the worst calamity. For really to think about someone means thinking about that person every minute of the day, without letting one's thoughts be diverted by anything—by meals, by a fly that settles on one's cheek, by household duties, or by a sudden itch somewhere. But there are always flies and itches. That's why life is difficult to live. And these people know it only too well."

The camp manager camp up; a gentleman named Othon, he said, would like to see them. Leaving Gonzales in the office, he led the others to a corner of the grandstand, where they saw M. Othon sitting by himself. He rose as they approached. The magistrate was dressed exactly as in the past and still wore a stiff collar. The only changes Tarrou noted were that the tufts of hair over his temples were not brushed back and that one of his shoelaces was undone. M. Othon appeared very tired and not once did he look his visitors in the face. He said he was glad to see them and requested them to thank Dr. Rieux for all he had done.

Some moments of silence ensued, then with an effort the magistrate spoke again:

"I hope Jacques did not suffer too much."

This was the first time Tarrou heard him utter his son's name, and he realized that something had changed. The sun was setting and, flooding through a rift in the clouds, the level rays raked the stands, tingeing their faces with a yellow glow.

Soon after, when the camp manager was seeing Tarrou and Rambert out, they heard a crackling noise coming from the stands. A moment later the loud-speakers, which in happier times served to announce the results of games or to introduce the teams, informed the inmates of the camp that they were to go back to their tents for the evening meal. Slowly everyone filed off the stands and shuffled toward the tents. After all were under canvas two small electric trucks, of the kind used for transporting baggage on railroad platforms, began to wend their way between the tents. While the occupants held forth their arms, two ladles plunged into the two big caldrons on each truck and nearly tipped their contents into the waiting mess-kits. Then the truck moved on to the next tent.

"Very efficient," Tarrou remarked.

The camp manager beamed as he shook hands.

"Yes, isn't it? We're great believers in efficiency in this camp."

Dusk was falling. The sky had cleared and the camp was bathed in cool, soft light. Through the hush of evening came a faint tinkle of spoons and plates. Above the tents bats were circling, vanishing abruptly into the darkness. A streetcar squealed on a switch outside the walls.

"Poor Monsieur Othon!" Tarrou murmured as the gate closed behind them. "One would like to do something to help him. But how can you help a judge?"

Questions

1. When the magistrate Othon and his wife are sent to the quarantine camp saying "we must do what we are told to do," do you think that this is an exhibition of example for the others, since it was Othon who helped instate the quarantine laws?

2. Camus makes a striking point about the rift between the rich and the poor. Is the quarantine, as set up in this novel, detrimental to the poor, while being a mere inconvenience to the rich? In a real-life quarantine instance, what issues should be discussed to alleviate this dichotomy?

3. Camus attempts to liken the camp to that of a prison, its deterministic nature infringing upon human rights; the camp goers must be in bed by sunset, and are told when to eat, all under the guise of "efficiency." When does "efficiency" encroach upon the freedom of humanity?

4. The walls of the stadium serve two purpose: they prevent escape, and they also provide a shield for those who are not quarantined from seeing the despair of the camp. Should the public be aware of these less-than-stellar accommodations? What should be done to ensure that a quarantine situation is not so similar to a prison situation?

CASE 8.4

"Culture of Life": Politics at the Bedside — The Case of Terri Schiavo

George J. Annas

For the first time in the history of the United States, Congress met in a special emergency session on Sunday, March 20, to pass legislation aimed at the medical care of one patient—Terri Schiavo. President George W. Bush encouraged the legislation and flew back to Washington, D.C., from his vacation in Crawford, Texas, so that he could be on hand to sign it immediately. In a statement issued three days earlier, he said: "The case of Terri Schiavo raises complex issues.... Those who live at the mercy of others deserve our special care and concern. It should be our goal as a nation to build a culture of life, where all Americans are valued, welcomed, and protected—and that culture of life must extend to individuals with disabilities."[1]

The "culture of life" is a not-terribly-subtle reference to the antiabortion movement in the United States, which received significant encouragement in last year's presidential election. The movement may now view itself as strong enough to generate new laws to prevent human embryos from being created for research and to require that incompetent patients be kept alive with artificially delivered fluids and nutrition.

How did the U.S. Congress conclude that it was appropriate to attempt to reopen a case that had finally been concluded after more than seven years of litigation involving almost 20 judges? Has the country's culture changed so dramatically as to require a fundamental change in the law? Or do patients who cannot continue to live without artificially delivered fluids and nutrition pose previously unrecognized or novel questions of law and ethics?

The case of Terri Schiavo, a Florida woman who was in a persistent vegetative state and who died on March 31, was being played out as a public spectacle and a tragedy for her and her husband, Michael Schiavo. Mr. Schiavo's private feud with his wife's parents over the continued use of a feeding tube was taken to the media, the courts, the Florida legislature, Florida Governor Jeb Bush, the U.S. Congress, and President Bush. Since Ms. Schiavo was in a medical and legal situation almost identical to those of two of the most well-known patients in medical jurisprudence, Karen Ann Quinlan and Nancy Cruzan, there must be something about cases like theirs that defies simple solutions, whether medical or legal. In this sense, the case of Terri Schiavo provides an opportunity to examine issues that most lawyers, bioethicists, and physicians believed were well settled—if not since the 1976 New Jersey Supreme Court decision in the case of Karen Quinlan, then at least since the 1990 U.S. Supreme Court decision in the case of Nancy Cruzan. Before reviewing Terri Schiavo's case, it is well worth reviewing the legal background information that was ignored by Congress and the president.

THE CASE OF KAREN QUINLAN

In 1976, the case of Karen Quinlan made international headlines when her parents sought the assistance of a judge to discontinue the use of a ventilator in their daughter, who was in a persistent vegetative state.[2] Ms. Quinlan's physicians had refused her parents' request to remove the ventilator because, they said, they feared that they might be held civilly or even criminally liable for her death. The New Jersey Supreme Court ruled that competent persons have a right to refuse life-sustaining treatment and that this right should not be lost when a person becomes incompetent. Since the court believed that the physicians were unwilling to withdraw the ventilator because of the fear of legal liability, not precepts of medical ethics, it devised a mechanism to grant the physicians prospective legal immunity for taking this action. Specifically, the New Jersey Supreme Court rules that after a prognosis, confirmed by a hospital ethics committee, that there is "no reasonable possibility of a patient returning to a cognitive, sapient state," life-sustaining treatment can be removed and no one involved, including the physicians, can be held civilly or criminally responsible for the death.[2]

The publicity surrounding the Quinlan case motivated two independent developments: it encouraged states to enact "living will" legislation that provided legal immunity to physicians who honored patients' written "advance directives" specifying how they would want to be treated if they ever became incompetent; and it encouraged hospitals to establish ethics committees that could attempt to resolve similar treatment disputes without going to court.

THE CASE OF NANCY CRUZAN

Although *Quinlan* was widely followed, the New Jersey Supreme Court could make law only for New Jersey. When the U.S. Supreme Court decided the case of Nancy Cruzan in 1990, it made constitutional law for the entire country. Nancy Cruzan was a young woman in a persistent vegetative state caused by an accident; she was in physical circumstances essentially identical to those of Karen Quinlan, except that she was not dependent on a ventilator but rather, like Terri Schiavo, required only tube feeding to continue to live.[3] The Missouri Supreme Court had ruled that the tube feeding could be discontinued on the basis of Nancy's right of self-determination, but that only Nancy herself should be able to make this decision. Since she could not do so, tube feeding could be stopped only if those speaking for her, including her parents, could produce "clear and convincing" evidence that she would refuse tube feeding if she could speak for herself.[4]

The U.S. Supreme Court, in a five-to-four decision, agreed, saying that the state of Missouri had the authority to adopt this high standard of evidence (although no state was required to do so)

because of the finality of a decision to terminate treatment.[3] In the words of the chief justice, Missouri was entitled to "err on the side of life." Six of the nine justices explicitly found that no legal distinction could be made between artificially delivered fluids and nutrition and other medical interventions, such as ventilator support; none of the other three justices found a constitutionally relevant distinction. This issue is not controversial as a matter of constitutional law: Americans have (and have always had) the legal right to refuse any medical intervention, including artificially delivered fluids and nutrition.

Supreme Court Justice Sandra Day O'Connor, in a concurring opinion (her vote decided the case), recognized that young people (such as Karen Quinlan, Nancy Cruzan, and now Terri Schiavo—all of whom were in their 20s at the time of their catastrophic injuries) do not generally put explicit treatment instructions in writing. She suggested that had Cruzan simply said something like "if I'm not able to make medical treatment decisions myself, I want my mother to make them," such a statement should be a constitutionally protected delegation of the authority to decide about her treatment.[3] O'Connor's opinion was the reason that the Cruzan case energized a movement—encouraging people to use the appropriate documents, such as health care proxy forms or assignments of durable power of attorney, to designate someone (usually called a health care proxy, or simply an agent) to make decisions for them if they are unable to make them themselves. All states authorize this delegation, and most states explicitly grant decision-making authority to a close relative—almost always to the spouse first—if the patient has not made a designation. Such laws are all to the good.

THE SCHIAVO CASE IN THE COURTS

Terri Schiavo had a cardiac arrest, perhaps because of a potassium imbalance, in 1990 (the year *Cruzan* was decided), when she was 27 years old. Until her death in 2005, she had lived in a persistent vegetative state in nursing homes, with constant care, being nourished and hydrated through tubes. In 1998, Michael Schiavo petitioned the court to decide whether to discontinue the tube feeding. Unlike *Quinlan* and *Cruzan*, however, the Schiavo case involved a family dispute: Ms. Schiavo's parents objected. A judge found that there was clear and convincing evidence that Terri Schiavo was in a permanent or persistent vegetative state and that, if she could make her own decision, she would choose to discontinue life-prolonging procedures. An appeals court affirmed the first judge's decision, and the Florida Supreme Court declined to review it.

Schiavo's parents returned to court, claiming that they had newly discovered evidence. After an additional appeal, the parents were permitted to challenge the original court findings on the basis of new evidence related to a new treatment that they believed might restore cognitive function. Five physicians were asked to examine Ms. Schiavo— two chosen by the husband, two by the parents, and one by the court. On the basis of their examinations and conclusions, the trial judge was persuaded by the three experts who agreed that Schiavo was in a persistent vegetative state. The appeals court affirmed the original decision of the trial court judge

> Despite the irrefutable evidence that [Schiavo's] cerebral cortex has sustained irreparable injuries, we understand why a parent who had raised and nurtured a child from conception would hold out hope that some level of cognitive function remained. If Mrs. Schiavo were our own daughter, we could not hold to such faith.

> But in the end this case is not about the aspirations that loving parents have for their children. It is about Theresa Schiavo's right to make her own decision, independent of her parents and independent of her husband.... It may be unfortunate that when families cannot agree, the best forum we can offer for this private, personal decision is a public courtroom and the best decision-maker we can provide is a judge with no prior knowledge of the ward, but the law currently provides no better solution that adequately protects the interests of promoting the value of life.[5]

The Supreme Court of Florida again refused to hear an appeal.

Subsequently, the parents, with the vocal and organized support of conservative religious organizations, went to the state legislature seeking legislation requiring the reinsertion of Ms. Schiavo's feeding tube, which had been removed on the basis of the court decisions.[6,7] The legislature passed a new law (2003–418), often referred to as "Terri's Law," which gave Governor Jeb Bush the authority to order the feeding tube reinserted, and he did so. The law applied only to a patient who met the following criteria on October 15, 2003—in other words, only to Terri Schiavo:

> (a) That patient has no written advance directive;
>
> (b) The court has found that patient to be in a persistent vegetative state;
>
> (c) That patient has had nutrition and hydration withheld; and
>
> (d) A member of that patient's family has challenged the withholding of nutrition and hydration.

The constitutionality of this law was immediately challenged. In the fall of 2004, the Florida Supreme Court rules that the law was unconstitutional because it violates the separation of powers—the division of the government into three branches (executive, legislative, and judicial), each with its own powers and responsibilities.[8] The doctrine states simply that no branch may encroach on the powers of another, and no branch may delegate to another branch its constitutionally assigned power. Specifically, the court held that for the legislature to pass a law that permits the executive to "interfere with the final judicial determination in a case" is "without question an invasion of the authority of the judicial branch."[8] In addition, the court found the law unconstitutional for an independent reason, because it "delegates legislative power to the governor" by giving the governor "unbridled discretion" to make a decision about a citizen's constitutional rights. In the court's words:

> If the Legislature with the assent of the Governor can do what was attempted here, the judicial branch would be subordinated to the final directive of the other branches. Also subordinated would be the rights of individuals, including the well established

privacy right to self determination.... Vested rights could be stripped away based on popular clamor.[8]

In January 2005, the U.S. Supreme Court refused to hear an appeal brought by Governor Bush. Thereafter, the trial court judge ordered that the feeding tube be removed in 30 days (at 1 p.m., Friday, March 18) unless a higher court again intervened. The presiding judge, George W. Greer of the Pinellas Country Circuit Court, was thereafter picketed and threatened with death; he has had to be accompanied by armed guards at all times.

Ms. Schiavo's parents, again with the aid of a variety of religious fundamentalist and "right to life" organizations, sought review in the appeals courts, a new statute in the state legislature, and finally, congressional intervention. Both the trial judge and the appeals courts refused to reopen the case on the basis of claims of new evidence (including the 2004 statement from Pope John Paul II regarding fluids and nutrition[9]) or the failure to appoint an independent lawyer for her at the original hearing. In Florida, the state legislature considered, and the House passed, new legislation aimed at restoring the feeding tube, but the Florida Senate—recognizing, I think, that this new legislation would be unconstitutional for the same reason as the previous legislation was—ultimately refused to approve the bill. Thereupon, an event unique in American politics occurred: after more than a week of discussion, and after formally declaring their Easter recess without action, Congress reconvened two days after the feeding tube was removed to consider emergency legislation designed to apply only to Terri Schiavo.

CONGRESS AT THE BEDSIDE

Under rules that permitted a few senators to act if no senator objected, the U.S. Senate adopted a bill entitled "For the relief of the parents of Theresa Marie Schiavo" on March 20, 2005. The House, a majority of whose members had to be present to vote, debated the same measure from 9 p.m. to midnight on the same day and passed it by a four-to-one margin shortly after midnight on March 21. The President then signed it into law. In substance, the new law (S. 686) provides that "the U.S. District Court for the Middle District of Florida shall have jurisdiction" to hear a suit "for the alleged violation of any right of Theresa Marie Schiavo under the Constitution or laws of the United States relating to the withholding or withdrawal of food, fluids, or medical treatment necessary to sustain her life." The parents "have standing" to bring the lawsuit (the federal court had previously refused to hear the case on the basis that the parents had no standing to bring it), and the court is instructed to "determine de novo any claim of a violation of any right of Theresa Marie Schiavo... notwithstanding any prior State court determination..."—that is, to pretend that no court has made any prior ruling in the case. The act is to provide no "precedent with respect to future legislation."

The brief debate on this bill in the House of Representatives (there were no hearings in either chamber and no debate at all in the U.S. Senate) was notable primarily for its uninformed and frenzied rhetoric. It was covered live on television by C-SPAN. The primary sponsor of the measure, Congressman Thomas DeLay (R-Tex.), for example, asserted that "She's not a vegetable, just handicapped like many millions of people walking around today. This has nothing to do with politics, and it's disgusting for people to say that it does." Others echoed the sentiments of Senate majority leader and physician Bill Frist (R-Tenn.), who said that immediate action was imperative because "Terri Schiavo is being denied lifesaving fluids and nutrition as we speak."

Other physician-members of the House chimed in. Congressman Dave Weldon (R-Fla.) remarked that, on the basis of his 16 years of medical practice, he was able to conclude that Terri Schiavo is "not in a persistent vegetative state." Congressman Phil Gingrey (R-Ga.) agreed, saying "she's very much alive." Another physician, Congressman Joe Schwarz (R-Mich.), who was a head and neck surgeon for 27 years, opined that "she does have some cognitive ability" and asked, "How many other patients are there with feeding tubes? Should they be removed too?" Another physician-congressman, Torn Price (R-Ga.), thought the law was reasonable because there was "no living will in place" and the family and experts disagreed. The only physician who was troubled by Congress's public diagnosis and treatment of Terri Schiavo was James McDermott (D-Wash.), who chided his physician-colleagues for the poor medical practice of making a diagnosis without examining the patient.

Although he deferred to the medical expertise of his congressional colleagues with M.D. degrees, Congressman Barney Frank (D-Mass.) pointed out that the chamber was not filled with physicians. Frank said of the March 20 proceedings: "We're not doctors, we just play them on C-SPAN." The mantras of the debate were that in a life-or-death decision, we should err on the "side of life," that action should be taken to "prevent death by starvation" and ensure the "right to life," and that Congress should "protect the rights of disabled people."

The following day, U.S. District Court Judge James D. Whittemore issued a careful opinion denying the request of the parents for a temporary restraining order that would require the reinsertion of the feeding tube.[10] The judge concluded that the parents had failed to demonstrate "a substantial likelihood of success on the merits" of the case— a prerequisite for a temporary restraining order. Specifically, Judge Whittemore found that, as to the various due-process claims made, the case had been "exhaustively litigated"; that, throughout, all parties had been "represented by able counsel"; and that it was not clear how having an additional lawyer "appointed by the court [for Ms. Schiavo] would have reduced the risk of erroneous rulings." As to the allegation that the patient's First Amendment rights to practice her religion had been violated by the state, the court held that there were no state actions involved at all, "because neither Defendant Schiavo nor Defendant Hospice are state actors."

Whittemore's decision was reasonable and consistent with settled law, and was, not suprisingly, upheld on appeal. The case of Terri Schiavo resulted in no changes in the law, nor were any good arguments made that legal changes were necessary. The religious right and congressional Republicans may nonetheless attempt to use this decision to their advantage. Despite the fact that Congress itself sent the case to federal court for determination, some Republicans have already begun to cite the ruling as yet another example of "legislating" by the courts. For they liken the action permitted—the withdrawal of a feeding tube—to unfavored activities, such as abortion and same-sex marriage, that courts have allowed to occur. All three activities, they argue, represent attacks on the "culture of life" and necessitate that the President appoint federal court judges who value life over liberty.

PROXY DECISION MAKERS, PERSISTENT VEGETATIVE STATES, AND DEATH

A vast majority of Americans would not want to be maintained in a persistent vegetative state by means of a feeding tube, like Terri Schiavo and Nancy Cruzan.[11] The intense publicity generated by this case will cause many to discuss this issue with their families and, I hope, to sign an advance directive. Such a directive, in the form of a living will or the designation of a health care proxy, would prevent court involvement in virtually all cases—although it might not have solved the problem in the Schiavo case, because the family members disagreed about Terri Schiavo's medical condition and the acceptability of removing the tube in any circumstances.

Despite the impression that may have been created by these three cases, and especially by the grand-standing in Congress, conflicts involving medical decision making for incompetent patients near the end of life are no longer primarily legal in nature, if they ever were. The law has been remarkably stable since *Quinlan* (which itself restated existing law): competent adults have the right to refuse any medical treatment, including life-sustaining treatment (which includes artificially delivered fluids and nutrition). Incompetent adults retain an interest in self-determination. Competent adults can execute an advance directive stating their wishes and designate a person to act on their behalf, and physicians can honor these wishes. Physicians and health care agents should make treatment decisions consistent with what they believe the patient would want (the subjective standard). If the patient's desires cannot be ascertained, then treatment decision should be based on the patient's best interests (what a reasonable person would most likely want in the same circumstances). This has, I believe, always been the law in the United States.[12]

Of course, legal forms or formalities cannot solve nonlegal problems. Decision making near the end of life is difficult and can exacerbate unresolved family feuds that then are played out at the patient's bedside and even in the media. Nonetheless, it is reasonable and responsible for all persons to designate health care agents to make treatment decisions for them when they are unable to make their own. After this recent congressional intervention, it also makes sense to specifically state one's wishes with respect to artificial fluids and hydration—and that one wants no politicians, even physician-politicians, involved in the process.

Most Americans will agree with a resolution that was overwhelmingly adopted by the California Medical Association on the same day that Congress passed the Schiavo law: "Resolved: That the California Medical Association expresses its outrage at Congress' interference with these medical decisions."

If there is disagreement between the physician and the family, or among family members, the involvement of outside experts, including consultants, ethics committees, risk managers, lawyers, and even courts, may become inevitable—at least if the patient survives long enough to permit such involvement. It is the long-lasting nature of the persistent vegetative state that results in its persistence in the courtrooms of the United States. There is (and should be) no special law regarding the refusal of treatment that is tailored to specific diseases or prognoses, and the persistent vegetative state is no exception.[13,14] Nor do feeding tubes have rights: people do. "Erring on the side of life" in this context often results in violating a person's body and human dignity in a way few would want for themselves. In such situations, erring on the side of liberty—specifically, the patient's right to decide on treatment—is more consistent with American values and our constitutional

traditions. As the Massachusetts Supreme Judicial Court said in a 1977 case that raised the same legal question: "The constitutional right to privacy, as we conceive it, is an expression of the sanctity of individual free choice and self-determination as fundamental constituents of life. The value of life as so perceived is lessened not by a decision to refuse treatment, but by the failure to allow a competent human being the right of choice."[15]

NOTES

1. President's statement on Terri Schiavo, March 17, 2005. (Accessed March 31, 2005, at http://www.whitehouse.gov/news/releases/2005/03/20050317-7.html.)

2. In re Quinlan, 70 N.J.10, 355 A2d 647 (1976).

3. Cruzan v. Director, Missouri Dept. of Health, 497 U.S. 261 (1990).

4. Cruzan v. Harmon, 760 S.W.2d 408 (Mo. 1988).

5. In re Guardianship of Schiavo, 851 So. 2d 182 (Fla. 2d Dist. Ct. App. 2003).

6. Goodnough A. Victory in Florida feeding case emboldens the religious right. New York Times. October 24, 2005:A1.

7. Kirkpatrick DD, Stolberg SG. How family's cause reached the halls of Congress: networks of Christians rallied to case of Florida woman. New York Times. March 22, 2005:A1.

8. Bush v. Schiavo, 885 So.2d 321 (Fla. 2004).

9. Shannon TA, Walter JJ. Implications of the papal allocution on feeding tubes. Hastings Cent Rep 2004: 34(4): 18–20.

10. Schiavo ex rel. Schindler v. Schiavo, No. 8:05-CV-530-T-27IBM (M.D. Fla. Mar. 22, 2005) (slip opinion).

11. Eisenberg D. Lessons of the Schiavo battle. Time, April 4, 2005:23.

12. Annas GJ. The rights of hospital patients. New York: Discus Books, 1975:81–4.

13. *Idem*. The health care proxy and the living will. N Engl J Med 1991;324:1210–3.

14. The Multi-Society Task Force on PVS. Medical aspects of the persistent vegetative state. N Engl J Med 1994;330:1572–9. [Erratum, N Engl J Med 1995;333:130.]

15. Superintendent of Belchertown State School v. Saikewicz, 373 Mass. 728, 742, 370 N.E.2d 417 (Mass. 1977).

Questions

1. The 1976 Karen Quinlan case set a precedent in determining end-of-life decisions. What basis did a contemporary Congress and president have in ignoring this court decision in the Schiavo case?

2. What ethical issues do proxy-decision makers have to deal with, beyond the legal issues? Does the legal system have jurisdiction over private family decisions?

CPSIA information can be obtained at www.ICGtesting.com
Printed in the USA
BVOW11s0353251113

337044BV00005B/8/P